The ATLAS *of* LITERATURE

General Editor
MALCOLM BRADBURY

Stewart, Tabori & Chang
New York

THE CONTRIBUTORS

We are very grateful to all our contributors, who are listed below together with the names of their pieces. All the other essays were written by MALCOLM BRADBURY.

RUDIGER AHRENS (*Weimar and the German Romantics*) Professor of English at the University of Würzburg in Germany, Rudiger Ahrens is a member of numerous University bodies and has lectured extensively on English and German literature throughout the world. Work includes books on Shakespeare, Francis Bacon and literary theory.

GUIDO ALMANSI (*Post-War Italian Fiction*) Guido Almansi, retired Professor of English and Comparative Literature at the University of East Anglia, is now a cultural journalist in Italy.

LOUIS DE BERNIÈRES (*Latin American Writing: A Literary Heritage Explored*) Louis de Bernières is the author of four novels. *The War of Don Emmanuel's Nether Parts* (1990) and *Captain Corelli's Mandolin* (1995) have both won the Commonwealth Writers Prize. *Don Emmanuel* won Best First Book Eurasia Region in 1991 and *Señor Vivo and the Coca Lord* (1991) won Best Book Eurasia Region in 1992. In 1993 he was selected as one of the 20 Best Young British Novelists and in 1995 he was given the Lannan Foundation Award.

CHRISTOPHER BIGSBY (*The South, Slavery and the Civil War, Depression America* and with Eric Homberger, *Harlem's Renaissance*) Christopher Bigsby is Professor of American Studies at the University of East Anglia, and Chairman for the British Council Annual Seminar in Contemporary Literature. Books include *The Black American Writer Vols I and II* (1971), *The Second Black Renaissance* (1980), *A Critical Introduction to 20th Century American Drama*, Vols I, II and III (1982–5) and *Modern American Drama 1940–1992* (1992). He is the author of three novels: *Hester* (1994), *Pearl* (1995) and *Still Lives* (1996).

PATRICK BOYDE (*Dante's Worlds*) Patrick Boyde is Serena Professor of Italian at the University of Cambridge. His numerous publications on Italian Literature include *Dante's Lyric Poetry* (1967), *Night Thoughts on Italian Poetry and Art* (1985) and *Perception and Passion in Dante's 'Comedy'* (1993). He is a Fellow of the British Academy.

MELVYN BRAGG (*The Lake District of the Romantics*) Melvyn Bragg was born in Cumbria, England. Since 1965 he has written 14 novels, many set in his native Lake District. He is also the author of several works of non-fiction including *Land of the Lakes* (1983). He is controller of Arts at London Weekend Television, where he has edited and presented the *South Bank Show* arts programme since its inception in 1978. He is President of the National Campaign for the Arts.

JUSTIN CARTWRIGHT (*South African Stories*) Justin Cartwright was born in South Africa and was educated there and at Oxford. His novels include *Freedom For The Wolves* (1982), *Interior* (1988), winner of a CNA award, *Masai Dreaming* (1994), winner of the 1994 M. Net award in South Africa and *In Every Face I Meet* (1995), shortlisted for the Booker and Whitbread prizes. The BBC televised his satirical novel *Look At It This Way* (1990) in 1992. His latest book *Not Yet Home: A South African Journey* was published in 1996.

RUPERT CHRISTIANSEN (*The Romantics Abroad*) Rupert Christiansen read English at King's College, Cambridge and later at Columbia University in the United States. He has published a number of books on opera and is opera critic for the *Spectator*. He also writes regularly for *Harpers and Queen* and the *Daily Telegraph*. Publications include *Romantic Affinities: Portraits from an Age 1780–1830* (1988) and *Tales of the New Babylon: Paris 1869–75* (1994).

JONATHAN COE (*London: The Dislocated City*) Jonathan Coe lives in London. He is the author of four novels: *The Accidental Woman* (1987), *A Touch of Love* (1989), *The Dwarves of Death* (1990), and *What a Carve Up!* (1994), winner of the 1995 John Llewellyn Rhys Memorial Prize and the 1996 Prix du Meilleur Livre Étranger.

JON COOK (*Dreaming Spires: Nineteenth Century Oxford and Cambridge*) Jon Cook is Senior Lecturer in English Studies at the University of East Anglia. Among his most recent publications are contributions to a collection of essays on *The Prelude* (1993) and to *The Penguin History of English Literature: the Romantic Period* (1994).

VALENTINE CUNNINGHAM (*The Spanish Civil War* and *Writers Go to War*) Valentine Cunningham is a Fellow and Tutor in English Literature at Corpus Christi College, Oxford. He is author and editor of a number of publications including *British Writers of the Thirties* (1988), *Spanish Front: Writers on the Civil War* (1986) and *The Penguin Book of Spanish Civil War Verse* (reprinted 1996).

FRANK DELANEY (*The Irish Revival*) Frank Delaney is a writer and broadcaster for BBC television and radio in Dublin and London. His publications include *James Joyce's Odyssey* (1981), *Betjeman Country* (1983), *The Celts* (1986), *A Walk in the Dark Ages* (1988) and a series of novels set in 20th century Ireland, beginning with *The Sins of the Mothers* (1992).

RISA DOMB (*Contemporary Israeli Writing*) Risa Domb is lecturer in Modern Hebrew Literature at the University of Cambridge. She is a Fellow and Director of Studies at Girton College, and Honorary Director of the Centre for Modern Hebrew Studies.

OWEN DUDLEY EDWARDS (*Eighteenth Century Dublin* and *Eighteenth Century Edinburgh and Scotland*) Owen Dudley Edwards is Reader in History at the University of Edinburgh. His books include writings on Macaulay and Eamon de Valera.

FADIA FAQIR (*In Search of Andalusia: Arabic Literature Today*) Fadia Faqir was born in Jordan and is the author of two novels: *Nisanit* (1990) and *Pillars of Salt* (1996). She lectures at the Centre for Middle Eastern and Islamic Studies at Durham University, and is the general editor of the Arab Women Writers Series for Garnet Publishing.

JOHN FLETCHER (*The France of the Enlightenment* and *Paris as Bohemia*) John Fletcher is Professor of European Literature at the University of East Anglia. He has written a number of books including *Alain Robbe-Grillet* (1983), and has made a prize-winning translation of Claude Simon's *The Georgics* (1989). He is working on a critical edition of Albert Camus' *Le Premier Homme*.

GREG GATENBY (*Canadian Images*) Greg Gatenby was born in Toronto where he graduated from York University. He has been Artistic Director of the Harbourfront Reading Series since 1975. His published writing includes poetry (*Growing Still*, 1981), anthologies (*Whales: A Celebration*, 1983) and literary histories (*The Very Richness of That Past*, 1995). He is working on a new collection of poems and a literary history of Toronto.

TERRY HANDS (*Shakespeare's Stratford and London*) Terry Hands, theatre and opera director, lives in London. He was Founder-Artistic Director of the Liverpool Everyman Theatre from 1964–66. He then joined the Royal Shakespeare Company, Stratford-upon-Avon, where he stayed for 25 years as Associate and Artistic Director.

GITHA HARIHARAN (*The Fantasywallas of Bombay*) Githa Hariharan grew up in Bombay but now lives in New Delhi. *The Thousand Faces of Night* won the Commonwealth Writer's Prize for Best First Book in 1993. Her most recent novel is *The Ghosts of Vasu Master* (1994).

DESMOND HOGAN (*James Joyce's Dublin*) Desmond Hogan lives in the west of Ireland and is the author of four novels: *The Ikon Maker* (1976), *A Curious Street* (1984), *A New Shirt* (1986) and *A Farewell to Prague* (1995). *A Link With the River* (1989) has been published in the United States and the collection *Elysium* in Germany (1995).

ERIC HOMBERGER (*The Beat Generation, Greenwich Village* and, with Christopher Bigsby, *Harlem's Renaissance*) Eric Homberger is Reader in American Studies at the University of East Anglia. His publications include *The Historical Atlas of New York City* (1994) and *Scenes from the Life of a City: Corruption and Conscience in Old New York* (1994).

HEINZ ICKSTADT (*Berlin: The Centre of German Modernism* and *Germany After the War*) Heinz Ickstadt is Professor of American Literature at the John F. Kennedy Institute für Nordamerikastudien at the Freie University of Berlin. He has published widely in German and English on postmodern fiction, modern poetry and urban literature.

DOUGLAS JOHNSON (*The Paris of the French Romantics* and *Stendhal's, Balzac's and Sand's France*) Douglas Johnson is Professor Emeritus of French History at the University of London. His publications include *Guizot and French History 1787–1874* (1964), *France and the Dreyfus Affair* (1967) and *A Concise History of France* (1970).

RUSSELL CELYN JONES (*Dylan Thomas's Wales*) Russell Celyn Jones grew up in Swansea, Wales, and now lives in London. He is the author of three novels: *Soldiers and Innocents* (1990) which won the David Higham Prize, *Small Times* (1992) and *An Interference of Light* (1995). He has written for a number of British national newspapers and broadcasts periodically on British BBC radio.

PAUL LEVINE (*Writers' Hollywood*) Paul Levine is Professor of American Literature at Copenhagen University in Denmark. He was born and raised in New York and educated at Wesleyan, Princeton and Harvard Universities in the United States. He has written extensively on literature, film and culture. Publications include *Divisions* (1975), *E.L. Doctorow* (1985), *Lynn Chadwick* (1988), and a collaboration with Doctorow on a volume of the novelist's screenplays.

IAN LITTLEWOOD (*Existentialist Paris and Beyond*) Ian Littlewood has taught at universities in France, Japan and the United States, and is now teaching English at the University of Sussex. Among his publications on France are *Paris: A Literary Companion* (1987) and *Paris: Architecture, History, Art* (1992).

JAMES McFARLANE (*Scandinavia: The Dark and the Light*) James McFarlane was Professor, now Emeritus, of European Literature at the University of East Anglia. He is author and editor of a number of publications including: *Scandinavia: an International Journal of Scandinavian Studies* (1975–91) and *The Cambridge Companion to Henrik Ibsen* (1994). He was awarded the Commander's Cross, Royal Norwegian Order of St Olav in 1975.

PAUL MICOU (*Manhattan Tales: Who's Afraid of Tom Wolfe?*) Paul Micou was born in San Francisco and graduated from Harvard University in 1981. He is the author of six novels including *The Cover Artist* (1990), *The Death of David Debrizzi* (1991), *The Last Word* (1993) and *Adam's Wish* (1993). He now lives in London.

ARTHUR MILLER (*Broadway*) Arthur Miller was born in Manhattan in 1915 and graduated from the University of Michigan. He has written numerous award-winning stage plays including *Death of a Salesman* (1949), *The Crucible* (1952), *A View from the Bridge* (1955) and *Broken Glass* (1994), which won the Olivier Best Play Award. He has also written and published various prose works, a collection of short stories, *I Don't Need You Any More* (1967) and four works of non-fiction. His latest novel, *Plain Girl*, was published in 1995.

MICHAEL MILLGATE (*Thomas Hardy's Wessex*) Michael Millgate is University Professor of English Emeritus at Toronto University. He is the author of a number of publications on Hardy, including *Thomas Hardy: A Biography* (1982), *The Life and Work of Thomas Hardy* (1985) and *The Collected Letters of Thomas Hardy* (1978–88).

ALASTAIR NIVEN (*The Writing of Africa Today*) Alastair Niven is Director of Literature at the Arts Council of England. Publications include *D.H. Lawrence: The Novels* (1978) and many articles on African Literature. He was Director General of the Africa Centre, London, for six years, edited *The Journal of Commonwealth Literature* for 13 years and has judged awards, including the Booker Prize in 1994.

ALEXS PATE (*Everywhere the Wind Blows: African-American Writing Today*) Alexs Pate is a writer, poet and performance artist. He teaches Creative Writing at Macalester College in Minnesota. His work has been published in *The Washington Post* and *Essence*. His first novel, *Losing Absalom* (1995), was published to great acclaim.

GLENN PATTERSON (*Divided Ireland*) Glenn Patterson is writer-in-residence at Queen's University, Belfast. His novels include *Burning Your Own* (1988), winner of the Rooney Prize for Irish Literature, *Fat Lad* (1992), short-listed for the GPA Book Award, and *Black Night At Big Thunder Mountain* (1995). He has also written a short play, and television documentaries on Northern Irish culture and politics.

ROY PORTER (*Eighteenth Century London*) Roy Porter is Professor of the Social History of Medicine at the Wellcome Institute for the History of Medicine in London. His books include *In Sickness and in Health: The British Experience 1650-1850* (1988) and *London: A Social History* (1994). He lives in London.

JANE SELLARS (*Wild Yorkshire: The Brontës of Haworth*) Jane Sellars was born in Yorkshire and graduated in art history from Manchester University. For ten years she worked at the Walker Art Gallery, Liverpool, where she established herself as an authority on Victorian women artists. She has been the director of the Brontë Parsonage Museum since 1989. She lectures and broadcasts on the Brontës, organizes exhibitions and was co-author of *The Art of the Brontës* (1995).

PATRICIA SHAW (*Cervantes' Spain*) Professor Shaw heads the Department of Modern Philology at the University of Oviedo in Spain. Her numerous publications on Spanish and English Literature include *Seventeenth Century English Views of Spain* (1981). In 1988 she was awarded an OBE for her services to English Studies in Spain, where she has lived for over forty years.

LUCRETIA STEWART (*The Writing of the Caribbean*) Lucretia Stewart was born in Singapore and lives in London. She is the author of *Tiger Balm – Travels in Laos, Vietnam and Cambodia* (1992) and *The Weather Prophet – A Caribbean Journey* (1995).

JAMES SUPPLE (*Montaigne's France*) James Supple is Professor of French Studies at Strathclyde University, Scotland. He lectures worldwide on Montaigne and contributes regularly to literary journals. His publications include *Arms Versus Letters: the Military and Literary Ideals in the "Essais" of Montaigne* (1984) and *Montaigne et la rhétorique* (1996).

ARCH TAIT (*The Sleeping Giant: Pushkin's, Gogol's and Dostoevsky's St Petersburg* and *Russia and Eastern Europe after the Second World War*) Arch Tait teaches Russian Literature at the University of Birmingham and is co-editor of the British magazine *Glas: New Russian Writing*. His translations include Vladimir Makanin's Russian Booker Prize-winning novel *Baize-covered Table with Decanter* (1995).

D. J. TAYLOR (*Depression Britain* and *Campus Fictions*) D. J. Taylor is the author of three novels including *Real Life* (1992), and two critical studies: *A Vain Conceit: British Fiction in the 1980s* (1989) and *After the War: The Novel and England Since 1945* (1993). He is currently writing a biography of William Makepeace Thackeray. He lives in London.

GAVIN WALLACE (*Precipitous City: Robert Louis Stevenson's Edinburgh* and *This Grey but Gold City: The Glasgow of Gray and Kelman*) Gavin Wallace is a course tutor in Literature with the Open University in Scotland. He has published widely on Scottish literature and Scottish cultural affairs. He was co-editor of *The Scottish Novel Since the Seventies* (1992), regularly reviews books for *The Scotsman* and is co-editor of the literary journal *Edinburgh Review*.

NIGEL WEST (*Cold War Tales*) Nigel West (Rupert Allason, MP) is European editor of the *Intelligence Quarterly* and has written extensively on the spy world. His non-fiction includes *MI6: British Secret Intelligence Service Operations 1909-45* (1983) and *Unreliable Witnesses: Espionage Myths of World War II* (1984). His fiction includes *The Blue List* (1989), *Cuban Bluff* (1990), and *Murder in the Commons* (1992).

MICHAEL WILDING (*Australian Images: Sydney and Melbourne*) Michael Wilding is Professor of English and Australian Literature at the University of Sydney. His publications of fiction and selected short stories include *Under Saturn* (1988), *Pacific Highway* (1982) and *Reading the Signs* (1984). He was elected Fellow of the Australian Academy of Humanities in 1988.

KAZUMI YAMAGATA (*Japan: Land of Spirits of the Earth*) Kazumi Yamagata is Professor of English and Comparative Literature at the University of Tsukuba in Japan. In 1988 he was awarded the 25th Culture of Translation Award for his translation of Susan Handelman's *Slayers of Moses*.

CONTENTS

8 *Introduction*

10 **Part One**
The Middle Ages and the Renaissance

12 Dante's Worlds
16 Chaucer's England
20 Shakespeare's Stratford and London
24 Montaigne's France
28 Cervantes' Spain
32 The Discovery of the New World:
Arcadia and Utopia

36 **Part Two**
The Age of Reason

38 The France of the Enlightenment
42 The Journeys of the Age of the Novel
46 Eighteenth Century London
50 Eighteenth Century Dublin
53 Eighteenth Century Edinburgh and Scotland

56 **Part Three**
The Romantics

58 The Lake District of the Romantics
62 The Romantics Abroad
66 Jane Austen's Regency England
70 The Paris of the French Romantics
74 Weimar and the German Romantics
78 Washington Irving's Europe
82 James Fenimore Cooper's Frontier

86 **Part Four**
The Age of Industrialism and Empire

88 The Sleeping Giant: Pushkin's,
Gogol's and Dostoevsky's St Petersburg
92 Stendhal's, Balzac's and Sand's France
96 Dickens's London
100 Steaming Chimneys:
Britain and Industrialism
104 Wild Yorkshire:
The Brontës of Haworth
108 Emerson's and Hawthorne's
New England
112 Dreaming Spires: Nineteenth Century
Oxford and Cambridge

116 **Part Five**
The Age of Realism

118 Mark Twain's Mississippi
122 The South, Slavery and
the Civil War
126 Paris as Bohemia
130 The European Apple:
Henry James's International Scene
133 Thomas Hardy's Wessex
137 Scandinavia: The Dark and the Light
140 Precipitous City:
Robert Louis Stevenson's Edinburgh
144 London in the 1890s
148 Dreams of Empire
152 The Irish Revival
154 Chicago's World Fair

158 **Part Six**
The Modern World

160 Wittgenstein's Vienna
163 Kafka's Prague
166 James Joyce's Dublin
170 Writers of the Great War
174 Paris in the Twenties
178 The World of Bloomsbury
182 Berlin: The Centre of German Modernism
186 Greenwich Village
190 Harlem's Renaissance
194 Main Street, USA
197 William Faulkner's New South
200 Writers' Hollywood
204 Depression America
208 Depression Britain
212 The Spanish Civil War
216 Writers go to War

222 **Part Seven**
After the Second World War

224 Existentialist Paris and Beyond
228 Germany After the War
232 Post-war Italian Fiction
236 London in the Fifties
240 Scenes From Provincial Life
244 Broadway
248 Dylan Thomas's Wales
252 The Beat Generation
256 Cold War Tales

260 **Part Eight**
The World Today

262 Russia and Eastern Europe After
     the Second World War
266 The Fantasywallas of Bombay
270 Japan: Land of Spirits of the Earth
274 Campus Fictions
276 Divided Ireland
280 The Writing of the Caribbean
284 Australian Images: Sydney and Melbourne
288 Contemporary Israeli Writing
291 In Search of Andalusia:
     Arabic Literature Today
294 South African Stories
298 Latin American Writing: A Literary
     Heritage Explored
302 The Writing of Africa Today
306 Canadian Images
310 Everywhere the Wind Blows:
     African-American Writing Today
314 Manhattan Tales: Who's Afraid of Tom Wolfe?
318 "This Grey But Gold City"
     The Glasgow of Gray and Kelman
320 London: The Dislocated City
324 The World After the Wall

326 Authors and their Works
333 Places to Visit
343 Further Reading
346 Index
352 Picture Credits and Acknowledgments

INTRODUCTION

"The Great Khan owns an atlas in which are gathered the maps of all the cities: those whose walls rest on solid foundations, those which fell in ruins and were swallowed up by the sand, those that will exist one day and in whose place now only hares' holes gape."

Italo Calvino, *Invisible Cities* (1972)

The truth is, fiction depends for its life on place," the American writer Eudora Welty once observed, "Location is the proving ground of 'what happened? who's here? who's coming?' – that is the heart's field." Place, travel and exploration have always been among the most fundamental elements of literature. Our poetry, our fiction, our drama is itself a mapping of the world, wide-ranging, highlighted in some parts, dark in others, always changing in space and time. A very large part of our writing is a story of its roots in a place: a landscape, region, village, city, nation or continent. Much more of it is an odyssey of travels: of adventure, discovery, exploration, pilgrimage, journeys to new worlds. What's more, places themselves are changed by what is written of them, and take some of their meaning and mythic character from literature.

Thus literature itself is an atlas, an imaginative map of the universe, and as Herman Melville wrote in *Redburn*: "nearly all literature, in one sense, is made up of guide-books." The aim of *The Atlas of Literature* is to bring this idea fully alive. It explores the many different connections that, since medieval times, have existed between writers and books, and landscapes, cities, islands, continents. It looks at many of the revealed and hidden maps of literature, past and present, real and imagined. It considers writers and works that are intimately connected with a place or landscape, capturing a town, a city, a region in its fictional texture or its literary heyday.

The *Atlas* is devoted to real places so vivid they have become part of literature's great crowded scene, the imaginary ones imposed over them, and the intricate connections between the two. It acknowledges the way that our maps of the world have been shaped by literary writings: America, the New World, was imagined in European books long before Europeans ever explored, conquered or settled there. In our modern world, the globe has both shrunk and widened. Now important books and great writers come and go between many regions, continents and cultures. In consequence our own mental and imaginary maps of the world have been transformed.

We show here the key places related to the making of literature: the houses and communities where writers worked, the theatres they worked for, the cafés they met in. We also show the impact of their writings on those places, and some of the settings and scenes from the books themselves. We follow the growth of literary cities, locate writers' houses and landscapes. The book concludes with an extensive bibliography, a listing of further writers associated with particular places and societies (inevitably many writers and places jostled for entry, and there have been some sacrifices) and a list of writers' houses and settings that can be explored.

The four years of work on this *Atlas*, taking me through many travels, maps and guide-books, have deepened my longfelt conviction that literature and geography are intimately related. Thus the book has been a pleasure to make, and this is not least because of the co-operation of those who worked on what is a collective endeavour. Frances Gertler conceived and developed the project, Tim Foster established the design, and they and their dedicated team of editors, designers and researchers, especially Alison Macfarlane, Blânche Harper and Zoë Goodwin, explored cities and landscapes, books and their illustrations, graphic possibilities and cartographic byways, in careful detail. Our contributors provided not simply text and enthusiasm, but detailed geographical information and illustrations. I am particularly grateful to Eric Homberger, Heinz Ickstadt and Arch Tait for their informed assistance, which applies to more entries than they are credited with. Thanks to their help, it can be hoped that *The Atlas of Literature* will offer a novel international history of literature since the medieval period, as well as a source of reference and enjoyment.

Malcolm Bradbury
Norwich 1996

NOTES ABOUT THE BOOK AND A KEY TO THE MAPS

Translated works are given their English title with the date of first publication in the original language. The maps use modern bases and street names. Locations are in the vernacular of the country they represent. The key, right, applies to all the maps, but in certain cases, individual keys are also given. City and town dots vary in colour, according to the colour of the map. Birth dates appear when a person was born in a place indicated on the map; other dates refer to the period of time a person or institution was there, or the date of a visit. A date is not given if something or someone was in a place sporadically, or if the information is not known. Authors and titles keyed into an area indicate the work was set there.

Place with literary associations: STILL THERE
Place with literary associations: NO LONGER THERE

Place featuring in author's life: STILL THERE
Place featuring in author's life: NO LONGER THERE

Real place featured in a work: STILL THERE
Real place featured in a work: NO LONGER THERE

Jefferson Fictional place
Oxford Real place

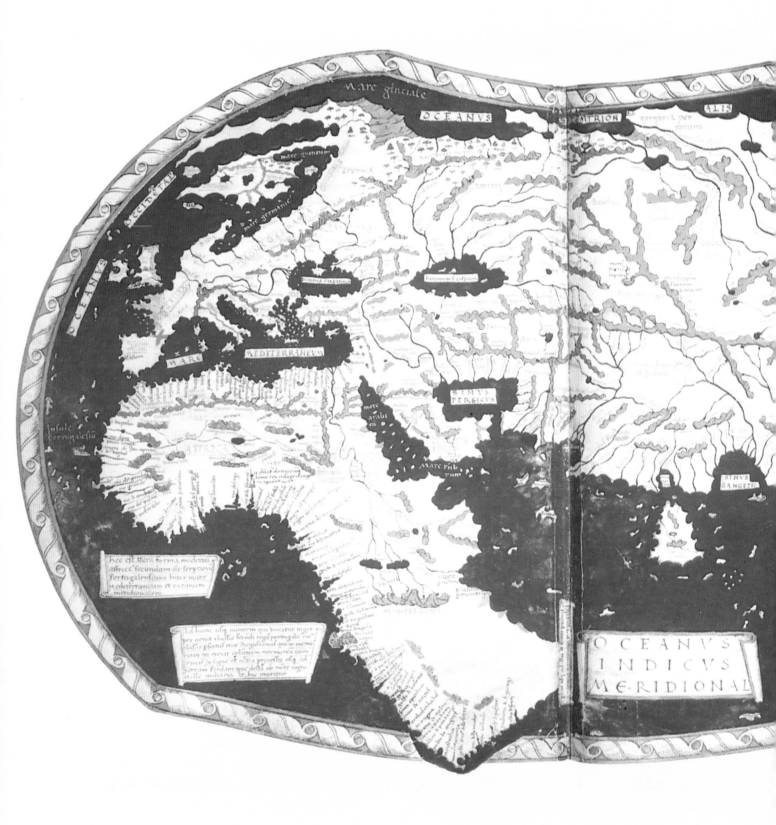

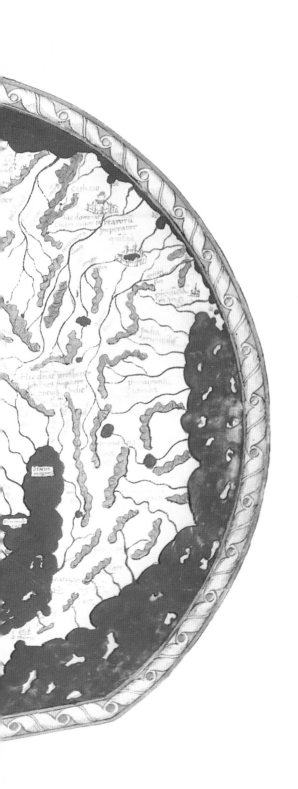

PART ONE

THE MIDDLE AGES AND THE RENAISSANCE

In the beginning was the Word. It was divine, and it was secular. Human beings had always told each other stories, transmitting the revelation of their faiths, their legends of adventure and exploration, their stories of cities and kings, war and love. In the classical Mediterranean world, the great religious books – the *Bible*, the *Talmud*, the *Koran* – were joined by the myth-making of poetry, epic narrative and drama. When Johannes Gutenberg, working in Strasbourg and Mainz in the 1440s, invented (or re-invented) moveable type, the great revolution of the book occurred. Now tales formerly passed by word of mouth, told from the pulpit, transmitted in illuminated manuscript, became public print. The world about which stories were told was in no less fundamental change. Its pilgrims and seafarers, explorers and discoverers, theologians and philosophers, extended its fringes, mapped its unknown spaces, drew a new cartography, made fresh cosmologies relating human geography and the divine. According to British politician and writer Francis Bacon, three mechanical inventions had changed "the whole face and state of things throughout the world" – printing, gunpowder and the magnet – which permitted literature, conquest and navigation, and let the Renaissance spirit flourish...

Henricus Martellus's map of the world, c.1490, is based on the earlier Ptolemy map, but draws on the voyages of Portuguese discoverers to illustrate the newly-found Cape of Good Hope.

DANTE'S WORLDS

"Florence bore me, Ravenna holds me." This modern adaptation of the famous epitaph for Virgil (70–19BC) is a fair summary of the six rhyming hexameters that appear on Dante's (1265–1321) sarcophagus, and takes us to the very heart of the poet's work. Many other places were important in Dante Alighieri's life, but they can all be plotted along the trajectory connecting these two cities.

Born in 1265, Dante spent most of his first 35 years in the place of his birth. Florence was then a powerful and self-governing city-state, at the height of an economic and demographic boom that was to bring the population up to about 100,000 (a megalopolis by contemporary standards). Incessant factional struggles for power in the period between 1250 and 1293 led to successive reforms in the constitution, such that the older "noble" families were excluded from government. Participation became limited to those who created and administered its wealth – the members of the major guilds, chief among them the merchants who had control of the wool trade.

In Domenico di Michelino's fifteenth century painting, above, Dante stands holding his Comedy, *with Florence to his left, the gates of Hell to his right, the mountain of Purgatory behind him and the celestial spheres above his head.*

Despite the fact that he was born into the minor nobility, Dante joined the guild of physicians and apothecaries in 1295, and served as one of the six Priors of the city in a difficult two-month period in 1300. Friends, including the poet Guido Cavalcanti, were exiled. Eighteen months later, in consequence of a political coup, Dante himself was banished on pain of death. He remained an exile in various courts of Italy for the last twenty years of his life, finally settling in Ravenna from about 1318 until his death at the age of 56 in September 1321.

The poems and prose of the *Vita nuova* (1292–3), celebrating his youthful love for Beatrice, are studiously vague and dream-like about himself, his fellow citizens and his city. But once he had gone into exile, and "saw his native land only in his dreams," Florence came to obsess his memory and imagination. He began to write a poem, completed only shortly before his death, entitled simply *The Comedy of Dante Alighieri from Florence.*

Although this is a story of a journey into the other world (Hell, Purgatory and Paradise), it is dominated, paradoxically, by constant detailed reference to this one – thanks to hundreds of closely-observed similes and to reminiscences of the individual souls whom the narrator, guided by Virgil, meets as he passes through the realms of the dead.

As a result, his *Comedy* gives us vignettes of life in a late medieval Italian city-state which are as vivid as those in Ambrogio Lorenzetti's allegories of *Good and Bad Government in Siena* and, like them, depict a Heaven or Hell on earth. Nothing and no one is seen dispassionately. On the one hand Florence is the city of St John the

Lorenzetti's Good Government, above, *presents an ideal vision of a Tuscan city-state, the narrow streets filled with traders, the piazza dominated by young people dancing, as a symbol of harmony.*

Baptist, its narrow streets and encircling wall dominated by the Baptistery, its religious and civic centre, a city which Dante believed to have enjoyed a golden age of sobriety, peace and justice in the time of his great-great-grandfather Cacciaguida, before the coming of trade, wealth, immigration, envy and political turmoil. On the other, it is the strife-torn city of its first patron, the war-god, Mars; and most of the great names among the Florentines of his youth are charged with self-indulgence, violence, sexual depravity, corruption and treachery.

During the first months of his banishment Dante remained in Tuscany, hoping to return with his fellow-exiles by force of arms. Then he "became a party by himself" and travelled to "almost every part where this language extends." In these years he acquired his astonishing familiarity with the dialects of Italy, and set himself the task (in his *De vulgari eloquentia* of c.1304) of defining a supra-regional language in which to write the *Comedy*. There are countless allusions to the cities and regions of central and northern Italy in his poem. Some are invectives against misrule and discord (the Montagues and Capulets in Verona were already proverbial for their feuds). Some add little to what you might find in a gazetteer; but at their best they have the power to evoke, for example, a vast expanse of plain, river and sea, together with the passionate longing of the damned for the earth where they had known happiness, as in the opening words of Francesca: "The city where I was born lies on the shore where the Po descends with his followers to find peace."

Between 1308 and 1313 Dante's hopes of return to Florence were revived by the election of the Count of Luxembourg as the Holy Roman Emperor Henry VII.

The detail of a medieval fresco, above, shows how in Dante's time the densely-populated city of Florence was dominated by church towers, imposing palazzi and, above all, the Baptistery in the centre.

Aligning himself with the Ghibellines (the imperial party), this former Guelph (Florence traditionally supported the Papacy) wrote passionate open letters to the Cardinals and Florentines urging them to accept Henry. His euphoria following the Emperor's coronation in Milan (1311) was soon extinguished by military defeats and Henry's death in 1313. But the experience led Dante to lift his sights yet again, and to embrace imaginatively not just Tuscany or Italy, but Europe, the whole inhabitable world and the whole of mankind.

The *Comedy* repeatedly condemns the Popes of his day for their involvement in politics and pretensions to supreme temporal power. A critique of recent European rulers (not forgetting Henry III in England and Ottocar IV

in Bohemia) is matched by celebration of some of the Nine Worthies of the past, including Judas Maccabeus and Charlemagne. Dante's *Monarchia* (c.1313-18) argues that God intended there to be one supreme ruler, a "mon-arch" (the Emperor, not the Pope) and draws on Virgil's *Aeneid* to celebrate the conquests of the Roman people which culminated in the reign of Augustus who brought peace to the whole world in preparation for the birth of the Saviour. In Dante's ideal vision, Rome was meant to be the seat of both God's "Vicars" on earth. In *Questio de situ aque et terre* (1320), Dante went on to investigate the distribution of land and sea over the surface of the globe – taking data from the *Bible*, ancient geographers and the contemporary *Mappae mundi* and making them the basis of some of his most daring fictions.

In Dante's view, the globe we live on is at the centre of a spherical universe, and has a circumference of 20,400 miles. All the "dry land that appeared above the waters" (cf *Genesis 1: 9–10*) is found in the Northern hemisphere. This Pangeia (as modern earth scientists call it) extends through 180 degrees of longtitude from Cadiz in the West to the mouth of the Ganges in the East. The most favoured of its seven "habitable climes" lies on the shores of the sea in the "middle of the earth," the "Mediterranean," thought to extend through fully ninety degrees of longitude (a monumental error). In the very middle of the "dry land" (*in medio terrae*, as the *Bible* says) lies Jerusalem, site of the Crucifixion, the redemptive sacrifice at the centre of human history.

Such are the accepted "facts" onto which Dante will graft his poetic fictions. In the *Comedy* he makes the Fall of Lucifer the cause of three cataclysmic shifts. All existing land in the southern hemisphere fled to the North; a huge volume of earth was dislodged when Satan (as we now know him) came to rest in the very centre of our globe, gouging out a vast hollow cone which would be the site of Hell; the displaced earth rushed to the surface to form an immensely high mountain island exactly at the antipodes to Jerusalem. On top of this mountain is the Garden of Eden – where Adam and Eve would be created to make good the defection of the fallen angels. In

On the Anglo-Saxon Mappa mundi, *above, east is presented at the top, Asia takes up the whole of the upper half, and the Mediterranean with its many islands separates Europe, to the left, from Africa on the right. The Pillars of Hercules are clearly indicated at the bottom.*

the fullness of time its slopes would become the place where the souls of penitent sinners are cleansed of sin (Purgatory). And at the end of the process the purified souls ascend from Eden (the "earthly" paradise) into heaven proper (the "celestial" paradise), which lies beyond the outermost of the nine concentric spheres that carry the planets and fixed stars round the Earth.

So the redemptive journey of Dante-the-Pilgrim takes him not from London to Canterbury, but down to the earth's centre, up into the southern hemisphere, all the way up the mountain of Purgatory to the Garden of Eden, thence in free space-flight into each of the ætherial spheres, and finally beyond space and time into the presence of God. For the first two parts of his *Comedy* (*Inferno* and *Purgatorio*), Dante-the-Poet prepared a detailed map which is just as meticulous as the map of the celestial bodies he took from the astronomers and used in *Paradiso*. He had become a "moral cosmographer," whose vantage point allowed him to plot both actions and places in their true relationships. So he could imagine himself looking down on earth from the outermost of the planets, seeing the whole of the landmass spread out before him from India to Spain, and reflecting that the cause of all our conflicts is no more than a patch of dry ground, "a threshing-floor which makes us so ferocious."

Six hours later, the pilgrim looked down to earth once more. Now he was over the meridian of Cadiz; to the East he could see almost as far as Jerusalem, to the West the ocean over which he could visualize the "mad crossing of Ulysses." This striking phrase is a reference back to his meeting in Hell with Ulysses' shade, who tells the story of his last voyage and death. Dante's Ulysses never returns to Ithaca. From Circe's realm, not far from Naples, he continues to sail westward till he comes to the Atlas Mountains in Morocco, known as the Pillars of Hercules, thought to have been placed there as a sign from the gods that men should venture no further. His few remaining crewmen are "old and slow," but he persuades them to set forth in quest of a "world without people, behind the sun," since they were "not made to live like brute beasts but to follow virtue and knowledge." For five months they ply their oars southwest over the Ocean, till one day they catch sight of a high mountain. But just as they are rejoicing, a whirlwind rises from the New Found Land and the ship is swallowed by the sea.

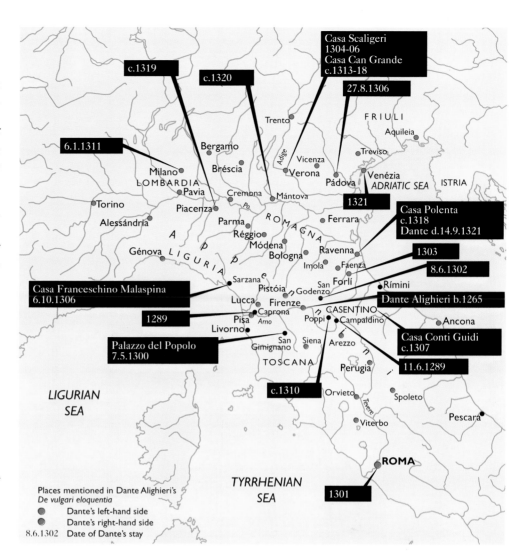

DANTE'S ITALY: *In the twenty years of his exile Dante lived in or visited many places. The dialects of the cities with coloured dots are discussed in his* De vulgari eloquentia, *which shows he was aware of the generic differences caused by the watershed of the Appennines.*

Dante makes it clear later that they had travelled 5,100 miles and had come within sight of Purgatory, which is indeed the place where men will finally gain "virtue and knowledge." But this is a voyage without divine sanction, and in any case premature. Ulysses consciously neglects his duty to society. He thinks knowledge lies in the accumulation of sense-data, and sets out at a time of life when Dante thought men should "lower the sails of their activities in this world." Within the moral co-ordinates Dante uses to draw a map of our relationship with God (for our final "haven" is "Heaven"), Ulysses stands convicted on at least five counts. But most readers fail to grasp why Dante should consign to Hell a figure with whom he felt such deep affinity. Dante's "mad flight" of invention ("folle volo" is Ulysses' own phrase) shows at once his unique grasp of the integrated cosmology, moral philosophy and religious faith of his own age, and a prophetic insight into their disintegration in the age to come.

[15]

CHAUCER'S ENGLAND

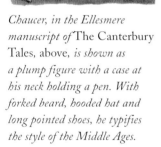

It's in April, when the showers are sweet, that people go on pilgrimages. Then "palmers long to seek the stranger lands/And specially, from every shire's end/In England, down to Canterbury they wend." The writer who tells us this (in Neville Coghill's modern adaptation) is Geoffrey Chaucer (1340–1400), England's first major poet, in his "Prologue" to *The Canterbury Tales*. Set down in the 1390s, the tales constitute 24 wonderful stories supposedly recounted by a band of chattering pilgrims as they travel down from London to the Thomas-à-Becket shrine at Canterbury. The result was one of the most important poems ever written in English – not only because of its poetic art, which is great, but because it gives us an incomparable portrait of medieval society.

Chaucer, in the Ellesmere manuscript of The Canterbury Tales, above, *is shown as a plump figure with a case at his neck holding a pen. With forked beard, hooded hat and long pointed shoes, he typifies the style of the Middle Ages.*

Chaucer was well placed to understand his England and exploit its living language. Son of an influential vintner, the young Chaucer became a page at the court of King Edward III. He married one of the Queen's attendants, related to John O'Gaunt, and went on a campaign to France, where he was captured and ransomed. Several diplomatic missions to Spain, France and Italy followed. On one of these journeys, to Genoa, Pisa and Florence, he is reputed to have met two of the greatest Italian writers of the day, Boccaccio and Petrarch. In post-Norman times, Chaucer spoke French, and knew French courtly love poetry (he made a noted translation of *The Romance of the Rose*). But when he wrote his own poetry, he chose the English of the London he lived in. The first great poet to use post-Norman English as a poetic language, he took the stories he told from the literature of the age, and from the Classics.

Chaucer's medieval London was a dense and crowded city. Some 40,000 people lived inside the square mile of its city walls. Just after Chaucer's birth it was swept by the Black Death of 1348–9; in 1381 it was faced with the Wat Tyler Rebellion. Its port was busy, its streets full, severed heads of criminals and traitors stood on pikes on London Bridge. The only river crossing, the bridge's 19 arches were covered with fine stone houses, merchants' shops and a chapel devoted to the English martyr Saint Thomas-à-Becket.

It's not far across London Bridge, at the Tabard Inn in Southwark, just south of the river, that Chaucer has his pilgrims gather one April day. In the poem, he claims to have met them just as they set out: "nine and twenty in a company/Of sundry folk happening then to fall/In fellowship, and they were pilgrims all." Pilgrimage was an ideal literary device for Chaucer, letting him construct a gallery of some of the most interesting and exotic types from the English life of the day. It also provided (as the Florence plague had for Boccaccio in *The Decameron*, 1348–58) a perfect framework for the telling of a great variety of stories. Different pilgrims are given tales to tell, in this style or that, epic or comic, devout or vulgar, British or European, creating a fund of narrative that also weaves itself into being something like an epic of medieval life.

Although the stories stand as self-contained tales, the pilgrimage device is crucial.

Dominated by the Tower of London, the medieval panel, left, shows the capital Chaucer knew so well. He first lived in Aldgate, then moved to Greenwich, along the Thames, and finally had a house in the garden of the Lady Chapel of Westminster Abbey. He enjoyed the patronage of three kings in his lifetime, Edward III, Richard II and Henry IV.

Thomas-à-Becket (1118-70) became Archbishop of Canterbury in 1162, and challenged Henry II over his subordination to the state. The illustration, left, from a Latin manuscript shows the "turbulent priest" being murdered by four of the King's Knights on 29 December, 1170 – to become England's greatest Saint.

Chaucer's Tabard Inn, depicted in the engraving below, was probably destroyed by fire in around 1676. The Talbot, a later inn on the same site, was also demolished – in 1875.

Pilgrimages were central to medieval life. A mixture of adventure and religious observance, a kind of domestic crusade, the pilgrimage had fixed routes, fixed devotions, fixed penances and fixed rewards in heaven. By following the rituals, and obtaining the indulgences, sins and crimes were purged, illnesses cured, miracles produced and souls saved for eternity. The journey was difficult and long, but there were various ways of relieving the hardship, and telling stories was one.

The Canterbury Pilgrimage was also one of the great trails of Christendom. It stood next in importance to the pilgrimages to the Holy Land, Rome and Santiago de Compostella in Spain. It displayed the significance of Saint Thomas-à-Becket, former Archbishop of Canterbury, murdered by four knights on the altar of his own cathedral in 1170 at the King's instigation. The tale has been told and retold, its modern version being T.S. Eliot's poetic drama, *Murder in the Cathedral* (1935). As they should, many miracles followed Becket's death. Within two years he was canonized a saint. The shrine with his martyred corpse was placed in Canterbury Cathedral in 1220. Thereafter vast numbers of pilgrims – kings and princes, commoners and criminals – made their way there, on penances voluntary or obligatory, from various starting points, but above all from London.

Over the years the journey, as Chaucer shows, had acquired a spirit of jollity. Pilgrims were supposed to walk on foot, abase themselves, beg food and shelter on the way. In Chaucer's 17,000-line narrative the pilgrims make

a gayer journey of it: they ride on horseback, stop at inns, and indulge themselves in various ways, all under the encouragement of their ever cheerful host, Harry Bailly, from the Tabard Inn. Some are old, experienced pilgrimage hands. There's a "perfect gentle Knight," whose son is his squire, and who has been on Crusades to the Holy Land to fight the "infidel." The shifty Pardoner, who carries a bag of dubious relics and trades in indulgences, has been to Rome. But tourist among tourists is the notorious, cheerful, much-married Wife of Bath, who has made all the pilgrim journeys. She has "thrice been to Jerusalem," and has visited Rome, Cologne (going to the shrine of the Magi), as well as Santiago de Compostella.

Telling stories to cheer themselves on their way, Chaucer's pilgrims cross medieval Kent on what would have been a three or four day journey. They would go down the main Dover Road that links England with the coast and the further

The Wife of Bath, right, in an illustration from the Ellesmere manuscript, is Chaucer's greatest comic character. As John Dryden later said of the pilgrims, they are important as "their general characters are still remaining in mankind, and even in England, though they are called by other names...."

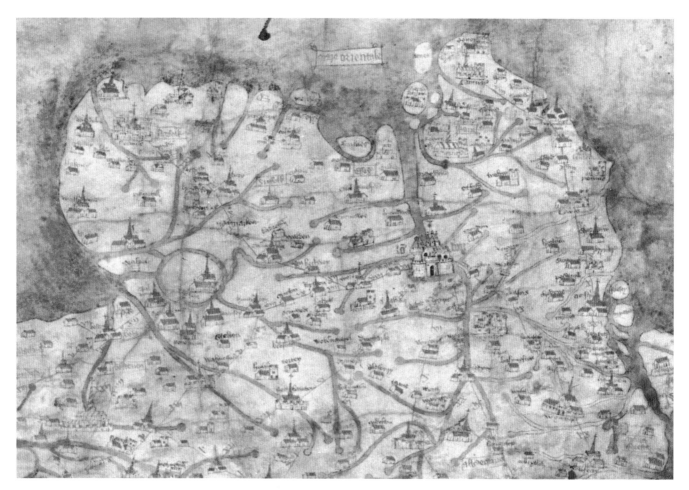

CHAUCER'S PILGRIM ROUTE: *There were two main pilgrim routes to Canterbury in Chaucer's day. The journey Chaucer's own pilgrims took from London* (below) *followed the old Roman Way* (*Watling Street*) *down to Canterbury and the Kent Coast. The alternative route was from Winchester, the site of the older shrine of St Swithin, across southern England. The section of the medieval Gough map above covers the area of Kent through which the pilgrims would have travelled, and reveals how differently these contours were perceived from today.*

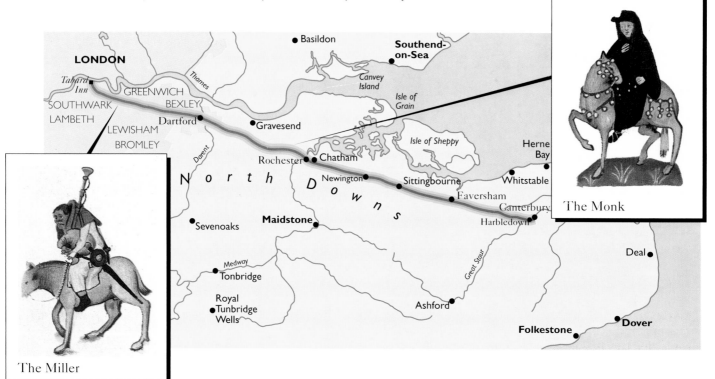

kingdom of France. Going from South-wark down the Old Kent Road, they'd cross Blackheath and look down on the port at Greenwich (where, Chaucer tells us, the women were shrews). Further on they would find many inns and travellers, although they would also be faced with danger from highway robbers. They would stay overnight at Dartford, then go to Rochester, where another British writer of social abundance, Charles Dickens, would spend part of his youth. Dominated by its cathedral and Norman keep, Rochester was the place where a great bridge crossed the Medway. Perhaps there was one more night stop at Faversham, where the prosperous monastery greatly benefited from the pilgrimage.

Although Chaucer's Pilgrims enjoy themselves telling tales on the way, medieval pilgrimage was a serious business. Pilgrims travelled to purge their sins, express their thanks to God, or seek health, as Chaucer tells us:
"from every shires ende
Of Engelond, to Caunterbury they wende,
The holy blisful martir for to seke,
That hem hath holpen, whan that they were seke."

Chaucer never completed his tale, told all his stories, got his pilgrims to the shrine, nor brought them back home. The last place he mentions is the village of Harbledown, tantalizingly close to Canterbury, where his pilgrims get their first view of the vast cathedral dominated by a gilded statue of the Archangel Michael. A later, anonymous poet added the *Tale of Beryn*, suggesting what might have happened next. Chaucer's band would ride into Canterbury through its new West Gate (still there), and stay at the pilgrim inn, the Chequer of Hope, beside the cathedral (the Inn has gone, but the site remains). In the cathedral they would find the shrine of Saint Thomas decked with wealthy gifts, and be offered a piece of his skull to kiss. (This place of miracles, where sins were purged and the sick were healed, was later removed by Henry VIII in his own battle with the church.) The pilgrims would perform their devotions, seek indulgences, then, like any modern tourist, buy pardons and pilgrim badges to take home as proof of where they'd been.

As other later writers like John Bunyan in his *Pilgrim's Progress* (1684) showed, a pilgrimage was not simply a journey but a parable or allegory of human life itself. For Chaucer, it was rather a parable of society and the times. His pilgrims – men and women, soldiers and civilians, clerics and layfolk – are general representatives of their age.

We see men of rank (the Knight), and working people like the Merchant, Miller, Shipman and Cook. We see representatives of the law, and above all of the pervasive church: the prim Prioress and her Nun, the Pardoner, the Summoner, the poor Oxford Clerk. And as for the 24 tales they tell (some unfinished), these emerge naturally from their characters, but also come from the literature and folklore of Europe, and an age of poetic discovery also represented by Petrarch, Dante and Boccaccio, all of whom Chaucer echoes. *The Canterbury Tales* is an honest record of real lives and experiences, a rich anthology and sourcebook of literature. And as critics have noted, it's distinguished by Chaucer's "humanity" – his humour and fascination with ordinary people and common things.

Chaucer's ambitious narrative was far from complete when he died in 1400. The pilgrims never reach their journey's end; some tell no tale at all. Still, *The Canterbury Tales* has been seen to mark the start of true English literature, the first national epic. Chaucer was buried in Westminster Abbey, in Saint Benet's Chapel which became Poet's Corner, now itself a place of literary pilgrimage. Traces of Chaucer's journey are to be found in Southwark and along the "Pilgrim Way" to Canterbury itself. Chaucer's influence, his comic love of place and character, can be seen in English writing ever since.

THE WORKING LIFE OF GEOFFREY CHAUCER

1357	*Page at court to Elizabeth, Countess of Ulster*
1359	*Squire (apprentice knight) serving in France with Edward III. Prisoner in the Ardennes*
1367	*In the King's service as yeoman, valet and a diplomat*
1374–86	*Controller of the Wool Custom in London*
1385	*Justice of the Peace in Kent*
1386	*Enters parliament as Knight of the Shire of Kent*
1389	*Royal Clerk of Works under Richard II*
1391	*Forester in the King's forest at Petherton, Somerset*

SHAKESPEARE'S STRATFORD AND LONDON

I used to live just outside Stratford-Upon-Avon in Clifford Chambers, a tiny hamlet where reputedly the poet and dramatist Ben Jonson once lived – or was it the poet Michael Drayton? Maybe they just frequented the hostelry there. Across the fields it is a twenty-minute walk to Stratford, part bridle-path, part field-way, the earth and stones trodden into a track by centuries of informal passage. At night, with the sheep dim silhouettes in the mist rising from the river, it was easy to imagine Shakespeare (1564–1616) himself stumbling home from a convivial evening with Ben, breathing in the night vapours, to die of a chill – an ague – on the very day 52 years later that he had been born. The story of his death is probably apocryphal. But it is in the nature of Shakespeare's life – its mystery and its symmetry – that probability should grow so effortlessly from possibility.

Heminges and Condell's First Folio of Shakespeare's collected works, the frontispiece of which is shown above, *first appeared in 1623, and was reprinted three times in the seventeenth century.*

Shakespeare began his life in Stratford-Upon-Avon, Warwickshire, and he ended it there. That at least we know. He was baptized on 25 April, 1564, in Holy Trinity Church, and buried there on 25 April, 1616. The church still stands: not too big, not too small, sweetly proportioned to its place by the river Avon, and like most English churches fairer without than within. Did Shakespeare go there often? It's difficult to say. His plays are witness both to a careful Christianity and a passionate Existentialism. In later life, prior to her marrying the strictly Protestant Dr John Hall, his first daughter Susanna is cited as absent from church at Easter – a criminal offence at the time. Like father, like daughter? On her gravestone, it says she was "witty above her sex," and attributes that quality to her father. Perhaps she shared his ambiguity too.

Shakespeare's birthplace in Henley Street, Stratford, depicted in the engraving right, *still exists. Once the house of a wealthy man, the farmer and glover John Shakespeare, it is large for the time, two houses in fact, growing naturally from the rich earth in which they were set.*

For the rest of the community, the church was the natural centre – the place to meet, mourn or celebrate, the house of its identity. Shakespeare's Stratford was a prosperous Midlands market town, already well established by his day. The people were mainly of peasant stock, risen to yeoman and aspiring to Master. "Whosoever studieth the laws of the realm, who studieth in the universities, who professeth liberal sciences, and to be short, who can live idly and without manual labour, and who will bear the port, charge and countenance of a gentleman, he shall be called Master," wrote Sir Thomas Smith in 1588. Their concerns are somewhat unimaginatively defined by the street names: Sheep Street, Bull Lane, Swine Street, Bridge Street, Church Street. But there was a Grammar School, and education was the key to a new middle class, which, if not educated itself, was determined that its children should be. Protestantism might provide a work ethic, later a political purpose, but education encouraged aspiration and escape. This is the Stratford where William Shakespeare seems to have spent his early years.

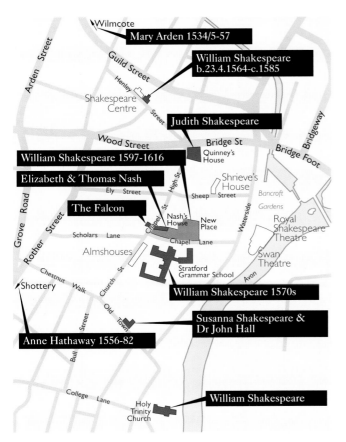

Mary Arden 1534/5-57
Wilmcote

William Shakespeare
b.23.4.1564-c.1585

Judith Shakespeare

William Shakespeare 1597-1616

Elizabeth & Thomas Nash

The Falcon

William Shakespeare 1570s

Susanna Shakespeare &
Dr John Hall

Anne Hathaway 1556-82

William Shakespeare

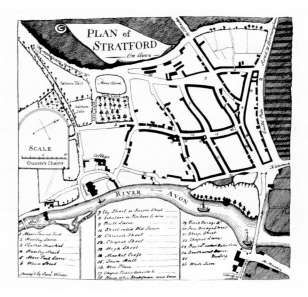

SHAKESPEARE'S STRATFORD: *Shakespeare spent his first twenty years almost entirely in Stratford. He went to the Grammar School (the King's New School) in Church Street, married there, probably at the Holy Trinity, and later moved to New Place – all of which can be visited today. Samuel Winter's seventeenth century map of Stratford, above, very little changed from Shakespeare's time, shows how the town was then just a clearing in the forest.*

Shakespeare went to the Grammar School (the King's New School) in Church Street, where he would have learned reading, writing, arithmetic and enough Latin to have been "in his younger yeares a Schoolmaster in the Countrey." He married in Stratford – Anne Hathaway, a farmer's daughter – and his children were born in Stratford. A fine house on the corner of Chapel Street and Chapel Lane, New Place, later became his home.

But for the first twenty years we can only guess at what his life may have been, or what influence Stratford itself had on him. Certainly nature was very close. The town looked, and must have felt, like a clearing in a forest: the Forest of Arden. The houses would have reflected the countryside in their construction and colour. Wooden frames, exposed beams, wattle and daub, flagstones, reeds on the roofs and rushes on the floors. And colour. Not the black and white of today, but ochre, pink and blue: soft hues in harmony with the soft light.

Places don't make plays; people do. And Stratford must have seen many of the people who subsequently enrich the plays. Shakespeare's characters are just too detailed, too eccentric – sometimes

Anne Hathaway's cottage, right, *in Shottery, just a mile or so outside of Stratford, can be visited today.*

too improbable – to have been purely inventions: Petey, Davey, Justice Shallow (from neighbouring Charlecote, perhaps), Silence, Audrey, the Young Shepherd, Baptista, Sly, Costard, Holofernes, Dull, Dogberry – the list is endless. Shakespeare's Comedies are a teeming tapestry of English country life; but it is probably *The Merry Wives of Windsor* (1602) which most closely chronicles life in Stratford. Master Ford and Master Page represent the class Shakespeare himself aspired to: wealthy, landowning, professional. The Comedy has a happy ending, but the darker overtones of Halloween suggest a community still in touch with a pagan past. To this day dolls may be found up trees on nearby Dover's Hill; and although the community in *The Merry Wives of Windsor* celebrates its energy through fun and practical jokes, these same people would, only a few years later, cut off the King's head, and establish a Commonwealth.

Perhaps the influence of Warwickshire on Shakespeare is subtler still. I remember sitting on the steps of the Arden Hotel one morning with Karolos Koun, the great Athenian director who had come to Stratford to direct *Romeo and Juliet*. It was very early, the day's traffic not yet begun, and we looked out at the sun rising, Holy Trinity, the river with its willows, the countryside beyond. "You see you can only do Shakespeare in England," he mused, "You need this light, the low hills, the grey, the green – the nature that bred him. We cannot do Shakespeare in Greece. Our shadows are too black, our light is too white...." "Does that mean," I asked tentatively "that therefore we cannot do Greek tragedy in England?" He left the question unanswered.

The Elizabethans had their feet in the mud, their eyes on the stars and a joke on their lips. Shakespeare, the supreme Elizabethan, grew up in the mud and reality of Stratford, jokes were everywhere. But for the stars – the intellectual intoxication of curiosity and debate, aspiration and vision, philosophy, politics, the court, danger, excitement – for these he had to go to London. And he did. Though we don't know quite when.

Late sixteenth century London was in full turbulent growth. Together with Naples and Paris, it was already one of the three great cities of Europe, and with a rising population of 300,000 (about a tenth of the nation) soon to be the largest. Above all, London was the political and commercial centre of a country unifying under Elizabeth I all levels of society within a shared view of nationhood. It was Shakespeare's genius to provide this new nation with a new language through his plays. He reinvented the prose he used and refined the existing verse into the most flexible dramatic poetry the world has ever known.

London was a city of ideas, Shakespeare its great communicator. By 1592 he was established in London as an actor and playwright, so he must have been there earlier, probably from about 1590. How he got there we don't know. Nor what he did from his last recorded presence in Stratford, at the christening of his twins Judith and Hamnet in 1585. Travelling theatre companies passed through Stratford: Leicester's Men in 1586, the Queen's Men in 1587. He may have followed them. We know that *Henry VI, Part I* and *Titus Andronicus* were premièred in 1592, probably at the newly refurbished Rose Theatre, and Shakespeare belonged variously to Pembroke's Men, the

The Globe theatre, right, opened in 1599 with Shakespeare's Henry V, *and was burned down in 1613 during a production of* Henry VIII.

Admiral's Men, Sussex's Men, Strange's Men. In 1592 plague closed the theatres for two years, and again we lose sight of Shakespeare until 1594, when he re-emerges as a principal figure in the newly formed Chamberlain's Men. Did he go on tour for two years? Did he leave the theatre? Speculation links him with the Earl of Southampton, to whom he dedicated the narrative poems *Venus and Adonis* (1593) and *The Rape of Lucrece* (1594). Shakespeare by this time was not only an established playwright but also a serious poet and an actor: "a handsome well shap't man – very good company, and of a very readie and pleasant smooth Witt." It has always seemed to me entirely possible that early in his life he had to make a career choice – whether to become a serious writer/entertainer to the aristocracy, like Berowne in *Love's Labours Lost* (c.1595), or pursue the precarious rough-and-tumble of the public theatre. The theatre won. It was after all the new debating chamber for a new era, and booming. There, eventually, he learned to combine the exquisite poetry of *Richard II* (c.1595) with the ruder show-biz of *Richard III* (c.1595).

From 1594 we can track Shakespeare's theatres across London more easily than we can his lodgings. The Chamberlain's Men – for whom he wrote for the rest of his life – played first at The Theatre in Shoreditch. A roughly cylindrical building of three storeys with a thrust stage, it was built in 1576 by James Burbage (father of actor Richard), closed in 1597, and dismantled in 1598 to provide materials for the new Globe. In between came The Swan, but probably only for a season. These were open-air theatres, subject to wind and weather, and suitable only for short summer seasons. As soon as he could, and before the Globe burned down in 1613, Shakespeare had moved to the Blackfriars, an indoor theatre that premièred his Last Plays and probably revived some of the others.

Shakespeare appears to have lived close to his theatres. In 1596 he was assessed for taxes in Bishopsgate; later that year he moved to the southern suburbs. By 1600 he was in Southwark, close to the Globe in a neighbourhood called the Clink; and by 1604 he is recorded as a tenant of Christopher Mountjoy in Cripplegate. He probably returned to Stratford in 1610, but

in 1613 he bought the Blackfriars Gatehouse in London as a real-estate investment. So much – so little. And none of it of as great import as the taverns like the Mermaid where he thrashed out ideas with the greatest writers and thinkers of the time.

The London influence on Shakespeare's plays is obvious, particularly on the History Plays. Eastcheap existed, so too did a Boar's Head, and characters like Pistol, Bardolph, Quickly must have been there. The Court clearly lived cheek by jowl with the populace, and foreign observers comment, astounded, on the singularity of the English, calling England, among other things, "the Paradise of married women." It was a place where hair varied from long to short, punk to shaven, and beards and moustaches flourished in every shape and style – or not at all. Paul Hentzner, writing in 1598, talks of the English as "lovers of show...vastly fond of great noises...such as the firing of cannon, drums and the ringing of bells...." They are reproved for liking bright colours, getting drunk, and crying too easily. An optimistic, confident, exuberant people, they are in all the plays, even the darker "city" plays that characterize the more cynical age of King James 1 – *Measure for Measure* (1604), *All's Well That Ends Well* (1602–4), *Coriolanus* (1607–9). And, as Charlecote could become Illyria, so too could London be Venice or Vienna.

It was probably the Thames that counted for most in Shakespeare's development. Indeed it may have been the route of his five-year "disappearance." With Hawkins' new ships and Elizabeth's new policies, England rapidly became a nation of pirates. Down the river went the merchantmen and privateers, back came the booty of five continents. Not just tangibles like gold and silver, tobacco, but ideas, visions, stories, the Petrarchan sonnet, Neo-

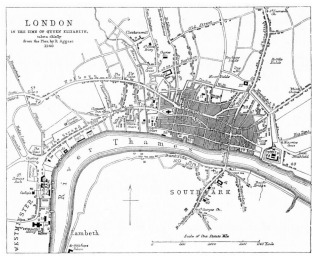

In sixteenth century London (shown in the 1560 map of London bottom), *suburbs were spreading out from the walled city to absorb the villages which give London to this day its unique quality of "agglomeration." For Shakespeare, the city still had a country feeling as he walked across the fields to Westminster Abbey, or rowed across the Thames to the Globe theatre – a feeling captured in Visscher's 1619 view of London,* top.

Platonism, alchemy, spies. It was Shakespeare's triumph to transform what he saw and heard into that passionate association of thought and feeling we call his plays. His life, what we know of it, was relatively simple. He lived, died and wrote in Stratford. He earned his living in London. His good fortune, and ours, was that his genius had all the inspiration of the English Renaissance behind it: the intoxication of Elizabethan London, and the nourishment of heartland Warwickshire. He was shaped by his time – and, in writing, shaped Time itself.

MONTAIGNE'S FRANCE

According to an inscription we can still read in his château at Montaigne near Bordeaux, Michel Eyquem de Montaigne (1533–92) retired from public service in 1571 to dedicate himself to a life of study. Retirement proved far from complete, but he was able to spend much of the next 21 years devoting himself to the kind of self-study and self-discovery which forms the basis for his *Essays*, published in various editions between 1580 and (posthumously) 1595. The title ("Try-outs") is deliberately modest. But the author was only too aware that he had created a new literary genre and that his decision to base his study of himself on a broader study of man was completely original: "Authors communicate themselves to the public by some peculiar mark foreign to themselves; I am the first to do so by my universal being, as Michel de Montaigne."

Montaigne, above, is an ideal guide to France during the Renaissance – a period of rapid and often violent change which saw the transition from medieval to more modern world-views.

One of Michel Eyquem de Montaigne's greatest discoveries was that, in the same way he could study himself in other men, others could see themselves reflected in him. As twentieth century British novelist Virginia Woolf would put it, people "standing before that picture gazing into its depths" see "their own faces reflected in it." It is not surprising, therefore, that Montaigne played a central role in the French tradition, attracting the attention of writers as different as Pascal, Descartes, Flaubert and Gide. He stands at the junction between the Ancient World and the Modern – simultaneously looking back at the Greek and Roman historians and philosophers who so fascinated him, and prefiguring literary and philosophical developments that still preoccupy us today.

A visitor to Montaigne's château will find the library much as he describes it (without, alas, the books): "It is on the third storey of a tower. The first contains my chapel; the second a bed-chamber with a dressing-room.... My library is round in shape, squared off only for the needs of my table and chair and, as it curves round, it offers me a single glance at all my books." The inscription in the adjoining room shows his decision to devote himself to study was in part a compensation for the death of his friend

Etienne de la Boétie (1530–63). Like Montaigne, la Boétie was an eminent member of the law courts at Bordeaux, though probably far happier in the role: his discourse *On Voluntary Servitude* (1574) indicates a willingness to deal directly with the political issues of the day. His house in the centre of Sarlat with its richly carved façade shows a man happy to flaunt his influence and social status. Montaigne preferred his secluded library in a secluded château. The beams are inscribed with a rich collection of maxims showing a deep-rooted scepticism tinged with pessimism: "For I see that all of us, however great we are, are but ghosts or insubstantial shadows." (Sophocles).

This might reinforce the view that Montaigne's reasons for taking up the pen resembled those of other noblemen in the region of Bordeaux and the Dordogne. Pierre Brantôme (1540–1614) wrote of great captains, and retold anecdotes of the women of the French court, to compensate for the fact that a riding accident had put a premature end to his career. Monluc, based in Agen, wrote his memoirs because he felt that his services to the crown had not been adequately recognized. Montaigne's retirement from the courts of Paris and Rouen into "the bosom of the learned virgins" (the Muses) was inspired by more philosophic reasons, and would never be as complete as he thought. He had still to become Mayor of Bordeaux in 1581–85; more importantly, his staunch loyalism, calm common sense and shrewd diplomatic skills made him an important

The first edition of Montaigne's Essays, *the frontispiece of which is shown left, was published in 1580.*

emissary during top-level negotiations between Henry III and Henry of Navarre.

Henry of Navarre (1553–1610) would be crowned Henry IV following the assassination of his predecessor in 1589. His accession was violently opposed by the Duke of Guise and other extremist Catholics, for he had been brought up as a Protestant. The origin of these problems went back to 1517, when Martin Luther embarked on the road that led to the split of Christendom into two opposed churches. The influence of Luther's thought is already apparent in the work of the great storyteller François Rabelais (c.1494–c.1553) (*Pantagruel*, 1532; *Gargantua*, 1534) and the poetry and short stories of Marguerite de Navarre (1492–1549) ("Mirror of the Sinful Soul," 1531; "Heptameron," posthumously, 1558). The fact that she was sister to King Francis I did not protect Marguerite from the attentions of the Sorbonne, charged with ensuring religious orthodoxy (one reason why she often found it prudent to spend time in the tiny court at Nérac, rather than in Paris). Less well-protected was Rabelais, who sometimes found his native Chinon, or Lyon where he worked as a doctor, too close to Paris, and chose to follow his patrons to Italy.

By the time Montaigne took up his pen, the situation had deteriorated. The turning point came in 1559, with the death of Henry II. His sons (one of them, Francis II, was husband to the future Mary Queen of Scots) were all young or weak kings. Two forces that conspired to increase the crisis were the existence of strong noble clans determined on a bid for power, and the growth of a much more militant, organized form of Protestantism, led by Jean Calvin (1509–64). Born in Noyon, north of Paris, Calvin was forced to flee to Geneva, where he helped train pastors who returned to spread the Word in France. Though Calvin is thought a master of French prose, Montaigne never mentions him, and displays throughout the *Essays* constant hostility toward the religion he represented, blaming it for the dismemberment of France. He was less open in his views of the various grandees exploiting the situation. But we can deduce he supported Henry of Navarre's claim on the throne, because he considered him the legitimate heir, and probably urged him to adopt the policy he chose in 1595, when he abjured Protestantism

Montaigne's château, above, near Bordeaux, remains much as it was when he was there, his presence not surprisingly felt: "I spend most days of my life there, and most of the hours of each day."

to secure his hold on the throne. Henry probably never did say "Paris is worth a mass," but Montaigne would have sympathized. He adored the capital; one of his main regrets in old age was that he would not live long enough to see the completion of the Pont Neuf. It was not finished until 1604, and now bears a statue of Henry IV. Montaigne would surely have approved; he was very proud of Navarre's two visits to his relatively humble château.

Montaigne's view of France was, however, darkened by his experience of civil war. Rabelais was able to present a comically epic picture of war, and transpose the Franco-Spanish wars to the countryside near his birthplace at La Devinière; Montaigne offers a more tragic vision, of peasants being tortured or massacred, leaving their grapes to rot on the vine, even digging their own graves. Brantôme can still praise the chivalrous deeds performed in early sixteenth century Italy; Montaigne is more concerned with the soldiers who tried to trick their way into his château, and with the Reasons of State given to justify the assassination of Henry of Guise during the Estates General at Blois in 1588. Visitors to the royal castle and the room where the deed was performed may be reminded that Montaigne was present in Blois at the time, or had only just left.

Montaigne was not the only writer whose vision was affected by the civil wars. We recall the greatest poet of the day, Pièrre de Ronsard (1524–1585), as author of delicate pastoral poems based on the countryside near his castle at La Possonnière, or as a love poet immortalizing Cassandre Salviati (*Amours*, 1552), the Marie whose name is forever associated

François Rabelais' satirical books about the giants Gargantua and Pantagruel, which appeared in his Oeuvres, above, were parodies of medieval epics.

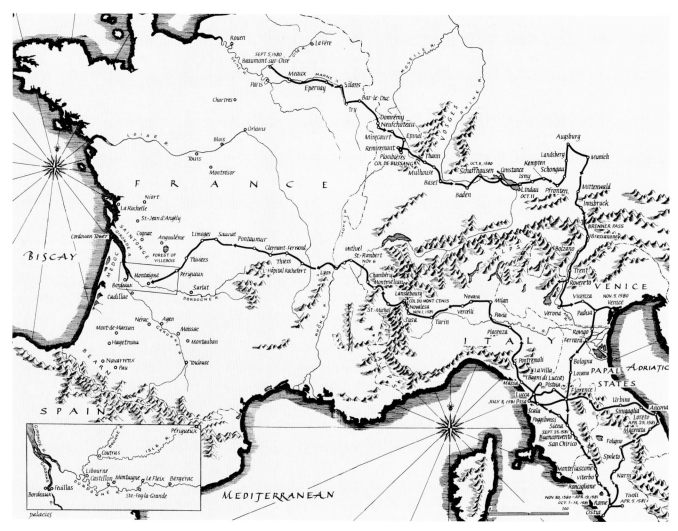

with the village of Bourgueil, or Hélène de Surgères, whose room at the top of the Louvre is the subject of the ageing poet's complaints in some of his most famous sonnets (*Sonnets For Hélène*, 1578). But he also wrote *Discourses on the Miseries of This Age* (1562), directed at the Protestants. Curiously, one of his staunchest Protestant foes, Agrippa d'Aubigné, met the object of his affections (Diane de Salviati) in the same château at Talcy where Ronsard had met Cassandre. But d'Aubigné abandoned love poetry and devoted most of his later years to recounting the story of the wars, or to mounting a bitter attack on the morals of his contemporaries (*Les Tragiques*, 1616–23).

Montaigne's dislike of the destruction he saw around him was enough to make him seek escape in Utopian dreams of purity, particularly represented by the natives of the New World. But even in the world of the Noble Savage, evil forced itself on his vision; he was convinced by the Spaniards' accounts of their conquests that they were destroying a culture much superior to their own. His interests in contemporary realities were such, in any case, that his mind kept returning to his sixteenth century

MONTAIGNE'S FRANCE: *The map shows the route of Montaigne's journey across Germany and Switzerland to Italy in 1580–81. The box shows the area around Montaigne's château. La Boétie lived at Sarlat and Monluc at Agen. North of Bordeaux is the area around Blois, where Rabelais was born at La Devinière near Chinon. Ronsard lived at La Poissonnière and du Bellay at Liré.*

France – whose vices were, he felt, greater than those being attributed to South American cannibals.

A more radical attempt to escape the conflicts of his age was his journey in 1580–81 to Italy. In one sense, his visit to Rome was a homage paid by a humanist to the city he, like his predecessors, considered as manifesting the fate of all human state-building. In another, it was a prototype of the Grand Tour in which many noblemen would indulge over the following centuries. But Montaigne was a special kind of traveller. He did not want to bring back information about the length of the Pantheon, or "the rich embroidery of Signora Livia's knickers." He wanted to know how other men's minds worked; travel became an analogue of reading. And reading was never bookish entertainment; it was conversation with other men. Recommending both travel and study for his ideal pupil, Montaigne argues: "In his commerce with men I mean him to include... those who live principally in the memory of books."

Montaigne was in Italy when he heard that, without seeking the honour, he had been elected Mayor of Bordeaux. We know he took time returning home. Was it because he no longer missed family and friends? This seems unlikely; he tells us absences made him fonder of them on his return. Was it because he welcomed freedom from the constant dangers caused by endemic civil war? Certainly. His account of the irritations of running his estate is convincing enough to show he was not inclined to follow Joachim Du Bellay (1522–60) in romanticizing from Rome the delights of home ("When, alas, will I see the smoke rising from my small village / When will I see the walls of my poor house?"). And unlike Du Bellay in his sonnet sequence *Antiquities of Rome* (1558), Montaigne seems to have felt the majesty of Rome he imagined in his reading of the classics outweighed any distress at seeing its current ruined state: "however often I revisited the tomb of that great and mighty city, I would feel wonder and awe."

We may surmise he delayed his return because he enjoyed the chance to visit the places where his favourite classical authors and the heroes of whom they spoke had lived. Again he shows an uncanny insight into modern psychology, asking: "Is it by nature or by an aberrant imagination that the sight of places which we know were frequented or lived in by people we admire moves us somewhat more than hearing an account of their deeds, or reading their writings?" Those who visit Montaigne's château today should remember that his universally admired wisdom, which so affected his age and later ones, and his sheer delight in being a living, thinking being, were virtues developed in the midst of bloody civil war, whose destructive effects disfigured the society of his age.

Following a failed political assassination in 1572, thousands of Protestants were killed in Paris and throughout France. Rather than ending the civil wars this St Bartholomew's Day massacre, depicted in the engraving above, *exacerbated hostilities.*

On Montaigne's return from his tour around Italy in 1581, he took up his new post of Mayor to the city of Bordeaux – whose gateway is depicted in the sixteenth century engraving, right.

CERVANTES' SPAIN

"In a certain place in La Mancha, whose name I prefer not to remember...." So runs the famous opening sentence of one of Europe's greatest books, *The History of the Valorous and Witty Knight-Errant Don Quixote*, by Miguel de Cervantes (1547–1616). Its first part appeared in 1605, when its author was 58, and was an amazing success, its fame spreading across Europe. When a spurious sequel appeared, Cervantes wrote a second part, completing the adventures. It appeared in 1615, a year before its author died, within days of his great contemporary, Shakespeare. In the book, Cervantes invents two of the most powerful characters in literature, Don Quixote, "the Knight of the Doleful Countenance," and Sancho Panza. The image of the tall, gaunt knight on his lean nag, the small squat squire on his donkey, both silhouetted against the Manchegan plain with the odd windmill in the distance, has become an emblem of Spain; and the book itself the first great novel.

The life of Cervantes, pictured above, mirrored the history of his nation, from her dominance as the greatest European power to the beginning of her seventeenth century decline, prefigured by the loss of the Invincible Armada in 1588.

La Mancha – the region of Spain to which the book lays claim, and whose geography it traverses – is in New Castile, southeast of Madrid, the largest stretch of dusty and these days treeless plainland in that mountainous country. Extending some 183 miles from east to west, some 114 miles from north to south, it is enclosed by chains of mountains. The most noted range is Sierra Morena, where the deluded knight retires to do amorous penance and meets many a "rare adventure." Today the two most important Manchegan towns are the provincial capitals Albacete and Cuidad Real. Cervantes ignores the first, but Sancho Panza is quick to recognize some excellent wine from the latter, while the fulling mills that so terrify him are probably nearby.

Miguel de Cervantes Saavedra led an adventurous life himself, but in a much wider world. The son of a surgeon-apothecary, he was born in Alcala de Henares, an ancient university town near Madrid, where two different birthplaces claim him. He went to Italy in 1569, then enlisted as a soldier in the army of Philip II. His finest hour was in 1571 at the Battle of Lepanto, where he took part in the victory over the Turks that secured Spain's pre-eminence in the Mediterranean. Aged 24, he served under the King's half-brother, the gallant and charismatic Don Juan de Austria, and lost the use of his left hand, gaining the nickname "The One-Handed Man of Lepanto." It was, he wrote, the "most memorable and greatest of occasions, the like of which was never seen in past centuries, nor can be hoped to be seen in those to come." The memory of this "most fortunate day" when the Mediterranean returned to Christendom is exalted in the Captive's Narrative in *Don Quixote*.

After more military operations, Cervantes was captured by Barbary pirates in 1575. Taken to Algiers as a slave, he made four attempts at escape, and was ransomed in 1580. Back in Madrid he wrote plays and a pastoral romance, *La Galatea* (1585). Plagued by poverty, he was forced to keep his family with dreary administrative posts in Madrid, Seville and Valladolid, in the service of Philip II. One involved the supply of provisions for the Invincible Armada, whose victory he prophesied, and whose defeat he lamented in verse. He applied for posts in the Indies, and was several times in prison for debt. It was probably when he was in prison in Seville that he began *Don Quixote*.

Broadly we can equate the Don's decline from sword-brandishing defender of idealistic causes to vanquished knight, bereft of arms and illusions, with Spain's own slide from a dynamic and expansionist

EL INGENIOSO HIDALGO
DON QUIXOTE
DE LA MANCHA
COMPUESTO
POR MIGUEL DE CERVÁNTES SAAVEDRA.

TERCERA EDICION
CORREGIDA
POR LA REAL ACADEMIA ESPAÑOLA.

PARTE PRIMERA.

TOMO I.

CON SUPERIOR PERMISO.
EN LA IMPRENTA DE LA ACADEMIA
POR LA VIUDA DE IBARRA, HIJOS Y COMPAÑÍA.
MADRID MDCCLXXXVII.

Cervantes' Don Quixote was originally published in Spain in 1605. The frontispiece of the third edition of the first part, revised by La Real Academia Española, is shown here.

fidei defensora to a spiritually disillusioned nation. The Don seeks to retire to the country and make his will as the nation too began to withdraw into itself. The sword was exchanged for the pen; the disenchanted mood of Philip II's later reign coincides with the "Golden Age of Spanish literature." The "Curious Discourse" the Don delivers on the time-honoured rivalry between Arms and Letters reflects the change, and *Don Quixote* itself was but one contribution to the rich cornucopia of literary works that poured from Spanish printing presses as the century turned.

This was when Lope de Vega (1562–1635), the first great Spanish dramatist, reigned supreme on the stage, producing some 1,500 dramas. Following the "picaresque" tradition founded by the anonymous *Lazarillo de Tormes* (1554), Mateo Alemán (1547–1615) wrote *Guzmán de Alfarache* (1559–1604), an international bestseller which developed the new Spanish genre with which the realities of *Don Quixote* have so much in common. The ornate sonnets of Luis de Góngora (1561–1627) from Córdoba became objects of admiration and controversy. Francisco de Quevedo (1580–1645) raised Spanish satire to heights of witty mordancy; he too wrote a picaresque novel, *La Vida del Buscón* (1626), translated as *The Rogue*. Most of these authors were graduates of the universities of Salamanca, Alcalá and Seville; Cervantes had no such education behind him, only a wealth of travel and experience.

The change is seen in the two remarkable characters Cervantes invented to carry us through his story, with its vast cross-section of contemporary life and culture. The Don, symbolizing the realm of romance and imagination, comes from the world of knight-errantry; Sancho, exemplifying the life of hard facts, from the world of picaresque. Both worlds imply that their heroes are constantly on the move, ripe for chance encounters, new adventures, meetings with strange human types. The double convention lets Cervantes present his story as a confrontation between literature and reality and create a series of unforgettable portraits comparable in

In Don Quixote *Cervantes created a rich tapestry woven from many strands – the tale of chivalry, the pastoral romance, the picaresque novel, the account of real-life adventures, captured in this sixteenth century title page illustration by Pedro de Medina.*

vividness and comic spirit only with Chaucer and Shakespeare.

Since the book appeared, innumerable scholars have tried to chart the routes taken by the Don on his three "sallies," identify the sites of his adventures, or unearth the foundations of the five inns that host his encounters. Much is surmise, but it is worth accepting their judgments to enjoy the book, or La Mancha itself, to the full. Argamasilla de Alba is considered the "certain place" where the Don lived and "did apply himself wholly to the reading of books of knighthood," and is said to be where Cervantes was imprisoned and the book conceived. The Don was knighted, it is said, at an inn some four miles away across the plain of Montiel.

On the second sally, when the Don acquires the loquacious, down-to-earth Sancho as companion, he has his most famous adventure – tilting against the windmills

Don Quixote *is the story of the little townships, villages and isolated inns of La Mancha that form the essence of Quixote's rural Spain.*

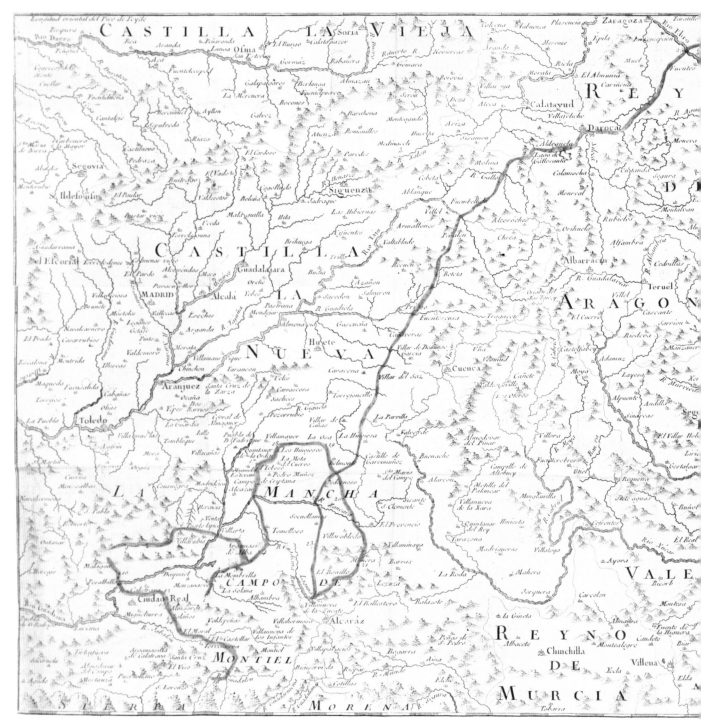

he mistakes for giants – near the picturesque village of Campo de Criptana. Now a mere handful of windmills remain, but there were 34 in 1752. Near Puerto Lápice he does "fearful battle" with the irate Biscayner, to save an "enchanted princess." A whole series of episodes is set around the little town of Malagón, including the excellent supper of goat flesh and hard Manchegan cheese, the encounter with the ruthless Yanguesian carriers, and the comic happenings at the inn the Don mistakes for a castle, which culminate in Sancho being tossed in a blanket by some "malicious and playsome" folk. Near the River Guadiana, the Don thinks he sees in a dust cloud a pagan

and a Christian army in battle. He charges forth, neglecting Sancho's warning that "those which you go to charge are but sheep and muttons." Close to the little town of Almagro the Don acquires the famous helmet of Mambrino, which Sancho observes to be "for all the world like a barber's helmet." Near Torrenueva, Quixote releases the galley slaves, and must retreat to the Sierra Morena for fear of reprisals from the Holy Brotherhood. While Sancho sets out for El Toboso, the Don does extravagant penance in the vicinity of El Viso del Marqués, until brought safely home by his friends. In the Don's third sally he and Sancho cover even more ground, travelling

MAPA DE UNA PORCION DEL
REYNO DE ESPAÑA
QUE COMPREHENDE LOS PARAGES POR DONDE ANDUVO
DON QUIXOTE,
Y LOS SITIOS DE SUS AVENTURAS

THE PICARESQUE NOVEL

picaresque (adj) *of or relating to a type of fiction in which the hero, a rogue, goes through a series of episodic adventures. Sp pícaro = a rogue*

Key picaresque works

1553	Anon *Lazarillo de Tormes*
1594	Thomas Nashe *The Unfortunate Traveller*
1599-1604	Mateo Alemán *Guzman de Alfarache*
1605	Francisco Lopez de Ubeda *La Picara Justina*
1626	Francisco de Quevedo *La Vida de Buscon*
1669	H.J.C. von Grimmelshausen *Simplicissimus*
1715	A.R. LeSage *Gil Blas*
1722	Daniel Defoe *Moll Flanders*

DON QUIXOTE'S SPAIN: *This map, reproduced from the Third Edition of Cervantes'* Don Quixote *for La Real Academia Española, is just one of the many attempts made by scholars to plot the intricate route taken by the Don on his three sallies across the rural roads of Spain.*

from Argamasilla to coastal Barcelona, and crossing large stretches of Castile, Aragón and Catalonia. The Don's new feats of chivalry start close to El Toboso, the home of his "peerless" mistress Dulcinea. Today it has a Casa de Dulcinea, housing a Don Quixote museum. The Don meets the morality players near Osa de la Vega, battles with the Knight of the Wood near Belmonte, encounters the marriage of Camacho and has "the famous adventure of the Montesinos Cave" near the Lagoons of Ruidera. In Aragón, he passes the "braying village" of La Peraleja, visits the Duke's Palace (probably in Pedrola) and reaches Sancho's ungovernable kingdom, the Isle of Barataria

(possibly suggested by the water-locked Alcalá de Ebro). He crosses the Ebro near Osera; thence to Barcelona and the fatal encounter with the Knight of the White Moon.

The interested traveller can still retrace the Don's journey, passing through a rich variety of Spanish landscapes and a series of small towns, many keeping their seventeenth century flavour. He, however, who would retrace the footsteps of the "onlie begetter" of these adventures will have to add visits to some larger cities: to Alcaá de Henares, where Cervantes was born, to Seville where he was imprisoned for debt (and where it is generally believed Don Quixote was conceived), to Valladolid, where he followed the Court, and to Madrid, scene of his earliest literary endeavours, and where he spent the last years of his life, writing the second part of *Don Quixote*. Here he died in 1616, and was buried in the Convent of the Trinitarian Nuns – in the street named, ironically, after his greatest literary rival: the Calle de Lope de Vega.

As for *Don Quixote*, it is now considered to be the first work of Modern literature, to which almost all writers have felt indebted. The Czech novelist Milan Kundera expresses its importance best: "As God slowly departed from the seat whence he had controlled the universe and its order of values, told good and evil, and given a sense to each thing, then Don Quixote came out of his mansion and was no longer able to recognize the world. In the absence of the supreme arbiter, the world suddenly appeared a fearsome ambiguity.... Thus was born the world of the Modern Era, and with it the novel – the image and model of that world – sprang to life."

THE DISCOVERY OF THE NEW WORLD:
ARCADIA AND UTOPIA

"The discovery of America and that of a passage to the East Indies by the Cape of Good Hope are the two greatest and most important events recorded in the history of man." So wrote Adam Smith in his great work of economic theory *The Wealth of Nations* – which ironically appeared in 1776 as Britain's North American colonies declared their Independence. Smith was right. Throughout the Middle Ages the European imagination grew ever more familiar with a wider world elsewhere. Thanks to crusades and seafaring exploration, the map of the earth widened, challenging the older world picture. But with the discoveries in the New World the power, prospects and wealth of European states transformed. So did their vision of the universe, and the spirit of thought and literature. Indeed it can be said these discoveries released the Renaissance imagination itself.

The New World was hardly new. Great civilizations existed on the American continent long before the Europeans came, and this encounter was fatal in their history. The New World wasn't even new in Europe. From Plato onwards the idea of a great unknown land to the west had flourished – as Atlantis, Avalon, Eldorado, Paradise Regained, the Hesperides, or else Arcadia, the unfallen world, where, perhaps, there were great cities of gold, fountains of eternal youth. Its wonders would be strange, its society new, its people different, its animals never before seen. When Columbus with the support of the "Catholic Kings," Ferdinand and Isabella of Spain, sailed west looking for a route to Cathay he believed he had found his earthly paradise. Early explorers and discoverers, from Vespucci and Magellan to Cortés and Diaz, shared these notions – even after the "new founde land" was mapped in 1507 by Martin Waldseemüller as a distinct continent named "America," and became the adventure of the day.

It's been said that America was not discovered, but invented by the European imagination. An external vision was imprinted on the continent, to be lived out by its inhabitants, its colonists and the many migrants who came over the following centuries. Of course the discoverers and conquistadores soon met with hard American facts. But

When Christopher Columbus reached the Americas he reported he'd found a New Heaven and a New Earth. The fifteenth century tapestry, above, depicts the adventurers' much celebrated journey into the unknown.

if some myths were disproved, others weren't. As Spaniards exploring or conquering the southern continent found, there really were wonders: golden cities, strange creatures, "savages" and amazing splendours of nature. There was also disease, peril, warfare and conquest for European kings. Europe was imposed on the many Americas, suppressing native accounts. It was not until 1810 in what is now Latin America that the European yoke began to be thrown off.

Meantime the galleons sailed back with plunder for European coffers: gold and silver, artefacts, even "savages" for inspection. Reports from the New World flooded home too, to spread excitement throughout Europe. They fed an American myth that fascinated the age, and survives in the "American Dream" which still draws many migrants to the continent. For Europeans, they constituted the first American literature, transforming the reach of the European imagination and influencing the work of Tasso, Ariosto, Spenser, Shakespeare, Cervantes and Camoëns.

Amerigo Vespucci's reports encouraged Sir Thomas More to invent an ideal society in his *Utopia* (1515). Sir Philip Sidney's *Arcadia* (1590), while praising Queen Elizabeth for restoring the golden age, reflects on America. The "brave new world" in Shakespeare's *The*

Christopher Columbus (1451–1506), right, landed on a Caribbean island in October 1492. Thinking he'd found the Indies, he named the natives Indians. In his three next voyages he may never have touched the shore of continental America.

The New World was named, not after Columbus, who arrived there first, but after Amerigo Vespucci, shown in the engraving, below, on the seas.

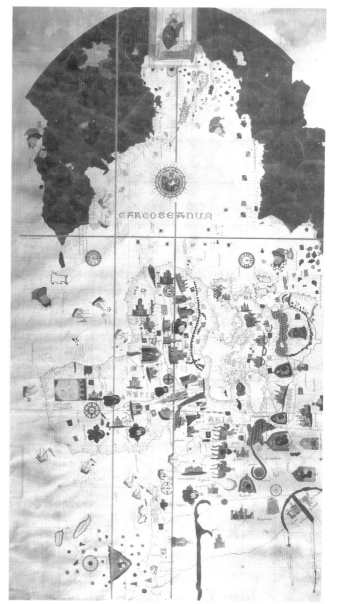

When Christopher Columbus's pilot, Juan de la Cosa, drew the first map of the emerging outlines of the New World, above, in around 1500, the shape was partly dictated by the shape of the hide on which it was drawn. However, when the map is turned on its side, the shape of the World as we know it becomes more recognizable.

Tempest (1611) refers to the first British settlement in the New World, Jamestown, Virginia, and Miranda's words reflect the Renaissance sense of wonder.

New World stories now spread through all the adventuring nations – Spain, Portugal, France, Italy, the Netherlands and Great Britain. Volumes of voyages (true or false) exist in all their literatures. In Britain, readers thrilled to Richard Hakluyt's *Principal Navigations, Voyages and Discoveries* (1589), recording voyages by the Cabots, Francis Drake, Sir Walter Raleigh and Sir Martin Frobisher. Intended to encourage exploration and colonization in North America, Hakluyt's several volumes have influenced the fantasies of many writers of the Elizabethan age and thereafter.

And every nation had a different America, depending where on the continent they landed, whether the aim was navigation or conquest, trade or plunder and whether the region was arctic or tropical, forest or desert, wilderness or settled landscape. Each took a distinct domain. Cortés took Mexico for Spain, Magellan explored the seas for Portugal, the Cabots and Verrazano sought a North-West passage for Britain and France. Each nation had its own travellers' tales. In the Southern continent were great jungles, strange tribes, ancient cities and empires. The Northern continent had its own wonders: great inland rivers and lakes, vast virgin forests, Indian tribes, the great Mississippi river, tropical Florida and, perhaps most amazing of all, the torrent of Niagara Falls.

The English came late, but by the end of the sixteenth century they too were looking for trade and plantations, or colonies. Michael Drayton's "Ode to the Virginian Voyage" (1606) celebrates "ours to hold/Virginia/Earth's onely paradise." Settled in 1607, Virginia began as a disaster, but soon became an effective colony. Captain John Smith, one of the first founders, gave a realistic account of the promise and the dangers in his *General History of Virginia* (1624). He also provided the first romantic American tale, the story of how the Indian princess Pocahontas saved him from death at the hands of her father, the chief Powhatan. England now had its first noble savage.

America soon gained its own printed literature (oral Indian legend and poetry was already abundant). In 1620 the Pilgrim Fathers settled the Plymouth Plantation and in 1630 came Massachusetts Bay, a group of religious colonies founded by English Puritans who thought they were led by "wonder-working providence" to found a new society in the new American Canaan. More British colonies developed down the eastern seaboard: Catholic Maryland (1634), Rhode Island (1636), New York (1664), Quaker Pennsylvania (1681). New England diarists like William Bradford and John Winthrop told of the founding of the "City on the Hill." They also brought with them the printing press. The book had now come to America, letting those on American soil tell their story, with the *Bay Psalm Book* (1640) often named as the first work of American literature. By contrast in Latin America most books were suppressed, the power of language remaining with Europeans and the church. Meantime the French explored the vast inner

According to John Smith's account, Pocahontas (1595–1617), above, rescued him from death by Indian hands in 1607, when she would have been about 12 years of age. She converted to Christianity, married the colonist John Rolfe and came to England in 1616, where she was presented to Queen Anne.

region from the Great Lakes down the Mississippi to the Gulf of Florida, known as New France or Louisiana. Samuel de Champlain (1567–1635) explored Nova Scotia, founded Quebec, opened the Great Lakes and recorded what he saw: remarkable nature and Indian "savages." Jesuit missionaries explored, converted and reported home in their *The Jesuit Relations and Allied Documents* (1610–1791), and Father Louis Hennepin's *Description de la Lousiane* (1683) became an international classic. This stimulated French philosophers to debate about the "noble savage" and the "social contract." Between 1550 and 1600 Spaniards came to California and Florida, and in 1609, under the Englishman Henry Hudson, the Dutch entered the Hudson Valley. All imprinted their culture, perceptions and writings on the ever opening continent.

The impact of American discoveries and the New World on literature is immeasurable. It is one of the most visible signs of travel on the human imagination. European arts and writing were transformed, and it has even been claimed that the novel, the most important modern literary genre, grew from this new age of adventuring. From this date on, America was endlessly recorded. American writers described their encounter with the so far unwritten land. Eventually they claimed cultural, finally political, independence: the British northern colonies in 1776, followed by the countries of Latin America.

There are many American literatures, some written throughout the Americas themselves, some written in Europe. Fundamental human ideas, myths and fantasies were shaped by the experience: of Arcadia and Utopia, the New Life and the American Dream, eventually some of the fundamental ideas of modernity itself, as Columbus's New World came to include skyscraper cities, space technology, and, in other parts of the continent, lost cities and tribes, which are still being explored.

The Mayflower, *left, came ashore on Cape Cod on 21 November, 1620, an event commemorated on America's Thanksgiving Day, the last Thursday in November. The boat's leader William Bradford recorded the event in* Of Plymouth Plantation.

VOYAGES OF DISCOVERY: *In the fifteenth century Britain, France, Holland, Portugal and Spain all sent people to explore the Brave New World of what is now known as America.*

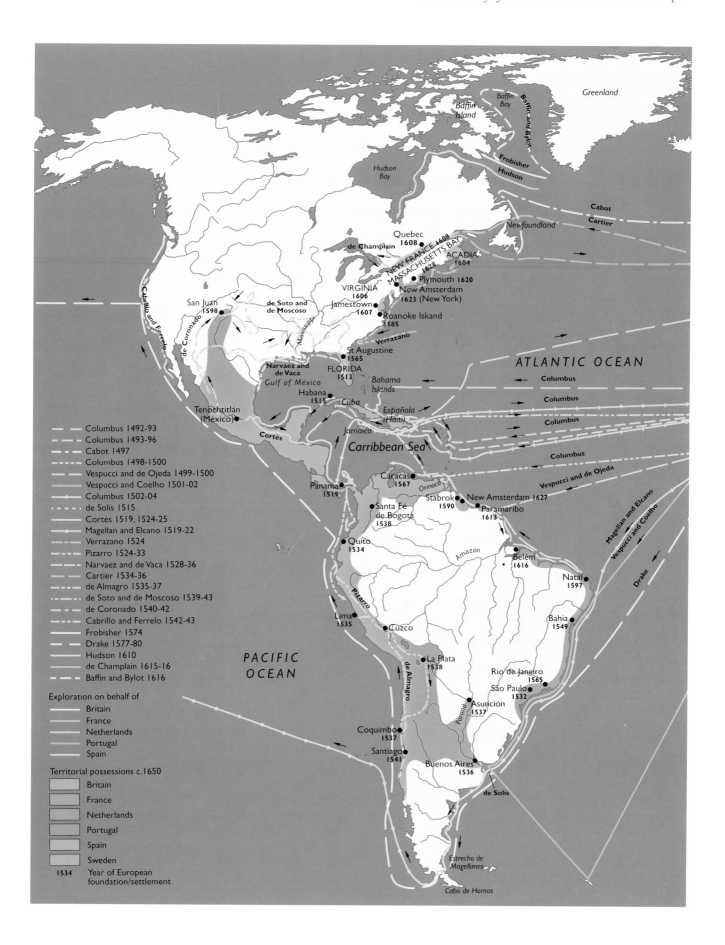

Greenland

Baffin
Island

Baffin
Bay

Baffin and Bylot

Frobisher

Hudson

Cabot

Cartier

Newfoundland

Hudson
Bay

Quebec
1608
de Champlain
NEW FRANCE 1608
MASSACHUSETTS BAY
1628
ACADIA
1604
Plymouth 1620
New Amsterdam
1623 (New York)
VIRGINIA
1606
de Soto and
de Moscoso
Jamestown
1607
Roanoke Iskand
1585
San Juan
1598
de Coronado
Verrazano
St Augustine
1565
Cabrillo and Ferrelo
ATLANTIC OCEAN
FLORIDA
1513
Bahama
Islands
Columbus
Narvaez and
de Vaca
Gulf of México
Habana
1515
Cuba
Columbus
Tenochtitlán
(México)
Española
(Haiti)
Columbus
Jamaica
Cortés
Carribean Sea
Columbus
Caracas
1567
Vespucci and de Ojeda
Panama
1519
Orinoco
Stabrok
1590
New Amsterdam 1627
Paramaribo
1613
Santa Fé
de Bogota
1538
Magellan and Elcano
Quito
1534
Amazon
Belêm
1616
Vespucci and Coelho
Natal
1597
PACIFIC
OCEAN
Pizarro
Drake
Lima
1535
Bahia
1549
Cuzco
de Almagro
La Plata
1538
Rio de Janeiro
1565
São Paulo
1532
Paraná
Asunción
1537
Coquimbo
1537
Santiago
1541
Buenos Aires
1536
de Solis
*Estrecho de
Magellanes*
Cabo de Hornos

--- Columbus 1492-93
--- Columbus 1493-96
--- Cabot 1497
--- Columbus 1498-1500
--- Vespucci and de Ojeda 1499-1500
--- Vespucci and Coelho 1501-02
--- Columbus 1502-04
--- de Solis 1515
--- Cortés 1519, 1524-25
--- Magellan and Elcano 1519-22
--- Verrazano 1524
--- Pizarro 1524-33
--- Narvaez and de Vaca 1528-36
--- Cartier 1534-36
--- de Almagro 1535-37
--- de Soto and de Moscoso 1539-43
--- de Coronado 1540-42
--- Cabrillo and Ferrelo 1542-43
--- Frobisher 1574
--- Drake 1577-80
--- Hudson 1610
--- de Champlain 1615-16
--- Baffin and Bylot 1616

Exploration on behalf of
--- Britain
--- France
--- Netherlands
--- Portugal
--- Spain

Territorial possessions c.1650
Britain
France
Netherlands
Portugal
Spain
Sweden
1534   Year of European
         foundation/settlement

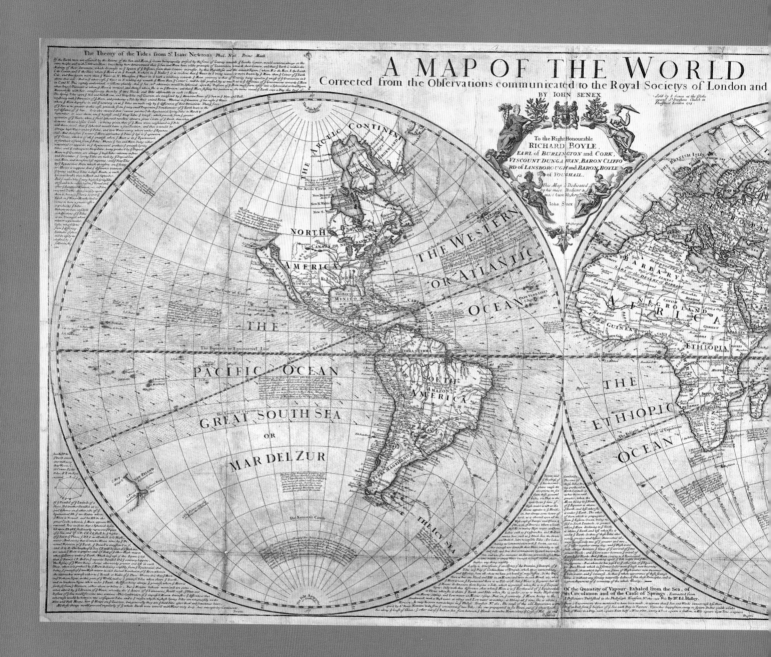

A MAP OF THE WORLD

Corrected from the Observations communicated to the Royal Societys of London and

BY IOHN SENEX

Sold by I. Senex at the Globe against St Dunstans Church in Fleetstreet London 1725.

To the Right Honourable
RICHARD BOYLE
EARL of BURLINGTON and CORK,
VISCOUNT DUNGARVAN, BARON CLIFFO
RD of LANSBOROUGH and BARON BOYLE
of YOUGHALL.

*This Map is Dedicated by his most Obedient &
Iohn Senex*

The Theory of the Tides from Sr Isaac Newton's *Phil. Nat. Princ. Math.*

THE ARCTIC CONTINENT

THE ARCTIC CIRCLE

NORTH AMERICA

THE WESTERN OR ATLANTIC OCEAN

THE PACIFIC OCEAN

THE

The Equator or Equinoctial Line

SOUTH AMERICA

GREAT SOUTH SEA

OR

MAR DEL ZUR

The Antarctic Circle

THE ICY SEA

THE BRITISH ISLES

BARBARY

AFRICA

NEGROLAND

GUINEA

ETHIOPIA

THE ETHIOPIC OCEAN

Of the Quantity of Vapour Exhaled from the Sea, of
its Circulation and of the Cause of Springs. Extracted from
a Differtation Published in the Philosoph. Tranfact. No 189. 1690 by Dr Ed. Halley.

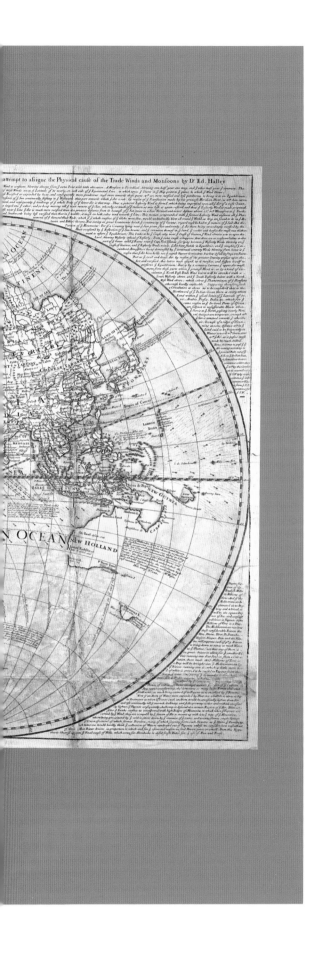

PART TWO

THE AGE OF REASON

In the eighteenth century, the texture of the Western world changed. It was an Age of Reason, and an Age of Improvement. The spread of discovery and the map of experience widened: Captain William Dampier circumnavigated the globe as the seventeenth century closed; Captain Cook followed him with new discoveries in the Pacific a hundred years later. The universe itself was seen through new eyes, above all those of Isaac Newton: in 1687 he published his *Principia Mathematica*, and all was light. The world became an object of study and science. Men of Reason and Enlightenment sought to devise the ideal social contract. Cities grew richer on trade, and were renewed in grand and imperial classical styles – for had not the spirit of Greece and Rome revived? The medieval mists cleared, theatre flourished, books and libraries prospered, writing became both a profession and a trade. A new form, aptly called the novel, began to fascinate the growing band of readers, whose eyes now focused less on the mysterious heavens or divine intentions than on the real, empirical, wide-flung world they lived in...

John Senex's 1725 map displays the move away from Classicism to scientific discovery. Rather than filling the borders with Classical motifs, he has added scientific texts: on the left is an extract from Isaac Newton's Principia Mathematica *and on the right an extract from Edmund Halley's Accounts of the Trade Winds and Monsoons from the Royal Society's* Philosophical Transactions.

THE FRANCE OF THE ENLIGHTENMENT

France's literary Golden Age ran from roughly 1629 – the date when King Louis XIII appointed Armand Jean du Plessis, Cardinal Richelieu, as his all-powerful Minister of State – to the French Revolution 160 years later. It ended as it began: with the destruction of fortresses. The ruined medieval castles we see on hilltops across France were blown up on Richelieu's orders, to show that newly-centralized royal authority would brook no challenge from local warlords. In present-day Paris the name "Place de la Bastille" is all that remains of the hated fortress-prison the mob tore down, stone by stone, in the turbulent and bloody days leading to the execution of the last absolute ruler, Louis XVI, and the foundation of the Republic.

Between these symbolic bloody demolitions France enjoyed a century and a half of internal peace. It permitted an unparalleled flowering of literature and ideas, which duly led to the birth of modern liberal democracy – and much else. The death of Louis XIV, the Sun King, in 1715 is often thought to mark a break, dividing seventeenth century Classicism from eighteenth century Enlightenment. Yet the movements glide almost imperceptibly into each other. *Philosophes* like Voltaire, Rousseau and Diderot – who inspired Tom Paine's *Rights of Man* (1791–2) and the American Declaration of Independence – would never have written with such authority without the transformation of the French language, the refinement of forms and ideas, forged by poets and dramatists like Racine and Corneille, whose neo-classical styles were so encouraged during the Sun King's long reign.

Richelieu loved theatre as much as court intrigue. When the contemporary comedies of Pierre Corneille (1606–84), a Rouen lawyer, won the attention of the actor-tragedian Montdory, he performed his work in Paris in 1629, the year of Richelieu's ascent. The King's adviser encouraged Montdory to settle his touring company in the Marais Theatre in Paris, a former tennis court in

The appointment of Cardinal Richelieu, top, *as Minister of State heralded the beginning of the Golden Age. The plays of Corneille, who wrote during the Cardinal's reign, were performed at the Comédie Française,* bottom.

the rue Vieille du Temple. Corneille became one of five playwrights who wrote under the Cardinal's direction, and his aim was to define a new age of classical taste. In 1635, Corneille produced his controversial but great tragedy *Le Cid*, which was distinctive for its alexandrine verse and formal method. With it, he became the founder of a new "classical tragedy," often dealing with Greek or Roman themes – *Horace* (1640), *Cinna* (1641), *Andromède* (1650), *Oedipe* (1659) – which nonetheless alluded to contemporary events. Corneille's plays were written either for the Marais or the Hôtel de Bourgogne in the rue Mauconseil, two theatres that later merged to become the Comédie Française.

Over a forty-year period Corneille shaped the making of a new drama well suited to the ambitions of Richelieu. But he witnessed the arrival of powerful rivals. Jean-Baptiste Poquelin (1622–73) was born in Paris, son of a court upholsterer. Like Shakespeare, he became an actor-manager, taking the name "Molière." After touring the provinces for 13 years writing plays for his own troupe, he won Paris fame by performing Corneille's *Nicomède* before the King, following it with a farce of his own, *Le Docteur Amoureux,* in 1658. The King

gave his support, and Molière was granted the use of court theatres: the Petit-Bourbon, then the Palais-Royal, built as a private playhouse in Richelieu's palace. If Corneille was tragedy, Molière was comedy. He wrote farces for the court, social satires on the age. He was a brave man, who, in an age when people were burnt to death for disrespect to religion or authority, could lampoon religious hypocrisy (*Tartuffe*, 1664) or the social follies of the time. He transformed the art of comedy, showed the power of irony, and died in harness, playing his own imaginary invalid.

Molière agreed to stage the plays of a yet greater rival, Jean Racine (1639–99). The orphan son of a customs official from La Ferté-Milon, Racine attended the Jansenist school, Port-Royal, then resolved on a literary career in Paris. Molière offered to put on his first two tragedies at the Palais-Royal, but Racine withdrew the second, *Alexander the Great* (1665) to the Hôtel de Bourgogne. In November 1667 his great tragedy *Andromaque* was performed at the Louvre. He became the new Corneille, to the dismay of the old one. The six tragedies that followed, including *Bérénice* (1670), *Iphigénie* (1674) and *Phèdre* (1677) were acknowledged as masterpieces. He was appointed to the Academy, made Historiographer-Royal along with Boileau, and became secretary to Louis XIV, who had attained the throne in 1661.

Racine's plays pursue the ideal of classical perfection and observance of the Aristotelian unities. A play written to such rules would be perfectly proportioned, just as the buildings of Athens and Rome were imitated in the design of great palaces like Versailles, built by the Sun King between 1676 and 1708. Architecture and drama mirrored the order and certainty of the age. The speech of the plays is courtly, reflecting the royal characters. Other writers were less restricted, telling of ordinary people. Jean de la

Fontaine (1621-95), from Château-Thierry, reworked classic fables into original forms, exploring contemporary morality through animal stories (*Fables*, 1668–94).

These writers laid the ground for the eighteenth century Enlightenment. So did the great seventeenth century thinkers René Descartes and Blaise Pascal. Descartes (1596–1650) was born in La Haye, travelled extensively, and died, of the cold, at the court of Queen Kristina of Sweden. *Discourse on Method* (1637) and other works set out the Cartesian philosophy, putting humankind at the centre of the universe with the famous proof of the existence of self: *cogito ergo sum*. He was buried in Stockholm, but his body was removed to Saint Germain-des-Près. Pascal (1623–62) was born in Clermont-Ferrand, moved to Paris in 1630, and published his *Pensées* in 1669. A devout Christian, a Jansenist, he tested religious belief with his famous wager: if God does

Left to right, Denis Diderot, Jean-Jacques Rousseau and Voltaire, the philosophes, were central intellectual figures of the Enlightenment.

not exist, we lose nothing by believing in Him; if he does, we win the jackpot. A less likely precursor of the Enlightenment is Cyrano de Bergerac (1619–55), born in Paris, the famous soldier and duellist, and author of fantastic Utopias, founder of science-fiction, and popularizer of the discoveries of Copernicus and Galileo.

Their successors were the great figures of the Enlightenment. All were born before the Sun King's death in 1715. The first to fame was Montesquieu (1689–1755), a provincial noble from La Brède, near Bordeaux. His *Persian Letters* (1721) is an "as-others-see-us" satire: what his Persian visitors find in France is the triumph of a centralized royal tyranny, untrammelled by the landed interests. *The Spirit of Laws* (1748), his masterpiece, contrasts France with England and its system of checks and balances; the work influenced the new 1788 constitution of the United States. But the great *philosophes* who transformed and "enlightened" the thought of their age and mapped the learning of their time were undoubtedly Voltaire, Jean-Jacques Rousseau, and Denis Diderot.

Voltaire (François-Marie Arouet) (1694–1778), born in Paris and educated by Jesuits, displayed the problems of the age: a freethinking satirist drawn to court society, he was ever at odds with church, the regent Duke of Orléans, or the new king, Louis XV. His commentaries earned him a year in the Bastille (1717–18) and exile in England (1726), where he met the poet Alexander Pope and his circle. His *Philosophical Letters* (1734), a celebration of political, social and religious liberty, forced him into retreat at Cirey, home of his patroness the Marquise du Châtelet. In 1750 he became adviser and chamberlain to Frederick the Great of Prussia, but fell into disgrace. In 1755 he left court circles to settle at Les Délices, outside Geneva, then at Ferney, four miles away in France.

His great work is *Candide* (1759), a philosophical tale (he invented the genre), affected by the Lisbon Earthquake, which comes to the disenchanted conclusion that "we must cultivate our garden," not innocently seek to change the world. He died in Paris aged 82, following the excitement of the staging of his tragedy *Irène*. Writing a century on from Racine, who represents order and certainty, Voltaire heralds the decay of certainty, the rejection of intolerance, the dawn of modern anxiety.

Voltaire and Rousseau make a great contrast. Voltaire was patrician, rational, urbane, distinguished by wit and lucidity; Rousseau was plebian, excitable and erratic, marked by intuitive brilliance. Born in Geneva of Protestant background, Rousseau (1712–78) was orphaned early. He ran away to Turin, became a Catholic convert, and wandered through Switzerland and France. For a time he lived near Chambéry, much recalled in his *Confessions* (1765–70). He moved to Paris, collaborated (as did Voltaire) with Diderot on the great project of the *Encyclopedia*, then fell out with his fellow *philosophes*. He too had to flee from arrest after publication of his freethinking profession of faith, travelled in England, Switzerland and France, and returned at last to Paris in 1770. His greatest contribution to political theory comes in *The Social Contract* (1762), which holds that humankind only enjoyed true happiness in the pre-social state of nature, which can be recaptured only if the individual surrenders to the common good. American democracy, idealistic communism and fascism all owe debts to this influential book, as the Romantic movement owes much to his novel *Emile* (1762). He died insane in Ermenonville, and was buried beside Voltaire in the Panthéon.

Diderot (1713–84), born in Langres in Champagne, the son of a cutler, studied in Paris and became a tutor and

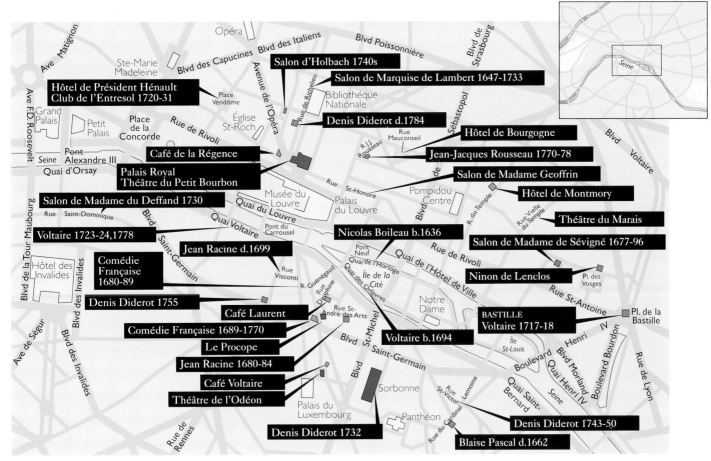

literary hack. He translated English philosophers, offered materialist reflections, and wrote for the new theatre, the *drame bourgeois*. Above all, in 1746 he began editing, with D'Alembert, the *Encyclopedia* (1751–76), one of the great collective achievements of the age. First intended as a translation of Chamber's *Cyclopedia* (1728), it became a 35-volume, all-embracing work covering contemporary knowledge. Inevitably it ran into trouble; in 1759 it was banned by the King. A work of rational humanism, Newtonian science, and new technical discovery, it drew on the services of the great thinkers of the day. It was the Enlightenment, leavened by Diderot's wisdom and wit. The wit was also in his literary writings: the brilliant *Rameau's Nephew* (1761), an ironic dialogue between a philosopher and a parasite, and the Sterne-like novel *Jacques le Fataliste* (1773). He died of apoplexy in Paris in 1784, the *Encyclopedia* battle won, his last words "The first step to philosophy is incredulity." He was buried at the Église Saint-Roche.

By now the *philosophes* were world influences. Voltaire had been at the court of Frederick the Great, Diderot lionized in Saint Petersburg by Cathe-

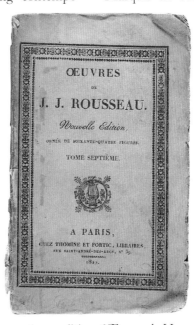

A new edition of Œuvres *de J.J. Rousseau, above,* was published in 1822.

rine the Great. But Enlightenment had another side, exemplified by Choderlos de Laclos (1741–1803) and the Marquis de Sade (1740–1814). Laclos, a career officer from Amiens who knew no citadel can withstand the siege of a resourceful enemy, applied the logic to the battle of the sexes in *Dangerous Liaisons* (1782), that cynical masterpiece of the arts of seduction. De Sade, another soldier, born in Paris, turned the Enlightenment on its head by expounding an ethic of sexual freedom and loveless cruelty as the one faith left in a godless universe in *Justine, Or the Misfortunes of Virtue* (1791), which coincided with the Revolution. Laclos was arrested during the Terror, but died serving Napoleon in Italy. De Sade died in Charenton Asylum in 1814. Now the kings had gone, the Enlightenment was overtaken by Romanticism. De Sade died a curiosity, a strange, perverse survivor from a bygone age.

THE JOURNEYS OF THE AGE
OF THE NOVEL

Over a short span of years in the early eighteenth century the novel established itself as a central literary form in Britain. From Aphra Behn's *Oroonoko* (1688), through the fiction of Daniel Defoe, to the death of Laurence Sterne in 1768, which brought his great anti-novel *The Life and Opinions of Tristram Shandy* (9 vols, 1760–67) to its untimely end, the novel became the most original and flourishing form in British writing. The chief founders were Behn, Defoe, Jonathan Swift, Samuel Richardson, Henry Fielding, Tobias Smollett, and Sterne. All had learned a key lesson from their European predecessors, above all Cervantes and Rabelais. This new form, the novel, if it was anything, was a tale of great travels and picaresque adventures.

Aphra Behn (1640–89), born in Kent, probably with the name Johnson, lived an adventurous life. She married a Dutch merchant in London, spied in Antwerp for Charles II and travelled to Surinam. She was also a much-esteemed poet, playwright and author of the satirical London comedy, *The City Heiress* (1682). However, she is best remembered for *Oroonoko* (c.1688), the story of an African royal slave taken to Surinam.

Women played an active role in the development of fiction – not surprisingly, as they were the main readers of it. Charlotte Lennox (1720–1804), daughter of a governor of New York, came to England and followed Behn with *The Female Quixote, or The Adventures of Arabella* (1752), which sought to capture the spirit of Cervantes in Britain.

Clockwise from top left, *Daniel Defoe, Aphra Behn, Laurence Sterne and Tobias Smollett all wrote tales of adventure in the eighteenth century, popularizing a genre which was to continue in literature for many, many years.*

producing what is thought to be some five hundred books, including his noted guidebook *Tour Through the Whole Island of Great Britain* (3 vols, 1724–26). It wasn't surprising that when he turned to writing novels, producing works like *Robinson Crusoe* (1719), *Captain Singleton* (1720), *Colonel Jack* (1722) and *Roxana* (1724), the spirit of journey and adventure was in them. Defoe could also deal realistically with London life, as he did in *The Fortunes and Misfortunes of the Famous Moll Flanders* (1722), which tells the (invented) tale of a woman born in Newgate, who was, says the title page, "twelve year a whore, five times a wife...twelve year a thief, eight year a transported felon in Virginia, at last grew rich, liv'd honest and died a penitent." But even this frank, realistic, very urban

Theirs were romantic tales. But Daniel Defoe (1660–1731) was made of plainer stuff. Son of a London butcher, he travelled as a merchant and probable spy around Britain and Europe before becoming a writer and a journalist,

story about rags-to-riches female entrepreneurialism is salted with adventures in the American colonies.

Defoe's great triumph was *The Adventures of Robinson Crusoe*, one of the classic tales of romantic adventure. It

Having been shipwrecked at the mouth of the Amazon, Robinson Crusoe, depicted in the eighteenth century book illustration left, *becomes the desert island castaway, forced to depend on ingenuity and the help of "noble savage," Man Friday.*

but no matter. What his book did was reveal the universal love for improbable and fantastic adventures, for imaginary voyages. Soon it was read "from the council chamber to the nursery," and it went on to influence alike children's fiction and the most bitter forms of dystopian satire, like those (later) works of George Orwell and Aldous Huxley.

In the eighteenth century, novels and journeys went together, and many early novels are described as *The Adventures of...* whoever. But picaresque adventures could happen in familiar places, as Henry Fielding (1707–54), playwright and London magistrate, showed. Following the vogue for stories of London crime, on which, as a founder of the Bow Street Runners, he was an expert, he wrote *The History of Jonathan Wild the Great* (1743), the story of a notorious criminal who ends up in Newgate and dies on the City gallows. But Fielding's greatest contribution to fiction was *The History of Tom Jones* (1749), a "comic epic," and one of the most warmly humorous and best British novels. Six parts of it are set in the country, six on the inns of the road, six in London, and Fielding presents us with a fine topography of country and city in the Britain of his day.

was based on the true story of the Scots sailor Alexander Selkirk, who was marooned on the island of Juan Fernandez in 1704. Defoe's story of Crusoe was much more than a romantic fictionalization; it was a classic myth of isolation, prudence and survival. Karl Marx called the book the prime example of entrepreneurialism in action; children over the centuries have simply enjoyed it as one of the greatest adventure stories written.

Jonathan Swift (1667–1745), that bitter Irish-born churchman, certainly did not write his *Gulliver's Travels* (1726) for the delight of children. His sailor Lemuel Gulliver sails to four fantastic places: Lilliput (where the people are six inches high), Brobdingnag (where they are giants), Laputa (a flying island) and the land of the Houyhnhnms, populated by civilized horses. He intended his exotic tales of imaginary lands to be a satire on the society he lived in, philosophy and human nature in general, as well as on colonization. However, he too drew on the vogue for travel tales, and based his work on one of the most popular books of the day, Captain Dampier's *New Voyage Round the World* (1697), intending to satirize tales of bold exploration as well –

Plainly, people in the eighteenth century loved to travel – with improved highways, a fresh romantic interest in the landscape, the growing popularity of the European Grand Tour. No writer explored this more than Tobias Smollett

Arthur Rackham drew the illustration, left, *for the 1939 version of Jonathan Swift's tale of fantastical and imagined worlds,* Gulliver's Travels. *Here in Lilliput the people are only six inches high.*

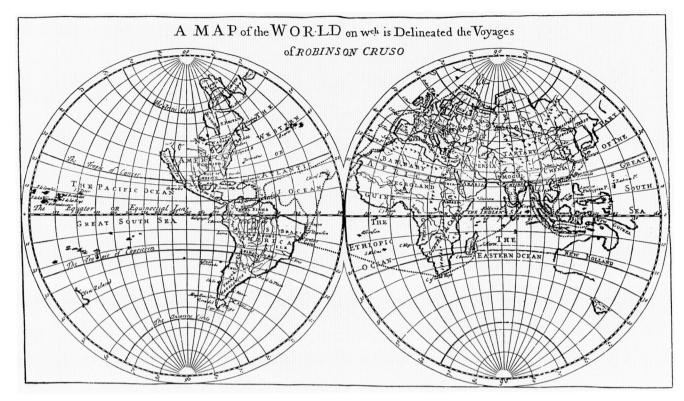

(1721–71), a Scot who fled abroad, travelled the world as a ship's surgeon, and died on the continent. He also translated Cervantes, so unsurprisingly his novels followed the picaresque fashion. The first, *The Adventures of Roderick Random* (1748), would lay down the pattern for all his fiction: a disinherited innocent sets off to make his fortune by travelling, randomly. There are adventures at sea, and he goes to South America, always in search of his missing father. *The Adventures of Peregrine Pickle* (1751) is Smollett's romping satire on the Grand Tour of Europe. *The Expedition of Humphry Clinker* (1771), mostly set in Britain, contains

Based on the real life story of the marooned Alexander Selkirk, Daniel Defoe's Robinson Crusoe became the most famous castaway in literature. The map, above, was drawn by Defoe for the novel.

some vivid London sights, like Sadler's Wells, Ranelagh Gardens and London's river life.

By Smollett's day, the novel had already acquired many of the qualities that have been exploited by fiction since. Some novels, like those by Samuel Richardson (1689–1761), a successful London printer in Fleet Street (*Pamela*, 1740; *Clarissa*, 1747–8), were sentimental, mostly concerned with a heroine's domestic and sexual adventures at home or in London. Others writers took the novel to be essentially about travels and adventures – across Britain, in Europe, around the wider world, even into the realms of fantasy. Cities and inns, ships and foreign wars became familiar subjects, expanding the imagination of the age.

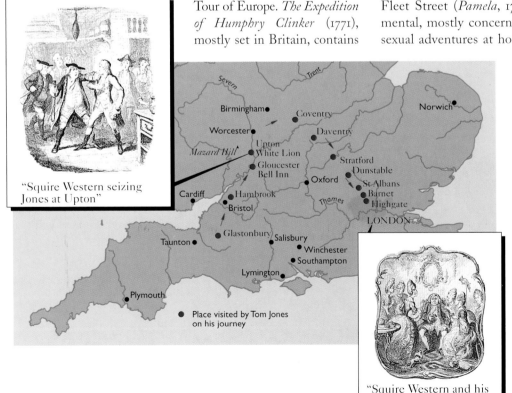

"Squire Western seizing Jones at Upton"

"Squire Western and his Lady Cousins in London"

THE JOURNEYS OF TOM JONES: *In* The Adventures of Tom Jones *Tom travels from Somerset, through Gloucester to social and steamy London where he is almost hanged during his search for his father and his true name. Shown here is the route he took and the inns he stayed at during his perilous journey across Britain.*

No sooner had the novel settled into this popular existence than it bred the anti-novel. Its creator was Laurence Sterne (1713–68), eccentric dean of York, vicar of Coxwold in Yorkshire. In 1760, when the first two volumes of *The Life and Opinions of Tristram Shandy, Gentleman*, appeared, this obscure parson shot to sudden fame. His novel was, he said, a "cock-and-bull" story, a work of "transverse zig-zaggery." If novels usually told the story of their hero from his birth, this one told it from his (botched) conception. The novel too is, deliberately, a botched conception. The preface is in the middle, some pages are blank or marbled. The author constantly announces the impossibility of telling the story, or finishing it, and indeed he kept it going through nine volumes until his death, when it was left unfinished.

Sterne was also a great traveller. Hence his book spawned a fascinating offspring, *A Sentimental Journey Through France and Italy* (1768). Based on his own visits, it's narrated by his idiosyncratic "Parson Yorick," a version of himself. Like other books of the day, it influenced many travellers thereafter, and "sentimental journeys," through both the landscape and ideas of the age, became common. When American writers like Washington Irving, or the British Romantic poets of the next century, set off on their own extensive travels, they often carried Sterne's book with them, and their works displayed its influence. As for

Samuel Richardson's Clarissa *was first published in 1748 in seven volumes. Shown here is the frontispiece to the 1787 edition, published by Harrison and Co. in London.*

Tristram Shandy, it influenced something else: the whole idea of the experimental novel, picked up again by writers like James Joyce and Samuel Beckett in the twentieth century.

With Sterne's death in 1768 an era of British fiction moved toward its close. Afterwards, the novel went in many directions. There was the comic novel of manners cultivated by Jane Austen, the historical romance of Sir Walter Scott, the Gothic fiction of Horace Walpole, Charles Maturin and Mary Shelley, the sentimental romance pursued by the many women writers of the day. But the fiction of comic adventure and picaresque wandering had made its mark. It lasted on, into the work of Charles Dickens, William Thackeray, Anthony Trollope and Wilkie Collins, taking in not the world of highwaymen and sentimental journeys, but the ever-changing face of industrial England.

The novel in Britain started by satisfying a new interest in readers in their own landscape and society, the topography of their cities and countryside, and the fascinating, often fantastic worlds that lay beyond their shores. Voyages, probable and imaginary, became the essential stuff of fiction. The connection between the novel and travel would endure, and the form long keep its fascination with strange characters, adventures, the wide panorama of society and geography. As a result, it has remained, to this day, one of the best maps we have of the life, manners, society and topography of its times.

English painter and engraver William Hogarth produced the illustration, below, *for the frontispiece of Laurence Sterne's* The Life and Opinions of Tristram Shandy *(1760–67).*

THE ADVENTURES OF...

1720 Daniel Defoe *The Life and Adventures of Mr Duncan Campbell*

1742 Henry Fielding *The Adventures of Joseph Andrews and his Friend Mr Abraham Adams*

1748 Tobias Smollett *The Adventures of Roderick Random*

1751 Tobias Smollett *The Adventures of Peregrine Pickle*

1752 Charlotte Lennox *The Adventures of Arabella*

1762 Tobias Smollett *The Life and Adventures of Sir Launcelot Graves*

1831 E. J. Trelawney *The Adventures of a Younger Son*

1843-4 Charles Dickens *The Life and Adventures of Martin Chuzzlewit*

1861-2 W. M. Thackeray *The Adventures of Philip*

1871 George Meredith *The Adventures of Harry Richmond*

EIGHTEENTH CENTURY LONDON

The relationship between the eighteenth century writer and the British capital resembles that between a married couple: intimate, emotional, yet often charged with tension. Samuel Johnson (1709–84) famously insisted that when a man was tired of London he was tired of life. Living in and around Fleet Street, that great nucleus of booksellers, publishers and authors, and founder of a "Club" – a brilliant gathering of artists and writers who included Sir Joshua Reynolds, Oliver Goldsmith and Edmund Burke – Johnson was the walking embodiment of the familiar Augustan claim that literature, the fine ornament of civilization, was essentially the product of the city.

This portrait of Dr Johnson is by fellow "Club" member, Sir Joshua Reynolds.

Johnson's prodigious and encyclopaedic literary output – he produced not just his pioneering *A Dictionary of the English Language* (1755), but the moral fable *Rasselas* (1759), two powerful coffee house magazines, *The Rambler* and *The Idler*, and the critical and biographical study *The Lives of the Most Eminent English Poets* (1779–81), not to mention his major edition of the plays of Shakespeare – would have been unthinkable outside the stimulus of London, the great metropolis, with its publishers and sophisticated readers. But it was Johnson who also penned one of the most damning attacks ever made on the capital, in his early satire "London" (1738), a gruesome vision of urban decay, destruction, crime and demoralization.

Johnson's love of London was certainly not incompatible with the thought that great cities spawn great corruptions. His poem hints at other ambiguities in the eighteenth century's literary vision of London: the city largely rebuilt after the Great Fire of 1666 and dominated by the new St Paul's of Christopher Wren. "Fleet Street" itself would soon turn from a simple street name into a metaphor for the newspaper press. The Georgians laid down another important association between a street and a particular type of writing. Grub Street was the name of an actual lane near Moorfields, just north of the City Wall – which, according to Johnson's *Dictionary*, was "much inhabited by writers of small histories, dictionaries, and temporary poems." As he suggests, "Grub Street" had started to be a collective term of abuse for all the dregs of authorship the new age of print, periodicals and coffee house readers produced. Here lived botchers of hack work, mercenary journalists, woeful versifiers, writers of shoddy catchpenny effusions. The great city might be the cradle of literature, but the infants it nursed were mostly monsters.

Indeed, some suggested they were raving lunatics. Moorfields, just a stone's throw from Grub Street, was the site of the Bethlem Hospital (popularly known as Bedlam), for long the nation's only lunatic asylum. The implication was clear: the writing spewed out by Grub Street hacks was symptomatic of delirious brains. This satirical connection proved close to the bone; a fair number of the literary figures of Georgian London did end up crazy. The Restoration playwright Nathaniel Lee (c.1649–92) was confined to Bethlem itself; the sublime religious poet Kit Smart (1772–71) – whom Johnson befriended – had to be lodged in St Luke's Asylum (founded 1751), just down the road from Bethlem. As John Dryden (1633–1700) warned, great wits were sure to madness near allied.

The infamy of Grub Street, its threat to an authentic literature, was never pronounced more fiercely than by Pope, that dean of Augustan poets, who himself struggled in the London literary marketplace. His *Dunciad* (1743) vilified the plague of

The first edition of Dr Johnson's infamous English Language Dictionary – the frontispiece is shown left – was published in 1755.

A
DICTIONARY
OF THE
ENGLISH LANGUAGE:
IN WHICH
The WORDS are deduced from their ORIGINALS,
AND
ILLUSTRATED in their DIFFERENT SIGNIFICATIONS
BY
EXAMPLES from the beſt WRITERS.
TO WHICH ARE PREFIXED,
A HISTORY of the LANGUAGE,
AND
AN ENGLISH GRAMMAR.
BY SAMUEL JOHNSON, A.M.
IN TWO VOLUMES.
VOL. I.

LONDON
Printed by W. STRAHAN,
For J. and P. KNAPTON; T. and T. LONGMAN; C. HITCH and L. HAWES;
A. MILLAR: and R. and J. DODSLEY.
MDCCLV.

penmen infesting the metropolis. The plot of this venomous satire rang the changes on all the associations between London, lunacy and pseudo-literature. It culminates in a cavalcade through the city by the "dunces" – the hack writers – which parodies the Lord Mayor's Day parade. It also

anticipates the progress through London of the painter William Hogarth's "idle apprenctice" who, having idled as a boy, takes up crime, and is finally hanged at Tyburn Tree gallows by the spot now occupied by Marble Arch.

In his pastoral poem "Windsor Forest" (1713) Pope implied that peace, beauty and goodness were really rural virtues. But for all this Pope had no intention of burying himself in the countryside – ridiculed by all the Restoration wits and playwrights as hopelessly hayseed, dull as ditchwater. He compromised by settling in 1718 in Twickenham, where his friend Jonathan Swift joined him for a time. Similarly, Hogarth, born in Smithfield, chose after a lifetime in London to settle in nearby Chiswick.

Alexander Pope's Twickenham home, above, was an eligible residence for those who sought both easy access to London and a semblance of tranquillity.

Pope, right, a Catholic Tory, looked to the past for great men and great art.

John Roque's 1748 map of London, below, shows eighteenth century London in detail.

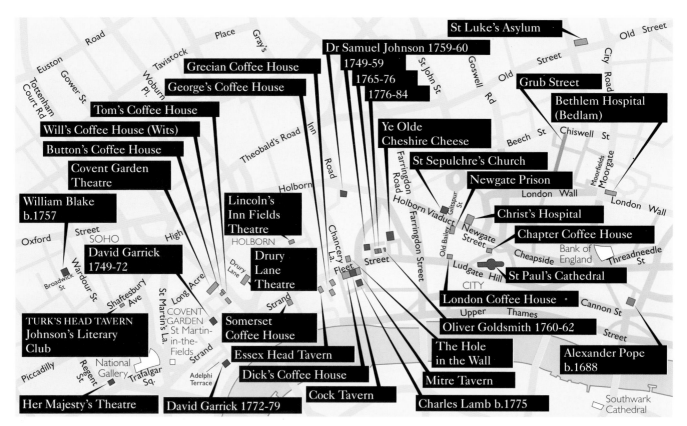

St Luke's Asylum

Old Street

Dr Samuel Johnson 1759-60

1749-59

1765-76

1776-84

Grecian Coffee House

George's Coffee House

Tom's Coffee House

Will's Coffee House (Wits)

Button's Coffee House

Covent Garden Theatre

William Blake b.1757

David Garrick 1749-72

TURK'S HEAD TAVERN Johnson's Literary Club

Her Majesty's Theatre

David Garrick 1772-79

Cock Tavern

Dick's Coffee House

Essex Head Tavern

Somerset Coffee House

Lincoln's Inn Fields Theatre

Drury Lane Theatre

Ye Olde Cheshire Cheese

St Sepulchre's Church

Newgate Prison

Christ's Hospital

Chapter Coffee House

St Paul's Cathedral

London Coffee House

Oliver Goldsmith 1760-62

The Hole in the Wall

Mitre Tavern

Charles Lamb b.1775

Grub Street

Bethlem Hospital (Bedlam)

Bank of England

Threadneedle St

Alexander Pope b.1688

Southwark Cathedral

National Gallery

Trafalgar Sq.

COVENT GARDEN St Martin-in-the-Fields

Roads/places labels: Euston Road, Gower St, Tottenham Court Rd, Tavistock Place, Gray's, Woburn Pl., Theobald's Road, Holborn, Inn Road, Chancery La., Fleet Street, Strand, Oxford Street, High, Wardour St, Broadwick St, Shaftesbury Ave, St Martin's La., Long Acre, Drury Lane, Piccadilly, Regent St, Adelphi Terrace, SOHO, HOLBORN, CITY, St John St, Goswell Rd, Old Street, City Road, Beech St, Chiswell St, Moorfields, Moorgate, London Wall, Farringdon Road, Holborn Viaduct, Giltspur St, Old Bailey, Newgate Street, Ludgate Hill, Cheapside, Upper Thames, Cannon St, Farringdon Street, Old Street

---

Hogarth was as ambivalent about London as Johnson was – celebrating it in his Beer Street, *censuring it in* Gin Lane, *above.*

Ambiguity about London life permeated eighteenth century writing. Daniel Defoe had dubbed it "the monstrous city," the Reverend Josiah Tucker "a kind of monster...no better than a wen." This diagnosis of London as diseased and parasitic echoed through the century. In the fine London scenes of his novel *Humphry Clinker* (1771), Tobias Smollett (1721–71) has his hero Squire Matt Bramble complain "the Capital has become an overgrown monster which, like a dropsical head, will in time leave the body and extremities without nourishment and support."

Such images of London as disease, physical and mental, were reinforced by the notion of it as a slum or moral sewer. London's actual sanitary, or insanitary, arrangements readily suggested the comparison. According to the poet William Cowper (1731–1800), London flowed "as to a common and most noisesome sewer/The dregs and feculence of every land." Cowper's broad message was "God made the country, and man made the town." His bitterness may

EIGHTEENTH CENTURY LONDON: *It was in the coffee houses of London, within the shadow of the newly-built St Paul's, that Dr Johnson and his friends met to discuss issues of literature and politics.*

be explained by the fact that he was yet another casualty of the Georgian capital. A young lawyer, poet and man-about-town from Hertfordshire, living in chambers in the 1760s, he too became unhinged and suicidal – and was finally confined in a lunatic asylum in St Alban's.

Still, the many evocations of London's evils should be taken with a fair pinch of salt. They were, partly, exercises in traditional politically correct literary nostalgia. Poets in Augustan London were trying to assume the mantle of the great tradition, whereby the urban poet displayed the countryside as beautiful and noble, and the town as corrupted, dissolute and vulgar. In the "improving" eighteenth century, there was endless literary mileage to be had in visions of bucolic bliss, and in anti-bourgeois, anti-plebian snobberies. But for all such expressions of disdain, we can always find a counterbalancing writer, seeing Georgian London as a great new Athens or Rome, or waxing lyrical over the phenomenal vitality of the capital.

A genre of London journalism grew up – Ned Ward got the ball rolling with *The London Spy* (1699), which delighted in sketching common people, everyday urban

Londoners lapped up John Gay's delightful rogue story The Beggar's Opera – *portrayed here in a painting by Sir Joshua Reynolds.*

Hospital, the ancient City of London charity school. He earned a living by office work, lived in Islington and Edmonton and wrote essays in his spare time. Close as he was to the new Romantic poets, London was his first love. For him, as for Johnson, it was, with its infinite variety, a place of which one would never tire. "I have passed all my days in London until I have formed as many and intense local attachments, as any of you mountaineers can have done with dead nature," he explained to those Lake District dwellers Dorothy and William Wordsworth.

If, with the Romantics, the battle of country and city entered a new phase, the contradictions of London found expression in the work of William Blake (1757–1827), whose references to the city are closely observed. He thundered against the moral degradation created by its brutal, avaricious, competitive ways. He drew attention to its victims: chimney-sweeps, street-walkers, orphans, beggars. He laid blame at the door of the City fathers.

Blake's solution to the problem of the city and its "mind-forged manacles" wasn't a Romantic exodus to the country or the mountain. It was – to evoke a contrast drawn by Saint Augustine – to render the hellish city holy, and substitute for the *civitas Diaboli*, the City of the Devil, he saw round him the *civitas Dei*, the City of God.

sights, smells and sounds. Theatre, too, reviving after the 1660 Restoration, also focused on the drama of the city. The theatres of London filled again and were improved, and public entertainment grew popular. The task of the Restoration comedies of Sir George Etherege, William Wycherley, Sir John Vanburgh and William Congreve was to set the absurd excesses of St James, Covent Garden and Ranelagh Gardens wittily onto the stage. Town life was depicted as fast, loose, smart and lecherous. "I have got the London disease, they call Love, I am sick of my Husband, and for my Gallant," ominously says Wycherley's (1641–1715) Mrs Pinchwife, in *The Country Wife* (1675). Londoners relished the topographical references that filled the novels of Defoe and Henry Fielding, and loved George Lillo's tragedy, *The London Merchant, Or the History of George Barnwell*, produced at Drury Lane Theatre in 1731, which for the first time turned City apprentices and harlots into tragic figures.

Besides writing *The Beggar's Opera* (1728), John Gay (1685–1732) also produced a work very typical of the times, *Trivia, or Walking the London Streets* (1717), a versified walking tour of the city, warning strollers of, for instance, the street-walkers of Covent Garden. Simple in form and diction, gently mocking, it was a hymn to London, to the joys of sauntering around, soaking up the atmosphere, and it reinforced the feeling of belonging to the city.

By the end of the century, with the rise of the Romantic movement, feeling against the city and for nature rose. Still, love of the metropolis persisted, and it was never better expressed than by Charles Lamb (1775–1834), born in Crown Office Row and a pupil of Christ's

London has always been loved by some writers, hated by others. The crucial fact was that, in an age when printing and publishing prospered, newspapers and magazines flourished, reading grew, and the theatre delighted a leisured and fashionable public, writing became as never before a profession and a trade. There was no doubt that, during the eighteenth century, the profession of letters became a thoroughly urban career.

Son of a hosier, William Blake, above, was a keen observer of the London he was born in.

EIGHTEENTH CENTURY DUBLIN

Dublin was a Norse city until 1171 when Asculf, the last jarl, was routed by the invading Normans; it was a Norman city, by lineage at least, until 1534, when "Silken Thomas," last of the Kildare Fitzgerald rulers, threw off his allegiance to Henry VIII (in what is now Abbey Street), only to be defeated the next year and then executed; it was an English city until the Union of the British and Irish Parliaments of 1800. During this time, its beggars, hod carriers, street cleaners, chairmen and unskilled workers were normally Irish Catholic, although from time to time nominally excluded by security-conscious rulers as late as the eighteenth century. By the mid-century Catholics may have been the majority of the 100,000 population, although, as a High Court judge remarked at the time, the law did not suppose such a thing as an Irish Roman Catholic to exist.

The Irish Parliament, built on College Green by two of its own members, Edward Lovell Pearce and Arthur Dobbs, between 1728 and 1739, excluded Catholics and Presbyterians. But the English government administrators who controlled the Kingdom of Ireland under Queen Anne, George I, George II and George III regarded all Irish-born persons as security risks, and gave the plum jobs in Church and State to Englishmen, who loyally drew their salaries, whether they ever came to Ireland or not.

So our eighteenth century literary map begins with Dublin Castle, seat of Government just south of the Liffey. Until the reign of George III, Viceroys rarely remained on duty for more than a few months at a time; nor did their Chief Secretaries, who handled the dirtier work of bribery and security. But, following the tradition of Edmund Spenser, who stayed in Ireland to write *The Fairie Queene* (1596–99), Joseph Addison (1672–1719) began his immortal work as an English essayist while Chief Secretary at the Castle from 1708–10, working on the essays of *The Tatler* with his Oxford friend and playwright Richard Steele, who was Dublin-born (in Bull Alley, near Saint Patrick's Cathedral) and then London-resident. Addison returned to the Castle again in 1715, and he and Steele continued

The New Musick Hall in Fishamble Street, depicted in the engraving above, showed the first performance of Handel's Messiah on 12 April, 1742.

their collaboration with their even more famous and popular periodical *The Spectator*.

Addison served initially under the Viceroy Thomas, Earl of Wharton, a ferocious Whig, whom Jonathan Swift would call "the most universal villain I ever knew," and help overthrow by his London pamphleteering. Literary traffic between the two capitals was constant and two-way. The Viceroyalty itself blazed without literary light until 1745, when Philip Dormer Stanhope, Earl of Chesterfield (1694–1773), famous for the elegance of the almost daily letters on polite living he wrote to his bastard son, steered a very smooth ship through the reefs of threatened Jacobite rebellion. His Viceroyalty coincided with the death in 1745 of Jonathan Swift, whose name outshines all others in St Patrick's Cathedral, despite its near eight hundred years of existence under Catholics and Protestants. It shines too in his posthumous endowment of St Patrick's Hospital in Bow Lane ("He gave the little wealth he had/To build a home for fools and mad/To show by one satiric touch/No nation wanted it so much"). Swift was born in Dublin, on 30 November, 1667, at 7 Hoey's Court (which no longer exists), and went, like William Congreve, to Kilkenny Grammar School. As a Protestant churchman he had hopes of an English bishopric. Instead he was appointed

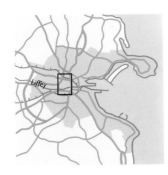

EIGHTEENTH CENTURY
DUBLIN: *The Wide Streets
Commission of 1757 made
Dublin the second city of
Empire in beauty as well as
size. In Dame Street the
Commission produced the great
highway that linked the Castle
with the Irish Parliament.*

Dean of St Patrick's, where
he remained for 32 years,
writing prolifically and satir-
ically on numerous Irish
and ecclesiastical questions.
He is buried in the church,
beside his beloved "Stella."

Swift was an Irish
writer. Irish Court and
Irish Parliament refreshed
his memories of flattery
and treachery, jobbery and
snobbery from his great
London days under Queen
Anne. It was enough to
touch the deadly point of
every satiric dart when in

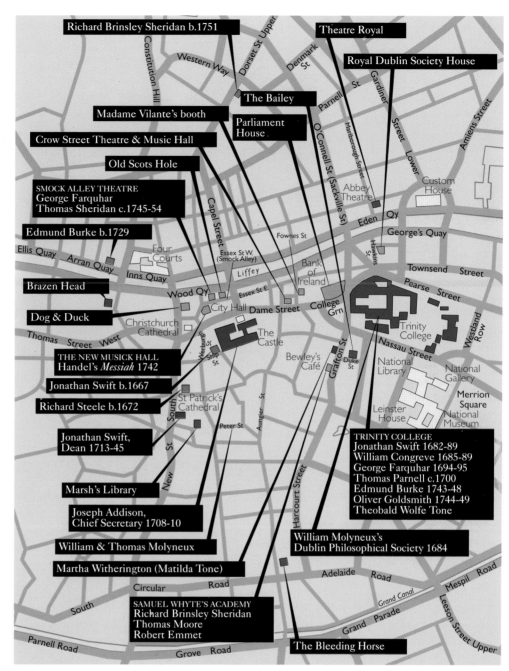

the mid-1720s he fashioned Lilliput for his *Gulliver's
Travels* (1726). Irish beggars, swarming in ever greater
numbers as Dublin increased from the 60,000 of 1690 to
the near 200,000 of 1800, became the hideously magnified
mendicants of Brobdingnag. Irish scientific and scholarly
enquirers like William and Thomas Molyneux of Peter
Street augmented his Laputa mockery of the London
Royal Society, on which the brothers modelled the Dublin
Philosophical Society, begun in 1684, refounded in 1733,
made the "Royal" Dublin Society in 1820, flourishing
today in Ballsbridge (where like much else in Dublin it
remains "Royal" without the expense of Royalty). The
problems of the Gaelic Catholic lower classes, English
Protestant ruling classes and the Irish Protestant resident
classes caught between them, are the basis of the Yahoos,

Houyhnhnms and Gulliver himself – though only one of
their many meanings. Swift's sources for Gulliver include
Irish servants; in its earliest, Gaelic form the book makes
Lilliputian-style fairies meet and even copulate with mortals (as Gulliver unconvincingly denies on his own behalf).

Irish-language poetry was still being composed in
Swift's Dublin. Sean O Neachtain (John Neville), the
most prolific Dublin Gaelic poet, acted as a sort of poetic
disseminator of coded Jacobite news and propaganda.
His most famous work was the romantic *Rachainn Fo'n
gCoill Leat*, in which the poet promises the female audience a full orchestra with birds playing the instruments.
Had he lived till 1742, his feathered friends would have
found themselves competing with the choirs of St
Patrick's and Christ Church in the New Musick Hall

as Handel conducted them in the first performance of his *Messiah*.

Still in the Castle neighbourhood at Essex Bridge was the famous Smock Alley Theatre. George Farquhar (1678–1707) acted here at the close of the seventeenth century before emigrating to London, where he would cough himself to death in poverty as the audience revelled in his new play *The Beaux' Stratagem* (1707). Thomas Sheridan was the great mid-century impresario; he would tour Britain as a leading authority on how to speak English, thus anticipating the exhortations of another Dublin Protestant, Bernard Shaw, in *Pygmalion*. We don't know if his sense of linguistic rectitude extended

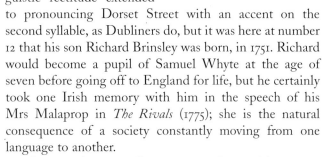

Clockwise from top left, *Jonathan Swift, Richard Steele, Oliver Goldsmith and Edmund Burke are all writers who left their mark on Dublin.*

to pronouncing Dorset Street with an accent on the second syllable, as Dubliners do, but it was here at number 12 that his son Richard Brinsley was born, in 1751. Richard would become a pupil of Samuel Whyte at the age of seven before going off to England for life, but he certainly took one Irish memory with him in the speech of his Mrs Malaprop in *The Rivals* (1775); she is the natural consequence of a society constantly moving from one language to another.

Oratory, however fleeting, is a form of literature, and while wholly justifying Swift's "Tell us what the pile contains/Many a head that holds no brains," the College Green Parliament became as famous for entertainment and high drama as Smock Alley. Glorious patriotic utterances defied Whitehall tyranny in language enviable to Cicero and Demosthenes, until the government came through with the necessary job and the patriot rejoined the herd. The struggle for legislative independence may only have resulted in Whitehall being forced after 1782 to bribe a little more and bully a little less, but John Philpot Curran and Henry Grattan showed quality above their posturing contemporaries, as advocates for Catholics no less than Protestants, and as (ultimately vanquished) opponents of the Union. In London, Grattan would have found himself intellectually outranked by an Irishman who may well have studied College Green oratory but

limited his Parliamentary career to Westminster: Edmund Burke (1729–97). Burke, who reflected so seriously on the state of the English nation, was born at 12 Arran Quay, of a Protestant father and Catholic mother. His Dublin public life was that of a student in the 1740s at Trinity College, where he founded an Addisonian paper, *The Reformer*, and the Historical Society. He was a more diligent student than the contemporary whose statue now complements his own in front of their *alma mater* Oliver Goldsmith (1730–74), author of the comic play *She Stoops to Conquer* (1773). His poem "Retaliation" contains the finest portrait of Burke ever painted; ironically, he wrote it as a mock-epitaph, but unfortunately he predeceased his subject by over twenty years.

Burke's education was better than England could have given him, but the great College founded by Elizabeth I in 1592 had lost some of its intellectual vigour since 1707 when philosopher George Berkeley (1685–1753) wrote his *Essay Towards a New Theory of Vision, Treatise Concerning Human Knowledge and Dialogues between Hylas and Philonous*. Berkeley saw the building of the Jacobean College Library, with its 209-foot Long Room, which houses the Book of Kells. The College's Corinthian façade arose in the 1750s to confront the grandeur of Parliament House; it has remained, but the Parliament is now the Bank of Ireland. The great statue of William III is gone, but Dublin unconsciously commemorates that Prince of Orange-Nassau in Nassau Street (1756).

Perpendicular to Nassau Street is Grafton Street, where in 1785 Theobald Wolfe Tone saw Martha Witherington seated in the window of number 68. He quickly named her Matilda, married her in St Ann's, Dawson Street, and involved her in his horrendous adventures which included exile, imprisonment and suicide. She and her son were left to publish his autobiography, whose charm, scapegrace wit and keen observation conquer readers far beyond the dim circle of modern ideological votaries.

EIGHTEENTH CENTURY
EDINBURGH AND SCOTLAND

Eighteenth century Scotland declares its divisions ruthlessly: Gaelic Highlands defying Protestant Lowlands, ancient oral tradition versus bookish Enlightenment, country against city. A reading of Robert Louis Stevenson's *Kidnapped* (1886) – with its Lowland Whig Presbyterian David Balfour confronted by the Highland Jacobite Catholic Allan Breck – sets it up well. Stevenson's superb topography revives both his own nineteenth century Highlands, and guestimates those of the eighteenth century: all the better for modern readers, for whom much of both are lost.

This eighteenth century world becomes yet more vivid when we look at the decorum, controlled spaciousness and high respectability of the Stevensons' New Town family residence, in Heriot Row. Its survival, and the vanishing of the world of Allan Breck, say so much. The New Town, with its ordered streets, planned by mid-eighteeenth century Freemasons, spoke of Edinburgh's determination to enlist in Progress and

The Heart of Midlothian, depicted in the eighteenth century engraving, above, *is central to Scott's book of that name.*

civilize the future, pursue the rational and the verifiable and dispose of the counter-productive. The old Nor' Loch was drained at this time, the Bridges thrown over its bed, the great Mound created from its dredged soil.

But it is not so easy. Stevenson's Edinburgh was already outstripped in population by rival Glasgow (in the 1790s Edinburgh had twice Glasgow's population; both had six women to every five men). For all that nineteenth century Edinburgh was improved, it was now driven back onto the nostalgia its Era of Enlightenment had officially rejected. Eighteenth century Edinburgh looked like a literary city more in retrospect than in its own day. In its own time its pre-eminence was scientific, educational, medical, philosophical. We stand in front of St. Giles's Cathedral and look at the Heart of Midlothian, knowing from Walter Scott's (1771-1832) *The Heart of Midlothian* (1818) that this pattern in the stones designates where the jail stood, whence in 1736 the iron-disciplined mob took

Captain Porteous of the City Guard to hang him in the Grassmarket for shooting at the citizenry. He had been convicted and sentenced, but Whitehall had deferred the date and looked like remitting it, leaving the Edinburgh mob free to be fired on whenever the Guard might please.

That was the Old Town. The New Town does not have things like the close opening off the scene of the execution called "Porteus Pend." But it's simply not a New Town story. Not that Scott, for all his love of gracious society, was a New Town boy. Born near the Cowgate, he grew up at 25 George Square, hearing from Old Town bodies how the city was taken by the forces of Charles Stuart in 1745 – as he would tell in *Waverley* (1814) – or confronting in himself the duties of legal apprenticeship around Parliament Square while his heart was leaping toward folklore research, a dichotomy that determines the nature of *Redgauntlet* (1824).

In his novels, poems and collections of Border ballads, Scott sought to rescue the social history of the past from the oblivion where his old teacher, Principal William Robertson, pioneer scientific historian of the Scottish Enlightenment, with a real belief in scientific source-use, cast what fell below "the dignity of history." Moderate Church of Scotland minister at Greyfriars' Kirk, Robertson called for toleration against Catholics, and had his house wrecked by the mob in 1779. Knowing as a descendant of a Highland clan what emotions could do, he sought judicious objectivity in his histories of Scotland, Europe and the Americas. With far more art and assurance his friend, David Hume (1711–76) imposed his Tory views on his *History of England* (1754–61).

The University of Edinburgh (founded 1583) refused Hume a chair, for which mistake it compensates with a hideous tower in George Square. But he worked happily in Parliament Square, as Advocates' Librarian, and died in residence at the southwest corner of the New Town's richest square, St Andrew, just off St David Street (Hume persuaded the city authorities so to name it, in covert allusion to himself and the scepticism which aborted his professorship). In St Andrew Square is the house where Henry Brougham was born in 1778, whence he grew into the most literary and most loathed Lord Chancellor of England in the nineteenth century. Brougham was co-founder of the *Edinburgh Review* in 1802 (or a contributor so early he thought he was) and his mordant pen did much to make the quarterly an object of universal interest and frequent execration. It was his cruel dismissal of Byron's first volume that led to the poet's vituperative *English Bards and Scotch Reviewers* (1809).

The *Review*'s editor until 1829 (after which he became a judge) was Francis Jeffrey (1773–1850), who carried out his

Robert Burns had a series of love affairs, and many of his lovers feature in his poems. He is depicted in the engraving above *with Highland Mary, subject of his poem "To Mary in Heaven."*

Walter Scott, above, *wrote most of his Waverley novels at 39 Castle Street, before moving to Abbotsford.*

business in his house at 18 Buccleuch Place. His skill brought a superb team into action, including Sydney Smith, Thomas Macaulay and Thomas Carlyle, and defined the style and nature of nineteenth century British literary criticism. It was an old tradition; Edinburgh had learned to speak Enlightenment to the nation. An even more influential and long-lasting pioneer was William Smellie (1740–95) of Anchor Close, who published the *Encyclopaedia Britannica* in three volumes in 1771. He was fired by the

example of Diderot and the French *Encyclopèdists*. The second edition of the *Britannica* (1777–84), under James Tytler, was notable for the editor's making the first hot-air balloon flight in Britain, as research for the relevant article. But if Tytler is thus an example to all future scholars, Smellie too should also be a household word. It was he who printed the Edinburgh edition of the poems of Robert Burns in 1787, which sold 3,000 copies, copyright and profits being collared by the publisher William Creech. Although Burns spent time here, Edinburgh associations still seem inappropriate for the man whose revolutionary impact on British poetry derived from his use of Scots language and his ploughman experience. It was Ayrshire and Alloway that gave him his data, his homespun wisdom, his philanthropy, his fine theological ironies revealed immortally in "Holy Willie's Prayer" and the grand mock-horror of "Tam O'Shanter" (1790).

Still, Burns owed much of his craftsmanship to poet Robert Fergusson (1750–74). He died young and neglected in the Edinburgh Bedlam (now a theatre) despite the patriotism of his *Auld Reekie* (1773) and the sounds and voices of the Edinburgh of his day kept alive in his work. Burns raised a monument to him over his grave in the Canongate Cemetery. Edinburgh made Burns himself too self-conscious, inducing too much English language work, where he had less originality. It also brought the unfulfilled love duet with Mrs Agnes McLehose ("Clarinda") which ended with his haunting "Ae Fond Kiss and then We Sever," as well as his marriage to Jean Armour.

Burns echoes the dual pressure of Scots reality and English polite literariness which had beset Allan Ramsay's (c.1685–1758) earlier work, including his play *The Gentle Shepherd* (1725). But although later writers – Scott among them – spoke Scots as their natural tongue, they wrote in English, knowing they lost a major market if their Scotticisms alienated the parochial people south of the Border. "Wandering Willie's Tale" in *Redgauntlet* is one of the few revelations of Scott's power in the vernacular.

Gaelic was generally spoken in the Highlands well beyond the eighteenth century, and Edinburgh too had its Gaelic craftsmen. Donnchadh Ban Mac-an-t-Saoir (White Duncan Macintyre, 1724–1815) was actually from

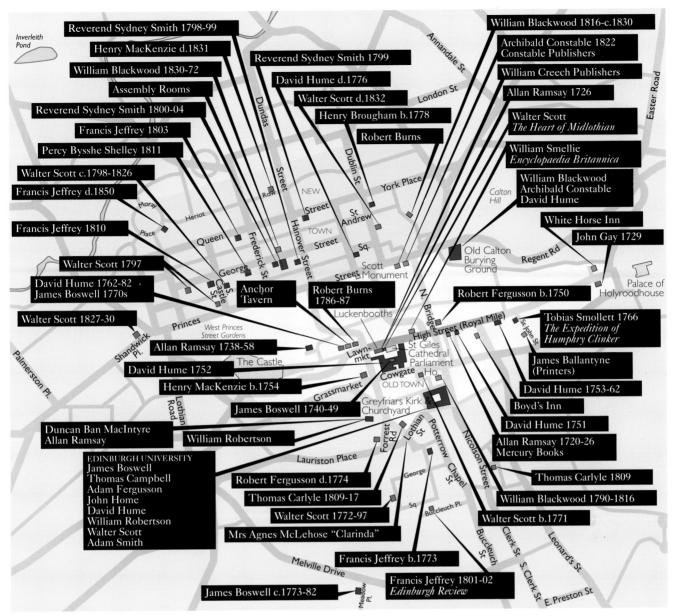

Inverleith Pond

Reverend Sydney Smith 1798-99
Henry MacKenzie d.1831
William Blackwood 1830-72
Assembly Rooms
Reverend Sydney Smith 1800-04
Francis Jeffrey 1803
Percy Bysshe Shelley 1811
Walter Scott c.1798-1826
Francis Jeffrey d.1850
Francis Jeffrey 1810
Walter Scott 1797
David Hume 1762-82
James Boswell 1770s
Walter Scott 1827-30
Allan Ramsay 1738-58
David Hume 1752
Henry MacKenzie b.1754
James Boswell 1740-49
Duncan Ban MacIntyre
Allan Ramsay
William Robertson

EDINBURGH UNIVERSITY
James Boswell
Thomas Campbell
Adam Fergusson
John Home
David Hume
William Robertson
Walter Scott
Adam Smith

Robert Fergusson d.1774
Thomas Carlyle 1809-17
Walter Scott 1772-97
Mrs Agnes McLehose "Clarinda"
Francis Jeffrey b.1773
James Boswell c.1773-82
Francis Jeffrey 1801-02
Edinburgh Review

Reverend Sydney Smith 1799
David Hume d.1776
Walter Scott d.1832
Henry Brougham b.1778
Robert Burns

Robert Burns 1786-87
Luckenbooths

Anchor Tavern

William Blackwood 1816-c.1830
Archibald Constable 1822
Constable Publishers
William Creech Publishers
Allan Ramsay 1726
Walter Scott
The Heart of Midlothian
William Smellie
Encyclopaedia Britannica
William Blackwood
Archibald Constable
David Hume
White Horse Inn
John Gay 1729

Robert Fergusson b.1750
Palace of Holyroodhouse

Tobias Smollett 1766
The Expedition of
Humphry Clinker
James Ballantyne
(Printers)
David Hume 1753-62
Boyd's Inn
David Hume 1751
Allan Ramsay 1720-26
Mercury Books
Thomas Carlyle 1809
William Blackwood 1790-1816
Walter Scott b.1771

NEW TOWN
Dundas Street
Dublin St
London St
Annandale St
Easter Road
York Place
Row
Heriot
Moray Place
Queen
George
Castle St.
Frederick St
Hanover Street
Street
St Andrew Sq.
Scott Monument
Calton Hill
Old Calton Burying Ground
Regent Rd
St John St
High Street (Royal Mile)
Lawn-mkt
St Giles Cathedral
Parliament Ho.
Cowgate
OLD TOWN
The Castle
Grassmarket
Greyfriars Kirk & Churchyard
West Princes Street Gardens
Princes
Shandwick Pl.
Palmerston Pl.
Lothian Road
Forrest Rd
Lothian St
Potterrow
Chapel St
Nicolson Street
George Sq.
Buccleuch Pl.
Buccleuch St
Clerk St
S. Clerk St
Leonard's St
E. Preston St
Lauriston Place
Melville Drive
Meadow Pl.
N. Bridge

1766 to 1793 one of what Fergusson called the "black banditti, the City Gaird," whose inclusion of Gaelic-speaking Highlanders, however poetic, would hardly have increased the public confidence. His poems were published in Edinburgh in 1768. A bard of the Campbells, he followed them into battle in support of the Hanoverians in 1745, but his work reflects the tension of supporting the victors, whose conquest was at the expense of Gaelic culture. His great influence was Alastair Mac Mhaighstir Alastair (Alexander Macdonald, c.1695–c.1770), a captain in the forces of Charles Stuart and cousin to Jacobite heroine Flora Macdonald. Alastair's collection of poems, *The Resurrection of the Ancient Scottish Tongue* (1751), was the first non-religious printed work in Gaelic.

These tensions in the Gaelic world were seminal, if unpredictable, in their impact on Scottish literature. Most cataclysmic of all in its effects on European and American Romanticism was the curious artefact *Ossian* (1762) –

perpetrated by the great scholar James Macpherson, who drew on existing traditions, fragmentary manuscripts and oral evidence to produce a genteel version of the ancient myths of Gaeldom. It was denounced by Dr Johnson as a forgery, and by Irish scholars as plagiarism: but it was simply an appallingly vulgarized version of arcane, psychologically complex Gaelic material, homogenized for weaker Enlightenment palates.

The past and the Highlands could be made acceptable to Lowland and Anglocentric critics if they were sanitized. Scott, who knew the more realistic ancient texts on which Macpherson based his epics, made the same point when in *Rob Roy* (1817) he made his loveable Bailie Nichol Jarvie express the hope, in the name of improvement, that it would prove possible to drain Loch Lomond.

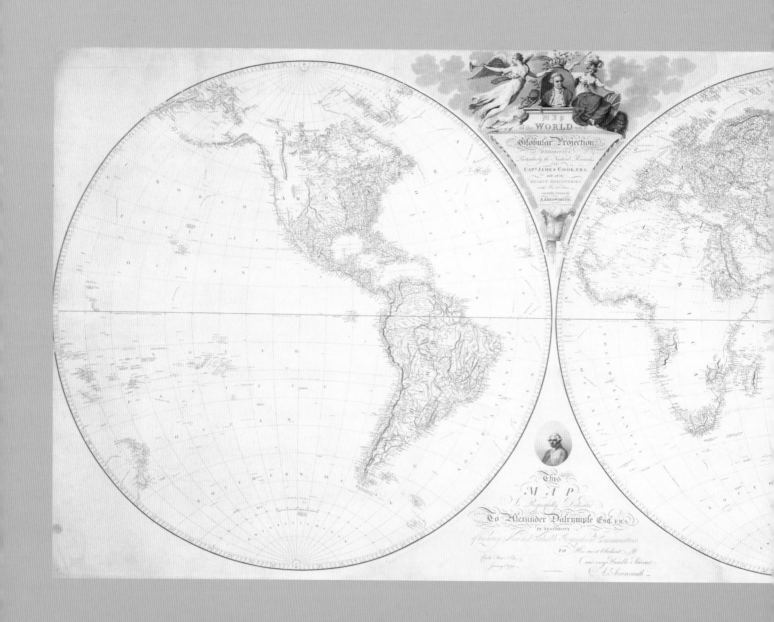

PART THREE

THE ROMANTICS

The eighteenth century closed in a sequence of revolutions: the American Revolution (1776–83); the French Revolution (1789–99); the Industrial Revolution, marked by the invention of the steam engine; and – in the realm of literature, thought and sensibility – the Romantic Revolution. The Romantic sensibility was drawn to travel, and by the end of the eighteenth century it seemed much of the world had been clearly mapped. The Romantic Revolution itself was distinguished by an emphasis on the creative imagination, on feeling, on the power of nature, landscape, the foreign, the distant and the picturesque, the fascination of geography and history of the world at home and abroad, including the polar regions. Many conflicting definitions of Romanticism have been given, yet no-one doubts the fundamental change of feeling that swept through the arts as the nineteenth century began. Seeing the world and nature in a fresh and different way, this new spirit released the energies of poetry, the drama of the imagination, the conviction that, as the English poet Shelley said, the poet was the "unacknowledged legislator" of mankind. The Romantic mind determinedly mapped the changing world afresh. It found very different sites of feeling – in nature, mountains, torrents and lakes; in national folklore, representing the spirit of the people; in travel itself, a lesson in sensibility; in fantastic journeys in space and time...

Aaron Arrowsmith's map of the world, 1794, draws on Captain Cook's three voyages of discovery, which had dispelled many of the geographical myths, and removes many imaginary lands from the world's oceans (though many still survived in literature).

THE LAKE DISTRICT
OF THE ROMANTICS

William Wordsworth (1770–1850) alone would be sufficient to guarantee the Lake District a place in such a book as this. Britain's third poet, after William Shakespeare and John Milton, he was born and nourished and educated in the Lakes, he walked the valleys and fells ceaselessly, lived most of his life there, and wrote great poetry in and about the Lake District. He also attracted other writers of genius. Samuel Taylor Coleridge swung north to be near him. Thomas de Quincey began as a besotted disciple, and stayed for the rest of his life. John Keats and Charles Dickens, like many others, visited the district solely because of Wordsworth and stayed to write memorable prose. And there was his sister, Dorothy, who gave him eyes, who gave him ears and humble cares and delicate fears, and who gave us the *Journals*, largely written for her brother.

It was Wordsworth's Lake District. But from him, as from the massive grip of the mountains at the centre of the area, many other peaks and valleys radiate. And still do, from the twentieth century genius and children's storyteller, Beatrix Potter, to the saturated local landscape of Norman Nicholson's verse, and the man who wrote and illustrated the books of Common Prayer of the walking man, A.W. Wainwright.

In the middle of the eighteenth century when, for reasons scientific, industrial and philosophical, the sensibility of the West European intelligentsia was engaged in a momentous expansion, the study of landscape became an object of interest and

Dorothy Wordsworth in the painting above by Margaret Gillies, was as necessary a companion to her brother on the page as she was in life.

then a passion. The Lake District was central to this. John Dalton (1709–63), born in the north of the District, came from one of a group of well-educated families whose intellectual interest encompassed a wide range of Enlightenment knowledge. His "Descriptive Poem Addressed to Two Young Ladies at their Return from Viewing the Mines near Whitehaven" (1755) was the earliest poem to celebrate at length the beauties of the Lakeland landscape: *"Horrors like these at first alarm / But soon with savage grandeur charm / And raise to noblest thoughts the mind..../ I view with wonder and delight / A pleasing, though an awful sight...."*

Much of what later and far greater writers would discover and explore about the district is in this poem. The capacity of the close contemplation of nature to educate the mind; the emerging conjunction of "horror" and "grandeur" and "noble thoughts;" the connection between awe and pleasure. Another local man, Dr John Brown – from Wigton, my home town – published *A Description of the Lakes and Vale of Keswick* in 1767. After much rather breathless detail, Brown wrote that "The full perfection of Keswick consists of three circumstances, beauty, horror and immensity united."

Dalton and Brown were read by writers interested in picturesque travel – men such as Thomas Gray, Arthur Young, Father Thomas West, Gilpin and Hutchinson. By the late 1780s, the Lake District was discovered for the bolder members of the middle classes and the Romantically inclined young. The long war with France which began at the start of the 1790s and continued almost uninterruptedly until 1815 sealed the future of the Lakes in the affections of the zestful bourgeoisie, largely unable to escape the island because of war.

THE LAKE DISTRICT: *Nearly every river and mountain in the Lake District inspired someone to write a poetic response during the nineteenth century.*

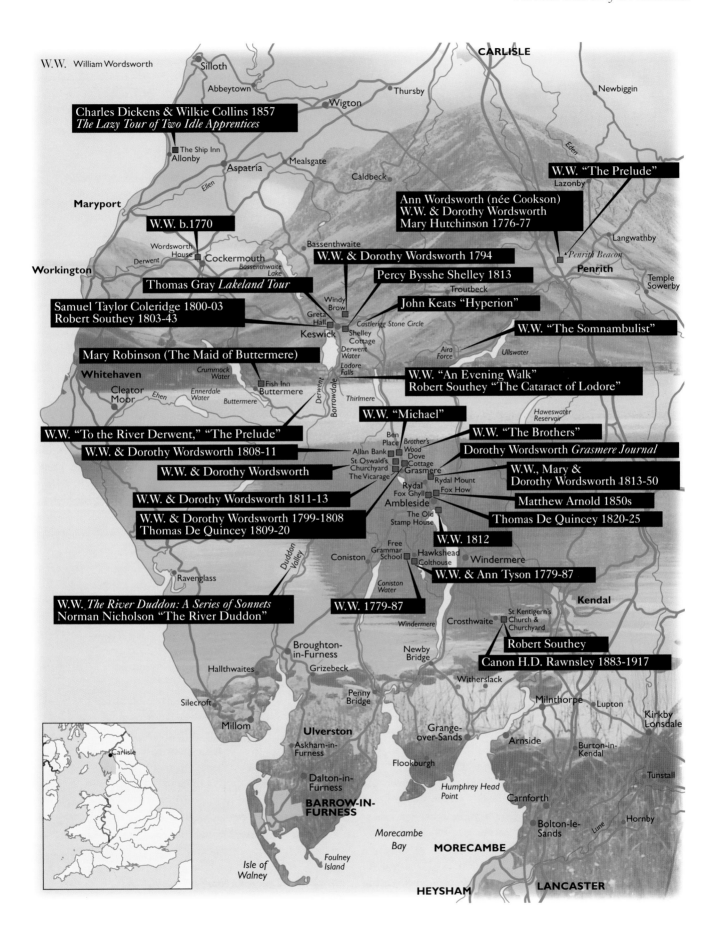

W.W. William Wordsworth

CARLISLE

Silloth

Abbeytown

Wigton

Thursby

Newbiggin

Charles Dickens & Wilkie Collins 1857
The Lazy Tour of Two Idle Apprentices

The Ship Inn
Allonby

Aspatria

Mealsgate

Caldbeck

Eden

W.W. "The Prelude"

Lazonby

Maryport

Ann Wordsworth (née Cookson)
W.W. & Dorothy Wordsworth
Mary Hutchinson 1776-77

Langwathby

W.W. b.1770

Penrith Beacon

Workington

Wordsworth
House

Derwent

Cockermouth

Bassenthwaite
Lake

Bassenthwaite

W.W. & Dorothy Wordsworth 1794

Penrith

Temple
Sowerby

Thomas Gray *Lakeland Tour*

Percy Bysshe Shelley 1813

Troutbeck

Windy
Brow

John Keats "Hyperion"

Samuel Taylor Coleridge 1800-03
Robert Southey 1803-43

Greta
Hall

Castlerigg Stone Circle

Keswick

Shelley
Cottage

Aira
Force

Ullswater

W.W. "The Somnambulist"

Mary Robinson (The Maid of Buttermere)

Derwent
Water

Whitehaven

Crummock
Water

Lodore
Falls

W.W. "An Evening Walk"
Robert Southey "The Cataract of Lodore"

**Cleator
Moor**

Ennerdale
Water

Ehen

Fish Inn
Buttermere

Derwent

Borrowdale

Thirlmere

Haweswater
Reservoir

Buttermere

W.W. "Michael"

W.W. "To the River Derwent," "The Prelude"

Ben
Place

Brother's
Wood

W.W. "The Brothers"

W.W. & Dorothy Wordsworth 1808-11

Allan Bank

Dove
Cottage

Dorothy Wordsworth *Grasmere Journal*

St Oswald's
Churchyard

Grasmere

W.W. & Dorothy Wordsworth

The Vicarage

W.W., Mary &
Dorothy Wordsworth 1813-50

Rydal Mount

W.W. & Dorothy Wordsworth 1811-13

Rydal

Fox How

Matthew Arnold 1850s

Fox Ghyll

Ambleside

W.W. & Dorothy Wordsworth 1799-1808
Thomas De Quincey 1809-20

The Old
Stamp House

Thomas De Quincey 1820-25

W.W. 1812

Free
Grammar
School

Coniston

Hawkshead

Colthouse

Windermere

W.W. & Ann Tyson 1779-87

Kendal

Coniston
Water

W.W. 1779-87

W.W. *The River Duddon: A Series of Sonnets*
Norman Nicholson "The River Duddon"

Windermere

Crosthwaite

St Kentigern's
Church &
Churchyard

Duddon Valley

Ravenglass

Robert Southey

Broughton-
in-Furness

Newby
Bridge

Canon H.D. Rawnsley 1883-1917

Hallthwaites

Grizebeck

Witherslack

Silecroft

Penny
Bridge

Milnthorpe

Lupton

Millom

Ulverston

**Grange-
over-Sands**

Arnside

Burton-in-
Kendal

Kirkby
Lonsdale

Askham-in-
Furness

Flookburgh

Tunstall

Carlisle

Dalton-in-
Furness

Humphrey Head
Point

Carnforth

**BARROW-IN-
FURNESS**

Bolton-le-
Sands

Hornby

*Morecambe
Bay*

Lune

Foulney
Island

MORECAMBE

Isle of
Walney

HEYSHAM

LANCASTER

William Wordsworth, born in 1770 (at Cockermouth, in what is now called Wordsworth House) was part of the well connected local intellectual elite, educated at Hawkshead, near the heart of the Lake District. His formal education was in the hands of Charles Farish, a brilliant teacher many of whose pupils became successful. His informal learning came from intense interactivity with the landscape as a roving boy. These foundations – high thinking and "natural" living – underpinned his strength and sensitivity. When with his sister he returned at the end of 1799 to the Lakes where he would spend the last fifty years of his life, he was in every way prepared for the place, as it could be said to have been prepared – by other previous writers – for him.

The first childhood memory recorded by Wordsworth in *The Prelude* (1805–6) – his epic poetic autobiography – is the sound of the River Derwent, which ran behind the family home at Cockermouth:

"One, the fairest of all rivers, loved/to blend his murmurs with my nurses son/And from his alder shades and rocky banks/And from his fords and shallows, sent a voice/That flowed along my dreams.../Oh! many a time have I, a five years' child/A naked Boy, in one delightful Rill/A little Mill-race sever'd from his stream/ Made one long bathing of a summer's day...."

This began a lifetime's work built on the place. It was both the "little unsuspected Paradise" described by Thomas Gray and also a lost Eden: as shown most concretely in the narrative poem "Michael" (1800), and most spiritually in "Intimations of Immortality based on Recollections of Early Childhood" (1807). The joy – at

From 1800–03 Dorothy Wordsworth wrote an almost daily record of her days at Dove Cottage, above: Wednesday, 16th (June 1802): "The swallows come to the sitting-room window as if wishing to build, but I am afraid they will not have courage for it.... They twitter, and make a bustle, and a little cheerful song, hanging against the panes of glass with their soft white bellies close to the glass and their forked fish-like tails."

its simplest and, for the majority of readers, most memorable in the poem "Daffodils" (1807) – and the loss – seen in the several tales of tragedy of the poor – and the intricate neurotic compulsions of memory wound the poet into the essence of the place.

Dorothy Wordsworth's *Journal* written at Dove Cottage was an invaluable source of information for her brother, who drew on the quiet and unstrained accuracies of her observation for many of his poems.

Samuel Taylor Coleridge, above, was one of the many poets drawn to the Lake District by William Wordsworth.

Samuel Taylor Coleridge came to live nearby in 1800, and can be credited with the first-ever description of fell walking in the district. On an eight-day tour in 1802, he wrote almost as indefatigably as he strode out. Writing at the top of the great mountain of Scafell in 1802, he says:

"I ascended Sca'Fell by the side of a torrent, and climbed and rested, rested and climbed, 'till I gained the very summit of Sca'Fell – believed by the Shepherds here to be higher than either Helvellyn or Skiddaw. Even to Black Coomb, before me all the Mountains die and three parallel Vales with their three Rivers, seen form their very Sources to their falling into the Sea, where they form...the Trident of the Irish Channel at Ravenglass. O my God! what enormous Mountains these are close by me, and yet below the Hill I stand on."

Thomas de Quincey (1785–1859) was another genius who came to the Lake District because of Wordsworth. After two visits in which he had failed at the last fence, he was still determined to meet "that man whom, of all the men from the beginning of time, I most fervently desired to see." With a little help from Coleridge he finally made it, and this is how he came to meet his hero:

"Had Charlemagne and all his peerage been behind me, or Caesar and his equipage, or Death on his pale horse, I should have forgotten them at that moment of intense expectation, and of eyes fascinated to what lay before me, or what might in a moment appear...no longer clearly conscious of my own feelings, I passed on rapidly; I heard a step, a voice, and, like a flash of lightning, I saw the figure of a tallish man, who held out his hand, and saluted me with most cordial expressions of welcome."

Just as Coleridge was drawn into Wordsworth's power and circle, so de Quincey (*The Confessions of an Opium Eater*, 1822), came, saw and was conquered. He was to take over Dove Cottage in Grasmere, the most resonant of Wordsworth's many houses. As one of the very few to read Wordsworth's *Prelude* in his lifetime – it was not published till after the poet's death in 1850 – de Quincey enjoys the unique distinction of being influenced in his prose style by an unknown and unread poem. Later he edited the *Westmoreland Gazette*, a local paper, and with such verve that it continues to be published to this day.

Still in this massif central of the Wordsworth circle must be included such lesser figures as Robert Southey (1774–1843), Poet Laureate and, from 1800, recognized as a "Lake Poet," best-remembered in verse for some playful lines written for his children about a waterfall, "The Cataract of Lodore" (1820):

"The Cataract strong / Then plunges along / Striking and raging / As if a war waging / Its caverns and rocks among / Rising and leaping / Sinking and creeping / Swelling and sweeping / Showering and springing / Flying and flinging / Writhing and ringing / Eddying and whisking / Sprouting and frisking / Turning and twisting / Around and around / With endless rebound / Smiting and fighting / A sound to delight in / Confounding, astounding / Dizzying and deafening the ear with its sound."

To Matthew Arnold (1822–88), a generation on, Wordsworth was the Godfather. Arnold's memorial verses (1850) begin:

"Goethe in Weimar sleeps, and Greece / Long since, saw Byron's struggle cease / But one such death remain'd to come / The last poetic voice is dumb – / We stand today by Wordsworth's tomb."

Even John Ruskin – who fully came to live in the Lake District he had visited so many times – can be seen as part of the Wordsworth archipelago, as many more poets have been ever since. Norman Nicholson (1914–87) is a later twentieth-century example. One of his best poems, "The River Duddon," begins with a wonderful reference to Wordsworth:

"I wonder, Duddon, if you still remember / An oldish man with a nose like a pony's nose / Broad bones, legs long and lean but strong enough / To carry him over Hard Knott at seventy years of age / He came to you first as a boy with a fishing-rod / And a hunk of Ann Tyson's bread and cheese in his pocket / Walking from Hawkshead across Walna Scar."

Of all the many friends and visitors, Dickens's account of his painful and sleet-blinded ascent of Carrock fell in 1857 is the funniest, and Keats' tour the most moving. In "At a Merry Meet at the Sun Inn in Ireby," Keats writes:

"There was as fine a row of boys and girls as you ever saw; some beautiful faces, and one exquisite mouth. I never felt so near the glory of patriotism, the glory of making, by any means, a country happier. This is what I like better than scenery. I fear our continued moving from place to place will prevent our becoming learned in village affairs: we are mere creature of rivers, lakes, and mountains."

It is impossible to write in the Lake District now without working inside the mind of Wordsworth. A novel of my own, *The Maid of Buttermere* (1987), set in 1802, found its way back inevitably to Wordsworth's description of Mary Robinson – the "Maid of Buttermere" of the title

In the Lake District, there are almost 300 mountains and about 33 lakes (Grasmere Lake is depicted in the painting above by Francis Towne), with paths between them which 250 years ago would have been narrow and regarded as perilous.

– and the comments on her by William and Dorothy were as pertinent a guide to the character and the story as any information you could wish for.

Wordsworth, at 16, wrote "Dear Native Regions," in anticipation of leaving school. The lines well summarize the feelings of so many, and the deep feelings the Lake District still provokes:

"Dear native regions, I foretell / From what I feel at this farewell / That, whersoe'er my steps may tend / And whensoe'er my course shall end / If in that hour a single tie / Survive of local sympathy / My soul will cast the backward view / The longing look alone on you."

THE ROMANTICS ABROAD

"Abroad" was one of the most potent words in the vocabulary of the British Romantics, obsessed as they were with what John Keats called "the viewless wings of poesy" – the realm beyond immediately visible reality, the limitless world of the imagination, the dream of the infinite elsewhere. But "abroad" also had more specific – and problematic – connotations. Between 1792 and 1815 Britain was largely engaged in waging a bitter war against Revolutionary France, and then the Napoleonic Empire. The fighting and blockades rendered much of mainland Europe inaccessible, travelling was dangerous. "Abroad" was not just a place of escape into poetic fancy, Grand Tour or innocent holiday, but a political minefield as well.

For the young Wordsworth and his generation, the first months after the Bastille fell in 1789 were a time of exhilarating hope that a better future had dawned. In 1790, while still a Cambridge undergraduate, Wordsworth (1770–1850) spent the summer vacation walking down the east of France to the famous monastery of the Grande Chartreuse and the splendours of the Alps. Carrying his belongings in a bundle on his head, he was greeted everywhere as a brother, and joined in the fun. "Bliss it was in that Dawn to be alive," as one of his most famous lines would have it. Later the following year, he returned to France seeking work as a tutor. By then the party was over: the promises of Liberté, Fraternité and Egalité were not being fulfilled, there was terror and violence on the streets, and a disastrous love affair in Blois with Annette Vallon added to his disenchantment. He returned to England in 1793 sadder and wiser – later recording the episode in his epic autobiographical poem *The Prelude* (written in 1805 but published posthumously in 1850). Apart from a brief trip in 1802 to visit his daughter by Annette Vallon, he would not return to France for nearly thirty years, by which time he had become patriotic to the point of xenophobia, his mind closed off to foreign influence, his genius as a poet dried up.

Between 1809 and 1811 Byron visited Portugal, Malta, Albania, Greece and the Levant – a tour which gave him the opportunity to swim the Hellespont, in emulation of Leander, the legendary lover of Hero. The event is recorded in the painting of Byron, above, by Sir William Allan.

His contemporary, Samuel Taylor Coleridge (1772–1834), directed his dreams across the Atlantic. In 1794, with another fledgling poet, Robert Southey, he planned to escape the oppressively reactionary atmosphere of William Pitt's England by emigrating to the United States, where he and a group of friends would establish a Utopian community on the banks of the Susquehanna. The scheme soon foundered, but Coleridge remained fascinated by travellers' tales – as we can read in "The Rime of the Ancient Mariner" (1798) and "Kubla Khan" (1816).

Coleridge's first taste of real abroad came between 1798 and 1799, when he visited Germany with Wordsworth and his sister Dorothy on a trip that lasted ten months. His motives were mixed: in part he needed to separate from his wife Sara; he also wanted to learn the language and make contact with the influential new Romantic philosophers of the University of Göttingen, who shaped his poetic theories. Back in England, he was soon miserable again, and proposed another abortive community, this time in the West Indies. Eventually, in 1804, he went to Malta and took a job as secretary to the High Commissioner. Poor health, opium addiction and desperate homesickness forced him to return, via Rome in 1806. He never left England again, except to tour the Rhine with Wordsworth in 1828.

The warmth of Rome came too late to save Keats, who spent his last few weeks in an apartment just off the Spanish Steps, right.

Following the fall of Napoleon, and the re-opening of the Mediterranean, Italy would become the country with the strongest allure for a younger generation of Romantics. For John Keats (1795–1821), its dry sunny climate also represented a last hope in his fight against tuberculosis. But after a difficult sea voyage from London to Naples with his friend Joseph Severn, he died on 23 February 1821 in Rome, and is buried in the Protestant Cemetery there. It was his only trip abroad, and it is tragic to think how in happier circumstances this most exotic of poets might have been thrilled and stimulated – as were so many other Romantic writers – by the Italian landscape and its ruins.

Lord Byron (1788–1824) was the best-travelled of the great Romantics. As a young nobleman, fresh out of Cambridge, who had made a stir with the publication of his satirical ode "English Bards and Scotch Reviewers"(1809), he embarked on a version of the Grand Tour so common in the eighteenth century. Soon he had become one of the most famous and glamorous men of Romantic Europe, the author-hero of the sensational poem "Childe Harold's Pilgrimage" (1812), loosely based on his own travels, and a great figure in fashionable society.

Byron described Shelley's funeral on the beach near Viareggio, above: "You can have no idea what an extraordinary effect such a funeral pile has, on a desolate shore, with mountains in the background and the sea before, and the singular appearance the salt and frankincense gave to the flame. All of Shelley was consumed, except his heart, which...is now preserved in spirits of wine...."

All this made the scandalous break-up of his marriage to Annabella Milbanke of such public interest that he was forced to leave England, never to return. Having dawdled through the Low Countries, passing Waterloo and sailing down the Rhine, he settled in 1816 for some months on Lake Geneva. The celebrated French intellectual Madame de Staël was a neighbour; his house-companions included Claire Clairmont, soon to be mother of his illegitimate daughter, and her half-sister Mary, recently married to a wild young poet called Percy Bysshe Shelley (1792–1822). During the day, Shelley and Byron boated on the lake, discussing Wordsworth's poem "The Excursion" (1800). In the evening they told ghost stories, causing Mary Shelley the nightmare which gave her the germ of *Frankenstein* (1818). Among the poems to emerge from this fascinating creative episode in literary history are Shelley's "Mont Blanc," Byron's "The Prisoner of Chillon" and the climax to the third canto of "Childe Harold's Pilgrimage."

Shelley, Mary and Claire had already travelled *à trois*, when Shelley and Mary eloped in 1814. They had found France shattered by the War; but, as Claire's diary records, Shelley (like Wordsworth before him) was enraptured by the glory of the Alps. "How great is my rapture he said, I a fiery man with my heart full of youth and with my beloved at my side, I behold these lordly immeasurable Alps." Meanwhile their cart-driver annoyed them by talking of "how good the pasturage was for cows." For a few weeks they settled near Lucerne, but soon lost heart and decided to return to England, via the water-buses which ferried up and down the Rhine. Priggish and fastidious,

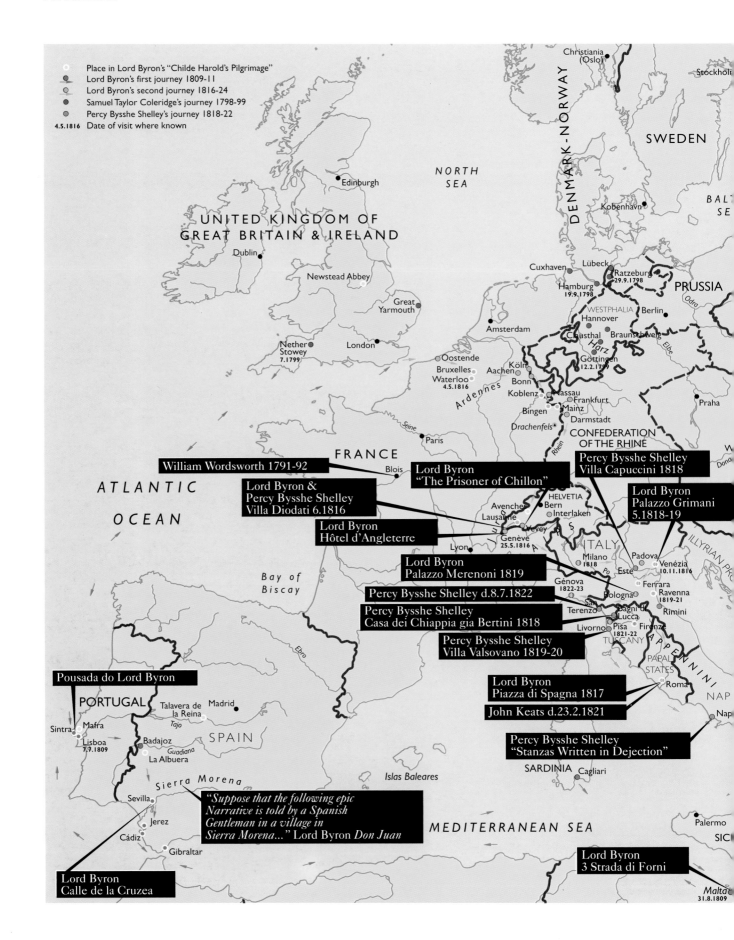

Place in Lord Byron's "Childe Harold's Pilgrimage"
Lord Byron's first journey 1809-11
Lord Byron's second journey 1816-24
Samuel Taylor Coleridge's journey 1798-99
Percy Bysshe Shelley's journey 1818-22
4.5.1816 Date of visit where known

Christiania (Oslo)
Stockholm
DENMARK-NORWAY
SWEDEN
NORTH SEA
BALTIC SEA
Kobenhavn
Edinburgh
Cuxhaven
Lübeck
Ratzeburg 29.9.1798
PRUSSIA
UNITED KINGDOM OF GREAT BRITAIN & IRELAND
Hamburg 19.9.1798
Hannover
WESTPHALIA
Berlin
Odra
Dublin
Newstead Abbey
Clausthal
Braunschweig
Harz
Elbe
Great Yarmouth
Amsterdam
Köln
Göttingen 12.2.1799
Praha
Nether Stowey 7.1799
London
Oostende
Bruxelles
Aachen
Bonn
Koblenz
Nassau
Frankfurt
Bingen
Mainz
Darmstadt
Waterloo 4.5.1816
Ardennes
Drachenfels
CONFEDERATION OF THE RHINE
Seine
Paris
Rhein
Dona
William Wordsworth 1791-92
FRANCE
Blois
Lord Byron "The Prisoner of Chillon"
Percy Bysshe Shelley Villa Capuccini 1818
ATLANTIC OCEAN
Lord Byron & Percy Bysshe Shelley Villa Diodati 6.1816
HELVETIA
Avenches
Bern
Interlaken
Lord Byron Palazzo Grimani 5.1818-19
Lausanne
Vevey
Lord Byron Hôtel d'Angleterre
Lyon
Genève 25.5.1816
ITALY
ILLYRIAN PRO
Milano 1818
Padova
Bay of Biscay
Lord Byron Palazzo Merenoni 1819
Po
Este
Venézia 10.11.1816
Percy Bysshe Shelley d.8.7.1822
Génova 1822-23
Ferrara
Ravenna 1819-21
Percy Bysshe Shelley Casa dei Chiappia gia Bertini 1818
Bologna
San Terenzo
Bagni di Lucca
Rimini
Livorno
Pisa 1821-22
Firenze
Percy Bysshe Shelley Villa Valsovano 1819-20
TUSCANY
Ebro
APPENNINI
Pousada do Lord Byron
Lord Byron Piazza di Spagna 1817
PAPAL STATES
Roma
NAP
PORTUGAL
Talavera de la Reina
Madrid
John Keats d.23.2.1821
Sintra
Mafra
Tajo
SPAIN
Nap
Lisboa 7.7.1809
Badajoz
Guadiana
La Albuera
Percy Bysshe Shelley "Stanzas Written in Dejection"
SARDINIA
Cagliari
Sierra Morena
Islas Baleares
Sevilla
"Suppose that the following epic Narrative is told by a Spanish Gentleman in a village in Sierra Morena..." Lord Byron *Don Juan*
MEDITERRANEAN SEA
Palermo
Jerez
Cádiz
SIC
Gibraltar
Lord Byron 3 Strada di Forni
Lord Byron Calle de la Cruzea
Malta 31.8.1809

they were shocked by the "horribly disgusting" behaviour of their fellow-passengers. "Having travelled and viewed the follies of other nations, my own country appears the most reasonable and the most enlightened," concluded Claire: a most un-Romantic sentiment.

The further dramas of Shelley's life have often been chronicled. From 1818 he moved permanently abroad, and was a great wanderer round Italy: Florence (where he wrote "Ode to the West Wind," 1820), Venice, Lucca, Livorno, Rome and Pisa, where Byron joined him. His last home was a quiet villa on the edge of the Bay of Lerici, near the modern resort of La Spezia. His brief life had been endlessly turbulent; here the exquisite landscape, and the presence of the enigmatic beauty Jane Williams, inspired him to some of his most serenely beautiful lyric poems. The almost eerie calm of "Lines written in the Bay of Lerici" and "With a Guitar, to Jane" preceded a storm. In July 1822 he went out sailing in the bay with friends; their boat, the Ariel, went down in a summer squall. Shelley's body was washed up some days later, unrecognizable except for a copy of Keats' "Hyperion" (1818–19), folded in his jacket pocket.

Byron too had spent the previous years living in various Italian cities: notably Venice, where his promiscuous involvements with women of all social stations won him further notoriety, and Ravenna, Pisa and Livorno. Although he found writing "a great pain," he wrote at a high speed, and continued to be astonishingly prolific. These were the years in which he produced turgidly serious "chamber-dramas" such as *Cain* (1821) and *The Two Foscari* (1821), now largely forgotten – and, as a pendant to their heavy-handedness, the light-fingered *Don Juan* (1819-24), which transports the reader not just through amorous adventures but on a "tour of Europe," through a variety of colourful European locations, from Seville to Saint Petersburg to London. Criticized in Britain, it was much admired by Goethe, among others.

His last journey brings us to another side of his multifarious personality. Always a "friend of liberty," he had spoken in the House of Lords on behalf of the Luddite cause. In Italy he supported the Carbonari, who were fighting the occupying Austrians. In 1823 he turned his attention to Greece, and the Greeks' revolutionary attempt to rid the country of oppressive Turkish rule. He agreed to lend the provisional government the then massive sum of £4,000, and sailed to Cephalonia to join the campaign, noting "I have a presentiment I shall die in Greece." His arrival boosted morale, but he found himself increasingly exasperated by Greek in-fighting. His health suffered in the dreadful conditions; three years after Keats, two after Shelley, he died of fever at the besieged town of Missolonghi in 1824. Thus, like so many of the English Romantics he ended his life abroad, in the European landscape that so deeply imbues much of their poetry and sensibility. Refused by Westminster Abbey, his embalmed body was returned home to Hucknall in Nottinghamshire. His heart remained, and today his name is still honoured in the modern Greece for which he fought.

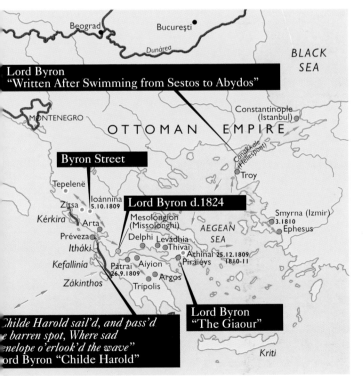

During Byron's stay in Switzerland in 1816 he stayed at the Villa Dodoti, above, from where he toured Lake Geneva (on whose banks it stood) with fellow Romantic poet, Shelley.

THE EUROPEAN TOUR: *The Romantic poets frequently travelled to the Mediterranean, with its sunny climate, romantic views and freedom from English political constraints and social conventions. The Romantic Grand Tour became central to their writing.*

JANE AUSTEN'S REGENCY ENGLAND

The image of Jane Austen's (1775–1817) world as confined is so famous we sometimes forget she was a citizen of the Regency world, and lived through its great transitions – not least the French and Romantic Revolutions, the Luddite Riots and the Napoleonic Wars. Likewise the view of her novels as romantic tales filled with marriageable girls and pantomime mamas has been so encouraged by film and television adaptations it is hard to remember she was one of the finest social observers of English writing, and one of the greatest comic ironists. True, she lived much in the country, never married, never left British shores. But as Mrs Bennet says in *Pride and Prejudice*, "I assure you there is as much of *that* going on in the country as in town."

Like the Georgian country houses and Regency terraces generally seen as the background to her work, Austen belonged to the transition from the eighteenth century, with its emphasis on sense, reason and improvement, to the nineteenth, with its emphasis on "sensibility" and romantic excitement. It was an age of new styles and exoticisms. When the Prince Regent turned a Sussex fishing village into smart Brighton and put up an Oriental Pavilion, and "Beau" Brummell walked through the modern streets of Bath, they displayed a new self-consciousness and a fascination with art and excess. They were also in Jane Austen's eyeline. She lived for six years in Bath – the city features strongly in three of her novels. Lydia goes to smart Brighton in *Pride and Prejudice*. And Austen dedicated *Emma* to the Prince Regent, who admired her work.

Jane Austen was born at the parsonage in Steventon, near Bath, in 1775, the sixth of seven children in an academic family. Until he became vicar of Steventon her father, the Reverend George Austen, had been an Oxford don, with a good library well-used by his daughter. She went to school back in Oxford (Brasenose college), which features in *Northanger Abbey* and *Mansfield Park*, and then to Abbey School, Reading. By the time she was twenty, and before the eighteenth century was over, she'd begun writing novels. Three of her famous six – *Pride and Prejudice*, *Sense and Sensibility* and *Northanger Abbey*, her sharp parody of the highly fashionable Gothic romances of the day – and also *Lady Susan*, were drafted at Steventon.

Jane Austen, above, *was one of the finest social observers of her time.*

In 1801, when her father had turned seventy, the family decided to move to the elegant spa town of Bath in Somerset. Jane is said to have fainted at the news. Like Anne Elliot in *Persuasion*, she "persisted in a very determined, though silent, disinclination" for that famed social meeting place and health farm. "The first view of Bath in fine weather does not answer my expectations; I think I shall see more distinctly through rain," she says. The family went to live at 1 The Paragon, then 4 Sydney Terrace, near very fashionable Pulteney Street. Here Catherine Morland lodges in *Northanger Abbey*, and in *Persuasion* Laura Place, Milsom Street, Gay Street, Westgate Buildings and the Pump Rooms are all used to effect.

Bath reached the height of its fame in the mid-eighteenth century, and had many literary personalities (among them, William Congreve, Richard Sheridan, Oliver Goldsmith, Fanny Burney). Although by now somewhat supplanted for fashion by Brighton, it kept a great air of Regency splendour and style. "Bath shoots out into new crescents, circuses and squares every year," Horace Walpole reported in 1791. Mostly they followed the grand architectural plans of the John Woods, father and son, who over the eighteenth century laid out Queen Square, the great curving Crescent (now the Royal Crescent), the Circus and the North and South Parade, so shaping one of Britain's finest cities.

Bath's routines were unforgiving: "Every morning now brought its regular duties," reports *Northanger Abbey*,

Milsom Street, left, plays a central role in Jane Austen's Bath novels. In Northanger Abbey *it is on this road that Isabella Thorpe goes shopping and General Tilney has lodgings.*

Jane Austen carefully learned the social map of Bath. She followed the season around the Upper and Lower Assembly Rooms and the Pump Room, below, ("In the Pump Room one who was so newly arrived in Bath must be met with") and recognized her own role in the marriage market – an important part of what Bath was for.

> "Do you know I get so immoderately sick of Bath, your brother and I were agreeing this morning that, though it is vastly well to be here for a few weeks, we would not live here for millions."
>
> Isabella Thorpe,
> *Northanger Abbey*

"shops to be visited; some new part of town to be looked at; and the Pump Room to be attended, where they paraded up and down for an hour, looking at everybody and speaking to no one" – a wise precaution. Following royalty and the latest "dandies," "Society" itself gathered, but many classes travelled across the country to take the health-giving (if not always clean) waters, enjoy the fashions, the notions, the season. "You may depend upon it, that they will move in the first set in Bath this winter, and as rank is rank, your being known to be related to them will have its uses in fixing your family (our family let me say) in that degree of consideration we all wish for," explains Mr Elliot in *Persuasion*.

At the spa resort, created around a Roman spring, assemblies and amusements were plentiful. Plays were performed at the old Theatre Royal in Orchard Street. There was a Circulating Library. Frailer figures came to bathe, take a health cure or just spend their last days. As in eighteenth century drama, spas and resorts became key settings for many of Austen's novels. Bath is in

Mansfield Park, *Northanger Abbey* and *Persuasion*. The unfinished *Sanditon* is about an itself unfinished speculators' seaside spa. *The Watsons*, the one novel Jane Austen wrote (but didn't finish) during her time in Bath, was initially set in a Sussex coastal resort, but then changed to the town of Dorking, Surrey.

Jane now submitted *Northanger Abbey*, under its original title *Susan*, to a publisher who took it but put it in a drawer; it would appear only after her death. In 1804, the Austens visited another popular resort, Lyme Regis on the Dorset coast. Here Jane engaged in fashionable sea-bathing, and walked on the famous Cobb, the harbour wall that projects out into the sea near the Undercliff. On their return to Bath, the family moved nearer the Pump Room on a six month lease to 27 Green Park Buildings. The Reverend Austen was ill, and in 1805 he died.

The Reverend's death, one of several that had occurred within the family, marked a tragedy and a sharp break in Jane Austen's life. She was thirty, had no income (she told her sister Cassandra to "prepare...for the sight of a sister sunk in poverty") and, despite proposals, was still unmarried, in a world where, as her novels acknowledge, for a woman marriage was all. With her mother and Cassandra she removed to the smaller 25 Gay Street and, later, in 1806, to unfashionable Trim Street. They then went to Southampton, sharing a house at 3 Castle Square with one of her naval brothers. In 1809 they moved again, to Chawton in Hampshire, where her brother Edward, adopted by a rich relative, had a handsome estate and a substantial cottage.

In this early illustration from Northanger Abbey *Henry Tilney proposes to Catherine Morland and, against his father's wishes, is accepted.*

Chawton Cottage, close to Alton, and near the London-Winchester high road, is nowadays the place most associated with Jane Austen. A seventeenth century red-brick house with "six bed-chambers," it is now a museum devoted to her work and her family. It was where she lived for the remaining eight years of her life, and where she rose to literary fame. Edward was often close by at Chawton Manor House and there was other society in the neighbourhood, but it was a quiet retreat, and became her chief writing place. She took pains to conceal her work, a creaking door warning her to hide it under the blotter when friends, relations and visitors entered.

In the era of the Romantic Revolution, when Byron and Scott dominated, her books seemed as modest and domestic in subject as she seemed quiet in life. In fact they owed everything to what had already happened to her, and to her sharply comic observations of the social world and her sense of the economic circumstances that governed real lives. Three had been drafted already, but were now rewritten. The later novels (*Mansfield Park*, *Emma* and *Persuasion*), were begun at Chawton but drew on previous experiences. In 1811 her first published book, *Sense and Sensibility*, *A Novel By a Lady*, appeared to acclaim. In 1813 *Pride and Prejudice* was an even greater success. In 1814 came *Mansfield Park*, in 1815 *Emma*.

In 1816 she revised the manuscript of *Northanger Abbey*, and completed surely her best book, *Persuasion*, about a heroine who had been forced into prudence in her youth and learns romance as she grows older. It is also about sea captains like her own brothers, who had triumphed against the French, and who represent a rising class in society. But her final illness – probably Addison's Disease – prevented work on her next, most modern book, *Sanditon*. In May 1817 she was moved to Winchester for medical treatment. At 8 College Street, now part of Winchester College, she died on July 18. She was buried in Winchester Cathedral, where her tomb is to be seen.

The map of Jane Austen's world is not wide, reflecting her class, gender, and unmarried state. She always spoke of it modestly, remarking on "the little bit of ivory on which I work with so fine a brush as produces little effect after much labour." Small wonder that, for all the admiration her books won, it took critics much time to see the hidden scale behind them. In

The Cobb at Lyme Regis, left, *provides the setting for a key scene in* Persuasion. *(Much later it would return in fiction as the place where the hero of John Fowles'* The French Lieutenant's Woman, *1969, first sees the figure of Sarah Woodruff, the Woman of the title.)*

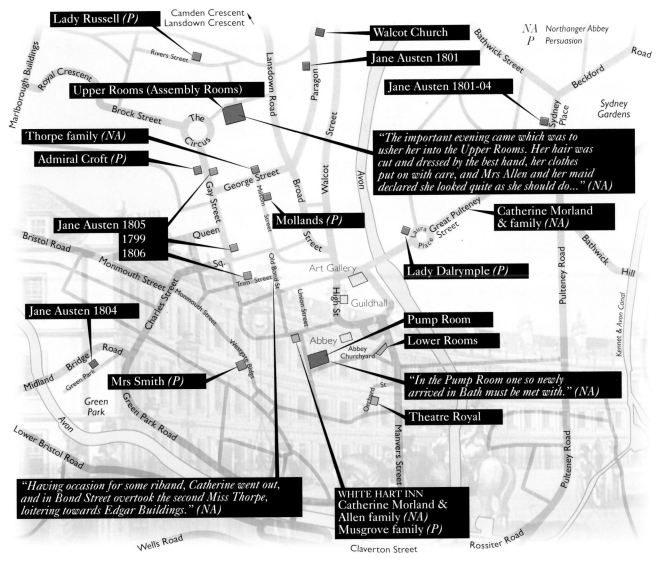

Camden Crescent
Lansdown Crescent

Lady Russell *(P)*

Walcot Church

Jane Austen 1801

NA Northanger Abbey
P Persuasion

Marlborough Buildings

Royal Crescent

Rivers Street

Upper Rooms (Assembly Rooms)

Brock Street

The Circus

Jane Austen 1801-04

Bathwick Street

Beckford Road

Sydney Place

Sydney Gardens

Thorpe family *(NA)*

Admiral Croft *(P)*

Gay Street

George Street

Milsom Street

Broad Street

Walcot Street

Avon

"The important evening came which was to usher her into the Upper Rooms. Her hair was cut and dressed by the best hand, her clothes put on with care, and Mrs Allen and her maid declared she looked quite as she should do…" *(NA)*

Jane Austen 1805
1799
1806

Queen Sq.

Mollands *(P)*

Laura Place

Great Pulteney Street

Catherine Morland & family *(NA)*

Bristol Road

Monmouth Street

Charles Street

Monmouth Street

Trim Street

Old Bond St.

Art Gallery

Lady Dalrymple *(P)*

Pulteney Road

Bathwick Hill

Jane Austen 1804

Wood Street

High St

Guildhall

Union Street

Abbey

Pump Room

Lower Rooms

Kennet & Avon Canal

Bridge Road

Green Park

Westgate Bldgs

Mrs Smith *(P)*

Abbey Churchyard

Orchard St

"In the Pump Room one so newly arrived in Bath must be met with." *(NA)*

Midland

Green Park Road

Avon

Lower Bristol Road

Theatre Royal

Manvers Street

"Having occasion for some riband, Catherine went out, and in Bond Street overtook the second Miss Thorpe, loitering towards Edgar Buildings." *(NA)*

WHITE HART INN
Catherine Morland & Allen family *(NA)*
Musgrove family *(P)*

Wells Road

Claverton Street

Rossiter Road

Austen's work the domestic is never far from the great, the country never distant from the town. Her books contain a real working society, and are precise on the sources of wealth and reputation. If they avoid the political riots and ironically observe the gothic romanticism of the day, they tell fundamental truths about the world she lived in.

They track rank and gradation, position and distinction, with a profound sense of that extraordinary pecking order, the English class system. They do so under the gaze both of ironic moral judgement and sensible compassion. They see life in the country is filled with echoes of the life of the world, that even in romance and marriage-making great patterns of social change are happening. As Sir Walter Scott said, "That young lady has a talent for describing the involvements and feelings and characters of ordinary life, which is to me the most wonderful I ever met with. The big Bow-Wow strain I can do myself like any now going; but the exquisite touch which renders ordinary common-place things and characters interesting from the truth of the description and the sentiment is denied to me." Today's readers still agree.

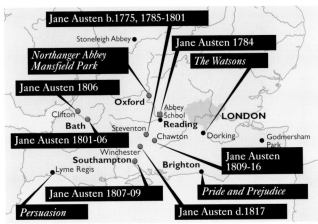

Jane Austen b.1775, 1785-1801

Stoneleigh Abbey

Jane Austen 1784

Northanger Abbey Mansfield Park

The Watsons

Jane Austen 1806

Oxford

Clifton

Bath

Abbey School

Reading

LONDON

Steventon

Chawton

Dorking

Godmersham Park

Jane Austen 1801-06

Winchester

Southampton

Brighton

Lyme Regis

Jane Austen 1809-16

Jane Austen 1807-09

Persuasion

Jane Austen d.1817

Pride and Prejudice

BATH AND SOUTHERN ENGLAND: *Bath features prominently in Jane Austen's* Northanger Abbey *and* Persuasion, *the main locations of which are plotted on the map of Bath above. Jane Austen's world was not very wide; she was born in Steventon, went to school in Oxford and Reading, spent six years in Bath, leaving only occasionally for visits to the seaside (Lyme Regis), and then lived her last years in Chawton Cottage near Alton.*

THE PARIS OF THE FRENCH ROMANTICS

The rue Chateaubriand in Paris leads into the rue Lord Byron, and is joined by the rue Balzac. Thus Paris commemorates literature; and thus the map of its street names evokes a great period of Romantic writing. Some people also find significance in the fact that the rue Chateaubriand is approached from the rue Washington – for the first American President was approached in the White House by the young Chateaubriand and informed that he single-handedly meant to discover the North-West Passage. This story was probably invented by Chateaubriand, whom Stendhal called the most consummate hypocrite in the whole of France. But it reminds us that one characteristic of the Romantic writers was not just they were fantasists, but that they often travelled far and wide in search of their fantasies.

In the wake of the French Revolution, literature in France as elsewhere grew more concerned with the emotions and the senses. Breaking free of the rules of eighteenth century Classicism, with its stress on reason, clarity and objectivity, it put new emphasis on nature and the transitions and mutability of history. It questioned the relation of self to society, the perplexities of being and emotion. The Revolution itself played a major role. The great figures of the age were brought down, ordinary people walked the stage of history, the world began anew. Then there was Napoleon: all Europe had been swept up in the dreams of a little man in a green-grey coat.

In France the term Romanticism was made widely known by Madame de Staël (1766–1817) in her book *De l'Allemagne* (1810). In this study of Germany, she distinguished the Romantic from the Classical, urged art to be more profound and sincere, and claimed the French should be open to foreign literature, especially German. The term Romantic stuck; the Romantics seemed a school with an agreed programme. That seemed especially so in Paris, where printing and publishing were undergoing a technical

Clockwise from top left: *Madame de Staël, Vicomte François-René de Chateaubriand, Alfred de Musset and Prosper Mérimée were among the leaders of the Romantic movement in Paris.*

revolution, great literary and philosophical journals were being founded, daily newspapers were circulating as they never had before, and the salon system linked those of similar political or artistic allegiance. Madame de Staël's own salon at 102 rue du Bac was one such famous meeting place, where the liberal minds of a generation met, among them the novelist Benjamin Constant, also her lover.

Madame de Staël offended Napoleon with her book, which compared France with the decline of the Roman Empire (appropriately her Swiss mother had nearly married English historian Edward Gibbon). The antipathy was mutual. On one occasion Madame de Staël danced with the Emperor. "Who," she asked him, "do you you think is the greatest woman who ever lived?" "I don't know her name, but she is the woman who has had the most children," Napolean replied. Not the answer the intellectual woman wanted. Staël was wife of the Baron de Staël-Holstein, Swedish Ambassador to Paris, from whom she legally separated in 1798. She was also daughter of Baron Necker, the Swiss banker in charge of French government finance from 1776 to 1781 and again at the dawn of the Revolution. At her father's house at

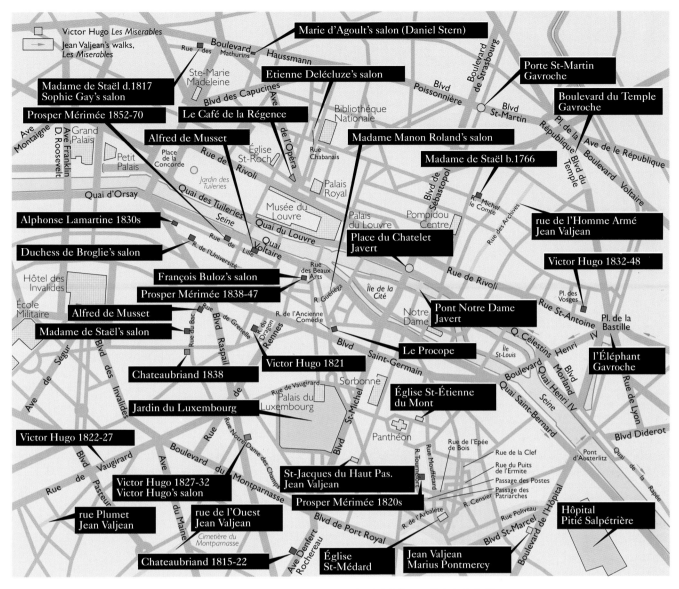

Map labels (clockwise / by region):

Victor Hugo *Les Miserables*

Jean Valjean's walks, *Les Miserables*

Marie d'Agoult's salon (Daniel Stern)

Etienne Delécluze's salon

Madame de Staël d.1817
Sophie Gay's salon

Prosper Mérimée 1852-70

Le Café de la Régence

Alfred de Musset

Madame Manon Roland's salon

Porte St-Martin
Gavroche

Boulevard du Temple
Gavroche

Madame de Staël b.1766

rue de l'Homme Armé
Jean Valjean

Alphonse Lamartine 1830s

Duchess de Broglie's salon

François Buloz's salon

Prosper Mérimée 1838-47

Place du Chatelet
Javert

Victor Hugo 1832-48

Alfred de Musset

Madame de Staël's salon

Pont Notre Dame
Javert

Le Procope

l'Éléphant
Gavroche

Victor Hugo 1821

Chateaubriand 1838

Jardin du Luxembourg

Église St-Étienne
du Mont

Victor Hugo 1822-27

Victor Hugo 1827-32
Victor Hugo's salon

St-Jacques du Haut Pas.
Jean Valjean

rue Plumet
Jean Valjean

rue de l'Ouest
Jean Valjean

Prosper Mérimée 1820s

Chateaubriand 1815-22

Église
St-Médard

Jean Valjean
Marius Pontmercy

Hôpital
Pitié Salpétrière

Map street and place names: Rue des Mathurins, Boulevard Haussmann, Ste-Marie Madeleine, Blvd des Capucines, Bibliothéque Nationale, Rue Chabanais, Ave de l'Opéra, Rue de l'Opéra, Ave Montaigne, Ave Franklin D. Roosevelt, Grand Palais, Petit Palais, Place de la Concorde, Rue de Rivoli, Église St-Roch, Jardin des Tuileries, Palais Royal, Musée du Louvre, Blvd de Sébastopol, Michel le Comte, Pompidou Centre, Rue des Archives, Boulevard de Strasbourg, Blvd Poissonnière, Blvd St-Martin, Pl. de la République, Blvd du Temple, Ave de le République, Boulevard Voltaire, Quai d'Orsay, Quai des Tuileries, Seine, Quai du Louvre, Quai Voltaire, Palais du Louvre, Rue de Rivoli, Pl. des Vosges, Rue St-Antoine, Pl. de la Bastille, Hôtel des Invalides, R. de l'Université, Rue de Lille, Rue des Beaux Arts, R. Guénéga, Île de la Cité, Notre Dame, École Militaire, R. de l'Ancienne Comédie, Rue du Bac, Rue de Grenelle, R. du Dragon, Blvd Raspail, Blvd de Rennes, Blvd Saint-Germain, Île St-Louis, Q. Célestins, Quai Henri IV, Blvd Morland, Henri, Quai Saint-Bernard, Rue de Lyon, Ave de Ségur, Blvd des Invalides, Rue de Vaugirard, Palais du Luxembourg, Sorbonne, Blvd St-Michel, Panthéon, Boulevard Diderot, Pont d'Austerlitz, Ave de Vaugirard, Rue de Pasteur, Boulevard du Montparnasse, Rue Notre Dame des Champs, Rue de l'Epée de Bois, Rue de la Clef, Rue du Puits de l'Ermite, Passage des Postes, Passage des Patriarches, R. Censier, Rue Poliveau, Rue de l'Hôpital, Blvd St-Marcel, Boulevard de l'Hôpital, Rue du Maine, Cimetière du Montparnasse, Ave Denfert Rochereau, Blvd de Port Royal, R. de l'Arbalète, R. Mouffetard, R.Tournefort

---

Coppet, Lake Geneva, or her mother's salon in Paris, she had met such men as Gibbon, Diderot and Talleyrand, and was thought a likely bride for William Pitt the Younger.

The rue du Bac was one of Madame de Staël's favourite places (she once said she would give all the world's rivers for the little stream there). She wrote two noted novels, *Delphine* (1802) and *Corinne* (1807), both portraits of the modern woman. Her tragedy was that Napoleon repeatedly exiled her: she was forced to live outside Paris, or at Coppet, or travel through Europe. "I do not dissemble that a residence in Paris has always appeared to me the most agreeable," she wrote in her travel record, *Ten Years of Exile* (published posthumously in 1821). "There only could I meet the generation which had known my father and the friends who had with us passed through the horrors of the Revolution.... French conversation exists nowhere but in Paris."

In 1788 Madame de Staël caused a scandal by writing enthusiastically (in *Lettre sur les ouvrages et le caractere de J-J Rousseau*) of the works of Jean-Jacques Rousseau, often

THE PARIS OF THE ROMANTICS: *The Paris of the Romantics was a city of private salons, restaurants and cafés – meeting places for generations of writers.*

seen as Romanticism's founding father. Now she and Chateaubriand were its chief exponents. Like his famous predecessor, Vicomte François-René de Chateaubriand (1768–1848) also led a roving life. Born in Combourg near Saint-Malo and presented at court at the age of 19, he began to move in literary circles before becoming a great traveller and diplomat. The Revolution disrupted his life, and in 1791 he went to the United States, travelling through French Louisiana, which Napoleon would sell in the Louisiana Purchase of 1803. He returned to France, fought for the Royalists, and was exiled to England. The impact on him of American nature and Indians led to some of the most influential tales of Romanticism. "Atala" (1801), "René" (1805) and "Le Natchez" (1826), his "epic of natural man," combine exoticism with a love of the Indians, whilst *The Genius of Christianity* (1802) shows his melancholy religious bent: man's desire for the infinite can only be satisfied by Christianity. The Romantic heroes he depicts are endowed with boundless desires, imagination, loneliness, the *mal de siècle* of changing times.

Chateaubriand followed Napoleon's adventures in Egypt, writing of the magic "Orient." But falling out with him after the Duc of Enghien's assassination in 1804, he settled at La Vallée aux Loups, a country home south of Paris. After the Bourbon Restoration in 1815, he moved to 88 rue d'Enfer (now the rue Denfert-Rocherau), near the Observatory, then to the Hôtel de Clermont Tonnerre (now the Hôtel de Chateaubriand) in the rue du Bac, near Madame de Staël. A noted Parisian figure, Chateaubriand daily visited Madame Recamier, whose famous salon was held in the Abbaye-aux-Bois in the Faubourg Saint-Germain. Here he met Benjamin Constant (1767–1830), whose novel *Adolphe* (1816), its anguished hero tortured by conflicting emotional and social obligations, is a psycho-portrait of the Romantic hero. Chateaubriand himself was buried on the Grand-Bé, a tiny rock of an island off Saint-Malo in Britanny. Although now a tourist centre, it is cut off when the tide comes in, leaving Chateaubriand appropriately

Prosper Mérimée's short story, "Carmen" – the frontispiece of the 1884 edition is shown above *– provided the inspiration for Bizet's famous opera of the same name (1875).*

isolated there, in touch only with the infinite.

Napoleon did have his adversaries, but the age of the Napoleonic wars became remembered as a time of particular intensity and enthusiasm. "Even if one had to die, what did it matter?" wrote Alfred de Musset (1810–57) in his novel *Confessions d'un enfant du siècle* (1836). "Death itself was so beautiful in those days, so great, so splendid in its steaming crimson cloak. It was as if it had become the very stuff of youth, as if no-one believed any longer in old age." Musset, playwright, poet, lover of George Sand, was everyone's idea of the Romantic ("It is the heart which speaks and sighs when the hand writes," he said), but he was too independent to belong to a school. Plays like *Fantasio* (1834) and his sequence of night poems (1835–7) are among the famous works of the period. A noted Parisian figure, he lived for a long time at 25 Quai Voltaire.

Musset was one of a generation linked together by Paris. He and Mérimée attended the Lycée Henri IV on the Boulevard Saint Michel. Victor Hugo studied at Louis-le-Grand, by the Panthéon; Théophile Gautier and Gerard de Nerval were together at the Lycée Charlemagne, where Balzac was a pupil. But salons were the main influence. Charles Nodier (who travelled to Scotland to meet Sir Walter Scott, and became a specialist in fantastic tales) was Librarian at the Arsenal, where he brought the leading Romantic writers of the day, along with painters like Delacroix. Later in the 1820s, the most famous salon, known as the *cénacle*, was that of Victor Hugo, meeting at his house in the rue Notre Dame des Champs, Montparnasse. Madame de Staël's daughter, the Duchess of Broglie, held a salon in her house at 90 rue de l'Université, the editor François Buloz at 10 (now 6) rue des Beaux Arts; Etienne Delecluze gathered Romantics to his house in the rue de Chabanais. No less important were the cafés (the Procope, the Café de la Regence, near the Palais Royal), and restaurants (especially in the Montorgeuil area). Parisian writers must have spent much of their time

THE REVOLUTIONARY WARS

- **1789** *French Revolution begins; abolition of feudal system and proclamation of Rights of Man*
- **1792** *French Republic proclaimed; beginning of Revolutionary Wars*
- **1799** *Napoleon becomes First Consul*
- **1804** *Napoleon becomes Emperor of France*
- **1805** *Napoleon defeats Austria and (1806) Prussia*
- **1812** *Napoleon invades Russia*
- **1815** *Napoleon defeated at Waterloo and exiled to St Helena*

there, but the Romantics still managed to write prolifically, particularly prose fiction.

Prosper Mérimée (1803–70) was among the most gifted. Influenced by Scott, he wrote a play about Cromwell before Hugo had the same idea, and encouraged interest in Russian writers like Gogol and Pushkin. His most famous works were the novellas "Carmen" (1845) and "Colomba" (1852). He lived for many years at 10 rue des Beaux Arts, for a time in the rue Jacob, finally at 52 rue de Lille. All are on the Left Bank, favoured as much by the Romantics as by the expatriates of the 1920s.

Alfred de Vigny (1797–1863), born in Loche, also won his fame amongst the Paris Romantics. Brought to the city by his parents at the age of seven, he lived first in the Elysée Bourbon, then in the Marché d'Aguesseau, where he wrote many poems and an important historical novel, *The Spider and the Fly* (1826). Disillusioned by the July Revolution of 1830, he retired to the family château, La Maine Giraud, near Angoulême, and wrote his play *Chatterton* (1835), about a classic *poète maudit*.

Alphonse Lamartine (1790–1869) grew up near Mâçon, Burgundy. In 1820 he wrote "Le Lac," a poem of lost love and despair which stays for many the epitome of Romanticism. *Jocelyn* (1838) and *Le Chute d'un Ange* (1838) are part of a mystical personal epic poem, but they also show the social preoccupations which led him into a life in politics. Elected a Deputy in 1833, he played a leading part in the Revolution of 1878 and in the creation of the Second Republic. In Paris he lived at 123 rue de Lille, and Napoleon III presented him with a chalet at Passy. However, burdened with debt, he retired home to the Mâçon country, to Saint-Point.

Victor Hugo (1802–85) was the most famed and versatile of the Romantics. He was born in Besançon, but his success may be measured in his Paris ascent from his room in the rue Vaugirard, the lodging he rented in the rue Notre-Dame-des-Champs, to his great residence at 6 Place des Vosges. Hugo could claim to have marked the start of Romanticism with the anti-Classical preface to his play *Cromwell* (1827), and secured it by the famous, tumultuous Comédie Française performance of his play *Hernani* (1830). Between 1851 and 1870 he was a political exile in the Channel Islands. When he arrived in Jersey his son asked him what he intended to do there. "Contemplate the ocean," replied Hugo. "And you?" "I shall read Shakespeare," came the reply. "It's the same thing," Hugo said. And he published his Shakespeare in 1864. He wrote some of his greatest works in Guernsey. Novels, such as the outstanding *Les Misérables* (1862) and *Toilers of the Sea* (1866) as well as a number of poems. He returned to Paris a hero. For many in France he remains the inescapable symbol of French Romanticism.

When the greatest of the Romantics, Victor Hugo, returned to Paris from exile in 1870, it was in triumph. He was elected to the national assembly and the senate and lived his last years in veneration. His state funeral in 1885, top, was attended by two million people. His novel, Les Misérables – *the frontispiece is shown above – was an epic tale of the sufferings of humanity and is today one of the most important works to have come out of the Romantic period.*

WEIMAR AND THE GERMAN ROMANTICS

In 1776, as America's Continental Congress celebrated the Declaration of Independence, German literature set out on an expedition from Classicism to Romanticism, from a commitment to perfectability to a vision of infinity. Politically this journey came to a conclusion when Germany's constitution was created in 1848, at the Frankfurter Paulskirche. Its first draft was laid out in 1816, at Weimar. (So was the constitution of 1919 which created the Weimar Republic.) It must sometimes seem that Weimar was the hub of Germany – especially as it is also associated with Christoph Martin Wieland (1733–1813), Johann Gottfried Herder (1744–1803), Johann Wolfgang von Goethe (1749–1832) and Friedrich von Schiller (1759–1805), some of the greatest figures of German literary and philosophical culture.

In fact Weimar was the small seat of government of the twin Duchies of Weimar and Eisenach in Thuringia, on the River Ilm. In Goethe's day it had a population of six thousand, and was a market town for the surrounding country, which at the first census of 1785 had 106,398 inhabitants in some seven hundred square miles of territory. Its main feature was the beauty of the surrounding coun-

Madame de Staël, in her famous book on Germany (De l'Allemagne, 1810), saw Weimar "not as a small town, but a large château," as most of it was part of the palace of Duke Karl August – Karl Kraus's painting of the Duchy, above, from c.1785 shows this perfectly.

tryside, which tempted philosophers and writers to extended walks: at least, that is, until the Duke, with much help from Goethe, created a more inviting alternative by laying out a large park in the town's centre.

Friedrich von Schiller, above, attempted to balance the ideals of Classicism and Romanticism.

It was Wieland who first prepared the ground, when, on the invitation of the Duchess Anna Amalia, niece of Frederick the Great, he went as tutor to the young princes Karl August and Bernhard. In his famous Bildungsroman, *Agathon* (1766–7) – the first philosophical novel of its kind – he had tried to bridge the gap between personal feelings and dialectical reasoning, so laying the foundation stones of *Sturm und Drang* (Storm and Stress), the literary movement which was to lead the way to German Romanticism. In 1776

another representative of this movement, Herder, followed. As historian and literary critic, he became Goethe's mentor, and drew his attention to Shakespeare's art, as well as to the importance of national sensibility in literature. Their friendship began in Strasbourg from 1770, declined when they met again in Weimar, then recovered in later years.

It was in 1775 that Goethe, still only 26, moved to Weimar as a busy court official to the new young Duke Karl August. He had already become famous with his play *Götz von Berlichingen* (1771–3) and his novel *The Sorrows of Young Werther* (1774). Werther is the typical genius, who perishes of disappointed love and his inability to find sufficient sympathy in his surroundings. The book started a literary and sentimental revolution right across Europe. It is among the first to make a personal effort to express emotion. Here writing starts to make experiments, language no longer follows strict rules. Christian belief loses importance, nature is idealized, the artificial life of the Baroque court condemned, and feeling, as the young Goethe has it, is everything.

Schiller, who from 1788 taught history at the University of Jena, which lies only a few miles away, came to Weimar soon after. He too became established as a great playwright with *Die Räuber* (1781), a drama of political revolt, and in Weimar he would write more major plays, including *Wilhelm Tell* (1804). The two men distrusted each other at first, but came to recognize that they were complementary as poets, playwrights and thinkers. Both tried to balance the claims of Classicism and Romanticism. Classicism had found its renaissance in the speculative aesthetics of Johann Winckelmann (1717–68), whose sensitive insights into Greek and Roman art became the foundations of modern archaeology. Unlike the French Enlightenment, which emphasized social and rational rather than aesthetic ends, the German Enlightenment (*Aufklrung*) sought a comprehensive understanding of the modern world.

Goethe and Schiller were instrumental in developing the idea of culture as something more than material, an ideal to live by. What Weimar writers share is a humanistic philosophy of life, an invincible optimism concerning the perfectability of man. Man should be capable of shaping his own nature and identity, and thereby culture and society too. Goethe strove for an organic harmony of form and content, science and art, man and nature, reason and feeling. His plays, poems and novels win the confidence of their readers not through logic or style alone, but through the integrated beauty of their form. Their protagonists impress us through the fulfilment of their duties, which are no longer given by God but by man to himself. The idea of Culture (*Kultur*) was central. It resurrects from generation to generation, handed down by word or through institutions. This philosophy found literary expression in Goethe's own great Bildungsroman, *Wilhelm Meister's Apprenticeship* (1796), which became the great source book for the early Romantics.

The page, above, *is taken from the earliest illustrated edition of Goethe's* Faust, *which appeared in 1854, with sketches by Engelbert Seibertz.*

Schiller too had close contact with this new school (the *Neue Schule*, as members called their movement), until a quarrel divided him from the group that had gathered in Jena. He remained closer to the idealistic principles of Immanuel Kant (1724–1804), the great philosopher of his generation. The Kantian "Categorical Imperative" and his own rational idealism govern the actions of his dramatic protagonists, who perish in the attempt to reconcile personal longing and ethical duties, sacrificing the first to fulfil the second. Goethe for a time fled Weimar for Italy, where he acquired a taste for the Italian Renaissance and where his artistic excitement quickened. In 1788 he returned, re-designed his house on Frauenplan, and entered the later period of his writings. For most of his life he worked on his drama *Faust* (*Part One*, 1808; *Part Two*, 1832). But he also wrote the remarkable and symbolic novel *Elective Affinities* (1809) and took up extensive scientific, medical and botanical interests.

New visitors arrived in the Duchy of Weimar. In 1796 Johann Friedrich Richter, alias Jean Paul (1763–1825), was invited. He met Herder, Goethe and Schiller, and wrote his own comic Bildungsroman, *Siebenkäs* (1796–97), which followed the newly-beaten track. The poet Friedrich Hölderlin (1770–1843) was received at Goethe's house; by contrast the dramatist and storywriter Heinrich von Kleist (1777–1811) never recovered from the depression resulting from his rejection by Goethe. By now many of the Romantics of the *Neue Schule* had gathered round the University of Jena. August Wilhelm Schlegel (1767–1845) from Göttingen, became a professor, and laid down many

In Werther *and* Faust, *Johann Wolfgang von Goethe,* above, *created figures of almost mythical significance.*

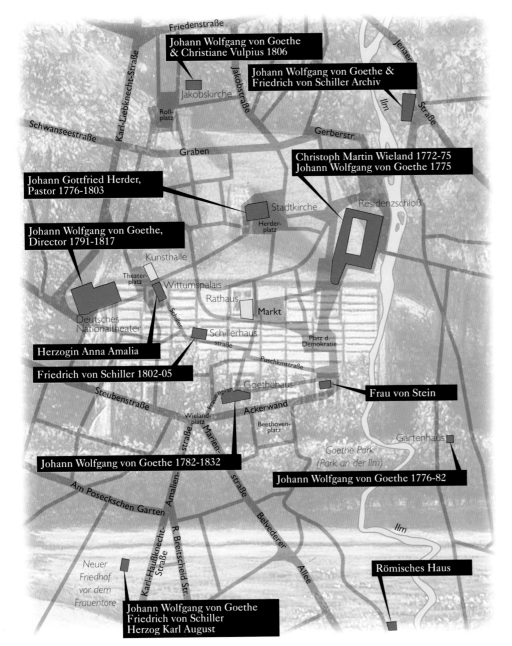

Friedenstraße

Johann Wolfgang von Goethe
& Christiane Vulpius 1806

Johann Wolfgang von Goethe &
Friedrich von Schiller Archiv

Jakobskirche

Jakobstraße

Jenaer

Straße

Roll-
platz

Schwanseestraße

Karl-Liebknecht-Straße

Gerberstr.

Ilm

Graben

Christoph Martin Wieland 1772-75
Johann Wolfgang von Goethe 1775

Johann Gottfried Herder,
Pastor 1776-1803

Stadtkirche

Residenzschloß

Herder-
platz

Johann Wolfgang von Goethe,
Director 1791-1817

Kunsthalle

Theater-
platz

Wittumspalais

Rathaus

Deutsches
Nationaltheater

Markt

Schiller-

Schillerhaus

Herzogin Anna Amalia

straße

Platz d.
Demokratie

Friedrich von Schiller 1802-05

Puschkinstraße

Steubenstraße

Goethehaus

Frauenplan

Frau von Stein

Ackerwand

Wieland-
platz

Beethoven-
platz

Marien-

Johann Wolfgang von Goethe 1782-1832

straße

Gartenhaus

Goethe Park
(Park an der Ilm)

Amalien-

Johann Wolfgang von Goethe 1776-82

Am Poseckschen Garten

straße

Ilm

Belvederer

Neuer
Friedhof
vor dem
Frauentore

Karl-Haußknecht-
Straße

R.Breitscheid Str.

Allee

Römisches Haus

Johann Wolfgang von Goethe
Friedrich von Schiller
Herzog Karl August

*The Grimm brothers − Jacob and
Wilhelm, above − produced what is
now the most famous collection of fairy
tales in the world.*

achievement, by departing from Classicism altogether. Friedrich Schlegel denied the desirability of Classical works, seeing their idealized and fixed forms as barriers to perfectability. Greek literature became not the artistic ideal but something to challenge and overthrow. This was a philosophy that offered scope for the enormous creativity which became the great characteristic of German Romanticism. Now it was no longer enough to live in harmony with nature; the Romantics wanted to live in unison with it. The sense of life was found by turning away from reality. Johann Fichte (1762−1814) was a leading philosopher, developing a form of idealism where the *Geist*, the spirit, commands. According to Friedrich Schelling (1775−1854), the Romantic perception of art was the one force that could reconcile the eternal dualism of nature and consciousness.

Although the Romantics divided in several directions, a new spirit of experiment emerged − in painting (Philipp Otto Runge, Casper David Friedrich) and music (Robert Schumann, Felix Mendelssohn). The fixed rules of the past were broken. Nationality, language theory and etymology became important concerns; so did myth and

of the tenets of Romanticism. His brother Friedrich (1772−1829) wrote for Schiller's literary reviews, and he was to produce an essay on *Wilhelm Meister* which confirmed the importance of the novel as a genre. With their literary theory they prepared the ground for the new school. Other Romantics came too, including the poet Friedrich von Hardenberg, alias Novalis (1772−1801), the dramatist and novelist Ludwig Tieck (1773−1853), and his friend the poet Wilhelm Wackenroder (1773−98). They aimed to create the Romantic book that could combine all the arts, appeal to all the senses. Unfortunately their attempts usually led to such fragmentations as Novalis's *Heinrich von Ofterdingen* (1802), which integrated music and painting, poetry and prose. It also gave the *Neue Schule* its key symbol, the blue flower. It was Novalis who declared the goal of the movement: to surpass Goethe's literary

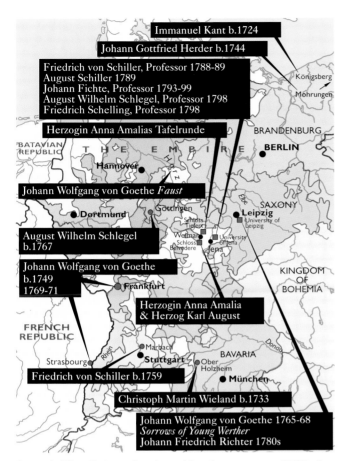

Immanuel Kant b.1724

Johann Gottfried Herder b.1744

Friedrich von Schiller, Professor 1788-89
August Schiller 1789
Johann Fichte, Professor 1793-99
August Wilhelm Schlegel, Professor 1798
Friedrich Schelling, Professor 1798

Herzogin Anna Amalias Tafelrunde

Johann Wolfgang von Goethe *Faust*

August Wilhelm Schlegel
b.1767

Johann Wolfgang von Goethe
b.1749
1769-71

Herzogin Anna Amalia
& Herzog Karl August

Friedrich von Schiller b.1759

Christoph Martin Wieland b.1733

Johann Wolfgang von Goethe 1765-68
Sorrows of Young Werther
Johann Friedrich Richter 1780s

GERMANY: *When Goethe moved to Weimar in 1775, it became the centre of German Romanticism, attracting writers, philosophers and artists from the surrounding areas.*

With the work of Joseph Freiherr von Eichendorff (1788–1857), that ever restless figure, the Romantics began to deplore the impact of industrialism on nature, society and the individual. In the fantastical tales of Ernst Thomas Amadeus (E.T.A.) Hoffman (1776–1822), story-teller and composer, an admirer of Beethoven and an interpreter of Mozart, imagination combined with reality, and began to indicate the way toward realism. Romanticism is famous for its escapism. But it showed more political awareness than Goethe, who preached ethics and the duty of the individual, and came to distrust the movement he himself had helped to create.

Yet by the time he died, aged 82, Goethe had himself explored most of the issues – Classicism, Romanticism, nature and science, psychological conflict – which would preoccupy the revived romantic German literature of the nineteenth century. He and Schiller (who died over a quarter of a century earlier) are buried together, in a mausoleum in the ducal cemetery at Weimar – which itself came to be seen as one of the great and ideal meeting places of European art and culture. It later attracted more great figures, including Nietzsche. The Goethe House (Goethes Gartenhaus) and the Schiller House (Schillerhaus) stand in the town, and their two statues are outside the National Theatre, signifying the influence they had not just on German but world literature.

legend. The Grimm brothers (Jacob, 1785–1863; Wilhelm, 1786–1859) were philologists, who simply collected fairy tales and folk songs, and presented Germans with their first dictionary and a comprehensive grammar. At their request they provided the poets Clemens Brentano (1778–1842) and Achim von Arnim (1781–1831) with folk songs they had gathered, and a new collection (*Des Knaben Wunderhorn*, 1805–8) appeared in which old tales and songs were adapted to Romantic sensibility: not quite what the Grimms had intended. Tieck too wrote fairy and supernatural tales (*Der Runenberg*, 1804). The Grimm brothers presented their own collection of tales in three volumes between 1812 and 1815.

German Romanticism became of international interest and influence for writers like Walter Scott and Washington Irving. New centres of Romanticism appeared at Heidelberg and Stuttgart. Many of the *Neue Schule* (Tieck, Schelling, the brothers Schlegel), had moved on to Berlin.

Johann H Füssli, like his contemporaries, took inspiration from the supernatural for his painting The Nightmare *(1781), right.*

WASHINGTON IRVING'S EUROPE

"I was always fond of visiting new scenes, and observing strange characters and manners. Even when a mere child I began my travels, and made many tours of discovery into foreign parts and unknown regions of my city, to the frequent alarm of my parents, and the emolument of the town-crier." So starts Washington Irving's (1783–1859) *The Sketch Book of Geoffrey Crayon, Gent* (1819–20), one of the first important books of American literature. Most of it is set in Europe, especially Britain, a place where he indulged what he called his "rambling propensity," and in the process created a large literary map that was to have vast consequences for Europe itself.

As his Christian name suggests, Washington Irving was a child of the American Revolution. The youngest son of a Scottish merchant who had settled in New York, he grew up in the "Knickerbocker" city, still close to its Dutch past. In 1809 the 26-year-old Irving, now a lawyer, provided it with an extravagant history when under the penname of Diedrich Knicker-bocker, he published his comic *A History of New York* (1908). It fired his ambition to be a professional writer – but the role scarcely existed in the newly independent America. With the war of 1812 hostilities with Britain resumed. No sooner had they ended in 1815 than Irving took the month-long sailing ship voyage over the Atlantic to Britain, hoping to satisfy his literary ambitions. It was to be the start of a 17-year expatriation.

The trip had a practical aim. His family's transatlantic import-export business, which had a base in Liverpool, was hit by the war, and eventually went bankrupt. Though he tried to save it, his ambitions were larger. "I am determined not to return home until I have sent some writings before me," he wrote, noting the writer's problems in a new country: "Unqualified for business, in a nation where everyone is busy; devoted to literature, where literary leisure is confounded with idleness; the man of letters [in America] is almost an insulated being, with few to understand, less to value, and scarcely any to encourage his pursuits."

In Britain tastes were changing. The Romantic revolution of Wordsworth, Byron, Shelley, Keats and Walter Scott was well under way. Irving learned from all of them,

Irving, above, was the first professional American writer. Trained as a lawyer, he much preferred to write, and became the leading American literary figure of his day, as well as a literary ambassador between the United States and Europe.

and realized too that in Britain a writer could now actually live by his writing. Adopting a new literary character – Geoffrey Crayon, a travelling artist – he wrote *The Sketch Book*, a spirited collection of essays and stories drawn from his English travels, and based on his "rambling propensity."

To modern tastes *The Sketch Book* may not seem a very original work. It was. In effect it invented Europe, above all England, seen from the eyes of an American who had come from the New World future to pay his respects to the Old World past. As Irving said, an American did not need to cross the Atlantic for wonders of scenery; they were there in the United States. "But," he wrote, "Europe held forth the charms of storied and poetical association. There were to be seen the masterpieces of art, the refinements of highly-cultivated society, the quaint peculiarities of ancient and youthful custom. My country was full of youthful promise; Europe was rich in the accumulated treasures of age. Her very ruins told the story of times gone by, and every mouldering stone was a chronicle." The American Grand Tour of Europe had begun.

Irving's book delighted readers on both sides of the Atlantic. It hailed the American promise; it celebrated the European past. Irving's New World idea of Europe was novel even to Europeans themselves. It had taken two revolutions – American and French – to suggest to them that theirs was an ancient culture, Greece to America's Rome. It showed America as a land without antiquity, but much in need of one. This was why Irving (Geoffrey

Crayon) had come over, looking at things "poetically, rather than politically." "I longed to wander over the scenes of renowned achievement – to tread, as it were, in the footsteps of antiquity – to loiter about the ruined castle – to meditate on the falling tower – to escape, in short, from the commonplace realities of the present, and lose myself among the shadowy grandeurs of the past," Crayon says in his "Author's Account of Himself." If America was futuristic New World, Europe was now charming Old World.

In Britain the Industrial Revolution had begun, as Irving, living in Liverpool and Birmingham, well knew. But the 34 English sketches he drew in his book dwell on a different, romantic Britain – of misty, labyrinthine English cities, quaint churches, the enduring life of the countryside and the village, the persistence of folk customs. His "poetic pilgrimage" takes in Westminster Abbey, Stratford-Upon-Avon and Oxford, places with literary or rural associations. Irving in effect invented romantic or tourist England. It is particularly to him that Britain owes an essential image of itself, as a land of quaint country Christmases, forelock-touching peasants, jolly journeys by stage coach, and of the benign American tourist, who, drawn by "an ancient tie of blood," delights in these romantic and poetic associations.

If quaint and touristic, the result is remarkably vivid. For Irving sentimentalized the romantic past when people on both sides of the Atlantic wanted to see history made legendary. His book established a "poetic" English landscape that would become literary and popular folklore.

He hadn't finished. Encouraged by Scott, who had himself largely invented Romantic Scotland, Irving next

set off to the heartland of folklore and legend, Germany. He toured the Rhine, collecting legends, went to Salzburg, Vienna and Dresden, and met the great German folktale writers, like Tieck and Jean Paul. A couple of the stories he collected he Americanized in *The Sketch Book*, and they became two of the most famous of all American tales – "Rip Van Winkle" and "The Legend of Sleepy Hollow." He reset them in the timeless Hudson valley, where the sense of legend could endure.

Irving had now created a romantic, thatched-cottage England and, with *Tales of a Traveller* (1824), a legendary Germany and Mittel-Europe. But the quest went on: "I am on the wing for Madrid!," he announced. It was a natural development, for through American diplomatic contacts Irving had been given access to the Columbus archive, and just at a time when the United States was expanding into the Spanish West. In 1828 he produced

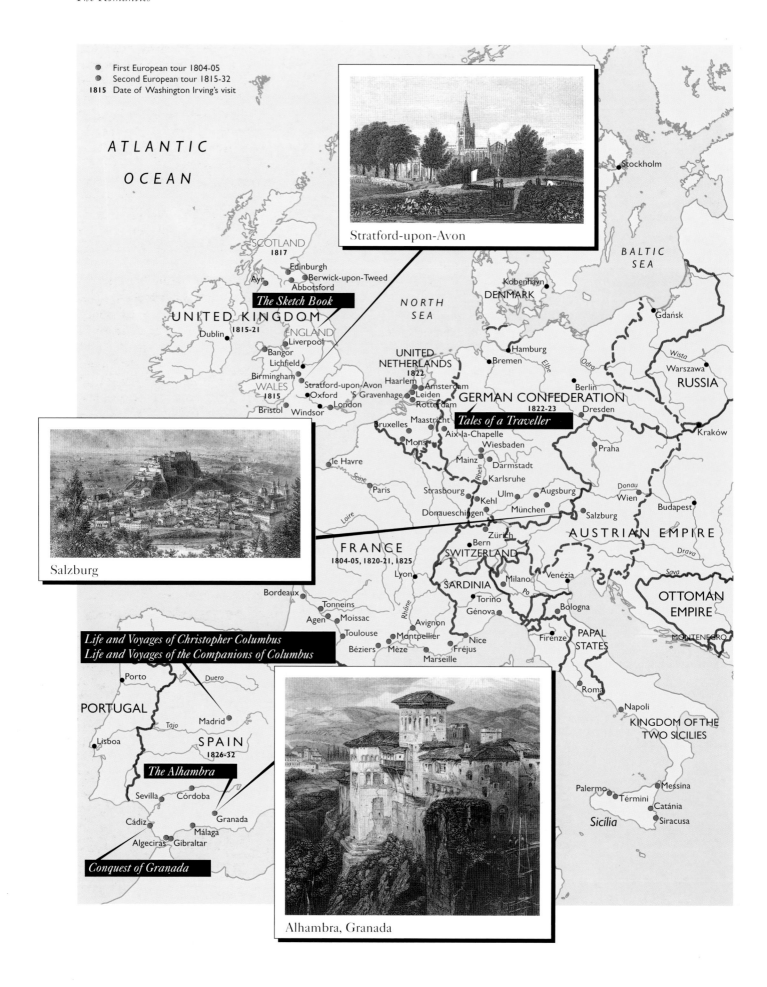

First European tour 1804-05
Second European tour 1815-32
1815 Date of Washington Irving's visit

ATLANTIC
OCEAN

Stratford-upon-Avon

BALTIC
SEA

Stockholm

SCOTLAND
1817

Edinburgh
Ayr   Berwick-upon-Tweed
       Abbotsford

NORTH
SEA

DENMARK

København

Hamburg

The Sketch Book

UNITED KINGDOM

Dublin **1815-21**
              Liverpool
         Bangor
         Lichfield
       Birmingham
WALES   Stratford-upon-Avon
1815   Oxford
       Bristol   Windsor London

ENGLAND

Bremen

Gdańsk

UNITED
NETHERLANDS
1822
Haarlem Amsterdam
'S Gravenhage Leiden
         Rotterdam
Maastricht
Bruxelles
         Aix-la-Chapelle
   Mons   Wiesbaden
         Mainz Darmstadt
         Karlsruhe

GERMAN CONFEDERATION
1822-23
Tales of a Traveller

Berlin

Dresden

Praha

Warszawa

RUSSIA

Kraków

le Havre

Salzburg

Seine

Paris

FRANCE
1804-05, 1820-21, 1825

Loire

Strasbourg
Kehl
Donaueschingen

Ulm   Augsburg
München

Zürich
Bern

SWITZERLAND

Lyon

SARDINIA

Rhône

Milano

Po

Torino

Génova

Wien

Donau

Salzburg

AUSTRIAN EMPIRE

Budapest

Drava

Sava

Venézia

Bologna

OTTOMAN
EMPIRE

MONTENEGRO

Bordeaux

Tonneins
Agen Moissac
Toulouse
Béziers Mèze

Avignon
Montpellier
Nice
Fréjus
Marseille

Firenze

PAPAL
STATES

Roma

Life and Voyages of Christopher Columbus
Life and Voyages of the Companions of Columbus

Porto

PORTUGAL

Duero

Madrid

Tajo

Lisboa

SPAIN
1826-32

The Alhambra

Sevilla Córdoba

Cádiz   Granada
       Málaga
Algeciras Gibraltar

Conquest of Granada

Napoli

KINGDOM OF THE
TWO SICILIES

Palermo
       Términi
Sicilia

Messina
Catánia
Siracusa

Alhambra, Granada

The Life and Voyages of Christopher Columbus, which portrayed the Genoan as a poetic, tragic explorer and completed the circle, linking the dusky mysteries of the Old World to the discovery of the New. Internationally translated, the book did much to win Columbus (and Irving) his mythic fame. With that and its sequel *Life and Voyages of the Companions of Columbus* (1831), Columbus fully became an American hero, a founding father of the nation. And Irving became the great chronicler of the transatlantic story.

Meanwhile, taken by the Moorish history of Spain, Irving was plunging deeper into history, above all legend. He went to live in the Moorish palace of the Alhambra in Granada, where he wrote *Legends of the Alhambra*. The book appeared in 1832, the year he returned to the United States and was fêted as the greatest American writer of the day. He had been to Europe, earned a great reputation, returned, and had not grown "un-American" by going. In fact he had brought Europe and the United States together on a single literary map.

Now the great American man of letters, Irving set himself up at Tarrytown in his beloved Hudson River valley, and turned his attention to the great Westward adventure. He wrote *Astoria* (1836), about William Astor and the fur trade, and *The Adventures of Captain Bonneville, USA* (1837), about the explorations of the desert. But his heart was not in it; in any

> "How many legends and traditions, true and fabulous – how many songs and ballads, Arabian and Spanish, of love and war and chivalry, are associated with this Oriental pile!"
>
> Washington Irving,
> *Legends of the Alhambra*

case, the American West had already been mastered by his great rival, James Fenimore Cooper. His true achievement was complete. He'd invented "Europe," a new romantic landscape for American eyes. He'd invented the "international theme," to be followed by many later American writers, from Henry James to Ezra Pound, T.S. Eliot and Ernest Hemingway – who also came to Europe for poetry, the falling tower, or just experience, and to contrast the European past and the American future. And he'd invented "the Old World," as a new and touristic landscape for American eyes. It's not too much to say that Irving had really invented the very idea of "Europe" itself, as the great European space best seen from the West. It's the space we live in today, when an idea of something like a "United States of Europe" exists.

In Irving's day, the people and regions of Europe hardly recognized that they were "European." The idea of a broad Old World continent with much in common was a dream best seen from the New World. If, today, people now think of themselves as Europeans, that owes quite a bit to Irving's wanderings and writings, which made two continents, Old World and New, mythically interdependent. Which only goes to prove that literary maps can have a very remarkable power.

Arthur Rackham's illustration, right, *vividly depicts a scene from Irving's "Rip Van Winkle": "Passing through the ravine, they came through a hollow, like a small amphitheatre, surrounded by perpendicular precipices, over the brinks of which impending trees shot their branches so that you caught glimpses of the azure sky and the bright evening cloud."*

WASHINGTON IRVING'S EUROPEAN TRAVELS: *Irving's first youthful European tour started in Bordeaux on 25 June, 1804. Eleven years later he was to make the journey that provided him with the valuable material for his fascinating tales of European myth and legend*

Washington Irving was fascinated by German Romanticism and legend. During his European travels he translated the opera Der Freischütz, The Wild Huntsman.

JAMES FENIMORE COOPER'S FRONTIER

"Twenty and the wilderness!" That is how one of the most famous of American literary heroes, Natty Bumppo, also known as Hawkeye, Deerslayer and Leatherstocking, describes the ideal life in James Fenimore Cooper's (1789–1851) *The Prairie* (1827), one of five novels in which the great frontiersman appeared. Cooper himself was the first major American novelist, and after some false starts he created a remarkable fictional mythology of the American experience in its greatest and defining testing place, the Wilderness. *The Leatherstocking Saga* was actually just one part of a literary career that produced over thirty books, but the stories are Cooper's most memorable to this day, because they reach to the heart of the great and ambiguous American adventure, the mapping and the settlement of the once Wild West.

James Fenimore Cooper, above, became a novelist when he threw down a British novel he was reading to his wife and said he could write a better one. Precaution (1820) was a weak imitation of Jane Austen, but with The Pioneers *(1823) Leatherstocking was born.*

Fenimore Cooper was born in 1789 immediately after the War of Independence from which the United States emerged as the world's first New Nation. The son of a judge who had acquired large tracts of frontier land in Upper New York State, he grew up at manorial Otsego Hall in what was to become Cooperstown – a settlement near the Great Lakes and the source of the Susequehanna River. This land, settled by Indians and fought over in several wars, stayed mostly virgin forest, until Judge William Cooper arrived. He was a squire-pioneer who claimed to have put more land under the plough than any other American. And over the next forty years he and his kind opened the entire region to development, industry, agriculture and profit.

"Only forty years have passed since this territory was a wilderness," Cooper wrote in his third novel *The Pioneers* (1823) of this quick-changing frontier. He tells us how "beautiful and thriving villages," "roads...in every direction," and "academies and minor edifices of learning" quickly sprang up to show "how much can be done in even a rugged country." But even while he records the progress, Cooper clearly yearns and mourns for the disappearing wilderness. He gives it a representative in the worn, elderly man of the woods, Natty

Bumppo, known as Leatherstocking. Ever in conflict with Judge Temple (based on Cooper's father) and his new pioneers, he stands as protector of the older wilderness, of the Indian, of the simpler world of natural law.

Although only a minor character in *The Pioneers*, the figure of Leatherstocking quickly attracted public interest. The frontiersman was starting to be a romantic American hero, representing the free spirit of the nation. Americans thrilled to the adventures of trapper, Daniel Boone, and his predecessor, Coonskin-hatted Davy Crockett. Pioneer, Indian fighter, and teller of frontier tales, Crockett died fighting for the Texans on the Alamo. His *Narrative of the Life of Davy Crockett* appeared in 1834.

Seeing both the romantic and historical importance of his hero, Cooper brought him back again in *The Last of the Mohicans* (1826). But now the setting is around Glen Falls, in New York State, and the time of the French and Indian wars of 1757. The French under Montcalm were taking their last stand against the British, and the frontier is a land of forest and forts. Leatherstocking is now Hawkeye, and not an elderly backwoodsman but a brave young fighter and a mediator between the white and the native American. The portrait of Uncas, the

The Deerslayer (1841), left, is one of five Cooper novels which deal – not in chronological order – with the different stages in Leatherstocking's life, from his experiences in the colonial wilderness of the Indian and Franco-British wars to his death on the prairies west of the Mississippi. The illustration, opposite, is from The Prairie *(1827), about Leatherstocking's final days.*

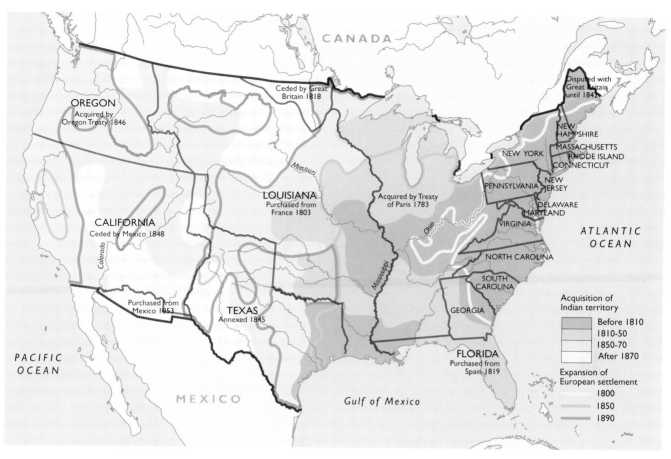

OREGON
Acquired by
Oregon Treaty 1846

CALIFORNIA
Ceded by Mexico 1848

Purchased from
Mexico 1853

TEXAS
Annexed 1845

LOUISIANA
Purchased from
France 1803

Ceded by Great
Britain 1818

Acquired by Treaty
of Paris 1783

Missouri

Colorado

Ohio

Mississippi

PACIFIC
OCEAN

MEXICO

Gulf of Mexico

CANADA

Disputed with
Great Britain
until 1842

NEW
HAMPSHIRE

NEW YORK

MASSACHUSETTS
RHODE ISLAND
CONNECTICUT

PENNSYLVANIA

NEW
JERSEY

DELAWARE
MARYLAND

VIRGINIA

NORTH CAROLINA

SOUTH
CAROLINA

GEORGIA

FLORIDA
Purchased from
Spain 1819

ATLANTIC
OCEAN

Acquisition of
Indian territory

Before 1810
1810-50
1850-70
After 1870

Expansion of
European settlement

1800
1850
1890

The Last of the Mohicans

Mo h a w k

O n e i d a

O n o n d a g a

Lake
George

Lake Ontario

Fort Oswego

Fort
Ontario

Fort William Henry

Fort
George

Glens
Falls

Fort Niagara

S e n e c a

C a y u g a

*Oneida
Lake*

Fort Stanwix

Fort Herkimer

Mohawk

Fort
Hunter

Cooperstown

Albany

The Pathfinder

The Pioneers

NEW   YORK

Hudson

The Deerslayer

Kingston

Newburgh

S u s q u e h a n n a

Susquehanna

The Spy

Fort
Montgomery

PENNSYLVANIA

Sunbury

New York

NEW
JERSEY

Settlement c.1750

British

French

J. Fenimore Cooper
b.1789

Delaware

Trenton

Philadelphia

Burlington

THE WESTWARD EXPANSION ACROSS AMERICA: *With
westward expansion,* top, *native Indian territory was almost
wiped out by the end of the nineteenth century. James Fenimore
Cooper's Leatherstocking novels, set around his native homeland
of Burlington,* above, *chart the beginning of this progression
from Indian wilderness to European settlement.*

courageous and loyal Mohican, is just as important. In fact Leatherstocking owes his virtuous natural instincts as well as his hunting prowess to his considerable relations with the Indian tribes, and his understanding of their natural and spiritual wisdom.

In *The Prairie* (1827) Cooper returned Leatherstocking to old age, and took him to another, crucial part of the frontier, and another era of history – to the flat plains newly opened by the Louisiana Purchase. In 1803, in "the biggest bargain in history," the American president, Thomas Jefferson, engineered the Louisiana Purchase, buying from Napoleon the French territories down the Mississippi, from the Great Lakes to the Gulf of Mexico – for only 15 million dollars. At once the New Nation tripled in size, and the entire frontier of settlement shifted to the other side of the Mississippi River. Dreaming of a trade route to Asia, a "passage to India," Jefferson now

The Kentucky pioneer, Daniel Boone (1734-1820), above, became the image of the fugitive backwoodsman and trapper, seeking the freedom of the wilderness, and always in flight from the advance of "civilization."

sent explorers west to find the passage to the Pacific. The West was opening up.

In *The Prairie*, the old Leatherstocking, now in his eighties, is still fleeing from "the march of civilization." The arid "rolling prairie" is just beginning to fill with new settlers. Natty resents their encroachment, trying to keep his pact with nature and the plains Indians. At the end, he dies "as he had lived, a philosopher of the wilderness, with few of the failings, none of the vices, and all of the nature and truth of his position."

Cooper actually wrote the book in Paris, on a seven-year expatriation to Europe. Here Balzac and other French and European writers of the day recognized his significance. The frontiersman became a great Romantic figure, the dying Indian a hero and the whole Western theme an international myth. Cooper set it aside for a time to write of Europe, but late in his career returned to his Leatherstocking novels with *The Pathfinder* (1840) and *The Deerslayer* (1841), now disillusioned with Jacksonian democracy and the arrogant new cult of the West. The frontier as he had known it was in the distant past, so once more these are novels of Leatherstocking's early days now a hundred years back.

The three illustrations, below, appeared in Meriwether Lewis and William Clark's History of the Expedition to the Sources of the Missouri *of 1814. Their journey was a success story: in 1805 they completed the Northwest Passage, and caught sight of "this great Pacific Ocean we have been so long anxious to see." Thereafter settlement proceeded rapidly, opening up the West.*

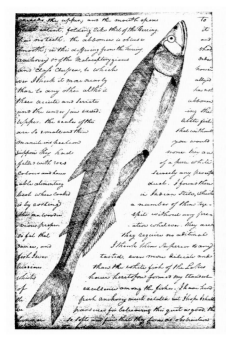

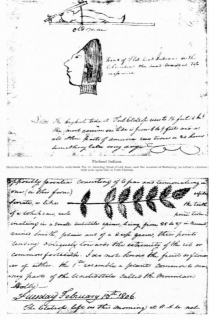

For Cooper and Romantic nature painters like Thomas Cole, whose The Last of the Mohicans *is shown,* right, *the American wilderness represented sublimity. Cooper wrote of it with ever growing intensity as the great romance, but his novels are also historical tales – a serious analysis of American history and social development as well as a romantic vision of the dying wilderness, mapping the often destructive process that came as the "march of civilization" prospered.*

In *The Pathfinder* Natty is 35, and choosing between love and the solitary life in "the solemn obscurity of the forests of America," where everything began. *The Deerslayer* goes back even earlier, to 1740 and the age of "twenty and the wilderness!" For Cooper and Natty alike this was now the legendary time when "a bird's-eye view of the whole region east of the Mississippi must have offered one vast expanse of woods." The story is set around romantic Lake Otsego; the first spoken words are "Here is room to breathe in!" It tells how the young Deerslayer has been raised by Delaware Indians and makes his bond of friendship with the noble Mohican Chingachgook, now being harried across the plains, the deserts and the mountains.

The West had become America's destiny, and "plotting the Golden West" became one of the chief tasks of Americans as they travelled and recorded what lay on or beyond the familiar limits of the wide continent. Travellers like John Charles Fremont, painters like John James Audubon, recorded or illustrated the experience. Washington Irving gave his account of the western fur trade in *Astoria* (1836), Francis Parkman's *The Oregon Trail* (1849) is rightly held as an American classic.

In Cooper's lifetime the dream that the United States represented a growing new western empire became reality for more than just Americans. It was a romantic dream of a Golden-Age democracy of freeborn men and women, close to nature and the sublime. But, as Cooper also shows, the realities were generally grimmer: the destruction of forests, the humiliation and murder of the Indian, the slaughter of the buffalo, the erosion of soil, the westward spread of slavery. Yet his myth had compelling power. "If anything from the pen of the writer of these romances is at all to outlive himself, it is, unquestionably, the series of *The Leatherstocking Tales,*" Cooper wrote when they were finished. He was right. His virgin forests, shining lakes, his Indians and his hunter-trapper with his forest skills, joined the great stock of international popular literature.

With Cooper the West became as literary a place as Europe or the Orient. Trappers and pioneers, cowboys and Indians, became the stuff of mythology. His books became classic boys' adventures, imitated in dime novels and Wild West Shows. When the movies began the books entered film. As America's first significant novelist he felt it the task of American fiction to explore the conflicting, often destructive and even genocidal energies of his new nation, even as he set its distinctive and wonderful wilderness on the map of literature.

CHRONOLOGY OF JAMES FENIMORE COOPER'S LEATHERSTOCKING NOVELS

The Deerslayer (1841)
   Set in 1740 around Lake Otsego in the age of the wilderness
The Pathfinder (1840)
   Set in c.1755 at the time of the French and Indian wars
The Last of the Mohicans (1826)
   Set in 1757 when the French under Montcalm were taking the last stand against the British, the frontier still a forest
The Pioneers (1823)
   Set in 1793 when settlements started growing
The Prairie (1827)
   Set just after the Louisiana Purchase of 1803

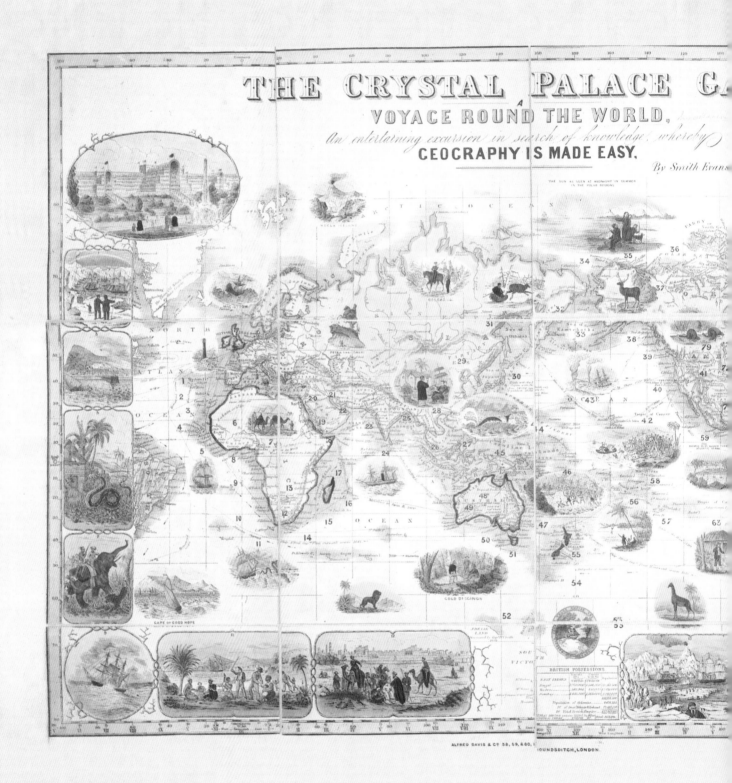

THE CRYSTAL PALACE GAME

VOYAGE ROUND THE WORLD,

An entertaining excursion in search of knowledge, whereby

GEOGRAPHY IS MADE EASY.

By Smith Evans

ALFRED DAVIS & Cº 58, 59, & 60, HOUNDSDITCH, LONDON.

PART FOUR

THE AGE OF INDUSTRIALISM AND EMPIRE

When the Great Exhibition was opened by Prince Albert in 1851 in the Crystal Palace in London's Hyde Park, it did not only signal Britain's proud, pioneering role in the technological revolution that was starting to transform mid-nineteenth century Europe and America. It also pointed the way to the vast developments in invention, science and commerce that would transform most of the world over the rest of the century. By now steamships had opened up world travel and created vast new shipping routes, and international tourism had begun. Not all the consequences were so engaging or delightful. In the West, cities were spreading like some great disease, factory chimneys rose on the skylines, mills clanked, masses of workers streamed through dark streets, a new class of industrialists and capitalists influenced the social order. "Things are in the saddle, and will ride mankind," worried transcendental poet Ralph Waldo Emerson. In an unsettled and ever more nationalistic Europe old regimes gave way to new ones, and the liberal revolutions of 1848 sent clear warning that the age of improvement would need to be accompanied by political reform. The writers of the day were confronted with new social relations and formations, fresh human types who emerged from the urban fog and struggled with more atomized lives...

The Great Exhibition inspired the Crystal Palace Game, 1854, where "Geography is made easy," and travel is fun.

THE SLEEPING GIANT:
PUSHKIN'S, GOGOL'S AND
DOSTOEVSKY'S ST PETERSBURG

St Petersburg was Russia's Palmyra of the North, raised on the shores of the Baltic so near the Arctic Circle that, in Aleksandr Pushkin's (1799–1837) words, "One twilight hastens to relieve another/ Giving the night a bare half-hour." Its waters are still infected by the bones of the slaves who built it, and not only the characters of Dostoevsky expected it to dissolve at any moment back into the mists of the Finnish swamps on which its construction had been willed. Ivan Turgenev (1818–83) was acutely aware of its unnatural location: "The flush of the evening twilight, a consumptive flush, has not yet faded and will not fade before morning from the white, starless sky; it stripes the silky smoothness of the Neva, which imperceptibly gurgles and swells, hastening onwards its cold blue waters."

Soon after arriving in St Petersburg from sunny Ukraine in 1828, Nikolai Gogol (1809–52) wrote home: "The stillness here is uncanny, no spirit sparkles in the people, all the clerks and civil servants talk ceaselessly about their departments and colleges, all is depression, everything is stuck in a rut of aimless, pointless labours in which their life is frittered fruitlessly away...." In *A Raw Youth* (1875) Fyodor Dostoevsky's (1821–81) raw youth Arkady Dolgorukov reacts even more strongly: "I often asked and still ask myself a really totally senseless question: they are all hasten- ing and rushing about their business, but who is to say that all this is not some person's dream, and there is not a single actual person here, not a single real action. That somebody may suddenly wake up who is dreaming all this, and it will all suddenly disappear."

The dreamer was, of course, Peter the Great (Tzar and Emperor, 1689–1725), who in 1702 reconquered from the Swedes the land on which his future capital would be built. The foundation stone of the Peter and Paul Fortress (Petropavlovskaya krepost) was laid the next year. An army of 40,000 workers from all parts of the Empire, their numbers "frequently decimated by the poisonous exhalations of the swamps and the enormous strain of the

Peter the Great, above, started the building of St Petersburg, his future capital, in 1703.

work," toiled to raise it from the sea. On Peter's death the new capital, initially centred around the Fortress, had 75,000 inhabitants. In the reign of his daughter Elizabeth the focus shifted to the needle-like spire of the Admiralty (Admiralteystvo) she built. From here radiated great avenues or "Prospekts". By 1784, under Catherine the Great, the population was 192,000. The city saw another burst during Pushkin's time, when much of its finest architecture appeared. The population was 425,000 when Gogol came. By 1881, the year of Dostoevsky's death and Alexander II's assassination, it had doubled again, to 861,000, still barely a fifth of the size of London.

St Petersburg was the European capital of a Byzantine autocracy. After the French Revolution, with dangerous ideas about, Tzar Alexander I (1801–25) and his successor Nicholas I (1825–55) kept a wary eye on their volatile and often artistic and liberally-inclined subjects. Pushkin and Lermontov suffered lengthy banishment. Gogol fled abroad after the dangerous success of *The Government Inspector* in 1836. Dostoevsky was subjected to a mock-execution by firing squad, then exiled. Even Turgenev was exiled for a year and a half for his obituary of Gogol, and spent most of his life abroad, dying in Paris. During his schooldays at the

Lyceum at Tsarskoe Selo, south of the city, Pushkin met the major literary figures of the day. Vasily Zhukovsky urged fellow writers to "unite to help the growth to maturity of this future giant who will outstrip us all." Their protection was soon needed. Barely had he left school than Pushkin – contemplating the gloomy Mikhailovsky Castle (Mikhailovsky zamok), its moats and drawbridges constructed for the rightly paranoid Paul I, who was murdered there soon after its completion – was penning his ode "Liberty." The poem circulated widely, and came to the attention of the Tzar, who told the Lyceum's headmaster: "Pushkin must be exiled to Siberia. He has flooded Russia with his outrageous poems. All young people are reciting them by heart." Pushkin's influential patrons interceded. He was exiled instead to the south of Russia in May 1820, not to return for seven years.

Meantime a Ukrainian schoolboy dreamt of a future life of loyal service in the capital: "I already picture myself in St Petersburg, in that merry little room whose windows look out on the Neva...," wrote Gogol. "From years long, long past, almost since before I understood anything, I have burned with an unquenchable zeal to make my life necessary to the good of the state." Arriving a year later he was frankly disappointed. He wrote home: "Every capital derives its character from its people, who set the seal of nationality on it. St Petersburg, however, has no such character: the foreigners who have moved here have settled down and now bear no resemblance to foreigners, while the foreignness has rubbed off on the Russians, and they have become neither one thing nor the other." In late

Pushkin's monument is his epic The Bronze Horseman *(1833). It conveys Peter the Great's vision and genius in creating the St Petersburg,* above, *that Pushkin,* right, *plainly loves, even while acknowledging the inhumanity behind its construction, and the authoritarianism on which the Russian state depends. The book was banned by the Tzar personally.*

1829 Gogol settled in the house described by Poprishchin in "Notes of a Madman" (1835): "We crossed to Gorokhovaya St, turned into Meshchanskaya, and stopped before a great house. 'I know this house', said I to myself, 'This is Zverkov House. What a warren! What manner of people are there indeed who do not live here: how many cooks and Poles, and clerks like ourselves, piled one on top of the other like dogs. I have a certain friend lives here who plays remarkably on the trumpet.'" Gogol's aspirations to be useful were restricted to working as a civil service clerk. But he was writing *Evenings on a Farm near Dikanka*. In 1830 his first stories brought immediate recognition, and he was introduced to Zhukovsky and Pushkin.

Pushkin's St Petersburg was the fashionable capital where members of the gentry lived before returning to their estates for the summer. His hero in *Eugene Onegin*

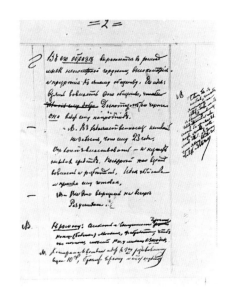

(1823–31) wanders down Nevsky Prospekt in the morning, visiting Talon's restaurant on the corner of the Moika Embankment, taking in the Bolshoi Theatre before whirling on to a ball. He describes "How often in the summer time / When the night sky over the Neva / Is transparent and light... / We delighted unspeaking in / The balm of a smiling night." However, Pushkin absented himself from the unveiling of the Alexander Column (Alexsandrovskaya kolonna), Nicholas I's huge monument to his predecessor, in August 1834, responding instead with a poem. "I have raised myself a monument not built by men." It ends memorably: "And on the shattered fragments of wanton power our names shall be inscribed."

Pushkin's *The Queen of Spades* (1834), is almost contemporaneous with his *The Bronze Horseman*, with its ambitious, unbalanced hero, Hermann – described by Dostoevsky as "a colossal type, an extraordinary wholly Petersburg character...." With his Napoleonic hubris, and rationalistic determination to gamble only if the outcome is guaranteed, he is a precursor of Raskolnikov in Dostoevsky's *Crime and Punishment* (1866).

In the summer of 1833 Gogol moved to Malaya Morskaya Street. In his wonderful play *The Government Inspector* (1836) the writer of trifles, Triapichkin, lives in "House number 97, turning into the courtyard, on the second floor, to the right." Here Gogol wrote an invocation to the New Year: "Mysterious, unfathomable 1834! Where shall I dignify you with great works? Shall it be amid this heap of houses piled one

Dostoevsky (above left) wrote Crime and Punishment, *an early draft of which is shown* above right, *while living at the intersection of Stoliarny Lane and Meshchanskaya Street,* centre.

atop the other, these clattering streets, this teeming mercantilism – this ugly heap of fashions, parades, clerks, weird northern nights, glitter and sordid colourlessness? Do it I shall!" In his cramped apartment in Lepen House over the next two years, Gogol wrote *Nevsky Prospect, Notes of a Madman, The Portrait, The Nose, Taras Bulba, The Government Inspector* and the first chapters of his great comic novel *Dead Souls* (1842). The initial idea for these last two came from Pushkin, who, in 1835–6, lived not far off, on the French Embankment, in Batashov House, which Gogol frequently visited.

In 1837 Pushkin was fatally wounded in a duel, and died on 29 January, sparing the Tzar and his establishment further vexation. Crowds soon gathered at his house. Zhukovsky wrote to Pushkin's father: "the room where he lay in his coffin was constantly thronged with people. Assuredly more than ten thousand came to visit him, many were crying...." Turgenev asked the valet to cut off a lock of the poet's hair; the locket containing it, along with Turgenev's annotation, can be seen today in the Pushkin Memorial Apartment (Muzei-kuartira A.S. Pushkina). The novelist and poet Mikhail Lermontov (1814–1841) also went to pay last respects, and immediately wrote *Death of a Poet*: "And you who stand a greedy mob around the

"The pensive bard looks out upon
The tyrant's monument forlorn
Menacingly asleep amid the mists
His palace abandoned to oblivion.
The untrustworthy sentry utters no word
Silent the lowered drawbridge
The gates yawn open in the dark of night
And at the hand of a hired traitor
The crowned villain perishes."

"Liberty" Alexsandr Pushkin

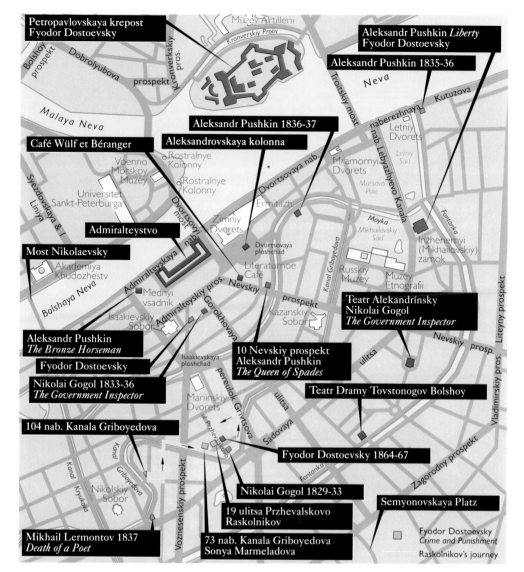

Petropavlovskaya krepost
Fyodor Dostoevsky

Aleksandr Pushkin *Liberty*
Fyodor Dostoevsky

Aleksandr Pushkin 1835-36

Aleksandr Pushkin 1836-37

Café Wülf et Béranger

Aleksandrovskaya kolonna

Admiralteystvo

Most Nikolaevsky

Aleksandr Pushkin
The Bronze Horseman

Fyodor Dostoevsky

Nikolai Gogol 1833-36
The Government Inspector

104 nab. Kanala Griboyedova

Teatr Alekandrínsky
Nikolai Gogol
The Government Inspector

10 Nevskiy prospekt
Aleksandr Pushkin
The Queen of Spades

Teatr Dramy Tovstonogov Bolshoy

Fyodor Dostoevsky 1864-67

Nikolai Gogol 1829-33

19 ulitsa Przhevalskovo
Raskolnikov

73 nab. Kanala Griboyedova
Sonya Marmeladova

Mikhail Lermontov 1837
Death of a Poet

Semyonovskaya Platz

Fyodor Dostoevsky
Crime and Punishment
Raskolnikov's journey

St Petersburg: *The cityscape of* Crime and Punishment *is affirmed by Russian scholar V.E. Kholshevnikov: "It is clear that Raskolnikov left the old woman's house...through the gates facing the Catherine Canal, walking along Yekateringofsky Prospekt to Bolshaya Podiacheskaya St, and continued along it to the Catherine Canal by Fonarny Bridge in the vicinity of Stoliarny Lane. Only after reaching the canal did he decide to 'make a loop.' Until this point he had been following the shortest route home...."*

throne / You executioners of Freedom, Wit and Honour." It brought him instant fame and, when drawn to the Tzar's attention, exile to Georgia. He died in a duel near Piatigorsk, aged 26.

When Pushkin died, Dostoevsky was 15 – and 27 when, on the night of 22–23 April, 1849, he and other members of the "Petrashevsky Conspiracy" were arrested. He was incarcerated in the Peter and Paul Fortress as a dangerous criminal, and on 22 December, 1849, at 7.00 a.m., the 21 condemned men were led to Semyonovsky Platz. The firing squad loaded their rifles and took aim. The rifles were lowered, the Tzar's "commuting" of the sentences read out. Dostoevsky was given four years' hard labour, followed by drafting into the army, and allowed to return to the capital only after Nicholas's death, in 1859.

He wrote *Crime and Punishment* (1866), perhaps the greatest of the many St Petersburg stories, while living in a peculiar area, of which local historian Vladimir Mikhnevich wrote in 1874: "Voznesensky Prospekt, Gorokhovaya and Kazanskaya Streets have concentrated between them predominantly the activities of tradesmen

and craftsmen: clockmakers, tailors, cobblers, cabinemakers, upholsterers, locksmiths, seamstresses and the like. Indeed the name Meshchanskaya (Townsfolk) previously given to one of them best characterizes the class of population in these parts...." This gives the setting of *Crime and Punishment*, with its images of urban poverty and the attempt to act heroically in a world of moral disorder.

In writing his great novel, Dostoevsky scarcely mentions the architectural splendours that dominate central St Petersburg. In *Crime and Punishment* the alienated hero Raskolnikov, presentiment of the resentful, rationalistic forces that would later destroy the Tzars, stands alone on Nikolaevsky Bridge (Nikolaevsky Most): "When he was walking to the University it would usually happen, most often on his way home, that perhaps a hundred times he would stop at just this spot, peer intently at what was truly a magnificent panorama, and wonder almost every time at the vague and unresolved impression it made on him. An inexplicable coldness always came over him as he contemplated its magnificence: the soul of the sumptuous vista was deaf and dumb for him."

STENDHAL'S, BALZAC'S AND SAND'S FRANCE

The high point of the French Romantic movement is often said to be 1830, when the July Revolution removed many remnants of the old regime, and made Louis-Philippe "Citizen King." The date is purely notional, as can be seen from the life span of many of the representative Romantics. Alfred Musset, playwright and poet, died in 1837; Alfred de Vigny in 1863; Alphonse de Lamartine in 1869; Alexander Dumas in 1870; and Victor Hugo in 1885. But, certainly, 1830 did mark a period of change.

Louis-Philippe displaced the Bourbon dynasty, and was made King by popular consent, even if that consent was limited to a restricted section of the people. France was altering quickly, as the impact of the industrial revolution grew, cities expanded, railways appeared. There was greater awareness of crime and poverty, the importance of science, the value of progress. Opportunities for wealth increased, and there was talk of the "career open to talents." Attitudes to religion and the church were shifting. There were writers emerging – especially a new band of novelists – who sought to enlarge their vision, and were concerned not just with traditional Romantic preoccupations (individuals and their sentiments) but society as a whole: families, businesses, communities. Nor did they confine their attention to the city of Paris, which many of them disliked; they chose to write of the French regions, and of other countries, too.

It was Henri Beyle "Stendhal" (1783–1842) who became the first of a new age of novelists whose fiction coincided with Romanticism, but led the way toward the later movement of Realism. Born in Grenoble, he hated the bourgeois spirit of the town. When he later returned after 14 years away to defend it in war, he still found it "this headquarters of pettiness." When he went to Paris in 1804 to settle with relatives at 505 rue de Lille (on the corner of the rue de Bellechasse) he was no more impressed. Paris was ugly; the surrounding countryside, lacking in mountains, made it worse. Only when posted to Milan with the Napoleonic army did he find the place he wished to be. Reason might say that real beauty was to be found in Naples, Dresden or Lake Geneva, said Stendhal, "but my

The work of Stendhal, left, *and Balzac*, right, *combined Romantic values with a new Realism.*

heart feels only Milan." After the defeat of Napoleon, he returned to Italy (1814–21). Later, following the Revolution of 1830, he would return to represent France in the small papal state of Civita Vecchia. In 1821 he came back to Paris, living for a time in the Hôtel de Bruxelles on the rue de Richelieu, later settling at the nearby Hôtel de Lillois, at 63 rue de Richelieu, on the Right Bank. He attended literary salons, and was delighted to meet Victor Hugo at one of them; but he advised Prosper Merimée not to attend them on the grounds that Parisian society was fatal to a young writer.

Two visits to London in 1821 and 1826 filled Stendhal with enthusiasm. Not only did he see two performances of Shakespeare's plays, which confirmed his belief that the English dramatist was superior to Racine, but he also found a landscape that delighted him, reminding him of Lombardy. He stayed at the Tavistock Hotel in Covent Garden, wandered round Chelsea, admired the Thames at Richmond, went to church in Windsor. He also found a spirit of reform. In France he read works of political economy and developed ideas similar to Saint-Simon's. All should be able to make their contribution to society, conquering nature and increasing wealth. "Civilization" as practised in Paris was refinement that sapped vitality, and society depended on the determination of natural leaders to carry out reforms.

His major novels recognize these themes. *The Scarlet and the Black* was published in 1830. It deals with Julien Sorel, a carpenter's son whose heart is greater than his fortune, an *arriviste* who seeks the higher social place he feels he deserves, only to become society's victim. *Lucien Leuwen* (written 1834–5, published posthumously 1890) is

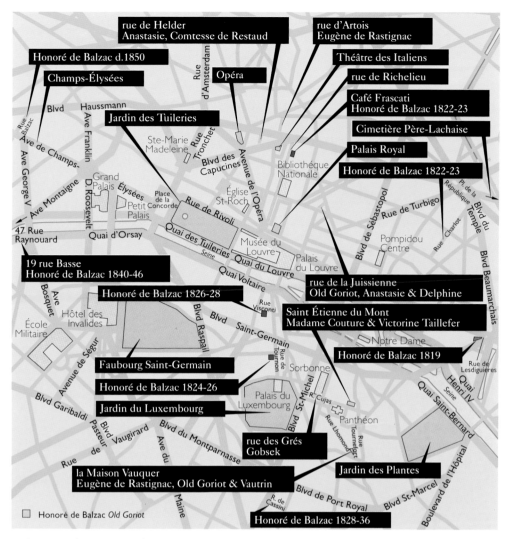

rue de Helder
Anastasie, Comtesse de Restaud

rue d'Artois
Eugène de Rastignac

Honoré de Balzac d.1850

Champs-Élysées

Théâtre des Italiens

rue de Richelieu

Café Frascati
Honoré de Balzac 1822–23

Cimetière Père-Lachaise

Palais Royal

Jardin des Tuileries

Honoré de Balzac 1822–23

19 rue Basse
Honoré de Balzac 1840–46

Honoré de Balzac 1826–28

rue de la Juissienne
Old Goriot, Anastasie & Delphine

Saint Étienne du Mont
Madame Couture & Victorine Taillefer

Faubourg Saint-Germain

Honoré de Balzac 1819

Honoré de Balzac 1824–26

Jardin du Luxembourg

rue des Grés
Gobsek

Jardin des Plantes

la Maison Vauquer
Eugène de Rastignac, Old Goriot & Vautrin

☐ Honoré de Balzac *Old Goriot*

Honoré de Balzac 1828–36

Vie
De Rossini,
PAR
M. De Stendhal,
Ornée des Portraits de Rossini et de Mozart.

PREMIÈRE PARTIE.

Paris,
CHEZ AUGUSTE BOULLAND ET Cⁱᵉ, LIBRAIRE
RUE DU BATTOIR, N° 12
1824.

another portrait of a corrupt society run by a governing
class that bows only to money. *The Charterhouse of Parma*
(1839) is set in his beloved Italy, apart from when the hero
Fabrice goes on an excursion to Napoleonic France, where
he witnesses the Battle of Waterloo with the French army.
The defeat of Napoleon reduces Fabrice to a state of futility, part of the Romantic sensibility. In his unfinished
autobiography *The Life of Henry Brulard* (written 1835–6,
published 1890), Stendhal tells us he has *"le coeur italien"*
and that his heart beat faster when, at 17, he first set eyes
on the plain of the River Po. Still, he died in Paris in 1842,
and is buried in the cemetery of Montmartre.

The Scarlet and the Black appeared at almost the same
time as *The Chouans* (1829), the first novel Honoré de
Balzac (1799–1850) published under his own name.
Focusing on the loyalist guerrillas who had fought against
the Republic in 1800, it became the first volume of a
remarkable fictional project, an interlocking sequence of
novels that in 1841 Balzac called his *"Comédie humaine."*
He researched the book on a visit to Fougères in Brittany
in 1828; but such fact-finding journeys would prove rare
in his career. Often complimented on the accuracy of
his descriptions of place, he frequently wrote of regions

*Paris in the 1830s, above, was dominated by the Palace and gardens
of the Tuileries, and the Louvre behind it.*

and places he had never visited. In fact, Balzac gives an
impression of France rather than an exact description.

Balzac was born in Tours and educated at Vendôme, a
short distance away. He made a brief visit to Paris in 1813,
and was for a time a pupil at an annexe of the Lycée
Charlemagne, in the Marais district, boarding in the
Hôtel de Salé (now the magnificent Musée Picasso). The
Marais was dirty and uninspiring, and he was glad to

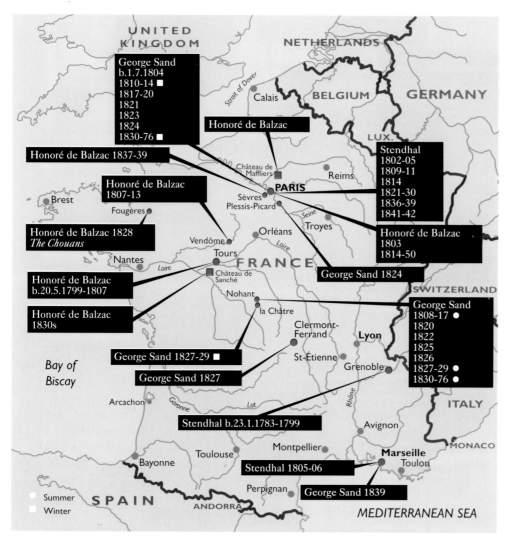

THE FRANCE OF THE REALISTS:
Although Stendhal, Balzac and George Sand lived a lot of their time in Paris, they all felt a greater affinity towards the countryside, staying in the locations shown on this map.

The illustration, below, is from the 1848 edition of Cousin Bette, *one of the 91 works Balzac wrote in his massive* Comédie humaine *series.*

return to Tours, rediscover the Loire, walk its valley. But he would always vividly remember his Parisian experience and use it in his many novels. He was there in the Marais again, living with his family at 90 rue du Temple, when Napoleon was overthrown. He never lost his admiration for the leader and recorded indignantly how curses had rained on him in his hour of defeat.

In 1816 he became a student at the Law Faculty, in the Latin Quarter, where he heard Guizot lecture, would walk by the Seine browsing among the booksellers, then return to the Marais, where – like other noted nineteenth century novelists, including Charles Dickens – he worked as a lawyer's clerk, a world much described in his books. Like Dickens, too, he acknowledged his passion for going out on the streets late at night and observing life. "In listening to these people I could espouse their lives. I felt their rags upon my back. I walked with my feet in their tattered shoes; their desires, their wants – everything passed into my soul...." In 1819 his family moved for financial reasons to the small town of Villeparisis, about 12 miles northeast of Paris. He announced he wanted to be a writer, moved back to Paris, and was installed in a shabby room at 9 rue Lediguières, on the edge of the Marais again, near the

Bibliothèque de l'Arsenal, which he describes in *La peau de chagrin* (1831). From here he wrote novelettes under assumed names, worked as a journalist, and engaged in a disastrous publishing venture.

Balzac often worked in the château at Le Saché, near Tours, where his desk was placed in a small bedroom on the top floor. From here came some of his finest novels, including *Old Goriot* (1834–5). But it was in Paris that the greater part of the work was done. From 1828–36 he lived at 1 rue Cassini (demolished around 1900), near to the Observatory on the edge of the city. But to escape creditors he had to leave the city, and settled between Sèvres and Ville d'Avray in a hermitage called Les Jardies. In 1847 he moved back to Paris to the rue Fortunée. That year he also spent some six months in the Ukraine, returning there to marry in 1850. This voyage did not create literary inspiration, possibly because of his preoccupation with financial affairs. Tragically he died on his return to the rue Fortunée, which is now called rue Balzac in his honour.

Balzac's great ambition, his ultimate achievement, was to describe French society as a whole: make sense of it, explore its governing values, in essence explain it. Many of his books – they include *Eugénie Grandet* (1833), *Lost*

Illusions (1837-43) and *Cousin Bette* (1846) – have recurrent characters, creating a rich and interlocking world, one part of his massive influence on the fortunes and future of the novel. They cover a world from Paris to the provinces, and form a multiple, dense yet coherent analysis of bourgeois French society.

One of his characters, Eugène Rastignac, is often seen as the most representative figure of Balzac's *Comédie humaine*. He appears in several volumes, thus helping to create a unity in the work. From an impoverished provincial family Rastignac comes to Paris in 1819 from Angoulême. He mixes with the nobility, pursues wealth, has many mistresses, gambles and is a successful politician. At the climax of *Old Goriot* he makes a much quoted theatrical declaration:

When George Sand, above, moved into the provinces her writing heralded the start of the regional novel in France.

"As daylight waned, he walked up to the highest part of the Père Lachaise cemetery and saw Paris spread out below him, along the two banks of the winding Seine. Lights were beginning to shine. His eyes fastened themselves almost greedily upon the space that lay between the column of the Place Vendôme and the dome of the Invalides. There lay the glittering world he had hoped to conquer. He stared at the humming hive as if sucking out its honey in advance and pronounced these impressive words 'It's you, or me, now!'"

Precision also comes with the setting of novels. Thus, in *Cousin Bette* there are 19 different houses in Paris, all of them carefully appropriate to the social context. The Hulot's family home is in the rue de l'Université, the political and administrative quarter, and when the Baron Hulot buys Valérie Marneffe a flat it is in the rue Vaneau, in the same administrative, aristocratic quarter. After his disgrace Hulot hides in the eastern Marais, then moves to the poverty stricken district of the Place Maubert, just outside the Latin Quarter, before going to the rue de Charonne, the working class area which goes from what is now the Place de la Bastille to the Père Lachaise cemetery.

Balzac's huge ambitions to make the novel an inclusive social record were matched by George Sand (1804–76). Her real married name was Aurore Dudevant, but she adopted her masculine pseudonym from one of her early lovers, the novelist Jules Sandeau. Separated from her husband Baron Dudevant, she settled in Paris in 1831 and led an independent life as a writer, also conduct-

George Sand spent many of her summers in the family home, right, *at Nohant in the Berrichon region of the department of Indre, which provided the inspiration for the pastoral settings of her novels.*

ing a famous liaison with Alfred de Musset, and later one with Chopin. Her highly successful early novels – they include *Indiana* (1831), *Valentine* (1832) and *Lelia* (1833) – were love stories, but they contested many of the social and moral conventions of the day, and supported women's independence. From 1836 her writings became more socially and politically inspired. In 1839 she returned to her family home in Nohant. Now her socialist ideals became expressed as a love of the peasantry, and she detailed their work and their pleasures, their sentiments and their fraternity. Sand today is best remembered for these novels, which include *The Foundling* (1847-8), and *The Pool of Evil* (1846) her attempt to render peasant life as "noble." The sight of a young man ploughing is treated as a ceremonial picture. The peasant world, though a struggle against nature, is tranquil, the story sentimental. The farmer is a widower with two children whose parents-in-law wish him to marry again. On the way to the woman they have chosen he meets a poor servant girl and they wander lost around the "Pool of Evil," a pool supposed to be the haunt of the devil. The girl refuses his offer of marriage, since she is too poor. But her gentleness moves everyone; she is accepted. As Balzac had listened to the stories of workers and their wives in Paris, Sand listened to those of villagers – and so gave birth to the regional novel in French literature.

DICKENS'S LONDON

No writer's imagination was more haunted by London than Charles Dickens's (1812–70). And no writer has more haunted the spirit of London itself since, or had such an effect on literary treatments of it. The Dickensian vision of London – city of bustle and cross-sweepers, the foggy river and the marshes, debtor prisons and old crooked lodging houses, ancient inns-of-court and smoky counting houses, ship-chandlers' stores, taverns and coaching inn yards – is the strongest literary vision of the capital we have. Its sights, smells and human collisions fill the sweeping reach of his novels. The voice of London – the cockney speech of Sam Weller and Mrs Gamp, the chatter of Mr Jingle – has never been more vividly set down.

So strong are the images in Dickens's novels, many drawn from a London observed in childhood, that we sometimes forget he was not born there.

Dickens was born in Portsmouth in 1812, at 387 Mile End Terrace, Portsea (now the Dickens Birthplace Museum). In 1816, his father, a clerk in the Naval Office at the end of the Napoleonic Wars, was sent to London, taking lodgings at 10 Norfolk Street (now 22 Cleveland Street) for two years, until he was moved to the dockyard town of Chatham, Kent, that "mere dream of chalk, and drawbridges, and mastless ships, in a muddy river" Dickens would often use in his novels.

In 1822 the family returned to London, to Camden Town, still on "the outskirts of the fields." Now aged ten, Charles would associate the house with genteel poverty. This is the residence of Mr Micawber in *David Copperfield* (1849–50) and Tiny Tim in *A Christmas Carol* (1843). From its windows the city and its spires and domes could be seen. Charles soon began to wander around London, imbibing both its magic and its darkness. In 1824, with his improvident father in financial difficulties, he went out to work pasting labels at Warren's Blacking Factory, a rat-filled warehouse at 30 Hungerford Stairs, by the mud-filled Thames and its grimy coal barges. For young Dickens this was "grief and humiliation," especially when his father was put in Marshalsea Debtors' Prison in Southwark with his wife and younger children.

The variety and contrast of London – gentility and beggary, great spaces and cramped crooked streets, leisure and brute work, families and orphans, "strange experiences and sordid things" – would add to his humiliation. They would fill his imagination, stock his memory, shape his psychology, become his education, feed the "quite astonishing fictions" he began to tell to others. The streets he wandered between the Blacking Factory, the Marshalsea and his lodgings on Lant Street today bear the names of the characters who sprang out of them (Pickwick Street, Little Dorrit Court). The cityscape, as Peter Ackroyd says in his brilliant biography, was still largely an eighteenth century one, and "the London of his novels always remains the London of his youth."

When Dickens's father was released from prison the family moved to Little College Street, then to 29 Johnson Street in Somers Town. After some schooling, Dickens became a lawyer's clerk in Gray's Inn. He began writing for the theatre and magazines, and became a shorthand reporter in the law courts and at the House of Commons. He produced *Sketches of London* for the *Evening Chronicle*, striking for

Some of the most remarkable scenes in David Copperfield *and* Little Dorrit *are drawn from Dickens's experience of his father's stay in Marshalsea Prison, depticted in the engraving, left.*

The Old Curiosity Shop in Portsmouth Street, Lincoln Inn Fields, above, *was the inspiration for Dickens's novel of the same name.*

In this illustration from A Christmas Carol, *the miserly Scrooge is visited on Christmas Eve by the ghost of Marley.*

their portraits of working people, vagrants, circus performers, poor and criminal districts, prisons like Newgate, amusement places like Vauxhall.

In the 1830s, the young reporter became the wonder writer of the day. Living in Marylebone, he wrote and published his first book *Sketches by Boz* (1836), a vivid collection of London scenes accompanied by illustrations from the great caricaturist George Cruikshank. Invited to follow up its success, he developed *Pickwick Papers* (1836–7) in twenty monthly parts, which grew in scale as the public fell in love with each new episode. Here, with the Pickwickians and Sam and Tony Weller, was Cockney London in full voice; he had created new, deeply English comic characters who fascinated readers of every kind.

In 1836 Dickens married Catherine Hogarth, and they rented lodgings at Furnival's Inn. In 1837 they took a 12-roomed house at 48 Doughty Street, Bloomsbury. He'd signed contracts for five novels, produced at enormous speed in monthly parts. First came *Oliver Twist* (1838), with its portrayal of London orphans, the criminal den of Fagin, the slum of the Rookery where Bill Sykes meets his end. Then followed *Nicholas Nickleby* (1838–9), *The Old Curiosity Shop* (1840–1) where Quilp dies dramatically in the Thames, and *Barnaby Rudge* (1841). Finished before he was thirty, these books form a great vision of the new Victorian age. With them he became a world famous writer. When in 1842 he toured the United States, he was fêted as no visiting author had been before.

The death of Catherine's younger sister Mary darkened the Doughty Street idyll. In 1839 the Dickens family moved to 1 Devonshire Terrace, by Regent's Park. Dickens also acquired Fort House, Broadstairs, to take his family out of London. His comic imagination was beginning to darken, the "giant phantom" of London taking more complex shape. He wrote works of social and moral criticism like *Martin Chuzzlewit* (1843), which probed the selfishness and fraudulent corruption of his day.

By now it was plain that Dickens was the great novelist of the earlier Victorian age, an engrossing tale-teller who also captured its social problems, its growing spread and sprawl, its Utilitarian philosophies, the rise of the age of steam and commerce. He represented its conscience, its sympathy for those who suffered or endured. He was concerned with the state of prisons, the problems of education, the nature of poverty, the cruelty and indifference of the bureaucracy and the law.

The Great Exhibition of 1851, housed in the Crystal Palace in Hyde Park, was a vast image of Victorian change and "improvement." Dickens had already recognized this expansion. *Dombey and Son* (1847–8) shows the jerrybuilding of what's been called "Stuccovia," the coming of the railways that transformed his old Camden Town. *Bleak House* (1853) deals with the growing problem of slums, as well as with the victims of the Court of Chancery. *Hard Times* (1854), an industrial novel dealing with northern mill-town life in "Coketown," was inspired by a strike in

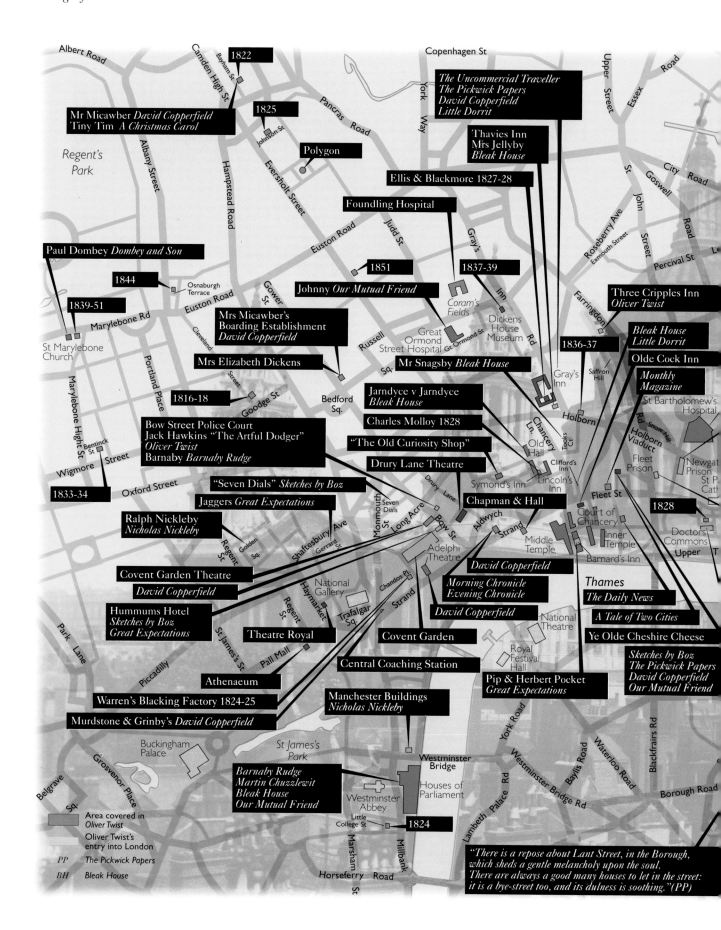

1822

The Uncommercial Traveller
The Pickwick Papers
David Copperfield
Little Dorrit

1825

Mr Micawber David Copperfield
Tiny Tim A Christmas Carol

Thavies Inn
Mrs Jellyby
Bleak House

Regent's Park

Polygon

Ellis & Blackmore 1827-28

Foundling Hospital

Paul Dombey Dombey and Son

1844

1851

Three Cripples Inn
Oliver Twist

1839-51

1837-39

Johnny *Our Mutual Friend*

Osnaburgh Terrace

Bleak House
Little Dorrit

St Marylebone Church

Mrs Micawber's
Boarding Establishment
David Copperfield

1836-37

Olde Cock Inn

Monthly Magazine

Mrs Elizabeth Dickens

Mr Snagsby *Bleak House*

St Bartholomew's Hospital

1816-18

Jarndyce v Jarndyce
Bleak House

Charles Molloy 1828

Bow Street Police Court
Jack Hawkins "The Artful Dodger"
Oliver Twist
Barnaby *Barnaby Rudge*

"The Old Curiosity Shop"

Drury Lane Theatre

Fleet Prison

Newgate Prison
St P. Cath

"Seven Dials" *Sketches by Boz*

1828

Jaggers *Great Expectations*

Chapman & Hall

1833-34

Doctors' Commons
Upper

Ralph Nickleby
Nicholas Nickleby

David Copperfield

Covent Garden Theatre
David Copperfield

Morning Chronicle
Evening Chronicle

Thames

The Daily News

Hummums Hotel
Sketches by Boz
Great Expectations

David Copperfield

A Tale of Two Cities

Theatre Royal

Covent Garden

Ye Olde Cheshire Cheese

Sketches by Boz
The Pickwick Papers
David Copperfield
Our Mutual Friend

Athenaeum

Central Coaching Station

Pip & Herbert Pocket
Great Expectations

Warren's Blacking Factory 1824-25

Manchester Buildings
Nicholas Nickleby

Murdstone & Grinby's *David Copperfield*

Buckingham Palace

St James's Park

Westminster Bridge

Barnaby Rudge
Martin Chuzzlewit
Bleak House
Our Mutual Friend

Houses of Parliament

Westminster Abbey

Borough Road

Little College St

1824

Area covered in *Oliver Twist*

Oliver Twist's entry into London

PP   The Pickwick Papers

BH   Bleak House

"There is a repose about Lant Street, in the Borough,
which sheds a gentle melancholy upon the soul.
There are always a good many houses to let in the street:
it is a bye-street too, and its dulness is soothing."(PP)

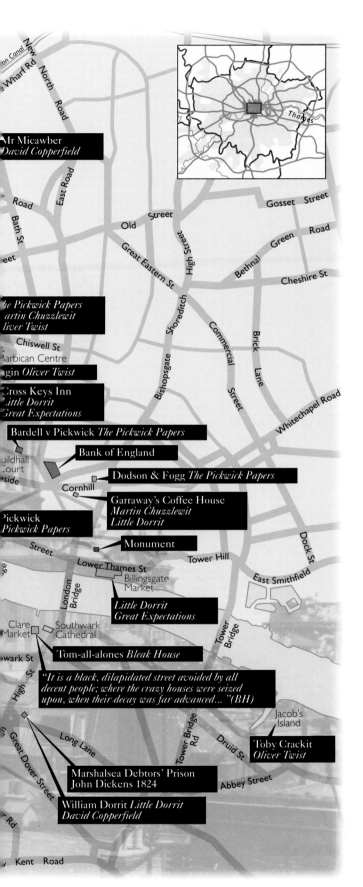

Mr Micawber
David Copperfield

Road

Bath St

eet

East Road

New Wharf Rd

on Canal

North Road

Gosset Street

Old Street

Street

Great Eastern St

High Street

Shoreditch

Bethnal Green Road

Cheshire St

Brick Lane

Commercial Street

Whitechapel Road

he Pickwick Papers
artin Chuzzlewit
liver Twist

Chiswell St
Barbican Centre
gin *Oliver Twist*

Cross Keys Inn
Little Dorrit
Great Expectations

Bishopsgate

Bardell v Pickwick *The Pickwick Papers*

uildhall Court
side

Bank of England

Dodson & Fogg *The Pickwick Papers*

Cornhill

Garraway's Coffee House
Martin Chuzzlewit
Little Dorrit

Pickwick
Pickwick Papers

Street

Monument

Lower Thames St

Tower Hill

Dock St

London Bridge

Billingsgate Market

East Smithfield

Little Dorrit
Great Expectations

Clare Market

Southwark Cathedral

wark St

Tom-all-alones *Bleak House*

Tower Bridge

"It is a black, dilapidated street avoided by all
decent people; where the crazy houses were seized
upon, when their decay was far advanced..." (BH)

High St

Jacob's Island

Long Lane

Tower Bridge Rd

Druid St

Toby Crackit
Oliver Twist

Great Dover Street

Marshalsea Debtors' Prison
John Dickens 1824

Abbey Street

William Dorrit *Little Dorrit*
David Copperfield

Rd

Kent Road

Preston. *Little Dorrit* (1855-7) is dominated by the collapse of a railway tycoon and City financial scandals, though the Marshalsea is one of the chief settings. So is the Circumlocution Office, the bureaucracy which stifles invention and emblemizes the official Britain of the day.

In 1851 Dickens moved again, to Tavistock House in Bloomsbury. Here he wrote many of the later novels, put on theatricals, entertained friends from Wilkie Collins to Hans Christian Anderson. By now he had lived in or wandered around many very different Londons, from the world of the wealthy or famous to that of the poor, from Georgian energy to Victorian sprawl. His novels covered the city's great spread, from the East End to Hampstead and Richmond, and depicted the change to an ever more industrial age. His portrait was growing more gloomy, the urban life he saw grimmer and more mechanical.

In 1857, now the most successful and popular writer of the age, he bought Gad's Hill, near Rochester in Kent, a house he had coveted as a boy. *Great Expectations* (1860), *Our Mutual Friend* (1865), and the unfinished *Edwin Drood* (1870) were all written here. On 8 June, 1870, exhausted by another reading tour of the United States, he died on the couch, aged 58. He had hoped to be buried nearby, without a memorial. But the funeral became a national occasion, and he was interred in Poet's Corner at Westminster Abbey. Huge crowds came to see his coffin.

Dickens was certainly not the only writer to create and construct the magic and the darkness of London. Peter Ackroyd has rightly called him a "Cockney Visionary" along with William Blake and the painter Turner. "All," he says, "were preoccupied with light and darkness in a city that is built in the shadows of money and power; all of them were entranced by the scenic and the spectacular, in a city that is continually filled with the energetic display of people and institutions." For Dickens, as for Blake, the map of the city became an underlying code, a symbolic universe, for his prolix and various art, both comic and tragic, popular and sophisticated.

Novelists ever since have tried to capture the variety of a city ever in movement and growth, change and contrast. George Gissing and H.G. Wells did so; to this day Angela Carter, Justin Cartwright, Ian Sinclair and Peter Ackroyd have sought to, in a city that has changed profoundly, yet in many respects remains the same. Dickens's London is still visible not only in the places or scenes associated with him, but in its living characters, and in it we can still recognize much of the metropolis of today.

DICKENS'S LONDON: *The city's river, the bridges and barges, Marshalsea prison, Spitalfields, Covent Garden, much of London "from Bow to Brentford," became a ground-plan for Dickens's sketches, and for his massive and crowded novels.*

STEAMING CHIMNEYS:
BRITAIN AND INDUSTRIALISM

The Great Exhibition of 1851 said it all. Beneath Paxton's vast glass dome, set up at Prince Albert's behest in London's Hyde Park, the engineering wonders and merchandise on display marked Britain's status as "the workshop of the world." It represented "the march of progress," the engine of change forging the modern era. It showed the achievements of a land that turned out two-thirds of the world's coal, half its iron and cotton goods. It affirmed Britain's leadership in the industrial revolution. 1851 was, said the historian Macaulay, "a singularly happy year of peace, plenty, good feeling, innocent pleasure and national glory."

The England celebrated under the Great Exhibition's amazing iron frames was certainly changing at speed. Railway building fever had swept Britain in the 1840s, recorded by Charles Dickens in his first truly and wonderfully Victorian novel, *Dombey and Son* (1848). In the end the villain is crushed by a panting train. But if Dickens's London was changing fast, the northern and midland cities that had been shaped by the industrial revolution, over half a century old, were in explosive growth. Between 1821 and 1841 London had grown by twenty per cent, changing from a Georgian to a Victorian city. Manchester, Sheffield, Leeds and Birmingham had grown by forty per cent, Bradford by sixty five per cent. These were the Victorian "shock-cities," emblems of the age.

The nineteenth century anonymous painting of Old Hetton colliery on the outskirts of Newcastle, above, captures the time of London's "Steaming Chimneys."

Dickens was one of many who disliked the Great Exhibition. In *Chartism* (1839) Thomas Carlyle (1795–1881) warned of a new era in which people were becoming slaves to mechanical process, and called on all to ponder the "Condition-of-England Question." Many Victorians did. Tennyson in his optimistic poem "Locksley Hall" might celebrate "the ringing grooves of change," but Matthew Arnold doubted the value of poetry in a time when "The complaining millions of men / Darken in labour and pain."

It seemed the form best-suited to facing this new urban and industrial world was the novel. Walter Pater called it "the special and opportune art of the modern world." It could travel freely and record frankly, could tell contrasting, multiple stories and relate different parts of society to the whole. It could draw on detailed research into social problems. Harriet Martineau (1802–76) wrote her story "A Manchester Strike" (1835) as part of a study of political economy. Mrs Frances Trollope visited the northern textile mills to see child labour and write *Michael Armstrong, Factory Boy* (1839). It could lay claim to realism and compassion. "The only effect I ardently long to produce by my writings," wrote George Eliot (1819–80), the great voice of realism, "is that those who read them should be better able to imagine and to feel the pains and joys of those who differ from themselves in everything but the broad fact of being struggling, erring human creatures."

Charles Dickens visited the 1851 Great Exhibition, left, twice, disliked it, and was moved to suggest another exhibition, "of England's sins and negligences."

In the industrial north weavers worked long hours at upstairs windows. Mill whistles blew early and late. In the huge cotton, wool and silk mills, like the one shown below, babies slept beneath noisy spinning frames where the older children worked.

The "Condition of England" was to become a main theme of Victorian fiction. Its motto came from the subtitle of politician-novelist Benjamin Disraeli's (1804–81) *Sybil, or The Two Nations* (1845). The two nations Queen Victoria rules are the rich and the poor; the book deals both with the "saloons of the mighty" and the Lancashire mill towns and a Chartist riot. Like Thackeray and Anthony Trollope, Disraeli wrote of "Society" – but also society in a wider sense, drawing on Parliament's famous Blue Books to look at child employment and low wages. The England of contrasts concerned many novelists of the day. In *Mary Barton* (1848), Elizabeth Gaskell (1810–65) sets Manchester mill-owning wealth against working-class poverty. In *North and South* (1855), she examines another crucial contrast, between Southern England and fictional "Milton" in "Darkshire" in the industrial north.

"Miltons" were the cities that were beginning to impinge on the consciousness of the nation: the northern mill towns, the coke towns, the factory towns, the spinning towns, the iron towns, the pottery towns, the cotton towns, the silk towns. The mill owners and ironmasters – upstart industrialists and a new class in themselves – lived on moors above the smoke, while the mills below churned at all hours. Factory chimneys, late-Georgian mill sheds, pottery banks rose over streets of back-to-back dwellings, filled with those who had fled poverty on the land for ill-paid, insecure work in the towns.

There was Manchester where Mrs Gaskell lived and many more wrote of. It was, said the government observer Sir James Kay-Shuttleworth in the 1840s, "the metropolis of the commercial system," made up of "great capitalists," the rich and ingenious merchants who were "monuments to fertile genius and successful design," and a vast labouring population "like a slumbering giant at their feet." However the giant did not always slumber. Machine-

breaking, riots (the Peterloo Massacre in Manchester, 1819; Chartist Riots in the 1830s and 1840s; strikes in the 1850s) and cholera epidemics interrupted the grand ingenious design.

"Sooty Manchester – it too is built on the infinite Abysses," Carlyle wrote in his *Past and Present* (1843), "and it is every whit as wonderful, as fearful, unimaginable, as the oldest Salem or Prophetic City" – and just as worthy of study. "Manchester is as great a human exploit as Athens," said Benjamin Disraeli in his novel *Coningsby, or The New Generation* (1844). "Even his bedroom was lit by gas. Wonderful city!" But it had a darker side, which Frederick

Mrs Elizabeth Gaskell, above, was one of the many novelists to write about the society she lived in, often contrasting rich and poor, north and south.

Mills in Leeds, Bradford and on the Tyne flourished. William Bell Scott's The Industry of the Tyne: Iron and Coal, *above, depicts a typical scene.*

Benjamin Disraeli, left, once declared that his novels were his life. Many, like Coningsby (*1844*) *and* Sybil (*1845*) *are concerned with the conditions of the urban and rural poor that he was so interested in.*

A CHRONOLOGY OF EVENTS

1831 *"Swing Riots" are staged in rural areas against the mechanization of agriculture*

1832 *First Reform Bill is passed*

1833 *Factory Act forbids child labour under the age of nine*

1834 *The Tolpuddle Martyrs are transported for trying to form a trade union*

1834 *Poor Law Amendment Act sets up workhouses for the poor*

1836 *The first train service is opened in London*

1838 *The Chartist movement begins in the north of England*

1838 *The Anti-Corn Law league is founded in Manchester*

1842 *Lord Ashley's Mines Act prohibits the employment of child or female labour underground*

1842 *Chartist riots erupt in the industrial north*

1844 *Railway mania begins; over 5,000 miles of track are laid*

1846 *The Corn Laws are repealed*

1848 *The Public Health Act is introduced in an attempt to clean up slums*

1851 *The Great Exhibition opens in Hyde Park*

Engels, a radical German mill-owner, came to observe. He wrote *The Condition of the Working-Class in England in 1844* (1845) about Manchester mill-organization ("Since commerce and manufacture attain their most complete development in these great towns, their influence upon the proletariat is most clearly observable here"), before collaborating with Karl Marx on his influential study, *The Communist Manifesto* (1848).

In 1853 Dickens arrived in nearby Preston, to see a strike of 20,000 cotton mill workers, chanting the slogan "Ten per cent and no surrender." He found Preston "a nasty place," but spoke in sympathy with the strikers. In his harsh Northern industrial novel *Hard Times* (1854) – an attack on Utilitarianism dedicated to Carlyle – "severely workful" Preston features as "Coketown." "Coketown... was a triumph of fact," he writes. "It was a town of machinery and tall chimneys, out of which interminable serpents of smoke trailed themselves for ever and ever, and never got uncoiled. It had a black canal through it, and a river that ran purple with ill-smelling dye, and vast piles of building full of windows where there was a rattling and a trembling all day long, and where the piston of the steam-engine worked.... It contains several large streets all very like one another, and many small streets still more like one another, inhabited by people equally like one another...."

Dickens's "cities of fact" – the new industrial and mercantile cities – were becoming mythic literary places of their day. Down the Mersey was Liverpool, a lively Lancashire manufacturing city as well as the major transatlantic port. Here the young American writer Herman Melville came as a common sailor, describing his experiences in *Redburn* (1849). The novel shows Liverpool as an apocalyptic Babylon, filled with noise, disease, poverty, starvation, human despair. The very myth of Old England is upset by such realities. "Ah me, and ten times alas!" cries Redburn, "am I to visit Old England in vain? In the land of Thomas-a-Becket and stout John of Gaunt, not to catch the least glimpse of priory or castle? Is there nothing in all the British Empire but these smoky ranges of old shops and warehouses? Is Liverpool but a brick-kiln? 'Tis a deceit – a gull – a sham – a hoax!"

Lancashire was cotton. Yorkshire, across the Pennines, was wool (treated by Charlotte Brontë in *Shirley*, 1849). Sheffield had iron foundries. "Engine of Watt! unrivall'd is thy sway / Compared with thine, what is the tyrant's power?" wrote Ebenezer Elliott, the Yorkshire Corn Law poet, in "Steam at Sheffield" (1840). In Birmingham, in the workshop of the West Midlands, James Watt developed much of the steam engineering that powered the ironbound Industrial Revolution. Dickens takes us to Birmingham in his early novel *The Old Curiosity Shop* (1841): "Why had they come to this noisy town, when there were peaceful country places, in which, at least, they might have hungered and thirsted with less suffering than in this squalid strife! They were but an atom, here, in a mountain heap of misery.... In all their journeying, they had never longed so ardently...for the freedom of pure air, and open country, as now."

In novel after novel – Charles Kingsley's *Yeast* (1848) and *Alton Locke* (1850), Charles Reade's *It's Never Too Late to Mend* (1856), Mark Rutherford's *The Revolution in Tanner's Lane* (1887) – writers explored and challenged the new industrial landscape, the iron age, the spectacle of what Carlyle called "man grown mechanical in heart and head." But the new system was changing not just England but the novel itself. Dickens's later novels may be more pessimistic than his earlier ones, but they are more vivid, more experimental, grasping at the energies of change and the new types – the Dombeys and the Merdles, the indus-

trialists and financiers the new system brings into play. For the writers of the next generation – like George Eliot (1819–80) from Nuneaton near Coventry in Warwickshire, or Thomas Hardy (1840–1928) – the change has happened. In books like *Felix Holt the Radical* (1866) and *Middle-march* (1875), George Eliot can take what has happened to middle England since the First Reform Bill of 1832 to comment on the world of the Second.

By now industry had prospered, railways networked the land. The Midlands and North were the workshop of England, England the workshop of the world. Life had changed inexorably as people moved into cities; the cities had been transformed by the goods and machines they produced. Disraeli saw gas-light in Manchester; another generation saw electric trams. Victorian cities became places of civic pride and architectural grandeur. Before the century ended, writers from such places – George Gissing (1857–1903), from Wakefield, Arnold Bennett (1867–1931), from Stoke – would be literature themselves. And the city (old and new, southern and northern) rather than old rural England would be the forcing house and setting for most modern writing.

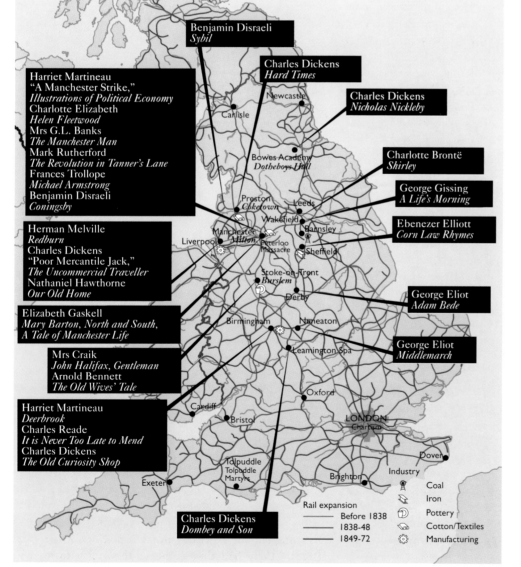

Benjamin Disraeli
Sybil

Charles Dickens
Hard Times

Charles Dickens
Nicholas Nickleby

Harriet Martineau
"A Manchester Strike,"
Illustrations of Political Economy
Charlotte Elizabeth
Helen Fleetwood
Mrs G.L. Banks
The Manchester Man
Mark Rutherford
The Revolution in Tanner's Lane
Frances Trollope
Michael Armstrong
Benjamin Disraeli
Coningsby

Charlotte Brontë
Shirley

George Gissing
A Life's Morning

Ebenezer Elliott
Corn Law Rhymes

Herman Melville
Redburn
Charles Dickens
"Poor Mercantile Jack,"
The Uncommercial Traveller
Nathaniel Hawthorne
Our Old Home

George Eliot
Adam Bede

Elizabeth Gaskell
*Mary Barton, North and South,
A Tale of Manchester Life*

George Eliot
Middlemarch

Mrs Craik
John Halifax, Gentleman
Arnold Bennett
The Old Wives' Tale

Harriet Martineau
Deerbrook
Charles Reade
It is Never Too Late to Mend
Charles Dickens
The Old Curiosity Shop

Charles Dickens
Dombey and Son

Newcastle
Carlisle
Bowes Academy
Dotheboys Hall
Preston
Coketown
Leeds
Wakefield
Manchester
Milton
Barnsley
Liverpool
Peterloo
Massacre
Sheffield
Stoke-on-Trent
Burslem
Derby
Nuneaton
Birmingham
Leamington Spa
Oxford
Cardiff
Bristol
LONDON
Chartism
Tolpuddle
Tolpuddle
Martyrs
Brighton
Dover
Exeter

Industry

Rail expansion
——— Before 1838
——— 1838-48
——— 1849-72

🏭 Coal
⚒ Iron
Ⓟ Pottery
🧵 Cotton/Textiles
⚙ Manufacturing

Marian Evans (1819–80), above, as George Eliot, wrote about rural and industrial middle England.

INDUSTRIAL BRITAIN: *The Great Exhibition of 1851 celebrated the industrial prowess of Britain. Railways now linked all the major towns and cities; factories in the north grew and grew.*

WILD YORKSHIRE:
THE BRONTËS OF HAWORTH

"Wuthering Heights is the name of Mr Heathcliff's dwelling, 'Wuthering' being a significant provincial adjective, descriptive of the atmospheric tumult to which its station is exposed in stormy weather. Pure, bracing ventilation they must have up there, at all times, indeed: one may guess the power of the north wind, blowing over the edge, by the excessive slant of a few, stunted firs at the end of the house; and by a range of gaunt thorns all stretching their limbs one way, as if craving alms of the sun."
Emily Brontë, *Wuthering Heights* (1847).

No tourist walks with more certain tread than the visitor to Haworth, West Yorkshire, the grim grey village which in the mid-nineteenth century was home of Charlotte (1816–55), Emily (1818–48) and Anne (1820–49) Brontë. The extraordinary mix of fact and fiction that means "Brontë" is understood all over the world. Here great novels were concocted in the imaginations of three lonely sisters who lived disappointing lives in miserable isolation in a remote moorland village. In October 1847 the literary world was set alight by a disturbingly frank tale of the passion of a plain little governess for her Byronic employer. Hot on the heels of Charlotte's *Jane Eyre* (1847) came Emily's *Wuthering Heights* (1847), the story of a violent love set on the moors, creating in Heathcliff the darkest soul in British fiction. Thereafter Brontë pilgrims found the path to Haworth parsonage.

After the deaths of Maria and Elizabeth Brontë in 1825, the surviving children (left to right: *Anne, Charlotte, Branwell and Emily*) *stayed together for six years, living in a world of make-believe.*

Add Elizabeth Gaskell's romanticized biography of Charlotte, published within two years of her death, and the myth grows inescapable. This is Brontë Country, a landscape of many planes, visited by millions.

Today's visitor arrives loaded with emotional expectations, and is rarely disappointed. Up the steep Main Street with its wide stone setts, rounding the corner by the church where Reverend Patrick Brontë sermonized his rough-hewn parishioners, and all the Brontë family are buried (except Anne, laid in St

Charlotte began writing Jane Eyre (*manuscript shown above*) *in 1846, while nursing her father in Manchester.*

Mary's Churchyard in Scarborough). Along the narrow lane, between the low-roofed Sunday school on the right where Charlotte taught village children, and the melancholy graveyard on the left, through the gate to the square walled garden which separates the Georgian parsonage from the graves that surround it. Through the front door, into the narrow, quite ungothic hallway, recreated as Mrs Gaskell described it: "Everything about the place tells of the most dainty order, the most exquisite cleanliness. The doorsteps are spotless: the small old-fashioned window panes glitter like looking-glass. Inside and outside of that house cleanliness goes up to its essence, purity."

In the dining room to the left, the Brontë sisters would each evening get out their writing desks. Round and round the table, arm in arm, they would walk, discussing ideas for stories, criticizing each other's work. The sofa is said to be where Emily died. To the right, the study

THE BRONTËS' YORKSHIRE: *In the landscape of the Brontës, fact and fiction are blended together. Many of the books' settings are based on the sisters' own life experiences.*

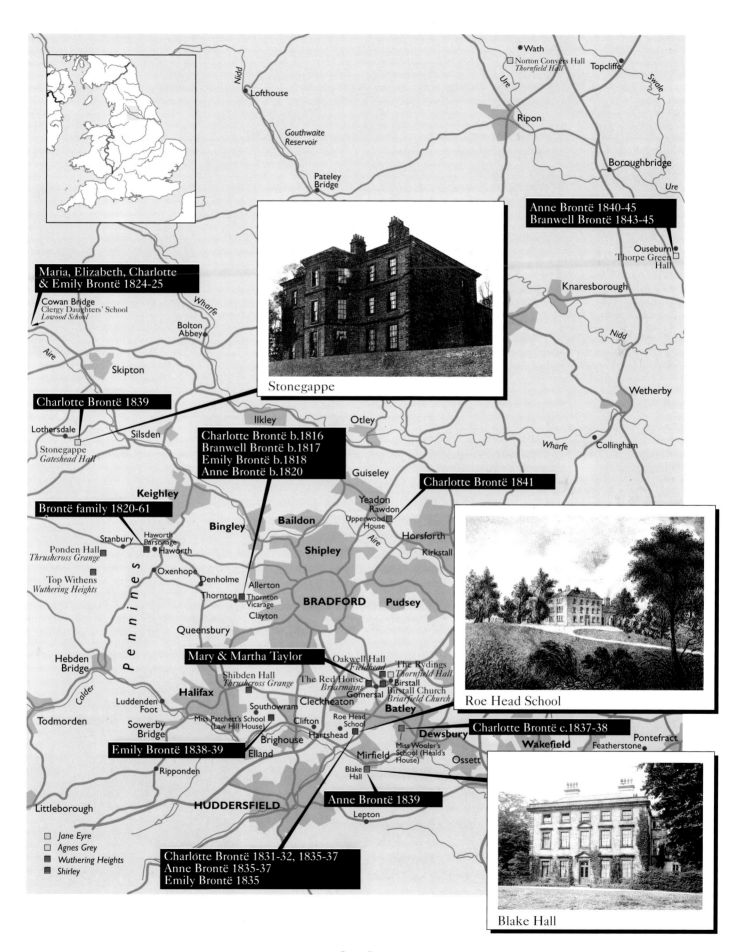

Wath

Norton Conyers Hall
Thornfield Hall

Topcliffe

Ure

Swale

Ripon

Boroughbridge

Ure

Nidd

Lofthouse

Gouthwaite Reservoir

Pateley Bridge

Anne Brontë 1840-45
Branwell Brontë 1843-45

Ouseburn
Thorpe Green Hall

Knaresborough

Nidd

Maria, Elizabeth, Charlotte & Emily Brontë 1824-25

Cowan Bridge
Clergy Daughters' School
Lowood School

Wharfe

Bolton Abbey

Wetherby

Aire

Skipton

Stonegappe

Charlotte Brontë 1839

Lothersdale

Silsden

Stonegappe
Gateshead Hall

Ilkley

Otley

Wharfe

Collingham

Charlotte Brontë b.1816
Branwell Brontë b.1817
Emily Brontë b.1818
Anne Brontë b.1820

Guiseley

Charlotte Brontë 1841

Keighley

Yeadon
Rawdon
Upperwood House

Horsforth

Kirkstall

Brontë family 1820-61

Stanbury

Haworth Parsonage

Haworth

Bingley

Baildon

Aire

Ponden Hall
Thrushcross Grange

Oxenhope

Shipley

Top Withens
Wuthering Heights

Denholme

Allerton

Thornton
Thornton Vicarage

BRADFORD

Pudsey

Clayton

Queensbury

Roe Head School

Hebden Bridge

Mary & Martha Taylor

Oakwell Hall
Fieldhead

The Rydings
Thornfield Hall

Birstall
Birstall Church
Briarfield Church

Shibden Hall
Thrushcross Grange

The Red House
Briarmains

Gomersal

Halifax

Cleckheaton

Batley

Charlotte Brontë c.1837-38

Luddenden Foot

Southowram

Calder

Clifton

Roe Head School

Dewsbury

Pontefract

Wakefield

Featherstone

Todmorden

Sowerby Bridge

Miss Patchett's School
(Law Hill House)

Hartshead

Miss Wooler's School (Heald's House)

Ossett

Emily Brontë 1838-39

Brighouse

Elland

Mirfield

Ripponden

Blake Hall

Littleborough

HUDDERSFIELD

Lepton

□ *Jane Eyre*
□ *Agnes Grey*
■ *Wuthering Heights*
■ *Shirley*

Charlotte Brontë 1831-32, 1835-37
Anne Brontë 1835-37
Emily Brontë 1835

Anne Brontë 1839

Blake Hall

of the Reverend Patrick Brontë, generally depicted as an unhappy, blind old man who survived all his intelligent family to live into blighted old age. By the wall, the piano which Emily played with "brilliancy," above the fireplace the black and white prints of John Martin's apocalyptic visions, which inspired the young Brontës' imaginations.

The warm heart of the household, the kitchen, failed to survive the Reverend John Wade, Rector of Haworth in the 1870s. However, when the Brontë Society (founded in 1893) acquired the parsonage in 1928 to make it a museum, memorabilia found its way back home; the longcase clock in the alcove on the stone stairs; Charlotte's poignant personal relics – tiny-waisted dresses, narrow pointed boots; Branwell's stilted portraits of local worthies; Emily's sparse mementos – watercolours of her pets and a scrap of a diary paper; Anne's collection of carnelian stones, souvenirs of stays in Scarborough; the hundreds of leaves of paper covered with words that made the Brontës famous.

The Brontës came to Haworth in 1820, when Patrick was made Rector. He brought his Cornish-born wife Maria and their six children: Maria, Elizabeth, Charlotte, Branwell, Emily and Anne, still a babe-in-arms. Misfortune soon struck. Mrs Brontë died on 15 September, 1821, and was buried in the family vault. Her sister Elizabeth Branwell came from Penzance to look after the family. In 1824 the four older daughters went to the Clergy Daughters' School at Cowan Bridge, fifty miles away (the grim Lowood School of *Jane Eyre*).

In May 1825 Maria, sent home ill from school, died aged eleven. The other three daughters were withdrawn, but it was too late for ten-year-old Elizabeth, who died at home on 15 June. For the next six years the surviving children were at home together. Their extraordinary imagination and intelligence began to flourish. Busy with

his parish, their father encouraged them to pursue an education; they found it in whatever literature came into the household, the study of art, the pursuit of their own imaginative creations. A famous gift of toy soldiers sparked their invention, inspiring the writing of tiny illustrated books. From 1826 they wrote tales of imaginary worlds, about places called Gondal and Angria.

In Victorian fashion, all three girls served as governesses, with various degrees of success and loathing. In 1831 Charlotte went to Miss Wooler's school at Roe Head, Mirfield, where she met her lifelong friends Ellen Nussey and Mary Taylor, who wrote "She looked like a little, old woman, so short-sighted that she always appeared to be seeking something.... She was very shy and nervous, and spoke with a strong Irish accent." Later she became a teacher at Roe Head, and Emily and Anne joined her as pupils. Taught at home by his father, Branwell joined social life in Haworth, and gave much cause for concern. He took art lessons in Leeds, but failed to apply to the Royal Academy of Arts in London as planned; a stint as a portrait painter in Bradford failed within a year.

Emily had one stab at a teaching job – at Miss Patchett's School for Girls in Halifax – then came home. In 1839 Charlotte and Anne left disastrous governess posts. Anne survived in the outside world longest, taking a five year post as governess to the Robinsons at Thorp Green Hall, near York. This ended ignominiously when Branwell became the son's tutor, only to leave in disgrace after his love affair with Mrs Robinson was discovered.

Charlotte and Emily came home from a year studying French in Brussels after Aunt Branwell's death in 1842. By 1845 the family were together again at the parsonage. Charlotte went back to Brussels but returned, disconsolate in her unrequited passion for her teacher, Monsieur Heger.

All continued to write, and in 1846 their *Poems* appeared under the pseudonyms of Currer, Ellis and Acton Bell; the privately printed book sold three copies. That year Charlotte submitted *The Professor* to many publishers; it was rejected and appeared posthumously in 1857. Helping her father through a cataract operation in Manchester, she began

Charlotte and Emily Brontë both studied at the Pensionnat Heger in Brussels in 1842. The school is no longer there, but these plans drawn by Louise Heger, show exactly where the school was at that time.

WUTHERING HEIGHTS,
BY EMILY BRONTË;
AND
AGNES GREY,
BY ANNE BRONTË.

LONDON:
SMITH, ELDER AND CO., 15, WATERLOO PLACE.
1873.

In 1872 Charlotte's publisher George Smith wrote to her lifetime friend, Ellen Nussey, asking her help in producing an illustrated edition of the Brontë novels, the frontispiece of which is shown near left, top. "I have commissioned a skilful artist [E.M. Wimperis] to visit Haworth and its neighbourhood and make drawings," he said, "you may possibly know the real names of some of the places so vividly described in Jane Eyre, Shirley and Wuthering Heights." Ellen confidently directed Wimperis, to among other places, an old farmhouse on the moors above Haworth named Top Withens, near left, bottom, forever destined to take its place on the mythic map of Brontë country. However, the detail of Wuthering Heights is really thought to come from long-demolished High Sunderland Hall, far left, near Halifax.

Jane Eyre, published to instant acclaim in October 1847. Two months later Thomas Newby published Emily's *Wuthering Heights* and Anne's *Agnes Grey*. Anne's second novel *The Tenant of Wildfell Hall* followed in June 1848.

In late 1848 the death-knell again began sounding over the parsonage. On 24 September Branwell died of consumption, having spent his last months in drug-fuelled decline. Emily followed on 19 December, and Charlotte, fraught with grief, lost Anne to consumption on 28 May, 1849. Charlotte lived until 1855, publishing her novels *Shirley* (1849) and *Villette* (1853), and enjoying, when shyness let her, the rewards of celebrity. She visited London, saw the Great Exhibition, met her hero William Makepeace Thackeray, made friendships with Elizabeth Gaskell and Harriet Martineau. She was sustained by the happiness of her marriage to her father's Irish curate, Arthur Bell Nicholls, but died in pregnancy. Mr Brontë survived his family to die in 1861 at the great age of 84.

Many of the settings in the Brontës' novels are real. There are the schools they attended (Cowan Bridge, Roe Head), the houses where they worked (Law Hill, Blake Hall, Stonegappe, Upperwood House, Thorp Green Hall), the homes of friends they visited. The house where

all the Brontës except Maria and Elizabeth were born still stands in Market Street, Thornton, just outside Bradford, but few go to its door. In writing *Shirley* Charlotte drew on her knowledge of the Batley-Dewsbury area, and Fieldhead was recreated from Oakwell Hall, now a museum standing incongruously in the shadow of a motorway.

The ruins of an old farmhouse named Top Withens, high on the moors over Haworth, are inextricably linked to the imagined Wuthering Heights, although the connection is doubtful. Today signs to Top Withens/ Wuthering Heights are helpfully translated into Japanese. Four miles away is Ponden Hall, thought to be the site of Thrushcross Grange in Emily's novel. Charlotte's sources are easier to find. A visit by her to Hathersage in 1845 provided both the name Jane Eyre and North Lees Hall, one of the inspirations for Mr Rochester's Thornfield Hall.

The real lure of Brontë country is the moorland, for readers the presumed landscape of nearly all the novels, although this too is somewhat erroneous. *Wuthering Heights* consists largely of dialogue; it is the reader who supplies most of the romantic setting. The world the Brontës truly occupied was the world within, and this can only really be entered by opening a Brontë novel.

EMERSON'S AND HAWTHORNE'S NEW ENGLAND

According to Bret Harte, if you shot an arrow into the air in Cambridge, Massachusetts – over the Charles River from Boston – you'd bring down a writer. In the nineteenth century Boston radiated education, culture and literature across expanding America. It hadn't always been so. Philadelphia had been the major centre of American thought; Hartford, Connecticut, an important publishing centre. But around 1840 something happened to Boston and surrounding New England. It became the "hub," the forcing ground of ideas, the centre of American intellectual independence.

John Winthrop's "City on a Hill" where the Puritans settled had stayed America's most Europe-facing city, even if tea from the East India trade had been dumped in its harbour at the famous "Tea Party" that prefigured the Revolution. It had stayed prosperous. Even when sea-trade diminished, there were the great textile mills of the hinterland to keep it going. Its bankers and merchant-princes lived on Beacon Hill, or in Cambridge. It boasted an ever-growing number of periodicals, publishers, concerts. "All Americans lecture, I believe," Oscar Wilde would say; they did in Boston. Lyceum Lectures started in 1826; and at the Lowell Institute one winter series attracted almost a sixth of the population (then around 80,000).

By the 1830s in Boston, culture was the new religion. "Frogpondium," Edgar Allen Poe (1809–49), born in Boston, but reared in Richmond, called it; there really were many croaking literary frogs. Over in Cambridge, around Harvard, America's oldest college, scholars, historians and writers gathered. Henry Wadsworth Longfellow (1807–82), Harvard professor of modern languages, lived at the Craigie House, fondly dreaming that Goethe might come to Cambridge, and duly wrote *Hiawatha* (1855). Everyone wanted to be a writer. Later, in the 1850s, they gathered together in the Saturday Club, based at Boston's Parker House Hotel, the great Boston Brahmins and the best of the "new America" – Longfellow and James Russell Lowell, John Greenleaf Whittier and Oliver Wendell Holmes, and some of the younger Transcendentalists.

Something had happened to the city of Puritanism and Paul Revere. Puritanism had yielded to Unitarianism, then to Transcendentalism. The chief figure was Ralph Waldo Emerson (1803–82), a renegade Unitarian Minister, born to the minister at Boston's famous First Church. Finding his faith waning, he visited Europe to see

New England was famously a region of ministers, colleges, black hatted Puritans, white-spired churches, town meetings and Minutemen.

Coleridge and Carlyle. Then between 1834 and 1835 he retreated to his family village home of Concord to "develop an original relation to the universe." He wrote the essay *Nature* (1836), which explained that "In the woods, we return to reason and faith." Bostonians called his writing Transcendentalism, even if what this meant was a little obscure. "'Transcendentalism means,' said our accomplished Miss B., with a wave of the hand, 'a little beyond,'" Emerson noted of a meeting of the Transcendentalist Club he and George Ripley started in 1836. It was

BOSTON IN THE NINETEENTH CENTURY: *Nineteenth century Boston (shown as it was then in the map, right) was "the Athens of America," and many writers were drawn there. New England wrote itself firmly onto the map of American literature, and from the 1840s it was the site of "the American Renaissance" – the place where powerful and original literary expression in America began. The heyday was the 1850s when some of America's greatest books –* The Scarlet Letter *(1850),* Moby-Dick *(1851),* Uncle Tom's Cabin *(1852),* Walden *(1854) and* Hiawatha *(1855) – appeared.*

BOSTON.

Henry David Thoreau 1834

Maturin Ballou 1847
The Boston Globe 1872

William Ticknor
1835-50s

Louisa M. Alcott 1852-55

William Dean
Howells 1883-84

Nathaniel Hawthorne
1839-42

Annie & James
Fields 1850s

Oliver
Wendell
Holmes
1858-70

Louisa M. Alcott &
Amos Bronson Alcott
1885-87

Julia Ward Howe 1863-65

Bellevue Hotel
Louisa M. Alcott 1950s

Science
Museum

Hayden
Planetarium

Charles

Charles St.

Blossom St.

Cambridge   Street

Charles

Pinckney

BEACON

Street

HILL

Louisburg
Square

St

Chestnut

Street

Beacon

Frog Pond

*Boston
Common*

Arlington

Beacon   Street

Park   St.

Street

Charlestown
Bridge

Old City
Hall

Boston Public
Latin School

King's Chapel

Tremont
House
Nathaniel
Hawthorne
*The Blithedale
Romance*

Athenaeum
Library

Massachusetts
State House

Granary
Burying
Ground

Park Street
Church

Masonic Temple

Elizabeth Peabody's
Bookstore & Publisher 1839
Sophia Peabody
Margaret Fuller's literary
salon
The Dial

West   St.

Washington

Haverhill

John F. Fitzgerald

Congress   Street

North St

Hanover St.

OLD CORNER BOOKSTORE 1829-65
Ticknor & Fields 1845-65-
publishers of:
Nathaniel Hawthorne
John Greenleaf Whittier
Henry Wadsworth Longfellow
Henry David Thoreau
Harriet Beecher Stowe

Paul Revere

Faneuil Hall
Nathaniel Hawthorne
Drowne's Wooden Image

Quincy
Market

Old City
Hall

First Church

Parker
House
Hotel

Milk   St.

Congress   Street

Expressway

Atlantic   Avenue

Long Wharf

Nathaniel Hawthorne 1939-41

Custom
House

State   Street

Old State House

William Emerson,
Preacher 1799

The Liberator Magazine

Governor Winthrop
Nathaniel Hawthorne
The Scarlet Letter

Old South Meeting House

THE SATURDAY CLUB
James Russell Lowell
Oliver Wendell Holmes
Henry Wadsworth Longfellow
John Greenleaf Whittier
THE MAGAZINE CLUB
The Atlantic Monthly
ed. James Russell Lowell

Boston

Inner

Harbor

Fort Point   Channel

Boston Tea Party
Ship & Museum

Congress Street

Summer Street

N

Nathaniel Hawthorne, below, set his greatest novel, The Scarlet Letter *(1850), in the Puritan Boston of two hundred years earlier. The protagonist, Hester Prynne, right, is condemned as a fallen woman and has a large "A" embroidered on her chest which has "the effect of a spell, taking her out of the ordinary relations with humanity and inclosing her in a sphere by herself."*

the mark of a new age. "Men grew reflective and intellectual," explained Emerson.

Not all New England was this way. On the windy Massachusetts coast at Salem a yet more obscure kind of writing was being done. Salem too had a Puritan history, unforgettable because of the Salem Witch Trials (where 19 witches were hanged). It grew rich on the East India trade, but had gone into decline. Sea widows lived in Gothic wooden houses. Legends from the past and distant places flourished. Here, on 4 July, 1804, at a house on Union Street, Nathaniel Hawthorne was born. After studying at Bowdoin College, he returned to an attic in his mother's house on Herbert Street, and started to write. For ten years he wrote obscure and unnoticed, until his *Twice-Told Tales* (1837) won him Boston interest. When Miss Elizabeth Peabody, now "godmother of Boston," found him a post at Boston Custom House and engaged him to her sister Sophia, Hawthorne came into the light.

Hawthorne, Emerson and the Transcendentalists now met. It was never a perfect match. Emerson and his friends wrote of nature, Hawthorne of history. Theirs was the optimistic world of the miraculous American present, his was stained with the guilts and brands of the past.

In 1841 Charles Ripley bought Brook Farm just outside of Boston to found one of those utopian experimental communities loved by the reforming New England spirit.

"A colony of agriculturalists and scholars," Emerson called it, and refused to go. But most of the best of Boston went, including Bronson Alcott, William Henry Channing and Margaret Fuller, formidable feminist author of *Women in the 19th Century* (1845). Hawthorne went too, looking for a marital home. It wasn't a success. Farming and writing didn't mesh, and Hawthorne spent a good part of the time up a white pine tree, before withdrawing from the experiment altogether. He didn't go far – to Emerson's Concord, a charming once-frontier village 17 miles northwest of Boston, first settled in 1635. It won its place in history on 19 April, 1775, when its "embattled farmers" fired at British Redcoats the shot "heard round the world," and the American Revolution began. Watching from the nearby Old Manse was Emerson's grandfather (another minister, of course). Hawthorne rented the cottage too and a happy stage in his life began, celebrated in his book *Mosses from an Old Manse* (1846).

As Hawthorne noted there, the fires of Transcendentalism burned as strongly here too: "Never was a poor little country village infested with such a variety of queer, strangely dressed, oddly behaved mortals, most of whom took it upon themselves to be important agents of the world's destiny, yet were simply bores of a very intense water." Among them was Bronson Alcott, now brooding on another utopian community in Cambridge, Fruitlands. Another was Henry David Thoreau (1817–62), who built himself a cabin on Walden Pond, and had an idea of writing an atlas of the place. "I went to the woods because I wished to live deliberately, to front only the essential facts of life," he explained in the book that came from this, *Walden, Or Life in the Woods* (1854). It was a remarkable record of his days, observations, speculations. For the Transcendentalists, the muddy pond became an ultimate emblem of nature, and its power over the self-creating American spirit. Like Emerson, Thoreau showed that the great New England subjects were nature, the self and the soul. But it did have a darker side, that sense of the Gothic and the tragic which Hawthorne himself embodied.

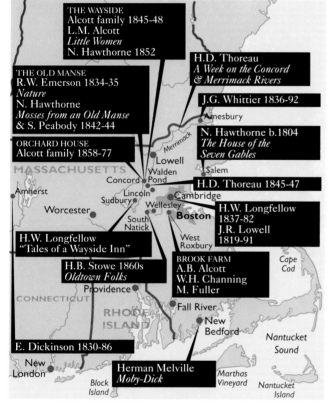

THE WAYSIDE
Alcott family 1845-48
L.M. Alcott
Little Women
N. Hawthorne 1852

THE OLD MANSE
R.W. Emerson 1834-35
Nature
N. Hawthorne
Mosses from an Old Manse
& S. Peabody 1842-44

ORCHARD HOUSE
Alcott family 1858-77

MASSACHUSETTS

Amherst

Worcester

Concord
Lincoln
Sudbury
South
Natick
Wellesley
Walden
Pond
Lowell
Merrimack

H.D. Thoreau
*A Week on the Concord
& Merrimack Rivers*

J.G. Whittier 1836-92
Amesbury

N. Hawthorne b.1804
*The House of the
Seven Gables*

Salem

H.D. Thoreau 1845-47

Cambridge
Boston

H.W. Longfellow
1837-82
J.R. Lowell
1819-91

H.W. Longfellow
"Tales of a Wayside Inn"

H.B. Stowe 1860s
Oldtown Folks
Providence

West
Roxbury

BROOK FARM
A.B. Alcott
W.H. Channing
M. Fuller

Cape
Cod

CONNECTICUT

RHODE
ISLAND

Fall River

New
Bedford

Nantucket
Sound

E. Dickinson 1830-86

New
London

Block
Island

Herman Melville
Moby-Dick

Marthas
Vineyard

Nantucket
Island

Concord, the "American Weimar," was one of many settlements around Boston that housed its expectant intellectuals and fed its literary, reformist spirit. There was John Greenleaf Whittier, Quaker and Abolitionist poet, in Amesbury up the Merrimack River (about which Thoreau also wrote). At South Natick out by Wellesley on the Charles was, for a time, Harriet Beecher Stowe (1811–96), who told its story in *Oldtown Folks* (1869). The book that gave her fame, her anti-slavery novel *Uncle Tom's Cabin* (1851), became a world bestseller, and helped stir the abolitionist sentiment that led to the Civil War.

At 28, Henry David Thoreau, who described himself as a "self-appointed inspector of snowstorms and rainstorms," built himself a cabin, which he called his "inkstand," on Walden Pond, above, just out of the village toward Lincoln, on land owned by Emerson, above left. Curious visitors inspected him as he stood in the water, played his flute, planted his beans. The Boston train chugged by, at night he often walked home for a meal.

NEW ENGLAND: *There were many New Englands: the academic world of Yale, the rocky shore of Cape Cod, the busy port at New Bedford where the whaling voyage of Melville's* Moby-Dick *begins, the grander harbour of Newport, where artists and the wealthy summered.*

There were other ways of "seeing New-Englandly." A hundred miles out of Boston, in the Connecticut Valley, lay Amherst, a small market town where a now-famous college had been founded. At the "Homestead" on Main Street lived Emily Dickinson, the "Nun of Amherst." She travelled even less than Thoreau, rarely leaving the house save to inspect the details of nature. In an upstairs room she quietly wrote some 1,775 poems, only seven published in her lifetime. "I'm Nobody! Who are you?" she challenged. In fact she was one of the most remarkable of nineteenth century American poets, intensely aware of the power of nature, death and the solitude of the spirit.

Only in the 1880s, when William Dean Howells, the Ohio writer who inherited the apostolic succession and edited *The Atlantic Monthly*, moved to New York, was Boston's dominance challenged. Maybe not even then. New England imprinted its spirit, landscape and culture onto the American imagination. "The landscape is democratic," Emerson explained, "not gathered into one city or baronial castle, but equally scattered into those white steeples, round which a town clusters in every place where six roads meet... Massachusetts is Italy upside down."

DREAMING SPIRES:
NINETEENTH CENTURY
OXFORD AND CAMBRIDGE

Oxford and Cambridge are Britain's two great university cities, small market towns with (mostly) ancient colleges that have played a large part in British religious, intellectual and literary life. In the nineteenth century, their literary story is linked with the great changes unfolding inside them during their adjustment to a reforming age. In the early 1850s a Royal Commission examined their organization; from 1853 dons were no longer required to be Anglican clerics. By 1871 tests of religious orthodoxy were largely abandoned; colleges opened their gates to Nonconformists and Catholics. From 1877 Fellows could marry. Around this time women's colleges were founded – Somerville and Lady Margaret (Oxford), Girton and Newnham (Cambridge). Both universities began the study of English literature, changing the status of the entire native tradition and its future.

A key moment came in 1833, when John Keble – fellow of Oriel and Oxford Professor of Poetry – gave a momentous sermon declaring the Anglican Church was being undermined by liberalism. It marked the birth of the "Oxford Movement," seeking to restore the influence of the Anglican Church. It was linked with a celebration of the medieval Gothic style, sign of an ordered and spiritual society. By the middle of the century several of the leading figures, including John (later Cardinal) Newman, converted to Catholicism; the Church's main religious influence was spent. Yet the mark on Oxford was indelible. Architect George Gilbert Scott designed the Martyrs' Memorial (1841) in its Gothic spirit. John Ruskin – an undergraduate at Christ Church (1836–42) supported the medieval style in his architecture, the Pre-Raphaelites supported it in their painting. The University Museum of Natural History epitomizes his architectural ideals; Pre-Raphaelite paintings by Edward Burne-Jones, Dante

Oxford's Christ Church, above, was home of learning to, among others, John Ruskin, Lewis Carroll, and later, the poet W.H. Auden.

Gabriel Rossetti and William Morris decorate the Oxford Union. The final accolade was near; the names Keble and Ruskin were themselves given to Oxford colleges.

The Oxford Movement was only one of the elite societies that flourished in the universities. Cambridge had its equal in "The Apostles." Founded in 1820 at St John's as the Cambridge Conversazione Society, it drew some of the most important young writers of the nineteenth, then the twentieth century. Alfred Lord Tennyson and his close friend Arthur Hallam – at Trinity in the 1820s – were leading lights. So too, much later was, among others, E.M. Forster, who evokes its atmosphere at the

"They very soon came upon a Gryphon, lying fast asleep in the sun." Lewis Carroll, Alice's Adventures in Wonderland

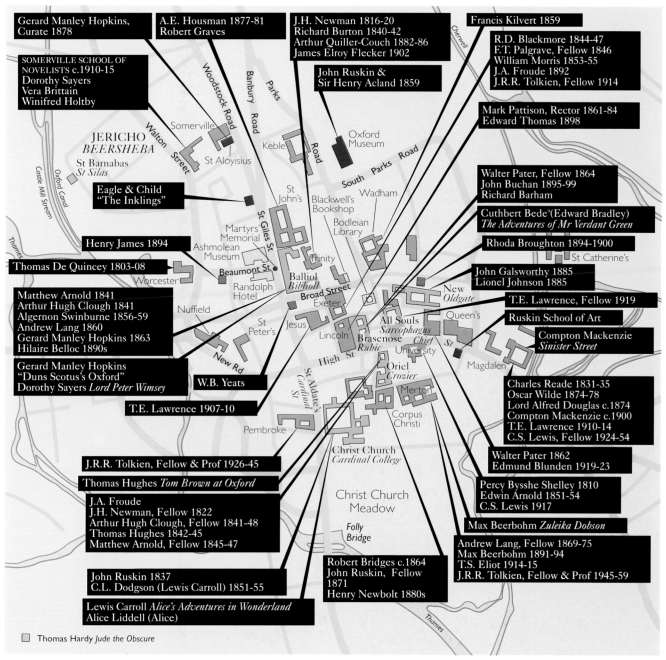

Gerard Manley Hopkins,
Curate 1878

A.E. Housman 1877-81
Robert Graves

J.H. Newman 1816-20
Richard Burton 1840-42
Arthur Quiller-Couch 1882-86
James Elroy Flecker 1902

Francis Kilvert 1859

R.D. Blackmore 1844-47
F.T. Palgrave, Fellow 1846
William Morris 1853-55
J.A. Froude 1892
J.R.R. Tolkien, Fellow 1914

SOMERVILLE SCHOOL OF
NOVELISTS c.1910-15
Dorothy Sayers
Vera Brittain
Winifred Holtby

John Ruskin &
Sir Henry Acland 1859

Mark Pattison, Rector 1861-84
Edward Thomas 1898

JERICHO
BEERSHEBA

Somerville

Woodstock Road

Banbury Road

Parks

Keble

Oxford
Museum

Walter Pater, Fellow 1864
John Buchan 1895-99
Richard Barham

St Barnabas
St Silas

Walton Street

St Aloyisius

South Parks Road

Wadham

Cuthbert Bede (Edward Bradley)
The Adventures of Mr Verdant Green

Castle Mill Stream

Oxford Canal

Eagle & Child
"The Inklings"

St
John's

Blackwell's
Bookshop

Bodleian
Library

Rhoda Broughton 1894-1900

St Catherine's

Henry James 1894

Martyrs
Memorial

Ashmolean
Museum

Trinity

John Galsworthy 1885
Lionel Johnson 1885

Thomas De Quincey 1803-08

Worcester

Beaumont St.

Balliol
Bibliol

New
Oldgate

T.E. Lawrence, Fellow 1919

Matthew Arnold 1841
Arthur Hugh Clough 1841
Algernon Swinburne 1856-59
Andrew Lang 1860
Gerard Manley Hopkins 1863
Hilaire Belloc 1890s

Randolph
Hotel

Nuffield

Broad Street

Exeter

Queen's

Ruskin School of Art

Compton Mackenzie
Sinister Street

Gerard Manley Hopkins
"Duns Scotus's Oxford"
Dorothy Sayers *Lord Peter Wimsey*

St
Peter's

Jesus

Lincoln

All Souls
Sarcophagus
Brasenose *Chief*
Rubic

University

St.

Magdalen

W.B. Yeats

New Rd

High St

Charles Reade 1831-35
Oscar Wilde 1874-78
Lord Alfred Douglas c.1874
Compton Mackenzie c.1900
T.E. Lawrence 1910-14
C.S. Lewis, Fellow 1924-54

T.E. Lawrence 1907-10

St. Aldate's
Cardinal
St.

Oriel
Crozier

Merton

Walter Pater 1862
Edmund Blunden 1919-23

Pembroke

Corpus
Christi

Percy Bysshe Shelley 1810
Edwin Arnold 1851-54
C.S. Lewis 1917

J.R.R. Tolkien, Fellow & Prof 1926-45

Christ Church
Cardinal College

Thomas Hughes *Tom Brown at Oxford*

Christ Church
Meadow

Max Beerbohm *Zuleika Dobson*

J.A. Froude
J.H. Newman, Fellow 1822
Arthur Hugh Clough, Fellow 1841-48
Thomas Hughes 1842-45
Matthew Arnold, Fellow 1845-47

Folly
Bridge

Andrew Lang, Fellow 1869-75
Max Beerbohm 1891-94
T.S. Eliot 1914-15
J.R.R. Tolkien, Fellow & Prof 1945-59

Robert Bridges c.1864
John Ruskin, Fellow
1871
Henry Newbolt 1880s

John Ruskin 1837
C.L. Dodgson (Lewis Carroll) 1851-55

Lewis Carroll *Alice's Adventures in Wonderland*
Alice Liddell (Alice)

Thomas Hardy *Jude the Obscure*

Cherwell

Thames

start of his novel *The Longest Journey* (1907). Meetings, held secretly behind locked doors at Trinity or King's, were full of intellectual earnestness and homoerotic flirting; such friendships bonded the British establishment – and even the spy rings that later corrupted it from within.

The Societies offered new freedoms of speech, thought and relationship. They also contributed to that distinctive Oxbridge sense that implied that the true intellectual and imaginative life isn't just invisible to outsiders, but most insiders too. Tennyson conveys this sense of a distinctive elite in his poem "In Memoriam," the elegy he composed on Hallam's death in 1833 (published 1850). In it he revisits Trinity, and moves "Up that long walk of limes" to New Court, where the Apostles had met: "Where once we held debate, a band/Of youthful friends, on mind and

OXFORD*: In the nineteenth and early twentieth century, the hallowed colleges of Oxford fostered some of the greatest writers of our time. For Thomas Hardy, the city was to become the "Christminster" Jude Fawley visits in* Jude the Obscure.

art/ And labour, and the changing mart/ And all the framework of that land."

If Cambridge had Tennyson (1809–92), Oxford had Matthew Arnold (1822–88), educated at Balliol, then Fellow of Oriel, before he became an inspector of schools. Two poems "The Scholar Gypsy" (1853) and "Thyrsis" (1866) return him to Oxford – or its surrounding, very pastoral countryside: Illsley Downs, the Cumnor Hills, Bagley Wood. Expressions of deep Victorian unease, these poems celebrate Oxford as a scholarly and pastoral

world of free-spirited life, which contrasts with "this strange disease of modern life/ With its sick hurry, its divided aims...." In *Culture and Anarchy* (1869), Arnold returns to this nostalgic Oxford again. It has, he says, many faults: "Yet we in Oxford, brought up amidst the beauty and sweetness of that beautiful place, have not failed to seize one truth – the truth that beauty and sweetness are essential characters of a complete human perfection. When I insist on this, I am all in the faith and tradition of Oxford."

The sunlit world of Oxford rivers and meadows provides the evocative opening for *Alice in Wonderland* (1865), written by C.L. Dodgson (1832–98) under the name of "Lewis Carroll," mathematics don at Christ Church from 1855, lover of logical puzzles, little girls, and photography. *Alice in Wonderland* and its companion *Alice Through the Looking Glass* (1871) are more than nostalgia – or children's literature. They satirize the intellectual and political controversies of the Victorian age, including Darwin's theory of evolution, published in *Origin of Species* (1859), while the strange rituals and eccentric and impassioned characters owe not a little to college High Table.

For all their traditions, both universities were rich in the production of new poetry and prose. The poetic roll-call includes not just Wordsworth, Coleridge, Byron and Shelley, Tennyson, Arnold and Arthur Hugh Clough, but Edward Fitzgerald, Gerard Manley Hopkins, William Morris, Algernon Charles Swinburne, Oscar Wilde, Robert Bridges, Edward Thomas, Rupert Brooke, Siegfried Sassoon. Prose writers include Charles Darwin, the historian Thomas Macaulay, J. A. Froude, John Ruskin, Walter Pater, Mark Pattison and later, Lytton Strachey. Only that great Victorian form, the novel, seems lacking. The wide-ranging imagination and social exploration of the great nineteenth century novelists – Charles Dickens, the Brontës, Mrs Gaskell, George Eliot – appear to have little to do with the Oxbridge milieu.

This would be misleading. William Makepeace Thackeray was an undergraduate at Trinity College, Cambridge, but left in 1830 without a degree, having gambled away his inheritance. His writing career started with contributions to an undergraduate magazine, *The Snob* – one of many produced in both universities to this day. If we still call the two universities "Oxbridge," that's because Thackeray invented the name for his novel *Pendennis* (1850). It shows the hero, Arthur Pendennis, coming up to college and, like his creator, getting into gambling debts until he's ignominiously "plucked" (sent down in disgrace for failing his examinations). It displays a university alive with sociability and comic episodes, where con-men and prostitutes gather to fleece naive undergraduates.

University fiction had something of a tradition, traced back to J.G. Lockhart's *Reginald Dalton: A Story of English University Life* (1823). Novelists from Benjamin Disraeli to Anthony Trollope wrote university scenes in their novels, presenting "Oxbridge" sometimes as social wonderland, sometimes as place of dissipation, sometimes as moral training for life – as in Frederic Farrar's *Julian Home: A Tale of College Life* (1859) or Thomas Hughes's *Tom Brown at Oxford* (1861). A different perspective was given by Charles Kingsley, in his "Condition of England" novel *Alton Locke* (1850). An undergraduate at Magdalene College, Cambridge (1838–42), Kingsley underwent a conversion from hard-drinking sportsman to dedicated scholar. In his novel, the protagonist Locke, Chartist, tailor and poet, visits Cambridge to find it the epitome of privilege and social injustice, a place for spoiled aristocrats who exclude those too poor to pay.

This was no new complaint. In *Rural Rides* (1830), William Cobbett surveys the Oxford colleges, and reflects on "the drones they contain and the wasps they send forth." In Thomas Hardy's *Jude the Obscure* (1895), poor Wessex countryman Jude Fawley travels to "Christminster" (Oxford) hoping to fulfil his intellectual aspirations by entering a college. Living in a district of terraced houses and corner shops (Jericho), he applies to "Cardinal College" (Christ Church).

Tennyson, right, *wrote many of his early poems at Cambridge.*

Unsuccessful, his dismissal is Hardy's message: he dreams of an open, intellectual Oxford that does not exist.

There were other outsiders in Oxford. In 1888 Mrs Humphry Ward (1851–1920) published *Robert Elsmere*, reviewed by Gladstone, and a great bestseller among serious nineteenth-century novels. Mrs Ward was niece of Matthew Arnold and wife of an Oxford don; she knew the web of Oxford interconnections well. The novel deals with the religious crisis of a young academic, Elsmere, and his encounter with rational doubt. The sceptics he encounters were based on real Oxford dons.

By the end of the century the universities became more associated with aesthetes and dandies. Oscar Wilde, at Magdalen, came under the influence of Ruskin and Walter Pater, and took the Newdigate Prize for poetry in 1878. When Max Beerbohm (1872–1956), an undergraduate at Merton from 1891 to 1894, wrote his Oxford novel *Zuleika Dobson* (1911), it was an Aesthete's rebuke to generations of morally earnest fictions. Oxford's male undergraduate world is completely upturned by the visit of a beautiful "new woman" – who ends the book checking the trains for Cambridge.

"New women" did more than upset Oxbridge undergraduates. Women's colleges were becoming important places of literary apprenticeship. Between 1910 and 1915 a fresh generation of women writers, including Dorothy Sayers, were all students at Oxford's Somerville College.

Oxford and Cambridge's literary associations are endless. From Shelley and Wordsworth, Tennyson and Arnold, to Rupert Brooke and A.E. Housman, Oxbridge was a source for much of British poetry, and turns up in a list of novels too. There are those who long to leave, and those who long to get in; sceptical rationalists and defenders of the old Anglican faith; sporting young gentleman and defiant aesthetes; old men and new women; those who stand for the old spirit and those who yearned for the new. It may have expelled

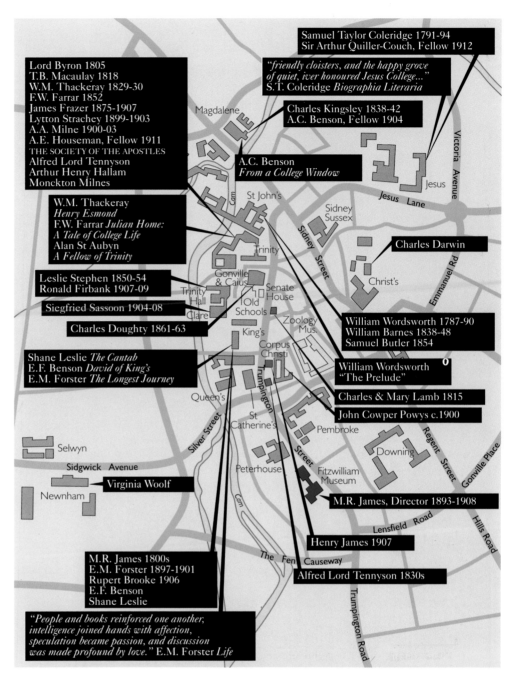

CAMBRIDGE: *As this map of colleges and their writers shows, the literary scene within the ancient dwellings was various and long.*

Shelley, offended Hardy – but it played an incomparable part in British literature.

Running through it all are vivid public and private events: Keble's sermon in 1833 and the public burning of *Nemesis of Faith* in 1849; the Apostles locked in conversation and Matthew Arnold's "Scholar Gypsy" wandering the Cumnor Hills; John Cowper Powys walking the Cambridge Fens, and the strange charm of Rupert Brooke and the young Virginia Stephen (Virginia Woolf) bathing naked in Byron's Pool on the River Cam. The dreaming spires of Oxbridge cast their image across nineteenth century writing; they continue to do so to this day.

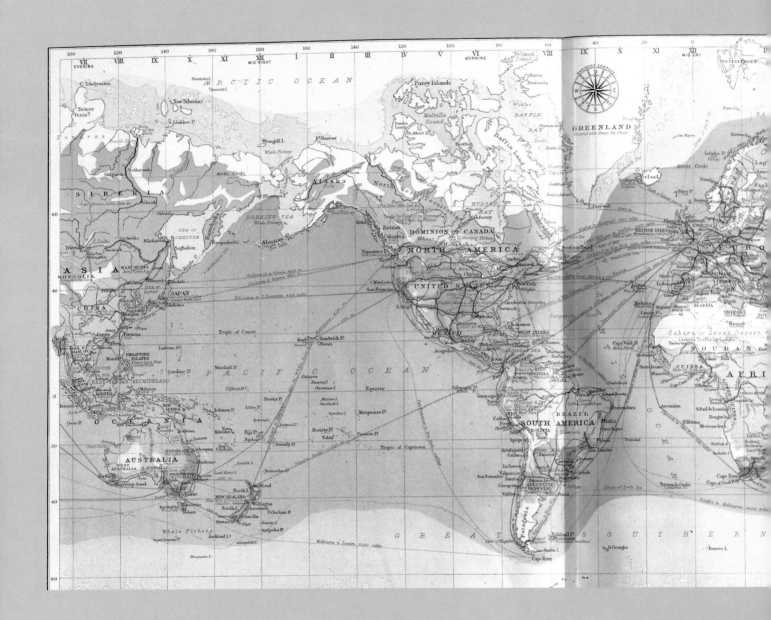

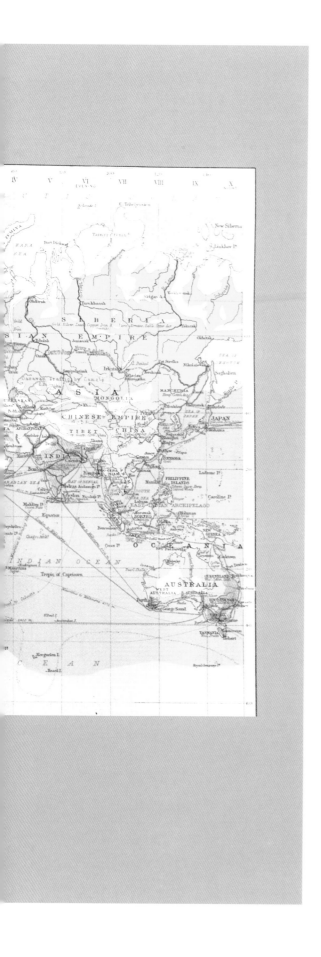

PART FIVE

THE AGE OF REALISM

"To enjoy the crowd is an art," wrote the French poet Charles Baudelaire, and by the second half of the nineteenth century the life of the city, the rush of the crowd, was moving to the centre of art and literature. It was clear that the pace of modernizing change was inescapable, and the world was growing more accessible and much more crowded. Now steamships linked the continents, moving a vast imperial trade. Europe, still at the centre of this busy and imperial traffic, experienced massive growth; America, its Civil War over, witnessed huge transcontinental expansion. The great cities were themselves being transformed by sanitation, gas and electric light. Many went through major rebuilding (Hausmann's Paris) and opened up to new styles of modern architecture and to modern forms of urban transportation. Education and literacy increased, and books and new journalism reached a much wider range of readers, who expected some account of their own lives. Writing now required an ever wider curiosity, a realistic social spread, a detailed observation, a more scientific understanding of social change, a vision of the future that was unfolding...

Bartholomew's Atlas of Commercial Geography, *1889, displayed a globe that was "open to, and available for, commercial enterprise," linked together by steamship routes (*in red*), international highways, railway tracks and telegraph cables.*

MARK TWAIN'S MISSISSIPPI

"When I find a well-drawn character in fiction or biography I generally take a warm personal interest in him, for the reason that I have known him before – met him on the river," wrote Samuel Langhorne Clemens (1835–1910), the writer who took his literary name from one of the sounding calls made by pilots on the Mississippi River, and became famous as "Mark Twain." In the years before the Civil War the Mississippi Valley and River was the American heartland: "the Body of the Nation," said *Harper's* magazine. It was the longest, crookedest river in the world, and "well worth reading about," said Twain in his evocative *Life on the Mississippi* (1883). Much of life was there, and here he really did meet many of his greatest characters: cheeky young Tom Sawyer and uneducated "Huck" Finn in *The Adventures of Tom Sawyer* (1876), Huck again in Twain's best work, *The Adventures of Huckleberry Finn* (1884), the idiosyncratic small-town philosopher "Pudd'nhead" Wilson and the mulatto slave Roxana in *Pudd'nhead Wilson* (1894).

Mark Twain, above, *drew on his experiences of childhood and of working as a pilot on the Mississippi for his novels of comic adventure.*

Mark Twain was America's greatest humourist, and one of her most interesting and original writers of fiction. What made him original was where he was born: in America's central heartland, close to the frontier, near the great river that formed the living artery of the nation. As the United States' "Manifest Destiny" spread West and trade grew, before goods roads or railroads, the river handled much of the life of early nineteenth century America. Ornate Gothic paddlewheel steamboats carried passengers from the cold north near the Canadian border to the tropical Southern swamps of Louisiana, where the French ruled till 1803, and the Gulf of Mexico. Flat barges hauled freight from 44 subordinate rivers. Going downriver, you passed not just through many climates and histories, but through two different Americas: the free states of the North, the slave states of the South. These were the states that went to war in 1861, when the union threatened to split forever.

The Mississippi linked the nation north-south; it was also the bridge to the West. The wagon trains formed at Independence, Missouri or Council Bluffs, then headed on, through flat plains, mountains, Indian country, to what lay beyond – a homestead, a new township, a silver lode or the prospect of gold. Up the North Platte River, past Fort Kearny, lay the Oregon Trail to the north, or the California Overland Trail to the southwest. It was contested territory; Oregon was held onto by the British, the Spanish and Mexicans held much of the South-West, and numerous Indians roamed or settled the plains and the pueblos to the south. Oregon was not acquired till 1846, California in 1848. The Mississippi Valley – bought from the French in the Louisiana Purchase of 1803 – was the last safe settlement. What lay beyond had been charted and written about by recorders Lewis and Clark and Francis Parkman, but it was still America's half-unknown frontier.

Sam Clemens was born on 30 November, 1835 in Florida, Missouri, on a tributary of the Mississippi. But, despite the opinion of Charles Dickens's Martin Chuzzlewit, this was no backwater. It had educated settlers; Sam's father was a Southern lawyer who had moved from Virginia, his mother was from Kentucky. Both were slave states, and so – despite its northern location – was Missouri.

In 1821 it had been grudgingly admitted to the Union as a slaveholding state under the "Missouri Compromise," and remained so until 1854; Twain grew up in a family with household slaves. In 1839, when he was four, they moved to Hannibal, Missouri, on the West bank of the mile-wide Mississippi. His father was justice of the peace; the house is still to be seen, and so is the small town atmosphere of

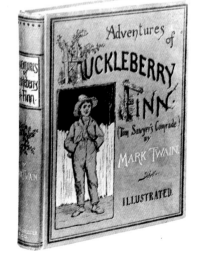

Huckleberry Finn, left, *is one of the great works of American fiction.*

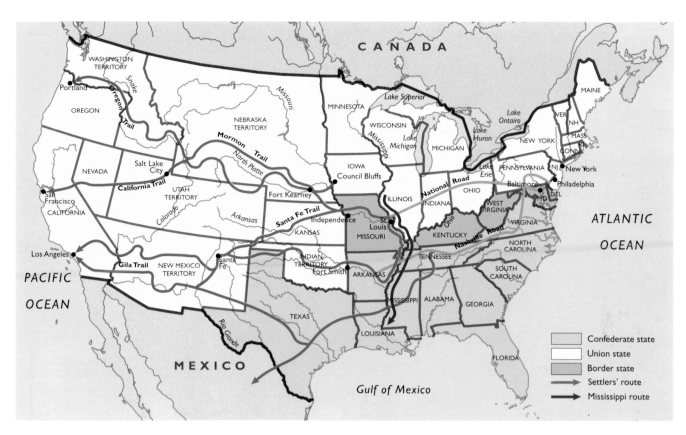

The Mississippi river linked North and South and provided a link to the west. Pioneers and travellers would trek to the river and then take one of the overland trails out to the Territories.

the place. Hannibal and the river became Twain's chief childhood experience and essential material. As one critic puts it: "Thanks to *Tom Sawyer* and *Huckleberry Finn*, its aspect in the forties has become the property of millions: the wharf giving upon the turbid waters where rafts and broad-horns, fast packets and gay showboats passed end-lessly, the plank sidewalks where Tom and Becky trudged to school, the tanyard where Huck's drunken father slept among the hogs, the steep slope of Cardiff (really Holliday's Hill), the surrounding woods of oak and hicko-ry and sumach, and a few miles downstream the cave where Injun Joe met his death."

Hannibal, 120 miles north of Saint Louis, was a thriving township with a population of over 1,000: part Northern and part Southern, part slave and part free. It was no longer the frontier; the emigrants and pioneers who disembarked here made their way further up to the West. An enormously busy river traffic, with boats every hour, linked it south to bustling Saint Louis, then down to Memphis and New Orleans. By branching up the Ohio River you could reach Cincinnati and the cities of the East. There was enough "sivilization" and Christianity in Hannibal ("Miss Watson she took me in the closet and

Many of the huge boats on the Mississippi River were captured in Currier and Ives' prints; the one above was published in 1866.

When Pudd'nhead Wilson *was serialized in* Century Magazine *it was advertised by a specially-drawn calen-dar for that year: June is reproduced here.*

JUNE.

S	M	T	W	T	F	S
··	··	··	··	··	1	2
●	4	5	6	7	8	9
☽	11	12	13	14	15	16
17	☉	19	20	21	22	23
24	25	☾	27	28	29	30
··	··	··	··	··	··	··

When I reflect upon the number of disagreeable people who I know have gone to a better world, I am moved to lead a different life.

3

prayed, but nothing came of it") to drive Huck Finn downriver on a raft. Recalcitrant slaves were sold "down the river" too, to the greater horrors of the cotton plantations further South. There were town drunks, cats sat lazily among the geraniums on the windowsills and Shakespearean actors came by.

The river, for Twain and his contemporaries, was a parade, but also a profession. After travelling a little, Twain in 1857 satisfied his boyhood ambition and trained with the famous Horace Bixby as a Mississippi riverboat pilot, the experience he recalls in *Life on the Mississippi*, a celebration of the river and those who worked it. It was, he said, a profession "I loved better than any I have followed since." In 1859 he was licensed as a riverboat pilot, but the great days of the river traffic were just about coming to a close. The Civil War finished it for ever; completion of the Union Pacific raiload linking Saint Louis to the West finally sealed its fate.

During the War Twain briefly joined the Confederate forces, but deserted after three weeks, "lighting out for the Territory," like Huck Finn. He headed West, went silver mining in Nevada and became a famous Western humorist. By the time his thoughts returned to the river, he was a leading literary figure, living in Hartford, Connecticut, and America was a leading industrial power. Twain recreated the great working river in *Life on the Mississippi*; and in *The Adventures of Tom Sawyer*, where Hannibal is Saint Petersburg, it becomes a boyhood idyll. Then in *The Adventures of Huckleberry Finn* he yielded to

what T.S. Eliot (another Missourian) calls "the strong brown god," and followed the myth of the river itself. Huck and the escaped slave Jim seek their independence and freedom on their raft as it floats downstream. Ironically it is moving toward slavery, and when they miss the turn up the Ohio river at Cairo they enter the darker South. But, celebrating the river and the spirit of freedom and innocence, and told in a fresh vernacular voice, the book shifted the entire language of American fiction.

Two things haunted Mark Twain. One was the memory of the Mississippi Valley in its heyday: a time of childhood, simplicity and American innocence. The other was the crime of slavery, which corrupted that idyll. In 1894 – just as the frontier officially closed and the United States declared itself an urban nation, just as the historian Frederick Jackson Turner explained that the American character had been formed by the frontier – Twain confronted slavery directly in *Pudd'nhead Wilson*. This book is set not in idyllic "Saint Petersburg" but in "Dawson's Landing," half a day's steamboat journey below Saint Louis, and so much closer to plantation slavery. The pessimistic story tells of a near-white slave, Roxana, who changes her baby for a white one in the cradle to save him from being sold, and so confuses black and white. Twain himself finally told the black and white story of life in the Mississippi Valley. He also made it a central piece of the geography of American literature.

MARK TWAIN'S MISSISSIPPI: *Illinois was not a slave state, but by law any Negro without freedom papers could be arrested and subjected to forced labour. Huck's intended journey with Jim down the Mississippi River and along the Ohio River would have guaranteed him greater safety, but the pair make a wrong turn and end up in the slave state of Arkansas.*

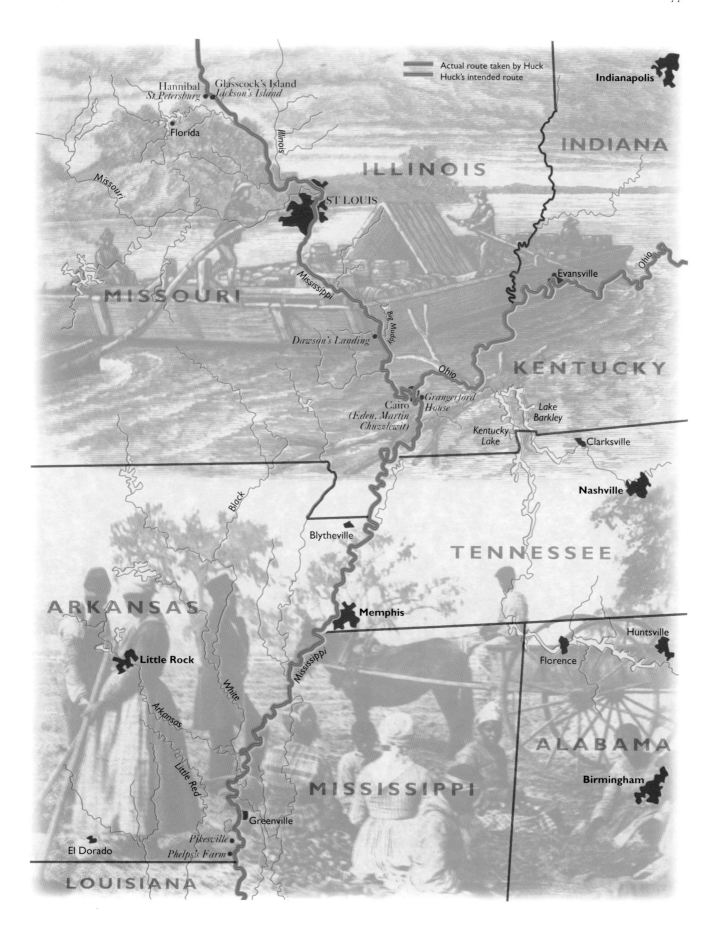

THE SOUTH, SLAVERY AND THE CIVIL WAR

As European visitors, or travellers coming down from the northern states of the Union often observed, the South was a very different part of America from the North. Here the writ of Puritanism hadn't run, some of the old cavalier attitudes of Europe lingered. Above all, they saw, in amazement or horror, that the South was the land of slavery. The Southern states – the states below the Mason-Dixon line, drawn in the 1760s between Pennsylvania and Maryland to settle a boundary dispute – gained their distinctive character and economy from the "Peculiar Institution," the import of black slaves from Africa to work its cotton or tobacco fields or serve its plantations. Eventually this became the great issue, the bone of national contention, the great challenge to American ideals of liberty and freedom: finally the most essential reason why North and South went to war with each other between 1861 and 1865.

The South was the land of Thomas Jefferson, author of *Notes on Virginia* (1785) and bred many leaders of the new nation. It bred Southern gentlemen and rivermen, share-croppers and poor whites, creoles and cajuns. It took pride in its distinctive culture, had its fair share of writers: not least Edgar Allan Poe (1809–49) – author of "The Raven" and "The Murders in the Rue Morge." He was born in Boston, the child of actor parents, but he grew up in Richmond, Virginia,

Only a few Southerners lived in white pillared mansions like Thomas Jefferson's home, above, on his plantation in Virginia.

went briefly to Jefferson's new University of Virginia at Charlottesville, and finally wandered as an editor through New York, Philadelphia, Boston and Baltimore, where he died. He set little of his writing in the South. Yet to this day his writing is associated with the spirit of "Southern Gothic," that went with the region's richer and more exotic atmosphere.

Inevitably, slavery flavoured much of the writing of the South (by 1861 there were four million slaves), as religion and its derivatives flavoured the writing of the North. It displayed itself in Southern fiction, in the work of writers like William Gilmore Simms (1806–70), from Charleston, South Carolina, whose work, like much southern writing, was influenced by Walter Scott and who

brought the historical romance to the region in novels such as *The Yemassee* (1835), about the Indian past. There was John Pendleton Kennedy (1795–1870), writing of Virginian plantation life (*Swallow Barn*, 1832), and the Kentucky writer Robert Montgomery Bird (1806–54), author of *Nick of the Woods* (1837), an Indian melodrama. There was a great tradition of Southern humour, expressed in Joel Chandler Harris's (1848–1908) famous "Brer Rabbit" stories, which came out after the Civil War. It was there no less in Southern music, like Stephen Forster's "My Old Kentucky Home" (1853).

The South was more than a vast half-tropical region with a mixed geography and culture. Settled largely by White Anglo-Saxon Protestants, it remained chiefly rural and conservative. For all the great plantations like Jefferson's Monticello in Virginia or William Byrd's Westover, few Southerners inhabited white-pillared mansions amid trees hung with Spanish moss, or even kept slaves. But there was a Southern myth that transcended these realities. This was royalist, un-Puritan, un-industrial, land-rooted America. Fiercely loyal to its own values, it sustained a coherent identity through its myths of regionality and chivalry, even when the truth of the matter was the harsh mountain life of the Appalachians or the bitter pains of sharecropping. Or above all, slavery.

Often the South's writers told another story: of big woods, frontier hardships (Daniel Boone), mountain-men, as well as of a troubled and often sexual fascination with darkness, blackness, miscegenation. Edgar Allan Poe took a Gothic imagination with him to New York when he left the South; Simms' historical fiction had a different flavour from more Utopian tales told about the North and the ever-opening West. "Southern Gothic" didn't just describe the mood of old cities like New Orleans, Charleston and Atlanta, or the plantation-houses hung with mosses and surrounded by slave cabins. It also described the spirit of the fiction and poetry that came from Southern writers, with its different sense of history, its greater awareness of social complexity.

Beyond all this was another story, yet harder to tell. It was illegal to teach reading and writing to slaves; even so, early on there was a black literature in the South. Black writers both used and subverted the language of their masters, in poetry and prose. Jupiter Hammon

Frederick Douglass (1818–95), bottom right, *was born a slave in Maryland, escaped to freedom in the North, and became an eloquent abolitionist and statesman. His* Fugitive Song *(1845)* top right, *campaigned against the slavery of the South, depicted in the painting,* The Slave Market, *top left, by Friedrich Schulz.*

(c.1739–1800) and Phillis Wheatley (1753–1784) wrote poetry in conventional English forms, though their work was touched with protest and suffused with irony. But only in time did their writing deal with the essential subject: the slave experience itself.

This came in the form of "slave narrative," some written by African-Americans themselves, some with the help of (usually Northern) white sympathizers. Frederick Douglass's *The Narrative of the Life of Frederick Douglass, an American Slave* (1845) raised the conscience of Northerners, and also had an important part to play in the Abolition movement that had emerged in New England and New York at the time. In turn his narrative fed back into early black novels: for example, William Wells Brown's *Clotel*, which was published in England in 1847, and Harriet E. Wilson's *Our Nig* (1859), the first novel by an African American writer to appear in America.

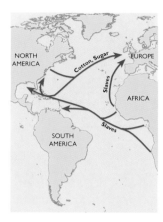

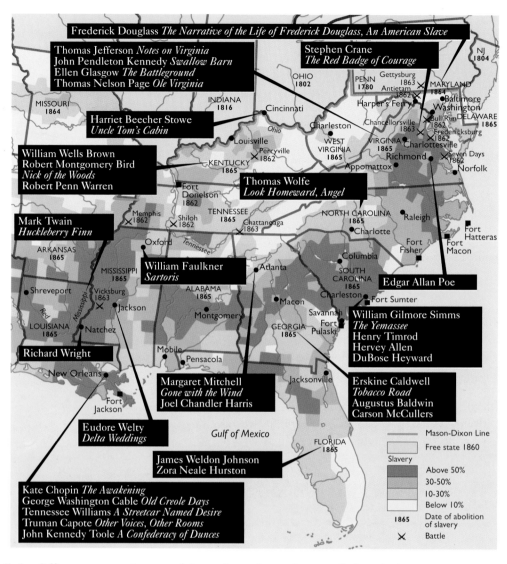

Frederick Douglass *The Narrative of the Life of Frederick Douglass, An American Slave*

Stephen Crane
The Red Badge of Courage

Thomas Jefferson *Notes on Virginia*
John Pendleton Kennedy *Swallow Barn*
Ellen Glasgow *The Battleground*
Thomas Nelson Page *Ole Virginia*

Harriet Beecher Stowe
Uncle Tom's Cabin

William Wells Brown
Robert Montgomery Bird
Nick of the Woods
Robert Penn Warren

Thomas Wolfe
Look Homeward, Angel

Mark Twain
Huckleberry Finn

William Faulkner
Sartoris

Edgar Allan Poe

Richard Wright

William Gilmore Simms
The Yemassee
Henry Timrod
Hervey Allen
DuBose Heyward

Margaret Mitchell
Gone with the Wind
Joel Chandler Harris

Erskine Caldwell
Tobacco Road
Augustus Baldwin
Carson McCullers

Eudore Welty
Delta Weddings

James Weldon Johnson
Zora Neale Hurston

Kate Chopin *The Awakening*
George Washington Cable *Old Creole Days*
Tennessee Williams *A Streetcar Named Desire*
Truman Capote *Other Voices, Other Rooms*
John Kennedy Toole *A Confederacy of Dunces*

THE SLAVE STATES: *The "African Trade" had become an essential part of the structure of the South, part of the triangular traffic between Europe, Africa and the Americas which kept its ports going. There was here a rough equivalence between cotton, sugar and human life. Captured in Africa, transported cruelly from its west coast, stored on board as you'd store a non-human commodity, the slaves were brought across the Middle Passage, before being put on the scaffold for sale to those who needed them for labour or as human investment.*

Yet the book that made all the difference was written by a minister's wife from New England, who was then living in Cincinnati, Harriet Beecher Stowe (1811–96). Her novel *Uncle Tom's Cabin* (1852) drew on the old slave narratives. It was a world bestseller, promoted Abolition, and presaged the end of the Old South. Slavery had divided the nation, become the great challenge to American ideals of liberty and freedom, and the chief reason why North and South went to war in 1861–65. When provoked by John Brown's attack on Harper's Ferry in Virginia, Southerners attacked the federal arsenal at Fort Sumter in April 1861, the death of the Old South began.

The Civil War was America's greatest crisis since the Revolution; the New Nation now nearly broke apart. The war provoked its own literature, from major oratory (Lincoln's speeches, above all his "Gettysburg Address"), poetry and song ("John Brown's Body" for one side, "Dixie" for the other). The greatest poet to write about the War was the Bohemian New Yorker, Walt Whitman

(1819–92), author of one of America's greatest poems "Leaves of Grass" (1855), who published *Drum Taps* in 1865, and the remarkable elegy on the death of Lincoln, "When Lilacs Last in the Dooryard Bloom'd."

Curiously, the Civil War was not much recorded in the fiction of the day, in part because many of the leading novelists (Nathaniel Hawthorne, William Dean Howells, Henry James among them) did not serve in it. Some, like Hawthorne, detested the demands for "unconditional loyalty:" "I have been publicly accused of treasonable sympathies – whereas I sympathize with nobody and approve of nothing..." he said.

Hence it was later novelists – Stephen Crane in *The Red Badge of Courage* (1895), Ambrose Bierce in *Tales of Soldiers and Civilians* (1993), Ellen Glasgow in *The Battleground* (1902), Upton Sinclair in *Manassas* (1923) and most famously Margaret Mitchell in her exotic *Gone With the Wind* (1935) – who treated it with glowing retrospect. In contrast, the War itself has been endlessly refought and recorded; it is said that some 100,000 volumes have been written about the conflict.

From early days the South contributed much to American writing. It might be in the form of Scott-influenced romance (Mark Twain, himself of Southern stock, had great fun with this tradition); it might be in the simple, suffering record of black slave narrative. But on these unhappily twinned relations a good deal of modern American writing began to rest. Some of the deepest American stories – coming from the sense of regional history, of racial complexity, indeed tragedy – passed from the South into the American tradition. Many of the most profound themes – romantic chivalry and black suffering, the struggle of a rural people first with their own compatriots and then with the new industrialization and modernity – came out of the South.

So did a different, darker awareness of history – a history that contained a grim knowledge of defeat. Even when, with the Civil War over, attention shifted to the West and the reconstruction of the nation, the Southern story continued to be explored. The Northerner John William De Forest explored the attempt at nation-rebuilding in *Miss Ravenel's Conversion from Secession to Loyalty* (1867), while George Washington Cable, from New Orleans, recalled *Old Creole Days* (1878), as well as telling his life as a Confederate officer in *The Cavalier* (1901). Also from New Orleans, Kate Chopin told of a woman's sexual awakening in the "chivalric," French-influenced society of the city in *The Awakening* (1899), while Ellen Glasgow from Virginia, the "Old Dominion," explored the bleak heritage the War had left in many novels.

Perhaps the greatest writer to emerge from the South was William Faulkner (1897–1962), who explored the psychic, moral and historical impact of the War, racial tension and miscegenation brought to the South, writing of the big woods, the dying plantations, the wounded aristocracy, the enduring slaves. "Southern Agrarian" writers

" Put us two up togedder, togedder—do, please, Mas'r," said the old woman, holding fast to her boy.

George Cruikshank's illustration from Harriet Beecher Stowe's Uncle Tom's Cabin, *above, shows Aunt Hagar being separated from the last of her children as they go off to become slaves.* Stowe, *right, said that the novel had been written by God himself. An international bestseller, it presaged the end of the Old South.*

in the 1930s reacted against the mechanization of American Society. Other writers like DuBose and Dorothy Haywood, James Weldon Johnson, James Branch Cabell, Thomas Wolfe, Carson McCullers, Katherine Anne Porter, Eudora Welty and Truman Capote captured the distinctive and very varied textures of Southern life, from cities like New Orleans (Tennessee Williams's *A Streetcar Named Desire*, 1947) to the bitter life of small farmers (Erskine Caldwell's *Tobacco Road*, 1932).

Those whose forebears had been slaves had a story too. It was told by many, from Paul Laurence Dunabar and Charles W. Chesnutt, to later writers like Zora Neale Hurston (*Jonah's Gourd Vine*, 1934) and Richard Wright (*Native Son*, 1940) who both moved North in the great twentieth century diaspora. African-American writing too, became an essential part of the American tradition, and is to this day – not least in the powerful, angry writing of Toni Morrison and Alice Walker, for whom the double imprint of the crime of slavery and the powerful tradition of folk-narrative and regional mythology that came out of it are important still. The anxiety and Gothicism often found in American writing owes much to the history of the South, the terrible war between the States that nearly broke the nation, killed millions and left one part of it defeated, and to the guilt and trauma of slavery that ended, at least officially, with the Thirteenth Amendment of 1865.

THE CIVIL WAR IN FICTION

1891 Ambrose Bierce *Tales of Soldiers and Civilians*
1895 Stephen Crane *The Red Badge of Courage*
1936 Margaret Mitchell *Gone With the Wind*
1938 William Faulkner *The Unvanquished*
1944 Joseph Stanley Pennell *The History of Rome, Hanks and Kindred Matters*
1970 Stephen Becker *When the War is Over*
1976 Alex Haley *Roots*
1976 Shelby Foote *Shiloh*
1980 Donald Honig *Marching Home*
1989 Allan Gurganis *Oldest Living Confederate Widow Tells All*

PARIS AS BOHEMIA

Gustave Flaubert (1821–80), like many of his generation, enthusiastically hailed the 1848 Revolution which abolished the French monarchy. But he was soon disillusioned; the new Republic lasted only three years, swept away by Napoleon III's Second Empire. France's greatest poet, Victor Hugo (1802–85), preferred exile on Guernsey to life under its authoritarian regime. The Empire had its achievements. With vision and determination Baron Haussmann undertook the massive reconstruction of Paris, to make it the beautiful city we know, with its long perspectives, measured proportions – and better social control. Finally, in the wake of defeat in the Franco-Prussian War of 1870–71, Louis Bonaparte's government collapsed. France acquired, in the Third Republic, its first stable regime for a hundred years.

The heavily moustached features and burly figure of Gustave Flaubert, above, *dominated later nineteenth century France.*

For writers and artists, the Second Empire meant nothing. The regime was boring and bourgeois; they felt rejected and persecuted. They became "Bohemians," taking the term from Henri Murger's novel *Scenes of Bohemian Life* (1851), immortalized by Puccini's *La Bohème* (1896). Bohemians, said Murger, were those "whose main business is to have no business at all." Theirs was a world of neglected sons, students, painters, writers, would-be writers, showgirls. It was poor life as rich life, poverty as excess, marked by a sense of *ennui*, alienation, a feeling of superiority. It became the world of art, of the *avant-garde*.

Bohemia was poverty incarnate – but it let artists be artists. "Nothing but art may be believed in, and literature is the only confession," Flaubert said. Born in Rouen, son of a surgeon, Flaubert (1821–80) went to Paris, failed his law exams and returned to devote himself to literature. Following the Bohemian rule that art was all, he even broke off an affair that interfered with his writing. He claimed to have no autobiography but his books, and spent much of his life in

Normandy. He followed the bourgeois virtues, but called Bohemia "the fatherland of my breed." The great work to emerge after five years was *Madame Bovary* (1857), meticulously set in Normandy, near Rouen. The story of a country doctor's wife who takes lovers from boredom, gets into debt and commits suicide when the creditors foreclose, Flaubert saw it as a work of pure style. The authorities saw it as an offence against public morals; he was tried but acquitted. It is one of his most realistic works. Emma Bovary (who was, Flaubert insisted, himself) is a maker of sad illusions in a world of futility. He neither romanticizes nor condemns her; he observes her, with the famous impersonality of new "realism." His most Bohemian work is *Sentimental Education* (1869), a satire on his younger more idealistic self. Its hero, Frederic Moreau, typifies a generation strong in artistic temperament, yet without real achievement. He goes to Paris as a painter. Disillusioned by Napoleon's seizure of power, he spends most of the Second Empire abroad. He returns to find the object of his unrequited passion has become a white-haired grandmother, and all hope of realizing his youthful dreams gone.

PARIS AS BOHEMIA: *Based in Montmartre or the Latin Quarter, Bohemia formed a culture that lasted into the experiments of Modernism.*

Jules Claude Ziegler's The Republic (1848), left, *celebrates the abolition of the French monarchy.*

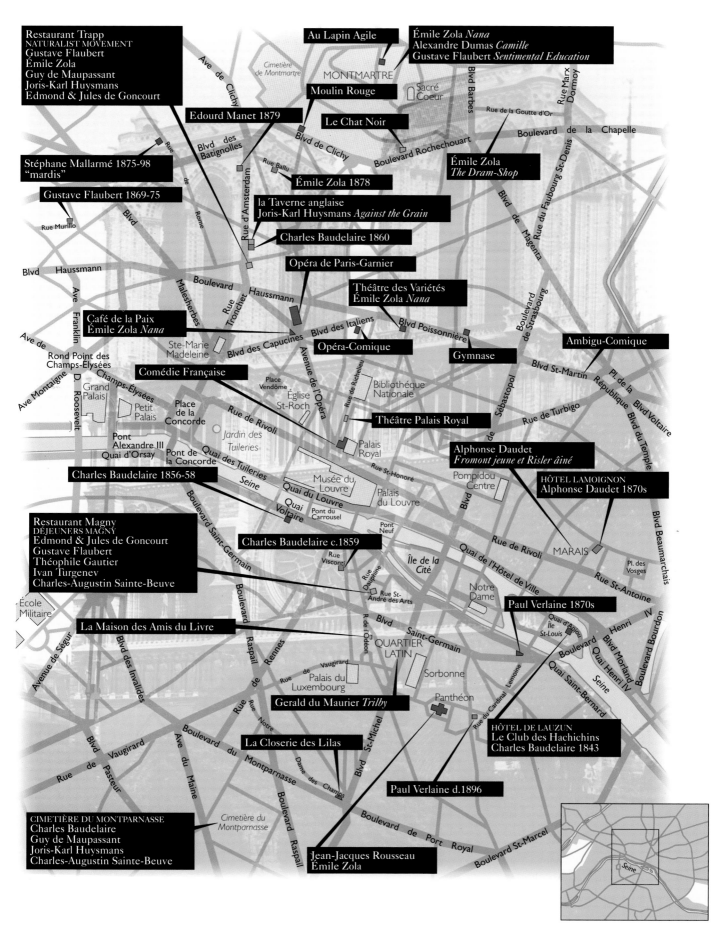

Au Lapin Agile

Émile Zola *Nana*
Alexandre Dumas *Camille*
Gustave Flaubert *Sentimental Education*

Restaurant Trapp
NATURALIST MOVEMENT
Gustave Flaubert
Émile Zola
Guy de Maupassant
Joris-Karl Huysmans
Edmond & Jules de Goncourt

MONTMARTRE

Sacré
Coeur

Moulin Rouge

Le Chat Noir

Edourd Manet 1879

Stéphane Mallarmé 1875-98
"mardis"

Émile Zola 1878

Émile Zola
The Dram-Shop

Gustave Flaubert 1869-75

la Taverne anglaise
Joris-Karl Huysmans *Against the Grain*

Charles Baudelaire 1860

Opéra de Paris-Garnier

Théâtre des Variétés
Émile Zola *Nana*

Ambigu-Comique

Café de la Paix
Émile Zola *Nana*

Opéra-Comique

Gymnase

Comédie Française

Bibliothéque
Nationale

Théâtre Palais Royal

Charles Baudelaire 1856-58

Alphonse Daudet
Fromont jeune et Risler âiné

HÔTEL LAMOIGNON
Alphonse Daudet 1870s

MARAIS

Restaurant Magny
DÉJEUNERS MAGNY
Edmond & Jules de Goncourt
Gustave Flaubert
Théophile Gautier
Ivan Turgenev
Charles-Augustin Sainte-Beuve

Charles Baudelaire c.1859

Paul Verlaine 1870s

La Maison des Amis du Livre

QUARTIER
LATIN

Sorbonne

Gerald du Maurier *Trilby*

Panthéon

HÔTEL DE LAUZUN
Le Club des Hachichins
Charles Baudelaire 1843

La Closerie des Lilas

Paul Verlaine d.1896

CIMETIÈRE DU MONTPARNASSE
Charles Baudelaire
Guy de Maupassant
Joris-Karl Huysmans
Charles-Augustin Sainte-Beuve

Jean-Jacques Rousseau
Émile Zola

Realism was the controversial movement that became a literary and painterly credo in the wake of the failed European Revolutions of 1848. The debate raged in Paris through the 1850s. Flaubert's friend Guy de Maupassant (1850–93), from near Dieppe, also in Normandy, became a disciple, in notable stories like *Tallow Ball* (1880). So did the Goncourt Brothers, Edmond (1822–96) and Jules (1830–70), who collaborated on documentary fictions like *Germinie Lacerteux* (1864), about one of their servants. Realism was characterized by painstaking documentation, transparency, exactitude of style. It dealt with representative individuals in their social setting, the urban world, the industrial revolution. Painters turned realist too, above all Gustave Courbet (1819–77), who created a Pavilion of Realism when the 1855 Paris Exposition refused his pictures. His huge canvases depicting everyday life hang in the Musée d'Orsay alongside his *The Origin of the World* (1866), a long-censored work which many think the most powerful representation of female sexuality ever produced.

"*Le naturalisme, c'est la nudité*," wrote Émile Zola (1840–1902), who sought to advance the movement of Realism on scientific lines. The son of an Italian engineer, he was born in Paris but brought up in Aix-en-Provence ("Plassans" in his novels) where he knew Cézanne. Impressed by Pasteur's discoveries and Darwin's theory of evolution, he saw the novel as a laboratory experiment (*Le roman expérimental*, 1880). His *Rougon-Macquart* series of novels (1871–93) offers a vast documentary history of the Second Empire, examined against the working of laws of social science and heredity. His books sold in hundreds of thousands, his house at Médan became a hive of activity. His social commitment was shown in *J'Accuse!* (1898), his defence of Dreyfus. Sentenced to imprisonment, he fled to England, and returned a hero. He died in Paris, accidentally suffocated by charcoal fumes in his apartment.

Society, politics, science weren't universal concerns in Bohemia. "Art for art's sake" was its banner, dissipation and disaster often the fate of its writers. Even Edgar Allan Poe (1809–49), that struggling figure from the American underside, was included, when Charles Baudelaire (1821–67) translated him into French. His infelicities disappeared and his impact became great, not least on Baudelaire. Baudelaire had spent an unhappy childhood in Lyon and Paris, travelled to India; by the time he went to college he had the venereal disease that would kill him. He joined Paris Bohemia, sinking ever deeper into debt. He worked in the studios of realist artists, wrote art criticism. Poe showed him another way. In 1857 he brought out his remarkable collection of Symbolist poems, *The Flowers of Evil* (it too was prosecuted). Baudelaire represented the anxious state of modernity, the appeal of Satanism, the hidden meanings of a chaotic city. His work looked to Romanticism: the idea that poety is a privileged means to explore a mysterious world normally hidden from us.

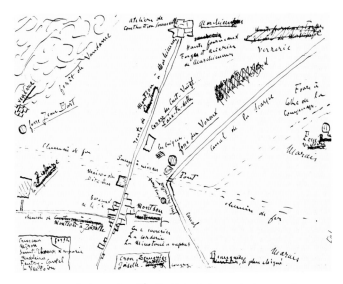

The "Naturalist" novels of Émile Zola, left, *can be heavy going, but his accounts of Haussmann's rebuilding of Paris (*The Priest, *1872*), *the work of Paris butchers and prostitutes (*Nana, *1880*), *his portraits of slum life (*The Dram-Shop, *1887*) *and mining life (*Germinal, *1885*) *make him the extraordinary recorder of fundamental aspects of late nineteenth century French society. He would even sketch maps, like the one above* showing the area covered in *Germinal, *to visualize the milieu of his novels.*

His most distinctive Bohemian successor was Arthur Rimbaud (1854–91), born in the industrial town of Charleville near the Belgian border. He began writing poetry early; indeed all his verse was written in his teens. He sent some to another important bohemian poet, Paul Verlaine (1844–96). They began a homosexual affair, and travelled to England and Belgium together. It ended in disaster. In a quarrel in a Brussels hotel, Verlaine shot and wounded Rimbaud, and was imprisoned. By now Rimbaud had composed some of the most haunting and original verse we have, publishing *A Season in Hell* in 1873, and writing *Illuminations*, printed by Verlaine, in 1886. But he gave up poetry, fled to Africa, and became a trader and gunrunner at Harar, Abyssinia. He was brought home dying to Marseilles in 1891.

Stephane Mallarmé's life (1842–98) was sober by contrast. He was a provincial school teacher who came to Paris to live a bourgeois life on the rue de Rome, where he held a salon. He too translated Poe (*The Raven*, 1875), and his own poetry was if anything more radical than that of his symbolist predecessors, displaying a compression and allusiveness not achieved before. His most famous poem, "L'Après-midi d'un faune," appeared in 1876, illustrated by his friend Manet. His *vers libre* and word music shaped the 1890s decadence, while his crystalline impersonality was hugely influential on twentieth century French poetry, especially on his greatest disciple Paul Valéry (1871–1945).

The Symbolist movement that flourished towards the century's end was an antithesis of Naturalism. Its doctrine of *l'art pour l'art* and of the veiled impression was shared by some prose-writers, the Decadents above all, who reacted against modern materialism by cultivating an exaggerated aesthetic brilliance. A key text was Villiers de l'Isle Adam's (1839–89) prose poem "Axel" (1890), which combined elements of gothic, horror and romance. It opened the final, "decadent" decade of the century in fine style, and appropriately provides the focus for *Axel's Castle* (1931), Edmund Wilson's brilliant book on Modernism and Symbolism.

In 1889 Paris celebrated the centennial of the Revolution. Gustave Eiffel's great iron tower rose above the city – an abstract modern monument shaped by the wind, claimed its creator, placed over a World Fair largely devoted to technology and science. But a revolt against science, materialism, history itself was growing. Religion was back. Rimbaud, who had advocated "debauchery of all the senses," repented on his deathbed. Paul Claudel (1868–1955) famously underwent conversion in Notre Dame on Christmas Day 1886. Joris-Karl Huysmans (1848–1907), author of the decadent bible *Against Nature* (1884), came to Catholicism via Satanism, a familiar course in the 1890s.

This was the age of the *belle époque*, and these have been called the "banquet years." Paris became a stage set

Against Eiffel's tower stood the new basilica of Sacre Coeur, above, the tasteless monument which gleams like icing sugar from the top of Montmartre, a focal point for Bohemia.

for the arts. There was the Offenbach craze, the can-can of the Folies Bergères. Bohemian cabarets (Montmartre's Chat Noir and Lapin Agile) flourished. Bohemia had triumphed: would-be painters, writers, models poured in from many countries to rent a handy garret and enjoy the life of artistic poverty. When Whistler arrived in Paris, he told the cab driver to take him to "Bohemia." In 1894 Gerald du Maurier's (1834–96) novel *Trilby*, set in the Latin Quarter, became an international bestseller, setting a new fashion in hats, smart cigarettes, trips to Paris. Bohemia had become a fantasy, but it had been real, and poor enough too. The source of modern art and poetry, the seedbed of fundamental debates between realism and aestheticism, materialism and experiment, it had created an *avant-garde* to stand against the bourgeois *belle époque*.

It took the genius of Marcel Proust (1871–1922) to square the circle. In a room at 102 boulevard Haussmann, lined with cork to fend off asthma attacks, he began his vast novel *Remembrance of Things Past* (1913–27). It is both a masterpiece of social realism and a symbolist exploration of time and memory. In the opening book two paths lead out of Combray. They seem to lead in opposite directions: art or society, Bohemia or wealth. In the last book they meet. Proust resolves the division that had run through French culture ever since Mima's tiny hand became

THE EUROPEAN APPLE:
HENRY JAMES'S INTERNATIONAL SCENE

"It's a complex fate being an American, and one of the responsibilities it entails is fighting against a superstitious valuation of Europe," Henry James (1843–1916) wrote. No novelist ever accepted their fate more willingly. James will always be famous for his treatment of the "international theme," the encounter between American innocence and European experience. Whenever we think of the writer as a transatlantic traveller, or the novel as a form that explores the encounter between the Old World and the New, we think of him. Some of his characters – Christopher Newman, the innocent businessman in Paris in *The American* (1877), Isabel Archer, the daring young American woman caught in the prison of a moneyed marriage in *The Portrait of a Lady* (1881), Daisy Miller, the young and bold American girl dying of malaria in Rome in *Daisy Miller* (1878) – belong to an essential folklore of modern transatlantic encounter. And there is no doubt it helped map America, Europe and their complex inter-relationship for the modern imagination.

Henry James, shown above *in a painting by John Singer Sargent, was taken early to Europe for his "sensuous education."*

"My choice is the Old World – my choice, my need, my life," James told his diary, after settling in London in 1876. This followed an extended tour in which he tested various locations of Europe to see how they suited him as a writer. He had a delirious year in the "golden air" of Rome – reflected in *Roderick Hudson* (1876), his early novel about an American artist drinking from the cup of experience in Italy. There was a year in Paris, when he lived at 29 rue de Luxembourg, near the Place Vendôme and met the great *literati* of Paris, including the new exponents of Realism: Flaubert, Maupassant, the brothers Goncourt, Turgenev. The first of several books that resulted was *The American* (1877), the story of the allegorically named Christopher Newman's encounter with the cunning French aristocracy, who defeat him in the end.

It was London – "the place in the world where there is most to observe" – that claimed him. He took lodgings at 3 Bolton Street, Piccadilly (later moving to a flat in Kensington, 34 De Vere Gardens West), tried himself in English society, and famously dined out 107 times one winter. By now the international theme was his main subject. He triumphantly displayed it in *The Portrait of a Lady* (1881), the story of Isabel Archer, the free-spirited American released by inheriting a fortune to travel where she likes. Isabel visits not one Europe but three: gentlemanly Britain (green lawns and afternoon tea), socialite Paris and artistic Italy. She marries a corrupted American expatriate, and her innocence and moral seriousness are deeply tested. But they aren't destroyed; James always believed in the value of experience and maturity.

James's "international theme" was no chance subject. It was an exploration of his culture. In the age of steamship travel and the *belle époque*, transatlantic contacts between Europe and the United States were growing fast. The world, said James, was shrinking to the size of an orange. Americans, rich from their vast natural resources and technological inventions, poured into Europe on the stately transatlantic steamships. Even transatlantic marriages were increasing; the House of Lords, noted the London *Times*, had acquired many American mothers. Many Americans who preferred *belle époque* social Europe to their own industrializing culture, came, like James's Adam Verver in *The Golden Bowl* (1903), to collect the treasures of European art, or decided it was worth wedding new American wealth to old European class.

For James, the important thing was that these were times of new artistic cosmopolitanism. The writer, he felt, owed allegiance not just to a nation but to the larger international republic of letters and art. He was, he said, not American, not British, but European and cosmopolite. He travelled constantly through Europe, recording his impressions in several striking travel books – *Portraits of Places* (1883), *A Little Tour in France* (1883), *English Hours*,

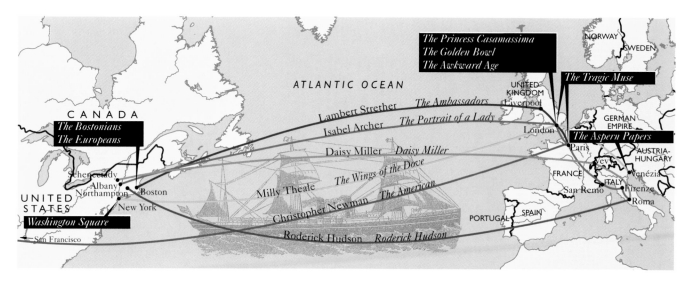

THE TRANSATLANTIC THEME IN HENRY JAMES'S NOVELS: *Henry James often sends the protagonists in his novels from New World America to Old World Europe, a journey which takes them from innocence to experience.*

1905 – still worth taking on journeys today. They show his vast curiosity, but also the underlying landscape of his great fiction – which reached its peak around the turn of the century in the famous "late works."

For if the international world was changing, the novel was too. That was due not a little to James himself. Ever responsive to the shifting art forms of the day – from painting, to the accelerating speed of life, the changing rules of society, the shifting sands of gender, the rise of material wealth, the new fascination with psychology and consciousness – his own novels grew more complex, some would even say obscure. James started as a Realist. He ended a Modernist; the international theme of the 1870s had merged with the interconnections and crises of modernity itself.

In the changeable 1890s, when there was a new Aestheticism and Decadence, and an acceleration of invention, James set the novel aside for a while to concentrate on theatre. But around 1897 he returned alike to the novel and the great "international theme." Now came his so-called "late works" – *The Ambassadors* (1903), *The Golden Bowl* (1903) – dictated to a secretary at Lamb House, Rye,

The Colosseum in Rome. Henry James set many of his works in the "golden air" of Italy, most notably Daisy Miller (1879), *the story of a young American girl who dies of malaria in Rome, and* The Aspern Papers (1888), *set in Venice.*

where he now mostly lived. Here he was part of an innovative literary community that included Stephen Crane, Ford Madox Hueffer (later Ford), Joseph Conrad. Now *belle époque* Europe was becoming a vulgar world of things, America – he revisited in 1905 and sharply recorded the experience in *The American Scene* (1907) – a modern "hotel civilization." By 1914, when the Great War started, James sensed that civilization was plunging into an abyss of blood and darkness, his world coming to an end. He died at Cheyne Walk in Chelsea in 1916, having become a British subject the year before.

In 1898 James bought delightful Lamb House, at Rye, Sussex, above left, a "little, becoming, high-door'd, brass-knockered façade to one's life." Here he entertained many literary figures, from Joseph Conrad to Stephen Crane, and wrote much of his finest late work.

In The Ambassadors, *France appears to the hero Lambert Strether as "a special series of impressions," needing to be gathered. As James put it in his preface, "people's moral scheme does break down in Paris." Here Strether experiences his "drama of discrimination," and learns the Jamesian lesson: "live – it's a mistake not to." James's distinctive technique was undoubtedly influenced by the French Impressionist painters, active from the late 1870s, such as Renoir, who painted the scene of the Seine at Argenteuil shown above right.*

James was one of the greatest of modern novelists. He was an expatriate not just to the charms of European society, but to the whole world of European art and culture, which by the end of the century was an art of new experiment. He aspired, he said, to write in such a way that no one could tell whether he was British or American. He looked with fascination and horror on the modern international landscape. His books are the product of intensive travel, not just through countries but moral states and modernizing culture. When he found his "international theme" it was simple, but he left it complex, for writers map not just geography, but the fast-changing history of their world.

The Modern movement has him as one of its chief founders. Modern fiction on both sides of the Atlantic would hardly have taken shape without him. Writers in America, Britain and across Europe listened to "the lesson of the master." Joseph Conrad and Virginia Woolf in Britain, Gertrude Stein and Ernest Hemingway in America, Marcel Proust and André Gide in France all owe much to James. He perfected the idea of the novel,

HENRY JAMES'S WORLD TRAVELS

1843 Born 15 April at 21 Washington Place, New York
1845 Lives in Europe for two years
1847 Returns to America
1855 Visits London, Paris, Geneva. Family takes a house in Berkeley Square, London
1856 Moves to Paris
1858 Returns to America
1859 Goes to Europe, visiting Germany and Switzerland. Educated in Bonn
1860 Returns to America
1875 Lives in Paris, 29 rue de Rivoli
1876 Moves to London, to 3 Bolton Street, Piccadilly
1879 Travels to Paris
1880 Visits Florence and London
1881 Moves to Venice, living at 4161 riva degli Schiavoni
1881 Returns to Boston, Quincy Street, then Brunswick Hotel
1882 Stays in Washington
1882 Visits London
1883 Stays in Europe
1884 Travels to Paris, London, Liverpool, Bournemouth
1886 Settles in London at 34 de Vere Gardens, Kensington
1891 Visits Italy
1895 Visits Ireland
1897 Moves to Lamb House at Rye, East Sussex
1913 Takes a flat at 21 Carlyle Mansions, Cheyne Walk, London where he dies in 1916

and the notion of the American writer eating the apple of Europe, the European writer eating the different apple of America, became part of the great literary diet. It wasn't just a complex fate being an American; it was a complex fate being a modern writer. And one of the responsibilities it entailed was to master the map of an intricate, changing, interdependent, mythical modern world.

THOMAS HARDY'S WESSEX

Thomas Hardy's (1840–1928) creation of his fictional Wessex is a supreme instance of the systematic imposition of the literary imagination upon an existing geographical location. Until Hardy first invoked the name early in 1874, during the serialization of his novel *Far from the Madding Crowd*, Wessex meant the ancient Anglo-Saxon kingdom of Alfred the Great. Within a few years it became the accepted designation for the area of southwest England where almost all of Hardy's early fiction had been set. By the end of the century, Dorset in particular was an established place of pilgrimage for devotees intent upon seeing the real settings of what had by then become an entire series of "Wessex Novels." As Hardy himself put it in 1895, his "dream-country" had "solidified into a utilitarian region which people can go to, take a house in, and write to the papers from." Today a distinct, if variously defined, regional entity called Wessex is recognized by geographers, governmental agencies and the National Trust, while local telephone directories list columns of Wessex businesses.

Thomas Hardy, above, *evoked a new regional identity in his novels.*

Thomas Hardy seems at first to have had no grand design in mind but to have wanted, quite simply, to provide his series of "local" novels with "a territorial definition" that would "lend unity to their scene." But as the novels and stories accumulated, each with its own topographical details, his conception of Wessex inevitably broadened. Because it sprang from an act of literary colonization rather than outright invention, his Wessex always maintained a close correspondence to existing natural and man-made features.

In the mid-1890s, Hardy's revision of his novels for a first collected edition provided an opportunity for his Wessex to be given tighter internal coherence. Names, locations and distances were made more consistent among the different texts as well as with actual maps. As this process continued in subsequent editions it became steadily easier to track down specific locations for fictional events – to trace, for example, the route of Tess's walk to Emminster (Beaminster) or the Christmas rounds of the Mellstock (Stinsford) "quire." Later still Hardy collaborated with his photographer friend, Hermann Lea, in the production of an authoritative illustrated guide called *Thomas Hardy's Wessex* (1913).

Even so, Wessex always remained a far more loosely constructed fictional world than, say, William Faulkner's Yoknapatawpha County. There is little recurrence of character, narrative or even setting among Hardy's novels and short stories, his preferred method being to focus intensively in each upon a single town, village or hamlet and its inhabitants' economically or environmentally conditioned lives. In *The Woodlanders* it is of central importance that the people of Little Hintock gain their livelihoods from the trees among which they live. In *The Mayor of Casterbridge* the tragedy of Michael Henchard is inseparable from his role in the town, itself described as "the pole, focus, or nerve-knot of the surrounding country life."

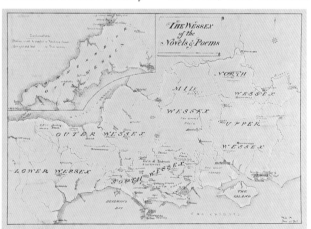

In drawing his own maps of the region, like the one, left, *Hardy became obliged to cover an area equivalent not just to Dorset and the adjoining counties but also to Berkshire, Devonshire and even parts of distant Cornwall, memorably the setting for the highly autobiographical novel* A Pair of Blue Eyes (*1873*).

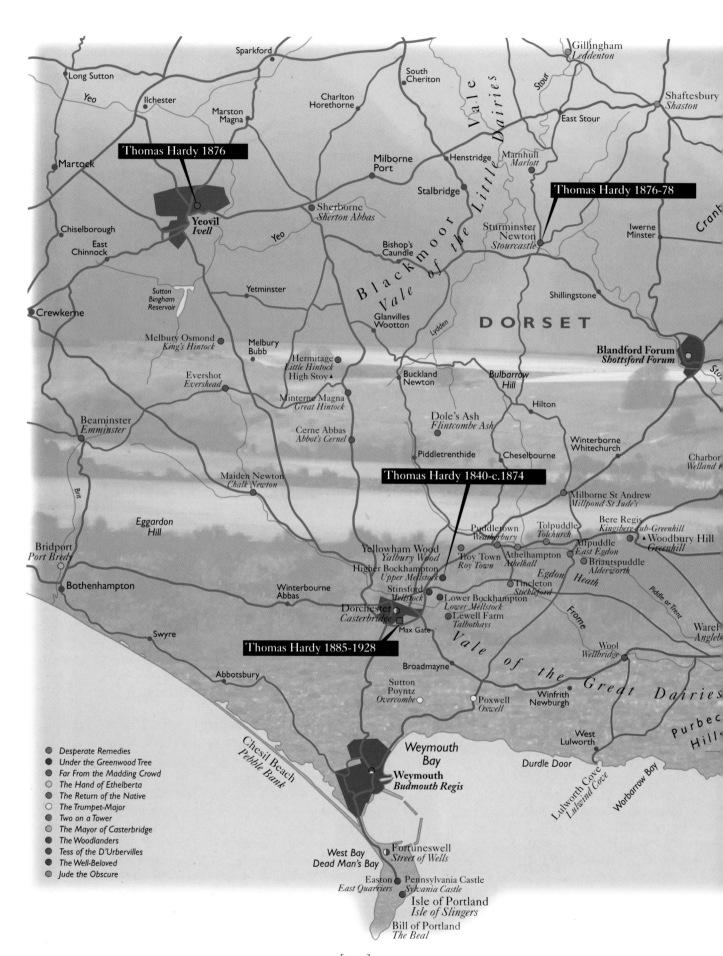

Sparkford

Long Sutton

Yeo

Ilchester

Martock

Marston
Magna

Charlton
Horethorne

South
Cheriton

Milborne
Port

Thomas Hardy 1876

Chiselborough

Yeovil
Ivell

Sherborne
Sherton Abbas

Stalbridge

East
Chinnock

Yeo

Bishop's
Caundle

Henstridge

Marnhull
Marlott

Thomas Hardy 1876-78

Sturminster
Newton
Stourcastle

Iwerne
Minster

Crewkerne

Yetminster

Sutton
Bingham
Reservoir

Glanvilles
Wootton

Lydden

Shillingstone

D O R S E T

Melbury Osmond
King's Hintock

Melbury
Bubb

Hermitage
Little Hintock
High Stoy ▲

Buckland
Newton

*Bulbarrow
Hill*

Blandford Forum
Shottsford Forum

Evershot
Evershead

Minterne Magna
Great Hintock

Dole's Ash
Flintcombe Ash

Hilton

Winterborne
Whitechurch

Charbor
Welland

Beaminster
Emminster

Cerne Abbas
Abbot's Cernel

Piddletrenthide

Cheselbourne

Brit

Maiden Newton
Chalk Newton

Thomas Hardy 1840-c.1874

Milborne St Andrew
Millpond St Jude's

Bere Regis
Kingsbere-sub-Greenhill

Bridport
Port Bredy

*Eggardon
Hill*

Puddletown
Weatherbury

Tolpuddle
Tolchurch

▲Woodbury Hill
Greenhill

Yellowham Wood
Yalbury Wood

Higher Bockhampton
Upper Mellstock

Troy Town
Roy Town

Athelhampton
Athelhall

Affpuddle
East Egdon

Briantspuddle
Alderworth

Bothenhampton

Winterbourne
Abbas

Stinsford
Mellstock

Tincleton
Stickleford

*Egdon
Heath*

Dorchester
Casterbridge

Lower Bockhampton
Lower Mellstock

Lewell Farm
Talbothays

Piddle or Trent

Max Gate

Vale

Frome

Ware
Angleb

Thomas Hardy 1885-1928

Swyre

Broadmayne

Wool
Wellbridge

Abbotsbury

Sutton
Poyntz
Overcombe

Poxwell
Oxwell

Winfrith
Newburgh

of

the

Great

Dairies

West
Lulworth

Purbec

Hill

*Chesil Beach
Pebble Bank*

**Weymouth
Bay**

Weymouth
Budmouth Regis

Durdle Door

Lulworth Cove
Lulwind Cove

Warbarrow Bay

- Desperate Remedies
- Under the Greenwood Tree
- Far From the Madding Crowd
- ○ The Hand of Ethelberta
- The Return of the Native
- ○ The Trumpet-Major
- Two on a Tower
- The Mayor of Casterbridge
- The Woodlanders
- Tess of the D'Urbervilles
- The Well-Beloved
- Jude the Obscure

West Bay
Dead Man's Bay

Fortuneswell
Street of Wells

Easton
East Quarriers

Pennsylvania Castle
Sylvania Castle

Isle of Portland
Isle of Slingers

Bill of Portland
The Beal

Gillingham
Leddenton

Stour

Shaftesbury
Shaston

East Stour

Vale

of

the

Little

Dairies

Blackmoor

Vale

Cran

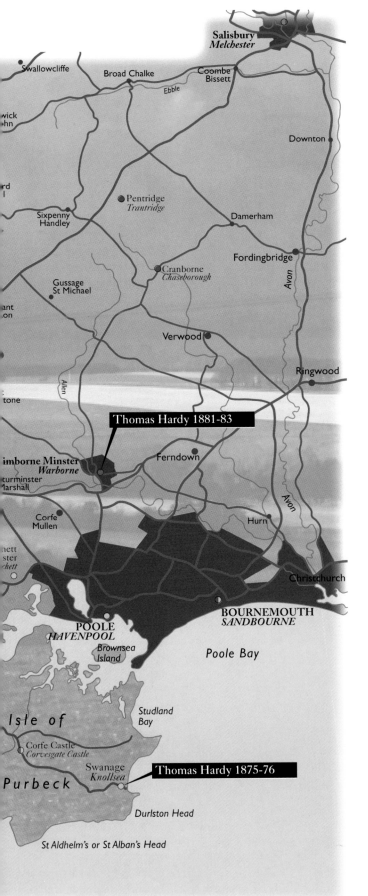

Salisbury
Melchester

Swallowcliffe

Broad Chalke

Coombe
Bissett

Ebble

Downton

Pentridge
Trantridge

Sixpenny
Handley

Damerham

Fordingbridge

Cranborne
Chaseborough

Avon

Gussage
St Michael

Verwood

Allen

Ringwood

Thomas Hardy 1881-83

Ferndown

imborne Minster
Warborne

Corfe
Mullen

Hurn

Avon

Christchurch

BOURNEMOUTH
SANDBOURNE

POOLE
HAVENPOOL

Brownsea
Island

Poole Bay

Isle of

Studland
Bay

Corfe Castle
Corvesgate Castle

Swanage
Knollsea

Thomas Hardy 1875-76

Purbeck

Durlston Head

St Aldhelm's or St Alban's Head

Although Hardy at the beginning of his career could scarcely have envisaged what Wessex would eventually become, the example of such novelists as Sir Walter Scott and Anthony Trollope – creator of the "Barsetshire" series of novels – doubtless encouraged him to anticipate commercial advantages from a strategy of sustained localization. To make such a choice was no less shrewdly to recognize where his richest and most accessible resources lay, and Hardy's most centrally regional work has traditionally been regarded as his best: *Under the Greenwood Tree* (1872), *Far from the Madding Crowd* (1874), *The Return of the Native* (1878), *The Mayor of Casterbridge* (1886), *The Woodlanders* (1887), *Wessex Tales* (1888), and *Tess of the d'Urbervilles* (1891). The only major absence from that list is *Jude the Obscure* (1895), a late novel largely devoted to the breakdown of the self-contained rural world, with its collective memory and distinctive economy and social values the earlier fiction had so richly recorded and celebrated. Wessex was less central to the poems Hardy turned his attention to in his last decades, but it remained both physically and allusively present as landscape, narrative setting and point of regional reference.

The sources of Hardy's familiarity with his region are readily identifiable. He was born on 2 June, 1840, the eldest of the four children of a master stonemason and his wife, in the hamlet of Higher Bockhampton (the Upper Mellstock of *Under the Greenwood Tree*), some three miles northeast of Dorchester. That Hardy identified "Egdon Heath" with the territory of his own childhood was implicitly acknowledged in the "Sketch Map of the Scene of the Story" which he drew for the novel's first edition.

As a child in Higher Bockhampton he was surrounded by the violin-playing, folk-singing, parish-pump gossiping and family-reminiscing of his parents and their friends. Growing up, he explored the neighbouring terrain of woods, heaths, rivers and farms, visited relatives in other Dorset villages, and walked daily to and from his school in semiurban Dorchester. In his teens and early twenties he travelled more widely as an apprentice and then as an assistant architect, inspecting houses, churches and churchyards. He broadened his local knowledge still

HARDY'S WESSEX: *In Hardy's novels the names of towns and villages were changed, Dorchester becoming Casterbridge, Weymouth Budmouth, but rivers and hills (the Stour, for instance, and High Stoy) retained their identity, as did ancient monuments such as Stonehenge. The locations correspond to Hardy's revised texts.*

Weymouth Bay, captured in the painting by John Constable, above, *features in several of Hardy's novels.*

rendered them so available to Hardy's pastoral purposes. Urban readers, moved by his persuasive presentation of rural habits, customs, speech and values, were intrigued to think that just a few hours' train ride away was a place unvisited, almost unheard of, where such a way of life had existed within living memory and might in remote recesses be surviving still.

It is a fascination not yet extinguished among Hardy's legions of contemporary readers, many of them drawn to his work as a record of a lost rural way of life, somehow quintessentially English, whose traces are even now faintly visible in the farms and churches, the lanes and trackways, the villages and small towns of a countryside still predominantly agricultural and in the contours of a topography essentially unchanged. The Frome, Stour, High Stoy, Bulbarrow and the other rivers and heights of land that Hardy adopted into his Wessex scheme remain as always the principal landmarks of Dorset, while such human relics as Maiden Castle, Corfe Castle, Stinsford Church and Hardy's birthplace stand very much as they were. Most remarkable of all, perhaps, is the continuing and ever-increasing use of the name Wessex throughout southwestern England and the resulting invocation, implicit yet automatic, both of Hardy himself and of that profoundly imagined world he so indelibly projected onto the landscape of an entire region.

further over the following decades by walking and cycling expeditions, membership of the Dorset Natural History and Antiquarian Field Club, familiarizing himself with such works as John Hutchins's *History and Antiquities of the County of Dorset* (1861–73) and immersing himself in the Napoleonic period in preparation for his vast blank-verse drama *The Dynasts* (three parts, 1904, 1906 and 1908).

Although he spent much of his time in London during his twenties and thirties, Hardy returned permanently to Dorset in his 42nd year and moved, in 1885, to Max Gate, the red brick house on the outskirts of Dorchester which he designed himself and which his father and brother built. There he lived with his first wife, Emma Lavinia Gifford, and his second wife, Florence Emily Dugdale, until his death in 1928 at the age of 87.

The geographical area corresponding to Hardy's Wessex saw many changes during his lifetime, the results of industrialization, urbanization, emigration and an expanding world economy. It has undergone no less significant changes since his death. The heath has largely been given over to forestry and to the Winfrith Atomic Energy Establishment. Dorchester has expanded greatly and is expanding still, under pressure from the housing schemes promoted by the Prince of Wales. The Frome water meadows just east of the town have been brutally bridged by a bypass that runs within a few yards of Max Gate itself. Other road works throughout the county have introduced new slabs of starkness into a landscape already in some measure depleted by the ploughing of uplands and the destruction of hedgerows.

Yet parts of Dorset and south Wiltshire can still communicate some sense of that beguiling illusion of timelessness and isolation which in the 1870s and 1880s

Hardy's birthplace, above, *stands among trees at the very edge of the wild heathland subsequently imagined as the lonely landscape "suggesting tragical possibilities" in* The Return of the Native.

SCANDINAVIA:
THE DARK AND THE LIGHT

When the obscure Norwegian playwright Henrik Ibsen (1828–1906) eventually found the courage and the resources to turn his back on his Nordic homeland and head for the South of Europe he was already 36. Hopeful as he was that the move would bring a great change to his life, he was unprepared for the immediate, overwhelming sense of release it brought, only dimly aware of the profound change it would have on his life and creative career. As he later put it, it was like breaking out of the lowering darkness, into the brilliant light: "I travelled down through Germany and Austria, and crossed the Alps on 9 May (1864). Clouds hung over the high mountains like great dark curtains; and we drove in under these and through tunnels and suddenly found ourselves at Mira Mare, where the beauty of the South – a wonderfully translucent gleam shining like white marble – suddenly opened up to me and left its stamp on all my later work...."

Ibsen's "escape" (originally meant as a limited study tour) extended into a 27-year period of self-imposed exile, spent mainly in Italy and Germany, until his eventual return as a world-famous old man, to Christiania, Norway's fine capital city at the head of the Oslo fjord, renamed Oslo in 1924. The exile was a revelation of a peculiarly Scandinavian kind. The Northern world he left was on the brink of profound social, economic, cultural and political change. Its literature, its arts, were on track to emerge, within a few brief decades, from virtual obscurity to a leading position in the Western world. And its major figures – the Danish philosopher Søren Kierkegaard, Danish critic Georg Brandes, the Swedish playwright August Strindberg, and, from Norway, Ibsen himself and the novelist Knut Hamsun (1859–1952), author of *Hunger* (1890) – would move into the vanguard of events.

It was a great cultural shift, but it drew on an unusual paradox for much of its creative excitement. Ibsen wasn't alone in feeling the urge to find fulfilment well beyond the immediate Nordic horizon. Even before Ibsen arrived, there was in Rome a significant small colony of Scandinavian writers and intellectuals, even an established Scandinavian Club to act as focus. Later on in the century, another Scandinavian-German group, which included Strindberg and Edvard Munch, gathered in Berlin, and gave immortality to the tavern where they met, Zum schwarzen Ferkel. Paris in the 1890s also had its regular component of Scandinavians, motivated by the same urge toward temporary or sometimes permanent escape.

The Norwegian artist Edvard Munch, famous for The Scream, *painted this portrait of Ibsen sitting in the Grand Café in Oslo.*

It wasn't uncommon for them to find that, once they had broken free of the Nordic and Lutheran climate, they could give uninhibited vent to hostile feelings about the society they'd left behind them, while exploring their true affection for some particular geographical region or landscape. For the tortured August Strindberg (1849–1912), author not just of great plays like *The Father* (1887) and *The Dance of Death* (1900), but of regional novels like *The People of Hemsö* (1887), it was the Stockholm Archipelago, with its many islands reaching out into the Baltic; for Ibsen it was the Molde Fjord. Yet more remarkable was the effect of the distancing; it lent to the view not enchantment, but an unexpectedly sharp focus. Geographic and cultural remoteness combined to hone the penetrative powers of the imagination, even when (perhaps particularly when) the fictional events of the authorship were wholly

Skien, where Ibsen was born, and Bergen, above, where he later worked, were modest-sized, hard-working communities close to the sea – the kind of places that could be found many times over on the coasts of Norway, Denmark, Sweden and Finland.

Scandinavian in their subject-matter. As Ibsen put it to his friend, the influential critic Georg Brandes: "Once I had been in Italy, I could not understand how I had been able to exist before." He found Mediterranean life intensely congenial, the culture of its people rich and rewarding, the whole situation conducive to work, and the contrast with what he called the "tepid-blooded" North was almost painful. What he probably had not anticipated was that, even so, he would always carry with him an inner Nordic landscape of total and undiminished clarity – and a capacity to capture, people and explore and re-explore it with a precision of recall that was astonishing.

In Italy the first thing he wrote, the dramatic poem *Brand* (1866) was quintessentially Scandinavian in atmosphere, message and location. It was set among fjords, mountains, storm-swept seas; it was doom-laden with the menace of Northern nature; it had a heavy symbolic weight of ice churches and avalanches. The contrast with the world in which he produced it couldn't have been greater; he wrote it in Genzano, in Arriccia, by the sun-drenched shorts of the Gulf of Naples. The same pattern was reinforced with his next work, *Peer Gynt* (1867), his greatest dramatic poem. Precisely set in the Norwegian valleys of Gudbrandsdal and the Dovre Mountains, specifically Nordic both in its social realism and its mythological material, he wrote it partly in Ischia, partly in Sorrento, in the Italian sun.

As the years of exile stretched to decades, Ibsen's sources of dramatic inspiration seemed inexhaustible. By the time he'd done, he'd written some 25 dramas; meanwhile the incongruity continued undiminished. *A Doll's House* (1879), that tale of Northern bourgeois crisis, Christmas

shopping, female independence, was written in Amalfi. The gloomy rain-drenched events of *Ghosts* (1881) were conceived in Sorrento. The Scandinavian small-town scandals of *An Enemy of the People* (1882) were imagined in Rome; so were the tragi-comic events that occur in the attic world of *The Wild Duck* (1884). When he lived for some years in Germany, the sharpness of vision stayed unimpaired. *Rosmersholm* (1886), *The Lady from the Sea* (1888) and *Hedda Gabler* (1890) all originated largely from his stay in Munich.

Ibsen put Norway and its crises of spirit on the stages of Europe. But from what was he – and other Scandinavians like him – fleeing? In the opening phrases of his unfinished autobiography, he explains his sense of constriction, oppression, anguish:

"I was born in a house by the market place [in Skien].... This house faced the entrance to the church with its high flight of steps and its imposing tower. To the right of the church stood the town pillory and to the left was the town hall with its jail and its 'mad house.' The fourth side of the market place was formed by the grammar school and the primary school. The church stood free in the middle. This prospect was the first view of the world to present itself to my eyes. Buildings on all sides; no greenery; no open country. But all the day long the air above the stone and wood of this town square was filled with the subdued thunderous roar from...many waterfalls. And piercing the roar of the waterfalls...was a sound like the whines of moaning and shrieking women. This came from the hundreds of saw-blades operating at those waterfalls. When I later came to read about the guillotine, I was always reminded of those saw blades."

In truth there was little remarkable about the Skien of 1828 except its typicality. Some eighty miles southwest of Oslo, down the great fjord, what made it typical was its will to survive in a harsh climate on what forests, sea, meagre land could yield. Ibsen's words make it clear how much Scandinavia was, always had been, a water-dependent society based on the sea as the international highway, the rivers and lakes for inland communication, the waterfalls for

JOHAN AUGUST STRINDBERG

1849 *Born in Stockholm, January 22*
1867 *Attends Upsala university*
1872 *Writes first major play,* Master Olof
1883-89 *Spends six years abroad in France, Germany, Switzerland and Denmark*
1887 *Writes* The Father *and* The People of Hemsö
1894-96 *Settles in Paris, where* The Father *and* Creditors *are staged. Poor and alone he suffers mental problems*
1896 *Returns to Sweden recovered*
1898-1909 *Writes 35 plays*
1907 *Founds his own Intimate Theatre in Stockholm for which he writes* The Ghost Sonata
1912 *Dies in Stockholm*

power. "The sea does not divide; it unites," goes an old Scandinavian saying; and the most enduring fact of Scandinavia was always the sheer length of its coastline – from beyond the North Cape, down to the Atlantic and North Sea seaboard, its shoreline ever penetrated by the inroads of the Norwegian fjords, then skirting the Skagerak and the Kattegat, taking in the jut of the Danish peninsula and island, before rounding the Baltic shores to Sweden and Finland.

When he chose his exile, Ibsen had already had some 12 years of theatre experience in Bergen and Christiania. He was regarded as rebellious, even dissolute. Having started as an apothecary's apprentice in Grimstad after his father had gone bankrupt, he produced nine plays whose public reception ranged from the mildly appreciative to the disastrous. He'd come on hard times, his spirits were at a low ebb, he drank heavily. He felt shame for his country's betrayal of Denmark in the recent war with Prussia, which seemed to deal a blow to his dream of Scandinavian unity. Above all, he'd come to regard all his work as having served false values and spurious ideals, those of romantic nationalism. He rejected the idea of a traditional literature of national pride, disliked the sentimental chauvinism of his early work. He demanded that he confront the realities of the world of modernity and the present.

The passion went into *Brand*. In the earliest version, he called on his countrymen ("fellows in guilt") to break free, told them the "heroic age" was a rouged and embalmed corpse, demanded that the nation's decomposition should serve as compost for providing "nourishment for new-sown seed." "See, this is why I have turned my sight and mind / away from the soul-dead tales of our past / away from the lying dreams of a bright future / and I go into the misty world of the present."

The words mark the beginnings of a new age. From 1864 onwards Ibsen shifted the rules of modern theatre. Decade by decade, his work shook the conventions, theatrical, social and sexual, of Europe. He was, as Brandes called

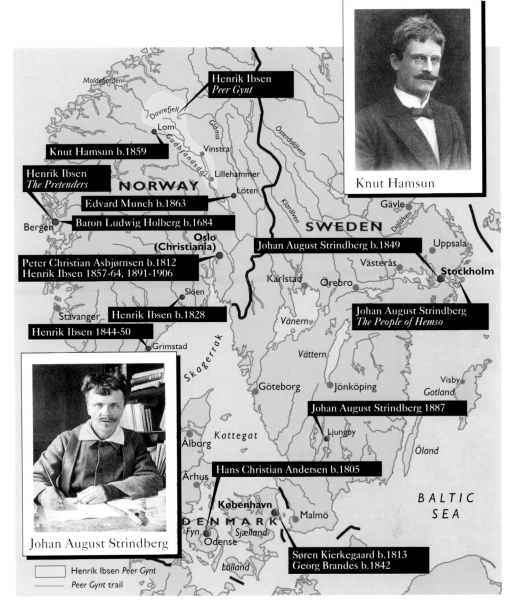

SCANDINAVIA: *The sea was a factor belonging to the collective unconsciousness of any Scandinavian of any epoch. More than anything, it had shaped its thinking and culture, attitudes and values.*

him, "a man of the modern breakthrough," who reshaped the ideas of his age. He spread the message of *Peer Gynt*: "To thine own self be true." Ibsen turned into Ibsenism, changing theatre and social thought everywhere.

In 1891 he returned in triumph to Christiania, to a different Scandinavia which now, in literature (Ibsen, Strindberg, Hamsun), music (Grieg, Sibelius) and art (Munch, Vigeland) was at the front of the modern movement. "Here among the fjords is my native land. But – but – but – where shall I find my home?" he asked Brandes. He wrote his final play, *When We Dead Awaken*, in 1899, just as the nineteenth century he sought to reform came to a close. A year later he had a stroke, and died in 1906.

PRECIPITOUS CITY:
ROBERT LOUIS STEVENSON'S EDINBURGH

Robert Louis Stevenson's (1850–94) bittersweet re-creation of Scotland from the distance of Samoa is one of the wonders of all literary exile. Born in a country whose turbulent history – permeated by the plangent motifs of emigration, exile and loss – was Stevenson's earliest obsession, it was Scotland's capital, his native Edinburgh, which would come to form the symbolic centre of Stevenson's understanding of the Scottish past; and, eventually, of his own. And there can be few cities which proclaim a nation's past with such thrilling palpability as Edinburgh.

Robert Louis Stevenson, above, spent his first 29 years in Edinburgh, and the city features in some of his greatest novels.

By the time Stevenson was born in Edinburgh on 13 November, 1850, the capital was, physically, an extremely unusual place. The town remained dominated by Old Edinburgh, the craggy ridge running downwards and eastwards from the Castle Rock to the Palace of Holyrood, upon which had evolved the Royal Mile – a mad dream of a medieval city, where teeming tenements towered to impossible heights, and were divided by tiny, narrow canyons of lanes known as wynds or closes, running downwards on either side, roughly at right angles.

In the eighteenth century, population density, the absence of sanitation and the shortage of building space made Edinburgh one of the filthiest and most overcrowded cities in Europe. But it was also uniquely energetic, exciting and egalitarian: a hotbed of genius, the city of Boswell, Hume, Smith and Ramsay.

With increased economic prosperity and a flourishing middle class following the controversial Union with England in 1707, the city's solution was to reinvent itself. To the north of the Old Town on the gentler slopes leading down to the Firth of Forth evolved a New Town: a systematic, rectilinear, symmetrical Georgian townscape which is one of the triumphs of European civic architecture, its elegant crescents, squares and gardens fashioned by an array of Britain's greatest neo-classical architects. It was a New Town for a newly-defined Edinburgh bourgeoisie of professional Anglo-Scots, who deserted the chaos of the old capital in droves to fill the Adam brothers' fashionable façades. Stevenson would inhabit both worlds, belonging fully to neither.

The divisions in Stevenson's Victorian Edinburgh were dramatic and deep, determined as much by history, class and conflicting national identities as stark architectural polarities. If his writing was to offer profound explorations of these native dualities, that is because the divisions within city and nation profoundly shaped him.

Almost as much as its weather, in fact. It is easy to underestimate the psychological significance of the city's pernicious climate upon the life-long invalid who, from the age of two, was daily in imminent danger of dying, but throughout the short epic of Stevenson's vain pilgrimage in search of health, the winds and rains of home accrued

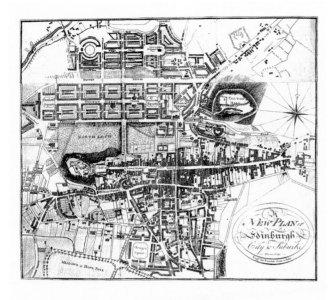

Early maps of Edinburgh, like the one above, *published in Thomas Brown's guide to the city in 1817, clearly display the city's resemblance to a long fishbone. In the eighteenth century it stank like one, too.*

boisterous in winter, shifty and uncongenial in summer, and a downright necrological purgatory in the spring...."

Ironically, the purchase by his parents in 1857 of 17 Heriot Row – one of the New Town's more elegant thoroughfares – was motivated partly by the mistaken assumption that the tall, south-facing windows promised increased doses of salubrious sunlight for their six-year-old son, already spending more time in the sick-bed than he did out of it (Stevenson was actually born in 8 Howard Place, on the northern fringe of the New Town; the second family home in Inverleith Terrace was soon abandoned because of damp). Doubtless, too, the couple were advertising their credentials as members of the capital's Victorian elite within this upmarket colony for the wealthy and professional classes. Stevenson's father, Thomas, was eminent in this respect, as a civil engineer whose firm had built harbours and lighthouses all over Scotland: Stevenson's grandfather had constructed the "impossible" light on the Bell Rock.

To begin with, Stevenson was destined to follow his ancestors, but it was a half-hearted 17-year-old who enrolled at Edinburgh University to study civil engineering (he later switched to law and qualified as an advocate in 1875, but he never practised). Although he would cut a memorable figure in the University's Speculative Society, Stevenson's priorities lay elsewhere: avid reading of literary classics, the camaraderie of Rutherford's Bar in Drummond Street, fittingly, almost directly opposite the massy portals of the University's Old College on South Bridge. The bar is pretty much as it was when Stevenson frequented it, cultivating new Bohemian acquaintances.

symbolic status as his oldest and deadliest enemy. Typically, he could make fun of the city which repeatedly tried to vanquish his puny frame and its ever-languishing lungs. An early work, *Edinburgh: Picturesque Notes* (1878), contains perhaps the most memorable vignette of the windy city ever penned: "Edinburgh pays cruelly for her high seat in one of the vilest climates under heaven. She is liable to be beaten upon by all the winds that blow, to be drenched with rain, to be buried in cold sea fogs out of the east, and powdered with snow as it comes flying southward from the Highland hills. The weather is raw and

Stevenson's Picturesque Notes (*a frontispiece is shown* above) *contains some of his finest writing about the windy city, depicted in the 1822 painting,* left, *drawn from the top of Calton Hill.*

"Velvet Coat," as he came to be known on account of a conspicuous sartorial statement of non-conformity, became a familiar sight in "insalubrious" Lothian Road, leading south to dingy Tollcross from the city's fashionable west end, or among the closes and howffs of the Old Town. Here, traversing whole vistas of the nation's past through the Grassmarket, the Lawnmarket or the graves of Greyfriars Kirk, was his romantic milieu *par excellence*, where he doggedly followed the antiquarian footsteps of Scott, or chased the reckless spirits of Robert Fergusson and Robert Burns in riotous dissipation. The rectitude symbolized by 17 Heriot Row was never far away, offering its veneer of respectability and comfort – a bolthole for the young Mr Hyde.

Stevenson wrote many of his early works from the family home at 17 Heriot Row (the house with the black door in the photograph above).

Stevenson's, like Burns's before him, was an argument with the status quo: the morality of an age which had abandoned the glorious legacy of the Scottish Enlightenment in favour of the starchy complacency of Victorian conformity which threatened to downgrade Edinburgh into the capital of "North Britain" – a term he came to detest. Thus while Stevenson remained dependent on the financial security advertised by his New Town milieu for virtually the rest of his life, it could not contain him. He captured the geometric and moral aridity of its grids and squares with characteristic brilliance: "draughty parallelograms" amidst "a wilderness of square-cut stone."

The argument became a revolt. But before the blow fell and Stevenson devastated his parents by confessing his agnosticism, there was, as ever, a role to be played out: that of apprentice civil engineer. Nothing is more paradigmatic of the tensions of the age, and the heady dualism brewing within the aspiring writer, than the series of inspection trips undertaken by Stevenson the younger and elder between the years 1863 and 1870, in which they encompassed every windswept harbour and battered lighthouse of the Scottish coast where the family had left its mark. Whether in the fishing villages of the Fife coast or off the shores of the Hebrides, the same division between convention and imaginative freedom dramatized by father and son is enacted: the former, rational and pragmatic, surveying for stress and strain in the names of safety, efficiency, material progress. The latter, thrilling to the rock girt, jagged Scottish coastline, devouring the lores of tides, winds and shipwrecks, storing atmosphere, topography and the telling detail, all of it to be deployed in retrospect, and with scintillating clarity, in the later fiction.

Closer to home, and this process of delayed imaginative distillation remains the same, whether it is the Hawes Inn in South Queensferry on the shore of the Firth of Forth where David Balfour is kidnapped, or the family's summer cottage at Swanston on the eastern slopes of the Pentland Hills, the home of the heroine of *St Ives* (1897), and the link between Edinburgh and the Borders, civic sophistication and older oral tradition which comprise the symbolic reading of Scottish society in *Weir of Hermiston* (1898). In each of the

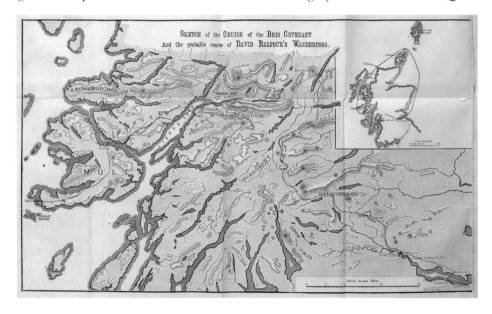

The map, left, from an 1891 illustrated edition of Kidnapped, *shows the wanderings of its protagonist, David Balfour, around Scotland.*

> "I saw rain falling and the rainbow drawn
> On Lammermuir. Hearkening I heard again
> In my precipitous city beaten bells
> Winnow the keen sea wind. And here afar,
> Intent on my own race and place, I wrote."
>
> Dedication, *Weir of Hermiston*

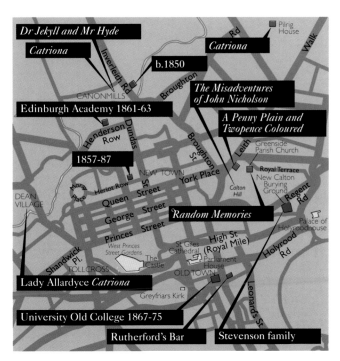

EDINBURGH: *Stevenson's experience of his city influenced even those novels, like* Dr Jekyll and Mr Hyde, *not set there.*

novels, place becomes incident, topography becomes adventure. The breathless plotting of *Kidnapped* (1886) and *Catriona* (1893) testify both to the unerring precision of Stevenson's memory, and to the fact that his historical understanding was, in an important sense, geographical. Not that his reliance on realistic setting is always so straightforward. *Dr Jekyll and Mr Hyde* (1886), that profound psychological parable anticipating modernist literature but disguised as a Gothic shocker, disguises other things too. Its disturbing vision of late nineteenth century urban anonymity owes far more to Stevenson's sensitivity to the duality inscribed upon the fabric of Edinburgh than to his knowledge of the streets of London: the setting is Edinburgh, stone for stone. Today, crossing the road from Stevenson's birthplace, 8 Howard Place, one comes to the unassuming Inverleith Terrace Lane, clearly the setting for the murder of Carew, with the high windows looming on the right through which the crime is witnessed.

While Stevenson is in exile in the South Seas, the intensity of his imaginative yearning and profound nostalgia for his native city is matched only by a lucidity in recapturing the past which is almost perversely accurate. His sensitivity to the flow and movement, too, of memory – often as it happens – is Proustian. The resulting emotions link the moving Dedications in *Kidnapped*, *The Master of Ballantrae* (1889), *Catriona* and *Weir of Hermiston* in their emphasis on the disparities between the writer's immediate exotic context, and his fictional subject-matter: elegies for the Scotland and Edinburgh Stevenson had lost. Dedicating *Catriona* to Charles Baxter, lifelong Edinburgh friend, he writes: "You are still – as when I first saw, as when I last addressed you – in the venerable city which I must always think of as my home. And I have come so far; and the sights and thoughts of my youth pursue me; and I see like a vision the youth of my father, and of his father, and the whole stream of lives flowing down there in the north, with the sound of laughter and tears, to cast me out in the end, as by a sudden freshet, on these ultimate islands. And I admire and bow my head before the romance of destiny."

This, two years before a brain haemorrhage robbed him of his life. "Like a vision." Here much is revealed about how far the later Scottish novels were passionate

creative compensations for – even denials of – their author's realization that he would never return. As he wrote those words, doubtless he could remember that younger Robert Louis Stevenson who loved to stand on the North Bridge – whose broad span connected Old Edinburgh across the divide of the valley of the Nor' Loch with the New – bowing his head not just before destiny, but also the violent buffetings of those vile Edinburgh winds, watching the trains smoke out of Waverley Station below to that "Somewhere-else of the imagination, where all troubles are supposed to end."

Sadly for Robert Louis Stevenson, the troubles never ended; nor was the past ever left behind. It was an equally fortunate thing for our literature that Stevenson could not forget his race, and place.

STEVENSON'S LIFE

1850 *Born 13 November in Edinburgh*
1867 *Enters Edinburgh University to study engineering*
1871 *Abandons civil engineering and takes up law*
1873 *Declares himself a non-believer*
1874 *Falls in love with Frances Sitwell ("Madonna")*
1876 *Falls passionately in love with Fanny Osborne*
1878 *Travels through the south of France on a donkey*
1879 *Sets sail for California*
1880 *Finally marries Fanny Osborne*
1883 *Writes* Treasure Island
1888 *Travels the South Seas*
1889 *Settles in his final home in Apia, in the Samoan Islands*
1894 *Dies of a brain haemorrhage*

LONDON IN THE 1890s

As the nineteenth century ended and the Victorian age began to close, London came to its peak. Already the world's biggest city, it was growing at an amazing rate; since 1860 its population had soared from three and a half to six and a half million. Its smart West End displayed the grandeur of a proud and wealthy nation, its middle class suburbs spread apace, its East End was a jungle of poverty. Capital of a still very United Kingdom, it dominated culture, communications, society, finance, politics and arts; drawing manufacturers and artisans, bankers and clerks, writers and artists into its ever-expanding metropolis. It was the great imperial capital of the age. From London Docks, by Limehouse and the Isle of Dogs, a vast shipping fleet brought the goods of empire back to the capital, and sent the manufactures of British cities out to the world in return. Over the river stood the Royal Observatory at Greenwich, the very mean and measure of the world's time.

London was an entrepôt of trade, a magnet for human migration – with more Irish than Dublin, Scots than Aberdeen, Jews than Palestine, Catholics than Rome. It was a modern city too, displaying the industry and technology in which Britain had been a nineteenth century leader. Everywhere were signs of rapid social change and development. Electric trams ran in its streets, underground trains beneath them. Offices filled with busy clerks, new suburban villas with prosperous businessmen, lodging houses and ghettos with exiles from the disorders and pogroms of Europe. The crossing in front of the Royal Exchange, in the City of London, was reckoned the busiest spot in the world. In 1876 Henry James settled in London, off Bolton Street near Piccadilly. "It is the biggest aggregation of human life – the most complete compendium of the world." And so it was. As one historian puts it, London was a "world city," at the height of its imperial, industrial and social power: a hub of energy, a magnet, a style-setter.

The modern city also bred its own modern literature – catching the complexity, fragmentation, the strange new surfaces and unimaginable depths. Since Chaucer, London had been at the centre of British writing. Now writers gathered there as never before, not just from the provinces – Thomas Hardy, George Gissing, Arnold

Writers, among them W.B. Yeats, gathered at the Rhymers' Club upstairs at the Ye Olde Cheshire Cheese off the Strand, above.

Bennett – but from all over the world. There were Scots like Robert Louis Stevenson, Irish like W.B. Yeats, Oscar Wilde and Bernard Shaw, Americans like Henry James and Stephen Crane, Poles like Joseph Conrad.

No wonder London prospered as source and subject for writing; it was the great literary challenge. In 1886 Henry James set aside his international theme to write a purely London novel, *The Princess Casamassima*, which dealt with revolutionaries and anarchists, but was a work of modern Impressionism. Its real theme, James explained in the preface, was "the attentive exploration of London, the assault directly made by a great city on an imagination quick to react." Capturing the labyrinthine city became the great task. "Then the vision of an enormous town presented itself, of a monstrous town more populous than some continents and in its man-made might as if indifferent to heaven's frowns and smiles, a cruel devourer of the world's light," wrote Conrad, explaining the idea of *The Secret Agent* (1907).

London equally lured the poets. In his brilliant *The 1890s* (1913), Holbrook Jackson, one of the survivors of the Aesthetic movement, noted that one mark of the new *fin-de-siècle* Aesthetes was their love affair with the metropolis. "When I look at a landscape I cannot help seeing its defects," Oscar Wilde (1854–1900) grandly announced, and turned from nature to art, country to city, in his novels and plays. The passion for urban scenes and sensations dominated the work of the Aesthetes – until, like Wilde, they ended up in Reading Jail, or fell off their bar stools at the Cheshire Cheese, as W.B. Yeats reported. In Wilde, Aubrey Beardsley, Max Beerbohm, Ernest Dowson, Lionel Johnson and more, metropolitan artifice flourished – just as it did in the paintings of James McNeill Whistler, with their foggy nocturnes and urban impressions.

New publishers and magazines flourished, and there was a boom in popular fiction. For the poor hack-writers of what Gissing called "New Grub Street," there were fresh literary careers, artistic or plain commercial, to be had. "Newspapers flap o'er the land / And darken the face of the sky," wrote John Davidson in his *Fleet Street Eclogues* (1893), which mocked the populist Yellow Press in the pages of the Aesthete's *Yellow Book*. But for Aesthetes and New Journalists alike, London scenes were all the rage. The gossipy newspapers told tales of the city – its pleasures, suicides, poverty, scandals, crimes – while poets like W.E. Henley wrote *London Voluntaries* (1893). In *The Soul of London* (1905), Ford Madox Ford, one of the best writers and editors of the day, wrote lovingly of the metropolis as a "vague kaleidoscopic picture" which was "the high-water mark of the achievement of the Modern Spirit." Ford's delightful and evocative book is also an impression: a vision of a city filled with detail, but just too random and culturally various to be grasped as a whole.

Not just Aesthetes and Impressionists took London as their subject. There were also the Naturalists, influenced by Émile Zola, who set out to explore and write about what George Gissing (1857–1903) called "the Nether World." Beyond the "civilized" London of Chelsea and Kensington and out beyond the financial world of the Royal Exchange there lay another, different, little-trodden London. This was the East End; an urban jungle as strange and dark as any in Africa – as General William Booth, founder of the Salvation Army, stressed when he titled his study of East End poverty, *In Darkest London and the Way Out* (1890). Here were the "lower depths," and writers stalked through them – like the American Jack London who recorded his Nietzschean reactions in *People of the Abyss* (1903). Naturalism aimed to be scientific and reforming – just like the missionaries and socialist reformers and sociologists who made their way to the East End. Gissing, struggling as a writer, knew lodging-house London and the world of poverty well. In books like *Workers*

For 1890s' writers and painters, London was mostly a series of shades – best seen in fugitive glimpses or "impressions." The images from the London night, the pervasive fog, the glittering Thames are captured by James Abbot McNeill Whistler in his view, above, of old Battersea Bridge (c.1872–5).

in the Dawn (1880) and *The Unclassed* (1884), he explored poor London from Soho to beyond the City of London, exposing social problems, harsh lives, drink, prostitution and the need for reform.

"East of Aldgate, another city begins, London flattens and sinks into its clay," writes V.S. Pritchett of the East End stories of Arthur Morrison (1863–1945), author of *Tales of Mean Streets* (1894) and *A Child of the Jago* (1896). Close by were Whitechapel and Stepney, with large immigrant communities, recorded by Israel Zangwill (1864–1926) in his *Children of the Ghetto* (1892), a powerful Naturalist work about the Jewish East End. Many serious writers explored the grim urban record – Arnold Bennett (1867–1931) in *A Man From the North* (1898), Somerset Maugham (1874–1965) in *Liza of Lambeth*

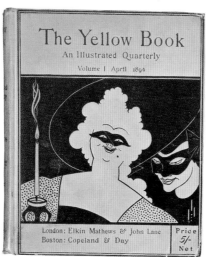

The Yellow Book *published essays by the Aesthetes and illustrations by Aubrey Beardsley.*

Morrison's Jago district, where he grew up, above, lay between Shoreditch and Bethnal Green: "His region smells of rabid little shops, bloated factories, sub-let workrooms and warehouse floors," comments fellow London writer V.S. Pritchett.

THE EAST END AND WEST END OF LONDON IN THE 1890s:
In the 1890s there was a great East-West divide, between wealth and poverty, colour and grey. Writers tended to describe their own locale, allowing the atmosphere to imbue their text.

(1897), George Moore in *Esther Waters* (1894), about a servant girl with an illegitimate child. Charles Dickens and the Victorian social novelists had written before of the "nether world," now it struck the public conscience. In writers like G. B. Shaw (1856–1950) and William Morris (1834–96), the spirit of Socialist reform grew.

In *News from Nowhere* (1890) Morris wrote a futuristic Utopian novel which saw a London without its factories and slums, its river clean and natural. Others, like G.K. Chesterton (1874–1936) in his *The Napoleon of Notting Hill* (1904), wrote even more extravagant fables of future London. H.G. Wells (1866–1946) made his name with future fantasies that came to be called science fiction (*The War of the Worlds*, 1898). Wells also wrote of ordinary, shopkeeper's London. In *Tono-Bungay* (1909) he celebrated the city, reflecting on how it confronted writers with its sheer scale and spread. Its most striking characteristic was tentacular growth and proliferation, which "teemed with suggestions of indefinite and sometimes outrageous possibility, of hidden but magnificent meanings." Already, in this richly comic novel, we have the motorcar, the aeroplane, the department store, advertising, the mass market: the "magnificent meanings" of the new urban age.

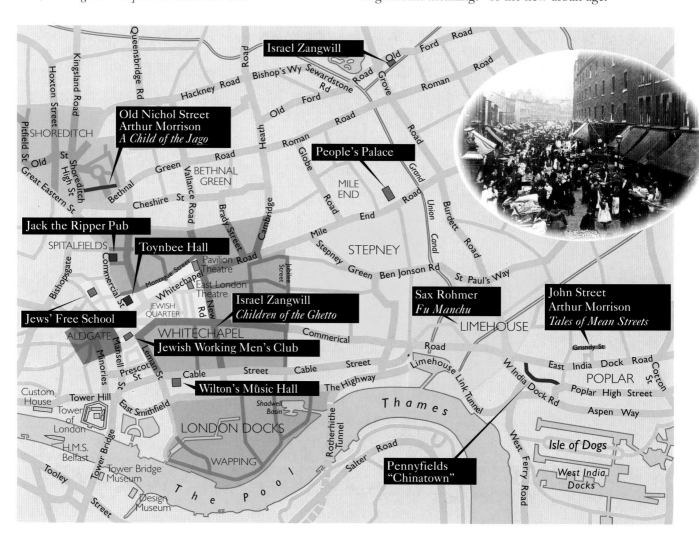

Contrast was what turn-of-the-century London was about. Tales of duplicity fascinated the times. Robert Louis Stevenson's *Dr Jekyll and Mr Hyde* (1886) presented two selves and two Londons: a daylight world of clean streets and professional respectability, a night world of shadows, back doors, crime. Although Charles Dickens and Wilkie Collins had told tales of crime and detection in the foggy city, the great inventor was Sir Arthur Conan Doyle (1858–1930), whose Sherlock Holmes appeared in *A Study in Scarlet* in 1887. "Look out of this window, Watson," he says. "See how the figures loom up, are dimly seen, then blend once more into the cloud-bank. The thief or murderer could roam London on such a day as the tiger does in the jungle, unseen until he pounces...."

The East End – Limehouse, "Chinatown" with its secret societies and "opium dens" – was Gothic space for the popular crime stories that flourished around the turn of the century, from authors like Edgar Wallace and Sax Rohmer, inventor of sinister oriental crime genius Fu Manchu. G.K. Chesterton (1874–1936) invented his priest-detective Father Brown (*The Innocence of Father Brown*, 1911), E.W. Hornung (1866–1921) his cracksman Raffles (*Raffles: The Amateur Cracksman*, 1899). With the work of E. Phillips Oppenheim and William Le Queux, the spy novel, another urban form suiting an age of political suspicions took shape.

From the 1880s to the dawn of the Great War in 1914, London was at its most imperial and expansive, and welcomed writers, movements and experiment on an unprecedented scale. These years saw not only a new celebration and exploration of London, but the birth, through these experiments, of the Modern movement. In prose and poetry, old forms shattered, new writing styles came in. After the War, London was never the same again.

This painting of Sherlock Holmes with pipe and deerstalker shows him as the archetypal detective.

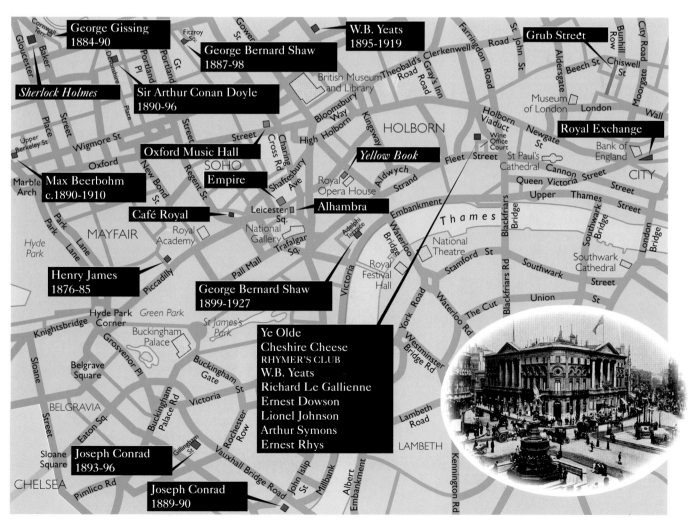

DREAMS OF EMPIRE

"We could not help remembering that no Sovereign since the fall of Rome could muster subjects from so many and so distant countries all over the world," said the Duke of Argyll, reflecting on the great celebrations held in London for Queen Victoria's Diamond Jubilee in 1897, as the spirit of British "jingoism" reached its peak. The nineteenth century had seen a revival of imperial adventuring, as the European nation states made not guns and armies but ships and railways, trade and technology, into the new instruments of empire. Now, as the century ended, it was leading to the rivalries that culminated in the "scramble for Africa." Soon the conflict over the Transvaal's gold and diamonds would turn into the Boer War that marked the century's end.

Of all the modern empires, Britain's was the greatest and most far-flung of all. Losing the American colonies in 1781 had not halted imperial growth. The empire grew apace, but in a different direction. Between 1815 and 1865, the British Empire enlarged, it was reckoned, by 100,000 miles each year. By 1820 it claimed dominion over a quarter of the world's population. It reached the islands of the Caribbean and of the Pacific, won during seventeenth and eighteenth century explorations and circumnavigations, above all Captain Cook's. It encompassed India, from 1858 another jewel in the Queen's crown. There were colonies in West and South Africa, Ceylon and Burma. Singapore was added in 1819, Aden in 1839, New Zealand in 1840, Natal and Hong Kong in 1843. These bases made it necessary to protect the Suez Canal, go to battle in Egypt and the Sudan. By the century's end the settler colonies of Canada, Australia and New Zealand were acquiring virtual self-government within the Commonwealth. In the Cape Colony, South Africa, Cecil Rhodes, despairing of getting the vote for British settlers from the Boers, was ready to go to war.

The spirit of Empire may have been built on Palmerstonian gunboat diplomacy, but it wasn't primarily to do with military conquest. At stake was trade, national wealth and resources, the spread of social and political development, Britain's prestige as a maritime commercial power. Its navies largely ruled the seas, a third of the

Britain first encompassed India in the early seventeenth century with the trading of the East India Company, officials of which are depicted, above, receiving the attention of British residents.

world's merchant shipping flew the Red Ensign, Britain handled two fifths of world trade in manufactured goods. Empire stimulated industrial growth and invention, enriched the merchant classes, gave the gentry a new role. Imperial wealth went into great estates, but equally factories and urban development. It held the nation together at home, provided new frontiers of settlement for expanding populations abroad. Imperialism had its bitter critics, especially in the Boer War. But, as never before or since,

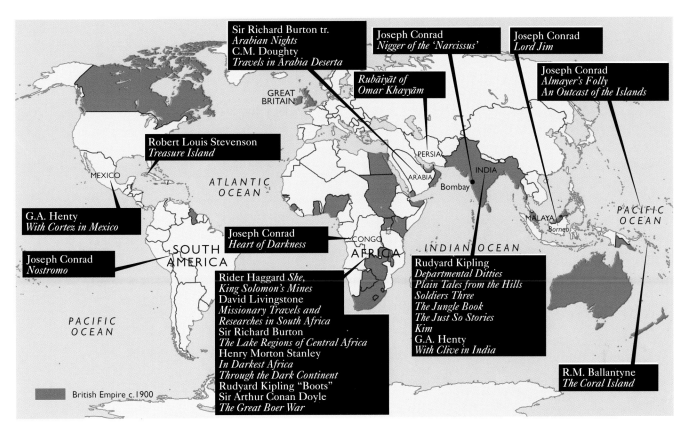

Sir Richard Burton tr.
Arabian Nights
C.M. Doughty
Travels in Arabia Deserta

Joseph Conrad
Nigger of the 'Narcissus'

Joseph Conrad
Lord Jim

Joseph Conrad
*Almayer's Folly
An Outcast of the Islands*

*Rubāiyāt of
Omar Khayyām*

GREAT
BRITAIN

Robert Louis Stevenson
Treasure Island

PERSIA

ARABIA

INDIA

Bombay

MEXICO

ATLANTIC
OCEAN

G.A. Henty
With Cortez in Mexico

PACIFIC
OCEAN

MALAYA

Borneo

Joseph Conrad
Heart of Darkness

CONGO

SOUTH
AMERICA

AFRICA

INDIAN OCEAN

Joseph Conrad
Nostromo

Rudyard Kipling
*Departmental Ditties
Plain Tales from the Hills
Soldiers Three
The Jungle Book
The Just So Stories
Kim*
G.A. Henty
With Clive in India

Rider Haggard *She,
King Solomon's Mines*
David Livingstone
*Missionary Travels and
Researches in South Africa*
Sir Richard Burton
The Lake Regions of Central Africa
Henry Morton Stanley
*In Darkest Africa
Through the Dark Continent*
Rudyard Kipling "Boots"
Sir Arthur Conan Doyle
The Great Boer War

PACIFIC
OCEAN

R.M. Ballantyne
The Coral Island

British Empire c.1900

most Britons, educated or uneducated, came to feel themselves citizens of the world – a world where Queen Victoria ruled supreme. Much of the map was coloured red, Britain had an empire on which the sun never set.

It now stuck its flag deep into British writing. Strange was the fact that it hadn't done so sooner. Nineteenth century British writers were indefatigable travellers, often escaping from the confined Victorian atmosphere of home. Explorer adventurers were many – from Charles Darwin, voyaging aboard the Beagle, C.M. Doughty and Richard Burton, explorers of Arabia, Mungo Park, Livingstone and Sir Henry Morton Stanley (*In Darkest Africa*, 1890), to the many hardy ladies who wandered the rarer places of the world – like Isabella Bird, whose travels took her to the United States, Hawaii, China and Japan (*Unbeaten Tracks in Japan*, 1880). Their tales fed a sense of the exotic, captured in such works as Burton's translation version of *The Arabian Nights* (1885-8) or Fitzgerald's *Omar Khayyam* (1859). The British explorer, doing abroad, was a world type – famously captured in Phileas Fogg, the intrepid English traveller celebrated in the fiction of Jules Verne.

The British explorer became a form of frontiersman, resourceful, bold, going where none had gone

The Empire: By the end of the nineteenth century many writers associated the spirit of Britain with the adventure romance. And all this was increasingly set within the conveniently spacious bounds of the imperial dominions – the red on the map.

before: haggling with the natives, climbing the highest mountain, hunting the largest game, seeking the lost mines of King Solomon or the source of the Nile, probably protesting about native cruelty to animals as well. Here the world became a different place, as civilization gave way to savagery, convention to freedom, boredom to wonder, and mad dogs and Englishmen – Englishwomen too – went out in the midday sun. Just as Cooper's stories of Leatherstocking, the great trapper following the ever-extending, ever-changing western frontier, became America's national myth, the flood of tales of exploration and imperial adventure became the British one. They were, says one critic, Martin Green, "collectively, the story England told itself as it went to sleep at night." Especially with male readers, they energized the instinct for travel, exploration,

Travellers' adventure tales, such as Livingstone's Life and Explorations, *left, became an essential part not just of British, but world, reading.*

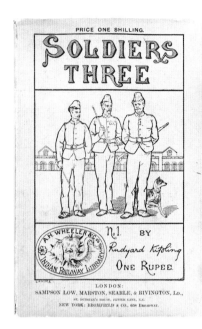

Rudyard Kipling, left, was born in Bombay, the son of a British art teacher. He came home to school, but returned to Lahore, worked as a journalist and begain to print his jingling poetry and stories, such as Soldiers Three, far left, *in The* Indian Railway Library *series, published by A.H. Allahabad.*

Robert Louis Stevenson, an inveterate traveller, died in the Pacific, ever in flight from his repressive Edinburgh upbringing. He is shown below playing a flageolet in bed in his final home, Apia in Samoa, where he was to die at the early age of 44 of a brain haemorrhage in 1894.

adventure, play, the will to rule. British adventure romance was not new: it went back to one of the first novels, Daniel Defoe's *Robinson Crusoe* (1719). In the age of nineteenth century travels, the tradition revived. Versions of the Crusoe story spread over Europe: the Swiss had theirs in Johann Wyss's *Swiss Family Robinson* (1814), Jules Verne did French versions at the end of the century. In Britain it shaped one of the most successful of all nineteenth century boys' books, R.M. Ballantyne's *The Coral Island* (1858) – the story of three resourceful British schoolboys cast away on an island in the Pacific, a clear myth of empire.

Toward the end of the century, as the popular book market grew, adventure romance, like the Empire, set its bounds ever wider. The great inventor was Robert Louis Stevenson (1850–94). "Fiction is to grown men what play is to a child," he said – and, revolting against the domestic confinement of the social novel, called for a new impulse to romance and adventure. He rewrote the *Arabian Nights* (1882), and proved his point with *Treasure Island* (1883), his remarkable tale of Long John Silver, Jim Hawkins, a parrot and the Spanish Main. The book deeply appealed to children; it still does. It also won the admiration of Henry James, who described it as a wonderful work of "murders, mysteries, islands of dreadful renown, hair breadth escapes, miraculous coincidences and buried doubloons."

Stevenson showed that the grim world of social Naturalism, the domestic romance, the spirit of aesthetic decadence were not all there was to fiction. Many learned the lesson; the success of *Treasure Island* encouraged H. Rider Haggard (1856–1925) to write *King Solomon's Mines* (1885), another instant bestseller. Born in Norfolk, Haggard was a public official in Natal and the Transvaal, and knew Africa at first hand. *King Solomon's Mines* not

only told of a quest for treasure across the great African landscape, but invented a British hunter frontiersman in Allan Quatermain, whose knowledge of nature and history is matched by his contempt for decadent civilization back home. "Ah! this civilization, what does it all come to?" he demands, noting that there is a savage in us all. Like Leatherstocking, he wanders his landscape with sympathy and understanding. Like Leatherstocking, he would return in book after book, a prototype of the Indiana Jones figure of today.

Haggard wrote 34 romances; the most famous is *She* (1887), about Ayesha, the beautiful and apparently immortal queen of Kor ("She Who Must Be Obeyed"). He was fascinated by the aeons of history, the great civilizations that had been in Africa, where most of his novels are set. But it was in India, "the jewel in the crown," that British imperial experience seemed deepest. Near the century's

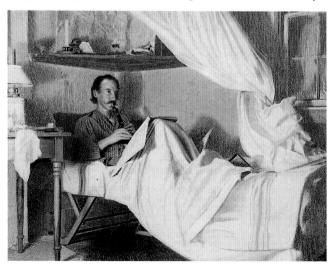

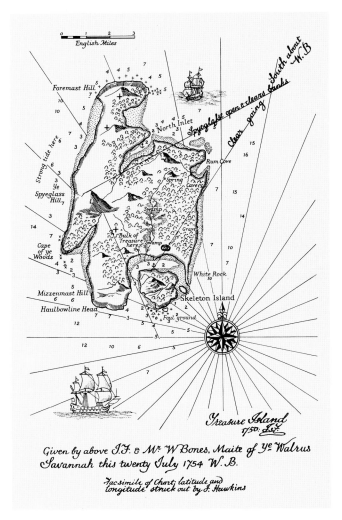

English Miles

Foremast Hill

Spyglass open clears banks W.B

North Inlet

Clear going

Rum Cove

Strong tide here

Ye Spyeglass Hill

Spring Cave

Swamp

Bulk of Treasure here

Cape of ye Woods

White Rock

Mizzenmast Hill

Skeleton Island

Haulbowline Head

Foul ground

Treasure Island
1750.

Given by above J.F. & Mr. W Bones, Maite of ye Walrus
Savannah this twenty July 1754 W.B.

Facsimile of Chart; latitude and
longitude struck out by J. Hawkins

In the introduction to Treasure Island, *Robert Louis Stevenson writes of the map, left, he drew for the book.* "It is, perhaps, not often that a map figures so largely in a tale, yet is is always important. The author must know his countryside, whether real or imaginary, like his hand; the distances, the points of the compass, the place of the sun's rising, the behaviour of the moon, should all be beyond cavil."

and *The Thirty-Nine Steps* (1915), the wartime spy thriller where Richard Hannay's life as an imperial adventurer is vital to his survival.

The greatest novelist of the Empire was not of British birth at all. Joseph Conrad (1857–1924), born Josef Korzeniowski of Polish parents in the Ukraine, moved to France, then joined the British merchant navy. He sailed the seaways of the imperial world from Malaysia to South America, East Indies to the Congo, for twenty years, before he eventually became a writer. His early novels were set in the Malayan Archipelago and the Pacific (*Almayer's Folly*, 1895; *An Outcast of the Islands*, 1986). His novella *Heart of Darkness* (1899) is a great allegory of the scramble for Africa, ending amid "the horror, the horror" of the Congo. *Nostromo* (1904) looks at what "material interests" have done to South America. The shadow of darkness, the endless hint of ambiguity, hidden in the imperial and marine sense of duty and fidelity, as well as a cunning literary technique, shapes all of Conrad's work.

In time the sun started setting on the British Empire. The Boer War was the beginning of the end. By the 1920s writers like E.M. Forster and George Orwell grew ever more critical of the imperial mission. Today the pink map of empire is faded, an old chart bought a century ago. Modern opinion has rejected much of this writing; this is to miss its meaning. The Empire was laced with ambiguity. Kipling might be the bard of the "White Man's Burden" but he was also an explorer of imperial uncertainty, aware of the challenge other peoples posed to Victorian confidence. In time the Empire would strike back, re-enter post-imperial Britain to form part of its culture. What shouldn't be forgotten is the power of the vast imperial geography, real and fantastic, digested into the British imagination – and its continued impact on its mythic history.

The work of Joseph Conrad, above, was mostly set aboard ship or in the world of seafarers sailing across the imperial map.

end it found its bard. Rudyard Kipling's *Departmental Ditties*, *Plain Tales From the Hills*, and *Soldiers Three* (all 1889) brought the Raj and the Indian frontier to sudden life. When he returned to Britain in 1890, he had seven books finished, and was greeted as the boy wonder.

To some Kipling (1865–1936) was "the bard of infantile jingoism," but he was one of the greatest writers of his day. He won the Nobel Prize; his books sold seven million copies in Britain, eight million in the United States. He was inventor of Mowgli and Tommy Atkins, Kim and Toomai of the Elephants. *The Jungle Book* (1894), *Captains Courageous* (1897), *Kim* (1901) and *The Just So Stories* (1902) cast their glow over the wonders of India, and fed the imagination of innumerable British children. He was the bard of the workaday India, ordinary soldiers, Indians themselves. He knew hard work, the streets, the jungle, the military camp, the engineers on tramp steamers.

Rudyard Kipling had many followers. There was G.A. Henty (1832–1902), who produced over a hundred books for the boys' market with titles like *With Clive in India* (1884) or *With Cortez in Mexico* (1891). There was John Buchan (1875–1940), later Baron Tweedsmuir, Governor General of Canada, who wrote Scottish, Indian and African romances, most successfully *Prester John* (1910),

THE IRISH REVIVAL

The sense of place always dominates in Ireland. "Where are you from?" remains the national enquiry. Land underpins all this. With the ocean on three sides and a dangerous neighbour on the fourth, native soil has always represented survival. And in survival and clay lies the greatest Irish identity. In Irish literature the tradition of earth and geography began in the natural world and had mutated elegantly by the time the Irish Revival was born at the end of the nineteenth century. Those tall Anglo-Irish windows always looked out over fields of passion. Ten centuries earlier, the monks in the limestone abbeys had found God in milk and honey and salmon and sky, and they praised Him with quills made of badger hair.

When Lady Gregory met Yeats, above, *she wrote to her cousin that he looked like "a starved Roman Catholic curate in seedy black clothes with a large black bow at the root of his long naked throat."*

Thus, Ireland's literary spirit developed from the earth itself and from the people who lived closest to it; and this spirit not only survives, but seems to continue eternally, as witnessed in the northern poems of Nobel Laureate, Seamus Heaney. The Irish Revival had an ambiguous relationship with the people of the land. Privileged but concerned landowners and Ascendancy scions brought forward its age-old oral cultures and mythologies and gave them a place at the core of the culture. This very ambiguity proved an energy source. Born in the Midlands and continued in urban salons, the Revival followed, almost like crop rotation, a period of romance and revolution, where poets were also song writers and soldiers were orators.

The Revival was chiefly motivated by an urban man with country experiences – William Butler Yeats – and his friend Lady Augusta Gregory, both of whom were privileged English-speaking Protestants, fascinated by the native culture of disadvantaged, often evicted, Irish-speaking Catholics. Yeats (1865-1939), raised in Dublin and London, had maternal stock in the northwest: the Pollexfens of Sligo. He explored Sligo as a boy and encountered the "little people," the faery host who rides out across the sky on May Eve from a door in the side of Ben Bulben to the top of Knocknarea, where they pay homage at the cairn-grave of their Queen Maeve (England's old Queen Mab). As an adolescent he roamed the shores of Rosses'

Point and asked the fishermen and the field labourers whether they had ever seen fairies. And the young Yeats was moonstruck by the Gore-Booth sisters ("two girls in silk kimonos, both beautiful, one a gazelle") in their château of Lissadell with "great windows open to the south." Throughout these moonings he practised a kind of cultural "slumming," in that he noted down a power among the natives ruled by his own class. The people in the thatched mud cabins had an ancient folklore with European overtones. They told sagas of cattle rustling, wars between royal husbands and wives in the west, great chess games and love stories in Ulster. In their speech the lower folk showed verve and originality. Even where they spoke English it had a unique colour, born of bringing Gaelic constructions forward by literal translation (now authenticated etymologically as Hiberno-English).

When the time came for him to express his art in more than poems, Yeats capitalized upon his understanding of the way of the people and their tradition. He needed an ally and the rain brought him one. Visiting that rare creature, a well-to-do upper-class Catholic landlord, Edward Martyn (1859–1923), Yeats was introduced to a neighbour, Lady Augusta Gregory of Coole Park. When this little Tweedledum met the tall, vague Tweedledee with his floppy bow tie, the Irish Revival was born. At that wet afternoon tea in Roscommon, when she told Yeats that "it was a pity we had no Irish theatre," she eavesdropped on his dreams. He believed a nation without

Sean O'Casey described Lady Augusta Gregory, left, *as "a blend of the Lord Jesus Christ and Puck [with her] sturdy, stout little figure clad in solemn black, made gay with a touch of something white under a long black silk veil" – Queen Victoria with a grin, perhaps.*

its own literature was no full nation, and he had long experimented with wrestling cultural nationalism from Ireland's ancient epics. Since Lady Gregory had translated some of those myth cycles and had encouraged the learning of the rebel Irish language among the *hauterie*, the marriage was made before the partners were introduced.

The Revival's greatest successes were perception of the natives' riches and the permission for those with education and connections to convert them into culture for all. With Coole Park as the heart and Dublin as the head, the possibilities spread island-wide. Soon writers of all castes and places flocked. Up stepped John Millington Synge (1871–1909) who wrote of the stony Aran Islands and the people of the west; James Stephens (1882–1950), whose fantasy worlds were everywhere and nowhere; George

Moore (1852–1933) with his great house in Mayo and his pretentious exile in Paris where he nonetheless produced fine novels of Ireland's landed people; George Russell, "AE" (1867–1935), sophisticated and innocent in Dublin; and Sean O'Casey (1880–1964), the playwright of tenement anguish. Synge found the plot for the *Playboy of the Western World* (1907) on Aran where they told him a tale of a mainland man who came over to hide among kinfolk after he had killed his father with a spade: the islanders hid him, then shipped him to America. In 1907, the Abbey Theatre audience rioted at the play: Ireland had no people heathen enough to cover up a patricide, they roared. And they rioted again when Sean O'Casey put a prostitute on the same stage as the national flag in *The Plough and the Stars* (1926). What O'Casey knew, though, was that a room in a Dublin tenement had as much atavistic power for its residents as any open acre.

Yeats and Gregory defined "Revival." The new writings updated that natural world so beloved of the medieval scribes. Even Yeats went to live close to the land, in County Galway; "An ancient bridge, and a more ancient tower/A farmhouse that is sheltered by its wall/ An acre of stony ground."

YEATS' LAND: *Yeats' imagery reflected the ancient force of the land: "I can see the Aran Islands, Connemara Hills, and Galway in the breaking light...."*

W.B. Yeats "Under Ben Bulben's Head"

W.B. Yeats' grave

Coleraine

Londonderry

Eva & Constance Gore-Booth

Rosses' Point

W.B. Yeats 1868-80s William & Elizabeth Pollexfen

W.B. Yeats "The Wanderings of Oisin"

John Millington Synge *Playboy of the Western World*

Lissadell House

Donegal

Omagh

Lough Neagh

Belfast

Bangor

NORTHERN IRELAND

Lurgan

Ballina

Knocknarea Colloney

Drumcliff

Sligo

Lower Lough Erne

Enniskillen

Upper Lough Erne

Armagh

Lough Gill Dooney Rock

George William Russell "Æ" b.1867-c.1877

W.B. Yeats "Ballard of Father O'Hart"

Westport

Moore Hall

W.B. Yeats "The Lake Isle of Innisfree"

W.B. Yeats "The Fiddler of Dooney"

Lough Mask

George Moore b.1852 *The Lake*

Renvyle House

W.B. Yeats & Lady Augusta Gregory

Oliver St John Gogarty

Lough Corrib

Edward Martyn

DUBLIN

Galway

Aran Islands

Galway Bay

Inishmaan

Durras House

Tullira Castle

Coole Park

Thor Ballylee

Lough Derg

Kildare

Liffey

Dun Laoghaire

George Moore 1901-11 *A Drama in Muslin*

Malahide

Cloughran

Portmarnock

ATLANTIC OCEAN

IRELAND

Shannon

James Stephens, Registrar 1919-24

W.B. Yeats 1880s

Sean O'Casey 1889 1897

Howth

Limerick

Castleknock

Clontarf

Tipperary

Chapelizod

Liffey

National Gallery

Sandymount

Tralee

W.B. Yeats 1917-48 "The Tower" "The Winding Stair"

Waterford

Grand Canal

Harold's Cross

Shelbourne Hotel

DUBLIN

Lady Augusta Gregory

Cork

Riversdale House

Rathgar

Booterstown

Blackrock

Monkstown

W.B. Yeats b.13.6.1865

W.B. Yeats

Tallaght

Rathfarnham

Dun Laoghaire

Sandycove

Bantry

Dalkey

John Millington Synge 1898-1902 *The Aran Islands* *Riders to the Sea*

John Millington Synge 1872 George William Russell "Æ" c.1877-1932

John Millington Synge b.16.4.1871

Kilternan

Shankill

CHICAGO'S WORLD FAIR (1893)

Probably nothing displayed the modern achievements of America more than Chicago's World Fair. Four hundred years (plus one) after the Discoveries, Americans celebrated with a World Columbian Exposition. The site was Chicago, a highly appropriate choice. A small village of only 250 people in 1833, it had exploded and was now the nation's Second City (New York being the First). Its population, which multiplied fivefold between 1870 and 1900, was over a million, mostly foreign-born. It was a business city, railhead of the plains, slaughterhouse to the nation, communications gateway to the west. But the frontier, largely cleared of its Indians, and highly-settled thanks to the railroads that met in Chicago, officially "closed" in 1890. There was no more free land, and the age of the Wild West was over. Shock cities like Chicago, modern mixtures of commerce, industry, wealth and immigration, were now the true America.

Supervised by the architect Daniel Burnham, the World Columbian Exposition's vast White City changed the face of Chicago. Four hundred temporary buildings faced with plaster of Paris and mostly built in neo-classical or beaux arts style, were set among artificial "Venetian" lagoons and canals. It was all lit by Edison's incandescent light bulb, powered in turn by two dynamos inside the Machinery Hall, said to be the largest building in the world. Millions came from all over to see the Fair – a demonstration of America's technological dominance.

For the 1893 Chicago Columbian Exposition, above, *a vast White City rose on seven hundred acres of swamp land by Lake Michigan.*

But the Fair's motto was "Make Culture Hum!" and it was its intention also to display American cultural potential. Writers and scholars were invited in great numbers to its huge congresses. "Chicago was the first expression of American thought as a unity," declared the historian Henry Adams, impressed by his visit. Meantime another great historian, Frederick Jackson Turner, announced his famous "frontier thesis" here, suggesting both that the American character had been shaped by its encounter with the West, and equally that the day of the West was done. And nothing made that more visible than Buffalo Bill Cody's *Wild West Show*, which displayed the tattered survivors of the Battles of Little Big Horn and Wounded Knee. The novelists came too. The young Theodore

Dreiser wrote his account of the fair; the realist Hamlin Garland pronounced on "Local Color in Fiction," claiming that the entire energy of American literature was moving to the Midwest – and, true to his message, he promptly took up residence in the Windy City.

Meanwhile a very unfairy world was unfolding downtown. In the Loop, flat-topped office "skyscrapers" of ten or more storeys, made possible by rock hard land and the elevator, rose up in the "Chicago style." They were a "proud and soaring thing," said Chicago architect Louis Sullivan; a new wonder of the world, thought

This Thanksgiving edition of Chicago's Bohemian magazine The Chap Book *had a cover illustration by Aubrey Beardsley who was commissioned to create a series of designs for the magazine.*

European visitors. Huge department stores (Marshall Field) and bank buildings appeared downtown. Dumbbell tenements rose round about to house the vast immigrant population – more Poles than in Warsaw, more Jews than in Lithuania. So bad were the social problems that Jane Addams founded her relief settlement Hull House, and a whole "Chicago school" of urban sociologists developed.

Chicago was, as everyone knew, a muscular business city. But it did stake its claim on culture. Enlightened patrons filled the Art Institute (founded 1879) with major purchases of the European Impressionists, and later the Modernists, still there to be seen in remarkable profusion. In 1893 John D. Rockefeller founded the University of Chicago, which became one of the major academic institutions of America. Lured by the cheap rent of housing built for the Fair and the mixture of tongues, writers poured into the city, and a new Bohemia began to flourish. There was a Bohemian Club, the Cypher Club, "where

Mrs Grundy has no sway," and a Chicago bohemian magazine *The Chap Book*. The *Chicago Tribune* and other papers attracted leading journalists, among them George Ade, F.P.A. Adams and Finlay Peter Dunne, inventor of the opinionated "Mr Dooley."

Helped by all this, from 1893 Chicago took its place on the literary map. Henry Blake Fuller (1857–1929), banker and novelist, published *The Cliff-Dwellers*, set around an office skyscraper, that very year, and told stories of Chicago Bohemia in *Under the Skylights* (1901). Theodore Dreiser (1871–1945) wrote *Sister Carrie* (1900), the scandalous tale of Carrie Meeber, who uses her body to advance in the world, depicting Chicago as a sexual "magnet" and more exciting than any human lover.

Frank Norris's The Pit *(1902) focuses on the capricious power of the Chicago Board of Trade,* below, *to destroy people's lives.*

Chicago-born Frank Norris (1870–1902) explored the world's largest grain exchange at the Board of Trade in *The Pit* (1903). And Upton Sinclair's (1878–1968) *The Jungle* (1903) recorded the Jewish-Lithuanian ghetto and the harsh world of the stockyards. He wrote of "pork-making by machinery, pork-making by applied mathematics" and changed the food laws of America.

Over the next twenty years the city would experience what came to be called the "Chicago Renaissance." Novelists like Henry Blake Fuller, Theodore Dreiser, Frank Norris, Floyd Dell and Sherwood Anderson, poets like Carl Sandburg, Vachel Lindsay and Edgar Lee Masters, told its story. In 1912 the wealthy patroness Harriet Monroe began *Poetry* (Chicago), which printed not only Sandburg and Lindsay, but also new experimental poetry by Wallace Stevens and T.S. Eliot ("Prufrock"), helped along by Ezra Pound, the London-based foreign editor. A year later Chicago saw the birth of Margaret Anderson's equally distinguished magazine, the *Little Review* – although it later moved to twenties' Paris.

Chicago was becoming America's Second City in literature, too. In 1912 Sherwood Anderson (1876–1941) left his paint factory in Elyria, Ohio, to join the writers and artists of Chicago bohemia, who included Floyd Dell, Maxwell Bodenheim and Ben Hecht. Here he wrote his *Winesburg, Ohio* (1919), a tale of the Midwest, but also an experimental

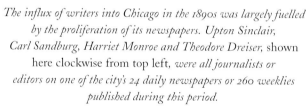

The influx of writers into Chicago in the 1890s was largely fuelled by the proliferation of its newspapers. Upton Sinclair, Carl Sandburg, Harriet Monroe and Theodore Dreiser, shown here clockwise from top left, were all journalists or editors on one of the city's 24 daily newspapers or 260 weeklies published during this period.

work influenced by Gertrude Stein, and by Chicago's Art Institute's showing of the modernist "Armory Show." In turn he influenced many Modernist writers of the twenties, among them Ernest Hemingway, whose home was in the Chicago suburb of Oak Park. Chicago-born James T. Farrell (1904–79) told a naturalistic fable of life on the South Side in the *Studs Lonigan* trilogy (1932–35). Richard Wright, one of many black writers to arrive from the South in the twenties, recorded his Mississippi experience in *Native Son* (1940).

Chicago's writing, like the city itself, generally had a hard, tough, material feel to it. Never as sophisticated as New York, as experimental as Greenwich Village, as cultured as Boston, the city's works were often naturalistic, or, influenced by the rural Midwest, folksy and vernacular. Its writers often left to go elsewhere. Hemingway went off to Paris, but still wrote tales of Chicago and the Michigan Woods. "Modernity," wrote Wallace Stevens, "is so Chicagoan, so plain, so unmeditative." Yet a major writing developed round the city; and to this day it houses fiction's chief laureate, Saul Bellow (b.1915), who portrays the postmodern city in *The Dean's December* (1982). The Chicago World's Fair set out to make Chicago culture hum. And so it did.

Chicago in the 1890s:
Chicago enjoyed a brief literary renaissance at the turn of the century. Its writers concentrated on working class protagonists and the colloquial language of the streets. Theodore Dreiser wrote about the area around the Loop in Sister Carrie, *James T. Farrell set his* Studs Lonigan *trilogy close to home, in Bohemia.*

> "Hog Butcher for the World
> Tool Maker,
> Stacker of Wheat,
> Player with Railroads and the
> Nation's Freight Handler;
> Stormy, husky, brawling,
> City of the Big Shoulders:
> They tell me you are
> wicked and I believe them,
> for I have seen your
> painted women under the
> gas lamps luring the
> farm boys...."
>
> "Chicago" Carl Sandburg

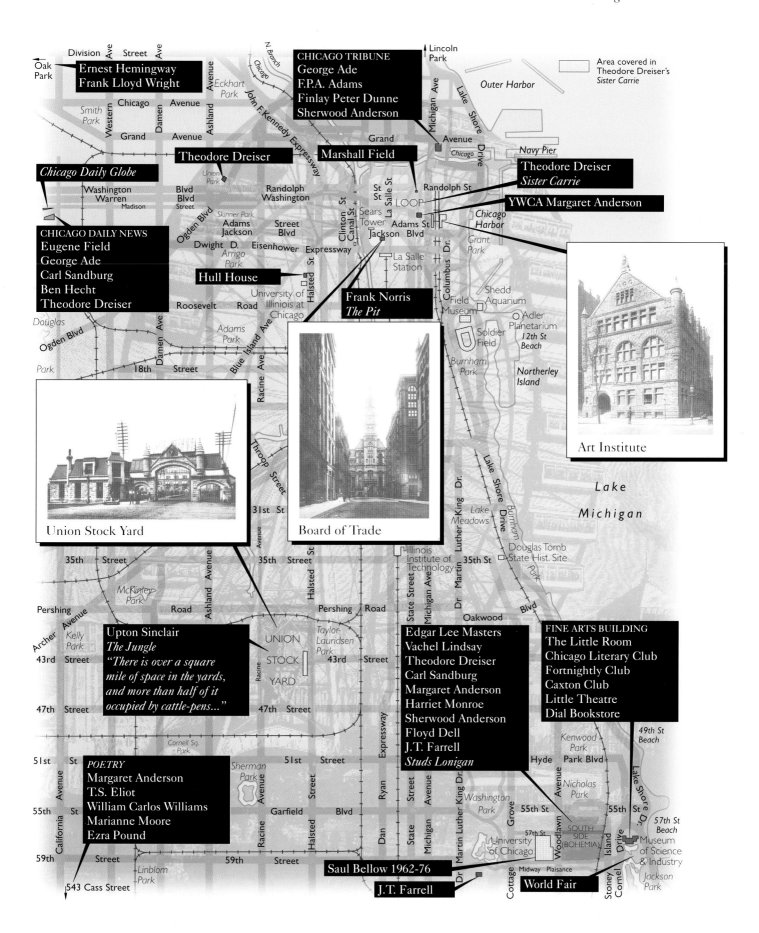

Division Ave Street Ave

Oak
Park

Ernest Hemingway
Frank Lloyd Wright

N. Branch

↑ Lincoln
Park

CHICAGO TRIBUNE
George Ade
F.P.A. Adams
Finlay Peter Dunne
Sherwood Anderson

Michigan Ave

Lake Shore Drive

Area covered in
Theodore Dreiser's
Sister Carrie

Outer Harbor

Smith
Park

Western
Damen
Ashland

Chicago
Avenue

Eckhart
Park

Chicago

John F. Kennedy Expressway

Grand

Avenue
Chicago

Navy Pier

Grand
Avenue

Theodore Dreiser

Marshall Field

Randolph
Washington

St
St

St La Salle St

Randolph St

Theodore Dreiser
Sister Carrie

Chicago Daily Globe

Union
Park

LOOP

Chicago
Harbor

YWCA Margaret Anderson

Washington
Warren
Madison

Blvd
Blvd
Street

Skinner Park

Adams
Jackson

Street
Blvd

Sears
Tower

Clinton St
Canal St

Adams St
Jackson Blvd

Grant
Park

Ogden Blvd

CHICAGO DAILY NEWS
Eugene Field
George Ade
Carl Sandburg
Ben Hecht
Theodore Dreiser

Dwight D.
Arrigo
Park

Eisenhower Expressway

Columbus Dr.

La Salle
Station

Field
Museum

Shedd
Aquarium

Hull House

Halsted St

○ Adler
Planetarium

Roosevelt Road

University of
Illinois at
Chicago

Frank Norris
The Pit

Soldier
Field

12th St
Beach

Douglas

Adams
Park

Burnham
Park

Northerley
Island

Ogden Blvd

Park

18th Street

Damen Ave

Blue Island Ave

Racine Ave

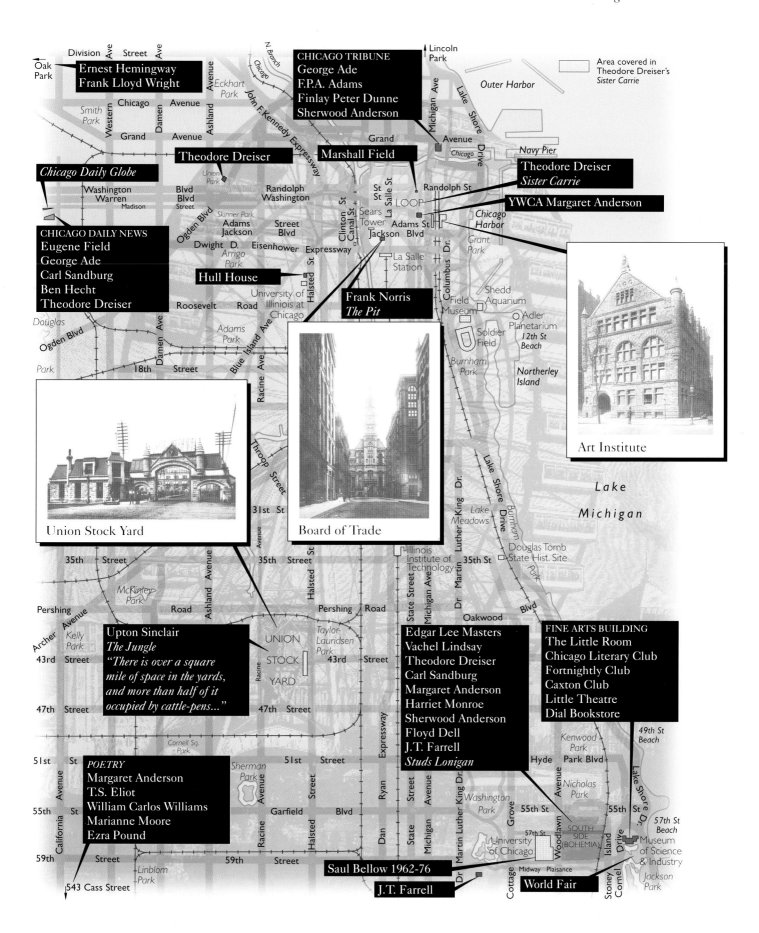

Union Stock Yard

Throop Street

31st St

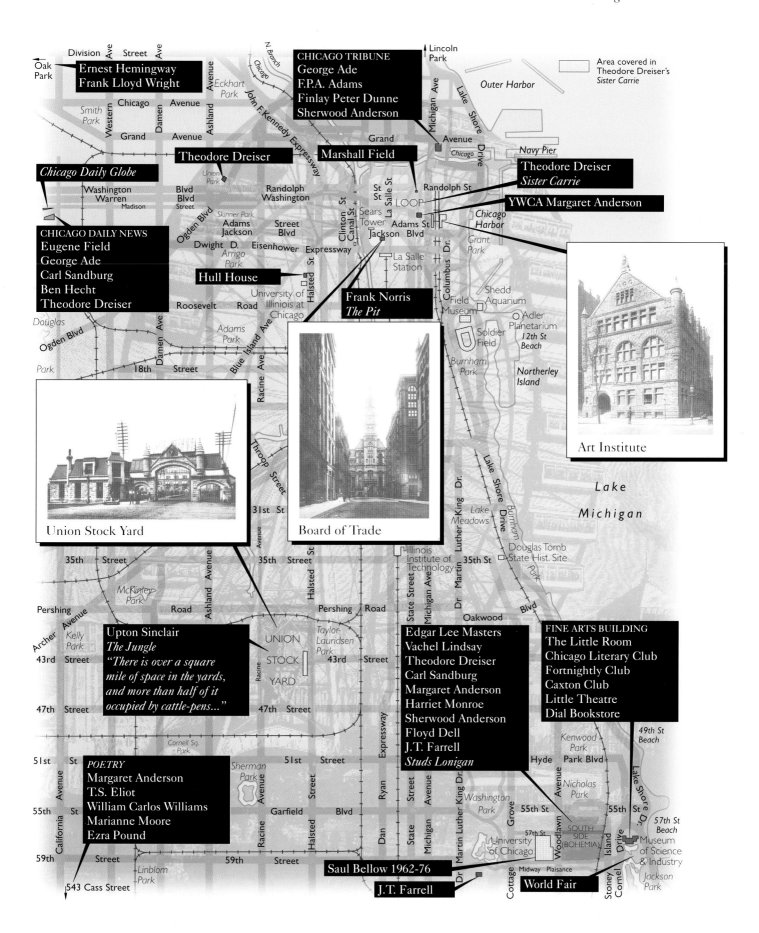

Board of Trade

Lake Shore Drive

Burnham Park

Lake

Michigan

Art Institute

Illinois
Institute of
Technology

Lake
Meadows

Dr. Martin Luther King Dr.

Douglas Tomb
State Hist. Site

35th Street
35th Street
35th St

Ashland Avenue

Halsted St

State Street

Michigan Ave

Park Blvd

McKinley
Park

Pershing
Avenue

Road

Pershing Road

Oakwood

Archer
Kelly
Park

Upton Sinclair
The Jungle
"There is over a square
mile of space in the yards,
and more than half of it
occupied by cattle-pens..."

UNION

Taylor-
Lauridsen
Park

Edgar Lee Masters
Vachel Lindsay
Theodore Dreiser
Carl Sandburg
Margaret Anderson
Harriet Monroe
Sherwood Anderson
Floyd Dell
J.T. Farrell
Studs Lonigan

FINE ARTS BUILDING
The Little Room
Chicago Literary Club
Fortnightly Club
Caxton Club
Little Theatre
Dial Bookstore

STOCK

43rd Street

YARD

43rd Street

Racine

43rd Street

49th St
Beach

47th Street

47th Street

Kenwood
Park

Cornell Sq.
Park

Hyde

Park Blvd

51st St

POETRY
Margaret Anderson
T.S. Eliot
William Carlos Williams
Marianne Moore
Ezra Pound

Sherman
Park

51st Street

Dan Ryan Expressway

State Street

Michigan Avenue

Dr. Martin Luther King Dr.

Washington
Park

55th St

Nicholas
Park

57th St
Beach

55th California St

55th Street

Garfield Blvd

Racine

Halsted St

Grove

Woodlawn

55th Lake Shore Dr.

59th Street

59th Street

University
of Chicago

57th St

SOUTH
SIDE
(BOHEMIA)

Island Drive

Museum
of Science
& Industry

Jackson
Park

Saul Bellow 1962-76

Linblom
Park

Midway Plaisance

57th St
Beach

543 Cass Street

J.T. Farrell

Cottage

World Fair

Stoney

Cornell

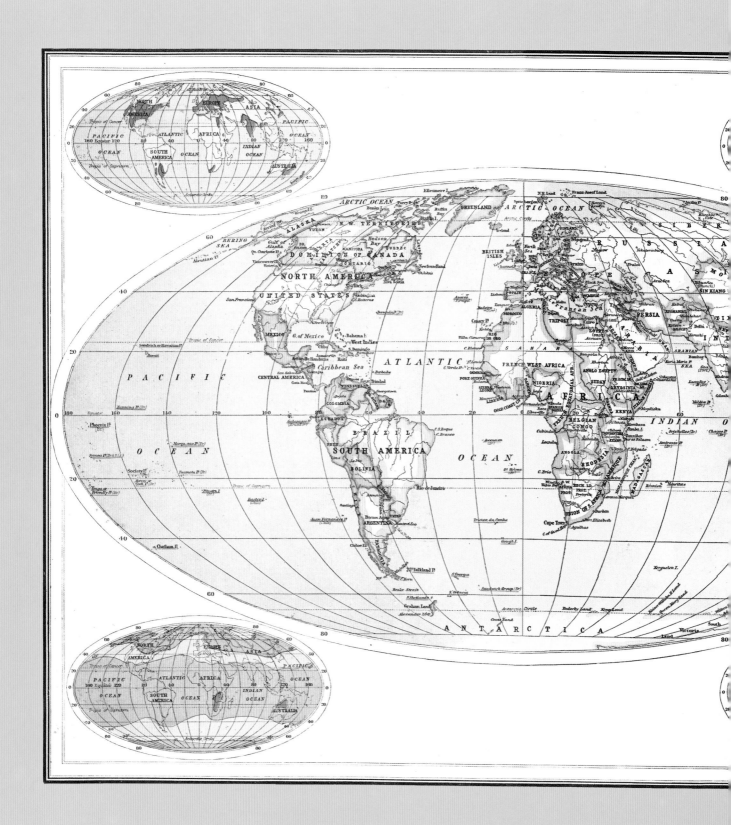

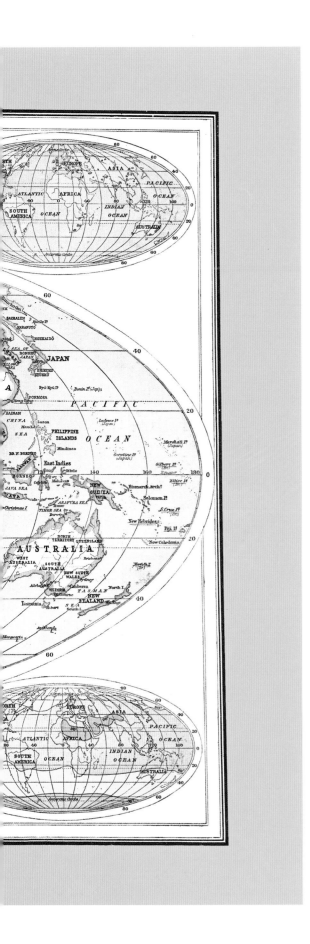

PART SIX

THE MODERN WORLD

Well before it rose over the horizon, the twentieth century had been foreseen. It was to be the "Modern Century," when the great developments occurring so rapidly in every sphere – science and technology, medicine and psychology, architecture and invention – would transform the human condition. The last years of the nineteenth century saw a tremendous acceleration, changing the very feel of reality. The new century quickly delivered its wonders (the internal combustion engine, film, X-rays, powered flight); and this had a rapid impact on the arts, challenging former ideas of reality and representation. Before 1914, in various cities of artistic experiment, Abstraction, Cubism, collage and the mechanical arts of Futurism had been established. But then the modern revolution turned first into a European and then a World War. Many of the European empires – in Austro-Hungary, in Russia, in Germany – collapsed or saw revolution. The map of the nations changed yet again. A new balance of European and world power ensued; a new ideology, Bolshevism, emerged to claim history as its own. In the arts there were really two "Modern" revolutions: the first the relatively optimistic one before 1914, a second more despairing one after 1918, when tumult left by war created the feeling that nothing was over, and turmoil would continue...

British cartographer Harmsworth's political map from their New Atlas (1920) *shows a world very different from before the First World War, with new boundaries and countries emerging.*

WITTGENSTEIN'S VIENNA

In his brilliant book *The Danube* (1986), Claudio Magris tries to capture the spirit of the beautiful ringed city of Vienna at its turn-of-the-century heyday. He goes to the Café Central, where a dummy of Peter Altenberg, who used to sit there writing his poems in these early modern years, sits still. Leo Trotsky – calling himself Bronstein – wrote here as well, planning revolution in Russia. Richard von Krafft-Ebbing came, no doubt to check the sexual distortions of the human mind; Robert Musil too, observing the stuff of his tale of truly modern man – *The Man Without Qualities* (1930–43). As Magris says, the Café Central tells us that reality in Vienna's great Modern moment was always a performance – a form of theatre, an everlasting mingling of real and unreal. Vienna was famous for illusions. Even the Blue Danube, which is not blue, is also not really in Vienna at all, but diverted to a channel beyond to let the great city grow.

Ludwig Wittgenstein, above, was one of many Austrian writers who left Vienna to live in exile in the late 1930s.

Somehow Vienna became the great modern city, although to look upon it even now one is not sure why. In the still torchlit Hofburg before 1914, Hapsburg Emperor Franz Josef sat in dusty splendour at the heart of a great, doubled, multi-cultural European empire that reached to the Adriatic, and held the soul of central Europe in its imperial hands. The Hofburg and the formal Ringstrasse showed the city in its glory, the culture in its place. However, 1 May, 1890 had seen the first Socialist parade along the Prater, part of the shape of things to come. Many thought to see Vienna go up in flames, reported Stefan Zweig (1887–1939). In 1895, on a walk in the Vienna Woods, the secret of dreams was revealed to young Doctor Sigmund Freud (1856–1939). At his consulting rooms at Berggasse 19, his "talking cure" began, along with the theory of modern Angst. In 1900 his first book *The Interpretation of Dreams* suitably opened out the civilization of the twentieth century to its underlying discontents.

1897 was the key year. Gustav Mahler, then only 37, was appointed to the Opera House (Operngasse), and began to upturn the great tradition of Mozart, Beethoven, Wagner, Strauss and the frothy, very Viennese Franz Lehar. Arnold Schonberg's work was first performed in that year.

Under the influence of architects Otto Wagner and Alfred Loos, the visual face of the city was remodelled; a modern transit system was being introduced. In 1897, in revolt against the grand Baroque of the recently constructed Ringstrasse, these new architects, and young painters who supported them, founded the Secession movement. A year on they opened their distinctive Secession building, and published *Ver Sacrum*. Meantime this "Jugendstil," which the French would call Art Nouveau, was transforming the Viennese streets – as well as the art galleries that showed the new ornate colour, half-abstract design and pure eroticism of Egon Schiele, Oscar Kokoshka, Gustav Klimt.

Partly because it was the hub of a vast empire of cultures and tongues that lay beyond, Vienna had always been a city of writers, musicians and artists. In the *fin-de-siècle* age of transition, this was truer than ever. Some of the key figures were Hugo von Hofmannsthal, Arthur Schnitzler, Hermann Bahr, the poet and essayist Stefan Zweig. From early youth, the Viennese-born Hofmannsthal (1874–1929) was an experimental poet, dramatist and brilliant essayist, capturing the modern spirit, the conflict of art and society. He went on to write libretti for the then quite outrageous Richard Strauss, and in 1912 created the

Kolomon Moser created the poster, left, for the promotion of the Secession magazine Ver Sacrum, *which campaigned to promote the "holy mission" of the modern arts. The poster's design is typical of the new Jugendstil.*

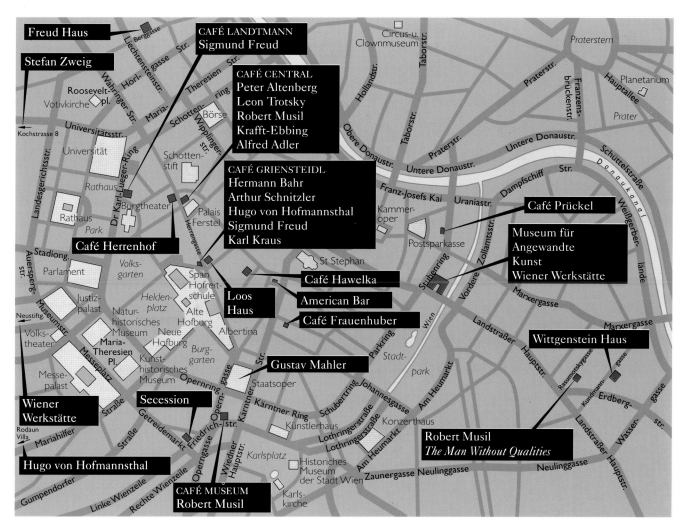

Map labels: Freud Haus · CAFÉ LANDTMANN Sigmund Freud · Stefan Zweig · CAFÉ CENTRAL Peter Altenberg Leon Trotsky Robert Musil Krafft-Ebbing Alfred Adler · CAFÉ GRIENSTEIDL Hermann Bahr Arthur Schnitzler Hugo von Hofmannsthal Sigmund Freud Karl Kraus · Café Herrenhof · Café Prückel · Museum für Angewandte Kunst Wiener Werkstätte · Café Hawelka · American Bar · Café Frauenhuber · Loos Haus · Gustav Mahler · Wittgenstein Haus · Secession · Wiener Werkstätte · Hugo von Hofmannsthal · Robert Musil *The Man Without Qualities* · CAFÉ MUSEUM Robert Musil

Everyman mystery play. But Hofmannstal stays most famous as the author of the remarkable *Chandos Letter* (1902), which beautifully and briefly captured the sense of a modern crisis in language and thought. It was very Viennese, a distillation of the anxiety about naming reality that many thinkers of Vienna – from Ernst Mach and Karl Kraus to Ludwig Wittgenstein – would refine and bequeath to the often word-silenced twentieth century.

Arthur Schnitzler (1862–1931), doctor and dramatist, exemplified a different side of Vienna – catching its bourgeois eroticism, its sense of neurosis, its war with itself. Now his most famous work is *Reigen* (1903), which became the film *La Ronde*; it shows the endless circle of sexual inter-relations that linked various parts of Vienna. But in *Leutenant Gustl* (1901) he brought the technique of interior monologue to the stage, and in *Professor Bernhardi* (1912) he showed the war of the generations. Freud wrote Schnitzler a letter to acknowledge him as a colleague in the investigation of the "under-estimated and much maligned erotic." Anxiety in early twentieth century Vienna wasn't only philosophical and linguistic; it was sexual, a crisis of body and the Id.

What helped feed the modern ferment – in which supposedly traditional, sentimental Vienna now seemed

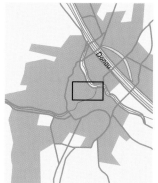

to specialize – was that the whole map of thought and sensation was changing, making the modern into a distinctive, special state. Karl Kraus (1874–1936), a Jew from Czech Bohemia, brought the great battle of the modern to the magazine pages in his *Die Fackel (The Torch)*, a periodical he started in 1899, and which ran for 992 issues. He filled it with an assault on hypocrisies and follies, the sentimental traditionalism and militarized bureaucracy, of a Vienna and an Austria still dominated by an imperial court. When the magazine collapsed in 1918, Kraus wrote a vast satirical play about the Great War and its consequences (*The Last Days of Mankind*, 1922).

The "Young Vienna" movement in literature came in a Viennese way. That is, it was born mostly in cafés: first the Café Griensteidl, depicted as it was in 1890 in the painting by Reinhold Volkel (1890), right, then the Café Herrenhof and the Altenberg-dominated Café Central.

There were other key names – not least those who, like Kraus, followed the story onward past 1918. There was Hermann Broch (1886–1951), author of the powerful *The Sleepwalkers* (1932) and the prose-poem *The Death of Virgil* (1946); Robert Musil (1880–1942), whose *The Man Without Qualities* (1930–43), deals with these same days of mankind in the death-year of Imperial Vienna, 1913–14; Joseph Roth (1894–1939), Jewish, from Galicia, who wrote *Flight Without End* (1927) and *Radetsky March* (1932).

And there was Ludwig Wittgenstein (1889–1951) – whose rich Jewish father financed the Secession building, who went to the same school as the young Adolf Hitler (that would-be painter from Brienz who changed everything in rage against the defeat of the Great War), who studied in Cambridge with Bertrand Russell before the War, returned home to fight in it, then became an Austrian elementary school teacher and architect. His house still stands at 19 Kundmann-gasse. It was his fate to explore not just the limits of a language but of a world. He returned to Cambridge, became its great philosopher (writing *Tractatus-Logico-Philosophicus*, 1922).

The studies in psychoanalysis made by Sigmund Freud, above, are today recognized throughout the world.

By the 1930s flight was everywhere. Hitler, himself an Austrian artist of sorts, returned in 1938; enthusiastic crowds filled the Heldenplatz. Freud had fled to London, Roth to Paris, Broch to Yale. Zweig died by his own hand in South America; many disappeared in the Nazi extermination camps. The anxiety of silence became a fact of history. Today Vienna is once more a beautiful city after the reconstructions of 1945. It holds in its great architecture, museums and galleries not just many of the chief creative discoveries and anxieties of the Modern, but also many of its deepest tragedies.

Vienna now shimmers through the many phases of its being: old imperial city, new city of the Ringstrasse, Secession Vienna, Freudian Vienna, the city of Anschluss and exile, the city of Occupation and *The Third Man*. Its past – the professors, writers, cafés, culture wars – are still there. So is the difficult border that lies between a great European grandeur, and another, even more fragmentary and plural Europe beyond, with a world that is not quite Europe waiting on its doorstep, sending the migrants from a mix of cultures across its anxious borders, to join a city still somehow in the process of formation.

Still, until the collapse of 1918 the Austrian writ, in power and art, ran wide. Even James Joyce, writing *Ulysses* in pre-war Trieste, wrote in Austrian territory. Budapest was one of the great cities of the double empire, its architectural and artistic imagination stimulated almost to excess by Viennese magic, replicated in its buildings, parks and river frontage at the time of the Hungarian millenarian celebrations in 1896. Budapest felt it was the mirror capital. However, perhaps the true twin city was not Budapest at all, but Prague....

KAFKA'S PRAGUE

Prague, the glorious ancient city spanning the Vltava, in the Upper Hungarian Kingdom, was the "city of a thousand golden spires," the "Dublin of the East." Language and culture rubbed together in a Central European profusion even greater than Vienna: there were Czechs and Slovaks, Germans and Jews. Prague had been Protestant and Catholic, Swedish and Austrian. It was capital and province, a centre of learning and a city of legend, fable and the past, the city of the Golem. Its unique Jewish ghetto (Josefov) was one of the richest and most rooted in the world, still shaped by the spirit of the alchemists and goldsmiths. It had one of the world's greatest castles, up on the hill (Hrådcany) – although few who ruled in it died a natural death. By the 1890s it looked toward two conflicting European capitals, Vienna and Berlin. Of its 25,000 Jewish population, about half spoke German and half spoke Czech.

The writing of Franz Kafka, above, *carried the cosmopolitan spirit of Prague.*

"If I look back at my native Prague, say at the beginning of this century, I am amazed by the marvellous mix of cultures and customs, by so many of the city's great men: Kafka, Rilke, Hasek, Werfel, Einstein, Dvorák, Max Brod," says Ivan Klima, one of Prague's most important writers today. But, he adds, Prague's past consisted not only of a great cultural surge; "it was also a time of hatred, of furious and petty and often bloody clashes," which entered the writing of the time. Hence many of its most famous writers left: Rainer Marïa Rilke (1875–1926) – "the Santa Claus of loneliness," according to W.H. Auden, and always the restless traveller – went in 1896, settling for a time in Paris and then at Castle Duino, near Trieste, where he wrote his great *Duino Elegies* (1923). Franz Werfel (1890–1945) became a leading Expressionist writer in his drama, fiction and poetry. Driven into exile in the Nazi years, he ended his days in Hollywood. Karel Capek (1890–1938), whose play *R.U.R.* (1920) invented the human machine, the robot, during the years of the fledgling republic, travelled widely in Europe, though he returned to Prague at the end.

The house in Prague where Kafka lived between 1916 and 1917, at 22 Golden Square (Zlatà ulicka), right, still stands today.

But the two writers who really dominated early modern Prague were Franz Kafka (1883–1924) and Jaroslav Hasek (1883–1923). Even though Kafka's work was twice virtually eliminated – first by the Germans for its Jewishness, then by the Communists for its portrait of the twentieth century "Kafka-esque," that sense of totalitarian obliteration in which they themselves specialized – he was not in the end a political writer (his diary for 2 August, 1914 reads: "Germany has declared war on Russia – swimming in the afternoon"). Rather his modernity lay in the way he succeeded in making political and psychic crises exactly equivalent. His father Hermann, a Jew from the Bohemian countryside who abandoned the Czech language for German, became a successful Prague haberdasher, moving to a number of addresses in the heart of the Jewish district and around the Old Town Square (Staromestské námestí).

The revolt of the delicate tubercular son against heartily aggressive father turned into what proved the most personal and the most universal of modern rebellions. Franz went to study at the Prague German university (Karolinum) and became a Doctor of Law. His father pushed him to work for

the insurance bureaucracy of the Austro-Hungarian government (Assicurazione Generali) – but the son sneaked off to the Café Arco to find the company of fellow writers, such as his university friend Max Brod. Unlike others, Kafka mostly stayed in Prague, apart from important trips to Vienna, Berlin and Bohemian spas. "This little mother has claws," he said of his native city. Instead of leaving, he became a self-exile. On the city's Laurenziberg Hill he defined his literary ambitions. "What will be my fate as a writer is very simple," he would explain. "My talent for portraying my dreamlike inner life has thrust all other matters into the background."

Kafka's novels – the early *Amerika* (written 1912, published 1927), *The Trial* (1914, 1925), begun in the week in 1914 the Great War started, *The Castle* (1922, 1926) – and his marvellous short fiction became a universal history of modern anxiety. In them he found his true role in a short life – becoming, in effect, a superfluous man, a universal nothing, no longer "I" but "K." "He over

Hasek's satire on the Austrian military bureaucracy and on war in general, The Good Soldier Schweyk (*an illustration from which is shown* above), *was inspired by the writer's experiences in the First World War.*

whom Kafka's wheels have passed has lost forever any peace with the world," the German critic T.W. Adorno once wrote, in a compelling phrase.

Strangeness in his writing is so matter-of-fact we easily forget how grotesque the events of his novels and stories – with their constant intersection of ordinary life and the extreme, the fantastic, the self-eliminating – actually are. At the time of his death in 1924, during the brief period of interwar independent democracy, he asked Brod to burn his novels. Against all odds they survived, and survive still as a universal modern myth. Visitors to Prague today, and present-day writers like Ivan Klima, Milan Kundera and Václav Havel, still define the city through Kafka. If ever a writer almost unintentionally imprinted a fiction onto a geography and a history, it was Kafka in Prague.

Jaroslav Hasek, that anarchic bohemian, was the second key figure of literary Prague. He was a drunk and a political gadfly: he was put in prison, threw himself once off the Charles Bridge (Chechuv most), and

The life of the Jewish population in Prague was centred around its synagogues, like the Altnai, below, now one of the oldest in Europe.

The tomb of Franz Kafka and his parents, Hermann and Julie, below, can be visited in the Jewish cemetery in Prague-Strasnice.

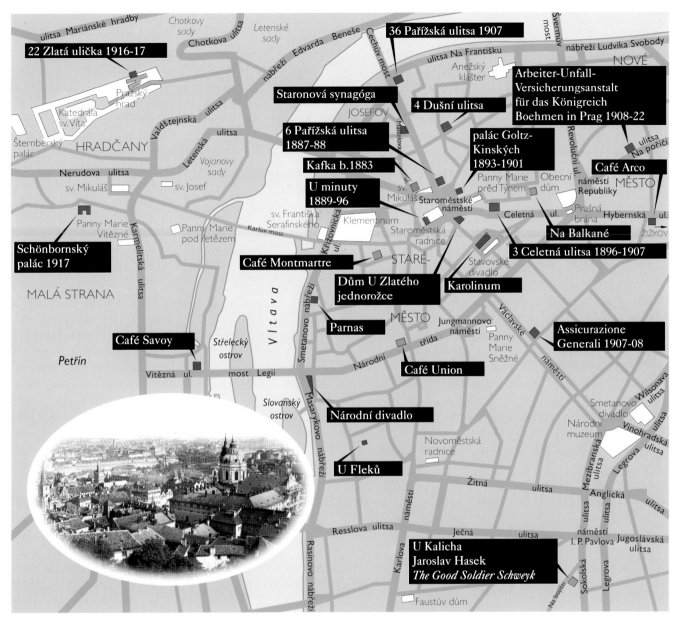

founded a political party ironically called The Party of Peaceful Progress Within the Limits of the Law. He fought in the Austro-Hungarian army in Galicia in the Great War, was taken prisoner by the Russians, became for a time a Communist, then a cabaret artist. All this became material for his brilliant black comedy *The Good Soldier Schweyk* (1923, published 1930), written not like Kafka's novels in German, but in common Czech. Here senseless war and Austro-Hungarian Imperial nonsense are satirized and seen through the mischievous eyes of the common soldier: the little man, the wise fool, a people's hero.

Like Kafka's work, Hasek's book took full form and acquired full fame only after his death. Between them, the writer of lonely inner exile and the rogue anarchist were

KAFKA'S PRAGUE: *Kafka's traces – his rebuilt birthplace (Uveze), several homes near the Old Town Square (Staromestské nàmesti), his tomb, shared with father and mother, in the Jewish cemetery, the distinctive atmosphere of the old ghetto – are visible again in contemporary Prague.*

key writers of modern Prague. Today's Prague, after the three betrayals of 1938, 1948 and 1968, is still a city of good writers, one of them, Václav Havel, was Czech president. But Prague still has the spirit of anxiety, strangeness and extremity that between them Kafka and Hasek left amid its ghettos, bars, breweries and golden spires.

JAMES JOYCE'S DUBLIN

"Take hold of it and keep hold and let it pull you where it will," Henry James said to Edith Wharton about New York. And if any writer was ever pulled by a city – by its Jacobs' biscuit tins, its Bolands' bread vans, its mixed penny cakes, its tasselled dance cards, its encaustic pub windows, the figureheads on its quaystones, its frequent pastiche of its own phrases, its immersion in a distinct nether dialect much like that of *Finnegans Wake* – it was James Joyce (1882–1941), by the city of Dublin.

James Augustine Joyce was born on 2 February, Candlemas Day, 1882, of a genteel Dublin mother and a father from Cork whose fortunes were sliding. This was the time when Maud Gonne rode to Donegal to alleviate the plight of the peasantry, accompanied by a Great Dane who wore leather shoes. In childhood there was already exile, if only from creditors. There was the "sudden flight" from South Dublin, from the stucco houses, the palm trees and the pavilions where you could peep at the sea, to North Dublin, to the disarray by the River Tolka, to streets of swan-neck lamp-posts by football pitches, to the lowing of country cows at the cattlemarts, to different views of the sea. In Fairview, where the Joyces lived at three different addresses, there was the old Jewish cemetery at Ballybough, once a burial place for suicides. There were shifts in school, from the elite Clongowes Wood, to the poor North Richmond Street School of the Christian Brothers, then back to the Jesuits at the Belvedere Day School.

Brendan Behan once said that when he moved from the slums to a housing estate it ruined his sex life. But for Joyce it brought him closer to Monto, the Dublin red-light district to which there were early journeys. In the Nighttown sequence of *Ulysses* it was recreated in dramatic form: the solicitings, jibes and insistence on its innocence were theatrical. It is where Bloom meets his dead son Rudy wearing an Eton jacket, just as Stephen does at Christmas dinner 1891.

Russian poet Osip Mandelstam's wife, Nadezhda, describes man's greatest asset as a sense of guilt, and for Joyce Ireland and the Jesuits supplied that guilt: the nights when the imagination was sexually riotous, balanced

Pre-eminently photographed in his youth in a peaked cap (a "spec cap" in Ireland) with tilted head, sharp, almost apologetic features, Joyce perceived a disease in Dublin – "a centre of paralysis."

between the days of school admonition and punishment, the dense populations of the churches in central Dublin, each with their own demands of devotion and confession, nourishing the guilt. If his nights of desire unmoored him from Catholicism, he still preserved the way Jesuits code and order the world. Albert Camus wrote of Proust's fiction that "it bears the resemblance of the world of dispersion...which gives it meaning on the very level of discord;" the same can be said of *Ulysses*. As Oliver St John Gogarty said, Joyce always adhered to the "ancient oligarchies:" Homer, Virgil, Euripedes, Seneca.

Take the Dart railway from Central Dublin and go to Sandycove, passing Booterstown where there is often a fair like the one in "Araby" (*Dubliners*), past the stucco houses of Blackrock and Monkstown, past Seapoint with its mesmerized figures in the tide. Only at the Forty Foot, near the Martello Tower with its "deep jelly of water," do people dare to be naked. There's a vulnerability about opening *Ulysses* here, reading about the place where Stephen lives with Buck Mulligan, looking at the "merrying sunshine," walking beside the snotgreen, scrotum-tightening sea, wondering how to write about his island. Coming here, we remember he isn't a strong swimmer.

In Joyce's *Ulysses*, published in Paris in 1922, Professor Maginnis, Mrs M'Guinness the pawnbroker, and the fictional Blazes Boylan, in socks with skyblue clocks, saunter simultaneously through a Dublin day like the boats crisscrossing the Irish Sea. Boats crossing the Irish Sea, seen from the Martello Tower at Sandycove at the start of the novel, took Joyce away. In a penultimate passage of *Ulysses*, a red-bearded sailor from County Cork breaks into a litany of reminiscence – the North Wall, sailors, the sea as threshold. Some, like Eveline in a story in *Dubliners*, never cross that threshold. Others, like Stephen Dedalus in *A Portrait of the Artist As a Young Man*, go and seem destined not to come back. Yet they stay bound to the inventory of its streets and its place-names, as if in Jewish convenant: "If I forget thee, O Jerusalem, let my right hand forget her cunning."

James Joyce attended University College, Dublin, where, like many of the young Catholic bourgeoisie, he chaffed at ideologies like Nationalism, movements like the Irish Literary Revival. He determined not just to leave but to bring a kind of birth with him from Dublin to Europe, like the wild geese who fled Ireland for Europe in the seventeenth and eighteenth centuries. The closing pages of *A Portrait* are fragmentary, journal-like, votive, charged with rain and sunshine; the streets like Grafton Street, where the crowds bring people together for their valedictory meetings, are then supplanted by other streets, the European esplanades and boulevards.

After brief exile in Paris, Joyce returned to Dublin, when his mother was dying. Then with a Galway girl, Nora Barnacle, he went into exile again: in Trieste for most of 11 years until the Great War came, in Zurich afterwards, and from 1920 in Paris, where he stayed for twenty years until the Germans came. He revisited Ireland in 1909, thinking of opening a cinema, and made his last visit in 1912. His books too came out in exile. *Dubliners* was published, belatedly, in London in 1914, *A Portrait of the Artist* in New York on 29 December, 1916. His play, *Exiles*, was performed in Munich in 1919. *Ulysses* (1,000 copies done by a Dijon printer) came out in Paris on his birthday in 1922, *Finnegans Wake* appeared in London on 4 May, 1939 — just as Europe collapsed again, so he was soon off into final exile in Zurich.

"Wherever you go, I will follow you," Bertha says in *Exiles*. Nora followed Joyce. They first went out together on 16 June, 1904 – the "Bloomsday" he set the events of *Ulysses* on. They went to Ringstead, at the mouth of the Liffey, the world-river that runs its way through *Finnegans Wake*. Nora's hair was "rousse-auburn;" Joyce makes the predominant colour of her city "Titian-red."

James Joyce had a strange idea of loyalty in sexuality. He pushed his wife to the point of adultery a number of times, and at that point he seemed to have a tremendous fear of betrayal and loss. Boys like the laminated ones on Dollymount Strand, in *A Portrait* ("Their bodies, corpse-white or suffused with a pallid golden light or rawly tanned by the sun, gleamed with the wet of the sea"), were both attraction and mortal foe for him. In the notes for *Exiles* he suggests that a sexual relationship between Richard and Bertha, Robert and Bertha, would fulfil a homosexual desire of the two men for each other. "Huer" (whore) was a bi-sexual word in Dublin. On a visit to Dublin in 1906, when it seemed his wife had had sexual relations with a young man like one of those on Dollymount Strand he was disconsolate, till reassured by another young man at 7 Eccles Street. This is Leopold's

James Joyce shared the Forty Foot near the Martello Tower, above, with his close friend, Oliver St John Gogarty, in September 1904.

and Molly's house in *Ulysses*, about which he was still enquiring from his Aunt Josephine Murray in Dublin two months before publication, "could you jump over the railings without injuring yourself?"

With Joyce, life and art are frequently the one sentence. Both Stephen Dedalus and Leopold Bloom prefer "a cisatlantic to a transatlantic place of residence." Joyce chose Europe early. When war came in 1939 he went into it ever deeper. The perilous train journey from Saint-Germain-des-Fosses to Geneva he took shortly before his death had a parallel in his fiction in the train journey in a third class carriage from Broadstone Station, near Fontenoy Street where his Verdi-singing father lived for a while, to Mullingar, at the close of *Stephen Hero*. The bundles tied in spotted handkerchiefs had an equivalent pattern to the polka-dotted bow-ties he wore in later life; the "smell of debased humanity" around him recalled the smell of peasants in the chapel in Clongowes Wood on the morning of his first early communion.

"He had the fidgets," Beckett said about German poet Rainer Maria Rilke. In the same spirit, Joyce often made light of profundities; yet if anything his work was about the soul and its flights. On the way from Broadstone Station to Mullingar, on the little platforms or in hotels like the Grenville Arms, he must have seen young women like the one Davin describes in *A Portrait*: "a batlike soul waking to the consciousness of itself in darkness and secrecy and loneliness." "When the soul of a man is born in this country," Stephen says, "there are nets flung at it to hold it back from flight." Joyce insisted to his publisher Sylvia Beach that until he wrote, Dublin had historical but not imaginative existence, and his history was in hock to the British Empire and the Italian church. It was his task to make Dublin the archetypal modern city – even if it took flight to do it.

"It's time for some great person of your country to come forward and hold out a hand to you and us," Joyce was told by his daughter in 1934. Indeed the Irish Minister for External Affairs Desmond Fitzgerald offered to propose him for the Nobel Prize, Yeats invited him into the Irish Academy of Letters. But Joyce was haunted by the fate of Parnell, who "went from country to country, city to city...like a hunted deer" after his affair with Kitty O'Shea was exposed. Quicklime was thrown in his eye in Castlecomer: Joyce feared a like fate if he returned. He tried to remake his Dublin, have it without living in it – and as F. Scott Fitzgerald saw, "the price was high." He ended less writer, more symbol, like Beckett – an Irishman in exile who can't be in Britain but can be in Europe, an unvanquished Dubliner opening the door in a house of neutral shades, smelling of disinfectant, in Switzerland, "the last *Naturpark des Geistes.*" Dead of a perforated ulcer, he was laid in Zurich's Fluntern Cemetery on 15 January, 1941.

A sense of place is so important in Joyce that it affected the way people read him. Cyril Connolly says: "For me any criticism of *Ulysses* will be affected by a wet morning in Florence when in the empty library of a villa with a smell of wood-smoke, the faint eaves drop, I held the uncouth volume dazedly open in the big armchair." And at the end of her *A Time In Rome* – the city where "The Dead" and *Ulysses* were conceived – Elizabeth Bowen writes what could be the epitaph for Joyce's Dublin: "My darling, my darling. Here we have no abiding city."

JAMES JOYCE'S DUBLIN: *The key settings of Joyce's novels, plotted on this map, encompass the whole city.*

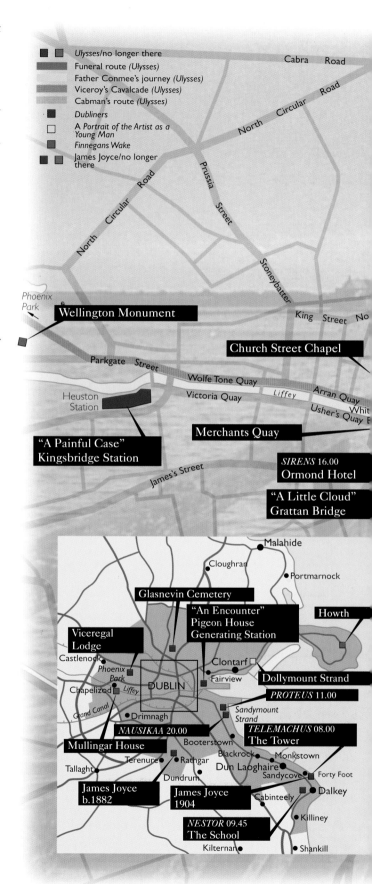

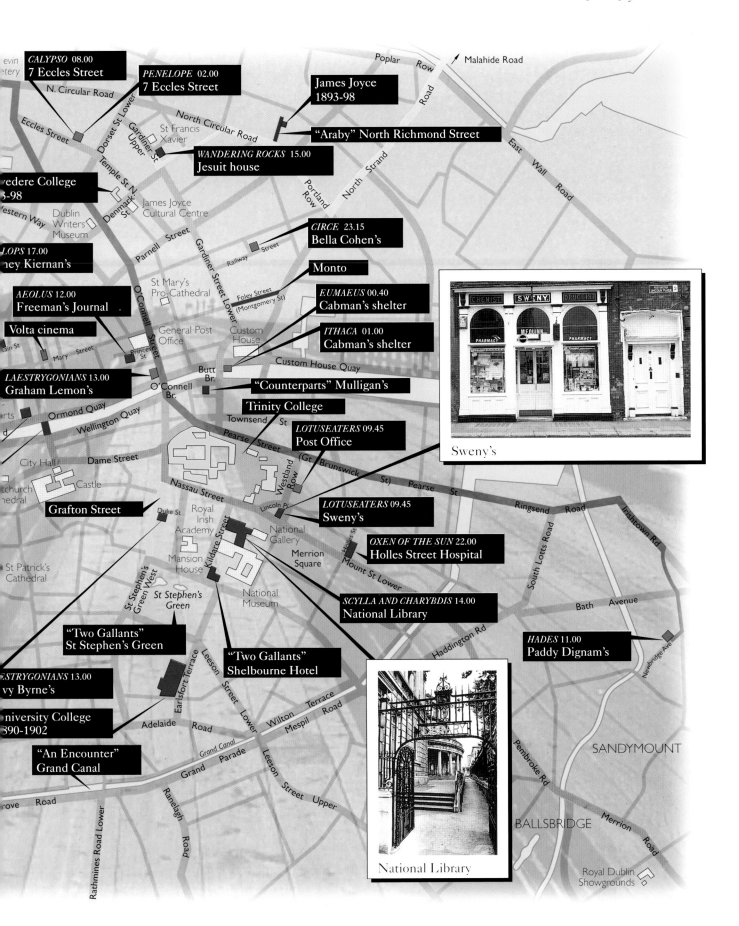

CALYPSO 08.00
7 Eccles Street

PENELOPE 02.00
7 Eccles Street

**James Joyce
1893-98**

"Araby" North Richmond Street

WANDERING ROCKS 15.00
Jesuit house

CIRCE 23.15
Bella Cohen's

Monto

EUMAEUS 00.40
Cabman's shelter

ITHACA 01.00
Cabman's shelter

LOPS 17.00
ney Kiernan's

AEOLUS 12.00
Freeman's Journal

Volta cinema

LAESTRYGONIANS 13.00
Graham Lemon's

"Counterparts" Mulligan's

Trinity College

LOTUSEATERS 09.45
Post Office

LOTUSEATERS 09.45
Sweny's

OXEN OF THE SUN 22.00
Holles Street Hospital

SCYLLA AND CHARYBDIS 14.00
National Library

HADES 11.00
Paddy Dignam's

Grafton Street

**"Two Gallants"
St Stephen's Green**

**"Two Gallants"
Shelbourne Hotel**

ESTRYGONIANS 13.00
vy Byrne's

**niversity College
890-1902**

**"An Encounter"
Grand Canal**

Sweny's

National Library

WRITERS OF THE GREAT WAR

At the end of Thomas Mann's (1875–1955) epic novel, *The Magic Mountain* (1924), the young hero Hans Castorp descends from the "magic mountain," the sanatorium at Davos where for seven years he's been a tuberculosis patient, onto the flatland. He enters a new world: "the moist air rent by a sharp singing whine, a raging, swelling howl as of some hound of hell, that ends its course in a splitting, a splintering and sprinkling, a crackling, a coruscation; by groans and shrieks.... It is the flat-land, it is the war." We aren't told whether Hans survives the Great War or not. But his pre-war bourgeois German world has gone to disaster. And Mann himself, who started the book as a social satire in 1912, would take ten years, in war and post-war crisis, to complete it – by which time it had changed into an apocalyptic post-war work.

The Magic Mountain was by no means the only modern work to be transformed by the crisis that struck Europe in August 1914. Many of the great Modernist epics – Joyce's *Ulysses* (1922), Proust's *Remembrance of Things Past*, 1913–27), Lawrence's *Women in Love* (1920), Forster's *A Passage to India* (1924) – were not just written over the War, but radically changed by it. But then all writing was changed by what happened to Europe between 1914 and 1918. From country after country, on both sides of the fronts and the barbed-wire, young men went into battle with notions of heroism, patriotism and sacrifice in their hearts and minds. Henry James, near his life's end, pessimistically warned that this was the close of the advance of civilization, and that the "war has used up words." But for many this seemed not true: to them, it all looked like a great twentieth century adventure: "a bright and jolly war," promised the German Crown Prince.

British Georgian poets like the promising young Rupert Brooke ("Now, God be thanked Who matched us with His hour/And caught our youth, and wakened us from sleeping") and Julian Grenfell celebrated the immortal moment. (Brooke died at Gallipoli on 23 April, 1915, Grenfell of wounds suffered near Ypres a month later.) But they were not the only patriots who looked to the War with expectation. "The war is the great remedy," wrote the sculptor Gaudier-Brzeska (died in action 1915) in *Blast*, the experimental Vorticist magazine which produced two issues, one just before and one just after the real blasts started. Likewise German Expressionist poets exhilarated in the great cleansing. "Celebrate the aeroplane, flood the museums," the Italian Futurist F.T. Marinetti had cried. And he too delighted in the great explosion of action and destruction that would purge the past and create the vitalist modern spirit, when he went to war against the Austrians after Italy entered the conflict in May 1915. The

It took the hideous stalemate of the trenches, the war of attrition, the battles for a few feet of mud, the rising toll of corpses, the horrors of poison gas and machine warfare, to question and quell most of the myths about the glory of war.

Henri Barbusse's Le Feu, *published in two volumes, right, was one of the first novels to tell of the horrors of trench warfare in France, and was read all over the world.*

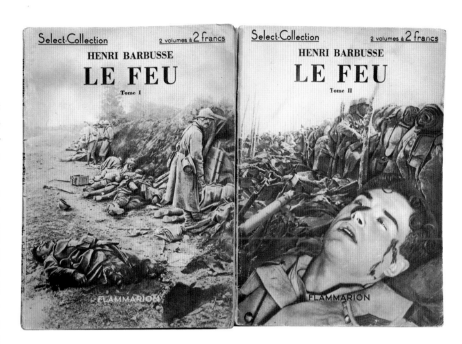

French experimental poet Guillaume Apollinaire felt himself attached to France by warfare as never before – even though he was seriously wounded in action.

It soon became clear to most that, as Edmund Blunden would put it, there was: "No road. No thoroughfare. Neither race had won, nor could win, the War. The War had won, and would go on winning." German writers like Herman Hesse withdrew to neutral Switzerland – where, out of the remnants of German Expressionism, the Dada movement was born, declaring the meaningless nature of the age. In Britain D.H. Lawrence, Siegfried Sassoon and others began to express pacifist sympathies. More common was just a sense of grim and tragic resignation. As H.M. Tomlinson put it in 1915, "the parapet, the wire and the mud" were now "permanent features of human existence."

Henry James had been right: one of the significant casualties of war proved to be language and literature itself. As Paul Fussell observes in his book *The Great War and Modern Memory* (1975), about the many writings troops sent home, "the presumed inadequacy of language itself to convey the facts about trench warfare is one of the motifs of all who wrote about the war." And, even after the myths of patriotism and sacrifice had subsided, language still felt powerless to capture the atrocity, the horror, the extremity. As Fussell ironically adds, writers like Pound, Joyce, Lawrence and Yeats were, after all, not at the front to teach those there how to do the job better.

The poets went in first. It was poetry, with its lyric or tragic brevity, that could first capture war's mythic prospects and then its true immediacy. We have numerous anthologies of war poetry now that trace the movement, over the terrible years and the quick-changing generations, from patriotic affirmation to rejection, disenchantment and rage. Poets like Ivor Gurney and Isaac Rosenberg distilled the fervour and the boredom, the excitement and the endless horrific moments, showing the horror, the pity, the endless spectacle of slaughter and wounding, the mental crisis, the ultimate rage. "God! how I hate you, you cheerful young men/ Whose pious poetry blossoms on your graves/ As soon as you are in them," wrote Arthur Graeme West (killed April 1917). Now

"In all my dreams, before my helpless sight,
He plunges at me, guttering, choking, drowning.

If in some smothering dreams, you too could pace
Behind the wagon that we flung him in,
And watch the white eyes writhing in his face,
His hanging face, like a devil's sick of sin;
If you could hear, at every jolt, the blood
Come gargling from the froth-corrupted lungs,
Obscene as cancer, bitter as the cud
Of vile, incurable sores on innocent tongues –
My friend, you would not tell with such high zest
To children ardent for some desperate glory,
The old Lie: Dulce et Decorum Est
Pro patria mori."

"Dulce et Decorum Est" Wilfred Owen

the poetry was in the pity, said Wilfred Owen (killed 4 November, 1918).

For most Europeans, the *belle époque* ended and the war started between 28 July and 4 August, 1914. "Heir apparent and his consort assassinated this morning by means of an explosive nature," the British Consul in Sarajevo cabled home on 28 July. Mobilization on the Eastern front started at once. On 4 August, Britain entered the conflict, after the Germans invaded France through Belgium. The horrors and carnage, the range and uncertainty of outcome, intensified for the next four years; the war spread right across Europe – France, Belgium, Mesopotamia, Turkey, Italy, the Eastern front. It became

a World War when, in April 1917, Woodrow Wilson brought the United States in on the Allied side. It became a larger historical crisis still when the Bolshevik Revolution succeeded later that same year, taking Russia out of the war. By mid-1918 Ludendorff's armies, relieved from the Eastern front, almost succeeded in invading Paris. They were repulsed, and on 11 November, 1918 the Armistice was signed.

Although poets like Siegfried Sassoon, left, and Rupert Brooke, right, began by praising the glory of war, they soon realized its horrors: Sassoon was invalided home in 1916 and became a virtual pacifist; Brook died of blood poisoning aboard a hospital ship in the Aegean sea when he was only 25 years old.

By the time it was done, the War had cost the Allies five million men and the Central Powers three and a half million. The impact on Western sensibility and writing was massive. As the German critic Walter Benjamin vividly put it: "men returned from the battlefield grown silent – not richer but poorer in communicable experience. A generation that had gone to school on a horse-drawn streetcar now stood under the open sky in a countryside in which nothing remained unchanged but the clouds, and beneath those clouds, in a field of force of destructive torrents and explosions, was the tiny, fragile human body."

The Great War killed much else beside a generation of young soldiers. It killed romanticism and sentimentalism, dreams of heroic action and imperial adventure. In the years after, the sensibility of the horror of what had happened seeped into the texture of Western literature. The War had upturned entire empires, overthrown ruling castes and classes, destroyed cities, changed the world balance of power. Europe was altered from a bastion of Western history and civilization into a shattered, unstable modern battlefield; an unwilling America inherited the baton of responsibility for new history. It

had shattered language, old ideas of progress, established faiths. It ushered in an era of what C.E. Montague called *Disenchantment* (1922), of what William Gerhardie, in a novel of the same year, titled simply *Futility*. It also created a crisis of artistic forms.

The *avant-gardes* that already had developed from the turn of the century in the great European cities like Vienna, Paris, Berlin and London had brought in major new movements in fiction, poetry, drama, architecture and philosophy. They had begun to break open the frame of realism, had celebrated vitalism and abstraction, rendered art more mechanical and fragmentary. But it took the War to ensure the inevitability of this revolt, and anchor it firmly to modern history. The twenties was the heyday of Modernism – of *Ulysses* and *The Magic Mountain* and *The Waste Land*, *The Duino Elegies* and *Mrs Dalloway* and *The Sound and the Fury*. But these books, with their fragments shored against the ruins, were all flavoured and shaped not just by new techniques but by the knowledge of crisis, the realization that the Modern spirit was now steeped in blood and disaster.

Perhaps the clearest imprint was on the war novel, which in the wake of the conflict became a dominant modern form over the course of the twenties. The novel is generally slower than poetry to react to the immediate moment, but there were realistic contemporary novels of the front and trench warfare. The most notable was Henri Barbusse's chilling *Le Feu*, about French troops in the mud of the line, which appeared in France in 1916. Its English translation *Under Fire* (1917) was soon being read by

British and American troops at the front, and influenced writers from Wilfred Owen to the young Ernest Hemingway, serving with the Red Cross Ambulance service in Italy, where he was seriously wounded. Thereafter a sequence of novels appeared which came fresh from the front and the field, capturing the life of troops in the trenches, on whatever side of the eternal mud or barbed wire they happened to be.

These included the American John Dos Passos's *One Man's Initiation* (1920) and his *Three Soldiers* (1921), e.e. cummings' *The Enormous Room* (1922), based on his experiences as an American ambulance man in a French military prison, Jaroslav Hasek's grotesque black comic novel about the little corporal in the Czech army, *The Good Soldier Schweyk* (written 1921-23), R.H. Mottram's *The Spanish Farm Trilogy* (1927), Ford Madox Ford's four-volume British epic of war and social collapse, *Parade's End* (1924–28), the German Arnold Zweig's anti-war *The Case of Sergeant Grisha* (1928). Over the twenties, the war novel became a central modern genre. By the end of the decade, when fears of yet another war grew, it became a flood.

In 1929 Erich Maria Remarque published his epic of doomed life in the German trenches, *All Quiet on the Western Front*, and Ernest Hemingway his account of the Italian campaign, including the famous retreat from Caporetto, *A Farewell to Arms*. The same year saw Richard Aldington's bitter satire of war and Victorian values, *Death of a Hero*, and Robert Graves's no less ironic memoir *Good-bye to All That*. In 1930 came Siegfried Sassoon's *Memoirs of an Infantry Officer*, Henry Williamson's *The Patriot's Progress*, Frederick Manning's vivid disturbing tale of the experiences of an ordinary British soldier, *The Middle Parts of Fortune*, also called *Her Privates We*. These did more than re-create horrific experiences; they displayed a war that had plainly failed to end war or create a world fit for heroes to live in. It's estimated some seven hundred war books were published in Britain alone by 1930. And in German and French literature too, the same horrifying subject dominated much writing.

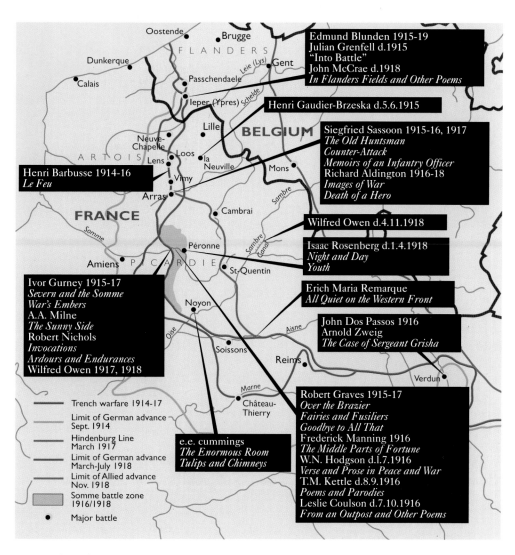

THE FIRST WORLD WAR: *The horror of war, described most poignantly in poetry, was made even more terrible because so many of the young poets were killed: this map shows the distribution of writers around the Front during the War.*

If western writing after 1918 feels fundamentally different from writing before 1914, that is surely because the shattering effect of the Great War radiated its effects right through literature. It fragmented, hardened and modernized the voice of twentieth century literature, shook its sense of language, changed its view of history and reality. In *The Great War and Modern Memory*, Fussell argues that the passage of writing during the Great War "from pre-war freedom to wartime bondage, frustration and absurdity signals just as much as does the experience of Joyce's Bloom, Hemingway's Frederic Henry or Kafka's Joseph K. the passage of one kind of writing from one mode to another," leading to a literature of irony. And in many ways the huge battle maps of the First World War were to be firmly laid over nearly all modern writing.

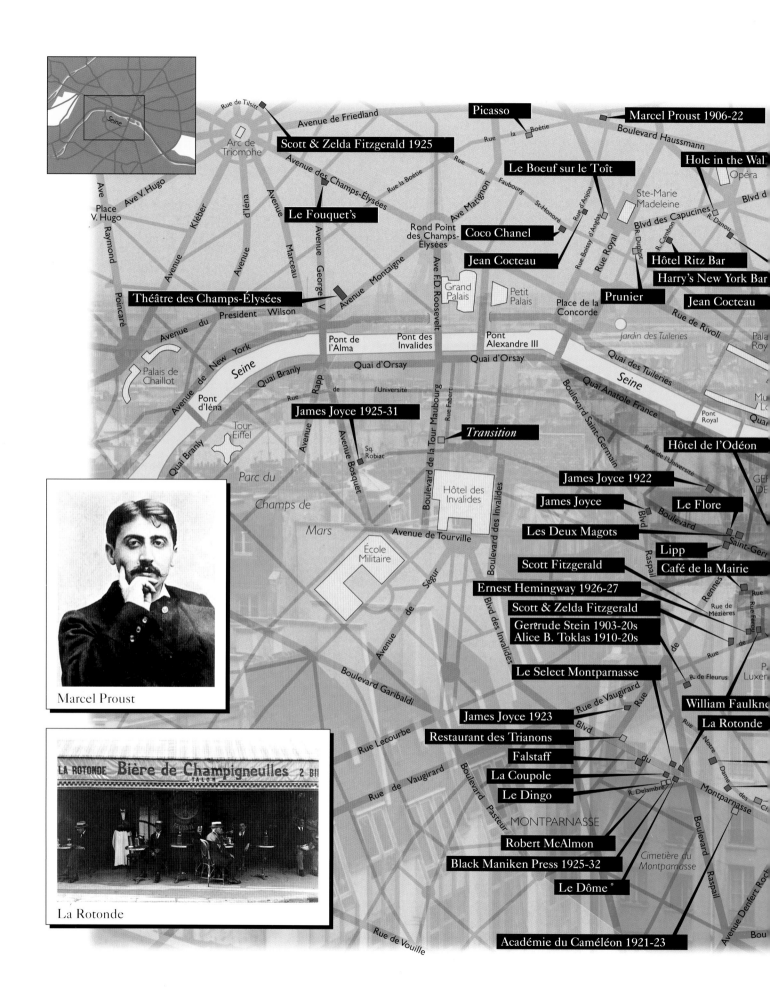

Picasso

Marcel Proust 1906-22

Scott & Zelda Fitzgerald 1925

Arc de Triomphe

Hole in the Wall

Opéra

Le Boeuf sur le Toît

Ste-Marie Madeleine

Blvd d

Le Fouquet's

Coco Chanel

Hôtel Ritz Bar

Jean Cocteau

Harry's New York Bar

Théâtre des Champs-Élysées

Grand Palais

Petit Palais

Prunier

Jean Cocteau

Place de la Concorde

Palais de Chaillot

Jardin des Tuileries

Tour Eiffel

James Joyce 1925-31

Transition

Hôtel de l'Odéon

Parc du

James Joyce 1922

Champs de

James Joyce

Le Flore

Hôtel des Invalides

Les Deux Magots

Mars

École Militaire

Avenue de Tourville

Lipp

Scott Fitzgerald

Café de la Mairie

Ernest Hemingway 1926-27

Scott & Zelda Fitzgerald

Gertrude Stein 1903-20s
Alice B. Toklas 1910-20s

Le Select Montparnasse

William Faulkner

James Joyce 1923

La Rotonde

Restaurant des Trianons

Falstaff

La Coupole

Le Dingo

MONTPARNASSE

Robert McAlmon

Cimetière du Montparnasse

Black Maniken Press 1925-32

Le Dôme

Académie du Caméléon 1921-23

Marcel Proust

La Rotonde

[174]

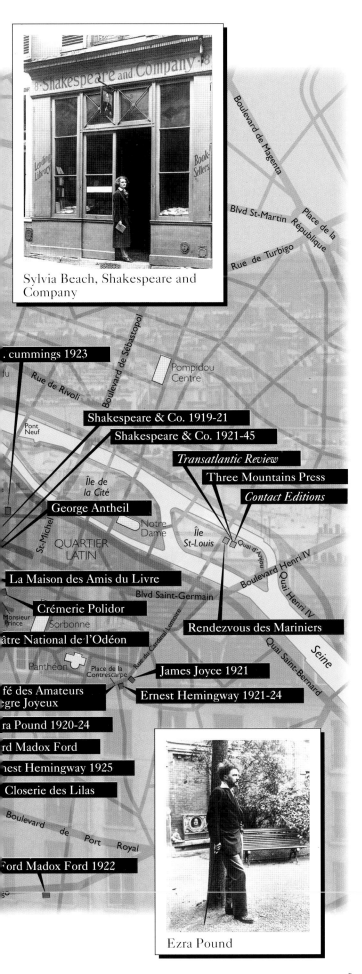

Sylvia Beach, Shakespeare and Company

. cummings 1923

Rue de Rivoli

Pompidou Centre

Boulevard de Sébastopol

Boulevard de Magenta

Blvd St-Martin

Place de la République

Rue de Turbigo

Pont Neuf

Shakespeare & Co. 1919-21

Shakespeare & Co. 1921-45

Transatlantic Review

Three Mountains Press

Contact Editions

Île de la Cité

George Antheil

St-Michel

QUARTIER LATIN

Notre Dame

Île St-Louis

Quai d'Anjou

Boulevard Henri IV

Quai Henri IV

La Maison des Amis du Livre

Blvd Saint-Germain

Crémerie Polidor

Monsieur Prince

Sorbonne

âtre National de l'Odéon

Rue du Cardinal Lemoine

Rendezvous des Mariniers

Quai Saint-Bernard

Seine

Panthéon

Place de la Contrescarpe

James Joyce 1921

fé des Amateurs gre Joyeux

Ernest Hemingway 1921-24

ra Pound 1920-24

rd Madox Ford

nest Hemingway 1925

Closerie des Lilas

Boulevard de Port Royal

ord Madox Ford 1922

Ezra Pound

PARIS IN THE TWENTIES

According to Ezra Pound (1885–1972), Paris in the 1920s was "the laboratory of ideas in the arts." The cosmopolitan city suffered badly in the Great War. The glowing *belle époque* ended, the wounded came home, the franc slid in value, the scars of the German bombardment of 1918 showed. But what Henry James called "the great literary workshop of Paris" continued to flourish. In fact, over the troubled yet gay twenties, Paris became the crucible of the Modern movement – a place of manifestos, wild exhibitions, and public outrages by the movements of Dada and Surrealism, which stopped traffic with parades asking "Do you want to slap a corpse?"

Even before 1914 the excitement began. In 1908 the Cubist movement in abstract painting was announced. In 1913 the Russian Diaghilev shocked Paris with his ballet of Stravinsky's *The Rites of Spring*, and Marcel Proust published the first book of *Remembrance of Things Past*, his great multi-volume novel of Modernist consciousness. A recluse in his famous cork-lined room at 102 Boulevard Haussmann, on the Right Bank, Proust wrote on through the First World War, recording not only the delicate world of childhood memory but the death of the old high society Paris. He was still writing on the day of his death. His great funeral in 1922 marked the end of one modern era, the start of another.

In 1919 André Breton and Louis Aragon had founded the magazine *Littérature*, and Surrealism was born. In 1920 the Romanian Tristan Tzara organized the first tumultuous festival of Dada. From 1922 to 1925 the postwar Modern movement peaked – and mostly in Paris. 1922 saw the publication of James Joyce's *Ulysses*, Paul Valéry's *Charmes*, and T.S. Eliot's *The Waste Land*, edited in Paris by Ezra Pound. In 1923 Jean Cocteau and François Mauriac published major works and Ford started the *Transatlantic Review*. In 1924 the review *La Revolution surrealiste* was founded and Cocteau's *Poems* and Ernest

PARIS IN THE TWENTIES: *Montparnasse became the centre for expatriates who came to Paris in the twenties, where life revolved around the cafés and bars like the Dôme and the Deux Magots.*

Gertrude Stein, left, and Alice B. Toklas, right, lived in an apartment on the Left Bank which had French and expatriate visitors alike: among them Picasso and Matisse, and a raft of fresh-faced young Americans hoping for literary fame.

Hemingway's *In Our Time* were published. And as Ford said, "there was never a day so gay for the Arts as any twenty-four hours of the early twenties in Paris."

So if you were a young unpublished writer with radical ambitions, like Ernest Hemingway, who arrived in December 1921, Paris was the only place to be. It was the centre of experiment, the creative writing class of the twenties, the university of Modernism. Major French writers – Breton and Aragon, Paul Claudel, Paul Valéry, André Gide, Jean Cocteau – were experimenting with new forms, genres, manifestations. It was, Hemingway explained later, a "moveable feast." Year after year, writers swarmed in from everywhere, driven by exile, post-war political upheaval, literary censorship, or just the need for a drink. London had grown depressed after the War. The United States had President Harding, Puritanism and Prohibition. They came in, said Ezra Pound, like "leaves in the autumn," while the American art collector and writer Gertrude Stein explained in *Paris, France* (1940): "they all came to France, a great many to paint pictures and naturally they could not do that at home, or write, they could not do that at home either, they could be dentists at home."

"A lost generation," Stein called them. But if they felt lost in history, they found themselves in Paris. Stein lived on the Left Bank with her companion Alice B. Toklas, in a studio apartment, filled with Cézannes and Picassos, at 27 rue de Fleurus, near the Luxembourg Gardens, and by the twenties her salon (Paris was all salons) was a required port-of-call for all the young expatriates. Ezra Pound moved from London to Montparnasse in 1920 and settled in a "*pavillon*" at 70 bis rue Notre Dame-des-Champs – very handy for the Dôme, Coupole and Rotonde cafés, literary meeting places, and the quieter Closerie des Lilas – where he trimmed and adjusted Eliot's *The Waste Land* and wrote his *Cantos* and an opera about Villon. He tempted James Joyce, already in exile in Trieste, to Paris because it was "the cheapest place last year." After he arrived in 1920, Joyce, who changed from address to address, soon became a key figure of the literary commu-

nity. In October 1921, he finished surely the greatest Modernist novel of the century, *Ulysses*, at 5 Boulevard Raspail. Ford Madox Ford, in flight from Britain for sexual as well as literary reasons, came in 1922, and rented a studio cottage at 65 Boulevard Arago.

Many more joined in. French hospitality to writers, a cheap exchange rate, the inspirational access to wine and spirits, even the post-war disillusion and the "lost generation" mood of gay despair all helped. Sherwood Anderson, Thornton Wilder, e.e. cummings, and more all came in from the States. F. Scott and Zelda Fitzgerald were often there, but preferred the Ritz and the other comforts of the Right Bank. Hemingway rented a small fourth-floor apartment with a shared squat toilet at 74 rue du Cardinal-Lemoine, behind the Panthéon, by a sawmill and lumberyard – all fondly remembered in his tart memoir *A Moveable Feast* (published posthumously in 1964). Later, in 1924, he would move to a larger apartment near Pound at 112 rue Notre-Dame-des-Champs. Pound helped him to write, he taught Pound to box. He met Sylvia Beach, owner of the English language bookstore Shakespeare and Company, who started at 8 rue Dupuytren, and later moved to 12 rue de l'Odéon. In 1922 she published from the bookstore James Joyce's *Ulysses* in an edition of 1,000 copies when it was banned elsewhere.

Within five years of the War, at a time when the Americanization of Paris was speeding up, a whole expatriate

CHRONOLOGY OF MAJOR PUBLICATIONS AND PERFORMANCES

1920 Ezra Pound *Hugh Selwyn Mauberley*
1921 John Dos Passos *Three Soldiers*
New York Dada *magazine (first and last volume)*
Jean Cocteau's ballet *Les Mariés de la Tour Eiffel*
1922 e.e. cummings *The Enormous Room*,
T.S. Eliot *The Waste Land*,
James Joyce *Ulysses*,
1923 e.e. cummings *Tulips and Chimneys*
1924 Ford Madox Ford's *Transatlantic Review* first published
Ford Madox Ford *Some Do Not*, Volume I of *Parade's End*
William Carlos Williams *The Great American Novel*
1925 Ernest Hemingway *In Our Time*
F. Scott Fitzgerald *The Great Gatsby*
Josephine Baker *La Revue Nègre*
1926 Ernest Hemingway *The Sun Also Rises*
1927 Ernest Hemingway *Men Without Women*
Last stage appearance by Isadora Duncan
Gertrude Stein Libretto of *Four Saints in Three Acts*
1928 George Gershwin *An American in Paris*
1929 Erich Maria Remarque *All Quiet on the Western Front*
Ernest Hemingway *A Farewell to Arms*

geography had developed in Paris. Montparnasse was the chief centre. Here were the smart well-lit cafés and the zinc bars where writers met, drank, talked, even wrote. Here were smarter bars and clubs like Cocteau's Le Boeuf Sur Le Toit, and the salons. There were English-language newspapers, magazines and bookstores. Small presses kept springing up to print the experimental work produced: Robert McAlmon's Contact Editions, which in 1923 printed Hemingway's first book *Three Stories and Ten Poems* and William Carlos Williams's *Spring and All*; McAlmon's and William Bird's Three Mountains Press, which printed *In Our Time* (1924), Pound's early *Cantos*, Stein's massive *The Making of Americans* (1925), Djuna Barnes and Nathanael West.

What was achieved in Paris in the twenties? In the boulevards and small tree-lined streets of Montparnasse, the Modern movement found a safe home in the post-war chaos. The writers came and left again, but the bars, the magazines, the movements stayed, providing a continuity. A busy multi-lingual artistic life developed. The movements multiplied, sometimes uniting, sometimes attacking each other fiercely: Symbolism, Futurism, Expressionism, Unanisme, Dadaism and Surrealism. Paris was a place of amusement and exile, experiment and disillusion, artistic gaiety and drunken depression. Radical artistic ideas flourished, and it was an era of major French works, of the later volumes of Proust's *Remembrance of Things Past*, of Valéry's "The Graveyard by the Sea" (1932), of Cocteau's *Poems* and Gide's *The Counterfeiters* (1927).

Just as importantly, modern American literature found itself linking up with many international movements. From Paris in the twenties and early thirties, Hemingway, Pound, William Carlos Williams, William Faulkner, Gertrude Stein, Anaïs Nin and Henry Miller opened American writing out to an experimentalism it had not had before. American writing became accepted in Europe, and French and American writers influenced each other. Many of the key American books of the experimental twenties were born in Paris: Hemingway's *In Our Time* and *A Farewell to Arms*, Stein's *The Making of Americans*, William Carlos Williams's *The Great American Novel*. New British and Irish writing too flourished there. Joyce's *Ulysses*, Ford's *Parade's End*, and later, the fiction of Jean Rhys, Lawrence Durrell and Samuel Beckett, all depended on Paris. The Modern movement that laid its imprint right across the most daring arts of the century owes nearly everything to Montparnasse.

Inevitably enough, expatriate Paris and its "lost generation" became itself the subject of literature. In 1926 Ernest Hemingway published *The Sun Also Rises*, set among the Latin Quarter expatriates, largely around the bars of the Dingo and the Select. It is a novel of smart but

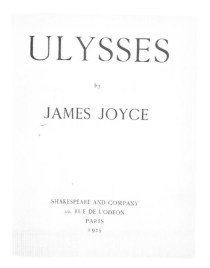

ULYSSES

by

JAMES JOYCE

SHAKESPEARE AND COMPANY
12. RUE DE L'ODÉON
PARIS
1925

James Joyce's Ulysses, *was completed in October 1921 and published by Sylvia Beach's bookshop, Shakespeare and Co. (which Beach and Joyce are shown sitting in,* below*), after being banned for obscenity in America and Britain. The title page disclaimed any typographical errors: proofing was rushed, as a succession of typists refused to type the most explicit chapters. The husband of one of the typists even threw several pages into the fire in disgust.*

jaded spirits, the post-war wounded, who chase life through an elaborate expatriate geography that can still be tracked round the streets and bars of Montparnasse. Many Americans travelled to Paris to live the life of the book. F. Scott Fitzgerald recorded more of the expatriate scene, in Paris and the South of France, in *Tender is the Night* (1934), noting "by 1928 Paris had grown suffocating. With each new shipment of Americans spawned by the boom the quality fell off, until toward the end there was something sinister about the crazy boatloads."

But it was in 1929, with the Great Depression, that the great creative era ended. Most of the exiles, their bankdrafts from home stopped, went home to write of a darker age, taking their Modernist instincts with them. This is one of the most vividly remembered eras of modern writing. But, as Hemingway said in *A Moveable Feast*: "Paris was always worth it, and you received return from whatever you brought to it. But this is how Paris was in the early days when we were very poor and very happy" – and when so much important work was written.

THE WORLD OF BLOOMSBURY

"I ask nothing better than that all reviewers, for ever, and everywhere, should call me a highbrow," Virginia Woolf wrote teasingly. "If they like to add Bloomsbury, WCI, that is the correct postal address, and my telephone number is in the Directory. But if your reviewer...dares hint that I live in South Kensington, I will sue him for libel." Bloomsbury, WCI, is a postal district of London: the area of grey Georgian houses, straight streets, long terraces and leafy squares, pubs, restaurants, small publishers and specialist bookshops around the elegant British Museum and Senate House. It was also, as Woolf implies, something more: the name of a cultural climate, a social and intellectual grouping, that challenged the age, asserted the spirit of art, and had a massive impact on the culture, arts and manners of modern Britain.

The photograph of Virginia Stephen, above, *was taken in 1903, before her marriage to Leonard Woolf in 1912.*

"Bloomsbury" stretched far beyond Bloomsbury. It was a style, a clubby club, a tone of voice, a social caste, a passion for intelligence, a taste for "beauty and truth," a narcissistic yet independent-minded elite. It was highly British, very cosmopolitan. It represented the post-Victorian, experimental, modern, not just in writing and painting, but in philosophy, politics, economics, interior design and sex. It was a web of family relations, intricate friendships, sexual liaisons, snobberies. It often resembled a family quarrel, sons and daughters at war with mothers and fathers. It was a campaign against the Establishment, which duly became an Establishment itself. Some loved it, some fell out with it, some hated it. But without "Bloomsbury" Britain would never really have had a Modern movement at all, or some of its best art and literature.

To be a "Bloomsbury" it helped to have gone to Cambridge at the turn of the century, and have joined the "Apostles" or the Mid-night Society at Trinity, as did Thoby Stephen, Leonard Woolf, E.M. Forster, Lytton Strachey and Clive Bell. It also helped to study with the philosopher G.E.

Moore, whose *Principia Ethica* (1903) urged "By far the most valuable things we know or can imagine are certain states of consciousness, which may roughly be described as the pleasures of human intercourse and the enjoyment of beautiful objects." Virginia Stephen, being not son but daughter of the great Victorian critic Sir Leslie Stephen, was the only one of the family not to go to Cambridge, which outraged her – but she thought and behaved exactly as if she had.

When papa died in 1904, Virginia, sister Vanessa, and brothers Thoby and Adrian, left the family home at 22 Hyde Park Gate in smart Kensington for a less fashionable, almost improper address: 46 Gordon Square.

In Georgian houses nearby, more "Bloomsberries" gathered, like writer David Garnett, biographer Lytton Strachey, painter Duncan Grant, economist John Maynard Keynes. Each Thursday their house was the meeting place for those interested in the new ideas and aesthetics sweeping the post-Victorian world.

In 1907, Forster published *A Room With a View*, Vanessa

Vanessa Bell's studio in 8 Fitzroy Square, left, *is depicted here in a painting by the artist herself.*

BLOOMSBURY: *When Virginia, Vanessa, Thoby and Adrian Stephen moved to 46 Gordon Square in 1904 Bloomsbury became famous as a community and a centre of the arts.*

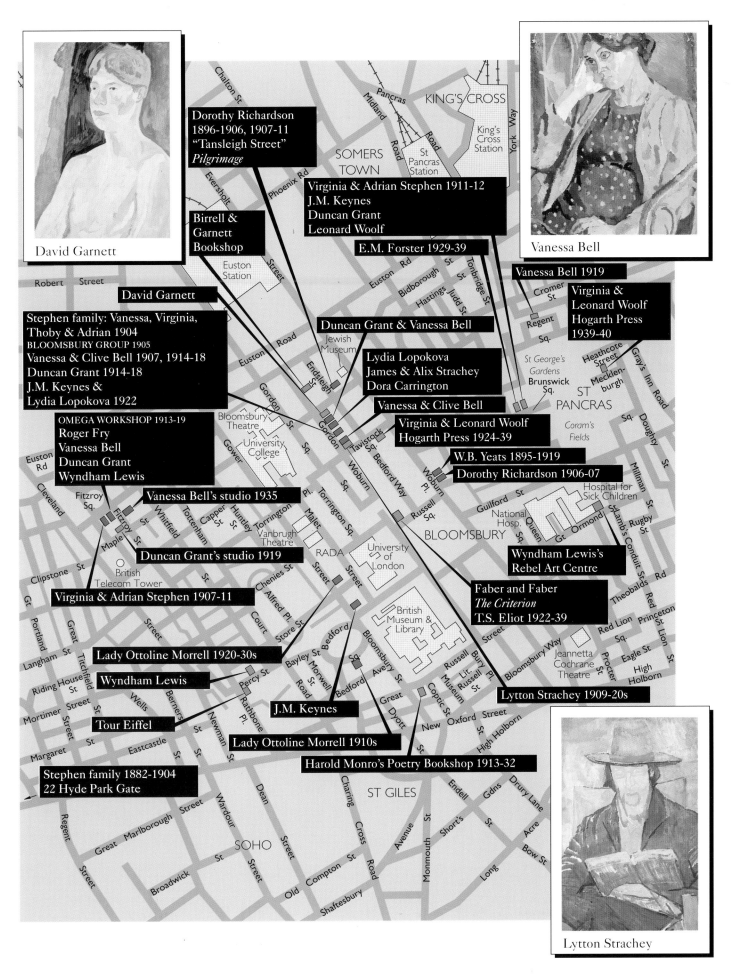

David Garnett

Vanessa Bell

Lytton Strachey

Dorothy Richardson
1896-1906, 1907-11
"Tansleigh Street"
Pilgrimage

Birrell &
Garnett
Bookshop

David Garnett

Stephen family: Vanessa, Virginia,
Thoby & Adrian 1904
BLOOMSBURY GROUP 1905
Vanessa & Clive Bell 1907, 1914-18
Duncan Grant 1914-18
J.M. Keynes &
Lydia Lopokova 1922

OMEGA WORKSHOP 1913-19
Roger Fry
Vanessa Bell
Duncan Grant
Wyndham Lewis

Vanessa Bell's studio 1935

Duncan Grant's studio 1919

Virginia & Adrian Stephen 1907-11

Lady Ottoline Morrell 1920-30s

Wyndham Lewis

Tour Eiffel

Stephen family 1882-1904
22 Hyde Park Gate

Virginia & Adrian Stephen 1911-12
J.M. Keynes
Duncan Grant
Leonard Woolf

E.M. Forster 1929-39

Duncan Grant & Vanessa Bell

Lydia Lopokova
James & Alix Strachey
Dora Carrington

Vanessa & Clive Bell

Virginia & Leonard Woolf
Hogarth Press 1924-39

W.B. Yeats 1895-1919

Dorothy Richardson 1906-07

J.M. Keynes

Lady Ottoline Morrell 1910s

Harold Monro's Poetry Bookshop 1913-32

Vanessa Bell 1919

Virginia &
Leonard Woolf
Hogarth Press
1939-40

Wyndham Lewis's
Rebel Art Centre

Faber and Faber
The Criterion
T.S. Eliot 1922-39

Lytton Strachey 1909-20s

Roger Fry's Omega Workshops, based in Fitzroy Square, fostered the work of the new post-impressionists.

married Clive Bell and took the Gordon Square house, Virginia and Adrian moved to nearby 29 Fitzroy Square. Virginia had assumed her father's mantle, writing criticism for the *Times Literary Supplement*, and had started the novel that became *The Voyage Out* (1915). 1910 was a key year. A new king, George V, took the throne, and Forster published *Howards End*, a portrait of a Britain split between male business persons and enlightened female intellectuals. In December Roger Fry rented the Grafton Galleries to mount an exhibition of French Post-Impressionist paintings by van Gogh, Cézanne, Picasso, Matisse. It shocked London into either rage or modernity – and marked the start of a new age of movements and manifestos. Up until the First World War movements multiplied: Edward Marsh's Georgianism, Ezra Pound's Imagism, born in a Kensington teashop, Wyndham Lewis's Vorticism. It was all, said one participant, Ford Madox Ford, "an opening world." The philistines fell, the *avant-garde* triumphed. Virginia sensed a new "modern" fiction, based not on plot but consciousness, Pound a new kind of poetry based on *vers libre*.

Bloomsbury played a central – but not the only – part. In 1911 Virginia moved to 38 Brunswick Square to form a suspiciously enlightened household with Grant, Keynes, and Leonard Woolf, whom she married in 1912. 1911 also saw another Post-Impressionist exhibition, and the founding of Imagism. In 1913 D.H. Lawrence published his controversial *Sons and Lovers*, Clive Bell announced "significant

form," Roger Fry founded the Omega Workshops for new artists and designers. Wyndham Lewis, a member at first, fell out with him and went off to found his own Rebel Art Centre, dubbing the Omega Workshops "Mr Fry's curtain and pincushion factory in Fitzroy Square."

The War dispersed the Bloomsbury group. Virginia and Leonard had moved to Clifford's Inn, but in 1913 after Virginia's attempted suicide, they sought a quieter life in Sussex, already known as a nest of singing birds (Henry James, Stephen Crane, Joseph Conrad, Ford Madox Ford, H.G. Wells and Rudyard Kipling had all lived here). They found an old cottage at Asheham, near Lewes. Soon Bloomsbury wintered in London and summered in Sussex. In 1915, the Woolfs found a delightful farmhouse at Charleston, near Firle, for Vanessa and Clive Bell. Duncan Grant, Vanessa's lover, came too; Lytton Strachey and Keynes were regular visitors. Bloomsbury acquired rival outposts. Lady Ottoline Morrell – Virginia called her "a Spanish galleon,

Sussex: As the First World War neared, Bloomsbury's first phase was over, and its inhabitants began to scatter, taking residences in the countryside around Sussex.

SOME BLOOMSBURY FICTIONS

1910	E.M. Forster *Howards End*
1911	Katherine Mansfield *In a German Pension*
1913	D.H. Lawrence *Sons and Lovers*
1915	D.H. Lawrence *The Rainbow*
1915	Virginia Woolf *The Voyage Out*
1915	Dorothy Richardson *Pointed Roofs*
1918	Wyndham Lewis *Tarr*
1919	Virginia Woolf *Night and Day*
1920	D.H. Lawrence *Women In Love*
1921	Aldous Huxley *Crome Yellow*
1922	Virginia Woolf *Jacob's Room*
1922	Katherine Mansfield *The Garden Party*
1923	Aldous Huxley *Antic Hay*
1924	E.M. Forster *A Passage to India*
1925	Virginia Woolf *Mrs Dalloway*
1925	Aldous Huxley *Those Barren Leaves*
1927	Virginia Woolf *To the Lighthouse*
1928	D.H. Lawrence *Lady Chatterley's Lover*
1928	Virginia Woolf *Orlando: A Biography*
1928	Aldous Huxley *Point Counterpoint*
1929	Virginia Woolf *A Room of One's Own*
1930	Vita Sackville-West *The Edwardians*
1931	Virginia Woolf *The Waves*
1931	Vita Sackville-West *All Passion Spent*
1937	Virginia Woolf *The Years*
1941	Virginia Woolf *Between the Acts*

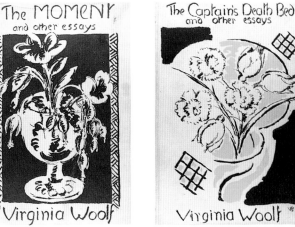

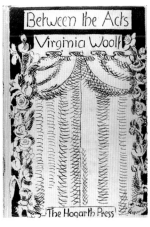

hung with gold coins" – was wife of Liberal member of Parliament, Philip Morrell, and a patroness and formidable salon hostess. In 1915 she acquired Garsington Manor, five miles outside of Oxford, where she held extravagant house parties, famed as nests of wartime pacifism and sexual intrigue. Bertrand Russell, Strachey, Carrington, the painter Mark Gertler, the Bells and Woolfs all came. So did a new generation: Siegfried Sassoon, Frieda and D.H. Lawrence, T.S. Eliot, Aldous Huxley. Like most things in Bloomsbury, the extravagant social and sexual climate soon entered literature. Set in its "dinted, dimpled, wimpled landscape," Garsington is Crome in Aldous Huxley's satirical novel *Crome Yellow* (1921). Russell, Gertler and Carrington are depicted. So

Virginia Woolf's Hogarth Press published her own novels: these first editions, above, *all have jacket illustrations by Vanessa Bell.*

is Lady Ottoline, already no stranger to fiction. She was Hermione Roddice in *Women In Love* (1920), Lawrence's vitalist attack on the sterility of modern culture.

The twenties marked the triumph of "Bloomsbury," and the "modern" spirit it affirmed. In 1915 the Woolfs leased Hogarth House in suburban Richmond, and established the Hogarth Press. It printed Virginia's own *Kew Gardens* (1919), T.S. Eliot's *The Waste Land* (1922), and many other "modern" works. In 1919, forced to leave Asheham, the Woolfs bought Monk's House in Rodmell. There was a fine garden with a lodge where Virginia wrote. Monk's House became Modern Literature; Charleston, its interior transformed by the art and design of the Bells and Grant, was Modern Art.

In 1924 the Woolfs returned to magic WC1, taking a ten year lease on a house at 52 Tavistock Square (now the Tavistock Hotel). The Hogarth Press was in the basement. Virginia was delighted, as her diary reports: "London thou art a jewel of jewels, a jasper of jocundity, music, talk, friendship, city views, publishing, something central & inexplicable, all this is within my reach, as it hasn't been since August 1913." The delight poured into the new novel, *The Hours*, published as *Mrs Dalloway* (1925). With that book, *To the Lighthouse*

(1927) and *The Waves* (1931), Virginia Woolf was seen as a major novelist who had opened out the framework of fiction. The modern novel, she said, came out of an age of new relations and connections, "a season of failures and fragments." In "Modern Fiction" (1919), she writes that life is not, as in older novels, "a series of gig-lamps systematically arranged; but a luminous halo, a semi-transparent envelope surrounding us from the beginning of consciousness to the end."

Bloomsbury was now not just friendships and attitudes, but literature. But personal relations always played a part. In 1922 Virginia met Vita Sackville-West, who grew up at the fifteenth century palace of Knole in Kent, and had married the diplomat Harold Nicolson; there was a love affair (Virginia celebrated Vita in *Orlando*, 1931). In 1930 the Nicolsons bought the abandoned castle of Sissinghurst in Kent, and transformed it and its gardens. In the tower is the press used to print the Hogarth books (including 13 titles by Vita). The most important work was a fragmentary poem by an Anglicized American who worked in Lloyd's Bank: *The Waste Land*. T. S. Eliot became a publisher at Faber and Faber in Russell Square, and editor of *The Criterion*. He helped bring the Woolfs into contact with new writers from the Gay Twenties and the Depression Thirties.

The War destroyed much of London. Bloomsbury's houses were hit; including 52 Tavistock Square and 37 Mencklenburg Square. Bombers flew over Monk's House; a German invasion was feared (and Leonard was Jewish). Shattered by this, and the death of James Joyce, Virginia felt madness returning. On 28 March, 1941 she wrote two letters, put stones in her pockets, and went to the river Ouse. Her body was found several days later. Her death marked the end of an era of British Modernism. After the War British writing would leave Bloomsbury behind, but the memorials Virginia left were great: her work provides some of the best accounts we have of literary insight.

BERLIN: THE CENTRE OF
GERMAN MODERNISM

Berlin became capital of the newly united German Reich in 1870. In the next forty years the provincial city, political and cultural centre of one of many German kingdoms, became what Mark Twain called the "German Chicago," and fourth largest city in the world. Only then did the Prussian capital become a cultural metropolis to compare with Paris or London. It had long been established as an intellectual centre when it had become a haven for fleeing French Huguenots, and Frederick the Great summoned Voltaire to his court. At the start of the nineteenth century, when Weimar and the court of Saxony were centres of German Classicism, it became

centre of German Romanticism. E.T.A. Hoffman lived (and died) here; so did Tieck, the brothers Schlegel, Achim and Bettina von Arnim, Schelling, Schopenhauer, Fichte, Clemens Brentano and Hegel. Later, in the Kaiserreich, its fame rested more on scientific achievement – although Germany's leading realist novelist, Theodor Fontane (1819–98), lived in Berlin.

The burning of 20,000 books in the Opera Square (Opernplatz) *on 10 May, 1933*, above, *symbolized the end of Berlin's literary prime.*

The city's breathtaking expansion, when it became the centre and symbol of Wilhemine Germany's modernizing push, made it the capital of German Modernism. Here as elsewhere, it started well before the First World War. If it took inspiration from Paris, it was fed by the experience of the booming metropolis, the shocks and contradictions, alienations and exhilarations of the modernizing process. What was later called "Expressionism" was a response to the city's "monstrous" yet creative energies. The poetry of Georg Heym and Ernst Stadler, the painting of George Grosz or Ernst-Ludwig Kirchner, showed an apocalyptic violence prophetic of that to come. It drew its energy from a sense of possibility and revolt against the rigidities of a restrictive culture. It was carried on by a generation that regarded the War as a liberation, fulfilling their desire for a more modern and intense life.

After the "defeat" of 1918, and the collapse of the Empire, Berlin life was chaotic, politically and culturally. Those who survived had lost the illusions and innocence of earlier Bohemia. It was a hard, fast-living place where fortunes were won and lost, careers made and destroyed, where bust followed boom and the new artistic scene had to adjust to the conditions of the market. Left against Right, Right against Left, struggled to control a new political order half-heartedly defended by a people only partially committed to the idea of democracy. In Berlin, 1918 saw a revolution and an abortive attempt to create a socialist republic. It continued with a rebellion on the left in 1919, costing more than a thousand lives, a year later with a no less futile coup on the right – until, in January 1933, Hitler and cohorts marched through the Brandenburg Gate. "I can't eat as much as I would like to puke," said the artist Max Liebermann when he watched from the balcony of his house. The twenties were framed by acts of violence. They opened with the murder of Karl

Georg Grosz, right, *in a self-portrait, was at the heart of German Expressionism.*

Bertolt Brecht, far right, *premièred his Threepenny Opera at the Theater am Schiffbauerdamm in 1928. He became a Marxist shortly afterwards and fled to Denmark in 1933.*

Berlin became the capital of Russian literature. Below right, *Aleksy Remisow* (front left) *and A.S. Jaschtschenko* (front right) *and Andrei Bely, Boris Pilnyak, Alexei Tolstoi and I.S. Sokolow-Mikitow* (left to right, back) *were all in Berlin in 1922.*

Liebknecht and Rosa Luxemburg (in 1919), then of Walter Rathenau, foreign minister, writer, Jew, keeper of the leading intellectual salon (1922). They ended in 1933, when the burning of the Reichstag was used to justify the political and ethnic cleansing of the capital's intellectual life. Many fled (Bertolt Brecht, Walter Benjamin, Alfred Döblin, Heinrich Mann). Others were imprisoned, tortured and killed (Erich Mühsam, Carl von Ossietzki).

Wilheminian Berlin had been a great national capital. The city of the disturbed and disturbing twenties was a cosmopolitan metropolis which rivalled Paris in energy and excitement, if not beauty and flair. Although W.H. Auden, Stephen Spender and famously Christopher Isherwood (*The Berlin Stories*, 1936) found it an important cultural (and sexual) centre in the early 1930s, British literary interest was directed on Paris when it focused on the continent at all. American expatriate life too was mostly a Paris affair. The exchange rate may have made life in Berlin less expensive than anywhere else in Europe, but for all its frantic excitement, it seemed a hard, graceless place. Djuna Barnes, Mina Loy and Malcolm Cowley came for brief periods, but then returned to Paris.

However, Robert McAlmon was fascinated by the city and published *Distinguished Air: Grim Fairy Tales* (1925), three precise, undeservedly forgotten studies of Berlin night-life. Josephson, editor of the expatriate magazine, *Broom*, moved it from Rome to Berlin in 1922. He dedicated an issue to the "angry city of Berlin" and its post-war *avant-garde*, publishing texts by Hülsenbeck, pictures by George Grosz and Paul Klee. Ernest Hemingway briefly came (to the opening of the dramatization of *A Farewell to Arms*). Sinclair Lewis in 1927 spent two months at the famous Hotel Adlon, where Thomas Mann stayed on his visits. Virginia Woolf came in 1919; Thomas Wolfe (*You Can't Go Home Again*, 1940) visited in 1925 and returned in 1936 to admire Hitler's Olympics.

Berlin was of far more importance to Eastern and Central Europe. Following the Bolshevik Revolution, many of Russia's emigré intelligentsia and bourgeoisie settled in the capital (360,000 at the beginning of the twenties). With 86 Russian publishing houses, daily newspapers and many bookstores, a historian could call Berlin "the capital of Russian literature." Among them was Vladimir Nabokov (1899–1977), whose father was murdered in the city by Russian fanatics in 1922. He stayed 15 more years, writing eight of his Russian novels before leaving in 1937. Andrei Bely (1880–1934), author of *Petersburg* (1913), spent two unhappy years (1921–3) there, pining for the freshness of revolutionary Moscow. Franz Kafka settled in Berlin's South West in 1923 and wrote his last stories there, before he was moved to a sanatorium near Vienna where he died in 1924.

For most Central Europeans, as for Germans, Berlin was attractive because it was the centre of a growing market for German language writing. Publishing houses like Mosse, Scherl, Ullstein, Samuel Fischer and Ernst

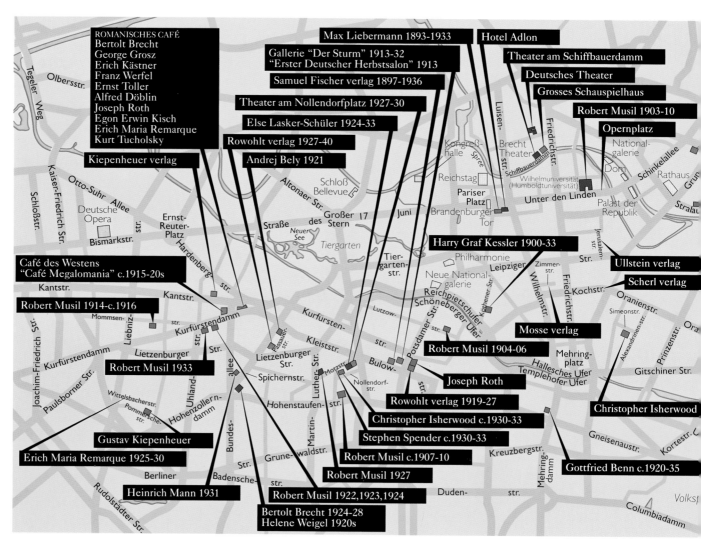

ROMANISCHES CAFÉ
Bertolt Brecht
George Grosz
Erich Kästner
Franz Werfel
Ernst Toller
Alfred Döblin
Joseph Roth
Egon Erwin Kisch
Erich Maria Remarque
Kurt Tucholsky

Max Liebermann 1893-1933

Hotel Adlon

Gallerie "Der Sturm" 1913-32
"Erster Deutscher Herbstsalon" 1913

Theater am Schiffbauerdamm

Deutsches Theater

Samuel Fischer verlag 1897-1936

Grosses Schauspielhaus

Theater am Nollendorfplatz 1927-30

Robert Musil 1903-10

Else Lasker-Schüler 1924-33

Opernplatz

Rowohlt verlag 1927-40

Kiepenheuer verlag

Andrej Bely 1921

Café des Westens
"Café Megalomania" c.1915-20s

Harry Graf Kessler 1900-33

Robert Musil 1914-c.1916

Ullstein verlag

Scherl verlag

Mosse verlag

Robert Musil 1933

Robert Musil 1904-06

Joseph Roth

Rowohlt verlag 1919-27

Gustav Kiepenheuer

Christopher Isherwood c.1930-33

Christopher Isherwood

Erich Maria Remarque 1925-30

Stephen Spender c.1930-33

Robert Musil c.1907-10

Robert Musil 1927

Gottfried Benn c.1920-35

Heinrich Mann 1931

Robert Musil 1922,1923,1924

Bertolt Brecht 1924-28
Helene Weigel 1920s

Rowohlt drew many writers, like the legendary Czech reporter Egon Erwin Kisch, and the Austrian novelist Joseph Roth, who wrote his novels (*Hotel Savoy*, 1924, *Radetzkymarch*, 1932) in Berlin's hotels and restaurants. "It's time to leave," he said prophetically in 1932. "They will burn our books and mean us." In 1933, the same year Hitler became Reichschancellor, Roth fled to Paris (where he later died in a poorhouse). Robert Musil (1880–1942) wrote his first novel, *Young Törless* (1906), in the city, where he met his wife Martha, and gave his famous speech on Rilke's death in 1927. Here he had one of his plays first performed, and wrote much of *The Man Without Qualities* (1931–33).

Berlin's theatrical life mostly centred in the East, at the Deutsches Theater, the Grosses Schauspielhaus, and the Theater am Schiffbauerdamm, all at one time or another under the directorship of the great Max Reinhardt. But artists, critics, writers and journalists usually met in the cafés and restaurants of the West (with the exception of Döblin's favourite, the Café Gumpert, near Alexanderplatz). Two cafés were legends of their time. In the Café des Westens met the Expressionist circle around Georg Levin (alias Herwarth Walden). He edited *Der Sturm*, which printed key German writers, lithographs by Kokoschka, Kirchner and Marc, and ran Berlin's foremost gallery (also *Der Sturm)* which exhibited Macke and Klee, Chagall and Kandinsky. His circle included poets Klabund and Mehring, Else Laske-Schüler, as famous for her poetry as her bohemian life-style, and Germany's greatest modern poet Gottfried Benn (1886–1956), whose first shocking collection *Morgue* appeared in 1912.

After the Great War the nearby Romanisches Café became the main meeting place. Here books were written, contracts signed, time whiled away with coffee, chess and gossip. Here came Bertolt Brecht, Georg Grosz, Franz Werfel, Ernst Toller, Alfred Döblin, Joseph Roth and Erich Maria Remarque. As political conflict and ideologi-

Der Sturm printed such writers as Gottfried Benn and Alfred Döblin.

Berlin in the 1920s was a cosmopolitan metropolis, attracting English, Russian and Americans to its streets, offering a rival to the beauty and flair of Paris at this time.

The Café des Westens, right, (on the corner of Kurfürstendamm and Joachimsthaler Strasse), which Berliners called the "Café Megalomania," was made famous by pre-war Bohème, attracting artists and writers of the Expressionist circle.

cal commitment deepened, experimentalism could no longer be an end in itself. It translated into politics, mostly of the left, sometimes of the right. Georg Grosz called for an art that detailed working class life. So did Bertolt Brecht (1898–1956), the playwright from Augsburg who came to Berlin in 1924. Alfred Döblin (1878–1957), a practising physician who wrote the powerful city novel *Berlin-Alexanderplatz* (1929), combined *avant-garde* experiment with left wing convictions. In 1933, when his books were banned, he fled to France, then, like Brecht and Thomas and Heinrich Mann, to the United States. "The mind is on the Left," said a motto of the twenties. It applied to most writers, from Walter Benjamin to Ernst Toller, Lion Feuchtwanger to Heinrich Mann.

There were exceptions. Ernst Jünger (b.1895) returned to Berlin in 1927 as nationalist publicist and writer. Aesthete, adventurer, war-time officer of the German army (Reichswehr), and uncompromising individualist, he celebrated war as a test of character, hated the softness of liberalism, longed for the coming of a "warrior state." He welcomed the seizure of power by the Nazis, but his fervent individualism rejected bonding. In Berlin he wrote two of his best works – *The Adventurous Heart* (1929) and

The Workers (1932) – but left in 1933, ironically just as his ideological opponents were forced to flee. Despite his ironic scepticism, Gottfried Benn identified, if only for a short time, his craving for a Nietzschean new order with the Nazis. But he shared friends with Brecht and George Grosz whom he knew from *avant-garde* days and continued to meet at the famous soirées of the publisher Samuel Fischer (who died in 1934) and of Harry Graf Kessler, a connoisseur and patron of the arts who left Berlin for Paris in 1933 (where he wrote his fascinating *Diaries: 1918-1937*). Benn called Heinrich Mann (1871–1950) – author of the trilogy *Das Kaiserreich* (1925) of which *Professor Unrath* was turned into the famous movie, *The Blue Angel* – his friend and gave the speech at his 60th birthday celebration in 1931. Nonetheless he condoned Mann's enforced resignation from the presidency of the Prussian Academy of Art two years later. He opposed anti-semitism, but must have known his former lover Else Lasker-Schüler was abused by the right-wing press when she won a literary award in 1932, then was beaten unconscious by Nazi thugs. He must also have known how many former friends (and enemies) had been forced from the city. Still, he hoped to profit from a creative new alliance of art and power, until he realized it was his very concept of art that offended the new regime. He was forbidden to write in 1938.

Berlin's intellectual and artistic life, no doubt, was burned in the actual and symbolic fires of 1933, before most of its protagonists would be murdered or, like Walter Benjamin, kill themselves in despair. On the surface, however, it seemed to go on without rupture. Absences were noted, regretted, perhaps even mourned. But each absence opened the possibility of a new career as Klaus Mann savagely demonstrated, with Gustav Gründgens in mind, in his roman à clef *Mephistopheles*, published posthumously in 1979. So, as Carl von Ossietzky grimly observed in 1930, the Romanische Café gradually gave way to a "germanisches café" – until it was destroyed beyond repair or reconstruction by fires of a different kind.

GREENWICH VILLAGE

Greenwich Village is a place – a significant slice of New York City's Lower Manhattan – but many have said it's also a state of mind. More than anywhere, "the Village" was home to the American arts, especially when radical or experimental. That's been so from the birth of the Republic to next week. Tom Paine, James Fenimore Cooper, William Jennings Bryant, Edgar Allan Poe and Herman Melville all lived here. Melville's Ishmael starts his quest for the white whale Moby-Dick from nearby Battery Park. Henry James was born in Washington Place. Mark Twain lived from 1900-1903 in Washington Square.

By the mid-nineteenth century New Yorkers were starting to move uptown, the Village becoming an Italian neighbourhood. By 1900 it was something else: Bohemia. Wannabe writers and painters took the cheap lofts. Radical dreams – socialism, feminism, world revolution – filled the cafés and clubs. Everyone – from Willa Cather to Theodore Dreiser, Sherwood Anderson to Marianne Moore, Floyd Dell to e.e. cummings, John Dos Passos to Eugene O'Neill – was around, eventually. "We came to the Village without any intention of becoming Villagers. We came because the living was cheap, because friends of ours had come already...because it seemed that New York was the only city where a young writer could be published," said Malcolm Cowley, recording the twenties' Lost Generation in *Exile's Return* (1934). South of Fourteenth Street you could still rent a hall-bedroom for $2 a week, a top floor for $30 a month – though rents boomed as young Americans grew ever more experimental. Now two Village generations coincided: the old pre-war movers and shakers, veterans of strikes, manifestations, the Armory Show; and twenties' moderns, glad to take the ship for Paris when the scene moved.

GREENWICH VILLAGE: *The Village runs from Fourteenth Street to Vandam, and west of Fifth Avenue to the Hudson River. Washington Square is the core; its south side was known as "Genius Row." Small family stores (see inset) were the norm.*

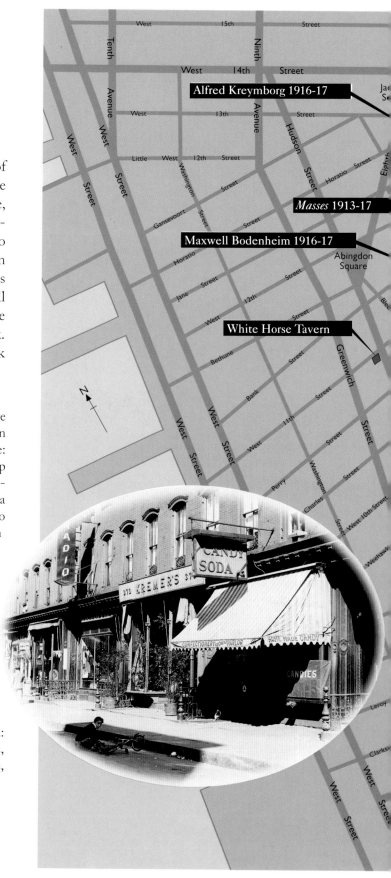

Alfred Kreymborg 1916-17

Masses 1913-17

Maxwell Bodenheim 1916-17

Abingdon Square

White Horse Tavern

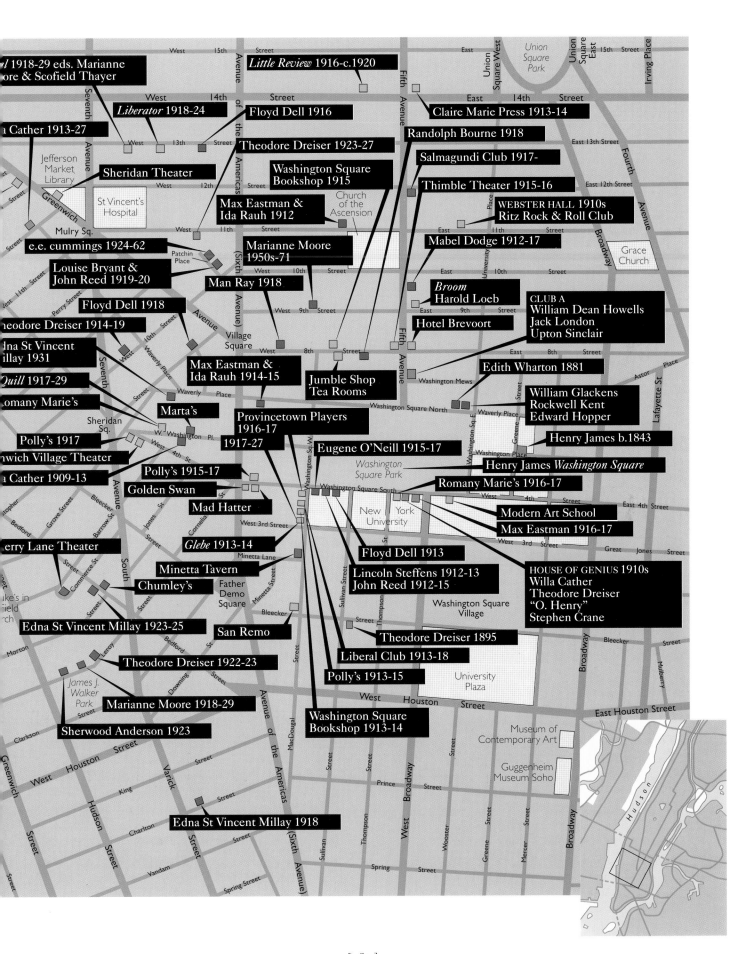

/ 1918-29 eds. Marianne
ore & Scofield Thayer

Little Review 1916-c.1920

1 Cather 1913-27

Liberator 1918-24

Floyd Dell 1916

Claire Marie Press 1913-14

Randolph Bourne 1918

Theodore Dreiser 1923-27

Salmagundi Club 1917-

Sheridan Theater

Washington Square
Bookshop 1915

Thimble Theater 1915-16

Max Eastman &
Ida Rauh 1912

WEBSTER HALL 1910s
Ritz Rock & Roll Club

Mabel Dodge 1912-17

e.e. cummings 1924-62

Marianne Moore
1950s-71

Louise Bryant &
John Reed 1919-20

Man Ray 1918

Broom
Harold Loeb

CLUB A
William Dean Howells
Jack London
Upton Sinclair

Floyd Dell 1918

Hotel Brevoort

heodore Dreiser 1914-19

Edith Wharton 1881

Ina St Vincent
illay 1931

Max Eastman &
Ida Rauh 1914-15

William Glackens
Rockwell Kent
Edward Hopper

Quill 1917-29

omany Marie's

Jumble Shop
Tea Rooms

Henry James b.1843

Marta's

Provincetown Players
1916-17
1917-27

Eugene O'Neill 1915-17

Henry James *Washington Square*

Polly's 1917

Romany Marie's 1916-17

nwich Village Theater

Polly's 1915-17

Modern Art School

1 Cather 1909-13

Golden Swan

Max Eastman 1916-17

Mad Hatter

Glebe 1913-14

Floyd Dell 1913

erry Lane Theater

Minetta Tavern

Lincoln Steffens 1912-13
John Reed 1912-15

HOUSE OF GENIUS 1910s
Willa Cather
Theodore Dreiser
"O. Henry"
Stephen Crane

Chumley's

Father
Demo
Square

Washington Square
Village

Edna St Vincent Millay 1923-25

San Remo

Theodore Dreiser 1895

Theodore Dreiser 1922-23

Liberal Club 1913-18

Marianne Moore 1918-29

Polly's 1913-15

Sherwood Anderson 1923

Washington Square
Bookshop 1913-14

Museum of
Contemporary Art

Guggenheim
Museum Soho

Edna St Vincent Millay 1918

The Village is "One of the most charming places in New York," said Willa Cather, who lived there; so did Stephen Crane, Dreiser, Dell, O'Neill. Nearby MacDougal Street runs south from West Eighth Street, past Washington Square, down to Spring Street. Barely eight blocks long, it was built when the downtown business and harbour districts became overcrowded. Quiet streets around New York University (begun 1833) were taken for merchants' homes, many near Washington Square. In the 1840s young Henry James could walk ten minutes down Fifth Avenue from his family's uptown home at 58 West Fourteenth Street to 19 Washington Square North, home of his grandmother, then across the park to MacDougal Street.

Here he found a second New York, of workers, craftsmen and artisans. Fashionable life was shifting uptown, the absence of broad avenues meant industry passed it by. The Village was becoming a backwater, lined with two and three storey brick dwellings, stores, stables, saloons,

When The Masses *needed funds, a costume ball was held, or a distinguished European lecturer shipped in; the illustration, above, was produced for the magazine for one such occasion.*

workshops. With the coming of the subway and the automobile, livery stables and carriage-repair shops closed. This created ideal space for artists' studios, but the Village's cultural flowering wasn't just a matter of real estate. Set at an oblique angle from the rigid grid of Manhattan's street plan, it offered diverse intangible things, like human scale, unmodernized saloons, flourishing cultural life. It was an ongoing rebuke to censors and cultural provincialism. As Martin Green puts it in his superb book *New York 1913* (1988) "The Village lived in perpetual secession from the rest of the country."

It always had. From the 1840s, when "Young America" in the arts battled with the Anglophile *Knickerbocker Review*, New York had partisan cafés, ideological saloons,

tendentious neighbourhoods. The Village held countless groups, some defined by immigrant origins, employment, radical politics, some by a magazine, an artists' cooperative, a saloon, a restaurant. Journalists gathered at Lincoln Steffens' apartment on Washington Square. Painters grouped around Robert Henri and John and Dolly Sloan, from Philadelphia. They created "The Eight," America's first great modern artistic grouping, who painted Village scenes and contributed political cartoons to the magazine *The Masses*, the Village's radical voice. Anarchists gathered at the East Thirteenth Street offices of Emma Goldman's *Mother Earth*, or the Ferrer Center at 104 East Twelfth, where Henri and George Bellows taught art classes and Lewis Mumford lectured on Kropotkin in 1917.

There was a university crowd near New York University; a snootier one at uptown Columbia where Max Eastman studied with John Dewey before he came to the Village in 1912 to edit *The Masses*. Feminists like Ida Ruah, Inez Milholland and Madeleine Doty met at Crystal Eastman's apartment to define the "New Woman." A Europe-influenced circle of artists, writers and photographers formed at Alfred Stieglitz's 291 Gallery on Fifth Avenue, chief home of experimental arts in pre-war years. Rich hostess Mabel Dodge – who helped organize the 1913 Armory Show which brought Cubism to New York – ran her salon at 23 Fifth Avenue.

The Village of cultural fame had many groups, few made up of native-born Villagers. Village culture was really shaped by incomers from the Midwest or Europe. Proud of its diversity and tolerance, it had no single type, no one cause. Relations, erotic, political, artistic, were ever fluid, alliances short-lived, tensions flourished, people moved in and out, the scene shifted every year.

A good model of Village complexity is 137 MacDougal Street, where Albert and Charles Boni opened the Washington Square Bookshop in the Armory Show year of experimental excitement. They aimed to make the bookstore a cultural nexus, publishing radical new books in a literary scene still run by Boston Brahmins. Alfred Kreymborg brought examples of the new Imagist poetry from London, sent him by the expatriate Ezra Pound. Kreymborg persuaded the Boni brothers to start *The Glebe* which ran for ten issues between 1913 and 1914, printing William Carlos Williams and James Joyce. He also became a fine talent scout, hunting up novels and poetry by Carl Sandburg, Vachel Lindsay, Marianne Moore.

The bookshop became an important centre; the Washington Square Players, later the Theatre Guild, performed their first play here in 1915. Next door was the Liberal Club, which Henrietta Rodman (Egeria in Floyd Dell's novel *Love in Greenwich Village*, 1926) founded in 1913 to provide local writers with a place of "creative gossip." Critic H.L. Mencken dubbed it the home of the "Washington Square mountebanks," and certainly, while Mabel Dodge brought Villagers together with Society and useful patrons, Rodman presided over a more informal world. But the groups interlinked. John Reed, Mabel Dodge's lover, was a regular at the Liberal Club. Reed was one of the leading socialists of the *New Review* and *The Masses*; he and Floyd Dell lived across from the club in Washington Square South.

Here Naturalist novelists like Theodore Dreiser, Upton Sinclair, Sherwood Anderson and Sinclair Lewis could meet artists like William Glackens, anarchists, socialists, journalists, free love advocates, Freud disciples, Cubist or Dadaist painters from Europe. "Pagan Routs," with artists and intellectuals dressed as bacchi, bacchantes, satyrs and nymphs were held, drawing much publicity. Floyd Dell wrote a play for them, *St George in Greenwich Village*, with Sherwood Anderson in a small part. The basement of the club housed Polly Holliday's restaurant, where the banter of Polly's lover, chef, head waiter and anarchist ideologue Hippolyte Havel, rivalled goulash as an attraction. Havel, who had been Emma Goldman's lover in London, settled in New York around 1909 and became a fixture at anarchist events. Described by Ben Reitman as someone who "thought in German, spoke in English, and drank in all languages," his jousts with the socialists of *The Masses* enlivened Village political life.

Soon the twenties' Lost Generation arrived, including Marianne Moore, Hart Crane, James Thurber, John Dos Passos, Elinor Wylie, Edmund Wilson, Thomas Wolfe, e.e. cummings. The Village became more self-conscious, and expensive. By 1929, when Lionel Trilling appeared, it was even respectable. Still, he said, "the Village was the Village, there seemed no other place in New York where a right-thinking person might live...."

The Village challenged the spirit of Middle America, yet over the 1920s something started to fade. The Red Scare of 1919 threatened its radicalism, and Prohibition its sustenance. Censorship struck: Margaret Anderson and the proprietor of the Washington Square Bookshop were arrested for distributing *Ulysses* via the *Little Review*. Montparnasse and New Mexico began to lure away many

The Liberator *magazine, a direct off-shoot of* The Masses, *was edited by Max Eastman, his sister Crystal and Floyd Dell.*

experimentalists. Perhaps the biggest threat was the sense that the Modernist revolution had done its work, the battle for the new arts was won – especially when in 1929 the Museum of Modern Art opened uptown.

Villagers were not always good political advocates; perhaps Max Eastman set the tone in *The Masses*, urging in 1913 "Tie up to no dogma whatever." *The Masses* itself was too irreverent for Socialists, too Bohemian for Communists, too depraved for the respectable intelligentsia, too intellectual for a mass readership. Yet Village aspirations flourished. Its impact on liberal American culture and politics and on acceptance of the whole Modernist spirit stays profound to this day.

Ezra Pound's famous injunction "Make It New!" probably far better applied to the Village than to the London he was living in. How deprived American culture would have been without the cultural radicalism, the Freudian advocacy, the passion for *avant-garde* experiment that typified the countless "little" magazines that emerged there. By the 1950s it was back with a new experimental agenda, mostly in different locations, south of Houston or in the East Village. But it was on MacDougal and round Washington Square between 1910 and 1930 that American culture had one of its greatest moments of energy.

The Washington Square Bookshop helped the New York launch of the Provincetown Players, above, *who drew on the talents of Eugene O'Neill, Susan Glaspell, Mina Loy and Edna St. Vincent Millay. For their 1916 winter season, a converted stables at 139 MacDougal Street was renovated. Two years later they moved to number 133, where premières of O'Neill's* The Hairy Ape *and* The Emperor Jones *were shown.*

HARLEM'S RENAISSANCE

Greenwich Village is downtown, Harlem is up. For a long time it remained a separate place, Nieuw Haarlem, settled by the Dutch in 1637. When New York began prospering after the Revolution, Dutch landowners had rural estates here. But, thanks to its harbour and vast immigrant population, nineteenth century Manhattan grew fast. In 1881 the elevated railway came to Harlem, in 1898 five boroughs joined in Greater New York. Fine apartment blocks rose north of Central park, and soon the area – largely inhabited by Jews and other immigrants who moved to Harlem in search of an escape from the slum tenements of the Lower East Side – was overbuilt. The young Henry Roth (1906–95) moved from the Yiddish Lower East Side to Harlem

in 1914 (*Call It Sleep*, 1934). In 1915 Arthur Miller was born on 111th Street. After the century turned, a new group, African-Americans, began to settle.

This followed the end of Southern Reconstruction in 1876 – an event that, of all the harsh years in African-American history, has probably been least understood. A vast black rural population was left to the mercy of white people who a dozen years earlier had been their owners, masters and overseers. The civil inferiority of former slaves was sustained, policed by a harsh legal system and – through the Ku Klux Klan – a regime of informal terror. Other minorities pouring into American cities in the great immigration influx of 1880 to 1914 might suffer economic inferiority and racial contempt; African-Americans remained in continued unfreedom.

In the South, significant leaders emerged – above all Booker T. Washington (1856–1915), founder of the Tuskegee Institute in Alabama, author of *Up From Slavery* (1901). Admired by fellow African-Americans in the South, where most of them still lived in rural poverty and illiteracy, he was often distrusted by those in the North, who thought his message simply "the old attitude of adjustment and submission." Critics led by W.E.B. DuBois (1868–1963), author of *The Souls of Black Folk* (1903), called for a political and cultural revolution against backwardness and discrimination. Within a single generation, a great diaspora began.

New York was the magnet. Between 1900 and 1940, the white population of the five boroughs of Greater New York rose from 2.1 to 4.9 million. The black population rose from nearly 60,000 to over 400,000, and then almost doubled again between 1940 and 1960. Like immigrants from Europe, they were self-exiles from distant home-

Between 1910 and 1920, 500,000 African-Americans, from a population of around ten million, moved out of the South, to settle in midwestern and northeastern cities. Most came to New York.

lands who had come to New York in hope of betterment. They were also redefining themselves as urban people, taking sides in the dispute between Booker T. Washington's vision of a contented Southern agricultural community and the modernizing vision offered by Northern African-Americans like DuBois.

In 1905 the brownstones and apartment blocks of Harlem were opened to black residents. Many of them were new arrivals from the South. New business opportunities were provided for black entrepreneurs and professionals, who mostly lived on "Striver's Row." But these were few enough, and jobs were hard: hotels, restaurants and theatres had racially restricted hiring policies. The Harlem concentration of blacks changed the situation. It created a lively culture, a new black consciousness, a revived interest in African origins, a black elite, and a determination to be assimilated into the

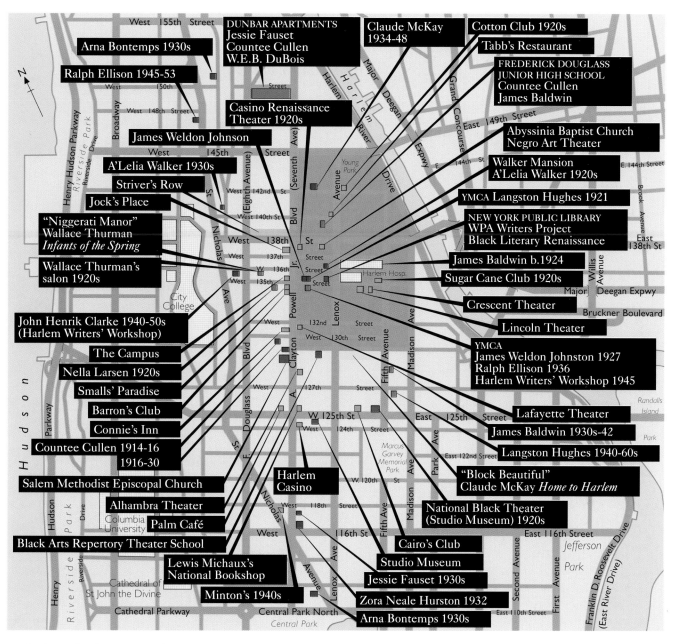

West 155th Street

DUNBAR APARTMENTS
Jessie Fauset
Countee Cullen
W.E.B. DuBois

Claude McKay
1934-48

Cotton Club 1920s

Tabb's Restaurant

Arna Bontemps 1930s

Ralph Ellison 1945-53

West 150th

FREDERICK DOUGLASS
JUNIOR HIGH SCHOOL
Countee Cullen
James Baldwin

West 148th Street

Casino Renaissance
Theater 1920s

Abyssinia Baptist Church
Negro Art Theater

James Weldon Johnson

West 145th Street

A'Lelia Walker 1930s

Walker Mansion
A'Lelia Walker 1920s

Striver's Row

West 142nd St

YMCA Langston Hughes 1921

Jock's Place

West 140th St

NEW YORK PUBLIC LIBRARY
WPA Writers Project
Black Literary Renaissance

"Niggerati Manor"
Wallace Thurman
Infants of the Spring

West 138th St

West 137th Street

James Baldwin b.1924

Wallace Thurman's
salon 1920s

W 136th Street

Sugar Cane Club 1920s

West 135th Street

Harlem Hosp.

Crescent Theater

John Henrik Clarke 1940-50s
(Harlem Writers' Workshop)

West 132nd Street

Lincoln Theater

West 130th Street

YMCA
James Weldon Johnston 1927
Ralph Ellison 1936
Harlem Writers' Workshop 1945

The Campus

Nella Larsen 1920s

Smalls' Paradise

West 127th Street

Barron's Club

Connie's Inn

W 125th St

Lafayette Theater

Countee Cullen 1914-16
1916-30

West 124th Street

East 125th Street

James Baldwin 1930s-42

Salem Methodist Episcopal Church

Langston Hughes 1940-60s

East 122nd Street

Alhambra Theater

Harlem
Casino

"Block Beautiful"
Claude McKay *Home to Harlem*

Palm Café

W 120th St

National Black Theater
(Studio Museum) 1920s

Black Arts Repertory Theater School

West 118th Street

Lewis Michaux's
National Bookshop

Cairo's Club

Studio Museum

Minton's 1940s

West 116th St

Jessie Fauset 1930s

East 116th Street

Zora Neale Hurston 1932

Central Park North

Arna Bontemps 1930s

East 110th Street

Central Park

professions. It also expressed itself in jazz and style – and above all in the "Harlem Renaissance."

The 1920s was the key decade. Black expression surged in jazz, dance, theatre, painting, sculpture, writing. Between the rural passivity of the South and the bubbling excitement of the Harlem streets, the twenties' Renaissance was born. When Alain Locke published *The New Negro* (1925), a striking anthology of creative work, essays and art, the movement acquired a cultural and artistic framework. The book was elegantly published by Albert and Charles Boni of MacDougal Street in Greenwich Village, who also published Jean Toomer's lyrical poem-fiction *Cane* (1923). There was no black publisher able to sell such books to white America,

HARLEM: *By the 1920s, the area between 130th and 145th Street, and Seventh Avenue and Madison (the shaded area on the map) had become known as "black Harlem." Harlem itself was the centre of African-American writing, and it continues to be so even now. Many of the famous meeting places of the twenties (shown here) have become the literary shrines and museums of today.*

and the people of Harlem were neither rich enough nor experienced enough to be the patrons of their own culture. The Jewish publisher Alfred Knopf published the poet-playwright Langston Hughes' first collection *The Weary Blues* (1926). Much of this was black writing for the white audience, and the traffic between Harlem and the rest of the city, and African-Americans and Jews, was intrinsic to the whole Renaissance.

Like other parts of New York, Harlem was a cosmopolitan community. African-Americans from the Deep South met blacks from the urban North. Rural farmworkers and elegant black professionals, musicians and hustlers, strolled along Seventh Avenue. A fresh generation of writers emerged. A few were Harlem-born, like the poet Countee Cullen (1903–1946), author of *Color* (1926). Most were migrants from the South, or the West Indies.

The Renaissance saw a new outburst of black writing (Countee Cullen and W.E.B. Du Bois are shown above top left and bottom). They led the way for later writers, like James Baldwin, top right, who was writing in Harlem in the 1960s.

James Weldon Johnson (1871–1938), author of *Black Manhattan* (1930), came from Jacksonville, Florida, Alain Locke (1886–1954) from Philadelphia. Claude McKay (1889–1948), author of *Home to Harlem* (1928), came from Jamaica, Zora Neale Hurston (1891–1960), who wrote *Jonah's Gourd Vine* (1934), from Eatonville, Florida. Jean Toomer (1894–1967) was born in Washington, DC, Arna Bontemps (1902–1973), author of *Black Thunder* (1935) in Louisiana. Wallace Thurman (1902–1934), who edited *The Messenger* and wrote the play *Harlem: A Melodrama of Negro Life* (1929), was from Salt Lake City. Langston Hughes (1902–1967), poet, story writer, dramatist and uniter of poetry and jazz, was born in Joplin, Mississippi.

A new cultural elite was emerging; DuBois' "Talented Tenth." Contributors to *The New Negro* included a lawyer, diplomat and professor (Johnson), a poet from NYU and Harvard (Cullen), a specialist in folklore and anthropology who had studied at Barnard and at Columbia with Franz Boas (Hurston). The editor, Alain Locke, was

the first African-American Rhodes scholar, and studied at Harvard and Berlin.

The hub of black Harlem was 135th Street between Fifth and Seventh Avenues. The 135th Street branch of the New York Public Library was a literary meeting place where fierce debates unfolded and plays were staged. The Walker Mansion at 108 West 136th Street – now the Countee Cullen branch of the New York Public Library – was a multi-racial meeting place for writers and artists, thanks to black heiress A'Lelia Walker. Nearby W.E.B. DuBois edited *Crisis* magazine for the NAACP (National Association for the Advancement of Colored People). The Lafayette Theatre at Seventh Avenue and 131st Street saw in 1920 a fantastic run of 490 performances of Eugene O'Neill's *The Emperor Jones*, a play by a white playwright with a black cast – though the atavism of the black central character showed old stereotypes had not died. Black theatre also flourished. DuBois founded the Krigwa Players, Abram Hill, author of the play *On Striver's Row* (1933), the American Negro Theatre, Langston Hughes the Harlem Suitcase Theatre.

Like much else in America, the Harlem Renaissance was battered by the Great Depression and shaped by the political swing to the Left. Writers travelled abroad, or worked for WPA Writers' Projects across the United States. Not all black writing came out of Harlem. Richard Wright from Natchez, Mississippi, knew Southern racism at first hand. Like many jazz musicians, he moved north to Chicago in the twenties, and in 1938 published *Uncle Tom's Children*, about the violence of race relationships in the South. In 1940, with *Native Son*, he produced the most influential black novel of the era. He lived in Harlem briefly, but, after the War, moved to the Left Bank in Paris, "where your color was the least important thing about you," to escape the

Music and jazz clubs – the Harlem Casino (*Seventh Ave and 138th*), the Sugar Cane Club (*Fifth Avenue and 135th*), above all the Cotton Club (*Lenox Ave and 143rd*), left, *where Duke Ellington and Count Basie played – were largely for white visitors from downtown.*

In the twenties, Striver's Row, below, *consisting of four blocks of attached houses, was one of Harlem's most fashionable homes; the "Row" appears in almost every work of Harlem's Renaissance literature.*

harsh racial climate, frequenting the Café Tournon and Chez Lipp. So did many other black writers (James Baldwin, Chester Himes, William Gardner Smith) of this and the next generation.

But the attraction of Harlem continued. Ann Petry came there in 1938 and published her novel centred around 116th street and the Harlem of her day, *The Street* (1942). Ralph Ellison, born in Oklahoma City, came to Harlem in 1936, at first sleeping on park benches; he captured its atmosphere in his compelling *Invisible Man* (1952). James Baldwin was born in 1924 in the Harlem Hospital, became a boy preacher, and evoked 1930s religious Harlem in *Go Tell it On the Mountain* (1953). Most of his later years were spent in Paris, but he returned to take a powerful if disputed part in the Civil Rights issues of the 1960s.

Harlem continued to play a major role in African-American writing and consciousness. The foundation of the Harlem Writers' Workshop, the Harlem Writers' Guild, the Black Arts Repertory Theatre School brought a second Renaissance. Many contemporary African-American writers from Maya Angelou to Louis Meriwether were involved in these groups. Though Chester Himes went to Paris, he set some of his crime fiction in the Harlem streets (*A Rage in Harlem*, 1965). *The Autobiography of Malcolm X* (ghosted by Alex Haley in 1976; filmed in 1993 by Spike Lee) explores how in Harlem the one-time Malcolm Little changed from small town crook to Black Muslim, and became a powerful influence on new African-American consciousness.

By the 1980s the United States had a major body of African-American literature. Few major black writers live there today; but Harlem has come to represent less a place than a spirit, fundamental to contemporary American Writing.

HARLEM LITERATURE

Novels

1923 Jean Toomer's experimental *Cane*
1928 Claude McKay *Home to Harlem*
1932 Countee Cullen *One Way to Heaven*
1936 Arna Bontemps *Black Thunder*

Poems and Plays

1933 Abram Hill *On Striver's Row*
1942 Langston Hughes *Shakespeare in Harlem*

MAIN STREET, USA

"Main Street is the climax of civilization. That this Ford car might stand in front of the Bon Ton Store, Hannibal invaded Rome and Erasmus wrote in Oxford cloisters." So writes Sinclair Lewis (1885–1951) at the start of *Main Street* (1920), his half satirical, half loving portrait of American small town life (which was instrumental in his winning the Nobel Prize for Literature in 1930). It's set in "Gopher Prairie, Minnesota" (Lewis was a Minnesotan who had fled to New York bohemia). But, as he says, it all would be the same in Ohio, Montana, Illinois or Upper New York State: "This is America – a town of a few thousand, in a region of wheat and corn and dairies and little groves."

Lewis wrote his observant book just as that world was changing for good. The United States had entered the Great War, and Woodrow Wilson had tried to make the world safe for democracy. But that was all over, Americans were back home again. The twenties boom was now under way – and "the business of America is business," announced President Calvin Coolidge. Interstate highways spread across the nation. The Rosebud Movie Palace brought its people images (still silent) of a bigger, glossier world that tempted many. Still, the small-town influence remained strong. It was there in the politics: in Prohibition, anti-immigration, Middle American values, "comfortable tradition and sure faith," also "dullness made God." But the small town was, as Lewis showed, becoming a "bewildered empire." It was losing touch with the frontier that had made it, and the American heartland was giving way to the great American city. As the seat of rural and puritan American culture, its influence was dying in the futuristic urban age.

In *Babbitt* (1922), Lewis moved his story forward, onward from small-town to bigger but still midwestern city. He set this satirical tale, his most famous, in "Zenith" (probably Minneapolis). Zenith is the small town grown

Sinclair Lewis, above, the great satirist of Middle America, was born in 1885 in Sauk Center, Minnesota, went to Yale and worked as a journalist until Main Street *won him fame.* Babbitt (1922) *and* Arrowsmith (1925) *followed. In 1930 he won the Nobel Prize, but his later works were weaker. He died in Rome in 1951.*

big, but here too, in the high new office buildings ("austere towers of steel and cement and limestone"), the business spirit reigns supreme. The book's small hero is George F. Babbitt, a 46-year-old realtor and "Prominent Citizen," "a God-fearing, hustling, two-fisted Regular Guy, who belongs to some church with pep and piety in it." He's really a hen pecked husband who vaguely dreams of a simpler life, far away from the gimmicks and the commercial hustle. A folkloric figure, he became the typical mid-American of the twenties. H.L. Mencken, the Baltimore scourge of American dullness, attacked "Babbittry" as the great American disease. And many a Babbitt populated twenties' American writing – in the stories of James Thurber, for instance. They also showed what it was revolting against; it was to get away from the Babbitts that many American writers fled, they claimed, to Paris.

If Lewis treated the midwestern small town and business city with satirical energy, Sherwood Anderson (1876–1941) treated it with delicate poetry. This former small-town Ohio paint salesman, who threw up his job to go to Chicago and write, took modern experiment seriously. He published his best book, *Winesburg, Ohio*, in 1919. Its 25 linked short stories form a very different account of

"Our railway station is the final aspiration of architecture. Sam Clark's annual hardware turnover is the envy of the four counties which constitute God's country. In the sensitive art of the Rosebud Movie Palace there is a Message, and humor strictly moral." The "small-townness" of Main Street, *from which this quote is taken, is captured perfectly in Edward Hopper's* Railroad Crossing, *above.*

small-town experience on or around Main Street. They construct a sad portrait of a group of isolated individuals – "grotesques" he called them – hungering to express and open out their lives, desires and dreams, but held down by the weight of old American puritanism, repression and solitude. Winesburg is a prison from which both lives and art seek to escape. Yet Anderson explores the delicate, twisted lives of the prisoners in a poetic, symbolist prose that set them in a Modernist gaze. One of his influences was Gertrude Stein; another was his Chicago friend Edgar Lee Masters, whose *Spoon River Anthology* (1916) told a similar story of lost midwestern lives.

There were two chief reasons why the Middle-American small town became such a major theme of the writing of the twenties. One was that the nation was changing so fast, as modernity and the post-war boom drove it forward, that it was already becoming a fading object. As the big cities flourished (the 1920 census revealed that for the first time most Americans lived in

The black Ford Model T motor car, shown above, *was appearing in every small town in the twenties, as the business boom started to spread right across the United States.*

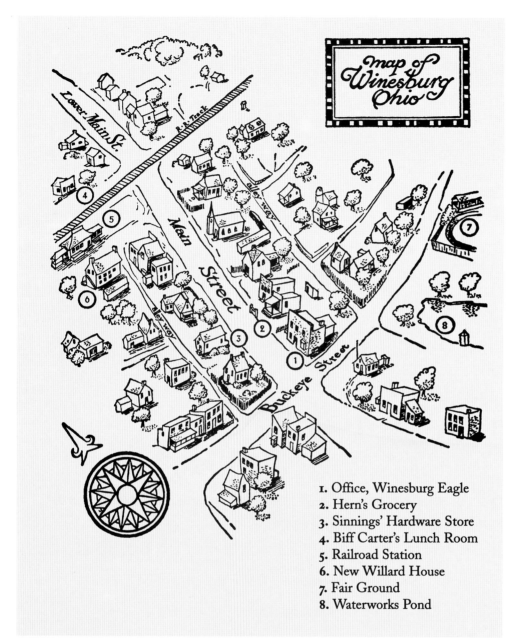

1. Office, Winesburg Eagle
2. Hern's Grocery
3. Sinnings' Hardware Store
4. Biff Carter's Lunch Room
5. Railroad Station
6. New Willard House
7. Fair Ground
8. Waterworks Pond

Writing of Sherwood Anderson's Winesburg, Ohio *in the* New Statesman, *Rebecca West says, "it delights in places where those who are not poets could never find delight...it seems persuaded there is beauty in anything. In such spirit Mr Anderson moves about his ugly little town and watches his dull ugly people. It lives, it glows, they exist as immortal souls." Its Main Street (and Lewis's), left, could be anywhere, its people, any small-town Americans.*

Up ahead was something else: the big city, literary experiment, the claims of art, the buzz of the fast-moving American future. Many writers – midwestern poets like Edgar Lee Masters, Carl Sandburg (*Good Morning, America,* 1928) and Vachel Lindsay (*Johnny Appleseed,* 1928) – tried to reconcile the two, as did powerful painters such as Edward Hopper and Andrew Wyeth.

So was small-town America just the home of what Mencken called the "booboisie," and the place of "dullness made God?" Or was it the real heartland, where Abraham

cities), industry took over, the age of mass communications was born, Americans started to look back on what they had lost, or were leaving behind. In one direction there was progress, in the other nostalgia. Was the small town, the frontier remnant, the old Middle American way, a provincial prison holding the nation back – or was it still a real source of American values?

But the other key reason was that so many new American writers came from there – Lewis and Anderson, Ernest Hemingway and F. Scott Fitzgerald – and felt the need to tell some version of the story. Behind them was what Thornton Wilder identified in his famous play *Our Town* (1938) as the simple domestic world of ordinary American life, where the yellow brick road started.

Lincoln and William Dean Howells came from, and which even self-created new men like Fitzgerald's Jay Gatsby tried to hold onto in the modern "waste land" age? Hemingway looked back from Paris to the Michigan Woods; and even Lewis confessed his secret love for the world of Main Street and the Bon Ton Store. As Fitzgerald's Nick Carraway confesses in *The Great Gatsby* (1925), "Even when the East excited me most, even when I was most keenly aware of its superiority to the bored, sprawling, swollen towns beyond the Ohio... even then it had always for me a quality of distortion." The small-town Middle West lived on, and still does – into the "Lake Wobegon" stories of Garrison Keillor and the local colour realism of today.

WILLIAM FAULKNER'S NEW SOUTH

"Beginning with *Sartoris* (1929), I discovered my own little postage stamp of native soil was worth writing about and that I would never live long enough to exhaust it." This is William Faulkner (1897–1967), "sole owner and proprietor," describing the birth of his new literary invention, Yoknapatawpha County, Mississippi, the setting of many of the novels which were to make him one of the most important of modern Southern writers. And Yoknapatawpha County, set over the area around Oxford, Mississippi, would become not just a remote American region, but an international myth about a part of America that might well have been a nation – until, that is, everything ended in 1865 with the South's defeat in the American Civil War.

It was never easy to be a Southern writer, as generation after generation in the post-Bellum South seemed to discover. The terrible defeat of 1865, the pains of Reconstruction which reconstructed very little, the wasting of cities and plantations, the rise of technological America in the North and the West, all suggested despair or withdrawal. Southern writers like Kate Chopin (*The Awakening*, 1899) appeared, but disappeared into obscurity. Poets like Sidney Lanier turned to mysticism. Novelists like Virginian Ellen Glasgow (*The Battleground*, 1902) wrote with grim despair of the region. Others like George Washington Cable (*The Grandissimes*, 1901) were so critical on the racial question they were driven from the South.

Encouraged by Sherwood Anderson, William Faulkner, above, drew on the landscape of his native region for his novels.

an airman) and then *Mosquitoes* (1927) about New Orleans twenties Bohemia.

But then came the great change. He decided to return home to Oxford, where he was once employed as postmaster at the University of Mississippi, relished the local whisky, and noticed that his true subject lay all around him. With *Sartoris* Faulkner's local world began to come alive. He created the fictional Yoknapatawpha County (founded on Lafayette County) with Jefferson (Oxford) its county seat. He took the name Yoknapatawpha from the Chicasaw word for "furrowed ground," found on old maps. Just like Thomas Hardy's Wessex, it was an imaginary place, but laid over real facts. It was 2,400 rural square miles of crossed destinies and complex genealogies, with a precise population of 6,298 whites and 9,313 "negroes." It also lay under a threefold curse: its land had been robbed from the Indians; it had taken up slavery and it had been defeated in the War Between the States.

According to Faulkner, born in New Albany, Mississippi, in 1897, it was far easier to write of the North or the West, because these areas were "young since alive," than it was to write from a South that was "old since dead...killed by the Civil War." Still, setting off to be a poet in New Orleans, he was determined to dispel the curse. Under Sherwood Anderson's guidance he wrote *Soldier's Pay* (1926), a novel about the impact of the Great War (in which he'd trained as

Faulkner called his stories of this world his "apocrypha," his alternative version of the Biblical history of the South. And the family history went in there too. The doom-laden, heroic Sartorises are his own family,

reliving the Civil War. The Snopes represent the depredations of carpetbagging and trade. Everywhere history seeps into the life of the present – but the literary technique is highly modern. "I discovered writing was a mighty fine thing," he reported. "You could make people stand on their hind legs and cast a shadow, and as soon as I discovered it I wanted to bring them all back."

For the next thirty years Faulkner did bring them back. His greatest novels and stories came from the thirties. These books – *The Sound and the Fury* (1929), *As I Lay Dying* (1930), *Light in August* (1932), *Absalom, Absalom!* (1936) – are filled with Yoknapatawpha history: the tale of a dying Eden declining, as virgin land becomes property, wood yields to the axe, nature to the machine, chivalry to trade. Decaying mansions, bear-hunts, segregation, miscegenation, lynchings, trips to Memphis, all fill the tales. They are also works of modern experiment, elaborately using stream-of-consciousness techniques – stories of the very Southern dislocation of human time.

In these books Faulkner told the Southern tale in many different lights, and in many different ways – through the lynching of Joe Christmas (*Light in August*), the great bear-hunt of one of his finest stories "The Bear" in the collection, *Go Down, Moses* (1942) and the lighter comedy of the "Snopes's Trilogy" in *The Hamlet* (1940), *The Town* (1957) and *The Mansion* (1959). His story – "the tragic fable of Southern history" – and his world became international, his experiment world-influential, and much admired by the French. He was recognized as a leading modernist, the equal of James Joyce or Virginia Woolf, and received the Nobel Prize for Literature in 1949.

Faulkner's work presaged a major revival of Southern writing. It was followed by the work of Robert Penn Warren (author of *All the King's Men*, 1946, inspired by the Louisiana demagogue Huey Long), John Crowe Ransom, Allen Tate, David Davidson – fine poets and

With its world of lost gentlemen and belles, sharecroppers, carpetbaggers (homeless travellers like those shown left*), poor whites, enduring blacks, and a Hardy-like chorus of town gossips, Yoknapatawpha echoed the South's history.*

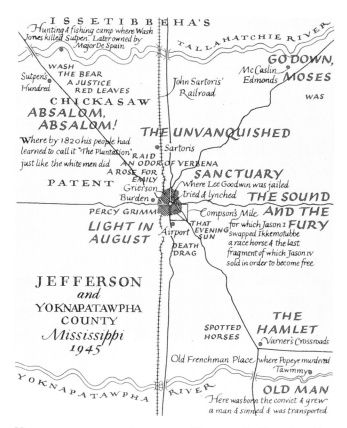

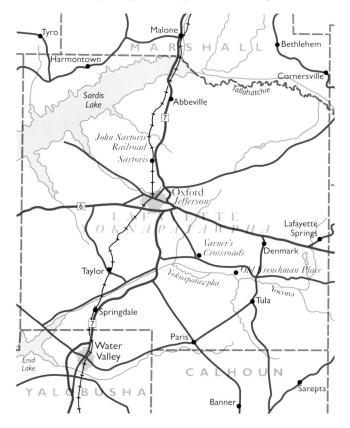

YOKNAPATAWPHA AND LAFAYETTE COUNTY: *Faulkner drew his own map of the fictional landscape he created for his novels, above, based on the area surrounding Oxford, below. Both are bounded by the Tallahatchie River. In the fictional county, the Yocona River becomes the Yoknapatawpha, and Jefferson becomes Oxford.*

William Faulkner helped to turn the South, with its plantations, cotton pickers, above, and farm workers, into one of America's most familiar literary landscapes.

critics, many of whom contributed essays to the anthology *I'll Take My Stand* (1930), the "Southern Agrarian" proclamation of a distinctive regional writing and culture. Erskine Caldwell grotesquely portrayed the Depression life of the Southern tobacco farmer in *Tobacco Road* (1932); while Margaret Mitchell's *Gone With the Wind* (1936) turned the story of the "lost" Southern cause into one of the world's great romantic weepies.

The plays of Tennessee Williams, Lilian Hellman and DuBose Heyward, and the text and photographs of James Agee's *Let Us Now Praise Famous Men* (1941) extended the story. With the work of Carson McCullers from Georgia (*The Heart Is a Lonely Hunter*, 1940), Eudora Welty from Mississippi (*Delta Wedding*, 1946), Flannery O'Connor from Georgia (*A Good Man Is Hard to Find*, 1955) the modern South acquired a new tradition of "Southern Gothic," taken further by Walker Percy, Truman Capote and James Dickie and still continuing today.

Like Edgar Allen Poe from the pre-Bellum years, Faulkner became the great presence. He was "Dixie Limited," as when fellow Gothic novelist Flannery O'Connor wrily complained that "Nobody wants his mule and wagon stalled on the same track the Dixie Limited is roaring down." Even in the powerful work of African-American women writers like Toni Morrison and Alice Walker his trace remains – above all in the mythic and historical ambition he gave back to Southern writing.

WRITERS' HOLLYWOOD

It's easy to condescend to Hollywood. Everyone has their favourite story about movie goucheries, and most concern writers. There's the one about Sam Goldwyn and Maurice Maeterlinck. Goldwyn hired the Belgian playwright and Nobel Prizewinner, who spoke no English, to adapt his novel *La vie des abeilles* and, when the screenplay was translated was shocked to find the hero was a bee, not knowing what the word *abeille* meant. In another instance Goldwyn showed his true feelings toward writers when he tried to hire the bestselling Louis Bromfield. "Sure, you're a great novelist, but how many people have heard of you?" asked Goldwyn, "If you write two or three successful pictures, the name of *Bloomfield* will be known all over the world!"

Writers often repaid the compliment. When F. Scott Fitzgerald returned from his first tour in Hollywood, critic H.L. Mencken wrote: "Thank God you have escaped alive! I was full of fear for you. If Los Angeles is not the one authentic rectum of civilization, then I am no anatomist. Any time you want to go out again and burn it down, count me in." When it comes to culture, Hollywood has always been different. Where writers were drawn to Paris in the twenties or New York

MGM producer Herman J. Mankiewicz wrote with actor/screen-writer Orson Welles what many consider the best film ever made, Citizen Kane *(1939), a still from which is shown* above.

in the forties because these were cultural capitals, writers first streamed to Hollywood in the thirties because of the new economic opportunities offered by the burgeoning movie industry. Even in the twenties writers had gone there to storyboard silent movies. But the advent of movie sound, and the industrialization of motion pictures under the studio system, required a new writing proletariat who could create stories and write dialogue.

Hence the second California Gold Rush. The novelist Ben Hecht telegraphed Herman J. Mankiewicz to come to write for Paramount: "Millions are to be grabbed out here and your only competition is idiots. Don't let it get around." Mankiewicz came – and stayed, together with an army of writers attracted to Hollywood in the 1930s and 1940s. First there were the Americans: hard-boiled novelists like James M. Cain, Raymond Chandler, Dashiell Hammett; proletarian writers like John Fante, Daniel Fuchs and Horace McCoy; solemn Broadway dramatists like Lillian Hellman, Clifford Odets and Maxwell Anderson; famous New York wits like Dorothy Parker and Robert Benchley. They met at Stanley Rose's Bookstore, Hollywood's answer to Shakespeare and Co., or drank at Musso and Frank, their counterpart to the cafés of Montparnasse.

Yet more illustrious writers came too. In 1934 John Dos Passos was invited by director Josef von Sternberg to write a Marlene Dietrich film, *The Devil is a Woman*. He was amazed by Hollywood's cultural pretensions, appalled by its display of wealth, and convinced that Austrian-born von Sternberg was really an impostor from Brooklyn. His screenwriting was a flop; but the experience went directly into his finest novel, The *Big Money* (1936), where he depicts Hollywood as the new power centre of mass culture, populated by opportunistic producers, corrupt artists, and cultural barbarians. Theodore Dreiser, author of *An American Tragedy* (1925), moved to Hollywood in 1940, and spent his last years writing *The Stoic* (1947). Although a self-proclaimed Communist, he was buried in an expensive section of Hollywood's celebrated cemetery, Forest Lawn, not far from the famous film cowboy Tom Mix. William Faulkner also laboured for long periods in Hollywood when his complex novels failed to find a wider audience. His disdain for the movies was legendary, his misadventures legion. He once asked a studio if he could work at home instead of in his office. It took MGM six months to discover he had moved back to Mississippi. He wrote only one story about Hollywood, "Golden Land." But he created some of his greatest fiction there, including parts of *Absalom, Absalom!*, while living in the Knickerbocker Hotel on North Ivar Street in 1936.

But the two novelists who wrote most perceptively about the movies were Nathanael West (1903–40) and Scott Fitzgerald (1896–40). West came to Hollywood in 1933 to work on a film version of his masterpiece, *Miss Lonelyhearts* (1933). He returned in 1935, in the depths of the Depression, and lived in a cheap hotel called the Pa-Va-Sed, on North Ivar Street, near Hollywood Boulevard, the setting for *The Day of the Locust* (1939). He was to remain there for the rest of his short life, working as scriptwriter for the smaller studios like Monogram on what was known as Hollywood's "Poverty Row."

Fitzgerald settled in Hollywood in 1937, when his literary career was in eclipse. In the twenties, the glamorous author of *This Side of Paradise* (1920) and *The Great Gatsby* (1925) had been one of the highest-paid writers in America. But with the break-up of his marriage, his wife Zelda's descent into madness, his own into alcoholism, and the fall of the country into Depression, he found himself struggling to remain economically solvent. He moved to the Garden of Allah – a legendary Hollywood housing complex built by actress Alla Nazimova in the twenties – and went to work for MGM. Although a failure as a scenarist, Fitzgerald used his film experience to create the richest portrait of Hollywood ever offered by a novelist. In his unfinished masterpiece *The Last Tycoon* (1941), Fitzgerald shows us the complexity of movie-making as a commercial and artistic activity. Unlike writers who mocked the pretensions of Hollywood culture, he saw the potential for greatness in his hero, the producer Monroe Stahr. Fitzgerald, who spent his final years in

In the thirties the streets around Hollywood Boulevard, above, *became the setting for* The Day of the Locust, *Nathanael West's surreal, apocalyptic novel about the backside of Hollywood life and the American Dream.*

Hollywood in the mistaken belief he could master screenwriting, became obsessed with the power of visual images: "I saw that the novel, which at my maturity was the strongest and supplest medium for conveying thought and emotion from one human being to another, was becoming subordinated to a communal art that, whether in the hands of Hollywood merchants or Russian idealists, was capable of reflecting only the tritest thought, the most obvious emotion. It was an art in which words were subordinated to images, where personality was worn down to the inevitable low gear of collaboration. As long past as 1930, I had a hunch that the talkies would make even the best-selling novelist as archaic as silent pictures...there was a rankling indignity, that to me had become almost an obsession, in seeing the power of the written word subordinated to another power, a more glittering, a grosser power...." By a bizarre coincidence, Fitzgerald and West died on the same weekend in December, 1940, Fitzgerald of a heart attack, West in an automobile accident. Only years later would a new generation of readers become aware that an era in writers' Hollywood died with them.

A new stream of writers began arriving in Hollywood in the late 1930s, as Europe moved closer to World War.

In The Last Tycoon, *Fitzgerald,* left, *describes brilliant studio executive Monroe Stahr teaching the rudiments of film-writing to snobbish British novelist Boxley, based on Aldous Huxley,* right.

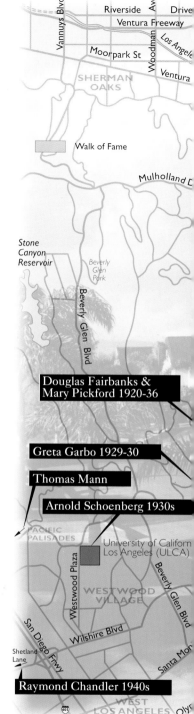

Some were British expatriates, among the most famous Aldous Huxley and Christopher Isherwood. Huxley arrived in 1937 for a visit, and decided to stay; he died there in 1963. In the 1940s he wrote screen adaptations of literary classics like *Pride and Prejudice* and *Jane Eyre*, but didn't like being lumped together with the hack writers mogul Jack Warner called "schmucks with Underwoods." Film wasn't a good medium to work in, he wrote a friend, because you were at the mercy of inferior collaborators: "What a disgust and a humiliation! It seems one worse, if possible, than the theatre. I shall stick to an art in which I can do all the work myself, sitting alone, without having to entrust my soul to a crowd of swindlers, vulgarians and mountebanks." He expressed his animus in a black comic novel, *After Many a Summer Dies the Swan* (1939), which deals with Randolph Hearst and also Forest Lawn Cemetery – later the setting for Evelyn Waugh's brilliant Hollywood and Los Angeles satire *The Loved One* (1948).

The last group of artists who came to Hollywood were exiles rather than expatriates: refugees from modern European history. Arnold Schoenberg took up a post at UCLA in the late thirties, where he taught composition, wrote 12-tone music, and played tennis with George Gershwin. Igor Stravinsky moved to Beverly Hills in 1940 and wrote such masterpieces as his *Symphony in Three Movements* (1946) and *The Rake's Progress* (1951). But the largest group were German writers – including Alfred Döblin, Heinrich Mann, Thomas Mann, Franz Werfel and Bertolt Brecht. Thomas Mann built a handsome

In The Day of the Locust, *Nathanael West describes a film studio (like* MGM *above) as a junkyard: "A Sargasso of the imagination! And the dump grew continually, for there wasn't a dream afloat somewhere which wouldn't sooner or later turn up in it, having first been made photographic by plaster, canvas, lath and paint."*

HOLLYWOOD: *In the 1930s an army of writers came to Hollywood to have their stories made into films or to become proficient screenwriters for one of the many studios there.*

house in Pacific Palisades, where he wrote his late masterpiece *Doctor Faustus* (1948). Brecht came in 1940. He failed to make a career in film, but wrote one of his finest plays, *The Caucasian Chalk Circle* (1955). Few German exiles mastered English and none made any substantial contribution to the movies, but they helped transform Hollywood into an international centre of high Modernism where Charles Laughton performed Brecht's *Galileo* and Theodor Adorno and Max Horkheimer brought the Frankfurt School of Social Thought to Southern California.

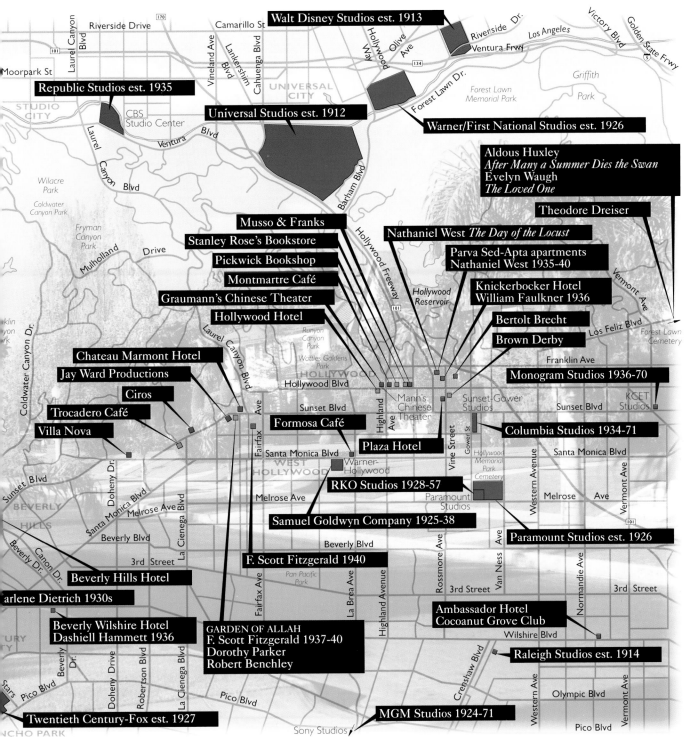

The Hollywood cultural renaissance barely survived the end of the War. With the death of the old Jewish moguls, the decline of the studio system, and the rise of television, the movie industry was irrevocably changed. The start of the Cold War and the rise of McCarthyism, the trial of the Hollywood Ten and the Hollywood blacklist, created a climate of intolerance, which drove out even a film genius like Charlie Chaplin. After providing a home for a generation of European refugees, Hollywood created its own generation of blacklisted American exiles.

When Norman Mailer came to Hollywood in 1949 for the film version of his *The Naked and the Dead* (1948), he found a movie community in disintegration. Significantly, he set his Hollywood novel *The Deer Park* (1955) in a desert resort. In 1951 producer David Selznick told a friend: "Hollywood's like Egypt. Full of crumbling pyramids. It'll never come back. It'll just keep on crumbling until finally the wind blows the last studio prop across the sands." Selznick was wrong. Hollywood would be reborn, in the sixties – but without its glittering cast of writers.

DEPRESSION AMERICA

One of the great images of American writing of the thirties is of a turtle struggling, again and again, to cross a busy interstate highway. The image – of nature and its struggle to survive and endure – comes in John Steinbeck's *Grapes of Wrath* (1939), a remarkable tale of the American Depression. It tells of the "Okies," poor farmers from the Southwest, driven off the land by depression, dust storms and the banks, trekking off with their possessions in broken jalopies, down the long harsh ride of Route 66 ("the mother road, the road of flight"), headed for California, last outpost of the American Dream.

On 24 October, 1929, the American stock market collapsed. For a few days, financiers fought to save the situation. By the fifth day the fight was lost. It was the "Great Crash." The twenties boom was over, the Jazz Age ending in a frenzy of selling. The collapse shook the foundations of the nation. People everywhere lost jobs, businesses, homes, farms. Many were on the move. They became nomads, migrating from ruined farms to jobless cities, riding freight cars as hobos, gathering in migrant camps ironically called Hoovervilles, after the do-nothing President – or going where Americans had always gone, West, like Steinbeck's "Okies," only to find that here too jobs were scarce and underpaid.

By 1930 unemployment was four million, a year later eight million, and by 1932 twelve million Americans were out of work. Beggars lined the streets, soup kitchens like the one above *fed the starving.*

When the Depression became world-wide and deep-rooted, American writers saw they had a new task: to tell the tragic story of their transformed, darkened nation. F. Scott Fitzgerald, laureate of the Jazz Age, saw that in a few weeks his twenties had become an unreal decade. The fantasy world – "The snow of 1929 wasn't real snow. If you didn't want it to be real snow you just paid some money and it went away," – was no more. With the thirties reality had arrived. Maybe not in Hollywood, which found a key role providing entertainment, like *Gold Diggers of 1933*, with its extravagant production number, "We're in the money." Few Americans were. Although Hollywood was there to remind Americans of values only temporarily suspended, there were many others, including a lot of writers, who thought the land had spent its promise. Maybe the American dream was over.

Writers reacted quickly. Theatre displayed the sense of crisis, a new-found need for political action. The left-wing New Playwrights Theater had staged its first production back in 1927. Now in 1929 Mike Gold – leading Communist and author of the protest novel *Jews Without Money* (1930) – founded the Workers' Drama League. Next year came the Workers' Laboratory Theater, later the Theater of Action, then the Theater Collective (1932–36). Agitprop theatre soon produced its classics, among them George Sklar's *Stevedore* and John Howard Lawson's *Marching Song* (both Theater Union). In 1935 Group Theater mounted two plays by Clifford Odets: *Waiting for Lefty*, the most famous thirties play, about a strike of New York cabbies; and *Awake and Sing!*, the story of the radicalization of a young Jewish boy. Like Odets, other young playwrights working in radical theatre of the day – Tennessee Williams in New Orleans, Arthur

Dorothea Lange (1895–1965) was one of a number of photo-journalists whose portraits and studies of the hardships of the Depression years among the migrant labourers of California (like her picture, right) became a telling documentary for the whole world. For many migrants home was a mobile shack in a field, with no water or sanitation, and the only future one of uncertainty and disappointment.

Miller in Michigan – would become the mainstay of Broadway in the post-war years.

Back from Paris, the expatriates came, to reckon with what had gone wrong at home. Some started travelling across the continent to recount the sufferings taking place, of cotton-pickers in Mississippi as much as Ford workers in Michigan. Writer James Agee and photographer Walker Evans, commissioned by the business magazine *Fortune*, spent four weeks in 1936 with Alabama tenant-farmers. Their photo-book *Let Us Now Praise Famous Men* didn't appear until 1941, but it remains an eloquent and poetic testimony to the suffering and endurance of poor whites when the rural economy collapsed.

Nearly everything written in the United States in the thirties reflected the Depression, in one light or another. The *avant-garde* writers of the twenties, like William Faulkner, changed direction. Depression is the "touch of disaster" lying behind Scott Fitzgerald's *Tender Is the Night* (1934), even though its subject is the high-living expatriate twenties. In *To Have And Have Not* (1937), set in Key West, Ernest Hemingway tells a Depression fable where his hero can no longer claim his separate peace. And in his vast trilogy *USA* (1930–36) John Dos Passos used montage technique to tell the whole story of twenti-eth century America as it moved from dream to disaster.

The thirties was an age of documentary and realism. Most books confronted the Depression head-on. Erskine Caldwell sensationally told of the poor tobacco farmers of the South in *Tobacco Road* (1932). James T. Farrell looked at the poverty of Chicago's South Side in the *Studs Lonigan trilogy* (1932–35). African-Americans, already the

> "The ancient overloaded Hudson creaked and grunted to the highway at Sallisaw and turned west, and the sun was blinding. But on the concrete road Al built up his speed because the flattened springs were not in danger any more. From Sallisaw to Gore is twenty-one miles and the Hudson was doing thirty-five miles an hour. From Gore to Warner thirteen miles; Warner to Checotah fourteen miles; Checotah a long jump to Henrietta – thirty four miles..."
>
> John Steinbeck, *The Grapes of Wrath*

victims of American life, suffered worst in the Depression. Richard Wright, who had migrated from Mississippi to Chicago, told the story of black rural Americans and life in the city, publishing his protest novel *Native Son* in 1940.

When Franklin D. Roosevelt was elected President in 1932 a "New Deal" began. The Works Progress Administration (WPA) was set up to provide funds for the arts. The Federal Theater founded in 1935, worked across the country staging plays about social and econom-ic circumstances. Its most famous contribution was the "Living Newspaper," drama-documentary designed to treat current events. Its black unit produced such works as *The Swing Mikado* and *The Black Macbeth*. A year earlier, in 1934, the Federal Writers' Project started to employ writers to write about America, with at one time up to 1,200 involved in its different projects, many to become famous later. Key projects were the 150-volume *Life in*

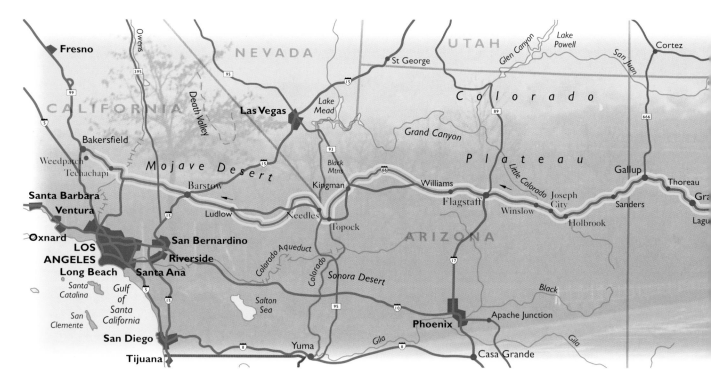

The Grapes of Wrath *made John Steinbeck,* above, *the most famous author of the 1930s.*

America, and a series of American Guides to states and regions. American writers looked afresh at their country, its landscape, people and social geography. Each segment of the nation was documented as it had never been before, by poets and novelists, historians and professors.

This was the climate in which John Steinbeck (1902–68) wrote most of his major fiction, much of it about California, where he had grown up and worked at a variety of jobs. *In Dubious Battle* (1936), about a strike of Californian fruit-pickers, and other works showed the great human battle to survive. But it was *The Grapes of Wrath* (1939), which takes his poor farmers, the Joads, on an epic journey across America, that brought him fame. Like many thirties' books, it was based on fact. The Joads are typical poor farmers of the Southwest. Three-quarters of Oklahoma farmers had been unable to pay interest on their mortgages, and in any case the mortgage companies went bankrupt. Poor farming methods and freak weather combined to create the Dust Bowl in which the topsoil blew away. The result of this disaster is faithfully recorded by Steinbeck.

The Joads travel from Oklahoma to California, in a parody of the great westward movement that had always offered the American promise of a new beginning. They drive down depression-troubled Route 66, across mountain and desert, to the Hoovervilles of California, trying to redeem themselves and their American ideals by becoming migrant fruit-pickers. Steinbeck researched this part of the book by visiting Californian squatter-camps himself, in 1936, and like him the Joads, when they arrive, now learn of the failure of the pieties that have sustained their American dream. There is no golden promise after all. Wherever they go, they are alien intruders, abused, harried by police, exploited. They cling to the importance of the family, and their notion of survival in dignity. The novel's heart comes when Ma Joad, who has sustained her family through the journey, realizes her devotion to the family must end; her duty is to human beings in general.

This was the common lesson of thirties' writing, the message in *Awake and Sing!* and many another book and play. It would return in Arthur Miller's *All My Sons* (1947), about corruption in wartime, written during the Second World War, performed in 1947, and still shaped by the values of the decade that had transformed American ideas and ideals. A generation of Americans was never to forget the Depression, which transformed modern American history in the twentieth century as powerfully as the surge toward technology had transformed the nineteenth.

But what ended the Depression was neither human solidarity nor a revival of capitalist energy and purpose. The war that began in Europe and then, in December 1941, brought Americans in to the conflict after the Japanese attack on Pearl Harbor, sent the nation back to

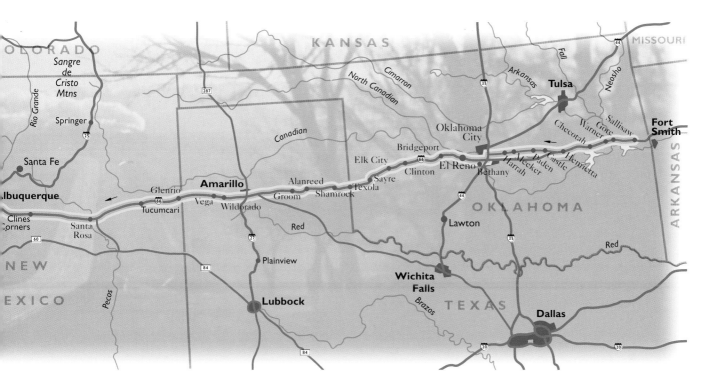

ROUTE 66: *"Route 66 is the path of a people in flight.... They come into 66 from the tributary side roads, from the wagon tracks and the country rutted roads.... Shamrock and McClean, Conway and Amarillo, the yellow. Wildorado and Vega and Boise, and there's an end of Texas.... there's the border of New Mexico...."*
The Grapes of Wrath

In 1940 John Ford made a film, left, of Steinbeck's The Grapes of Wrath.

work. The Okies who had fled to California soon stopped picking fruit and instead found well-paid work in the busy munitions factories and the navy yards. The wartime boom was followed, in 1945, by an era of unprecedented post-war prosperity, and Americans found themselves once more "the people of plenty."

But for those who had lived through the Depression of the thirties there could never be an easy acceptance that progress and plenty were the true American birthright.

"Nobody wants to remember painful things and so we have a tendency to deny that on the one hand we are afraid of it, and on the other that it might happen again," said Arthur Miller, about his play *The American Clock* (1980). "I want to tell them that this thing that seems to go on forever doesn't." For many American writers, the Depression was to remain not the central fact of modern American experience, but a lasting reminder of the fragility of American dreams and values.

DEPRESSION BRITAIN

From January to March of 1936, George Orwell (1903–50, real name Eric Arthur Blair) was sent up to the North by the Left Book Club to write his report on the depression-hit industrial northern areas of Yorkshire and Lancashire. He travelled from the Midlands to Manchester, to Wigan and Liverpool, then back to London by way of Sheffield, Leeds and Birmingham. The account he wrote of his journey, *The Road to Wigan Pier* (1937), was a searing, vivid and moving left-wing polemic. It was one of many journeys taken by thirties' writers into a Britain that seemed battered as never before by social division, class conflict, industrial crisis and what dominated it all, the Slump.

The post-war British economy had been in decline ever since the 1926 General Strike, but the date usually given for the start of the Depression is 1929, the year the American "Great Crash" sent its ripples across the economies of the world. That year unemployment in Britain stood at 1.2 million. By 1930 it had risen to two million and by 1931 it was nearly three. The impact of economic deterioration was profound. In 1931 Britain went off the Gold Standard; shortly after Ramsay Macdonald's Labour Government changed to a Conservative-dominated National administration; in 1932 Oswald Mosley founded the British Union of Fascists. The sense that some climacteric had been reached in Britain's post-war history was widespread.

In the wake of Labour's election rout, optimism briefly took hold; Alec Waugh's *Thirteen Such Years* (1931), a chronicle of the period 1918–31, ends on a note of hands-on-the-wheel resolve – only to be cast down by persistent economic gloom. As the market for industrial and manufactured goods dried up worldwide, entire communities, especially in the manufacturing North, existed on the brink of destitution. The human consequences of the Depression penetrated every stratum of thirties' literature. The post-1945 working class fiction of Alan Sillitoe, Philip Callow and Sid Chaplin is full of

Working class poverty grew, hunger marchers tramped across the nation. The "Means Test," by which benefit claims were assessed, became a potent symbol of degradation: the climax of Walter Brierley's Means-Test Man *(1935) comes immediately after the hated government inspector's monthly visit.*

anguished glances back to the world of jobless families living six to a room, or old man Seaton's face in Sillitoe's *Saturday Night Sunday Morning* (1959) turning "black from want of fags." Even the "upper-class" fiction of the period shows the surface frivolity undermined by the Slump. In Evelyn Waugh's (1903–66) bleakest novel *A Handful of Dust* (1934), Brenda Last's unappetizing boyfriend Beaver is a redundant advertising man, and the men of Anthony Powell's society novels are uneasily conscious of their shaky hold on paid employment.

Essentially the Depression prodded into existence a vast literature that not only reflected the social conditions of the time but the radical politics that seemed the one solution. Some of this was working class in origin, still more was written by middle class onlookers. A link between the two was provided by bourgeois patrons like Stephen Spender, Christopher Isherwood and John Lehmann, whose literary magazines – notably Lehmann's *New Writing* – supplied a vehicle for working class talent. Ironically, one odd effect of the Slump was to create new literary opportunities for figures like Leslie Halward from Birmingham, who began writing after losing his job as a plasterer, or Walter Greenwood (*Love on the Dole*, 1933), who turned to fiction and drama after being made redundant from a Manchester department store. From the early 1930s, nearly all the depression blackspots had a contingent of (mostly working class) writers exploring the crisis of the times. There was James Hanley in Liverpool, Harry Heslop, Sid Chaplin and J.C. Grant in Durham, "Lewis Grassic Gibbon,"

George Blake and James Barke in industrial Scotland, Joe Corrie and James Welsh in the Fife and Lanarkshire coalfields, Walter Brierley and F.C. Boden in the Nottinghamshire and Derby coalfields. South Wales was represented by Lewis Jones and B.L. Coombes, a miner who wrote his autobiography as *These Poor Hands* (c.1935). Such writing wasn't confined to obviously distressed industrial regions: Jack Lindsay's *End of Cornwall* (1937) charts the collapse of rural living standards in the agricultural South-West.

Working class writing now existed not to describe work but its absence. Harry Heslop, once a South Shields miner, records the view from Tyneside in his *Last Cage Down* (1935). "Not a battleship being built. Not a crane moving. Not a man hitting a rivet with a hammer. A great, stultifying death." Slump literature has several constants. It was keen to dramatize, from a left-wing standpoint, recent political and economic history. Grassic Gibbons' fine trilogy *A Scots Quair* (1932–34), a bitter commentary on the post-war decline of industrial Scotland, charts the move into radical politics. In the second volume, *Cloud Howe* (1933), Chris Colquohoun moves from the country to the urban jute mills, but before long the post-1929 slide takes hold, throwing men out of work and bankrupting the mills, leaving families sleeping in hovels built for livestock. In the final volume *Grey Granite* (1934), Chris's son Ewan, now in Glasgow, wakes to political reality after seeing policemen beat a young boy senseless and their horses trample an old man to death while breaking up a demonstration against the hated Means Test. The novel ends with him leaving Scotland altogether on a hunger march to the south, and as in many other thirties' novels, looking towards a future in the Communist Party.

Such end-of-tether journeys recur throughout thirties' writing. There was the "tramp autobiography," probably inaugurated by W.H. Davies's *Autobiography of a Super-Tramp* in 1908. Orwell plainly recorded what it was like to be out on the streets in Paris and London (*Down and Out in Paris and London*, 1933) or walking the road to Wigan's very unfamous Pier. As unemployed men wandered the country seeking employment the "tramp novel" became a

sub-genre, a newly-barbed version of the older picaresque, with doss houses and casual wards replacing the coaching inns of Dickens and Fielding. Even middle class novels of the period – Orwell's *A Clergyman's Daughter* (1935) or J.B. Priestley's *The Good Companions* (1929) – record the tramp around a darkened land.

If social conditions brought displacement in search of work, it also heightened the sense of place. The decade's most celebrated regional alliance, the "Birmingham Group," was not strictly speaking working class, but at least two of its members, Walter Allen and John Hampson, wrote novels that outlived the decade. Elsewhere Phyllis Bentley and Lettice Cooper wrote about the West Riding of Yorkshire, while the novels of Walter Greenwood and Louis Golding map out the terrain of tiny areas of the

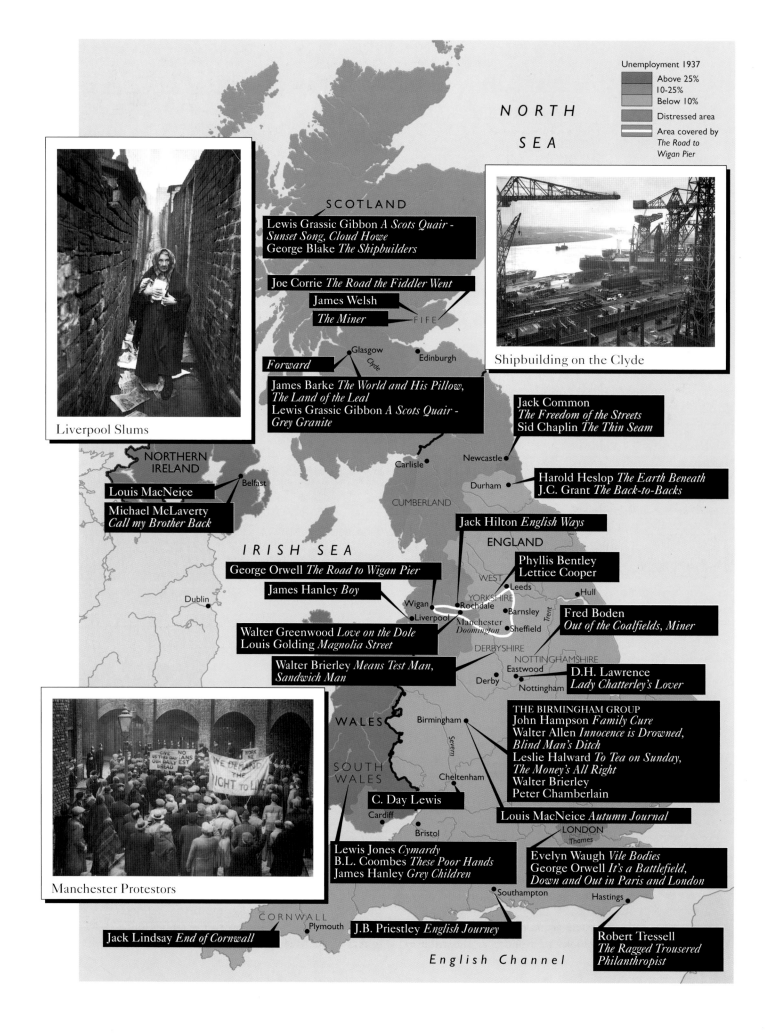

Unemployment 1937
- Above 25%
- 10-25%
- Below 10%
- Distressed area
- Area covered by *The Road to Wigan Pier*

NORTH SEA

SCOTLAND

Lewis Grassic Gibbon *A Scots Quair - Sunset Song, Cloud Howe*
George Blake *The Shipbuilders*

Joe Corrie *The Road the Fiddler Went*

James Welsh *The Miner* — FIFE

Forward

James Barke *The World and His Pillow, The Land of the Leal*
Lewis Grassic Gibbon *A Scots Quair - Grey Granite*

Glasgow
Clyde
Edinburgh

Jack Common *The Freedom of the Streets*
Sid Chaplin *The Thin Seam*

Newcastle
Carlisle

Durham

Harold Heslop *The Earth Beneath*
J.C. Grant *The Back-to-Backs*

CUMBERLAND

Shipbuilding on the Clyde

Liverpool Slums

NORTHERN IRELAND
Belfast

Louis MacNeice

Michael McLaverty *Call my Brother Back*

Jack Hilton *English Ways*

ENGLAND

Phyllis Bentley
Lettice Cooper

WEST YORKSHIRE
Leeds
Hull

IRISH SEA

George Orwell *The Road to Wigan Pier*

James Hanley *Boy*

Dublin

Wigan
Rochdale
Barnsley

Liverpool
Manchester
Doomington
Sheffield

Trent

Fred Boden *Out of the Coalfields, Miner*

Walter Greenwood *Love on the Dole*
Louis Golding *Magnolia Street*

DERBYSHIRE

Walter Brierley *Means Test Man, Sandwich Man*

NOTTINGHAMSHIRE
Eastwood

Derby
Nottingham

D.H. Lawrence *Lady Chatterley's Lover*

WALES

Birmingham

THE BIRMINGHAM GROUP
John Hampson *Family Cure*
Walter Allen *Innocence is Drowned, Blind Man's Ditch*
Leslie Halward *To Tea on Sunday, The Money's All Right*
Walter Brierley
Peter Chamberlain

Severn

SOUTH WALES

Cheltenham

C. Day Lewis

Cardiff

Louis MacNeice *Autumn Journal*

LONDON
Thames

Bristol

Lewis Jones *Cwmardy*
B.L. Coombes *These Poor Hands*
James Hanley *Grey Children*

Evelyn Waugh *Vile Bodies*
George Orwell *It's a Battlefield, Down and Out in Paris and London*

Southampton
Hastings

Manchester Protestors

CORNWALL
Plymouth

J.B. Priestley *English Journey*

Robert Tressell *The Ragged Trousered Philanthropist*

Jack Lindsay *End of Cornwall*

English Channel

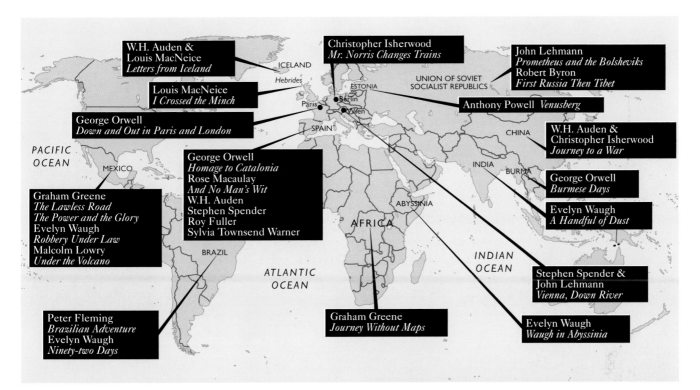

W.H. Auden &
Louis MacNeice
Letters from Iceland

ICELAND

Hebrides

Christopher Isherwood
Mr. Norris Changes Trains

UNION OF SOVIET
SOCIALIST REPUBLICS

ESTONIA

John Lehmann
Prometheus and the Bolsheviks
Robert Byron
First Russia Then Tibet

Louis MacNeice
I Crossed the Minch

Paris
Berlin
Wien

Anthony Powell *Venusberg*

George Orwell
Down and Out in Paris and London

SPAIN

CHINA

W.H. Auden &
Christopher Isherwood
Journey to a War

PACIFIC
OCEAN

MEXICO

George Orwell
Homage to Catalonia
Rose Macaulay
And No Man's Wit
W.H. Auden
Stephen Spender
Roy Fuller
Sylvia Townsend Warner

INDIA

BURMA

George Orwell
Burmese Days

ABYSSINIA

Evelyn Waugh
A Handful of Dust

Graham Greene
The Lawless Road
The Power and the Glory
Evelyn Waugh
Robbery Under Law
Malcolm Lowry
Under the Volcano

AFRICA

BRAZIL

ATLANTIC
OCEAN

INDIAN
OCEAN

Stephen Spender &
John Lehmann
Vienna, Down River

Peter Fleming
Brazilian Adventure
Evelyn Waugh
Ninety-two Days

Graham Greene
Journey Without Maps

Evelyn Waugh
Waugh in Abyssinia

UNEMPLOYMENT IN BRITAIN: *A good deal of the writing of the thirties is self-consciously small-scale and provincial. The majority of writers, says socialist literary historian, Andy Croft, focused on "a small locality, a family, a place of work, a street, or a short space of time." Many of the writers visited abroad, too, and again used their experience of travel,* above, *in their writing.*

Greater Manchester conurbation. Often province and capital found themselves at odds. As newspapers and magazines vied with each other to give accounts from the social and economic battlefront, a steady stream of established writers descended on distressed areas in what often seemed no more than a search for copy. J.B. Priestley's vivid *English Journey* (1934) is a powerful city-by-city record of a darkened England in the tradition of Defoe by a writer with deep Yorkshire roots. But it vied with works with titles like *Hungry England* or *Men Without Work*, part of the era's fascination with documentary. Orwell's *Road to Wigan Pier*, published, despite its own publisher's reservations, by the Left Book Club, had a circulation of 60,000 copies. But it also caused resentment. Jack Hilton, of the National Unemployed Workers Movement, to whom Orwell went for advice, felt the book a "travesty," and recorded a reverse journey, from Rochdale to Epsom in his *English Ways* (1938).

Fear of unemployment was not confined to the working classes. By 1934 the number of jobless "white-collar" workers was estimated at 400,000 out of a workforce of two million. The growing anxieties of professional and clerical employees ran through many a novel of lower-middle class life. Mr Smeeth, the dessicated accounts clerk of Priestley's *Angel Pavement* (1930), looks in wonder at the tribe of

The "Pylon Poets" (*Isherwood* left *and Auden* right) *travelled extensively throughout Britain and abroad.*

applicants for the single vacancy at the veneer distributing firm of Twigg & Dersingham. At the novel's close, thrown out of work when the firm is bankrupted by a charismatic swindler, Mr Smeeth contemplates his most ghastly nightmare – the loss of his livelihood.

The Depression was effectively ended by the Second World War: it took rearmament to solve the problems of the dole queue, fear of European conflict to transform the political mood. A more varied and troubled social map was drawn, a harder-nosed working class voice changed the note of British writing. From the standpoint of the unemployed miner or steelworker, scraping for food, living in fear of the Means Test, War at least did mean work.

THE SPANISH CIVIL WAR

The Spanish Civil War was the single most inflammatory political and military event in Europe in the run-up to the Second World War. It broke out in mid-July 1936, when right-wing elements in the Spanish Army – an uneasy coalition of anti-democrats, monarchists, Catholics and nationalists headed by General Francisco Franco – led a coup against the newly elected Republican, left-of-centre, Popular Front government of Manuel Azaña. Large parts of western, northern and southern Spain were soon under Francoist control. But attempted uprisings in Madrid and Barcelona were suppressed by ordinary working folk. The Basque country, Catalonia and large parts of eastern Spain stayed loyal.

A slow war of attrition set in which endured for three terrible years. From the start, the Civil War was recognized worldwide as an enactment and symbol of the struggles between Fascism and Democracy, dictatorship and freedom, right and left, that were leading Europe steadily toward a new World War. Overnight, Spain became the main focus of the ideological differences which dominated writing and culture in the inter-war years. Within weeks Spain turned into an international trial of military strength and strategy between Fascism and Communism. As France and Britain preached neutrality, tried to bring warring parties to the negotiating table and organized international Non-Intervention agreements, the Fascist governments of Italy, Portugal and Germany poured in material and men (90,000 or more) to help Franco. On the other side the Soviet Union – far less amply –

Called on by Republican posters like the one above, democrats, socialists, Communists – women as well as men – flocked to Spain to stop the spread of Fascism to yet another country, defend democracy and keep the Spanish revolution going.

sent in weaponry and personnel. The main effort of the Communist International, the Comintern, was to organize International Brigades of volunteer fighters.

Fifty thousand or so foreigners fought in the International Brigades and other republican units, such as the militias of the anarchist POUM (*Partido Obrero de Unificación Marxista*). The volunteers included scores of writers, artists, intellectuals, many of them exiles from Mussolini's Italy or Hitler's Germany. They offered their services and their lives as fighters, propagandists, advisers,

medical orderlies. Republican Spain also filled with writing observers, visiting poets, sympathetic artists and artistes. It was hard for self-respecting intellectuals to stay away; for those who did, the Civil War still became the main obsession of late thirties' writing. On the Left, it was the last chance to resist the closure of artistic expression that had happened under Fascist dictators (they often turned a blind eye to what had happened under Stalin). On the Right, Franco was perceived as Christianity's latest crusade against the spread of Satanic Communism. Few Rightist writers took up arms for Franco. The South African poet Roy Campbell boasted he did. But he was lying.

Modern warfare really came of age in Spain. The Nationalists deployed the latest tactics and horrors with relish – especially in the air, where they had superiority, with hundreds of German and Italian planes. The civilian populations of Madrid and Barcelona were bombed frequently, the ancient Basque capital of Guernica shattered by the bombers of the German Condor Legion. The vividness of the threat to modern freethinking culture was brought home when between 18 and 19 August, 1936, in the vengeful rightist terror in Granada, Federico García Lorca, one of Spain's leading modernist poets and playwrights, was shot dead by Nationalist gunmen (they also fired into his buttocks to signify their hostility to his well-known homosexuality).

Hemingway (third from left at the back in the trenches) was one of the many writers who went to Spain as a journalist.

Old Etonian socialist George Orwell (the tall fighter at the back of the queue below) went out for the British Independent Labour Party (ILP), enrolled in the POUM militia at its Lenin barracks in Barcelona, and fought on the Aragon front.

Leftist writers (and most of Spain's eminent writers and artists – Picasso, Casals, Machado, Hernandez – were Republicans) could now see plainly who the enemy was. "If we win here we will win everywhere," thinks Robert Jordan, hero of Ernest Hemingway's Spanish Civil War novel *For Whom the Bell Tolls* (1940). Fear of losing in Spain, and so losing everywhere, was in many volunteers' minds.

According to good estimates, some 27 German writers fought in Spain, including Communist novelist Gustav Regler (Commissar of the XII International Brigade) and Ludwig Renn, author of the pacifist novel *Krieg* (1929). The Commander of the XII Brigade was Hungarian novelist Mata Zalka, fighting under the *nom de guerre* "General Lukacz." The Brigade also had the renowned French Communist poet Louis Aragon. The French novelist André Malraux organized the tiny Republican air force in the first weeks of the coup. Other French volunteers were the novelist Claude Simon and the philosopher Simone Weil. The English Communist novelist Ralph Bates, resident in Catalonia for many years, became a Commissar. W.H. Auden, the best young

English poet of the day, volunteered knowing he'd make "a bloody bad soldier." Stephen Spender, a lesser poet but in all senses a bigger man, joined the British Communist Party to get its political sponsorship to fight, perhaps to die (the Party told him that Byronic martyrs would do the cause much good). Others who went included the Irish poet Ewart Milne, with the British Medical Unit for most of the conflict; the Irish Republican poet and activist, Charles Donelly; David Gascoyne, the Surrealist poet. Christopher St John Sprigg ("Christopher Caudwell"), novelist and literary theorist, drove an ambulance from London and stayed to fight. John Cornford, promising young poet, was on holiday in France in the Cambridge university vacation, crossed the border, and joined a Republican column of POUM fighters. Julian Bell, another new poet and nephew of Virginia Woolf, drove an ambulance to Spain and stayed as a driver. Others who saw active service include Communists Ralph Fox, Tom Wintringham and Clive Branson.

Not every writer was there to fight or participate. French novelist Antoine de Saint-Exupéry, Louis MacNeice, John Dos Passos and Ernst Toller all went as journalists. In July 1937 some eighty international writers were convoyed in a spectacular motorcade across Republican Spain (Madrid, Valencia, Barcelona) as part of the Second Congress of the International Association of Writers. "*Viva los intelectuales!*" cried the peasants in even the smallest villages. The mere presence of Julian Benda and André Chamson, Alexei Tolstoi and Octavio Paz, Sylvia Townsend

In 1937 the Left Review *declared "We are determined, or compelled, to take sides."*

As in so many Spanish fictions and images, the cruelty of bullfights and the crucifixion find their apotheosis in bodies smashed by bullets and bombs – most memorably in Picasso's painting Guernica, left, done in memory of the bombed and burned Basque town of that name, shown in the photograph, below.

Warner and Valentine Ackland all rooting for the Republic, was a significant propaganda coup. So were the 127 British writers who declared for the Republic ("¡UPTHEREPUBLIC!" was Samuel Beckett's terse contribution) in a *Left Review* survey of mid-1937, "Authors Take Sides on the Spanish War." And it was notable how few writers joined Ezra Pound and the Catholic Evelyn Waugh in supporting Franco. Graham Greene sat wryly on the fence; François Mauriac and Georges Bernanos were vocal against Franco and his Vatican supporters.

"How could this fight be lost now, with Hemingway on our side?" asked one American when the author spoke in New York's Carnegie Hall at a showing of Joris Ivens's documentary-propaganda film *Spanish Earth*, which Hemingway scripted, and John Dos Passos, Lillian Hellman and Archibald MacLeish sponsored. But even with Hemingway on its side, prospects for Republican victory leaked slowly but surely away. There was strong resistance; Madrid did not yield till the very end, in March 1939. But the great actions – on the Jarama, at Brunete, Teruel, on the Ebro – either brought stalemate or new Nationalist success. Barcelona fell in January 1939. By April Franco's victory was total.

The picture for writers was as grindingly dismaying as the war the volunteers had gone to assist. Orwell was badly wounded, nearly killed, by a bullet in the neck on the Aragon front. On the same front Regler was wounded, "General Lukacz" killed. John Cornford, now with the International Brigades, was wounded in the defence of Madrid, and killed in action on the Córdoba front at the end of December 1936. Ralph Fox died there days later. Christopher St John Sprigg and Charles Donnelly were killed in the Jarama fighting in February 1937. Julian Bell was killed in July 1937 when his ambulance was shelled in the Brunete offensive. Six thousand or so International Brigaders were killed in Spain, five hundred of them Britons. More were wounded, many severely.

Out of this bloody conflict came many notable works of prose and poetry: Auden's great poem "Spain" (1937), Malraux's *Days of Hope* (1937), Regler's *The Great Crusade*

(1940), Hemingway's *For Whom the Bell Tolls* (1940), Orwell's *Homage to Catalonia* (1938), Claude Simon's later, labyrinthine novel, critical of Orwell, *The Georgics* (1981). What they share with most leftist writings is a tone of unheroic muteness, defeat, failure, death, political numbness and human misery. The prevalent genre is elegy. The Spanish bears MacNeice saw in Barcelona Zoo epitomized the whole story: they were "99 per cent dead."

Triumphalist writing belonged to stay-at-home poets like Cecil Day Lewis and Edgell Rickword, or Roy Campbell and Hilaire Belloc on the other side. There might just be a future for friendship among comrades and lovers, but that would be tomorrow: "today the struggle," Auden keeps repeating. A persistent note is apocalypse, final days of reckoning: "On the last mile to Huesca / The last fence for our pride" (that's Cornford's poem "Heart of the Heartless World"). The story of Hemingway's Robert Jordan ends with the hero maimed and fallen, awaiting inevitable death. "No wars are nice," Cornford wrote to his girlfriend Margot Heinemann from hospital in Madrid, "and even a revolutionary war is ugly enough." In

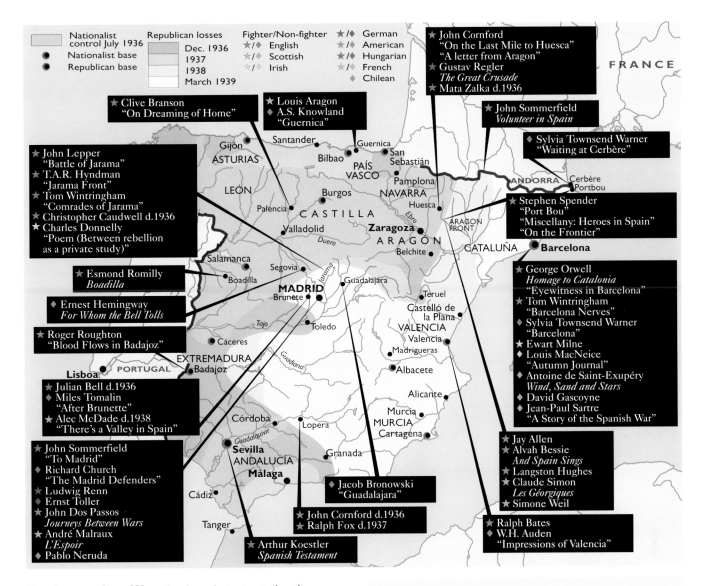

THE SPANISH CIVIL WAR: For the main part mapping the Civil War – and much of the writing is besotted with geography – is a mapping of pain.

fact a revolutionary and political war like this one was especially ugly, not least because of bitter conflicts on the Republican side. Anarchists, Trotskyites and socialists were all at war with the Communists, and the Communists with them. Stalin's men, it was soon clear, were exporting the neurotic Soviet obsession with Party purity, and using the terror tactics of the secret police to correct deviationism.

Western literature was reanimated by the Civil War. It would go on remembering it for years, mainly as the locale of lost socialist dreams, the taking of sides, the ending of innocence. As Louis MacNeice puts it in his autobiography, *The Strings Are False*: "The young men for whom the Spanish war had been a crusade in white armour, a Quest of the Grail open only to the pure in heart, felt as if their world had burst; there was nothing left but a handful of limp rubber rag; it was no good trying any more."

"Tomorrow for the young the poets
exploding like bombs,
The walks by the lake, the weeks
of perfect communion;
Tomorrow the bicycle races
Through the suburbs on summer evenings.
But today the struggle.
Today the deliberate increase in the
chances of death,
The conscious acceptance of guilt
in the necessary murder;
Today the expending of powers
On the flat ephemeral pamphlet
and the boring meeting.
The stars are dead. The animals will not look.
We are left alone with our day,
and the time is short, and
History to the defeated
May say Alas but cannot help nor pardon."

from "Spain" by W.H. Auden, 1937

WRITERS GO TO WAR

The Second World War was global and total. It happened on the ground, in the air, on the seas, under the waves. The fighting was terribly mobile; no front stayed fixed for long. The German word for a war that would strike like lightning, *Blitzkrieg*, entered the world's language once German forces burst into Poland in September 1939. Soon came advances into Norway and Denmark (April 1940), Holland, Luxembourg, Belgium (mid-May 1940), France (Paris fell 14 June, 1940), North Africa (March 1941), and Russia (June 1941). Lightning war seemed invincible. When Germany's ally Japan devastated the American fleet in a surprise attack on Pearl Harbor in December 1941, *Blitzkrieg* looked like an impressively exportable strategy.

Only slowly – with America now in the fray, and the Soviet Union turned on its former ally – did the tide turn. In North Africa Rommel's army was defeated in the tank battle at El Alamein in 1942; soon British, American and Commonwealth troops would push into Tunisia, across to Sicily. In the awful Russian winter of 1942–3 the German advance on Moscow foundered. General von Paulus's army surrendered (against Hitler's orders) at Stalingrad on 31 January, 1943; soon vast Russian armies would slowly drive German forces homeward. In the Pacific, American naval forces gradually made way against the Japanese, beginning with the battle of Guadalcanal (13 November, 1942). German cities (Cologne, Bremen, Hamburg, Berlin, Nuremburg, Dresden) were shattered from the air. The countdown to the end came with D-Day, 6 June, 1944. The British reached the Rhine on 15 February, 1945; next day Americans started huge air attacks on Tokyo. By 20 April, 1945, the Russians were in Berlin; on 8 May German forces surrendered. The Japanese war looked set to continue, but the atomic bombs on Hiroshima and Nagasaki on 6 and 9 August brought things to a horrific close.

It had indeed been total war. No-one in Europe or many other places was immune from its horrors. Distinctions between soldiers and civilians were obliterated; you were as likely to die in bed as on the battlefield. More than forty million lost their lives: over twenty million in the Soviet Union, three million Germans, three and a half million Japanese, some 300,000 Britons, the same number of Americans. In the ruthless Hitler-inspired war of extermination, six million Jews, and gypsies, homosexuals and other *Untermenschen*, perished in ghettos, prisons and extermination camps. Communities could be wiped out; massacres were not uncommon.

Japan's surprise attack on the American fleet at Pearl Harbor in 1941, above, brought the United States into the global conflict.

The War involved ordinary people – and writers and embryo writers – as never before. Young and not-so-young-writers were conscripted or volunteered to fight, on a scale unimaginable in the history of literary culture. John Pudney, Arthur C. Clarke, William Cooper, Roald Dahl, Christopher Middleton, Vernon Watkins, and Australian Patrick White were with the Royal Air Force. Americans like James Dickey, John Ciardi, Randall Jarrell, Howard Nemerov served with the USAF; Joseph Heller flew 65 bomber missions out of Corsica. William Golding, Roy Fuller, Alan Ross and Donald Davie were with the Royal Navy; Gore Vidal, Herman Wouk, J.P. Donleavy, Hubert Selby, Lawrence Ferlinghetti served in American fleets.

Soldier writers from Britain and the Commonwealth included Anthony Powell (Intelligence Corps), Anthony Burgess (Medical Corps), Kingsley Amis (Royal Corps of Signals), Brian Moore, Vernon Scannell, Spike Milligan, F.T. Prince and Edwin Morgan. Evelyn Waugh and Dan

Davin saw action in Crete, Brian Aldiss, Paul Scott, C.H. Sisson in India. American armies took Terry Southern, Isaac Asimov, J.D. Salinger, Richard Wilbur to Europe, Norman Mailer, Karl Shapiro, Kenneth Koch to the Far East. The vast number of poets in the Russian forces included Mikhail Dudin (siege of Leningrad), Alexsandr Tvardovsky, Mikhail Lvov and Mikhail Lukonin. German armies had Walter Bauer, Gottfried Benn, Günter Eich, Heinrich Böll (future Nobel Prizewinner). Günter Grass and Horst Bienek were boy recruits. Many were killed or imprisoned. Keith Douglas died in the Normandy landings, Sidney Keyes in Tunisia, Alun Lewis in Burma. Russian poet Pavel Kogan died near Novorossiik, Mikhail Kulchitsky near Stalingrad.

As writers recorded, total war touched all corners of life. Stephen Spender, Peter Quennell, William Samson and Henry Green were in the London Fire Service during the Blitz (see Green's *Caught*, 1943). Those not at the front were "backroom boys" (or girls), like Nigel Balchin (War Office), Cecil Day Lewis and Laurie Lee (Ministry of Information), Richard Hughes (Admiralty), Henry Reed, Mary Wesley and Angus Wilson (all codebreakers at Bletchley). In Occupied Europe, things were far grimmer. Jean-Paul Sartre, Albert Camus, Louis Aragon, René Char, Paul Eluard, Jean Tardieu, Francis Ponge, Nathalie Sarraute and Samuel Beckett were among those who risked their necks in the French Resistance, as did Ignazio Silone and others in the Italian. Polish poets Zbigniew Herbert, Czeslaw Milosz, Anna Swir, Tadeusz Rósewicz were involved in underground struggles. Krzysztof Baczynski died in the Warsaw Uprising of August 1944. Abba Kovner and Abraham Sutzkever escaped from the Vilna ghetto to fight with partisans against the Germans.

Many Jewish writers were compelled into forced-labour batallions, including Hungarians Miklós Radnóti and Istvan Vas. As a very young man, the Romanian Jewish poet Paul Celan escaped extermination (unlike his parents) but was held in a labour camp. Primo Levi (Italian) and Stanley Wygodski (Polish) managed to survive Auschwitz. Elie Wiesel and Aharon Appelfeld were sent to camps as mere boys; Wiesel survived Auschwitz and Buchenwald; Appelfeld, from Czernowitz, escaped detention and hid for three years in the Ukrainian countryside before joining the Russian army. The Berlin Jewish poet Nelly Sachs (another future Nobel Prize-winner) was ordered to a labour camp in 1940, but fled to Sweden. Luba Krugman Gurdus from Bialystock escaped

Elie Wiesel is shown above *at the far end of the middle row of a room in the concentration camp at Buchenwald, where he was sent as a boy and survived to relate the experience in his writing.*

shipment to an extermination camp when an SS guard recognized her from her college days; she wrote in hiding.

What unites such lives on both sides of the War is a shared sense of civilian existence disrupted by unimagined and unsought horrors. As Yuliya Drunina, a young Russian medical orderly who had to drag men to safety under fire, wrote: "Whoever says war is not horrible, knows nothing about war." Walter Benjamin, the great critic in exile in France from Hitler's Germany, committing suicide on the Spanish border because he couldn't get out of France; Irishman Samuel Beckett, on the run in occupied Paris, hiding out in Nathalie Sarraute's attic, driven into exile in the Vaucluse; the French poet René

AMERICAN WAR FICTION

1944 John Hersey *A Bell for Adano*
1946 Gore Vidal *Williwaw*
1947 John Horne Burns *The Gallery*
1948 Irwin Shaw *The Young Lions*
1948 James Gould Cozzens *Guard of Honor*
1949 John Hawkes *The Cannibal*
1951 Herman Wouk *The 'Caine' Mutiny*
1951 James Jones *From Here to Eternity*
1953 J.D. Salinger *Nine Stories*
1961 Joseph Heller *Catch-22*
1969 Kurt Vonnegut *Slaughterhouse-Five*
1973 Thomas Pynchon *Gravity's Rainbow*

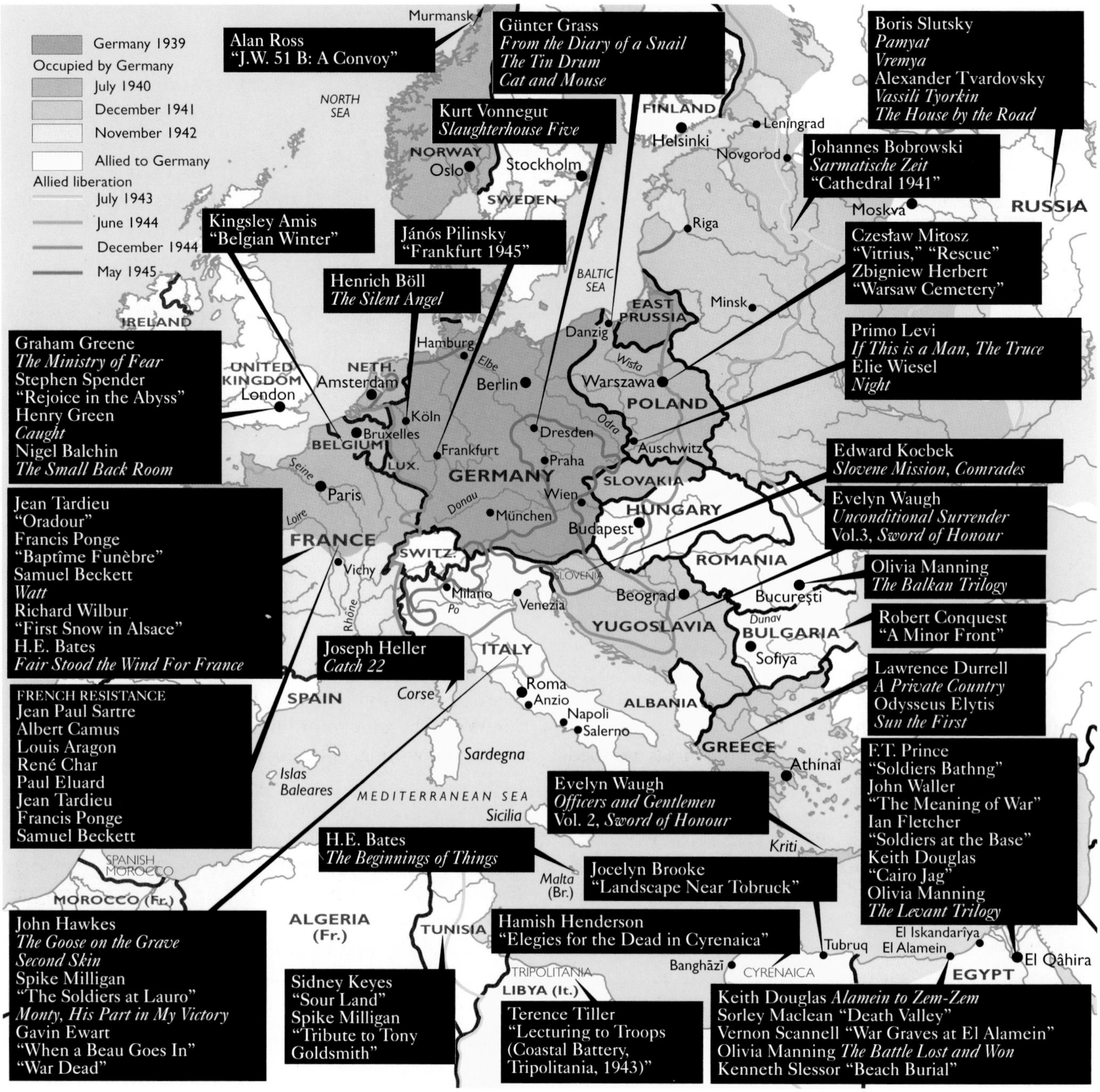

Germany 1939
Occupied by Germany
July 1940
December 1941
November 1942
Allied to Germany
Allied liberation
July 1943
June 1944
December 1944
May 1945
Alan Ross
"J.W. 51 B: A Convoy"
Günter Grass
From the Diary of a Snail
The Tin Drum
Cat and Mouse
Boris Slutsky
Pamyat
Vremya
Alexander Tvardovsky
Vassili Tyorkin
The House by the Road
Kurt Vonnegut
Slaughterhouse Five
Johannes Bobrowski
Sarmatische Zeit
"Cathedral 1941"
Kingsley Amis
"Belgian Winter"
János Pilinsky
"Frankfurt 1945"
Czesław Miłosz
"Vitrius," "Rescue"
Zbigniew Herbert
"Warsaw Cemetery"
Henrich Böll
The Silent Angel
Graham Greene
The Ministry of Fear
Stephen Spender
"Rejoice in the Abyss"
Henry Green
Caught
Nigel Balchin
The Small Back Room
Primo Levi
If This is a Man, The Truce
Elie Wiesel
Night
Edward Kocbek
Slovene Mission, Comrades
Jean Tardieu
"Oradour"
Francis Ponge
"Baptîme Funèbre"
Samuel Beckett
Watt
Richard Wilbur
"First Snow in Alsace"
H.E. Bates
Fair Stood the Wind For France
Evelyn Waugh
Unconditional Surrender
Vol.3, Sword of Honour
Olivia Manning
The Balkan Trilogy
Robert Conquest
"A Minor Front"
Joseph Heller
Catch 22
Lawrence Durrell
A Private Country
Odysseus Elytis
Sun the First
FRENCH RESISTANCE
Jean Paul Sartre
Albert Camus
Louis Aragon
René Char
Paul Eluard
Jean Tardieu
Francis Ponge
Samuel Beckett
F.T. Prince
"Soldiers Bathng"
John Waller
"The Meaning of War"
Ian Fletcher
"Soldiers at the Base"
Keith Douglas
"Cairo Jag"
Olivia Manning
The Levant Trilogy
Evelyn Waugh
Officers and Gentlemen
Vol. 2, Sword of Honour
H.E. Bates
The Beginnings of Things
Jocelyn Brooke
"Landscape Near Tobruck"
John Hawkes
The Goose on the Grave
Second Skin
Spike Milligan
"The Soldiers at Lauro"
Monty, His Part in My Victory
Gavin Ewart
"When a Beau Goes In"
"War Dead"
Hamish Henderson
"Elegies for the Dead in Cyrenaica"
Sidney Keyes
"Sour Land"
Spike Milligan
"Tribute to Tony
Goldsmith"
Terence Tiller
"Lecturing to Troops
(Coastal Battery,
Tripolitania, 1943)"
Keith Douglas Alamein to Zem-Zem
Sorley Maclean "Death Valley"
Vernon Scannell "War Graves at El Alamein"
Olivia Manning The Battle Lost and Won
Kenneth Slessor "Beach Burial"
Murmansk
NORTH SEA
NORWAY
Oslo
Stockholm
SWEDEN
FINLAND
Helsinki
Leningrad
Novgorod
Moskva
RUSSIA
Riga
BALTIC SEA
EAST PRUSSIA
Minsk
Danzig
IRELAND
UNITED KINGDOM
London
NETH.
Amsterdam
Hamburg
Elbe
Berlin
Wisła
Warszawa
POLAND
Köln
Bruxelles
BELGIUM
LUX.
Frankfurt
Dresden
Odra
Auschwitz
Praha
GERMANY
SLOVAKIA
Seine
Paris
Loire
FRANCE
Donau
München
Wien
HUNGARY
Budapest
SWITZ.
Vichy
SLOVENIA
ROMANIA
Milano
Po
Venezia
Beograd
București
Rhône
YUGOSLAVIA
Dunav
BULGARIA
Sofiya
ITALY
Roma
Anzio
Napoli
Salerno
SPAIN
Corse
ALBANIA
GREECE
Sardegna
Athínai
Islas Baleares
MEDITERRANEAN SEA
Sicilia
Kriti
SPANISH MOROCCO
MOROCCO (Fr.)
Malta (Br.)
ALGERIA (Fr.)
TUNISIA
Tubruq
El Iskandarîya
El Alamein
El Qâhira
TRIPOLITANIA
Banghāzī
CYRENAICA
EGYPT
LIBYA (It.)

Leynaud, imprisoned by the Germans at Fort-Montluc and shot in 1944 with 18 others – all longed to be elsewhere.

These are civilians who happen to be in war, clutching at sanity in writerly occupations reminiscent of peace. In Murmansk, destination of the harshest convoy route, poet Donald Davie learns Russian to read the poets. Before a desert tank battle, Keith Douglas makes sure he's packed Shakespeare's *Sonnets*. In India, Alun Lewis mails poems to the London magazines. Parachuted in on a mission to Tito's partisans in Croatia, Evelyn Waugh corrects the proofs of *Brideshead Revisited* (1945) – he told Graham Greene the book was his protest at "spam, blackouts and Nissen huts." On leave in Cairo and Alexandria, Keith Douglas and other poets find common literary cause with British Council and academic exiles there

THE WAR IN EUROPE AND NORTH AFRICA: *The Second World War was global and total. Writers fought and recorded the conflict throughout the world.*

> **"When a Beau goes in,**
> **Into the drink,**
> **It makes you think,**
> **Because, you see, they always sink**
> **But nobody says 'Poor lad'**
> **Or goes about looking sad**
> **Because, you see, it's war,**
> **It's the unalterable law."**
>
> "When a Beau Goes In" Gavin Ewart
> (A Beau was a Bristol Beaufort fighter airplane)

(Terence Tiller, Laurence Durrell, Bernard Spencer), as Olivia Manning records in her *Levant Trilogy* (1977–80).

"What in all worlds am I doing here?" asks Bernard Spencer's "Letter Home." Many of the war's most poignant literary moments are about its shocking impact on the ordinary. In Saul Bellow's *Dangling Man* (1944), a young Chicago intellectual awaits enlistment in existential agony. The first snow of winter falls

During the Second World War no-one was immune from the horrors: whole cities, like Coventry in England above, *were destroyed in the bombings.*

in Richard Wilbur's poem "First Snow in Alsace" – onto a dead man's eyes. Bomb flares like "clusters of spangles off a Christmas tree" descend onto a London street in Graham Greene's *The Ministry of Fear* (1943). Two lovers faithful unto death make love as the bombs get nearer in Zbigniew Herbert's poem "Two Drops." The soldiers in Alun Lewis's "All Day it Has Rained," shelter bored in their tents, smoking Woodbines, talking of girls and "dropping bombs on Rome."

A few militaristic souls like Keith Douglas relished the Army's drill and bull, but most saw military life as offensive and absurd. Evelyn Waugh's *Sword of Honour* trilogy (1952–61), the most substantial British novels to come from the War, professes to admire the "biffing" soldier Brigadier Ritchie Hook. But Waugh was too old and fat to be the soldier he'd have liked to be, and after the fiasco of the Crete withdrawal was kicked out of real soldiering. Like Kingsley Amis, Alun Lewis, Julian McLaren-Ross and Heinrich Böll, Waugh really belongs to the awkward squad these writers celebrate, as in Amis's mocking poem "The Voice of Authority: A Language Game." "Being in the Army is like being in the digestive processes of an immense worm," writes Randall Jarrell; and Henry Reed's poetic sequence "Lessons of the War" is about the mismatch between the Army's unselfconscious erotic jargon for weaponry and real lovemaking.

Little wonder that many of the most important works that record the experience are bitter or black-humorous classics of martinet caprice, military cock-up, and what was known in American slang as SNAFU (Situation Normal, All Fouled Up): Norman Mailer's *The Naked and the Dead* (1957) about battle in the islands of the Pacific, Pierre Boulle's satire on brass-necked English officer-class stickling for army regulations, *The Bridge on the River Kwai* (1952), and classic of them all, Joseph Heller's brilliant account of the air war over Italy, *Catch-22* (1961). In his *Memoirs* (1991) Kingsley Amis describes his experience

of British army life as akin to being in a Science Fiction world, possessed of its own logic, out of sync with the normal. Kurt Vonnegut, himself a prisoner-of-war in Dresden in 1945, agrees. His *Slaughterhouse Five* (1969) captures the absurdism of the city's destruction through a switching between historical present and Science Fiction time. A similar sense of the nightmare dislocation of the real runs through much of the writing on the Holocaust: the "ingeniously devised habitation of death" of Nellie Sachs' "O the Chimneys."

What writing does best in the face of global terror is to assume its basic task of bearing witness, telling the truth, subverting what the French Resistance poet Pierre Seghers called the "*fausse parole,*" the lying word. "How Did They Kill My Grandmother?" asks Boris Slutsky's poem: "I'll tell you how they killed her." Primo Levi and Elie Wiesel become recording angels; it's a traditional role for Jewish writing. The most important writings from the War tend to be marked by the imaginative strain of devising a radical mode of witness. Günter Grass's novel of growing up in Third Reich Danzig, *Cat and Mouse* (1961), wonders whether rubbing the narrator's typewriter with onion juice might just be the best way of bringing home the smell of that city, those years. The War's most memorable writings found their onion juice. Eugene Ionesco's plays *Chairs* (1952) and *Rhinoceros* (1960) are surreal allegories of the invasion of personal space; Beckett's

In The Caine Mutiny *Herman Wouk based his story on the battles in the Pacific, outlined in the map,* below, *from the book.*

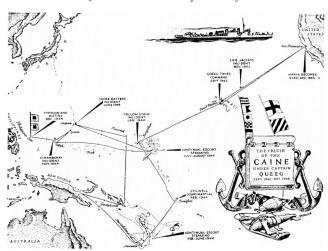

During the Second World War whole communities were wiped out; massacres were not uncommon. The photograph, left, shows the result of one such massacre: on 10 June, 1994 at Oradour-sur-Glanes near Limoges German soldiers shot 402 men and burned alive 240 women and children locked in the church. Jean Tardieu records the horror of this event in his poem, below.

"Oradour I shout and scream
each time that a heart bursts
under the assassins' blows
a terror-stricken face
two wide eyes, two red eyes
two serious eyes, two large eyes
like the night, madness
the two eyes of a small child
they will not leave me;
Oradour I no longer dare
read or pronounce your name"

"Oradour" Jean Tardieu

allegory of distress is in the Vauclause in the labyrinthine anti-novel *Watt* (1953) he wrote there, and in his parable of exile and displacement, *Waiting for Godot* (1952); Camus meditated on evil and fascism in his novels *The Outsider* (1942) and *The Plague* (1947), written in response to Nazism's "nihilist revolution."

Extreme times called for extreme and tangential measures, but less inventive writers settled for recording the moment of being quietly appalled. Much Second World War poetry captures private moments set in a "Personal Landscape" (the title of a poetry quarterly produced by the Alexandria group). A striking number of poems consider that private text of record, the photograph. "My photograph already looks historic," reflects Roy Fuller in "The Middle of a War." Keith Douglas's "Vergissmeinnicht," Vadim Strelchenko's "My Photograph," Zbigniew Herbert's "Photograph" – all sense there is time for no more than a postcard-sized jotting, a scene captured as if for a letter home (as in Douglas's "Cairo Jag," Spender's "Air Raid Across the Bay at Plymouth").

The geographical scale of war was vast. For many writers – refugees, prisoners, forced labourers, camp victims, soldiers and sailors far from home, always on the move – war experience was a grim odyssey, a farcical epic, a Vonnegutian set of Billy-Pilgrimages. The Welshman Alun Lewis despairs in India. The Jamaican-American Louis Simpson is frost-bitten in France, goes looting in Germany. Keith Douglas fights his way, like the other Desert Rats, from Alamein to Zem Zem, and from there to his death in Normandy. "This geography shrinks into sad/And personal trifles" is how Roy Fuller's "In Africa" puts it. There are few heroics. Herbert's "Farewell to September" mocks the suicidal heroics that sent Polish cavalry against the *Blitzkrieg* tanks. Tvardovsky's long poem "Vasily Tyorkin" is an extended version of the anti-heroic tropes Wilfred Owen and Siegfried Sassoon made the Great War's truthtelling norm. Simpson's "The Heroes" notes: "The heroes were packaged and sent home in parts." "Forward! Hurrah! The Red Dawn!!" writes Kulchitsky in his notebook, "I don't know how to write such verse." Fallen flyers are everywhere: in H.E. Bates's *Fair Stood the Wind for France* (1944), John Pudney's famous poem "For Johnny" ("Do not despair/ For Johnny-head-in-air"), Randall Jarrell's "The Death of the Ball Turret Gunner," Bernard Spencer's "Death of an Airman."

What does prevail is elegy. Elegies for massacred people, chums killed in battle, loved ones taken away and murdered: Primo Levi's poem "Epitaph," Vernon Scannell's "War Graves at El Alamein," Kenneth Slessor's "Beach Burial," Abba Kovner's "My Little Sister," Nellie Sachs' "In the Habitations of Death." Elegies, too, for destroyed cities: Heinrich Böll's Cologne (see his aston-ishing "lost" novel *The Silent Angel*, published only in 1992), Bobrowski's Novgorod ("Cathedral," 1941), János Pilinsky's Frankfurt ("Frankfurt 1945"), Spender's London, Hiroshima in the poems of Nobuyuki Saga, Tamiki Hara, who killed himself on learning he had radiation sickness and Sankichi Toge, who died of that sickness.

Elegies too, even more momentously, for God. Where God is in these terrible times is the question that unites Böll's narrative self, stumbling on Cologne's broken Catholic effigies in *The Silent Angel*; Günter Grass, brought up, as he puts it, "between the Holy Ghost and Hitler's photograph" ("Kleckerburg"); Elie Wiesel in his Auschwitz memoir *Night* (1958); Czeslaw Milosz in his "A Poor Christian Looks at the Ghetto;" and Richard Eberhart, who asks "Is God by definition indifferent, beyond it all?" ("The Fury of Aerial Bombardment").

F.T. Prince's much-anthologized North Africa poem "Soldiers Bathing" links the soldiers' naked bodies with the stripped, crucified Christ, but the note of redemptive suffering is rare in the writing. Much more typical is the

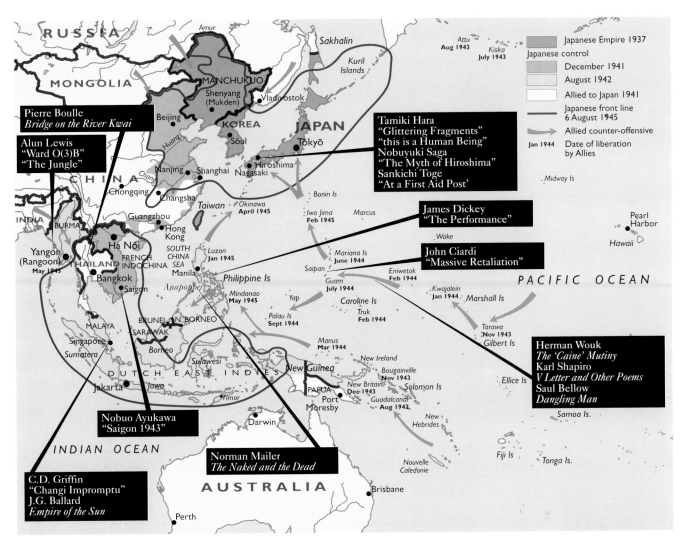

Map legend:
- Japanese Empire 1937
- Japanese control December 1941
- August 1942
- Allied to Japan 1941
- Japanese front line 6 August 1945
- Allied counter-offensive
- Jan 1944 Date of liberation by Allies

Map labels:

Pierre Boulle
Bridge on the River Kwai

Alun Lewis
"Ward O(3)B"
"The Jungle"

Tamiki Hara
"Glittering Fragments"
"this is a Human Being"
Nobuyuki Saga
"The Myth of Hiroshima"
Sankichi Toge
"At a First Aid Post'

James Dickey
"The Performance"

John Ciardi
"Massive Retaliation"

Herman Wouk
The 'Caine' Mutiny
Karl Shapiro
V Letter and Other Poems
Saul Bellow
Dangling Man

Nobuo Ayukawa
"Saigon 1943"

Norman Mailer
The Naked and the Dead

C.D. Griffin
"Changi Impromptu"
J.G. Ballard
Empire of the Sun

THE WAR IN THE PACIFIC: *The war in the Pacific seemed set to continue until the atom bombs were dropped on Hiroshima and Nagasaki in August 1945.*

existentialist stress on the randomness of suffering and mere human endurance, in Camus' *The Outsider* and Beckett's *Godot* – and, even more arresting, the recurrent sense of an unjudgmental refusal to hate the enemy and oppressor wherever they are. This is manifest in Primo Levi's distinguished refusal of condemnation in what he calls the "Grey Zone" of the Holocaust, in his *The Drowned and the Saved* (1986), or in James Dickey's use of an epigraph from Günter Eich, about "everybody disowning guilt in the great destruction," in his guilty poem "The Firebombing," about flying a mission over Japan.

Writerly brotherliness was one of the finest humane resistances: the voice offered to the evils, necessary or otherwise, history imposed. The War left a changed map of the world: politically, morally, artistically. Most writing since has been written in its shadow. Generation after generation of writers have returned to it as a subject; especially to the struggle for humanity, sanity, morality and linguistic meaning with which it burdened a grotesque century.

When the atom bomb was dropped on Hiroshima on 6 August, 1945 it brought death and radiation sickness to thousands of innocent civilians.

PART SEVEN

AFTER THE SECOND WORLD WAR

The Second World War ended in 1945 with a changed geo-political order, and an international crisis of conscience. In the last stages of the war in Europe, the fate of Jewish and other prisoners held in extermination camps like Buchenwald and Auschwitz made the genocidal nature of the Third Reich clear. Six million Jews had perished in the Holocaust. Then in the last days of the war against Japan in the Pacific, American planes dropped atomic bombs on Hiroshima and Nagasaki, and the "nuclear age," with its potential for global annihilation, began. By October 1945, some fifty countries combined to found the United Nations, with the aim of bringing peace, security, democracy and prosperity to the world. The unease, horror and anxiety were not allayed. The United States and Russia emerged as the two dominant Superpowers, effectively dividing world influence between them, and confronting each other with nuclear weapons in the 45-year Cold War that followed. For writers the crisis of war and its bitter ideological aftermath recast the "modern tradition," and sometimes made writing seem almost impossible. Post-war literature took on a very different character from the modern movement that went before...

This United Nations map of 1945 offers a glimpse of the perceived or hoped-for world order, emblematically showing the member nations, the images associated with them, the words of the Atlantic Charter and icons of human activities in the ancient and modern world, as well as symbols and roll-calls of the arts. The Axis Powers are largely omitted; over Japan is a tiny image of an exploding atom bomb.

EXISTENTIALIST PARIS AND BEYOND

"To be twenty or twenty-five in September 1944," wrote Simone de Beauvoir (1908-86), "seemed a tremendous piece of luck: all roads lay open." This was Paris in the weeks after the liberation. Certainly there was optimism, especially among the young, but there was also the bitter memory of the Occupation and all the compromises and humiliations it had involved. In another year there would be the shadow of the atom bomb and the looming spectre of the Cold War. What resulted was the hectic mixture of exhilaration and disillusionment that gave the Paris of the Existentialists its distinctive character.

The heart of the city's literary and intellectual life was the area round the ancient church of Saint-Germain-des-Prés. Off the boulevard, dotted along the still cobbled side-streets, were the small hotels where most of the denizens of Saint-Germain-des-Prés lived. They offered a bed, a basin and low rents, but not much more.

At the centre of this world was Jean-Paul Sartre (1905–80), whose *Being and Nothingness* (1943) had established him as the leading philosopher of Existentialism. After his return to Paris during the war, he had deserted Montparnasse for the café de Flore, which had the advantage of being only a few yards from the metro station of Saint-Germain-des-Prés. It was here, in the congenial café atmosphere, that he worked every day, gathering round him a group of like-minded writers and intellectuals who included Simone de Beauvoir, Maurice Merleau-Ponty, Raymond Aron and Raymond Queneau. Jean Genet (1910–86), the author of *Our Lady of the Flowers* (1944), was another familiar figure in the quarter, as was Albert Camus (1930–60).

In the post-war years this small area of Saint-Germain was a literary crucible out of which came a series of other important works. Among them were de Beauvoir's *The Second Sex* (1949) and *The Mandarins* (1954), Queneau's *Exercises in Style* (1947) and *Zazie in the Metro* (1959), and a stream of works by Sartre, including his trilogy of novels, *The Roads to Freedom* (1945–49), and plays such as *The Respectable Prostitute* (1946), *Crime Passionel* (1948) and *Lucifer and the Lord* (1951).

Existentialism in Paris was both a philosophy and a style. The cafés of Saint-Germain had their night-time counterpart in the neighbouring jazz cellars like the Tabou bar – noisy, thick with smoke and crowded with young people, dressed for preference in black, whom the popular press were quick to label Existentialists. The Tabou was run by Maria Cazalis, a poet who shared a room in the Hotel Louisiane at 60 rue de Seine with the singer Juliette Gréco, a celebrated muse of Saint-Germain and the

Clubs like the Tabou, above, *in the rue Dauphine and later the Saint-Germain in the rue Saint-Benoît became identified with a new post–war generation who, as one newspaper put it, were spending their lives in drinking, dancing and loving, "until the atom bomb drops on Paris."*

Existentialists. Another icon of the time was Boris Vian, whose versatile talents as writer and jazz trumpeter bridged the two worlds of this small area of Paris.

Sartre's increasing fame soon made it difficult for him to go on working at the Flore. Before long he moved to

the gilded cellar-bar of the Hotel Pont-Royal in the rue Montalambert, where the inconvenience of having to write on the barrels that served as tables was offset by the greater privacy. The Pont-Royal had another advantage. In October 1945 Sartre had launched his journal *Les Temps Modernes* from the offices of the publisher Gallimard in the little rue Sébastien-Bottin, just round the corner from the Pont-Royal. Designed as a platform for the views of Sartre and his associates, *Les Temps Modernes*, whose editorial board included many of the regulars from the Flore, was one of the dominant intellectual voices in post-war

Paris. The magazine lost its home at Gallimard after printing an article critical of André Malraux, the publisher's most valuable author. It was an episode characteristic of the time, when shifting political affiliations were the source of endless literary feuds. Since the war, Malraux had become closely identified with the anti-Communist politics of De Gaulle, which put him at the opposite end of the spectrum from *Les Temps Modernes*. Even Sartre and his friends, though they promoted the ideal of a politically committed *littérature engagée*, were under frequent pressure from hard-line Communists like Louis Aragon, who remained vigilant for deviations from the party line.

Political sniping may have been a permanent feature of the Paris scene, but to many outsiders it was a city remarkable above all for its tolerance. The American presence in post-war years was less distinguished and less flamboyant than in the twenties, but Paris nonetheless attracted a significant group of refugees from the political, sexual and racial intolerance of Cold War America. Richard Wright (1908–60), the author of *Uncle Tom's Children* (1938) and *Native Son* (1940) was one of the first. He had come over at the invitation of Gertude Stein, now back in her old apartment in the rue de Fleurus. Wright reached Paris in May 1946, a few weeks before Stein's death. "There is such an absence of race hatred," he informed his editor in America, "that it seems a little unreal." He settled in the rue Monsieur-le-Prince, between the boulevard Saint-Germain and the boulevard Saint-Michel, where he wrote *The Outsider* (1953) and made periodic contributions to *Les Temps Modernes*.

Other black Americans attracted to Paris over the next few years were James Baldwin (1924–87), who lived in the rue de Verneuil while working on early drafts of *Go Tell it on the Mountain* (1953), Chester Himes, creator of the Harlem detectives Coffin Ed Smith and Gravedigger Jones, who became a successful contributor to Gallimard's *Série noire*, and the novelist William Gardner Smith. The café de Tournon, opposite the north entrance to the Luxembourg Gardens, was a favourite resort of the black Americans and also of the group of young Ivy League expatriates, among them George Plimpton and Peter Matthiessen, who in 1953 founded the *Paris Review* which earned an enduring reputation for its interviews with literary celebrities like E. M. Forster, Evelyn Waugh and Graham Greene. Since the magazine's offices were in the rue Garancière, parallel to the rue de Tournon, the café made a convenient editorial base.

A rather different group of young Americans who settled temporarily in Paris in the 1950s were the Beat poets. Allen Ginsberg arrived in November 1957, and for much of the next year he, Peter Orlovsky and Gregory Corso lived together in the Hotel Rachou, later dubbed the Beat Hotel, at 9 rue Gît-le-Coeur, a decrepit little street just off the place Saint-Michel. They were joined there by

Already known for The Outsider *(1942) and* The Myth of Sisyphus *(1942),* Camus, *above, went on to write* The Plague *(1947),* The Fall *(1956) and the philosophical work* The Rebel *(1951), which led to his break with Sartre.*

William Burroughs, who had come from Tangier with the battered manuscript of *Naked Lunch*. In 1959 it was published by Maurice Girodias, whose Olympia Press, operating from offices in the nearby rue de Nesle, specialized in low-grade pornography but nonetheless achieved some spectacular literary coups, publishing not only *Naked Lunch* but also Pauline Réage's *Histoire d'O* (1954), Vladimir Nabokov's controversial *Lolita* (1955) and J.P. Donleavy's *The Ginger Man* (1955).

The importance of individual publishing houses is a recurring feature of these years. Les Éditions de Minuit had come into being as a Resistance publisher during the War, but in the 1950s it acquired a quite different sort of importance as the midwife of a new literary movement. From its offices at 7 rue Bernard-Palissy, a few yards from

the place Saint-Germain-des-Prés, came a series of novels which presented a radical challenge to conventional thinking about the genre. They were the work of a group of writers, including Nathalie Sarraute, Alain Robbe-Grillet, Michel Butor and Claude Simon, who came to be known as the *nouveaux romanciers*. In one year alone, 1957, Éditions de Minuit published Robbe-Grillet's *Jealousy*, Butor's *Second Thoughts* and Simon's *Wind*.

In its disregard for the traditional conventions of the novel, the *nouveau roman* was part of a more general literary earthquake whose shock waves had already passed through post-war Paris earlier in the decade. On 5 January, 1953 the Théâtre de Babylone on the boulevard Raspail earned a modest place in literary history as the scene of the opening night of Samuel Beckett's *Waiting for Godot*. There had already been productions of Eugene Ionesco's *The Bald Prima Donna* (1950) and Arthur Adamov's *La parodie* (1952), but though Ionesco's play went on to enjoy phenomenal success at the Théâtre de la Huchette, it was Beckett's bleak parable of the two tramps waiting forlornly for Godot that first brought this new kind of drama to popular notice. Its vision of a world of meaningless futility found a ready response in contemporary audiences. Later, these playwrights were grouped together as representatives of the Theatre of the Absurd, but they never presented themselves as a coherent movement. They colonized no particular cafés or districts of the city, and their work was internationalist rather than exclusively French in flavour. Its influence was felt across Europe as well as in Britain and the United States in the works of playwrights such as Edward Albee, Harold Pinter, Max Frisch and Václav Havel.

Both the Theatre of the Absurd and the *nouveau roman* marked a turning away from the notion of *littérature engagée*. They were raising theoretical questions about the relationship between literature and experience which became a vital stimulus for intellectual developments over the next two decades. In 1960 the Journal *Tel Quel*, published from the offices of the Éditions du Seuil at 27 rue Jacob, was co-founded by Philippe Sollers and a group of young *avant-garde* intellectuals. Over the next two decades its contributors, who included Tzvetan Todorov, Roland Barthes, Jacques Derrida, Michel Foucault and Julia Kristeva, were a powerful influence on developments in western thought. The ideas of structuralism which Claude Lévi-Strauss had begun to explore in the mid-1940s were taken up and adapted by these and other writers like Jacques Lacan and Louis Althusser in ways that were to transform contemporary intellectual life.

In recent years it is these figures – the academic theorists of structuralism, post-structuralism and modern feminist thought – who have tended to hold centre stage in literary Paris, rather than any group of imaginative writers. If we look for the geographical focus of new writing, we are less likely to find it in Saint-Germain than on the social margins of Paris, in the depressed suburbs where writers of African descent like Mehdi Charef and Farida Belghoul, the so-called Beurs, have grown up.

But for all the changes, there has been one element of continuity. From Existentialism to Postmodernism, Paris has always been intimately associated with the intellectual currents that have dominated the last half of the century. This is no coincidence. Ideas are welcome here. It may well be that the new superstars more often scribble their notes in an airport departure lounge than at a café table, but many of them still make Paris their home, not least because it remains a place where ideas matter and where people care passionately about the products of their culture. As long as this is the case, the French capital will continue to occupy a central place on the literary map.

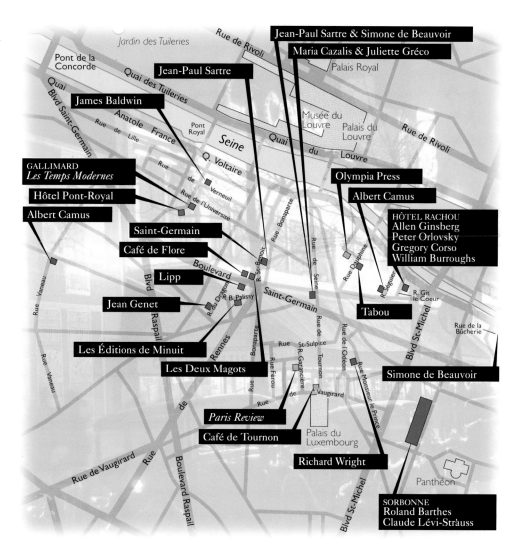

EXISTENTIALIST PARIS: *Along the boulevard Saint-Germain were ranged the bars and cafés where much of the literary business of the period was conducted – the Flore (shown in the photograph, left), the Deux Magots, the Brasserie Lipp are all plotted here.*

GERMANY AFTER THE WAR

Germany collapsed in 1945 but its literature had been destroyed much earlier through persecution and emigration. Nothing needs be said about those who stayed and were allowed to publish (all of them are second-rate figures at best). Of those who stayed and were forced into silence, only a few became prominent in the post-war literary scene; the poet and dramatist Günter Weisenborn, for instance, who worked with Bertolt Brecht in Berlin and had written songs for Viennese singer Lotte Lenya and then emigrated to New York in 1933 after his books had been burned. However, he returned to Berlin in 1939, later joined the resistance group "Rote Kapelle," became one of the very few who managed to survive its destruction in 1944, and made a modest literary career in post-war (West) Germany.

Among those who stayed but fell silent or withdrew into private life were Gottfried Benn (1886–1956) and Ernst Jünger (b.1895). Despite his dubious role in the early years of Nazi rule Benn became a living monument as Germany's master poet in the years before his death. Jünger's reckless intellectual adventurism marked his affinity for and yet his distance from the Nazis. He published his *roman à clef* against Hitler, *To the Marble Cliffs*, in 1939, without official imprimatur, and his books were promptly black-listed. After the War he was again forbidden to publish. But from 1955 on he was heaped with awards, as one of the most accomplished stylists of modern German prose. Shunned by the Left, embraced by a new intellectual Right, he continues to be a presence in post-war German literature, without really being a part of it.

Clockwise from top left: *Anna Seghers, Arnold Zweig, Gottfried Benn and Heinrich Böll were all writers in post-war Germany.*

Those who survived Nazism to reach exile – in the United States or the Soviet Union – were confronted with the eternal problem of Exile literature: they had to write for an audience that did not exist. Even the most famous exile of all, Thomas Mann (1875–1955), had his problems. Although he became, from the 1950s on, a central figure in modern German literature, his reception at home was ambiguous. Like many exiles, he suffered the right-wing calumny of having "betrayed" his people. He chose to live in Switzerland, where his friend Hermann Hesse had already moved as early as 1919. His brother Heinrich (1871–1950) was invited home to help rebuild a socialist Germany, but stayed in Santa Monica, California, where he died in 1950. Alfred Döblin, having fled to Paris, then to New York, returned to Germany as cultural adviser to the military government in the French zone. But he never regained his early literary status and died, almost forgotten, in Esslingen, near Stuttgart, in 1957.

For the Communist expatriates, the situation was different. Johannes R. Becher – who had moved from Expressionism to Communism in the twenties, and in 1933 fled Berlin for Moscow – returned in 1945 to East Berlin. Closely associated with Walter Ulbricht and Otto Grotewohl, he became Minister for Culture from 1954 until his death in 1958. In 1945 he founded the "Kulturbund for the Democratic Renewal of Germany," and persuaded Bertolt Brecht, Hanns Eisler, Anna Seghers and Arnold Zweig to return to the Russian occupied zone, which became the German

Democratic Republic in 1949. Brecht returned in 1947 to make the Theatre am Schiffbauerdamm the centre of post-war Germany's theatrical scene. He became its Director in 1954, two years before his death. He is buried in Berlin's Dorotheenstädtischer Friedhof – as were Friedrich Hegel, Theodor Fontane and Heinrich Mann before, and Helen Wegel, Zweig and Seghers after. Seghers fled Berlin in 1933 for Mexico City. In 1947 she came back to East Berlin and, a staunch defender of the Communist regime, acted as president of the GDR Writers' Organization from 1952 to 1978. Zweig (1887–1965) returned to Berlin in 1948 to become the GDR's leading novelist. For Communist Germany, Berlin continued as the major literary centre, if on a far smaller scale than two decades before.

In West Germany the literary and cultural scene was far more decentralized. To some extent this reflected the political structure of the new republic: Bonn was never intended to assume the role that had formerly belonged to Berlin. Nearly all the major publishing houses that had been in the nation's capital before the War now relocated elsewhere.

Group 47, the most significant post-war literary movement, was founded by Hans Werner Richter "to lay the foundation for a new democratic Germany, for a better future and a new literature that would be conscious of its responsibility for the political and social development." For more than twenty years it met in different places throughout West Germany. It comprised a changing circle of German and Austrian writers who had experienced the War and dreamed of a radically new beginning. Especially in its early period it proclaimed a literary language purified of all ideology and rhetoric, clean and precise enough to express a new experience. During its yearly meetings, the Group became a literary public in its own right, inviting young authors to present their work

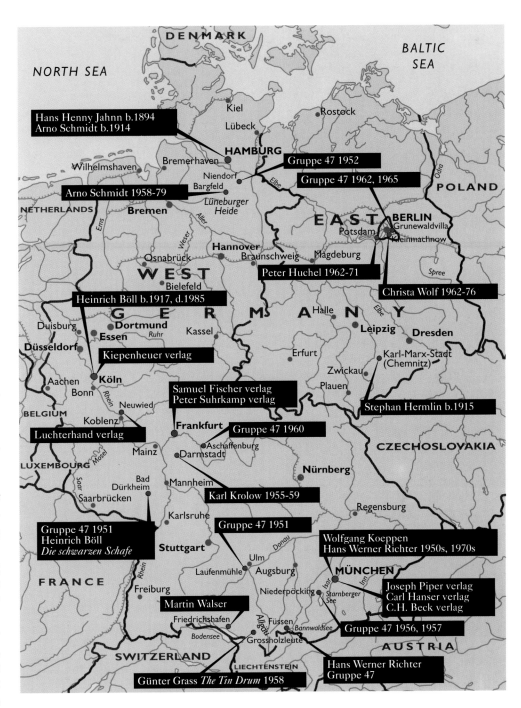

POST-WAR GERMANY: *After the Second World War the literary and cultural scene became far less centralized than in the 1920s and 1930s. As poet and critic Hans Magnus Enzensberger remarked, Group 47, which held meetings throughout Germany, had become "the central coffee house of a literature without a capital."*

and expose it to relentless critical scrutiny. To pass the test of the "electric chair" often meant the start of a new career – as with Günter Eich, Heinrich Böll, Martin Walser, Ingeborg Bachmann, Günter Grass and Uwe Johnson. With few exceptions the authors

The Wall changed life in Berlin fundamentally: it brutally made two cities out of one.

from the unfinished manuscript of *The Tin Drum*, published a year later. The Group was overwhelmed by Grass's power of baroque sensuousness. The book was followed by *Cat and Mouse* in 1961 and *Dog Years* in 1963. Later in the sixties Grass used his energies and reputation to support the Social Democrats and Willy Brandt. Grass's reading marked the dawn of the turbulent sixties in prose. A year later Hans Magnus Enzensberger's reading of his bitter poem "Schaum" (clearly an echo of Ginsberg's "Howl") did the same for verse. Uwe Johnson had already won critical acclaim when he read before the Group in 1960. Born in 1934 in Pomerania, he studied German and English

who gained reputations in the fifties and sixties were part of the Group or, like Paul Celan, Erich Fried and Peter Weiss (who chose not to live in Germany but wrote in German), affiliated to it.

Among the writers who succeeded with the Group, Böll, Grass, Johnson, and Enzensberger gained international reputations. Böll began his literary career with short stories that focussed on the chaotic experience of war and the post-war years. With every new book – *Tomorrow and Yesterday* (1954), *Billiards at Half Past Nine* (1959), *The Clowns* (1963) – he grew into the role of the "man of letters as public conscience," whose work became intensely popular, whose critical voice was heard in both Germanys (a rare achievement) and throughout Europe. After Hermann Hesse and the exiled poet Nelly Sachs, Böll became the third German author to win the Nobel Prize for Literature after the Second World War.

Günter Grass was born in 1927 in Danzig (Gdansk) and studied sculpture and graphic design before he turned to literature. He joined the Group in 1955, becoming instantly famous when, in 1958, he read

Literature at Rostock and Leipzig. Since his manuscripts were refused publication in the GDR his first novel *Speculations About Jacob* appeared with Suhrkamp in 1959. It is a dense meditation on Germany's bi-national existence, and the straddling of mental, political borderlines which eventually ruin Jacob's life. Johnson himself crossed the border to West Berlin later in 1959. There he lived for several years near Grass before moving to Rome, then to New York, finally to the Isle of Sheppey, where he finished his *magnum opus*, *Anniversaries* (1983) and died in 1984.

Group 47, although active and conspicuous, did not represent all of West Germany's literary life. Other significant names emerged: Karl Krolow, after Benn and Celan perhaps the most accomplished modernist German poet, or Wolfgang Koeppen who lived in Berlin in the 1930s then emigrated to Holland, settled in Munich after the War and wrote important novels of social criticism; or Hans

Bertolt Brecht returned to Berlin in 1947 to make the Theater am Schiffbauerdamm, left, the centre of post-war Germany's theatrical scene.

Henny Jahnn (1894–1959), dramatist, novelist, organ-builder, who fled Hamburg for Denmark where he wrote his monumental novel *Fluss ohne Ufer* in 1948 (Volume I translated in English as *The Ship*). Also from Hamburg came Arno Schmidt, who spent most of his literary life in Lüne-burger Heide, where he died in 1979. He is thought of by many as Germany's greatest contemporary writer – the Expressionist style of his early fiction later changed into the dense, hermetic prose of his gigan-tic *Zettels Traum* (1970), a novel in the tradition of Lewis Carroll and James Joyce. Although he became ever more reclusive, his house in Bargfeld became a centre of pilgrimage for a growing community of readers.

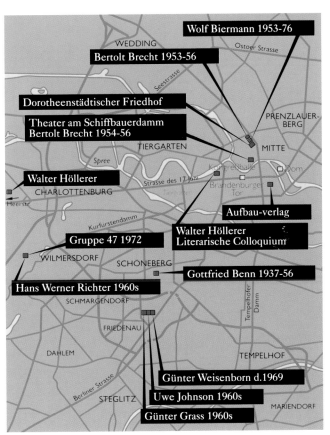

in English) decided to re-settle in East Berlin in 1951, and poet Stephan Hermlin, who left Germany in the late 1930s on a complex route of exile that took him to Palestine and Egypt, then Frankfurt, and back to East Berlin in 1947.

For these and other writ-ers of their generation, the affiliation with the GDR had been a matter of choice. For those who came to maturity after the Wall the choice to leave was no longer possible. Yet others had begun to see the GDR as home – to be criticized for its faulty implementation of socialism and yet, for all its faults, the "better" Germany. The regime was notorious for its suppression of adverse critical opinion, but it also managed to create loyalties. Thus, Christa Wolf, whose first novel *Divided Heaven* appeared in 1963, became a "national author" in a different sense than Brecht had been. Although her seventies novels received interna-tional acclaim, they were rooted in the realities of a specific GDR experience.

Each region of the Federal Republic thus contributed to its literary history. A lot happened in West Berlin, especially in the sixties, when Germany's political and intellectual life was once again focused on its fomer metropolis. After the Wall was built in 1961, Group 47 met several times in West Berlin. Richter lived there; so did Grass and Johnson. Poet and critic Walter Höllerer founded the influential magazine *Sprache im Technischen Zeitalter* and the forum "Das Literarische Colloquium," where the leading figures of contemporary European and American literature were introduced to a large public. But this burst of energy could not offset the impact of the Wall which made West Berlin a closed system that seemed subject to a slow but certain process of attrition.

The situation was different for East Berlin. Although always in competition with the larger and richer West Berlin, it could now increasingly assume the role of a capital. The powerful and prestigious Writers' Union was located there – as was the state-controlled Aufbau Verlag, which published, with few exceptions, all GDR literature. It had been dominated, in its first phase, by the older emigrant writers who, although not always in line with the regime's Stalinist policies, allowed themselves to be used as figureheads in the higher interest of Socialism. This was also true of such figures as novelist Stefan Heym, who after years of exile in the United States (his first novels were written

Today the literature of the GDR has vanished and many of its protago-nists (like Christa Wolf) have fallen silent, in a puzzled effort to redefine themselves in a changed political and literary land-scape. It's another chapter in the history of displace-ment which has marked German literature through-out the twentieth century. In one sense the political as well as the literary his-tory of post-war Germany ended with the unification in 1990. In another it has only just begun.

Members of Group 47 included Martin Walser, left, Heinrich Böll, right, and Ingeborg Bachmann, centre, shown at a meeting, above, in 1955.

POST-WAR ITALIAN FICTION

There's a golden rule about international literary fame. The writers best known abroad are not always the most interesting, but the most translatable ones. In the case of modern Italian literature, the gap has often been wide. The international fame enjoyed by Italo Svevo (1861–1928), James Joyce's friend from Trieste who wrote *The Confessions of Zeno* (1923), is justified by his originality, but is also due to his easily translatable style.

However, on the other hand, writers who in Italy are considered the most important of their time have scarcely crossed international boundaries to gain fame abroad. For instance, the experimental work of Carlo Emilio Gadda (1893–1973) is far too little known outside his own country (despite some excellent translations – for example *La Cognizione del dolore* (1963), a title marvelously rendered into English as *Acquainted With Grief*. This is also true of the work of Alberto Savinio (1891–1952), brother of the famous painter Giorgio di Chirico, and also of the *avant-garde* writer Giorgio Manganelli (1922–90).

This situation has led some writers to think of possible translations of their work even while they were writing their books. Italo Calvino, one of the greatest post-war Italian writers, was already wondering how the titles of his later books would sound translated into French and English before they were even finished. Umberto Eco is probably the most successful modern Italian writer throughout the rest of the world, primarily because, according to some critics, his novels can be read equally well in Italian or in any other language.

In the long Fascist years of the Mussolini dictatorship (1922–1945), literature and culture counted for very little, and there was strong censorship. Hence the arts developed either on the edges of official life (a situation encouraging hermetic writing) or, for many writers, in exile. Ignazio Silone (1900–78) wrote his early novels like *Fontamara* (1930), a study of peasant life in the Abruzzi, in Switzerland. During the *Resistenza* against the Nazis many of these efforts converged under the banner of the Left.

Post-war Italy was a battered, poor and politically divided country where literature had to struggle for a

The Second World War devastated many cities in Italy. Below is a photograph of one of the ruined houses of the city of Cassino, bombed because of its close proximity to the observation post behind.

The film still, right, *is from Roberto Rossellini's film* Roma città aperta (Open City). *In the leading roles here are Anna Magnani and Aldo Fabrizi.*

new identity. The late 1940s and early 1950s saw a great blossoming of Italian cinema, fiction, poetry and painting, encouraged in part by the efforts of publishers like Einaudi (founded in 1933). Already during the Fascist years, many leading writers had translated works of modern English and American literature into Italian. These translations continued after the War and exercised a considerable influence on the new Italian culture, whose most important phenomenon was the Neo-Realist movement, in film as well as in literature. Cinema saw such masterpieces as Roberto Rossellini's (1905–77) *Open City* (1945) and *Paisà* (1946) and Vittorio de Sica's (1901–74) *Bicycle Thieves* (1948).

In fiction, two writers, both known for their anti-Fascism, became seen as the best examples of the rebirth of Italian literature after the night of barbarity. Cesare Pavese, born in 1908 in Piedmont, attempted to develop a mythic vision of the world and of the Italian people, for instance in his novel *The Moon and the Bonfire* (1950). But the strain of being a compulsive myth-maker soon became apparent, and his fame has diminished somewhat since his suicide in 1950. Like Pavese, Elio Vittorini (1908–66), born in Sicily, was a translator of American literature and a major intermediary between Italian and foreign literatures as well as a writer of fiction. But he is noted for some brilliant short novels, above all *In Sicily* (1938–9).

Seen from today's perspective, the most important writer of the period probably remains Alberto Moravia (1907–90), already recognized and in full activity by 1945. He was born in Rome, and much of his writing is about his native city. He won fame in the Mussolini period for his first novel *The Time of Indifference* (1929), a pitiless description of the bourgeoisie during the early Fascist years, which was censored by the regime. After the War and the end of Fascism, he was seen as a leading literary figure, and produced a number of very successful novels including *The Woman of Rome* (1947), the story of a Roman prostitute, and *The Empty Canvas* (1960), which displays social realism but also shows the spirit of Existentialism (already present in *The Time of Indifference*).

The Second World War prompted a new boom in art and literature. Appropriating Land in Sicily *by Renato Guttuso, above, was painted in 1947.*

Moravia aimed to tell stories as plainly as possible, avoiding all stylistic and linguistic excesses: stories "that should tell themselves on their own" (as one critic puts it). He treated sexual themes with apparent eroticism, but he was fundamentally a social critic and moralist, and not just a morbid investigator of sex. His stories often seem to spring from a deep rancour toward life itself. *The Time of Indifference* remains his most original novel, perhaps because it was written before he started theorizing.

The Sicilian writer Leonardo Sciascia (1921–89) was almost as successful as Moravia, both in Italy and abroad.

In his novels like *Mafia Vendetta* (1961) and *The Council of Egypt* (1963), he explored the evils of his day and of his poverty-stricken and historic island, humiliated and tormented by the Mafia. Sicily produced another major novelist in Giuseppe Tomasi di Lampedusa (1896–1957). His novel *The Leopard* (1958) is a vivid portrait of a nineteenth century Sicilian prince. It became a remarkable posthumous success, not least because in 1963 Luchino Visconti turned it into a magnificent film. Another important writer of the period is Luigi Meneghello (b.1922), who taught Italian for several years at the University of Reading in England. In 1963 he published his best-known novel, *Libera nos a Malo*, in which, from his remote vantage point, he reconstructed, critically and yet sympathetically, the extraordinary evolution of his birthplace, Malo, a small village near Vicenza, from a traditional peasant culture to the twentieth century.

Significantly, a number of the post-war Italian writers were Jewish; for instance Alberto Moravia, Italy's best-known woman writer Natalia Ginzburg (1916–91), Carlo Levi (1902–75), author of *Christ Stopped at Eboli* (1945), and Giorgio Bassani, who wrote *The Garden of the Finzi-Continis* (1962). Among these, one of the most notable was Primo Levi (1919–87). He was born in Turin, and trained as a chemical engineer. He joined the Partisans in northern Italy in 1943 when the Nazis took over from the Fascists, was captured, deported to Auschwitz, and released in 1945. He recorded some of this atrocious history in his novel *If This is a Man* (1946), a book filled with suffering but written with great dignity, about his experience as a Jew in a death camp during the War. Other works, like *The Periodic Table* (1975), explore his experiences in a mixture of science, history and autobiography. Levi's death following a fall in the stairwell of his house in Turin was almost certainly suicide.

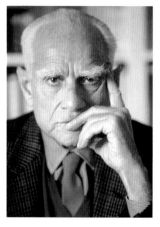

Clockwise from top left: *Alberto Moravia, Primo Levi, Italo Calvino and Umberto Eco have all achieved success in Italian and in translation.*

Italo Calvino (1923–85), born in Cuba and brought up in San Remo in Italy, wrote his early works in the form of "para-neo-realism" dealing with the Resistance, as in *Adam One Afternoon* (1949), or working class life in Milan. But there were already hints of the fantastic and fabulous elements that would appear in his works thereafter. His gift for elaborate fantasy is displayed in the trilogy *Our Ancestors* (1952–62), partly inspired by his beloved Robert Louis Stevenson, and translated into English as *The Cloven Viscount*, *The Baron of the Trees* and *The Non-Existent Knight*. The series of stories gathered together as *Cosmicomics* (1965) mixed science fiction with comic pastiche.

Along with Argentinian storyteller Jorges Luis Borges, Calvino is one of the great fable-makers of the twentieth century, and probably the Italian writer who will leave the greatest mark on modern literature. Beyond the concern with fantasy and folklore, he wrote short stories and novels which remain important reflections on contemporary society, and Italy's troubled passage from peasant to urban world. Later works include striking experiments (*If On a Winter's Night a Traveller*, 1979) and philosophical fictions (*Mr Palomar*, 1983), as well as important studies on the art of narration.

Two other significant writers who incarnated the spirit of comedy and carnival in the Italian culture of the 1960s and 1970s are far less known to foreign readers. The first is Luigi Malberba (b.1927) who published his great novel *Il serpente* in 1962, the other Gianni Celati (b.1937), who brought out his *Avventura di Guizzardi* in 1972. Many readers thought they would revive the great comic tradition of Italian Renaissance literature. But they both abandoned the comic form, and reverted to more solemn form: Malberba to the writing of grand historical-political myths, Celati to the search for a direct link between oral tradition and written literature.

Post-war Italy had other important novelists. Pier Paolo Pasolini (born in 1922 in Bologna and killed in 1975 by a mugger), for instance, was a novelist, poet, screenwriter and film maker, as well as a remarkable polemicist and essayist. He was perhaps the strongest and most original voice in modern Italian journalism. His two novels, *The Ragazzi* (1955) and *A Violent Life* (1959), both about life in the Roman slums, remain important, although they are perhaps over-shadowed by his wide-ranging activities in all fields of culture and art. Their plots are thin, but they show the extraordinary lin-guistic sensitivity of the man who wrote them. Although Pasolini was born in Bologna from a fami-ly originating from Fruili, a region in the North-Eastern part of Italy where a local language, *Friulano* dominates, he developed the crude language used by the bums and hooligans of the Roman suburbs into a form of literary art.

Last but not least, there is Umberto Eco (b.1932). Eco won intellectual recognition as a Professor of Semiotics, teaching at the University of Bologna as well as abroad, before he attracted world attention with his first novel *The Name of the Rose* (1980). A cunning crime tale set in a monastery, it was also a breathtaking synthesis of many of the intellectual themes and trends of the day. This many-faceted text can be read as a whodunnit, a histori-cal novel set in medieval times, a semiotic *summa* of culture, a journalistic hoax and an academic provocation. The book that succeeded it, *Foucault's Pendulum* (1988), no less ambitious, is an elaborate tale of conspiracies modern and ancient, and a plotter's compendium. In future, when the dust of his success has settled, Eco may well be revealed less as an important novelist than as one of the most versatile personalities of modern culture. Using literature as a space for infinite combinations of narrative and language, his contribution is perhaps less to the making of artistic form than to the invention of a new literary playfulness.

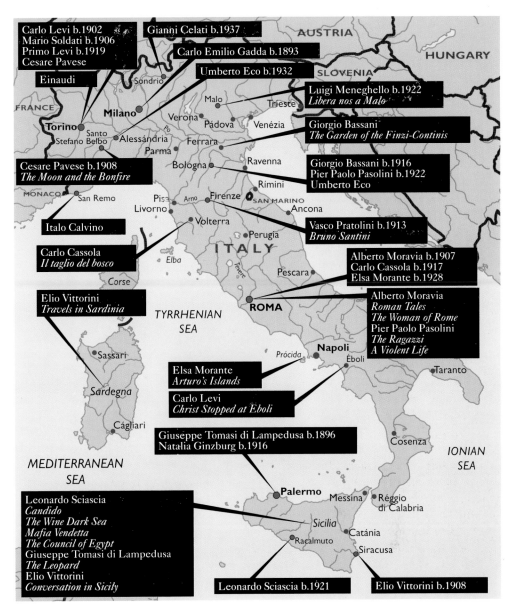

Umberto Eco's novel The Name of the Rose *was made into a successful film in 1986. This still from the film,* above, *shows Christian Slater,* left, *and Sean Connery,* right, *in front of an ancient monastery.*

LONDON IN THE FIFTIES

One hundred years after the Great Exhibition, London saw another great festival take shape. This one grew on the South Bank of the Thames, over the river from Westminster. A tall aluminium Skylon, a modernist equivalent of the Eiffel Tower, rose into the sky almost without visible moorings. A Dome of Discovery celebrated the triumphs of modern invention, especially British: radar, the jet engine. This was the Festival of Britain, the first great post-war event, held in 1951 to show the rising spirit of the nation after the horrors of war time.

The still foggy London of the Festival was a badly battered city. New tower blocks in brick or concrete hastily designed to rehouse Londoners displaced by six years of bombing began to sprout. In the war-scarred city, the great dome of Saint Paul's, symbol of national courage and survival, began to disappear behind grey office towers. But nearby was the new Barbican, later to become an important home for the arts.

The Festival itself was temporary; most of the buildings were pulled down. But the site was kept as an area for entertainment and the arts. A foundation stone for a National Theatre was laid. Although battered from the war, Britain was still hopeful, and politicians and planners did all they could to promote a sense of national and metropolitan pride. In 1953 the coronation of Queen Elizabeth II brought the nation together round their television sets and inaugurated the New Elizabethan Age. But the economic situation was desperate, the historic world-role of Britain in doubt. Old bastions of power, old habits of class, were disappearing. In the age of the Welfare State, cultural energy also seemed to be declining. The Festival was staged to suggest this was untrue.

In the fifties a new cultural climate did start to emerge. In 1956, the English Stage Company mounted a play by a young playwright, John Osborne, at the Royal Court Theatre in Sloane Square, near the King's Road. *Look Back in Anger* captured an era. Set in a Midlands town, it was an expression of youthful rage about the past, the complacent present, the uncertain future. The Royal Court (turned into

Set on London's South Bank, above, *the Festival of Britain was attended by over eight million people who saw sculpture by Henry Moore, Graham Piper and Jacob Epstein; the Skylon, designed by Powell and Moya; and the vast Dome of Discovery.*

a cinema in 1932, bombed in the War) was itself an emblem of the times. It started a striking series of new productions, with new British playwrights (Osborne, Ann Jellicoe, John Arden, Arnold Wesker), major works from radical Europeans such as Bertolt Brecht, Eugene Ionesco and Samuel Beckett. As for Sloane Square itself, it was, said the Royal Court's artistic director George Devine, rapidly becoming "the new Mayfair." In the nearby King's Road, Mary Quant opened her shop, Bazaar, inaugurating a new era of design and style that would peak in the 1960s. Across the city at the Theatre Royal in Stratford East, working class London had a new theatre too. In 1953 Joan Littlewood founded her Theatre Workshop, staging plays by Brendan Behan and Shelagh Delaney and popular musicals with a political edge like *O What a Lovely War!*

And from the other Stratford, Stratford-Upon-Avon, the Royal Shakespeare Company reached into London, putting on not only Shakespeare but new plays at the Aldwych, eventually finding a permanent home in the Barbican. The dream of the National Theatre, much encouraged by Sir Laurence Olivier, was slower to flourish. The foundation stone was in the wrong place. Not till 1963 did a National Theatre Company begin performing at the Old Vic, and the present South Bank complex, with its three theatres, built in the spirit of sixties concrete modernism, didn't open its doors until 1976. Still, *Look Back in Anger* proved that a new mood was emerging in British drama. There were many new drama companies and

In the original production of John Osborne's Look Back in Anger *at the Royal Court Theatre in 1956, Kenneth Haigh – shown* left *with Osborne* (smoking) *– played the now famous role of Jimmy Porter.*

venues, such as Arnold Wesker's Centre 42 project, a popular arts centre founded in the Round House in Camden.

The new mood went far beyond theatre: into fiction and poetry, popular art, fashion, style and design. The new culture was evident in many areas of British life: the rise of youth culture, jazz clubs, espresso bars, Teddy Boys, street style, the "New Look," and expressed by such things as street protests against the Suez and the Campaign for Nuclear Disarmament.

Well before Osborne's play was staged this new spirit had come into the novel. In 1954, three first novels appeared with a distinctive new flavour. One was William Golding's *The Lord of the Flies*, a metaphysical parable about moral crisis, set among schoolboys wrecked on an island after a nuclear holocaust. Another was Kingsley Amis's *Lucky Jim*, about a young, provincial university teacher in revolt against his elders and their culture. The third was Iris Murdoch's *Under the Net*, a philosophical comedy set in London and Paris and capturing the new age of Existential anxiety. Golding's book had a remote and distant setting. Amis's was set in the English provinces (almost certainly Leicester) but its hero pines for London. Murdoch's novel particularly captured the London mood of its day. "There are some parts of London which are necessary and others which are contingent," muses the streetwise narrator, Jake Donaghue. "Everywhere west of Earls Court is contingent, except a few places along the river." Jake hates contingency, and looks for the "necessary" places: Hammersmith Mall, Soho, Saint Paul's, at all hours and in all their moods.

Other novelists captured this London. Muriel Spark lived a Grub Street life in post-war London. She worked for *Poetry Review*, then started her own poetry magazine, living meantime in a Kensington hostel, then in Camberwell, south of the river. The climate of these places

The new angry mood of London in the 1950s was reflected not only in literature; it was the very essence of life and culture.

is captured in several of her wry and ironic novels: *The Ballad of Peckham Rye* (1960), *The Girls of Slender Means* (1963), set at the war's end, *Loitering With Intent* (1981) and *A Far Cry From Kensington* (1988), all dealing with this period with ever longer hindsight.

Such books capture a literary London made up of hacks, poverty stricken intellectuals, provincial hopefuls come to the city to live in bedsits and seek literary fame.

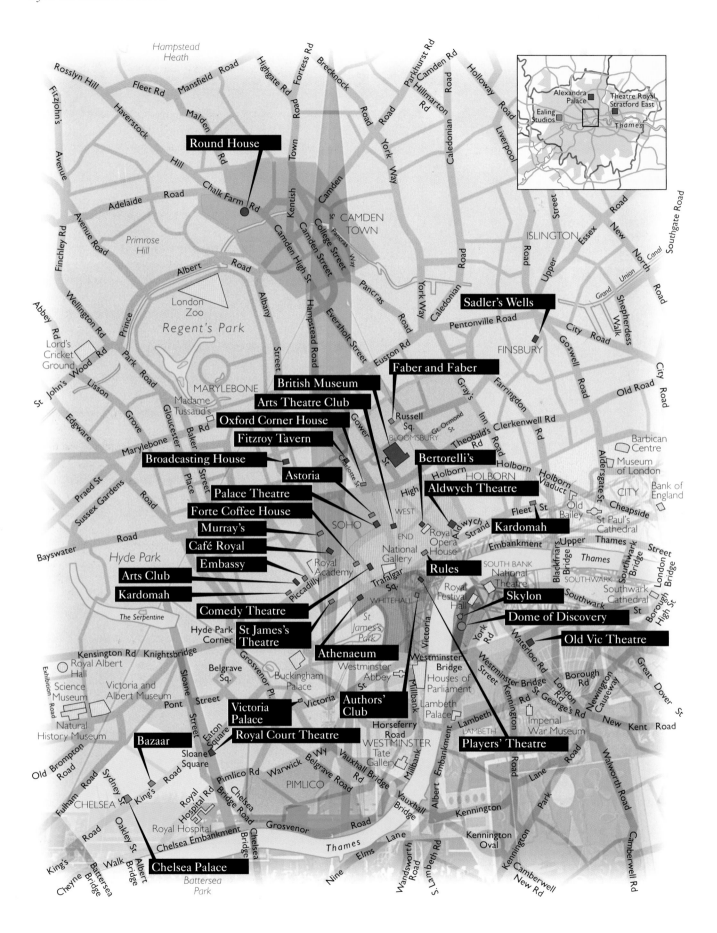

Hampstead
Heath

Rosslyn Hill
Fleet Rd
Mansfield
Road
Highgate Rd
Fortess Rd
Brecknock

Fitzjohn's
Haverstock
Malden
Road
Town
Road
Road
Parkhurst Rd
Camden Rd
Road
Holloway

Alexandra
Palace

Theatre Royal
Stratford East

Ealing
Studios

Thames

Avenue
Hill
Road
Hillmarton
Rd
Liverpool
Street

Finchley Rd
Adelaide
Road
Chalk Farm Rd
Kentish
Caledonian
Road

Round House

Camden
Camden High St.
College Street
Pancras Way
York Way
Caledonian Road
Upper
Essex
New
North
Road
Southgate Road

Avenue Road
Prince
Albert
Road
London
Zoo
*Primrose
Hill*
Camden Street
Pancras
CAMDEN
TOWN
ISLINGTON
Grand
Union Canal
Shepherdess
Walk

Abbey
Rd
Wellington Rd
Park
Road
Regent's Park
Eversholt Street
Hampstead Road
York Way
Euston Rd
Sadler's Wells
Pentonville Road
FINSBURY
City
Goswell
Road
Road

Lord's
Cricket
Ground
St John's
Wood Rd
Lisson
Grove
Gloucester
Place
Baker
Street
MARYLEBONE
Madame
Tussaud's
British Museum
Arts Theatre Club
Oxford Corner House
Fitzroy Tavern
Broadcasting House
Gower
St
Russell
Sq.
Gt. Ormond St.
BLOOMSBURY
Gray's
Faber and Faber
Theobald's
Rd
Inn
Clerkenwell Rd
Farringdon
Holborn
Holborn
HOLBORN
Holborn
Viaduct
Aldersgate St.
Barbican
Centre
Museum
of London
CITY
Bank of
England

Edgware
Road
Marylebone
Road
Praed St
Sussex Gardens
Astoria
Palace Theatre
Forte Coffee House
Murray's
Café Royal
Embassy
Arts Club
Kardomah
Comedy Theatre
Charlotte St.
SOHO
WEST
END
High
Bertorelli's
Aldwych Theatre
Royal
Opera
House
Aldwych
Strand
Kardomah
Fleet
St
Old
Bailey
St Paul's
Cathedral
Cheapside

Bayswater
Road
Hyde Park
The Serpentine
Royal
Academy
Piccadilly
National
Gallery
Trafalgar
Sq.
Rules
Embankment
Upper
Thames
Blackfriars
Bridge
Thames
Southwark
Bridge
Southwark
Cathedral
London
Bridge
Street

Kensington Rd
Knightsbridge
Hyde Park
Corner
**St James's
Theatre**
WHITEHALL
St
James's
Park
Victoria
Skylon
SOUTH BANK
National
Theatre
SOUTHWARK
SOUTHWARK
Southwark
St
Borough
High St
Great Dover St

Exhibition
Road
Royal Albert
Hall
Science
Museum
Victoria and
Albert Museum
Belgrave
Sq.
Grosvenor Pl.
Buckingham
Palace
Athenaeum
Westminster
Abbey
St
Westminster
Bridge
Houses of
Parliament
Royal
Festival
Hall
York
Rd
Waterloo
Road
Dome of Discovery
Old Vic Theatre
Westminster Bridge
Kennington
Rd
St George's Rd
Borough
Rd
Newington
Causeway

Natural
History Museum
Sloane
Street
Eaton
Square
**Victoria
Palace**
Royal Court Theatre
Pont
Street
**Authors'
Club**
Millbank
Lambeth
Palace
WESTMINSTER
Horseferry
Road
LAMBETH
Lambeth
Players' Theatre
Imperial
War Museum
London
Road

Old Brompton
Road
Bazaar
Sloane
Square
Royal
Hospital Rd
Pimlico Rd
Warwick
Belgrave Road
Wy
Vauxhall Bridge Rd
Tate
Gallery
Millbank
Albert
Embankment
Kennington

Fulham
Road
Sydney
Street
King's
Road
CHELSEA
Chelsea
Bridge Road
Chelsea
Grosvenor
PIMLICO
Road
Thames
Vauxhall
Bridge
Kennington

Old
Road
Oakley St.
Royal Hospital
Chelsea Embankment
Chelsea
Bridge
Chelsea Palace
*Battersea
Park*
Nine
Elms
Lane
Wandsworth
Road
S. Lambeth Rd
Kennington
Oval
Kennington
Park
Camberwell
New Rd
Camberwell Rd

King's
Road
Cheyne
Walk
Battersea
Bridge
Albert
Bridge

In 1956 one famous "outsider" appeared on the scene from Leicester: the 24-year-old Colin Wilson, who published a much-hailed philosophical study of Existentialism, simply called *The Outsider*. He was famed for sleeping out on Hampstead Heath, saying it was near the British Museum where he spent his time reading and writing. It wasn't, but the great domed Reading Room of the British Museum in Bloomsbury, where Karl Marx had written *Das Kapital*, was still one of the great lures of the day – celebrated in many works (Margaret Drabble's *The Millstone*, 1966, David Lodge's *The British Museum is Falling Down*, 1965). Its most famous denizen was Angus Wilson, superintendent there until he resigned to write his influential neo-Dickensian novels satirizing Anglo-Saxon attitudes (*Hemlock and After*, 1951, *Anglo-Saxon Attitudes*, 1956).

What such books and memoirs show is that the war had changed but not destroyed London bohemia with its poor poets, novelists, critics and painters, who drank at the Fitzroy Tavern, ate, when they could afford it, at nearby Bertorelli's, did hackwork for the publishers round

LONDON IN THE 1950S: "*Long ago in 1945 all the nice people in England were poor, allowing for exceptions,*" *Muriel Spark wrote in* The Girls of Slender Means. "*The streets of the city were lined with buildings in bad repair or no repair at all, bombsites piled with stony rubble....*" *But new cultural institutions were appearing and artistic confidence returned to the capital.*

In Central London in the 1950s the new culture was evident in many areas of life: the rise of youth culture, jazz clubs, espresso bars, Teddy Boys, street style and the "New Look."

Bedford Square, and sold their review copies for a meal in the dusty bookshops of the Charing Cross Road. In a time of small publishing houses and cheap books it was still possible to make a literary living. Publishers paid badly, but they were small firms run by determined individuals with clear literary tastes, and they liked writers. T.S. Eliot reigned over poetry at Faber and Faber, in Russell Square, just as Welsh born Dylan Thomas reigned over the pubs around Charlotte Street, until his death in 1953.

With Thomas's death, a romantic, apocalyptic generation died. A new poetry movement was revived with the publication of the anthology *New Lines* in 1956, but after the Coronation it was clear television was becoming the major force. When ITV opened in 1955 to rival the BBC television boomed. ITV started an Armchair Theatre; the BBC responded by increasing its drama output. A "writers' theatre" started in television, drawing in many new playwrights (Harold Pinter, David Mercer) and encouraging others, like Dennis Potter. And in those days, especially from the great Ealing Studios, even British films did well.

There were many Londons that overlapped each other. In *City of Spades* (1957) and *Absolute Beginners* (1959), Colin MacInnes vividly caught the London of Notting Hill and the black immigrant community. In *The Golden Notebook* (1962) Doris Lessing wrote of the Hampstead world of political intellectuals, reformers, therapists and feminists. In his vast *Music of Time* sequence (1951–75), Anthony Powell examined the dissolving world of clubs, great houses and the upper middle class, while C.P. Snow and William Cooper looked at the world of Whitehall, the Civil Service and the "Corridors of Power."

Fifties London was an exciting and anxious place. Culture was changing, perhaps shrinking. But a fresh writing was coming, from a new generation that saw the society differently and came from different places in it. In theatre, fiction and poetry, writing was finding new styles and energies. In the sixties, these distilled, as post-war London came to life, in the King's Road and Carnaby Street, in the jazz clubs and boutiques, in the theatres and recording studios, in sexual freedom and released political dissent.

Muriel Spark, above, writes about the 1950s with increasing hindsight.

SCENES FROM PROVINCIAL LIFE

In the 1940s and 1950s, after the Second World War ended, the British imagination seemed to shrink. One way to react to the horrific events that had been tearing the world to pieces for the last six years, sending servicemen and women to battle zones across the globe, was to pay fresh attention to life back home. Distant fields of conflict held terrible memories; the world continued to be a disordered, threatening place. But equally important was the question of what had been happening on the home front, to ordinary Britain. Now, many writers thought, it was time to look at scenes from provincial life.

Scenes from Provincial Life is the title of William Cooper's (b.1910) influential 1950s' novel. Set in Leicester in 1939 just as war clouds were gathering, it describes a world about to collapse. It's a wry, comic novel about the lives and loves of four provincial intellectuals. They think Hitler will soon invade Britain, putting their lives in danger, so they'd better escape to the United States. But love proves greater than Fascism, home more important than away and they stay until their lives dissolve into the war.

Cooper's book is a love affair with Leicester and regional life itself. In three sequels we follow the protagonist into the Civil Service, Whitehall and the grander scenes of London. Cooper's good friend C.P. Snow (1905–80) appears in the novels as Robert; and Snow himself, also from Leicester, wrote an eleven-volume sequence of novels, *Strangers and Brothers* (1940–70), following the hero Lewis Eliot from lower middle class Leicester to Cambridge, London and the Corridors of Power.

Such books marked a trend to return to provincial Britain as a literary subject. Philip Larkin (1922–85), born in Coventry, would become famous as a poet of provincial Englishness. But he first won notice with two novels which show the underlying landscape of his writing. *Jill* (1946) is about a young boy from Huddersfield who goes to Oxford and is torn between his lower middle

Barry Hines wrote about "people who live on council estates or in small terraced houses. The men work in mines and steelworks, the women in underpaid menial jobs."

class roots and the new world Oxford opens up. *A Girl In Winter* (1947) gives the reflections on ordinary England of a visitor to Britain ("Small fields, mainly pasture. Telegraph wires and a garage. That Empire Tea placard"), in what would become Larkin's half-loving, half-ironic tone. He shows the land in the way a whole generation would see it, in prose and verse.

These scenes from provincial life were something more than an experiment in local colour. They were explorations of Britain's changing culture, where its roots lay and what might renew it. In these books the young heroes (generally heroes, although Margaret Drabble born in 1939 Sheffield, follows a heroine's passage from north to south) are often doubly "outsiders." As provincials, they feel excluded from British metropolitan literary culture. As working or lower middle class young people, grasping opportunities afforded by new access to higher education, they feel conflict between their class and the larger metropolitan scene.

Some books were works of protest; others of celebration, exploring an unwritten Britain that had its own

PROVINCIAL BRITAIN: *The sense of place in post-war writing was helped by the growth in the 1950s and 1960s of regional civic theatres, which provided support for local writers, and grants from Regional Arts Associations.*

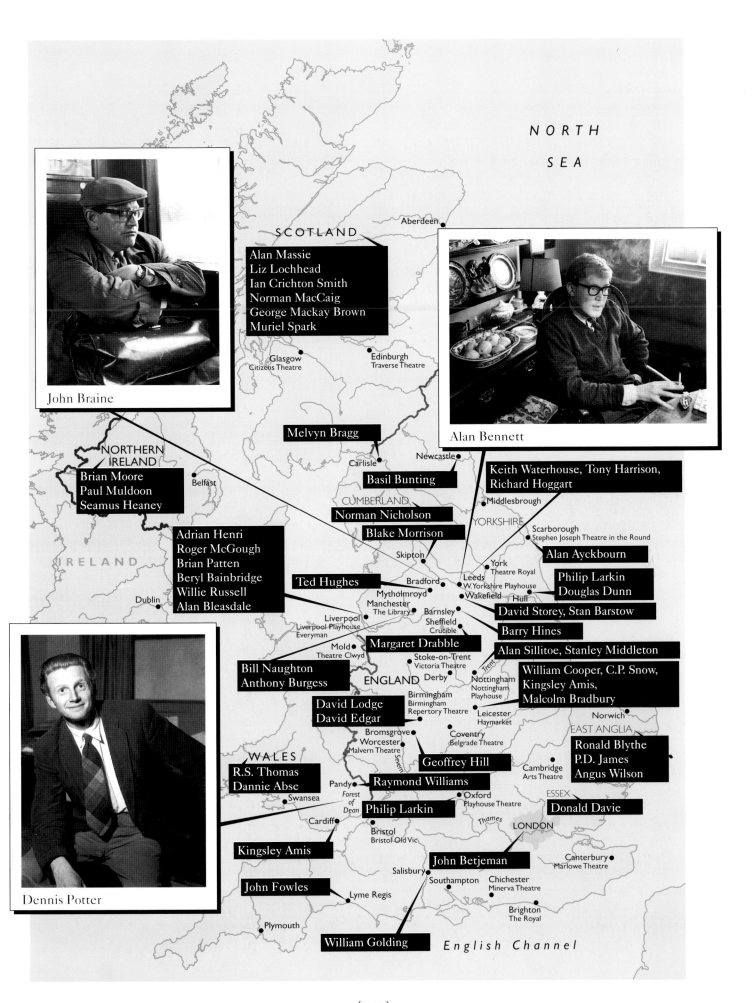

NORTH

SEA

SCOTLAND

Aberdeen

Alan Massie
Liz Lochhead
Ian Crichton Smith
Norman MacCaig
George Mackay Brown
Muriel Spark

Glasgow
Citizens Theatre

Edinburgh
Traverse Theatre

John Braine

Alan Bennett

Melvyn Bragg

Newcastle

NORTHERN
IRELAND

Belfast

Carlisle

Keith Waterhouse, Tony Harrison,
Richard Hoggart

Brian Moore
Paul Muldoon
Seamus Heaney

Basil Bunting

CUMBERLAND

Middlesbrough

Norman Nicholson

YORKSHIRE

Adrian Henri
Roger McGough
Brian Patten
Beryl Bainbridge
Willie Russell
Alan Bleasdale

Blake Morrison

Skipton

Scarborough
Stephen Joseph Theatre in the Round

Alan Ayckbourn

IRELAND

Ted Hughes

Bradford

York
Theatre Royal

Leeds
W.Yorkshire Playhouse
Wakefield

Philip Larkin
Douglas Dunn

Hull

Dublin

Mytholmroyd
Manchester
The Library

Barnsley
Sheffield
Crucible

David Storey, Stan Barstow

Liverpool
Liverpool Playhouse
Everyman

Margaret Drabble

Barry Hines

Mold
Theatre Clwyd

Alan Sillitoe, Stanley Middleton

Bill Naughton
Anthony Burgess

Stoke-on-Trent
Victoria Theatre

ENGLAND   Derby

Trent

William Cooper, C.P. Snow,
Kingsley Amis,
Malcolm Bradbury

Nottingham
Nottingham
Playhouse

David Lodge
David Edgar

Birmingham
Birmingham
Repertory Theatre

Leicester
Haymarket

Norwich

EAST ANGLIA

Bromsgrove
Worcester
Malvern Theatre

Coventry
Belgrade Theatre

Ronald Blythe
P.D. James
Angus Wilson

WALES

Severn

Geoffrey Hill

Cambridge
Arts Theatre

ESSEX

R.S. Thomas
Dannie Abse

Pandy
Forest
of
Dean

Raymond Williams

Oxford
Playhouse Theatre

Donald Davie

Swansea

Philip Larkin

Thames

LONDON

Cardiff

Bristol
Bristol Old Vic

John Betjeman

Canterbury
Marlowe Theatre

Kingsley Amis

Salisbury

Southampton

Chichester
Minerva Theatre

John Fowles

Lyme Regis

Brighton
The Royal

Dennis Potter

Plymouth

William Golding

English Channel

vigour and ways of life. But most were novels of social realism, reversing the spirit of Modern experiment that had grown in the pre-war years. Exploring in loving detail the texture of change, the shifting spirit of place, the gap between the generations, they amounted to a new post-war mapping of Britain and the detail of its ordinary lives – place by place, region by region, class by class; from them today's reader could construct a social history of Britain. Cooper and Snow wrote of the central Midlands, or one part of it: wealthy, smug Leicester, doing well from the hosiery trade. Alan Sillitoe wrote of rival Nottingham, city of D.H. Lawrence, lacemaking and bicycles, with its larger working class. David Lodge's novels show the Birmingham ("Rummidge") of entrepreneurs and

Alan Sillitoe's Saturday Night and Sunday Morning (*1957*) *is the story of Arthur Seaton, a worker in a Nottingham bicycle factory,* above, *whose only escape from his lathe is in the drunkenness and lovemaking of Saturday night and the regrets of Sunday morning.*

engineering factories. Many of the best books came from the North, from Yorkshire and Lancashire, the Victorian cities and towns of the industrial revolution. Bradford and Bingley already laid claim to J.B. Priestley. Now came John Braine (b.1922), whose *Room at the Top* (1957) was a brash tale about a young provincial opportunist determined to climb to success. Wakefield produced David Storey (b.1933) whose *This Sporting Life* (1960) is the tale of a young rugby player struggling between physical activity and mental life. Storey went on to become not only a powerful novelist – *Radcliffe* (1963) is a remarkable brooding meditation on the Yorkshire landscape – but a major playwright, author of *The Contractor* (1969) and other plays with Northern settings. Wakefield was also home to Stan Barstow (b.1928), whose striking working class novel, *A Kind of Loving* (1961) is set in fictional "Cressley."

This was mining Yorkshire, where a distinctive working class life and community sense had developed over generations. It was caught by Barry Hines from nearby Barnsley and a pit background in his early work. But as industrial patterns changed and their lives were threatened Hines devoted himself to writing of this experience. In *A Kestrel for a Knave* (1968) he told of a young boy growing up in such a community, when the rules were changing, the old occupations dying. It was brilliantly filmed as *Kes* (several of these novels became notable films and shaped the realist mood of British film and television drama).

Yorkshire now seemed to do as thriving a trade in writers as it once had in woollens. Leeds – the Victorian capital at the heart of the West Riding – had its comic laureate in Alan Bennett (b.1934), whose stage and television plays and revue performances conveyed the region's very ordinary tone of voice as well as its world view. Leeds also bred the prolific Keith Waterhouse, author of *Billy Liar* (1959), a fine comic novel about northern dreams and hopes, the playwright Henry Livings, and Richard Hoggart whose *The Uses of Literacy* (1957) – a social record of northern working class culture – was novel-like in its power of report and its cultural influence.

Poetry too was re-invigorated by a new sense of place. Some of the finest poets of the 1950s and 1960s also came from Yorkshire. Ted Hughes was born in 1930 in the aptly named Mytholmroyd on the Calder River in the Yorkshire Pennines near the Lancashire border, ancient, stoney and half-industrialized. His poetry converts this landscape into natural energy, mythic space and psycho-drama – above all in his "Moortown" sequence, illustrated by the photographer Fay Godwin (*Moortown*, 1979). Like the powerful poetry of Tony Harrison or Blake Morrison Hughes's poetry owes much to his Yorkshire roots.

Although Philip Larkin was a Midlander from Coventry, he became the poet of Hull, the ravaged seaport in the Yorkshire East Riding, over the Humber, at the end of the rail-line. Appointed University Librarian in 1955, he grew as distrustful of travel as he was of Modernist experiment. Place and people mattered to him, and he closely observed the detail of local lives, of Hull's "cut-price crowd, urban yet simple," the fish dock, the cemetery, the bombed old town near the harbour, the dull department stores put up after the air-raids, the once green landscape disappearing under motorways, shopping precincts, half-hearted urbanization. London seemed a world away, as his fine poem "Whitsun Weddings" (1964) shows – when he takes what seems a huge train journey from northern Hull to the capital, glimpsing the many small lives revealed on the way. At Hull Larkin was joined by other poets, including Andrew Motion and Douglas Dunn. The city also had significant playwrights like Alan Plater, leading television writer and dramatist for the Hull Truck theatre company. Further up the East Coast at the resort of Scarborough, playwright Alan Ayckbourn joined Stephen Joseph's small Theatre in the Round in 1959. In time he made it a major drama centre, both for first performances of his own cunning northern farces (*The Norman Conquests*, 1974) and new work by others.

Although it sometimes thought so, Yorkshire didn't stand alone. Across the Pennines in Lancashire, the opposite seaport, Liverpool, had its Poets (Adrien Henri, Roger McGough, Brian Patten), who linked verse with music, giving their own version of "the Mersey Sound" (*The Mersey Sound*, 1967), a fine comic novelist in Beryl Bainbridge, and important playwrights, including Willie Russell (*Educating Rita*, 1979) and Alan Bleasdale.

Other Northern cities and regions also found a new era of expression. Basil Bunting was the great bard of Newcastle. In Cumberland, Norman Nicholson celebrated his local habitation in powerful verse. Melvyn Bragg, born in Carlisle, reinvigorated the literary heritage of the Lake District in a series of novels. His first book *For Want of a Nail* (1965) deals in Hardy-like fashion with the familiar regional theme of wasted potential. His *Cumbrian Trilogy* (1969–80) is a social history of a Cumbrian family from the age of the hired farm hand to modern day. North of the border a new group of major Scots writers appeared, including Alan Massie and Liz Lochhead.

The North wasn't the only source of creativity; the cities weren't the only centres. The poet Geoffrey Hill, from Midlands Bromsgrove, celebrated his origins and the power of history and nature in *Mercian Hymns* (1971). Over in the "coloured counties," west of Birmingham, were the "blue remembered hills" of the ancient Forest of Dean. Dennis Potter, who was born here in 1935, used it as background and landscape for remarkable television plays. This was what Raymond Williams, novelist as well as cultural critic, called "border country." Williams was born in Pandy in 1921, on the border between Wales and England, region and metropolis, history and the future, working class and academic intelligentsia.

In East Anglia writers like Ronald Blythe (*Akenfield: Portrait of an English Village*, 1969) looked at the winds of change blowing through contemporary rural culture – while in 1969 Donald Davie published his *Essex Poems*. Wales had the poetry of R.S. Thomas and Dannie Abse, Scotland had the writing of Ian Crichton Smith, Norman MacCaig and George Mackay Brown, Northern Ireland Paul Muldoon and Nobel Prize-winner, Seamus Heaney.

The west coast seaport of Liverpool, above, *was another great literary centre, its cosmopolitan, streetwise culture regenerated by, among other things, the music of the Beatles.*

Even English suburbia found its laureate in the light and comic verse of John Betjeman.

Place is never everything in writing, but literature always owes much to the local. And this was made very evident in post-war Britain, helped to a great extent by the growth of civil theatres and regional independent television companies which encouraged local writers and regional stories. But the strongest force was the impact of cultural and social change itself. Today we can see many of these scenes of provincial life as snapshots of fast-fading ways of life. The industries that shaped the Northern cities were already starting to collapse – and with them the rooted, male-dominated communities and families, the work-shaped lives, the regional ways. Today post-war tower blocks have replaced the back-to-back terraces; supermarkets and malls have displaced the corner shop. Workplaces have gone, often work itself. So have many of the threads that connected people to place, generation to generation. Today's British authors writing scenes of provincial life (and many still do) have to write about a very different place.

For Kingsley Amis, left, *writing* I Like It Here *in the 1950s, "here" meant contemporary, ordinary Britain.*

BROADWAY

I'm afraid I don't know very much about Broadway. I'm even more afraid that nobody else does either. Half a century after I began writing plays in America I think I can say without risk, unfortunately, of contradiction, that I am not welcome on Broadway and never was. If this was not as I wished when I began, it was apparently my condition and, I knew it fairly soon. But, of course I was well inside an old tradition. Eugene O'Neill (1885–1953), a man born to show business, his father having been a vastly popular leading actor, called the place a "showshop," meaning that it had a tart's soul and the taste of a carnival barker. He hated it even as it acclaimed him our Number One playwright. Clifford Odets (1906–63), who had tried to make poetic plays for Broadway, cursed it finally and blamed it for his career ending so disastrously in Hollywood. I can't think of a writer who liked Broadway – a writer that is, who was trying to open up the country to itself.

Arthur Miller, photographed at the time of Death of a Salesman.

But how could it have been otherwise? Broadway is what it was supposed to be, the American equivalent of the French Boulevard theatre, a place of sheer entertainment, one or another version of the Folies Bergères and all that. Broadway, like American television, has always been suspicious of art when it was not openly hostile. Yet the myth continues that it is where the American theatre lives.

Mentioning television reminds me of a fairly unbelievable event; we were in the first day of production of the television version of my *Death of A Salesman* (1949) with Dustin Hoffman and John Malkovich, when a woman from the CBS Network, on which the show was to be broadcast, appeared in the studio and introduced herself to the director, Volker Schlondorf. She was quite civil and business-like and she said, "Now you understand, I'm sure, that we don't want any art."

What she meant was, no crazy scenery, no wild shots, just straightforward story-telling. "Don't worry," Schlondorf replied with a straight face, "we intend to stay as far

away from art as possible." No irony came through to her and she left reassured. I rather liked this hateful woman because of her candour, which was in such contrast to what one runs into on Broadway. There, like satire, art is what closes on Saturday night but nobody comes around telling you they don't want it. On the contrary, the reigning mythology has art as the crowning glory of Broadway; they are inextricable, one and the same thing. The point is that this hostility between artist and Broadway has been the case at least since I began, and if you read Eugene O'Neill's letters, was the bane of his life.

It was certainly the bane of Tennessee Williams's life, too. You know you're at a Broadway play – a serious one, that is – if you sense that the audience doesn't really want

Right, Mildred Dunnock, Arthur Kennedy, Cameron Mitchell *and* Lee J. Cobb *are shown,* left to right, *performing in the original production of* Death of a Salesman *in 1949 at the Morosco Theater on Broadway.*

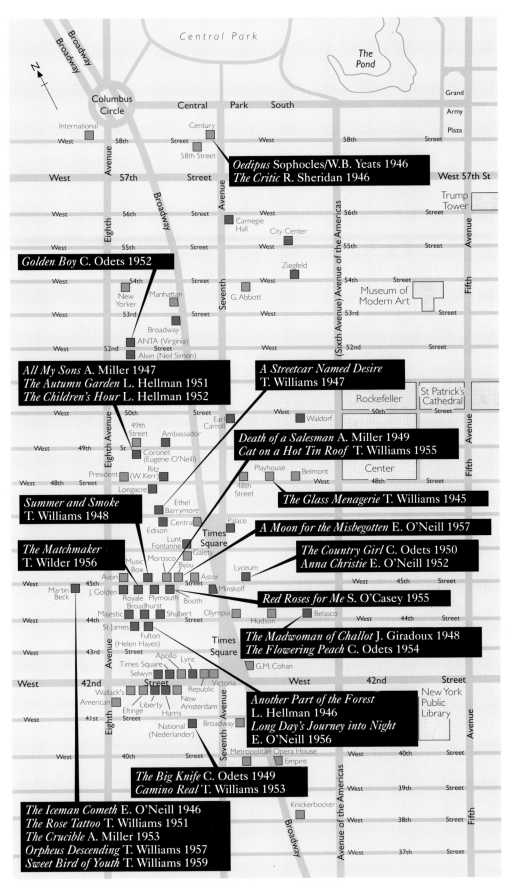

The programme, above, *is from
the original Broadway production of* Death of a Salesman.

BROADWAY IN THE 1950S:
*The map shows some key
productions at Broadway
theatres in the forties and
fifties. The names of the
theatres are those of the time,
with the present name (if the
theatre is still there) in
brackets underneath.*

Marlon Brando and Jessica Tandy, left, *in the Broadway production of Tennessee Williams's* A Streetcar Named Desire *at the Ethel Barrymore Theater in 1947.*

Tennessee Williams's Summer and Smoke, *in rehearsal*, below, *opened at the Music Box Theater in 1948.*

to be there. People read reviews of serious plays offered on Broadway and are ever so relieved when the review is bad – one more downer they don't have to see. Of course occasionally there is something they absolutely have to see, God knows why. In the past, great reviews for a serious play made the playwright, producer and director and even an actor or two fairly prosperous. Nowadays, *Angels In America*, surely one of the most praised pieces in decades, did not earn back its investment.

When I began trying to vault the wall around Broadway in the forties and into the fifties, I will admit it seemed a glamorous place. But that was because in any normal season there were two or three or even more plays, American and foreign, which were really interesting, and a few that had permanent significance. One wished to join the ranks of such authors.

There was Williams's *Glass Menagerie* (in 1944), Jean Giraudoux's *Madwoman of Chaillot* (in 1948) with its elegantly poetic sets; there was Yeats's translation of *Oedipus* and Richard Sheridan's *The Critic* (in 1946) played back to back on the same night by Lawrence Olivier; there was Thornton Wilder and Clifford Odets and Sean O'Casey and Lillian Hellman, plus pretty good – not great – work by a dozen other playwrights to keep the pot boiling. Above all, perhaps, there was the illusion (what's more important than illusion?) that you were addressing America when you opened on Broadway. The place, in

short, still wore its metaphor as a sort of platform from which one spoke to one's fellow Americans.

And it seemed so terribly important. The Sunday *New York Times* still had news of the theatre and pieces about theatre on the front page of the entertainment section instead of what they usually have now, the latest about television personalities, movie grosses, and anything peculiar enough about showbiz to warrant its momentary attention. Theatre is usually a few pages at the rear.

But if we can step way back, without falling off the cliff, we may have to confess that fundamentally not much has really changed. Broadway was always most comfortable with musicals, popular comedies and farces, and there was always a contradiction between its real nature and what eggheads think of as theatre. People go to theatre not to be improved but for a good time, to get away from the dishes and real life, while the serious theatre artist, now and in the past, is working in the opposite direction – trying to aquaint the audience with the armpits of reality. If a few of us have occasionally managed to force our way before the Broadway public, it does not mean the contradiction is resolved but merely pushed momentarily aside.

Is this to confess to the irremediable permanence of the decadent? But how long, really, did Ibsen run in Norway? A few weeks, and a few months perhaps in Germany, not more. The same probably goes for Chekhov, Strindberg *et al*. The big difference in the

[246]

Broadway system is the palpable atmosphere of outright rejection, more prevalent now than ever, of anything like a spiritual quest through theatre, the quest to discover what being human means in our time. Broadway consequently is now down to one or no serious works per season, relegating such oddments to the off-Broadway venues. Broadway, in a sense, has rather openly acknowledged what it was always about but sometimes pretended it wasn't. It isn't Gordon Craig's lay church where fundamentals of existence are contemplated in dramatic forms; it is entertainment, the trained bear, the tambourine, the exhilarating flash of the theatre art with an occasional charming tip of the hat to its spirit.

But who knows, maybe it will all turn out for the best. By having to confront such nugatory suspicion if not outright rejection, the serious writer may develop new aggressive forms through which to overwhelm the gum-chewers. Time was when Broadway, despite its cynicism, was in fact the very womb of all that was new in American theatre, rather than what it is now, the high-priced receptacle for inventions from abroad and across the country. I still believe that if a 15 or 20 dollar ticket were available (no doubt impossible without some kind of subsidy), an audience for drama might pop up again.

After an 18-year absence from Broadway, Judy Garland returns to the Palace Theater in 1951, right, *to a tumultuous welcome.*

Stephen Sondheim's and Leonard Bernstein's West Side Story, above, *first appeared on Broadway in 1959.*

But maybe not. A British producer recently reckoned that there are, in fact, about 40,000 British people who will buy tickets for a West End production of a serious play. Regardless of its enthusiastic critical reception, when that number has passed through the lobby, the game is basically a losing one for any serious work. I would think the same is more or less true of Broadway now.

Maybe the problem is that we have such wonderful memories. The Greek theatre at Syracusa had seating for 14,000 people.

DYLAN THOMAS'S WALES

Geography is also destiny for any writer in a small country like Wales. Some time during the nineteenth century, the culture of Wales split into two parts, still not quite synchronized, and into two languages: Welsh, the language of the rural north, and English, the language of the industrial south. This was the face of a conflict long fought in Wales, about who really has the moral right to define the soul of the nation. Dylan Thomas's (1914–53) Wales is just one Wales – and for a Welsh writer that is still part of the problem.

Had Dylan Thomas been raised in the North he would – through the conduit of the Welsh language – have been a very different kind of writer. For Welsh-language literature has generally been aligned with nonconformist religion, written by patriots creating propaganda for the Methodist chapel. And even though it has been used more freely today – there are some striking Welsh-language novels and poems – it was English that emerged as the language to express things forbidden in Welsh. Thomas could probably never have become what he said he was, a poet in conflict with the status quo, if Welsh had been his primary language.

Dylan Thomas's parents came from a Welsh-speaking country background in Carmarthenshire, but they adopted an English culture when they moved to urban and industrial Swansea, thinking English the more forward-looking, dynamic language. And while Thomas would certainly have been conversant with the strong tradition of bardic Welsh literature, he shunned the whole custom that saw the bard as a member of a community, answerable to the community. Thomas wrote for the English living outside of Wales. He was also a comic writer, and one target for his comedy was the Welsh lugubriousness that surrounded the chapel. He has been called a religious poet, and to a degree he was. But it was

The portrait of Dylan Thomas in his youth, above, *was painted by Augustus John in c.1937.*

the form rather than the content that he valued, the scriptural language rather than the supernaturalism. He went to chapel when young and enjoyed the fire and brimstone evangelists who solemnly warned the congregation about the sins of drink and the flesh. But, as his work showed, he responded more as an ironist than a believer.

Still, if Thomas denied his Welshness insofar as it meant provincialism and piety, he maintained all his life a fierce loyalty to a small geographic area in West and South Wales, the environs of Swansea and Camarthen, and to an even smaller number of settings – Cwmdonkin Park, Swansea Bay, Fern Hill, Rhosili and Laugharne. In fact nearly all the poems and stories he wrote, among them *Collected Poems, 1934–52* (1952); *Portrait of the Artist as a Young Dog* (1940); *Adventures in the Skin Trade* (1955) were set there. Even during the Second World War, when he was in London, and Europe was in flames, he continued doggedly to write about the lost Utopia of childhood in just these places.

DYLAN THOMAS'S WALES: *Thomas was born in Swansea in 1914 and spent the first twenty years of his life there. After a stay in London, he returned to Wales in 1949, this time to Laugharne to spend his final years at the Boat House with his wife Caitlin.*

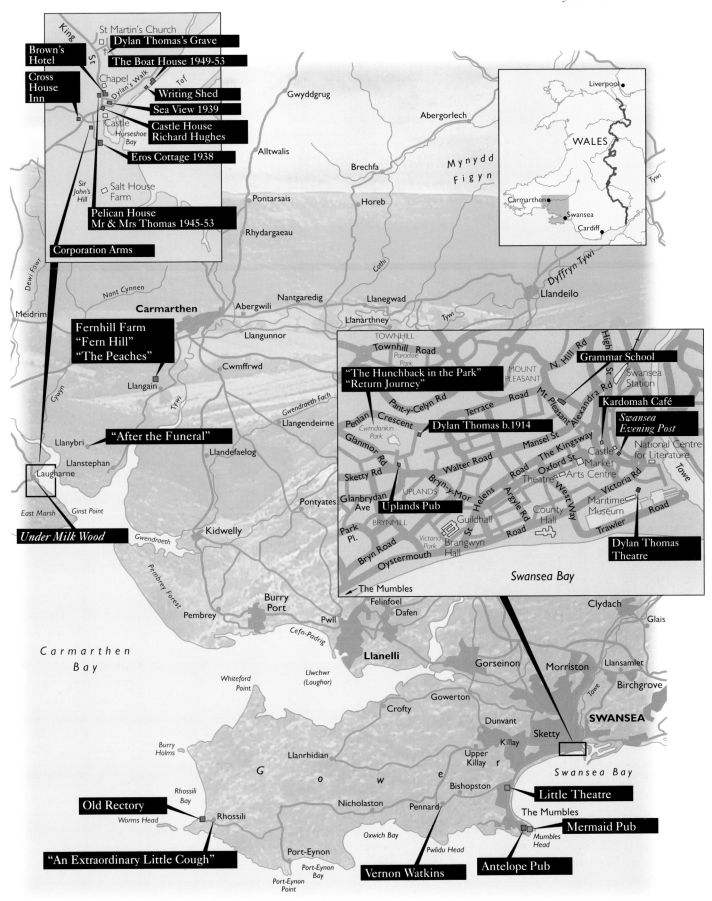

St Martin's Church
Dylan Thomas's Grave
Brown's Hotel
The Boat House 1949-53
Cross House Inn
Chapel
Writing Shed
Sea View 1939
Castle House Richard Hughes
Horseshoe Bay
Eros Cottage 1938
Sir John's Hill
Salt House Farm
Pelican House Mr & Mrs Thomas 1945-53
Corporation Arms

Gwyddgrug
Abergorlech
Mynydd Figyn

WALES
Liverpool
Carmarthen
Swansea
Cardiff

Dewi Fawr
Meidrim
Nant Cynnen
Carmarthen
Alltwalis
Brechfa
Pontarsais
Horeb
Rhydargaeau
Cothi
Dyffryn Tywi
Llandeilo

Fernhill Farm "Fern Hill" "The Peaches"
Cywyn
Llangain
Tywi
Abergwili
Nantgaredig
Llanegwad
Llanarthney
Tywi

Cwmffrwd
Llangunnor

TOWNHILL
Townhill Road
Paradise Park
MOUNT PLEASANT
N. Hill Rd
Grammar School
Swansea Station
High St
"The Hunchback in the Park" "Return Journey"
Pant-y-Celyn Rd
Terrace
Road
Mt Pleasant
Alexandra Rd
Kardomah Café
Penlan
Crescent
Cwmdonkin Park
Dylan Thomas b.1914
Swansea Evening Post
Glanmor Rd
Walter Road
Mansel St
The Kingsway
Castle
Market
National Centre for Literature
"After the Funeral"
Llanybri
Sketty Rd
Bryn-y-Mor
St Helens
Road
Oxford St
Arts Centre
Tawe
Llanstephan
Laugharne
Glanbrydan Ave
UPLANDS
Theatre
Victoria Rd
Uplands Pub
County Hall
West Way
Maritime Museum
East Marsh
Ginst Point
Park Pl.
BRYNMILL
Guildhall
Argyle Rd
Road
Trawler
Road
Dylan Thomas Theatre
Under Milk Wood
Gwendraeth
Bryn Road
Victoria Park
Oystermouth
Brangwyn Hall
Swansea Bay

Clydach
Glais
The Mumbles
Felinfoel
Dafen

Carmarthen Bay
Pembrey Forest
Pembrey
Burry Port
Pwll
Cefn-Padrig
Llanelli
Gorseinon
Morriston
Llansamlet
Birchgrove
Tawe

Whiteford Point
Llwchwr (Loughor)
Crofty
Gowerton
Dunvant
SWANSEA
Sketty
Killay
Upper Killay
Swansea Bay

Burry Holms
Llanrhidian
Gower
Nicholaston
Bishopston
Little Theatre
The Mumbles
Mermaid Pub
Mumbles Head
Old Rectory
Rhossili Bay
Rhossili
Worms Head
Pennard
Antelope Pub
Port-Eynon
Oxwich Bay
Pwlldu Head
Vernon Watkins
"An Extraordinary Little Cough"
Port-Eynon Bay
Port-Eynon Point

Dylan Thomas was born in 1914 in Swansea, at 5 Cwmdonkin Drive, a semi-detached house in the suburb of Uplands. He lived there till he was twenty, writing his early poems in his father's study. Cwmdonkin Park is nearby, with its regimented flowerbeds, wooded ponds, the bowling green, the bandstand, the "chained cup/That the children filled with gravel/In the fountain basin where I sailed my ship." Thomas's first playground, it was also the setting for the poem "The Hunchback in the Park," and the stories "Patricia, Edith and Arnold" and "Old Garbo" (in *Portrait of the Artist as a Young Dog*). It was the emblem of the innocence of childhood, where he felt the first tremor of encroaching adulthood in the form of the hunchback, "propped between trees and water," who "slept in a dog kennel."

It is to Cwmdonkin Park that the autobiographical narrator of "Return Journey" comes in search of lost childhood. When asked if he remembers the young Dylan Thomas, the Park Keeper replies: "I knew him well. I think he was happy all the time." And if today the park seems a lost Utopia, it's partly because of the impact Thomas's poetry has had on it, fact following fiction.

Thomas left Swansea for a writer's life in London Bohemia in 1934, but the Welsh imprint was heavy. The poetry he wrote is famed for its romantic feeling and its complex rhymed patterns, which surely owe something to traditional Welsh bardic forms like the *cynghanedd*, which use internal rhyme and alliteration within each line. And even though Thomas could not read Welsh, it is probable that he picked up these rhythms second-hand, since they permeate and poeticize Anglo-Welsh speech. He found a regional culture with Welsh friends and fellow-writers like Vernon Watkins, but equally protested that "Too many of the artists of Wales spend too much time talking about the position of the artists

Swansea Bay, depicted in the photograph, left, was a galaxy of parks, rugby grounds and guest-houses, stretching up the Mumbles Road and edging out onto six miles of moody beach. Sand blew across the tram lines and into the nexus of pubs like the Mermaid in the Mumbles or the Fishguard in Swansea.

"lying on Jack Stiff's slab near the pub in the Fishguard Alley, where the methylated-spirits drinkers danced into the policemen's arms and women like lumps of clothes in a pool waited, in doorways and holes in the soaking wall, for vampires or firemen...
We stood in the scooped, windy room of the arch, listening to the noises from the muffled town, a goods train shunting, a siren from the docks, the hoarse trams in the street far behind, one bark of a dog, unplaceable sounds, iron being beaten, the distant creaking of wood, doors slamming where there were no houses, an engine coughing like a sheep on a hill."

"Just Like Little Dogs"

of Wales." Even today the Welsh still go on arguing bitterly about how Welsh Dylan was, and certainly there have been plenty of Welsh writers, including poets writing in English, who have taken their Welshness more seriously. Yet one thing is certain: Dylan's lyricism, the melancholy and temperature of his language and his voice, is endemically Welsh.

One of the few observations Thomas made about how his writing worked was to stress how word and character, word and landscape, presented themselves together to him. His landscapes were half-invented ones: in *Under Milk Wood* (1954) Laugharne, where Thomas later on lived, becomes Llareggub ("bugger-all" in reverse). Like all his places, it is personalized, turned round, top-heavy with the transferred emotions of his characters. In the story "Just Like Little Dogs" the characters idle their time away on Swansea Bay, surrealistically observing strangers.

Swansea, too, has been written over by Thomas. Before the War it had a kinetic energy, strong in industrial, masculine identity and headstrong women. When the Luftwaffe targeted the docks, they destroyed much of this world and its architecture. "Return Journey" lists all the place names in an attempt at reclamation. "I went out of the hotel into the snow and walked down High Street, past the flat white wastes where all the shops had been. Eddershaw Furnishers, Curry's Bicycles, Donegal Clothing Company, Doctor Scholl's, Burton Tailors, W.H. Smith, Boots Cash Chemists, Leslie's Stores, Upson's Shoes, Prince of Wales, Tickers Fish, Stead and

Simpson – all the shops bombed and vanished." "Our Swansea is dead," he told his wife Caitlin, whom he married in 1937; and so, revisiting it today, it is.

There were other key landscapes. Fernhill, the smallholding farm in Carmarthenshire he visited as a child, was a tough little redoubt. In the 1920s when he visited it was worked by his aunt and uncle, Ann and Jim Jones, and he watched their struggle for survival there. Jim was a drunk, and model for Uncle Jim in "The Peaches." About a visit by a Mrs Williams, who arrives in a chauffeur driven Daimler, to bring a school-friend of Dylan's to stay at the farm, the story exposes the split between rural and urban, Welsh and English values. It's a darker account than that in Dylan's most famous poem, "Fern Hill," but like that poem it celebrates innocence and the moment in childhood "before I knew I was happy."

Thomas was out of Wales for many years, and his lyric and romantic style of poetry and his vast verbal energy won him worldwide success. He went on drunken reading tours to the United Sates, where some of his most admiring readers were to be found. However, on his return from an American visit in 1948, he and Caitlin came back to Wales to search for a house. He was interested for a while in the Old Rectory on the beach at Rhosili on the fine Gower Peninsula. But a year later the Boat House at Laugharne, 15 miles north of Rhosili near Camarthen, came onto the market. A small place of two hundred people in Dylan's day, Laugharne conveniently had seven pubs. In this "seashaken house /On the breakneck of rock," overlooking the estuary of the River Taf, Thomas settled and wrote his "play for voices" *Under Milk Wood* – first intended for radio, but frequently put on the stage since his death. Its "Llareggub" is a place for gossip and dreaming, and the work, with its rich variety of inhabitants, and its lyric alliterative prose, constructs not so much the tales of a place as a place of tales. During the four years the Thomases lived there, the Boat House took on a mythical significance. But it was cut short.

Thomas died suddenly, in New York in 1953, while he was on another wild American reading tour. His body was brought back to Laugharne, where he lies now, in comfortable walking distance of nearly every environment enshrined in his poetry, fiction and drama. For Welsh

Thomas described the four-mile long beach on the Gower Penisular as "The wildest place I know." Here he'd sit all day at Worm's Head (depicted in the painting, right), watching the Atlantic waves march silently leeward with headsets of pale spindrift.

The Boat House where Dylan Tomas lived became a mythical spot, not least for the flamboyance of Dylan's and Caitlin's four-year existence there. According to his biographer Paul Ferris, he completed only six poems over this period. One was the elaborately designed "Over Sir John's Hill," celebrating the topography he could see from the window of his writing shed at the bottom of the garden (shown in the photograph above). And across the estuary, two miles away, is Llanybri, where his ancestors were buried – including Ann Jones, who is deified in the lament "After the Funeral."

writing, Thomas remains both an heroic figure and a curse, his image powerfully laid over the topography of Wales. There are some other noted Welsh novelists, from Kate Roberts to Gwyn Thomas to Christopher Meredith, other major poets, like R.S. Thomas, all of whom have mapped a very different and more various Wales. "Land of my fathers," Thomas once said of his native land. "My fathers can keep it." Nonetheless Thomas keeps it too. His poetry and prose have written themselves onto the map of South Wales forever.

THE BEAT GENERATION

The American love affair with suburbia began in the 1950s. Americans increasingly thought of themselves as a handsome people with youthful, attractive Moms, wearing pretty white aprons, living in the suburbs. Nothing is easier to mock than the conformity of that suburban world. The sharpest edge of mockery and irony in the 1950s, which was largely the invention of Jewish stand-up comics like Lennie Bruce and Mort Sahl, scorned the racism, conservatism and affluent complacency of suburban America. Ralph Kramden, played by Jackie Gleason, lived in a grubby inner-city apartment far from the suburban ethos of *Papa Knows Best*. Nor did the great movie rebel-heroes of the decade (James Dean, Montgomery Clift, Marlon Brando) live in suburban

tracts. Elvis Presley did not become president of the debate club at Tupelo High School. The 1950s, that most conformist of decades, was rich in rebelliousness, sarcasm, idealism and indignation. Nowhere was this more strongly expressed than in the emergence of the Beat Generation.

The media myth of the "Beat Generation" was born in September 1957, alongside the publication of Jack Kerouac's (1922–69) second novel *On The Road*. The origins and derivation of the term were hotly debated. John Clellon Holmes claimed to have used it first in his jazz novel *Go* (1952, reissued 1959 as *The Beat Boys*). For Kerouac the term alluded to "beatitude," and the states of blessedness and happiness of the truly free spirit. "Beat" also appeared in Norman Mailer's influential essay "The White Negro" (1957), which set out the new vocabulary the "cool cat" had made his own: "The words are man, go, put down, make, beat, cool, swing, with it, crazy, dig, creep, hip, square." *Time* and *Life* carried articles on the Beats and lexicons of their jargon. Teenage followers were called "beatniks" when, just after Kerouac's book appeared, the first Russian satellite, "Sputnik," was launched in space.

"Beat Generation," "Beats" and "Beatnik" were additions to the modest nomenclature of American cultural dissidence. What set the Beats apart from previous *avant-gardes* was the sudden overwhelming glare of publicity. Overnight writers who had been unpublishable were interviewed, lionized, seduced. They were able to make a literary living, but the expectations greeting their subsequent publications were destructive. Success killed off the Beat Generation virtually at birth. A modest and sensible acclaim was denied them; at the moment they

The Beats and their lifestyle made good copy in Eisenhower's second term, and the brooding, handsome Kerouac, above, was everywhere in the media.

triumphed all went stale. By 1959 you could buy sweatshirts proclaiming "The Beat Generation." Beatnik jokes became a television fixture, high schools held Beatnik Parties. Maps and city guides identified the main attractions of the "Beat Scene" in San Francisco, Greenwich Village and Venice in California. No movement had gone so swiftly from obscurity to marketing strategy. But the Beats had skedaddled – to anywhere but the cafés,

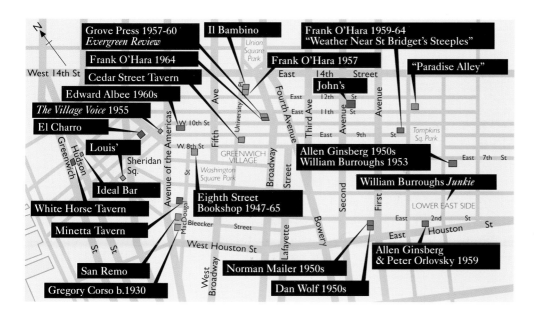

GREENWICH VILLAGE AND THE LOWER EAST SIDE: *The Beats travelled across Manhattan, from Greenwich Village to the Lower East Side to Morningside Heights. In the early 1940s Ginsberg and Kerouac had studied at Columbia University; in 1951 Ginsberg took an apartment at 206 East Seventh Street, and Kerouac and others followed him downtown.*

SAN FRANCISCO: *The Cassadys lived for a time in San Francisco, a traditional capital of American Bohemia since the nineteenth century. Kerouac often visited; Ferlinghetti's City Lights Bookstore was at its centre.*

galleries and poetry readings where the idea of Beat was watered down.

Seen as Bad Boys by the media, the Beats came to define themselves in hostility to the bland American mainstream. It was as though the counter-culture *zeitgeist* of the 1960s and 1970s was already being created in the cramped apartments of students at Columbia University, the candlelit coffee houses of Greenwich Village and the flop-houses of San Francisco in the decade after the end of the Second World War. The Beats took drugs, admired jazz, and exalted sex in most of its permutations and without neurotic inhibition. They loved life "on the road" and wrote poems entitled "In the Baggage Room at Greyhound" (Ginsberg), "Mexico City Blues" (Kerouac), "Vision of Rotterdam" (Corso). Their ability to shock is not what it was; but the Beats have never quite been tamed or made 'spectable. Beyond the myth of the movement is a canon of works that have survived: Allen Ginsberg's "Howl" (1956) and "Kaddish" (1960); Gregory Corso's "Marriage" (*The Happy Birthday of Death*, 1960); Kerouac's *On the Road* (1957); William S. Burroughs's *Junkie* (1953) and *The Naked Lunch* (1959); Gary Snyder's *Riprap* (1959). A slim harvest, but a real one.

Beyond the image lay a celebration of the amours and friendships a small group of men formed in the 1940s and 1950s. Ann Charters, Kerouac's first biographer, published *Scenes Along the Road* in 1970. It was an album of the Beats, containing photographs taken between 1945 and 1957, with a final image of Holmes, Ginsberg and Corso at Kerouac's funeral in 1969. The overwhelming maleness is unmistakable. Only one woman appears, Neal Cassady's wife Carolyn, with whom Kerouac had an affair in San Francisco (described in her book *Heart Beat*, 1977). The remaining images are of posed groups of buddies, arms

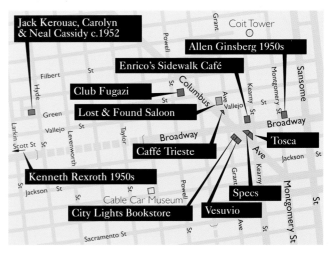

around each other, clowning on the beach in Tangier, in a park in Mexico City, in small rented rooms in New York or San Francisco. No literary movement in the United States since Huck Finn's gang has been so much of the boys, for the boys, by the boys. Corso's "Marriage" is a crucial text. Marriage was the nemesis, the closure of impulse, the defining of sexual roles:

"O God and the wedding! All her family and her friends/ and only a handful of mine all scroungy and bearded/just wait to get at the drinks and food..."

The literature of the Beats is about bonding between the boys, their amorousness, the sadness of the discovery that love and passions fade. All the rest – the zeal for Eastern religion, the flirting with Existentialism, the fascination with dreams, political radicalism, love of drugs, freewheeling sexuality – was merely decoration on a complex web of personal relations.

What held them together was a lifelong dedication to restlessness. They feared being trapped, in a relationship, a

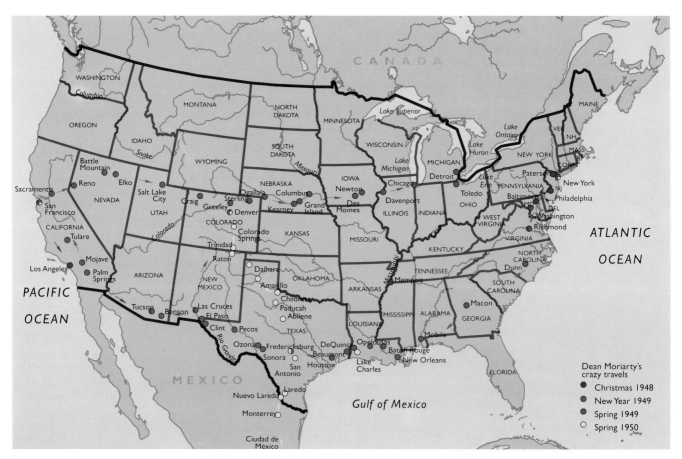

Dean Moriarty's
crazy travels
● Christmas 1948
● New Year 1949
● Spring 1949
○ Spring 1950

Gregory Corso's (above) *poems are
like Blakean footnotes scrawled in margins of entries on Paris, Stockholm or
Athens in Frommer's* Europe On Five
Dollars a Day.

style, a place. The message of
On the Road is clear: "*move.
And we moved.*" They travelled across the American
continent; to Europe and
the "Beat Hotel" in Paris; to
North Africa, to Asia; and
their biographies are travel
books, with brief interludes
where they met. They were
writers with a passion for
improvised "scenes," but no
more than provisional commitment to any given place.
The Beats travelled across
Manhattan from Greenwich
Village to the Lower East
Side. When friends moved
to Kansas City or Los
Angeles, the journeys grew
longer and more eventful.
But the rootless style perfected in New York in the
1940s scarcely changed for three decades. They wrote as
they lived: impulsive, with little patience for perfection of
style. Kerouac was indignant to learn that Ginsberg wanted to revise the first draft of "Howl" as nothing could be
less spontaneous.

ON THE ROAD: *Crossing the nation coast to coast several times in
the 1940s, Kerouac stored up the material which he poured into* On
the Road: *the novel's main journeys are shown on this map.*

Sense of place has often meant a great deal to
American writers, even when the place is a self-invented
Bohemia like Greenwich Village. There were still Villagers
when Ginsberg arrived who remembered the Pagan Routs
of *The Masses* and could tell you where John Reed lived
when he wrote *Ten Days That Shook the World* (1919). The
Beats made no such local commitments. They breezed
across Manhattan, carrying away little more than memories
of meetings, couplings, moments of dazzling illumination.
When Kerouac recorded his experiences of travelling
across the United States in *On the Road* he hoped it would
become part of a great novel, "Balzacian in scope." It was
a project on a scale missing from American writing since
the major works of Thomas Wolfe and John Dos Passos.
The presence of Neal Cassady, who appears as Dean
Moriarty in the novel, gave Kerouac's time on the road an
electric energy. Drink and drugs supplied whatever energy
sexual desire had failed to create. The book was mostly finished by 1950; by the time it appeared in 1957, Kerouac had
made it part of a vast "subterranean" sequence or legend
(*The Dharma Bums*, 1958; *The Subterraneans*, 1959) written
in jazz-like spontaneous bop-prosody, appropriate alike to
visionary awareness and constant movement, "adventuring
into the crazy American night."

"And on the way we drop in on Ferlinghetti at the bookstore and the idea suddenly comes to go to the cabin and spend a big quiet crazy weekend (how?) but when Larry hears this idea he'll come too...and we'll catch McClure at Santa Cruz and go visit Henry Miller and suddenly another big huge ball is begun."

Jack Kerouac

The Beats' contact with the West Coast poetry scene was uneasy, and became more strained over time. When Ginsberg went to San Francisco in 1954 he carried a polite letter of introduction from William Carlos Williams to Kenneth Rexroth. Rexroth read Ginsberg's poems, and was not impressed. "You went to Columbia University too long. You're too old to be going on with all this formal stuff like that. What's the matter with you?" It was a rebuke Ginsberg listened to. After enrolling on an MA degree programme at Berkeley, in July 1955 he moved to a little cottage near the Berkeley campus, and wrote "Howl for Carl Solomon," dedicating his first great poem to a New York friend then in an insane asylum. Through Rexroth, Ginsberg was introduced to Robert Duncan and Jack Spicer, two San Francisco poets, and looked up a 25-year-old Berkeley graduate student of Chinese and Japanese, Gary Snyder. In San Francisco he also met Kenneth Patchen and Michael McClure.

The famous poetry reading by Ginsberg at the Six Gallery on 13 October, 1955, at which he read "Howl Part I," was the first public reading for the poet, as well as for McClure, Snyder, Philip Whalen and Philip Lamantia. It was followed by a similar reading, to a wildly enthusiastic audience, at Berkeley. Within days there was an explosion of poetry readings across the Bay Area. Kerouac, just arrived from Mexico City, was in the Six Gallery audience, but, like poet Laurence Ferlinghetti, didn't read.

Ferlinghetti published his poems *Pictures of the Gone World* (75¢, 1955) as the first title in the City Lights "Pocket Poets" editions. The fourth title in the series was *Howl*, which appeared in October 1956. Threatened with prosecution, the poem soon achieved a stunning notoriety and by 1967 it had gone through 19 reprints. *Howl* was followed by Corso's *Gasoline* (95¢, 1958) and Lamantia's *Selected Poems* (1967). Ferlinghetti's own radical communitarianism wasn't quite "Beat," but he became their main publisher. Others in the Bay Area, like Duncan, felt resentment at the newcomers, who seemed to have an extraordinary flair for self-publicity. When the *New York Times* carried a piece by Richard Eberhart about the "San Francisco School," it was Ginsberg, from New Jersey, who received the lion's share of attention.

The San Francisco scene was soon gone. By September 1956, Snyder left to live in a Buddhist monastery in Japan. Ginsberg signed on a merchant ship sailing to Alaska, and on his return to California went to Mexico, New York, then Casablanca. William Burroughs was now a drug-exile in his "Delirium Hotel" in Tangier, writing *The Naked Lunch* (he was joined for a time by Kerouac). Corso left for Paris. North Beach gave way to Haight-Ashbury and the "Hippies." The memory of the electrifying poetry reading rapidly became part of a double myth, of the "San Francisco Scene" and the "Beat Generation." As Ginsberg read each line of "Howl," Kerouac called out "Go." One could hear the 1950s ending, and the 1960s being born.

The photograph below appeared in Ann Charters' pictorial record of the Beats, Scenes Along the Road. *Taken by Peter Orlovsky, it shows poet and publisher Lawrence Ferlinghetti* (far right) *outside of his City Lights Bookstore in San Francisco in 1956, together with* (left to right) *Bob Donlin, Neal Cassady, Alan Ginsberg and Bob LaVigne.*

COLD WAR TALES

Spy fiction as a genre in Britain developed just before the Great War (1914–18) and reflected the anxieties then prevalent about German espionage. A few writers like E. Phillips Oppenheim and William le Queux published sensational stories highlighting what they saw as the threat to England's southern coastline. As the Security Service quickly discovered, German intelligence operations were of an amateur nature and the invasion scares far removed from reality. Nevertheless, as the Security and Intelligence Services developed and expanded, virtually a whole generation of young fiction writers was drawn into the clandestine world of intelligence and counter-intelligence, providing them with a wealth of experience on which they later drew in their novels. A modern genre was born – which came to its peak in the Cold War.

Gleinicke Bridge, above, *was a key crossing point at the Berlin Wall, and was the route of escape for Karla in John le Carré's novel of espionage,* Smiley's People.

Even during the Great War the roll call of personnel recruited into MI5 and the Secret Intelligence Service (SIS) resembled the guest list of some prestigious literary award. Somerset Maugham, A.E.W. Mason, Valentine Williams, Compton Mackenzie and playwright Edward Knoblock – some of the most popular writers of the time – were all invited to serve in that most covert of British government departments, the SIS. Since its creation in 1909 it was headed by an eccentric, one-legged naval officer, Captain Mansfield Smith-Cumming, whose career had been cut short by chronic seasickness. His headquarters, located in a labyrinth of corridors and offices on the roof of a huge apartment block overlooking Whitehall, gave novice spies all the inspiration they needed. References to the mysterious chief, his handicap and his attic lair recur in numerous tales later offered as fiction.

The literary tradition established in the 1920s, with heroes like John Buchan's Richard Hannay, Somerset Maugham's Ashenden and Charles Williams's Clubfoot, gave the public a taste for a kind of adventure that was rather more authentic than it realized. Only when Compton Mackenzie (1883–1972) was convicted at the Old Bailey of the unauthorized release of his war memoirs, *Greek Memories* (1932), in which he described SIS activities in the East Mediterranean, did readers learn that confidential missions undertaken by Carruthers and his friend Arthur Davies – described thirty years earlier by Robert

Erskine Childers (1870–1922) in the hugely successful *The Riddle of the Sands* (1903) – might not have been completely imaginary. Annoyed by the prosecution, Mackenzie took his revenge the very next year, publishing his *Water on the Brain* (1933), a cruel satire on the real spy world.

The Second World War and its aftermath created a new generation of spy fiction. Its appetite whetted by authentic accounts of gallantry behind the lines, the public was quickly captivated by Ian Fleming's (1908–64) James Bond, the suave but ruthless spy who appeared for the first time in *Casino Royale* (1953), a swashbuckling yarn that blended Sapper's Bulldog Drummond with modern technology and a hint of pornography. The best-selling combination spawned plenty of imitators, but also set the foundations for a Cold War literary convention to which many highly acclaimed writers were to contribute and so

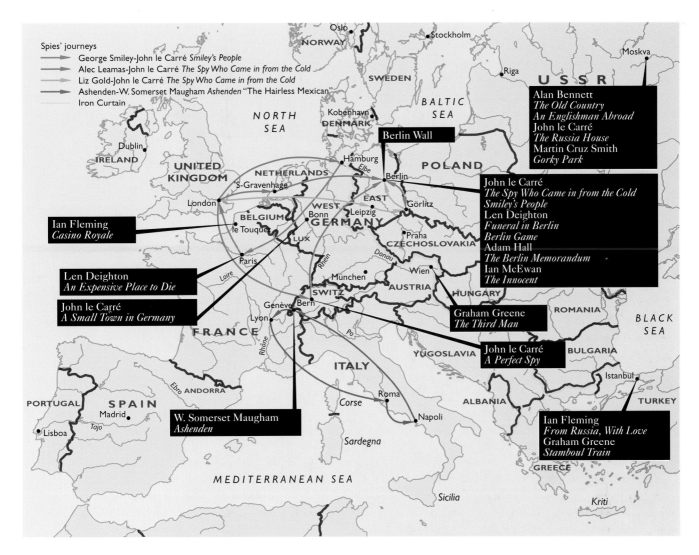

Spies' journeys
→ George Smiley-John le Carré *Smiley's People*
→ Alec Leamas-John le Carré *The Spy Who Came in from the Cold*
→ Liz Gold-John le Carré *The Spy Who Came in from the Cold*
→ Ashenden-W. Somerset Maugham *Ashenden* "The Hairless Mexican"
─── Iron Curtain

Alan Bennett
The Old Country
An Englishman Abroad
John le Carré
The Russia House
Martin Cruz Smith
Gorky Park

John le Carré
The Spy Who Came in from the Cold
Smiley's People
Len Deighton
Funeral in Berlin
Berlin Game
Adam Hall
The Berlin Memorandum
Ian McEwan
The Innocent

Ian Fleming
Casino Royale

Len Deighton
An Expensive Place to Die

John le Carré
A Small Town in Germany

W. Somerset Maugham
Ashenden

Graham Greene
The Third Man

John le Carré
A Perfect Spy

Ian Fleming
From Russia, With Love
Graham Greene
Stamboul Train

COLD WAR TALES: *Novels of espionage and intrigue were often set around the Berlin Wall. The spy journeys of several protagonists are plotted on this map.*

A still from Graham Greene's The Third Man, right, *which was originally written as a screenplay and filmed in 1949 by Carol Reed.*

build their own reputations. The climate of these Cold War Tales is that of troubled post-nuclear times. At its heart is the moral ambiguity of rival intelligence agencies, the West's own organizations showing betrayal and manipulation equal to their various Eastern Bloc counterparts.

Nowhere was the stark reality of post-war superpower confrontation more concentrated and contrasted than in the great cities of Austria and Germany, when after Allied victory they were under Four-Power control. Graham Greene (1904–91) – already the creator of the cosmic landscape of unease and betrayal called "Greeneland," and also a wartime SIS officer who worked as Kim Philby's subordinate – set his film and novel *The Third Man* (1950) in divided,

war-battered Vienna. Likewise John le Carré (b. David Cornwell 1931) wrote *The Spy Who Came in from the Cold* (1963) while serving in the looking glass world at SIS's Bonn station. Elleston Trevor (Adam Hall) also opted for Germany and the horrors of the Berlin Wall in his novel *The Berlin Memorandum* (1965), filmed (screenplay by

with Philby, le Carré could not have been unaffected by his own personal encounters with betrayal. His Bonn station commander was Peter Lunn, an SIS professional whose career was blighted by George Blake, the KGB mole whose Old Bailey trial in 1961 took place while le Carré was still operating under diplomatic cover in Germany. Working in the same building in Bonn was Frank Bossard, a scientific attaché who was arrested and convicted of espionage for the Russians a year after le Carré resigned from SIS after his success with *The Spy Who Came in from the Cold.*

Although Le Carré officially joined the SIS in 1960, his initiation into the real spy world had taken place earlier, when he had been recruited by MI5 to report on post-war Communist activity at Oxford University. During that period he had been run as a source by a legendary case officer, John Bingham, who worked as a Security Service handler in the War, and had taken to writing spy novels in 1952 with *My Name is Michael Sibley.* Bingham's own entry into MI5 had been facilitated by Maxwell Knight, another brilliantly intuitive MI5 agent-runner who wrote two crime thrillers in the early 1930s, while masterminding a network of agents to penetrate the Communist Party of Great Britain. One of his best sources was the London-based American novelist John Dickson Carr (*Top Secret*, 1964); while Bingham's stepson, William Younger, wrote murder mysteries (*The Skin Trap*, 1957) while working for MI5 as a molehunter.

Harold Pinter) as *The Quiller Memorandum* (1966), as did Len Deighton (who began his spywriter career with *The Ipcress File*, 1962) in *Funeral in Berlin* (1964). Although both authors seem to have achieved a high degree of verisimilitude, neither had first-hand experience of espionage. Deighton (b.1929) was a journalist and advertising man; Trevor began writing after leaving the RAF in 1945.

Graham Greene's experience of the nether-world of counter-intelligence, where concepts of allegiance and personal loyalty become blurred, are constant themes in novels like *The Quiet American* (1955), about American operations in Southeast Asia, and *The Human Factor* (1978). Even *Our Man in Havana* (1958) was a spoof entertainment that concealed the truth – that Greene had remained in contact with the SIS after the War and had undertaken various SIS assignments in Vietnam and Cuba long after his official departure from the organization in 1944. His relationship was terminated in 1968 when it was found he had volunteered an uncritical Foreword to defector Kim Philby's controversial autobiography, *My Silent War* (1968). There was also suspicion that Greene's long friendship with the traitor may have led him to carry the manuscript to a literary agent in Paris.

Just as Greene was influenced by his association

> **"In the higher ranges of Secret Service work the actual facts in many cases were in every respect equal to the most fantastic inventions of romance and melodrama. Tangle within tangle, plot and counter-plot, ruse and treachery, cross and double-cross, true agent, false agent, double agent, gold and steel, the bomb, the dagger and the firing party were interwoven in many a texture so intricate as to be incredible yet true."**
>
> Winston Churchill

The Security Service nurtured several other authors ("literary agents," they've been called), including Bingham's wife Madeleine, secretary at Blenheim Palace in Oxfordshire, the temporary headquarters of MI5 during the London blitz, and Charlotte Bingham, his daughter, who wrote *Coronet Among the Weeds* (1963) while typing in MI5's registry. Another important figure in war-time Security

Clockwise from top left: *Ian Fleming, John le Carré and Graham Greene drew on their experiences in the secret services for their novels.*

Service was John Masterman (1891–1977), an Oxford don who tried his hand at detective stories (*An Oxford Tragedy*, 1933, *Fate Cannot Harm Me*, 1935) before joining MI5 in 1940. After the War he exploited his acquired knowledge of counter-intelligence techniques in *The Case of the Four Friends* (1957), a detection classic, but insufficiently commercial to compete with his intelligence colleagues-cum-novelists, who turned the Cold War to great literary advantage.

For many modern readers, the spy novel and the world it created – of tension, betrayal, doubled roles, split loyalties – captured an age in which sinister forces governed, spy-scandals became a fact of life and defections and double-dealing grew common. Many works were of high literary quality. Len Deighton's research for detail, which mistakenly persuaded many he had been an insider, and le Carré's compelling creation of the post-war atmosphere of mystery, betrayal and dark complicity (focused in the chess-like confrontation between George Smiley and Karla) are only matched by one other thriller writer, Kenneth Benton (b.1909), whose long SIS career was but a prelude to literary success. On his retirement in 1968, after thirty years in the service, he put his experience to good use, producing spy novels – among them *The Twenty-fourth Level* (1969) and *Spy in the Chancery* (1972) – which boasted the hallmarks of a writer with a close knowledge of his subject, serving to confirm to the *cognoscenti* the true nature of his cover role as a diplomat.

The spy novel, particularly as it developed in Britain, became the form that best captured the Cold War era. A generation of writers took the dark realities of post-war superpower rivalry, ideological division and freeze and thaw to create a remarkable popular myth. The consistent common denominator of Cold War espionage fiction was attention to detail and fact. It was this that persuaded Ian Fleming to replace James Bond's Beretta, a puny weapon experts ridiculed, with a more plausible Walther PPK. Thus armed with suitable hardware, Fleming's Cold Warrior was transformed, albeit briefly, from romance hero to a semblance of reality.

The best novelists became so proficient in their art and research that some of their tradecraft and vocabulary – le Carré's invention of "the mole," "the Circus," "Moscow Centre" – influenced events themselves. Their terms and plots were adopted by genuine practitioners of the arcane arts on both sides of the conflict. Spy fiction was read behind closed doors in the Lubyanka, the CIA and Mossad. The genre reached its heyday in the era of suspicion that came from the darkest years of Cold War, when, effectively transferred to film and television, they powerfully reflected the threatening climate of the times. Today, it's been argued, the era of classic spy fiction is over, for the ending of the Cold War has destroyed one of our great modern myths. It seems too early to say. After all, conspiracy, terror, inhumanity, surveillance, betrayal and divided loyalties remain at the heart of the modern world.

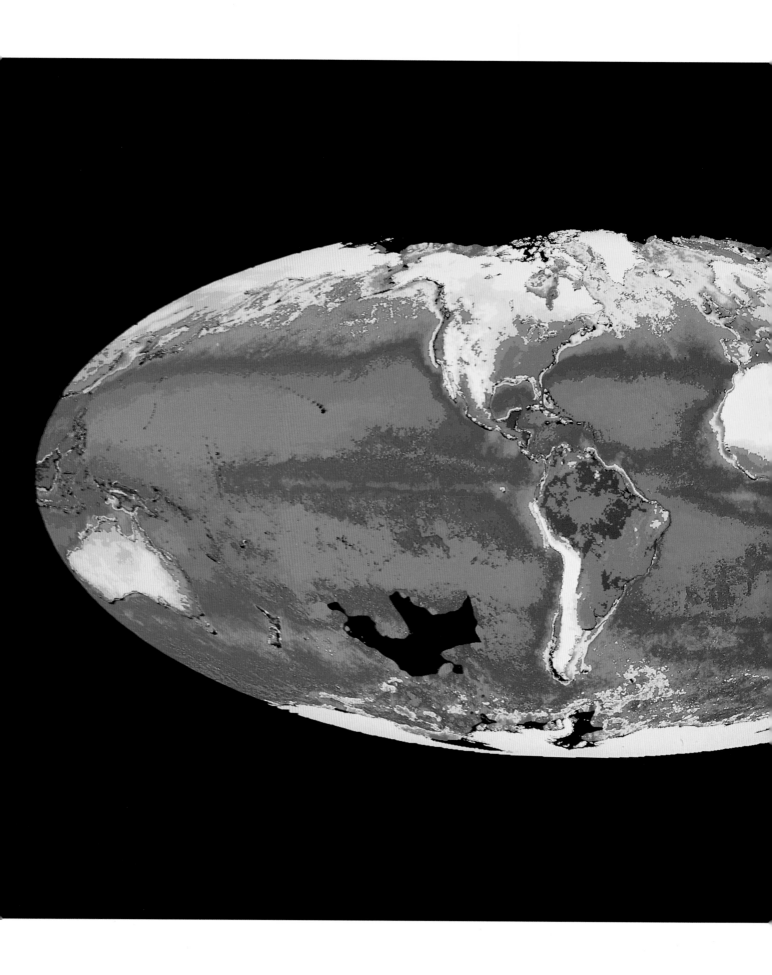

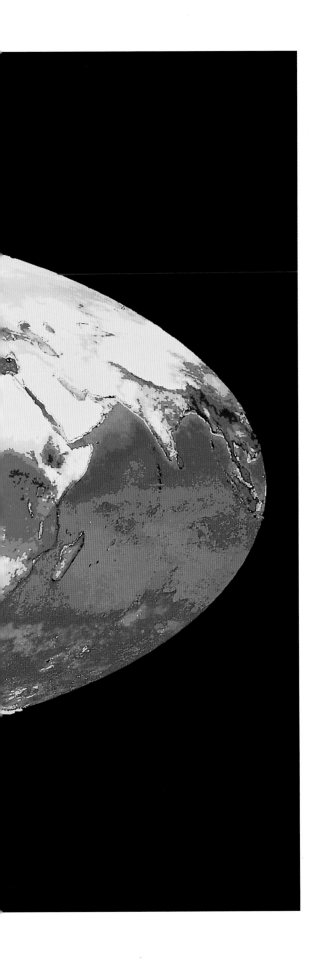

PART EIGHT

THE WORLD TODAY

Even before the coming of what political leaders called "the New World Order" after the collapse of Communism in 1989, the map of contemporary writing was taking on fresh shape – not least because, as every form of human contact and communication developed and expanded, the world was simply becoming a smaller, more interactive place. Global media systems brought instant news from all parts of the earth (and space) and allowed an international audience to share the same movies, music and fictions. The writer today lives in a "postmodern age" of screens, satellites, depthless history and virtual reality. The globalization of the world by its own new technologies has become a fact of history: weakening old nation states, generating new human movement and migration, creating cultural and literary pluralism. The new technologies have challenged not simply the old maps of the world but the Gutenberg Revolution – the era of the printed book, and therefore of a systematic literature. Our arts and images are themselves part of the new Information Superhighway. Our stories are already taking different shapes and appearing on new screens; yet the sheer energy and wonder of the widening world and its intersecting cultures continues to find vigorous literary expression...

This computer-generated "Satellite Map" of 1990 was produced by satellites continuously circling the earth taking pictures, and shows the way in which the mapping process itself has been reconceptualized by modern technology.

RUSSIA AND EASTERN EUROPE AFTER THE SECOND WORLD WAR

Literary matters are a "small cog in the totally integrated grand mechanism of social democracy," Lenin wrote in 1905. He meant journalism, but the Bolshevik state he founded did everything to ensure all writing should have just that status. Soviet Russia survived by crushing critical voices with ruthless terror. In 1924 Lenin's body lay in state in the Hall of Columns in the former Assembly House of the Gentry, now the Trade Unions' Club. Here seven years later playwright George Bernard Shaw, addressing a huge audience honouring his 75th birthday, told them: "We are going back [to England] much impressed." Three years on, Maksim Gorky (1868–1936) presided here over the First Congress of the Union of Soviet Writers, which defined the writer's task as to provide "a true and historically concrete depiction of reality in its revolutionary development." Reality and its development would be determined by the Party. The Hall of Columns also became the setting for Stalin's Show Trials, which started in earnest after Gorky's death (or murder) in 1936.

Reality had its revenge. In December 1991 the USSR finally ground to a standstill – as fifty years earlier Mikhail Bulgakov (1891–1940) metaphorically predicted in his fantastic novel *The Master and Margarita* (1929–40). Here Mikhail Berlioz, a leading functionary of the Writers' Union, tells a young poet that Jesus Christ never existed; the Devil arrives to say he did. They debate the matter at Moscow's Patriarch's Ponds; within the hour Berlioz is given conclusive proof of the Devil's existence – his head is cut off by a tram.

The Soviets did their best to sideline writers into penning copy for the Party's construction projects, while denouncing more ambitious work as inaccessible or alien to the people. Abundantly using the stick (many writers were murdered), they attempted to compromise others with a constant offer of carrots. Gorky's ill-advised endorsement of Stalin's industrialization drive was the most

Clockwise from top left *are Anna Akhmatova, Aleksandr Tvardovsky, Boris Pasternak and Yevgeny Yevtushenko.*

dramatic example. Returning to Russia in 1931, he was forbidden to leave the country, under virtual house-arrest in an art nouveau mansion he loathed (Dom muzei A.M. Gor'kogo).

The issue of carrots took place in the Writers' Union (Soyuz pisatelei SSSR), at 25 Tverskoy Boulevard. Bulgakov fictionalizes it in *The Master and Margarita*: "On the door of the first room on the upper storey was a large notice: 'Angling and Weekend Cottages,' with a picture of a carp caught on a hook. On the door of the second room was a slightly confusing notice: 'Writers' day-return rail warrants. Apply to M.V. Podlozhnaya.' The next door bore a brief and completely incomprehensible legend: 'Perelygino.' From there the chance visitor's eye would be caught by countless more notices pinned to the walnut doors: 'Waiting List For Paper – apply to Poklevkina', Cashier's Office,' Sketch-Writers:

Moscow: *The Writers' Union and Novy Mir struggle between themselves for the soul of Russian literature. Their locations can be seen here, together with those of other literary landmarks in the city.*

Personal Accounts.'" It was a greater distinction to be expelled from the Union than be admitted. Four of the five Russian Nobel Prize winners were expelled or never members.

The wartime years saw a loosening of the reins in many areas of Soviet life, including literature. In 1946 the reins were abruptly reapplied, with a campaign of vilification against Leningrad writers Mikhail Zoshchenko (1895–1958) and Anna Akhmatova (1888–1966), the censuring of the journal *Zvezda* (The Star) and the closing of *Leningrad*. The years from then until Stalin's death in 1953 were, on the surface, culturally dead. His demise produced immediate signs of literary revival, with a succession of articles appearing in *Novy Mir*, edited by Aleksandr Tvardovsky, a loyal Party member, but with fair awareness of literary values. Alexei Surkov, an indifferent poet but prominent Writers' Union official, conducted a whispering campaign, reminding the Kremlin that Tvardovsky's father, a blacksmith, was exiled for failing to pay punitive taxes imposed during the first Five-Year Plan. Tvardovsky had his class origins given as "kulak" (rich peasant) in the official file; and was removed from his position in August 1954.

As the post-Stalin power struggle continued within the Party leadership, events in society developed apace. The first annual Poetry Day in 1955 provided a focus, in Moscow and Leningrad, for liberal and oppositional forces. The young Yevgeny Yevtushenko (b.1933) made his first public appearance, reciting his verse from the steps of the old Moscow University building opposite the Kremlin. Krushchev secretly denounced Stalin's crimes at the twentieth Party Congress in 1956. That year the instability of the situation in Eastern Europe became apparent, with social unrest in Poland and a full-scale anti-Communist uprising in Hungary. Thaw reverted to freeze. In 1957 Yevtushenko was expelled from the Gorky Literary Institute (Literaturnyi institut imeni A.M. Gor'kogo). He

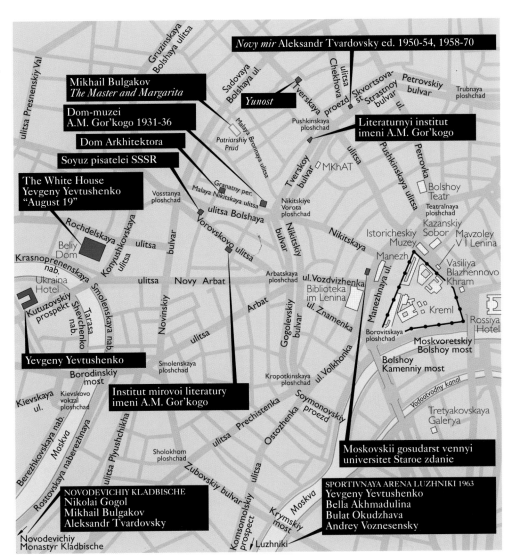

> "No,
> Never again shall Russia be on her knees.
> With us are Pushkin, Tolstoy.
> With us are people awakened forever
> and the Russian parliament,
> Like a wounded marble swan of freedom,
> defended by the people,
> swims into immortality."
>
> "August *19*" Yevgeny Yevtushenko

was also expelled from the Young Communist League, only to be reinstated to leading positions in both when the pendulum swung again. Restored to *Novy Mir* in 1958, Tvardovsky continued to lead what was seen as the main voice of the liberal intelligentsia.

Against this unstable background, the *Doctor Zhivago* affair was played out. Along with Akhmatova, Boris Pasternak (1890–1960) was one of the few survivors of the pre-revolutionary poets who stayed un-Soviet during the decades of Communist rule. Thinking the time

The judicial absurdity of the trial of Yuli Daniel and Andrei Sinyavsky, above, led to a marked increase in protests and open anti-government dissidence.

Publication of Pasternak's Doctor Zhivago *in Italy brought scathing criticism in the Soviet Union, as this cartoon depicting someone reading the book in the shadow of the newspaper offices of the "Daily Liar" shows.*

culminating in a grand procession down the new Peace Prospect. The engaging Yevtushenko was pressed into service as a youth ambassador, arriving in Britain in 1962. At home poetry readings became an important element of the political equation: the stars were Yevtushenko, Bella Akmadulina, Andrei Voznesensky and Bulat Okudzhava. The trend culminated in 1963 with an event before 14,000 spectators at the Luzhniki Palace of Sports. With the phenomenon of *magnitizdat* – publication by tape recorder – the Party stranglehold on literary outlets was beginning to slip.

In 1962 Tvardovsky won Krushchev's permission to print a novella by an unknown writer, Aleksandr Solzhenitsyn (b.1918), *One Day in the Life of Ivan Denisovich*. It caused a sensation: the subject was life in a Soviet prison camp. The barbaric repression of the secret police was an explosive topic: Solzhenitsyn, like Pasternak, found himself embodying one side of a struggle which could end only in renewed repression, or the demise of the Communist order. With Krushchev's overthrow in 1964, and his replacement by the unimaginative Leonid Brezhnev, the die was cast – for repression. So came the twenty geriatric years of what has since become called "the period of stagnation."

In 1965 two writers, Andrei Sinyavsky and Yuli Daniel were arrested by the KGB for publishing uninhibited, uncensored works abroad (they were smuggled out via the French Embassy). Hardliners consolidated their victory with a latter-day Show Trial, imposing maximum sentences of seven and five years' hard labour respectively. Sinyavsky had been a senior research fellow at the Gorky Institute of World Literature (Institut mirovoi literatury imeni A.M. Gor'kogo) and pall-bearer at Pasternak's funeral. But the trial showed times had changed; without physical torture and murder of opponents, Stalinism did not work. The defendants behaved very differently from their cowed, terrified predecessors of the 1930s, which encouraged more open protest.

The Brezhnev regime showed its resolve to die hard, above all with its forcible suppression of Aleksandr Dubcek's "socialism with a human face" in Czechoslovakia in 1968. *Novy Mir* stoutly refused public endorsement of the invasion; the Party did not fail to notice. Four members of the editorial board were removed in early 1970, bringing Tvardovsky's resignation. The continued rigid enforcement of Soviet values grew ever more ridiculous.

had come to take his novel of the Revolutionary years out of the drawer, Pasternak was wrong-footed by the fast changes of Party cultural policy. The novel's manuscript, apparently rejected by *Novy Mir* in 1956, had already been sent abroad. Surkov was instantly to hand, as leading light in the Writers' Union (his deeply compromised predecessor Aleksandr Fadeyev had shot himself after Krushchev's speech), and in 1957 spearheaded attempts to prevent Italian publication of the book. Pasternak's Nobel Prize in 1958 was represented as pure political provocation, and he was mercilessly persecuted till his death in May 1960.

Meantime, pursuing a new foreign policy aimed at minimizing the risk of atomic war while maximizing global Soviet influence, Krushchev undertook a "peace offensive." He visited western countries, including Britain. In 1957 a World Youth Festival in Moscow was permitted,

EASTERN EUROPE: *In the 1970s and 1980s many Russian writers were exiled from their native country, mainly settling in Western Europe and the United States.*

Uncensored Russian literature circulated in *samizdat* (self-publication) and *tamizdat* (publication over there), books which found their way back from the emigré Possev Press in West Germany, and others. The state adopted a grotesque policy of intimidation and furtive medical murder by incarcerating dissidents in psychiatric clinics, most notoriously the Serbsky Clinic.

In the 1970s any spark of originality was considered a political challenge. A raft of writers was packed off to the West: Valerii Tarsis (1966), Joseph Brodsky (1972), Andrei Sinyavsky (1973), Viktor Nekrasov, Aleksandr Galich, Solzhenitsyn (1974), Aleksandr Zinoviev (1977), Vasilii Aksyonov, Vladimir Voinovich (1980), Georgii Vladimov (1983). In 1979, in a gesture of open contempt, a large group of writers enraged Writers' Union apparatchiks by publishing eight copies of an anthology of uncensored work, *Metropol*. The Soviet literary establishment finally tottered into total farce by awarding the top literary prize to Leonid Brezhnev, for his war memoirs.

Cultural dementia was matched by economic sclerosis. The impossibility of matching the United States "Star Wars" challenge finally forced the Party down the fraught path of democratization. Mikhail Gorbachev in a cautious speech in the Palace of Congresses in 1987, upturned the cultural policy of decades: "Spiritual culture is not only an adornment of society: it is something which underlies its very viability, and determines society's intellectual and cultural potential. It is, if you like, the alloy which ensures its durability and the catalyst which ensures its dynamism." His *glasnost* (openness) policy led to a rash of works of critical realism, exposing hitherto-concealed ills and horrendous ecological irresponsibility. The works of emigrés appeared. Permitted subjects now included the greatest crimes of the Soviet regime, including the artificially induced famine in the Ukraine between 1931 and 1932 (of which Bernard Shaw blithely said he saw no evidence).

Writers proved much quicker than historians to show aspects of the past that left the Soviet government and the Party widely despised, as hardliners found in the coup of August 1991. Yevtushenko was to hand in the besieged Parliament Building, where his poem, "August 19" was read out to the parliament as part of his speech. Liberalization this time opened the doors not only for Russian writers but others right across the Eastern bloc – where formidable authors in countries like Czechoslovakia (Milan Kundera, Ivan Klima, Václav Havel) and Hungary (Peter Esterhazy, Georgy Conrad) had likewise struggled

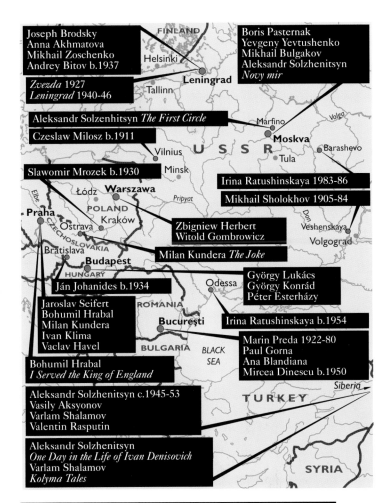

Joseph Brodsky
Anna Akhmatova
Mikhail Zoschenko
Andrey Bitov b.1937
Zvezda 1927
Leningrad 1940-46

Boris Pasternak
Yevgeny Yevtushenko
Mikhail Bulgakov
Aleksandr Solzhenitsyn
Novy mir

Aleksandr Solzenhitsyn *The First Circle*
Czeslaw Milosz b.1911

Slawomir Mrozek b.1930

Irina Ratushinskaya 1983-86
Mikhail Sholokhov 1905-84

Zbigniew Herbert
Witold Gombrowicz

Milan Kundera *The Joke*

Ján Johanides b.1934

György Lukács
György Konrád
Péter Esterházy

Jaroslav Seifert
Bohumil Hrabal
Milan Kundera
Ivan Klima
Vaclav Havel

Irina Ratushinskaya b.1954

Marin Preda 1922-80
Paul Gorna
Ana Blandiana
Mircea Dinescu b.1950

Bohumil Hrabal
I Served the King of England

Aleksandr Solzhenitsyn c.1945-53
Vasily Aksyonov
Varlam Shalamov
Valentin Rasputin

Aleksandr Solzhenitsyn
One Day in the Life of Ivan Denisovich
Varlam Shalamov
Kolyma Tales

RUSSIAN BOOKER PRIZE WINNERS

1992	Mark Kharitonov *Lines of Fate*
1993	Vladimir Makanin *Baize-covered Table with Decanter*
1994	Bulat Okudzhava *The Show is Over*
1995	Georgii Vladimov *A General and his Army*

to maintain freedom of expression and imagination. In Czechoslovakia Havel symbolically became President, only to see his country divide a little later.

The problems of writers did not die with the Cold War. In Russia the euphoria of 1987–89, when the shackles of seven decades were released, gave way to growing pessimism, as incompetent attempts to revolutionize the economy produced runaway inflation. In 1992 the number of fiction titles published was lower than in 1913. By 1993 book prices increased by twenty to fifty times; readers' incomes did not. In 1992 the new-founded Russian Booker Prize had to allow submission of works in manuscript, so complete was the publishing collapse. But the Prize's annual award marks a resurgence of public interest in the fate of Russian fiction, and has helped return some kind of normality to the judgement of literature.

THE FANTASYWALLAS OF BOMBAY

In the last fifty years, Bombay has grown in the Indian imagination into the fabulous, inescapable face of metropolitan India. With its plural, hybrid culture, the city is a little like the mixture that goes into one of its famous streetside delicacies, *bhelpuri*. In that irresistible dish, you can taste chutneys of garlic, dates and green chilies, the garnishing of raw onions and fresh coriander leaves. Bombay invades the palate with an equally wide range of tastes. It exemplifies best the kind of polyphonic chutney the modern Indian city is: commerce, myth, technology, revivalism – all add their unique, assertive flavours to its soul.

Many of "midnight's children" – Indian writers after the Raj – grew up in Bombay, in a city that was "Prima in India/ Gateway to India/ Star of the East/ With her Face to the West." In his vital, glittering novel *Midnight's Children* (1981), Salman Rushdie (b.1947) describes his Bombay and its boundaries in detail. The small strip of South Bombay Rushdie writes about nurtured several post-Independence children like him, filled them up with sights and sounds and smells and fabulous secrets – all of which would come tumbling out years later, thousands of miles away, as a very new kind of fiction.

This fiction was in English, but not in the English these writers had learned in England, or earlier in the hallowed portals of Bombay's Elphinstone College or St Xavier's College. Their English was a post-colonial invention, a language like Bombay, a hybrid creature with many heads and arms, guardian-goddess of an imaginary land that lives on and grows in the memory. Its assault of words, hopes, dreams and anguish all come together in these writers' portrayals of Bombay as Mother India: sometimes as a nostalgia for colour, at other times an indictment of the monstrous warts India has been afflicted by since "Mountbatten's ticktock," the midnight hour of Independence on 15 August, 1947.

Anyone who has lived in Bombay knows there are many Bombays. Even in the memories of the travelling midnight's children, these Bombays jostle for attention, flow together to make a large, almost amorphous metaphor. Salman Rushdie, Anita Desai, Shashi Tharoor, Amit Chaudhuri, Alan Sealey, Rohinton Mistry, Firdaus Kanga, the Pakistani writer Bapsi Sidhwa, author of *The Ice-Candy Man* (1992), all now live elsewhere, but they return time and again in their fiction to where many of their stories began – Bombay.

Of the many Bombays, it is Parsi Bombay that has lent itself to some particularly eloquent portrayals. The Parsis, who came to India from Persia in the seventh century to escape religious persecution, have a palpable sense

In their novels, Mistry and Sidhwa take their readers to a major landmark of Parsi Bombay: the Towers of Silence, above, home of a cemetery hidden amid green acres of landscaped gardens where the dead are left in dry wells for vultures to strip the bodies of flesh.

of community. The typical middle class Parsi colony, an almost self-contained enclave, is recalled in meticulous loving detail by Rohinton Mistry (b.1952) in *Tales from Firozsha Baag* (1987) and *Such a Long Journey* (1991). The apartments his Parsis live in are dilapidated, with peeling walls. There is little privacy: the smell of *dhansak* and *dhandar-paatyo* pervade the air. The Parsi map has this colony for its centre point. The outside world impinges selectively: there is the ubiquitous Irani restaurant across the road in an impoverished lane; the Parsi General Hospital, where the business of life – birth and death – is conducted. The children go to St Xavier's Boys School with its ornate gates, perhaps later to St Xavier's College.

Every Sunday morning there are visits to the Marine Drive maidan to play cricket. The culturally inclined go to the Cawasji Framji Memorial Library and to Western classical music concerts at the Max Müeller Society; for the simpler at heart, there is Chowpatty Beach nearby, its crowded sands, fat pigeons and the kerosene lamplit stalls selling a fiery *bhelpuri*. Visits to the Parsi Dairy Farm and Crawford Market are inevitable, in buses that meander "through narrow streets of squalor...crawling

In Baumgartner's Bombay (1988), Anita Desai, left, uses Bombay as a meeting point between East and West. For the German Jew Baumgartner, the underbelly of Bombay is as much a refuge as it is for the thousands who migrate year after year to its inhospitable pavements. Salman Rushdie, near left, draws on the fantastical aspect of Bombay film life that leaks into real life like a defective faucet. Radios blare out the latest film songs and hoardings with grotesque colours, below, loom into the sky.

painfully amidst the traffic of cars and people, handcarts and trucks" (*Tales From Firozsha Baag*). Right in the heart of this bustle is the refuge of the marble-lined fire temple and its "sacred fire, burning in the huge, shining silver *afargaan* on its marble pedestal."

Mistry, Sidhwa and Firdaus Kanga (*Trying to Grow*, 1990) have recorded their memories of Parsi Bombay with an affectionate microscope, paying attention to realistic detail. But the Bombay that attracts and engages most contemporary writers is a larger, wilder landscape, where memory and reality are often turned upside down. "If I seem a little bizarre, remember the wild profusion of my inheritance...," says Saleem in *Midnight's Children*. "Perhaps, if one wishes to remain an individual in the midst of the teeming multitudes, one must make oneself grotesque." The medium that has probably stood most often for post-Raj Bombay (a Bombay of the imagination that has grown to surreal proportions to match the city's identity) is its film industry. The Bombay popular film is a concoction of mirch-masala that caters, says Indian film-maker Shyam Benegal, to "what is probably the most pluralistic and diverse, multi-cultural, multi-lingual and multi-religious population group in the whole world."

The Hindi film, with its gallery of caricatures, is a rich source of material for all writers who turn their gaze on Bombay, or modern India. "Bollywood" is peopled with larger-than-life stars and hordes of smaller-than-life dreamers. In *East, West* (1994), Rushdie writes of the doomed-to-fail aspirant who sends word that he is spending "his days at the Sun 'n' Sand Hotel at Juhu beach in the company of top lady artistes...buying a big house at Pali Hill, built in the split-level mode and incorporating the latest security equipment to protect him from the movie fans...and life was filled with light and success and no-questions-asked alcohol."

In this fantasy-Bombay, Romeos cut their hair like Amitabh Bachchan, sweet young things wear Madhuri

Dixit saris. Sometimes you wonder if there is a shortage of heroes and heroines in real life, so powerful are those on celluloid. The film world and its crass commercial heart, surreal features, fantastic solutions to mundane problems, give new writers such as Shashi Tharoor (*The Great Indian Novel*, 1989), Alan Sealey (*Hero*, 1990) and Vikram Chandra (*Red Earth and Pouring Rain*, 1995) a prismatic view of India in all her ragged, magical glory.

Like the Hindi film, contemporary Indian fiction draws on India's vast resources of oral tradition – mythological and historical epics, ballads, poetry and music. Indian psychoanalyst Sudhir Kakar's description of Hindi film as "a collective fantasy," seems applicable to much of post-Raj fiction in English, which is also a "group daydream, containing...the hidden wishes of a vast number of people, unreal in a rational sense, but certainly not untrue." The result is a unique form which not only reflects old and familiar myths, but also creates contemporary ones.

There is of course the Bombay of residents – including those who have travelled and returned, like

poets Adil Jussawalla, and Dom Moraes (b.1938) – who after a lifetime of being "never at home," describes in his autobiography *Never At Home* (1992) how he was cured from writer's block on returning to the city after 17 years.

The pillar of English writing in Bombay was Moraes' mentor, the poet, critic and teacher Nissim Ezekiel. His Bombay is the University; the Oval maidan with its clock tower; Wilson College by Chowpatty Beach. He walks along the sands, waits for a bus, travels to Bellasis Road near Byculla, where he lives in "The Retreat," an old, high-ceilinged flat full of discreetly hanging cobwebs and piles of manuscripts. This landscape, he tells us in "Background, Casually" (*Hymns in Darkness*, 1976), has been his, by choice, for many years. He has been associated with at least two generations of Indian poets writing in English, including Gieve Patel, Eunice De Souza, Arun Kolatkar and Saleem Peeradina. Their poetry often tries to reconcile conflicting identities – as the title of Patel's poem tells us: "The Ambiguous Fate of Gieve Patel, He Being Neither Muslim Nor Hindu in India" (1972).

There is an important face of the city – some would say the real one – that is not often seen in South Bombay or well-known outside the country. Of its many voices Marathi is the principal one, but there is also the Babel of "immigrant" voices – Indians on the move within India, writing in Gujurati, Malayalam, Bengali, Tamil. The cosmopolitan city acts on these "regional language" writers to produce new streams of writing, creating work closer to Kafka, Camus, Neruda or Grass than to

For West-facing writers, the enduring symbol of Bombay is the Gateway of India, above, that hoary old arch that stands guard over the flotsam-filled waters leading to the sea beyond.

contemporary British writing. While those working in English may be engaged in a search for "the footprints of a forfeited language," these writers grapple with their own homegrown monsters of dismemberment and dislocation. Vilas Sarang, for example, writes stunning modernistic stories in Marathi (many translated in a wonderful collection, *Fair Tree of the Void*, 1990).

In the 1960s and 1970s dalit writers like Baburao Bagul and Namdeo Dhasal began to write of their first-hand experience of social evils. The dalits, the former untouchables of Hindu society, are virulently anti-upper-caste in their writing, anti-middle-class as well. Some of their work has been translated in the anthology *Poisoned Bread* (1992). As literature of protest, it corresponds best to African-American writing, or the revolutionary writing coming from Latin America, the Caribbean and Africa.

In the last two decades, though, it is Indian writing in English that has pierced Western scepticism about its literary viability and received international recognition. Since the late 1970s writers like Rushdie, Amitav Ghosh and Vikram Seth have made a cultural breakthrough that has altered the relationship between Indian writing in English and writing in the other Indian languages. They have produced work on a par with the best new writing in the British Commonwealth and in the Anglo-Irish and American traditions. The fantasywallas of Bombay are clearly here to stay.

> "Bombay was central, had been so from the moment of its creation: the bastard child of a Portuguese-English wedding, and yet the most Indian of Indian cities. In Bombay all Indias met and merged. In Bombay, too, all-India met what-was-not-India, what came across the black water to flow into our veins. Everything north of Bombay was North India, everything south of it was the South. To the east lay India's East and to the west, the world's West. Bombay was central; all rivers flowed into its human sea. It was an ocean of stories; we were all its narrators, and everybody talked at once."
>
> Salman Rushdie, *The Moor's Last Sigh*

POST-WAR BOMBAY: *In* Midnight's Children *Salman Rushdie wrote about his city in detail: "...along Marine Drive! On Chowpatty sands! Past the great houses on Malabar Hill, round Kemp's Corner, giddily along the sea to Scandal Point! ...on and on, down my very own Warden Road, right alongside the segregated swimming pools of Breach Candy, right up to huge Mahalaxmi Temple and the old Willingdon Club..." The map shows key settings from this novel and Rohinton Mistry's* Such a Long Journey.

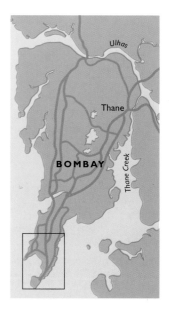

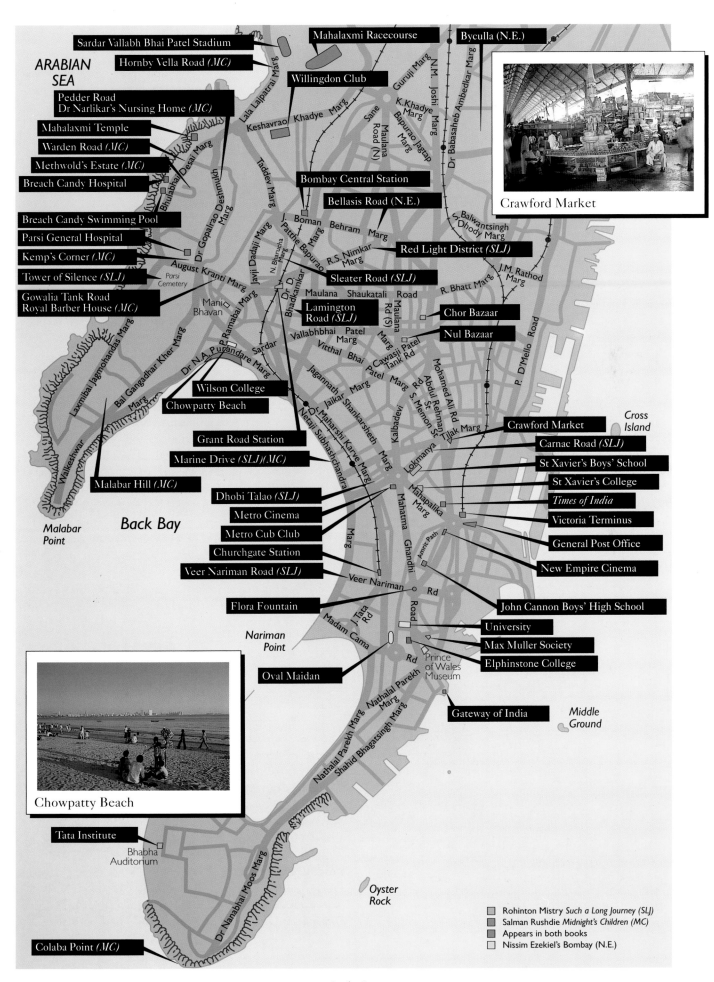

ARABIAN
SEA

Sardar Vallabh Bhai Patel Stadium
Hornby Vella Road *(MC)*
Willingdon Club
Mahalaxmi Racecourse
Byculla (N.E.)

Pedder Road
Dr Narlikar's Nursing Home *(MC)*
Mahalaxmi Temple
Warden Road *(MC)*
Methwold's Estate *(MC)*
Breach Candy Hospital
Keshavrao Khadye Marg

Bombay Central Station
Bellasis Road (N.E.)

Crawford Market

Breach Candy Swimming Pool
Parsi General Hospital
Kemp's Corner *(MC)*
Tower of Silence *(SLJ)*
Gowalia Tank Road
Royal Barber House *(MC)*

Red Light District *(SLJ)*
Sleater Road *(SLJ)*
Lamington Road *(SLJ)*
Maulana Shaukatali Road
Chor Bazaar
Nul Bazaar

Parsi Cemetery
Mani Bhavan

Wilson College
Chowpatty Beach
Grant Road Station
Marine Drive *(SLJ)(MC)*
Malabar Hill *(MC)*

Dhobi Talao *(SLJ)*
Metro Cinema
Metro Cub Club
Churchgate Station
Veer Nariman Road *(SLJ)*

Flora Fountain

Cross Island

Crawford Market
Carnac Road *(SLJ)*
St Xavier's Boys' School
St Xavier's College
Times of India
Victoria Terminus
General Post Office
New Empire Cinema

John Cannon Boys' High School
University
Max Muller Society
Elphinstone College

Malabar Point

Back Bay

Nariman Point

Oval Maidan

Prince of Wales Museum

Gateway of India

Middle Ground

Chowpatty Beach

Tata Institute
Bhabha Auditorium

Oyster Rock

Colaba Point *(MC)*

Rohinton Mistry *Such a Long Journey (SLJ)*
Salman Rushdie *Midnight's Children (MC)*
Appears in both books
Nissim Ezekiel's Bombay (N.E.)

JAPAN: LAND OF SPIRITS OF THE EARTH

Sense of place is central to Japanese culture. Shinto – along with Buddhism – has always been profoundly attached to distinctive settings: the mountains, rivers, bays and forests of the great island nation. And from early times the poets and chroniclers – often the same people – celebrated the holiness and mythic power of certain sites and shrines, or caught the "floating" spirit of the great Japanese cities.

The succession of capital cities – Nara, Kyoto, Kamakura and much later Edo (which became Tokyo) – were long-time centres of literary excellence in Japan. In the eleventh century the court of Kyoto produced three writers who became world-famous (though only in this century were they well translated into English). All were women and minor aristocrats. Lady Murasaki (c.980-1030) wrote the epic, psychological story *The Tale of Genji* (trans. 1935), amongst our first novels. More meditatively, the daughter of Takasue Sugawara (b.c.1008) wrote *The Diary of Sarashina* (c.1060), and Sei Shonagon (b.c.966) wrote the teasing *Pillow Book* (trans. 1928). But behind these sophisticated writings was a mass of earlier poetry and prose. As early as the eighth century, the great poetry anthology the *Manyoshu* (translated as *Ten Thousand Leaves*) was com-

The illustration, above, is from Sei Shonagon's The Pillow Book, *a teasing collection of love stories written in the tenth century.*

piled. It contains work by many kinds of Japanese – male and female, emperors and empresses, court officials, priests, unknown ordinary folk – and displays a great love of place. However, it was not until after the Battle of Sekigahara in 1600, when Ieyasu, the Tokugawa chief, began to suppress outside influence, that Japan, which was to be isolated from the world for two centuries, fully began to develop its own extraordinary and distinctive culture. Beside the aristocracy, the military and the priesthood a canny, inventive merchant class developed. Printed books

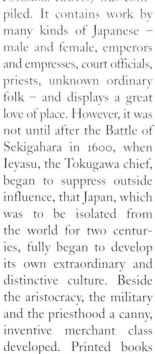

Hiroshige's eighteenth century painting of Mount Fuji, above, *captures the distinctive island feel of Japan.*

multiplied in volume and a large reading public appeared. It was not until the nineteenth century that Japan started opening up to outside influences as it discovered the West, and the West discovered it.

In the nineteenth century merchants, missionaries, engineers and teachers arrived. Among them was the strange Anglo-Irish-Greek-American Lafcadio Hearn (1850–1904), a delicate character who became a Japanese citizen (changing his name to Yakumo Koizumi). He also became the nation's chief interpreter to the West, in works like *Glimpses of Unfamiliar Japan* (1894), which show how Japanese art and life were stirring the imagination of modern Europeans and Americans.

His contemporary, Natsume Soseki (1867–1916), became a prominent modern Japanese novelist. Born in Edo in 1867, Sosekia was an avid scholar of foreign literature and spent two unhappy years studying in London at the turn of the century. Back home, he produced a range of novels, from the tragic and mysterious (*Kokoro*) to the comic (*Botchan*) – still the standard by which Japanese fiction is judged – which draws on his experiences as a

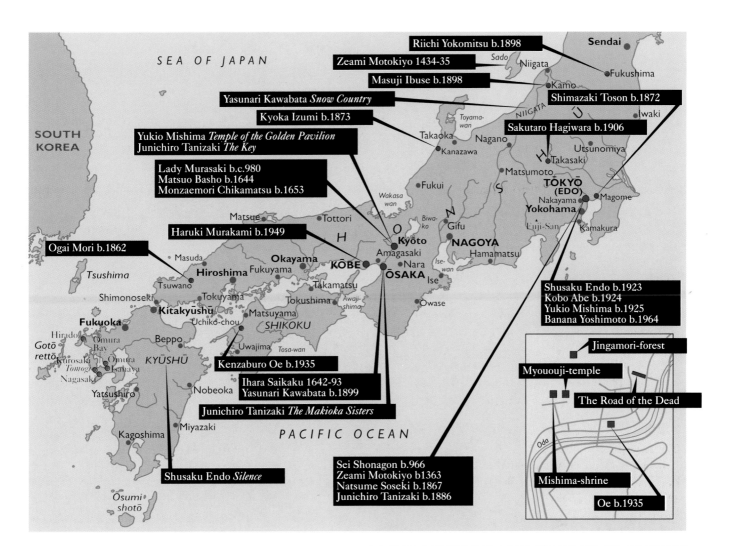

SEA OF JAPAN

SOUTH KOREA

Riichi Yokomitsu b.1898
Zeami Motokiyo 1434-35
Masuji Ibuse b.1898
Yasunari Kawabata *Snow Country*
Kyoka Izumi b.1873
Yukio Mishima *Temple of the Golden Pavilion*
Junichiro Tanizaki *The Key*
Lady Murasaki b.c.980
Matsuo Basho b.1644
Monzaemori Chikamatsu b.1653

Shimazaki Toson b.1872
Sakutaro Hagiwara b.1906

Haruki Murakami b.1949
Ogai Mori b.1862

Shusaku Endo b.1923
Kobo Abe b.1924
Yukio Mishima b.1925
Banana Yoshimoto b.1964

Kenzaburo Oe b.1935

Ihara Saikaku 1642-93
Yasunari Kawabata b.1899

Junichiro Tanizaki *The Makioka Sisters*

Shusaku Endo *Silence*

Sei Shonagon b.966
Zeami Motokiyo b1363
Natsume Soseki b.1867
Junichiro Tanizaki b.1886

PACIFIC OCEAN

Jingamori-forest
Myououji-temple
The Road of the Dead
Mishima-shrine
Oe b.1935

SOUTHERN JAPAN: *Sense of place has always been very strong in Japanese literature. Shusaku Endo meticulously plotted the settings of his novel,* Silence, *on the Island of Kyushu and the book's key locations are shown in green on this map. The inset shows Kenzaburo Oe's home village, Uchiko-chou.*

NOH PLAY

Zeami Motokiyo (1363–1443) developed the great ritual form of medieval Japanese drama, Noh plays, from its primitive origins to the highly purified art form that later influenced such Western poets as W.B. Yeats and Ezra Pound. At the age of seventy he fell from political grace and was exiled from Edo to the remote island of Sado, off the west coast.

KABUKI DRAMA

In Edo Monzaemon Chikamatsu (1653-1725) became the greatest of the Kabuki playwrights. Kabuki started as a secular offshoot of the religious Noh plays. Chikamatsu also developed another form of drama, Bunraku, the puppet plays. History, often recent history, provided many plots, as did dramas of love and love-suicide. Shinju ten no Aimijimi ("The Love Suicide at Amijima") dealt with events remembered by those who first attended the play, in an actual place, an island in Osaka Bay. Kabuki developed in the eighteenth and nineteenth century, and remains the most popular form of live theatre in today's Japan – adjusted, revitalized, moving and spectacular (and an influence on many modern Western playwrights).*

young schoolmaster in a remote part of the island of Shikoku, where he was a metropolitan "Lucky Jim" plunged into the backwoods of his own country.

Over the twentieth century, the Japanese novel has flourished powerfully. Two notable figures are Junichiro Tanizaki (1886–1965), who wrote with great subtlety of traditional Japan, contemporary Osaka (*The Makioka Sisters*) and the new metropolitan Tokyo, his native city; and Yasunari Kawabata (1899-1972), one of Japan's Nobel Prize-winners, whose *Snow Country* (1937), a masterpiece of poetic prose, journeys into the "deep north" that Basho encountered 250 years earlier. Then, famously, there was

沈 黙　遠藤周作

沈
黙

遠藤周作

Shusaku Endo, far left, *who was baptized a Catholic, belongs to the significant minority of Japanese Christians; his work as novelist and short story writer makes a central motif of the encounter between East and West. His finest novel* Silence *(1969), for which the Japanese cover is shown* left, *revisits the period of Tokugawa persecution of Christians on the island of Kyushu that took place 350 years ago.*

新潮社

Yukio Mishima (1925–70), whose shocking public suicide should not obscure his great literary achievement. His *The Temple of the Golden Pavilion* (1956), a modern story about the ancient religious city of Kyoto, is a classic contemporary tale of psychological obsession.

Japanese literature flourishes still, not least in the work of Shusaku Endo (b.1923) and Kenzaburo Oe (b.1935), two of Japan's finest contemporary novelists. Endo, author of *Stained Glass Elegies* (1984), was born in Tokyo, but visited Nagasaki and Hirado several times in 1965 to collect material for his novel *Silence* (1969) reporting his experiences in *The Native Places of the Christians* (1966).

Silence is the tale of two Portuguese Christian fathers who, in the 1640s, suffered under the official policy of the suppression of Christianity. It recalls the story of Father Christovão Ferreira, who is delegated by the Portuguese Jesuits to go to Japan, undergoes the "Torture of the Pit," and finally foreswears his faith, to the outrage of the Church. The book follows the story of Ferreira's pupil, Father Sebastian Rodrigues, who refuses to believe his much admired teacher had "grovelled like a dog before the

HAIKU POETRY

Matsuo Basho (1644-94) was born near Kyoto, then moved to Edo (now Tokyo), living as a recluse. He brought the three-line, 17-syllable Haiku form of poetry to the peak of refinement, inventiveness and suggestiveness. In his travel-diary Oku no Hosomichi (*translated as 'The Narrow Road to the Deep North'*), *he created in poetry and prose, fact and fiction, a journey through Japan that was both geographic and spiritual. Venturing to the remote northern parts of Honshu (Japan's main island) in 1694, Basho travelled with a loyal companion for more than two years, writing his "pilgrim's progress," recording history and legend, aware that he was looking for "something those before him had sought."*

infidel" instead of dying a martyr's death. With two other priests he sails from Lisbon and, after a fourteen-month voyage, reaches Tomogi, a fictional small fishing village near Nagasaki – modelled on the real Kurosaki, a small village in the Sotome ("Outer-Sea District") region, whose bleak scenery is very different from that of Nagasaki.

Endo chose Kurosaki – instead of the true place where Rodrigues landed – because he was attracted by its bleakness and the village of the Hidden Christians it contained. Endo himself travelled around Fukuda Harbour and climbed the mountain there to find a small village built by people from Kurosaki. Its little church where Endo sheltered from the rain became the cottage where Rodrigues too shelters, and the surrounding scenery was used as the landscape through which he flees when trying to escape the government authorities.

Rodrigues is joined by Christians from the Goto Islands, of which Kichijiro, his helper and then his betrayer, is a native. Rodrigues sails to do his missionary work in these islands; then on returning to Tomogi he is questioned by officials, and the martyrdoms begin. Later he wanders in the mountains, and meets Kichijiro in the cottage, where he is betrayed and taken to a cottage nearby, with other Christians who have already been captured. They are sent by ship to Yokose Inlet. Today there is nothing to remind us of that East-West encounter, except for a cross built in the mouth of the inlet.

Rodrigues's fate takes him on to Omura Bay, where the missionaries had begun building missions and seminaries, and then to Nagasaki, where he is cruelly questioned. He meets his apostate master Ferreira, who has been forcibly given a Japanese name, at the temple of Saishouji in Kami-machi, and is warned that "The country is a more terrible swamp than you can imagine." Finally, persuaded by Ferreira, Rodrigues stands in front of the *Fumie* (a Christian sacred image that Japanese

UKIYO-ZOSHI
("NOVELS OF THE FLOATING WORLD")

In the late seventeenth century, in Osaka, the writer Ihara Saikaku (1642-93) began to please the merchant class with novels that became known as Ukiyo-zoshi – "novels of the floating world." They were picaresque tales of ordinary life, concerned with money-making, greed, amorous adventures and the poorer townspeople who never achieved anything but disappointment. Saikaku was racy, entertaining, often very funny. A Japanese contemporary of English novelist Daniel Defoe, he created an observant comic realism (there were real disguised places, real disguised people), drawing on what might be called "the New Midlands" – which is what Osaka was.

Standing where 26 Christian saints, above, were executed for their faith Endo "felt awe and adoration for these strong-willed martyrs.

Kenzaburo Oe, right, author of The Silent Cry *(1987), was awarded the Nobel Prize for Literature in 1994.*

worshippers were required to stamp on as a sign of their abjugation of the Christian faith) and hears the words of Christ telling him to trample it down. He apostasizes his faith, is given the Japanese name Okada San-emon, and dies of illness at the age of 64. The settings of the novel can be seen today, an hour or so from Nagasaki by bus.

Like many of the newer Japanese novelists, Kenzaburo Oe writes of the confrontation of the old and new Japan. He was born not in one of Japan's great crowded cities but in a village in Shikoku, an island off the southeast coast of Honshu, the main island of Japan. The village is now called Uchiko-chou; a place which Oe himself describes as "a remote wooded valley" and "the depths of the forest." He has often returned there, creating many of his literary works out of the experiences he had of the village. In the process he has transformed it into a mythic place, and his work can best be read and understood from its landscape and perspective. His early novel *The Catch* (1958) begins with a description of the wooded village:

"Already the bottom of the valley was submerged in sunset and a mist cold as underground water gushing out in a wood. A light the color of grapes was pouring down on the small village, built along a cobbled road on the hillside facing the valley, where we lived."

The Silent Cry (1987) is today recognized as one of Oe's most successful books. In it a handicapped child is born to Mitsusaburo and Natumiko, who live in Tokyo. A friend of Mitsusaburo hangs himself, driven by strange wild forces. Another friend, newly back from America, advises him to leave Tokyo and return to Shikoku with him. The power of the woods is emphasized as they approach the wooded village, where Mitsusaburo feels himself to be alienated. His brother Takashi tries to revive the community, organizing a football team for the young people, and hoping to take over the role of an ancestor who has been a community leader and taken part in the Trouble of 1860.

The story becomes a quest into two dark secrets. One is that Takashi has committed incest with his retarded sister, who then killed herself. The other is that Mitsusaburo, confronted with this, denies the truth, saying that truth is Hell, but that Takashi cannot know it until he has completed his wanderings. He must return to the Purgatory of the human world and live in it – which he does, but not without committing suicide at the end.

In his great trilogy *The Burning Green Tree* (1993–5), Oe returns to his wooded valley once more. Here the hero – the Saviour – has been killed, but his death has reunited his believers. Again we see that this kind of mythic fable is possible only in Oe's chosen setting, which has the power to reveal both the hellish and the divine reaches of the human soul. Uchiko-chou lies about 25 miles south of Matsuyama, in a deep valley where water flows from the Nakayama, the Oda and the Fumoto Rivers. It is also rich in seasonal beauty; Oe's birthplace is still to be seen.

Today, Japanese writing – poetry, theatre and that form the Japanese may have invented, the novel – deals with a land of great contrasts. It is a world of advanced modernity and deep traditions, of vast high-rise cities and a rooted rural landscape of villages, mountains and shrines. Endo and Oe write of an "old" and a "new" Japan, of a land of vast economic energy which retains the subtlety of a long literary tradition.

CAMPUS FICTIONS

The university novel in Britain has very deep roots. It certainly goes back to Cuthbert Bede's *The Adventures of Mr Verdant Green* (1853–57), and reaches its height in the early years of the twentieth century with Max Beerbohm's *Zuleika Dobson* (1911) and Compton Mackenzie's *Sinister Street* (1914). Stylized, largely fantastic, such novels describe an ancient city drenched in sunlight and nostalgia. Their influence is pervasive. The early chapters of Evelyn Waugh's *Brideshead Revisited* (1945), set in the 1920s, are deeply indebted to the Beerbohm/Mackenzie view of Oxford. And the tradition endures: a representative "modern" Oxford novel might be Margaret Doody's *The Alchemists* (1980), in which two impossibly knowing undergraduates set up as brothel-keepers.

Malcolm Bradbury's campus novels take liberalism as their theme.

However, it is important to distinguish between "university novels" and the far more recent genre of "the campus novel." The latter is a post-Second World War phenomenon, tends to be written by university teachers (rather than reminiscing ex-students), and is probably set in a "new university," real or fictitious, in the period that follows the Robbins Report. It sees its horizon of modern breeze-block and concrete as a suitable environment in which to discuss some of the pressing social and intellectual questions of the times, or at least as a venue likely to encourage a particular type of comic writing: for the campus novel, it should be said, is nearly always comic in spirit.

Judged by these criteria, the most famous campus novel of all, Kingsley Amis's (b.1922) *Lucky Jim* (1954), which follows the progress of a harassed junior lecturer at a ghoulish "redbrick" provincial university which owes something to both Leicester and Swansea, is not a campus novel at all. It's a comic novel that happens to be set in a university, although it rehearses its author's stance on one of the great post-war educational issues, the debate about standards. Similarly C.P. Snow's (1905–80) *The Masters* (1954), while set in an ancient, firelit Cambridge college, is a part of a sequence more concerned with the idea of political and social power than with the daily lives of the Cambridge dons who exercise it. Perhaps the best early example of the kind of campus novel that by the 1970s would be filling the publishers' lists is Malcolm Bradbury's (b.1932) *Eating People Is Wrong* (1959), the work of a then junior lecturer at the University of Hull, who subsequently was involved in the development of English and American Studies at the "new" University of East Anglia in Norwich. Bradbury's theme is liberalism. His hero, a redbrick university professor, Treece, is a man adrift, ever searching for a moral compass point amid constantly shifting terrain. Bradbury's second novel *Stepping Westward* (1965) follows the uncertainty further, dealing with James Walker, a vacillating novelist of the fifties "Angry" school, who goes to a midwestern American university, where his tweedy English liberalism encounters a much sturdier American variant. In *The History Man* (1975) Bradbury confronts another theme: the encounter, in one of the "new" universities, between the movements of liberalism and radicalism that swept through British as well as American campuses at the end of the sixties.

In other novels, too, globetrotting academics come to (often comic) grief in far-flung lecture halls or conference venues. In David Lodge's (b.1935) *Changing Places* (1975), Philip Swallow, a timid English lecturer from the West Midlands' "University of Rummidge" (Lodge taught at Birmingham University) swaps jobs with Maurice Zapp, a much sharper and more formidable operator from

Birmingham University, above, *is one of the modern universities which was to spawn a number of campus fictions in the 1960s.*

Euphoria State University, USA. Lodge's *Small World* (1984) reworks a similar theme on the international conference circuit. His campus fiction is more straightforwardly comic than his other work. Caught on a tide of sexual misdemeanours and embarrassing accidents, his academics are more interested in jostling for power and precedence than staking out moral positions. Both books have much to say about intellectual faddishness, and Zapp's tireless pursuit of the latest theoretical orthodoxies is a running joke throughout.

By the late 1970s campus fiction had become a distinct and distinctive genre. A distinguishing mark was mordant comedy, often verging on farce. Tom Sharpe's (b.1928) *Porterhouse Blue* (1974), set in the most hidebound of Cambridge colleges, contains a graduate student who destroys himself in a gas explosion while trying to dispose of unwanted condoms. Howard Jacobson's (b.1942) *Coming From Behind* (1983), which takes place in and around a dismal Midland polytechnic (Wolverhampton?) aspiring to university status, is a jokey and neurotic dissection of personal and professional envy. Here though, amid drunken dons and libidinous lecturers, a serious point remains. No Cambridge tutor struggling to drag his college into the twentieth century could fail to read *Porterhouse Blue* without a tremor of recognition, while the reader of Sharpe's *Wilt* (1976) or Jacobson's novel would wonder if the polytechnic education was really a worthy use of human time.

Jokes about academic jealousy, poor educational standards and condoms were one thing. For the university also appeared as an appropriate stage on which to dramatize some of the key social and political concerns that had animated British society from the 1950s on. With their supposed commitment to excellence, liberalism and academic freedom (and in the newer universities widening educational opportunities and meritocratic advancement), universities were a key place for considering questions of standards, cultural values, the role of sixties radicalism and the emergence of the permissive society. Dacre Balsdon's Oxford dystopia *The Day They Burned Miss Termag* (1961) provides an early example. Simon Raven's (b.1927) *Places Where They Sing* (1970), set in "Lancaster

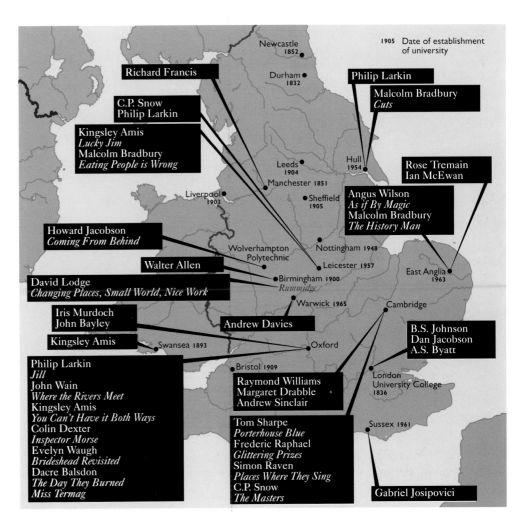

1905 Date of establishment of university

Richard Francis

C.P. Snow
Philip Larkin

Kingsley Amis
Lucky Jim
Malcolm Bradbury
Eating People is Wrong

Howard Jacobson
Coming From Behind

David Lodge
Changing Places, Small World, Nice Work

Walter Allen

Iris Murdoch
John Bayley

Kingsley Amis

Philip Larkin
Jill
John Wain
Where the Rivers Meet
Kingsley Amis
You Can't Have it Both Ways
Colin Dexter
Inspector Morse
Evelyn Waugh
Brideshead Revisited
Dacre Balsdon
The Day They Burned Miss Termag

Andrew Davies

Raymond Williams
Margaret Drabble
Andrew Sinclair

Tom Sharpe
Porterhouse Blue
Frederic Raphael
Glittering Prizes
Simon Raven
Places Where They Sing
C.P. Snow
The Masters

Philip Larkin
Malcolm Bradbury
Cuts

Rose Tremain
Ian McEwan

Angus Wilson
As if By Magic
Malcolm Bradbury
The History Man

B.S. Johnson
Dan Jacobson
A.S. Byatt

Gabriel Josipovici

Newcastle 1852
Durham 1832
Leeds 1904
Manchester 1851
Hull 1954
Liverpool 1903
Sheffield 1905
Wolverhampton Polytechnic
Nottingham 1948
Leicester 1957
Birmingham 1900
Rummidge
East Anglia 1963
Warwick 1965
Cambridge
Swansea 1893
Oxford
Bristol 1909
London University College 1836
Sussex 1961

BRITISH CAMPUSES: *The Robbins Report instigated the vast expansion of British universities in the 1960s and after. The locations of the new campuses and the novels written about them are shown on this map.*

College, Cambridge" (King's College, thinly disguised) depicts a student revolt that ends in an attack on the college chapel and the death of one of the main characters. Bradbury's *The History Man* sets the story of a predatory radical sociology lecturer, Howard Kirk, at the brand-new and very postmodern University of Watermouth, on the south coast.

By the 1980s, the genre of campus fiction was transforming, like British universities themselves. The radical Conservatism of Mrs Thatcher hit the university system hard. Budgets were pruned and teaching posts unfilled. The connection between the problems of universities and those in the wider economic landscape was explored in David Lodge's *Nice Work* (1988), a modern variant on the Victorian "Condition of England" novel which is one of the few university fictions to set the often narrow preoccupations of the academic world into the wider social context. Today the appeal of the Oxbridge universities has been revived – with the work, for example of Colin Dexter in his highly popular Inspector Morse novels.

DIVIDED IRELAND

For much of its history the island of Ireland has been a contested territory. When in 1921 a border was created, separating six predominantly Protestant counties of the historic nine-county province of Ulster from the remaining predominantly Catholic 26 counties of Ireland, long-standing political divisions took constitutional form. The existence, in the "administrative region" of Northern Ireland (it was not a state in its own right, any more than it was a Province), of a large minority aspiring to see a reunited Ireland free of British rule ensured further internal division. In time it led to the serious communal strife popularly known as "The Troubles." This was reflected in the literary development of both these Irelands and came to dominate the literature of the North.

In the new-founded Free State of Ireland – Eire from 1937, the Republic of Ireland since 1948 – the Civil War of 1922–23 was followed by a long period of cultural debate about what direction independent Ireland should take. The idealization of a rural Catholic society – promoted by Eamonn de Valera, enshrined in his 1937 constitution – conflicted with the cosmopolitan instincts of cities like Dublin or Cork, as well as the real hardships of rural life. It was this bucolic ideal Flann O'Brien (1911–66) lampooned in comic novels like *The Third Policeman* (1967) and his masterpiece *At Swim-Two-Birds* (1939).

When state censorship was introduced in 1929, this added to the atmosphere of cultural conflict. As late as 1965 the novelist John McGahern (b.1934), future winner of every major literary prize in Ireland, had his second novel *The Dark* (1965) banned, and was dismissed from his post as National School teacher. Little wonder that the Cork-born short story writer Frank O'Connor (1903–66),

writing the introduction to another banned book, Eric Cross's *The Tailor and Ansty* (1942), advised against taking up "a dangerous trade like literature in Ireland without developing the hide of a rhinoceros and renting a house in a strategic spot with direct access to the sea." The fact was that many did take up the dangerous trade; in fiction, drama and poetry Irish writing still flourished.

North of the border, similar tensions had arisen: between a Unionist government promising "a Protestant parliament for a Protestant people" and liberal, even radical writers. Throughout the 1920s and 1930s, the Progressive Bookshop in Belfast's Union Street sustained important links with writing and ideas from all over Britain and Europe. Two Belfast-born poets of this time, both Protestant, had a major influence on the growth of a new northern aesthetic. John Hewitt (1907–87) was for many years the keeper of the Fine Art collection in the Ulster Museum. A socialist and atheist, he explored the complexities of Ulster Protestant identity. His work celebrated the countryside, in particular the Glens of Antrim, heavily settled by Scots Presbyterians, who brought with them to Ireland a distinctive dissenting tradition.

Louis MacNeice (1907–63), meantime, was educated in England, spent most of his working life in Birmingham and London and returned rarely to Northern Ireland. But the links were strong. His father was a minister in Carrickfergus, then was appointed Bishop

Monagan poet Patrick Kavanagh, in his Ploughman and Other Poems (1936) *explored a rural existence far removed from Eamonn de Valera's notorious vision of comely maidens "dancing at the crossroads."*

"The Troubles" were to have far-reaching effects, on writing as on all other aspects of life, north and south of the border. The scene, right, shows fighting on the streets of Derry in 1972.

of Down and Connor. His anomalous position (too Irish to be British, too British to be Irish) as much as his engagement with contemporary world events made him an important figure for a whole new generation of Northern poets who emerged in the 1960s: among them Michael Longley and winner of the Nobel Prize for Literature in 1995, Seamus Heaney.

Irish nationalism and Ulster unionism seemed diametrically opposed, but they both fostered inward-looking, conservative societies against which writers reacted. The Northern version is chillingly evoked in *The Lonely Passion of Judith Hearne* (1957) by Belfast born novelist Brian Moore (b.1921), who left Northern Ireland to live in Canada and then the United States. The complacencies of both societies were shaken by the violence which broke out in Northern Ireland in 1969.

Faced by ever more militant northern Republicanism, the Republic of Ireland was forced to reflect on its long-standing aspirations for a United Ireland. The result was the emergence of a body of opinion hostile to the obsession with the North and critical of the extent to which the grail of a 32-county Ireland had been used to mask shortcomings in the 26-county republic. At the same time the expansion of the European Community offered a refocusing of Irish cultural energies that had long existed. So it could be fairly argued that a splendidly cosmopolitan, experimental novelist like Wexford-born John Banville (b.1945), author of *Doctor Copernicus* (1976) and *The Book of Evidence* (1989), is really extending the European-Irish tradition of James Joyce and Samuel Beckett.

In recent times, the Republic has successfully promoted itself as a centre of culture, even advancing the reputations of writers who suffered disfavour or chose exile in their lifetimes: G.B. Shaw and Oscar Wilde, Patrick Kavanagh and Flann O'Brien, Brendan Behan, and, of course, Samuel Beckett. Today James Joyce is omnipresent in Dublin's cafés and bars.

Recent novelists like Joseph O'Connor (b.1963) (*True Believers*, 1991) have written their way into the gap between the city's literary projection of itself and the changing reality of its present inhabitants. Some of this "new" Irish writing first found an audience via Dermot Bolger's Raven Arts Press, based in North Dublin. Bolger, a novelist of note as well as a dramatist, poet and critic, has been one of the most potent figures in current Irish writing. But it was the success of a fellow "northsider," Roddy Doyle (b.1958), which did most to draw national and international attention to the forces at work. Doyle's fourth novel *Paddy Clarke Ha Ha Ha* won the 1992 Booker Prize but before that, he had already entered public con-

Roddy Doyle's Barrytown novels – set in the fictional north Dublin district that bears close resemblance to the sprawling Ballymun estate – have all been admirably adapted to film. The Commitments, *right, was particularly successful at the cinema.*

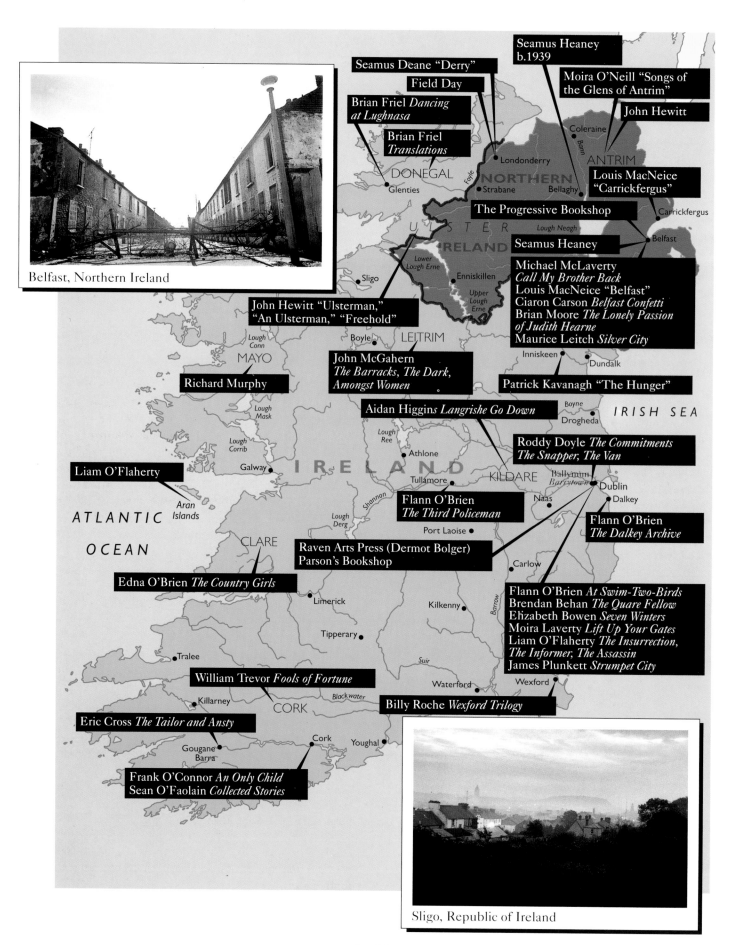

Belfast, Northern Ireland

Seamus Heaney b.1939

Seamus Deane "Derry"

Field Day

Moira O'Neill "Songs of the Glens of Antrim"

Brian Friel *Dancing at Lughnasa*

John Hewitt

Brian Friel *Translations*

Coleraine

ANTRIM

Londonderry

DONEGAL

NORTHERN

Strabane

Bellaghy

Louis MacNeice "Carrickfergus"

Glenties

ULSTER

Lough Neagh

Carrickfergus

IRELAND

The Progressive Bookshop

Belfast

Lower Lough Erne

Seamus Heaney

Sligo

Enniskillen

Michael McLaverty *Call My Brother Back*
Louis MacNeice "Belfast"
Ciaron Carson *Belfast Confetti*
Brian Moore *The Lonely Passion of Judith Hearne*
Maurice Leitch *Silver City*

Upper Lough Erne

John Hewitt "Ulsterman," "An Ulsterman," "Freehold"

Inniskeen

Dundalk

Boyle

LEITRIM

Lough Conn

MAYO

John McGahern *The Barracks, The Dark, Amongst Women*

Patrick Kavanagh "The Hunger"

Richard Murphy

Boyne

IRISH SEA

Drogheda

Lough Mask

Aidan Higgins *Langrishe Go Down*

Lough Ree

Lough Corrib

Athlone

Roddy Doyle *The Commitments The Snapper, The Van*

Liam O'Flaherty

Galway

Tullamore

KILDARE

Ballymun Barrytown

Dublin

Aran Islands

Shannon

Flann O'Brien *The Third Policeman*

Naas

Dalkey

ATLANTIC

Lough Derg

Port Laoise

Flann O'Brien *The Dalkey Archive*

OCEAN

CLARE

IRELAND

Raven Arts Press (Dermot Bolger) Parson's Bookshop

Carlow

Edna O'Brien *The Country Girls*

Limerick

Kilkenny

Barrow

Flann O'Brien *At Swim-Two-Birds*
Brendan Behan *The Quare Fellow*
Elizabeth Bowen *Seven Winters*
Moira Laverty *Lift Up Your Gates*
Liam O'Flaherty *The Insurrection, The Informer, The Assassin*
James Plunkett *Strumpet City*

Tipperary

Tralee

Suir

William Trevor *Fools of Fortune*

Waterford

Wexford

Killarney

Blackwater

CORK

Billy Roche *Wexford Trilogy*

Eric Cross *The Tailor and Ansty*

Cork

Youghal

Gougane Barra

Frank O'Connor *An Only Child*
Sean O'Faolain *Collected Stories*

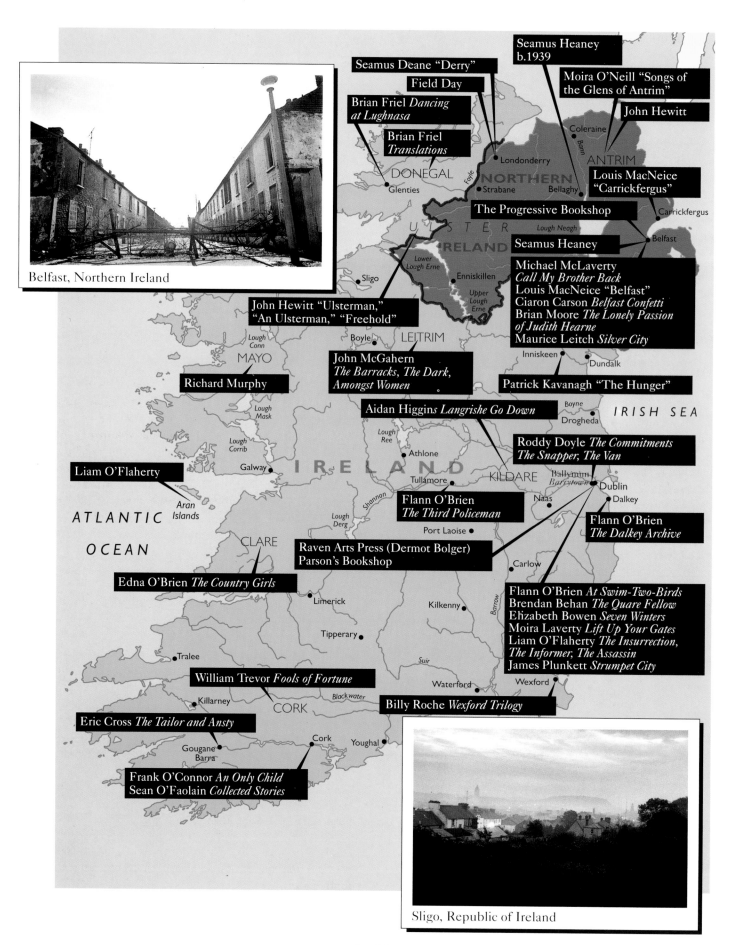

Sligo, Republic of Ireland

sciousness with his trilogy – *The Commitments* (1987), *The Snapper* (1990) and *The Van* (1991). With its strong reliance on regional dialogue, Doyle's work has added a new, urgent register to the Irish literary voice.

If young writing in the Republic has been burdened with the attempt to exploit Ireland's dead writers, writing in North Ireland has suffered from the image and exploitation of the political situation there. From 1969 on, Northern Irish fiction and drama have often been confused with fiction and drama set in Northern Ireland. Often the latter has taken Northern Ireland as a ready-made story, where the lines are drawn, the fundamentals agreed, the dramas obvious, the characters easily made black or white. Not surprisingly, thrillers and terrorist fictions have proliferated – but few have contributed any real insight into the society where the violence is actually occurring. Not that there has been any single response to the violence on the part of Northern Irish writers themselves. Jennifer Johnston's *Shadows on Our Skin* (1977), Maurice Leitch's *Silver's City* (1981), Bernard MacLaverty's *Cal* (1983), Mary Beckett's *Give Them Stones* (1987) and Danny Morrison's *West Belfast* (1989) are some of the novels that reveal the diversity of mood and opinion in the community at large.

Until recently at least, the most sustained attempt to register in serious literature the disruptions of these years has been made by Northern Ireland poets. Three – Seamus Heaney, Seamus Deane and Tom Paulin – were among the five founder-members of Field Day, set up in 1980 mainly to present the plays of the Londonderry-born, Donegal-based playwright Brian Friel (b.1929), author of *Translations* (1981) and *Dancing at Lughnasa* (1990). In 1991, under Deane's editorship, Field Day also produced a vast *Anthology of Irish Writing*. Critics north and south acknowledged its scope, though some questioned

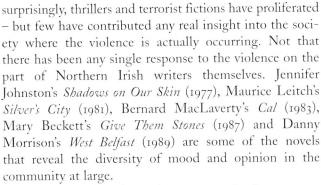

Clockwise from top left: *Tom Paulin, Roddy Doyle, Seamus Deane and Brian Friel all write of Ireland in their work.*

its implied political agenda, seeing its minimizing of the significance of Partition as denying the growth of distinct northern and southern experiences. But if history as read from the Field Day anthology seemed to represent an unbroken Irish line, for others in Northern Ireland it more resembled an unbreakable circle which imprisoned its inhabitants. Faced with the destruction of Northern Ireland's cities and towns in the 1970s, and the seemingly unending cycle of sectarian murders, such reactions were understandable, but only added to the impasse. As often in recent Irish literature, it took another poet to imagine a way out. In three remarkable volumes – *The Irish for No* (1987), *Belfast Confetti* (1989) and *First Language* (1993) – Ciaron Carson (b.1948) imagined new perspectives for familiar Northern Irish themes. The key notes are mutability and contingency; the dominant image is the map as unreliable fiction; the conflicting texts of opposed nationalisms are seen as of unreliable pedigree and open to revision. And Belfast, Carson's native city, becomes a city in process, constantly rebuilding itself on the landscape – a bewildering, at times a frightening place, but also a possible one. Aged 21 in 1969, the year the "Troubles" began, Carson represents a pivot between writers who found their literary voice before the violence and those shaped by it. The shifting urban focus of the literary landscape is clear in the work of novelist Robert McLiam Wilson (b.1964) who spent his early years on the West Belfast estate of Turf Lodge. His first novel *Ripley Bogle* (1989) expresses the rage of an entire generation with traditional politics. It's not an a-politcal stance, but an engaged, deeply humanist one.

Perhaps as at this moment a new hope for peace emerges, Irish writers are doing what many writers have long done: trying to update the imaginative map of the island to reflect its more complex society, and perceiving that rejection of the certainties of the past is not a trauma but an imaginative enterprise and the only freedom.

THE WRITING OF THE CARIBBEAN

Caribbean literature, which for our present purposes can be taken to mean primarily the work of writers from the English-speaking small islands that make up the daisy chain of the Lesser Antilles, is mainly a twentieth century phenomenon. It is also a literature of exile or, more precisely, of economic migration: very few of its writers actually live in the Caribbean. In the mid-1960s, London was the West Indian literary capital. Today many Caribbean writers are professors at North American universities: which may explain why Caribbean literature is so sophisticated when the newspapers of the islands, for instance, often seem crude and simplistic.

Slavery dominates Caribbean experience. It was abolished in the British islands in 1834, and in 1848 in the French islands, but it was not until the early twentieth century that a voice from the Caribbean began to be heard. Although this account concentrates on writers from the Anglophone Caribbean, it is impossible to ignore two key Francophone writers, Aimé Césaire (b.1913) and Frantz Fanon (1925–61). Both were born in Martinique: Césaire, poet, writer, politician, now in his eighties, still lives there. Césaire was the first person to use the term *négritude*; the name given to the movement that called for a resurrection of black values – an "Africa of the heart," a "heroic affirmation of blacks and their culture as other than the dominant Euro-American values that had enslaved and degraded them." In *Cahiers d'un retour au pays natal* (1939), the definitive expression of *négritude*, Césaire wrote: "et aucune race possède le monopole de la beauté, de l'intelligence, de la force" ("and no race has the monopoly on beauty, intelligence, or strength").

Césaire was almost contemporary with Frantz Fanon – who wrote in *Black Skin, White Masks* (1952) about the psychology of racism ("I wish to be acknowledged not as black but as white...who but a white woman can do this for me? By loving me she proves I am worthy of white love. I am loved like a white man.... When my restless hands caress those white breasts, they grasp white civilization and dignity and make them mine"). Slavery could never be forgotten, and cannot to this day. Yet, despite their common past, the early Francophone and Anglophone writers of the Caribbean actually had little in common. While the writing of the English-speaking writers generally dealt with the specifics of local experience, the French-speaking islands produced a largely political œuvre that was easily assimilated into the canon of French literature.

The Rastafarian movement evolved more or less simultaneously with *négritude*. Named after Ras Tafari, the original name for the Ethiopian Emperor Hailie Selassie, who compared "the heaven of Ethiopia" to the "hell of Jamaica," it originated in Jamaica, where for forty years it remained a popular religious cult, having little effect on the rest of the Caribbean. But, in the 1970s, its Back-to-Africa message, coinciding with the aims of the Civil Rights and Black Power

The dominant motif in Caribbean writing is a sense of place, inspired by the brilliant hues of the islands. D. Roosevelt's Eight Huts in Haiti, left, *captures this sensuousness perfectly.*

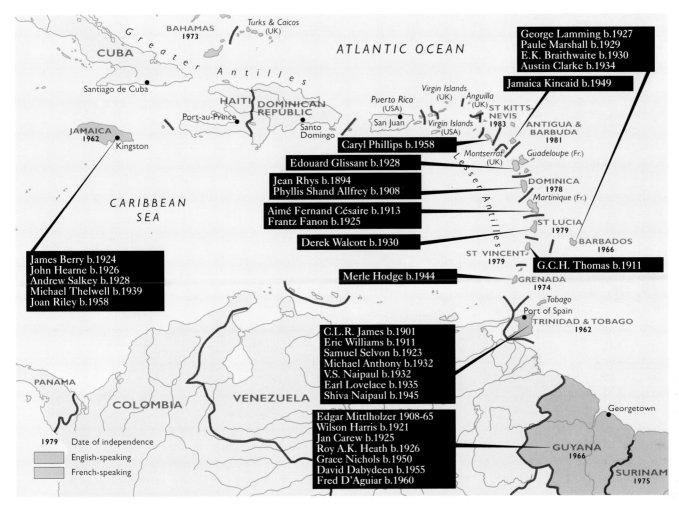

CUBA
Santiago de Cuba

Greater Antilles

BAHAMAS
1973

Turks & Caicos
(UK)

ATLANTIC OCEAN

George Lamming b.1927
Paule Marshall b.1929
E.K. Braithwaite b.1930
Austin Clarke b.1934

Jamaica Kincaid b.1949

HAITI
Port-au-Prince

DOMINICAN
REPUBLIC
Santo Domingo

Puerto Rico
(USA)
San Juan

Virgin Islands
(UK)
Virgin Islands
(USA)

Anguilla
(UK)
ST KITTS-
NEVIS
1983

ANTIGUA &
BARBUDA
1981

JAMAICA
1962
Kingston

Caryl Phillips b.1958

Montserrat
(UK)

Guadeloupe (Fr.)

Edouard Glissant b.1928

CARIBBEAN
SEA

Jean Rhys b.1894
Phyllis Shand Allfrey b.1908

DOMINICA
1978
Martinique (Fr.)

Aimé Fernand Césaire b.1913
Frantz Fanon b.1925

Lesser Antilles

ST LUCIA
1979

BARBADOS
1966

Derek Walcott b.1930

James Berry b.1924
John Hearne b.1926
Andrew Salkey b.1928
Michael Thelwell b.1939
Joan Riley b.1958

Merle Hodge b.1944

ST VINCENT
1979

GRENADA
1974

G.C.H. Thomas b.1911

Tobago
Port of Spain

C.L.R. James b.1901
Eric Williams b.1911
Samuel Selvon b.1923
Michael Anthony b.1932
V.S. Naipaul b.1932
Earl Lovelace b.1935
Shiva Naipaul b.1945

TRINIDAD & TOBAGO
1962

PANAMA

COLOMBIA

VENEZUELA

Georgetown

Edgar Mittlholzer 1908-65
Wilson Harris b.1921
Jan Carew b.1925
Roy A.K. Heath b.1926
Grace Nichols b.1950
David Dabydeen b.1955
Fred D'Aguiar b.1960

GUYANA
1966

SURINAM
1975

1979   Date of independence

    English-speaking

    French-speaking

movements in the United States, achieved more widespread favour. Rastafarianism has found its expression mostly in the sung word, but the lyrics of many of its reggae songs deserve to be regarded as poetry.

Césaire and Fanon, Edouard Glissant from Martinique, the great Trinidadian Marxist C.L.R. James, the "grand patriarch of contemporary West Indian culture," Eric Williams, who became first Prime Minister of Trinidad and Tobago – all were political rather than creative writers; their contribution is essential to an understanding of the post-slavery West Indies. But for a picture of everyday life in the small islands you need to turn to other writers: to Antigua's Jamaica Kincaid, Grenada's Merle Hodge, St. Kitts' Caryl Phillips, Jamaica's Michael Thelwell, or George Lamming from Barbados, whose classic novel *In the Castle of the Skin* (1953) follows his life from his ninth to his nineteenth year, and whose *The Emigrants* (1954) tells the story of those who, like the author, left the Caribbean to go to Britain in the 1950s.

V.S. Naipaul, his brother Shiva, Samuel Selvon and Earl Lovelace all came from Trinidad, the largest and most culturally prolific of the islands of the Eastern Caribbean. Like V.S. Naipaul, Samuel Selvon (1923–1994) moved to London in 1950, but spent his last years in Canada. In works like *The Lonely Londoners* (1956), the

THE CARIBBEAN: *Although most Caribbean writers were born on the islands, for the most part, their literature is a writing of exile, as many moved away in the 1950s and 1960s.*

definitive novel about London's West Indian community in the 1950s, he wrote from the perspective of exile, albeit voluntary, conveying the sense of missing and yearning so perfectly expressed in Keith Anderson's song:

"I've got to go back home/ This couldn't be my home/It must be somewhere else/Or I would kill myself/'Cos I can't get no clothes to wear/Can't get no food to eat/Can't get a job to get bread/That's why I got to go back home.../There is no gladness, nothing but sadness/Nothing like a future here.../That's why I got to, got to go back home/Even if I have to run..."

If politics – in that I include the tormented history of slavery and sugarcane, and the colonial era that

Bob Marley, above, *helped popularize the Rastafarian movement with his lyrical reggae songs.*

[281]

succeeded it – informs Caribbean non-fiction, the dominant motif in West Indian fiction is surely a sense of place. The heady perfume of the islands, the light, the colour, the dramatic shot-silk sunsets which precede a darkness that comes with the suddenness of a door slamming, the brilliant hues of the hibiscus and bougainvillaea, the burnished feathers of the humming-birds: all these illuminate Caribbean fiction. For black people, freedom from slavery meant the right to live in your own house, choose your own food, marry as you pleased: in other words all the things a free person, one who is not a prisoner or slave, takes for granted. Much of Caribbean fiction deals with the minutiae of everyday life because it was, in a sense, a novelty. One particular cruelty of slavery was that it removed people from their homes and transported them thousands of miles away. For generations, Africa was home (for a number of Afro-Caribbeans, it still is, in theory if not in practice). The notion of home is important in Caribbean life, and in the writing of the English-speaking Caribbean.

Trinidad, the home of calypso, and the scene of the mother of all carnivals, can be regarded as the cradle of modern Caribbean civilization. Considerably bigger than other Eastern Caribbean islands, it was the first to achieve independence. It has a racially mixed population (Africans, Indians, Chinese, Syrians, whites) and this, combined with its proximity to the South American mainland, gives it a flavour all its own. V.S. Naipaul (b.1932), best-known of all West Indian writers, is a Trinidadian from Port of Spain, but Indian rather than African by origin. Trinidadian Indians were the descendants of the indentured labourers brought to the Caribbean after the abolition of slavery; unlike in other islands, where problems tend to arise between black and white, in Trinidad it is the Afro-Indian divide that causes

V.S Naipaul, above left, draws on his experiences as an Indian in Trinidad for his novel A House For Mr Biswas *(1961). Jamaica Kincaid, above right, from Antigua, writes vividly of her home landscape in her novels. An earlier writer, Aimé Césaire, left, born in Martinique, was a key Francophone writer, who coined the term* négritude, *to assert the voice of the blacks.*

racial tension. Hostility between Africans and Indians keeps Indians out of government, away from major calypso triumphs, and in control of the business community.

Naipaul went to England on a scholarship at 18, and has lived there ever since. His novel *A House for Mr Biswas* (1961), drawing as it does on the experience of Indians in Trinidad, has a quite different sensibility from the novels of Afro-Caribbean writers. It is one of the great novels of the twentieth century, bearing comparison with *Great Expectations* and *Vanity Fair*. In it, Naipaul's father, a journalist in Port of Spain, provides the model for Mohum Biswas, who so wants a house of his own. Naipaul is as celebrated for his non-fiction, which led him to travel throughout Africa, India, the American Deep South and Latin America. But he is personally unpopular in the West Indies, having made no secret of his low opinion of his countrymen; he writes in *The Middle Passage,* his examination of five Caribbean societies: "History is built around achievement and creation; and nothing was created in the West Indies."

The blues skies and white sands of Barbados, left, were not a big enough hold for George Lamming, who left for London in the 1950s.

The high standard of Caribbean writing goes some way to disproving the assertion. In 1992 the poet and playwright Derek Walcott, born in 1930 in St Lucia and author of *The Castaway and Other Poems* (1965) won the Nobel Prize for Literature. Walcott has described himself as a "colonial upstart at the end of an empire." In his poetry you can hear the music of the islands, the "divine gurgling" of Creole. Although he is in the tradition of lyric poets like Robert Graves, Walcott's West Indian roots permeate every line. In the same way Edward Kamau Brathwaite, the Bajan poet, seeks out and uses in his poetry such aspects of African culture that are still to be found in the Caribbean.

The newer generation of Caribbean writers includes the novelist and playwright Caryl Phillips (b.1958), author of *The Final Passage* (1985) and *Cambridge* (1991) and Fred D'Aguiar and David Dabydeen, both from Guyana. Although on the South American mainland, Guyana, like Surinam, is culturally linked to the Caribbean rather than to Latin America. The one English-speaking country in South America, it too has a large Indian and hence culturally complex population. It has produced a number of notable writers, especially Wilson Harris (b.1921), author of the experimental *Guyana Quartet* (1985), and Roy A.K. Heath (b.1926), author of *The Georgetown Trilogy* (1979–81).

Perhaps the best-known of the younger generation of writers is Jamaica Kincaid (b.1949). Antigua, where she was born, is considered by many tourists the ideal Caribbean island, with its white sand beaches, warm turquoise waters, technicolour sunsets and balmy climate. But it also for many years had a government notorious for corruption (under the leadership of Vere Cornwall Bird, according to *Modern Caribbean Politics*, it "acquired the regrettable image of being the most corrupt society in the Commonwealth Caribbean, hosting a notorious amorality from top to bottom"). With the election of Bird's son Lester to Prime Minister in 1994, nothing much seems to have changed, despite fine promises. Kincaid, a sophisticated New Yorker writer, is author of two largely autobiographical novels, *Annie John* (1985) and *Lucy* (1990). She has also published a collection of short stories and a polemic, *A Small Place* (1988), a scathing indictment of what happened to Antigua as a result of colonial rule and the Bird regime. The book is virtually required reading for any visitor to the island; but it is for her lyrical fiction, which gives a vivid sense of the Caribbean landscape, that Kincaid is justly acclaimed.

St Vincent is (after Haiti) the poorest of the islands, with anything between 35% and 70% unemployment. People from other islands used to say that if Columbus ever returned to the Caribbean the only place he would recognize was St Vincent. This could explain why it has produced only one writer, G.C.H. Thomas (1911–94), author of the delightful *Ruler in Hiroona* (1972), a black comedy about West Indian politics and the decline of the arrowroot industry, almost entirely based on recent history.

White writers of the Caribbean are far fewer in number, and there is only one of real distinction: Jean Rhys (1894–1979), born in Dominica of Welsh descent. The island's spirit lingers in all her work. Her *Voyage in the Dark* (1934) describes the experience of exile: her heroine misses home, can't get used to the cold, and remembers an island "all crumpled into hills and mountains as you would crumble a piece of paper in your hand – round green hills and sharply-cut mountains." The largest and most moun-

Dominica, as well as Charlotte Brontë's Jane Eyre, *inspired Jean Rhys's* Wide Sargasso Sea *(1966), her haunting, heart-breaking evocation of the early life of the first Mrs Rochester. The still, above, is from the film of the book which was released in 1992.*

tainous of the Windward Islands, Dominica is often called a "dark place," where obeah is still much practised. It produced one other writer of note, Phyllis Shand Allfrey (1915–86), whose *The Orchid House* (1953) was compared on its reissue in 1990 to *Wide Sargasso Sea* but was actually written over ten years earlier.

If Caribbean writers have one single unifying them, it is a strong sense of place, and of home. There is also – always, beneath the humour, which is a West Indian characteristic – a sadness: an awareness of a past that can never really be forgotten, or forgiven.

AUSTRALIAN IMAGES:
SYDNEY AND MELBOURNE

When you think of Sydney you think of the harbour. Its history is that of a port city. Joseph Conrad, Jack London, Robert Louis Stevenson and D.H. Lawrence all sailed in at various times. So did Thomas Hardy's Arabella and Charles Dickens's Magwitch. Miles Franklin (1879–1954), who won fame with *My Brilliant Career* (1901), gives us a vivid description in *My Career Goes Bung* (1946): "The Harbour was divine in the full day sun, brilliant blue but with a breath of haze like a veil, and little grey cow tracks all across it like sashes on the tides. The small waves whispered of the tides on the rocks covered with oysters shells and draped in seaweed with a grand sedgy odour. The gulls rocked about like paper boats at play."

When you sail into the harbour, the first settlement on the South Head is Watson's Bay. Christina Stead (1902–83) lived at 10 Pacific Street from 1917–28, and here set her novels *Seven Poor Men of Sydney* (1934) and *For Love Alone* (1944). On the North side you see the imposing seminary of St. Patrick's College at Manly. Thomas Keneally (b.1935) trained for the priesthood there between 1952 and 1960 and used it as the setting for his first novel, the murder mystery *The Place At Whitton* (1964), and *Three Cheers for the Paraclete* (1968). The great Harbour poet was Kenneth Slessor (1901–71). His "Five Bells" (1939) laments the death of a cartoonist, Joe Lynch, who fell from a ferry. In "Captain Dobbin" he portrays a retired sea-captain who:

"Now sails the street in a brick villa/'Laburbum Villa.'/ In whose blank windows the harbour hangs/Like a fog against the glass/Golden and smoky, or stoned with a white glitter/ And boats go by, suspended in the pane/Blue Funnel, Red Funnel, Messageries Maritimes..."

Sydney's first major literary movement was in the 1880s and 1890s. A wave of radical and republican energy swept the city. The *Bulletin* magazine was founded in 1880

You're never far from the harbour in Sydney; the magazine publishers of the turn of the century had their offices close to the docks of Circular Quay, Darling Harbour and Woolloomoolloo. This district with its waterfront bars was to become a focus of Bohemian activity.

by J.F. Archibald with offices at 107 Castlereagh Street. The publishing house of Angus & Robertson started round the same time, in a corner shop on Market Street.

The literary bars were numerous and always changing. In the 1920s and 1930s there were Pellegrini's wine bar, Betsy Matthais's Café La Bohème in Wilmot Street, Theo's Club on Campbell Street; later decades saw various successors. Henry Lawson and Banjo Paterson were associated with the *Bulletin*. Both celebrated the bush, the outback, the country, Paterson with his poem "The Man from Snowy River" and the words of "Waltzing Matilda," the unofficial Australian anthem, Lawson with classic

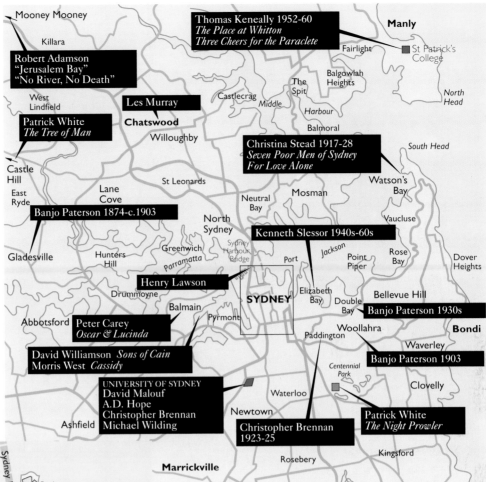

URBAN AND METROPOLITAN SYDNEY: *In Sydney literary life centres around the Harbour area, home of the* Bulletin *magazine and Angus & Roberston publishing house. However, many writers chose to live or work in the suburbs, including Thomas Keneally, who was educated at St Patrick's College in Manly; Kenneth Slessor, who lived in Elizabeth Bay; and Banjo Paterson, whose home was in the Woollahra area.*

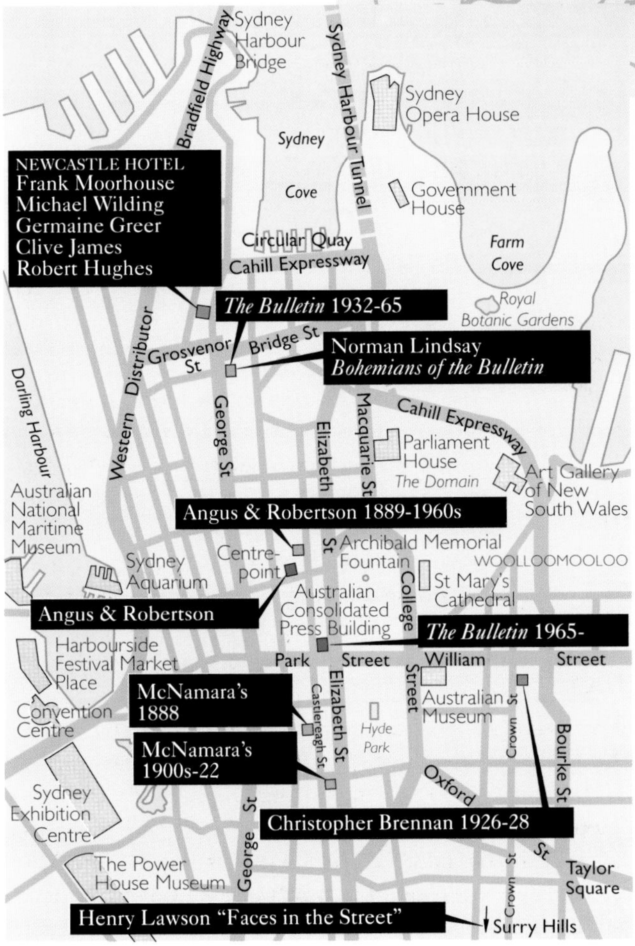

Map labels (upper map):

Mooney Mooney · Killara · Manly · Fairlight · St Patrick's College · North Head

Thomas Keneally 1952-60 / *The Place at Whitton* / *Three Cheers for the Paraclete*

Robert Adamson / "Jerusalem Bay" / "No River, No Death"

West Lindfield · The Spit · Balgowlah Heights · Castlecrag · Middle Harbour · Balmoral · South Head

Les Murray · **Chatswood** · Willoughby

Patrick White / *The Tree of Man*

Castle Hill · East Ryde · Lane Cove · St Leonards · Mosman · Watson's Bay · Vaucluse

Christina Stead 1917-28 / *Seven Poor Men of Sydney* / *For Love Alone*

Banjo Paterson 1874-c.1903 · North Sydney · Neutral Bay · Dover Heights

Gladesville · Hunters Hill · Greenwich · Sydney Harbour Bridge · Jackson · Point Piper · Rose Bay

Kenneth Slessor 1940s-60s · Parramatta · Port

Henry Lawson · Drummoyne · Elizabeth Bay · Bellevue Hill

SYDNEY · Double Bay · **Banjo Paterson 1930s** · **Bondi**

Abbotsford · Balmain · Pyrmont · Woollahra · Waverley

Peter Carey / *Oscar & Lucinda* · Paddington

Banjo Paterson 1903

David Williamson *Sons of Cain* / **Morris West** *Cassidy* · Centennial Park · Clovelly

UNIVERSITY OF SYDNEY / David Malouf / A.D. Hope / Christopher Brennan / Michael Wilding · Waterloo

Ashfield · Newtown · **Patrick White** / *The Night Prowler*

Christopher Brennan 1923-25 · Rosebery · Kingsford

Marrickville

Map labels (lower map):

Sydney Harbour Bridge · Bradfield Highway · Sydney Harbour Tunnel · Sydney Opera House · Sydney Cove · Government House

NEWCASTLE HOTEL / Frank Moorhouse / Michael Wilding / Germaine Greer / Clive James / Robert Hughes

Circular Quay · Cahill Expressway · Farm Cove · Royal Botanic Gardens

The Bulletin 1932-65 · Western Distributor · Grosvenor St · Bridge St · George St

Norman Lindsay / *Bohemians of the Bulletin* · Cahill Expressway · Macquarie St · Elizabeth St · Parliament House · The Domain · Art Gallery of New South Wales

Darling Harbour · Australian National Maritime Museum

Angus & Robertson 1889-1960s · Centrepoint · Archibald Memorial Fountain · WOOLLOOMOOLOO

Sydney Aquarium · College St · Australian Consolidated Press Building · St Mary's Cathedral

Angus & Robertson · Harbourside Festival Place · Park Street · **The Bulletin 1965-** · William Street · Bourke St

McNamara's 1888 · Hyde Park · Australian Museum · Crown St

Convention Centre · Castlereagh St · Elizabeth St

McNamara's 1900s-22 · Oxford St

Sydney Exhibition Centre · **Christopher Brennan 1926-28** · Taylor Square

The Power House Museum · George St · Crown St

Henry Lawson "Faces in the Street" · Surry Hills

---

stories like "The Drover's Wife" and "The Union Buries Its Dead." Both lived an urban life in Sydney. Lawson's early poem "Faces in the Street" commemorates the poverty of the inner-city suburb Surry Hills: "They lie, the men who tell us in a loud decisive tone/ That want is here a stranger, and that misery's unknown..."

Paterson (1864–1941), who lived on the inner harbour with his grandmother, duly became a respectable solicitor. Lawson (1867–1922) was a drifter who in the 1880s lived in various city doss-houses and, after an unhappy marriage, at addresses in North Sydney when not in jail for failing to pay his wife maintenance. He became one of the living icons of literary disaster, begging for a pint at the quay. Another was Christopher Brennan (1870–1922), correspondent of Mallarmé, and modernist poet, who was dismissed from the University of Sydney in 1925. He frequented the city bars, lived in Paddington, then in Woolloomooloo.

Sydney's Bohemian years are recorded by the Lindsays. Norman Lindsay (1879–1969), artist, cartoonist and novelist, wrote a classic memoir of the 1890s, *Bohemians of the Bulletin* (1965). His son Jack (1900–90) took the story on thirty years with *The Roaring Twenties* (1960). They lived at Lavender Bay, but when the Lindsay marriage broke up Jack and his mother moved to Queensland, Norman to Springwood in the Blue Mountains, where he painted fleshly nudes, laid his grounds out with sculptures and held court till his death in 1969. The Blue Mountains were a retreat for Eleanor Dark (1901–85), author of *The Timeless Land* (1941–53), a classic historical trilogy of Australian settlement. Springwood is now a museum of Lindsay's work, Dark's home in Varuna is a Writers' Centre.

Sydney's Bohemian world was still thriving in the 1960s and 1970s when a new wave of creative energy developed after the dull, puritanical Menzies years. Australia was always a heavily urbanized society; the myth was it was a rural one, and for decades this was the literary image too. In the late 1960s a fresh wave of writers began recording the urban life around them, challenging the official view with a more accurate portrayal of inner-city life. Bohemia was reinforced by post-war libertarianism which depoliticized Sydney by comparison with Melbourne, but encouraged a hedonistic life-style and "critical drinking." With publishing at a low ebb, writers found outlets in readings, and new literary journals sprang up: *New Poetry* (1971–82) edited by Robert Adamson, *Tabloid Story* (1972–80) edited by Frank Moorhouse, Michael Wilding, Carmel Kelly and Brian Kiernan. The George Hotel at Darling Harbour and the Newcastle Hotel near the quay became nightly venues for poets, novelists, journalists, film-makers. The young Germaine Greer, Clive James and Robert Hughes could all be found

Kings Cross, above, *was the nightlife centre of post-war Sydney and for a while a key place for writers to live.*

here in the late 1950s and early 1960s. At this time many writers moved from King's Cross to neighbouring Paddington. As that grew gentrified, they moved to Balmain, an old waterfront suburb further up the harbour from the Bridge. Balmain was where *Tabloid Story*, *New Poetry* and publishers Wild & Woolley were founded. Frank Moorhouse's (b.1938) *The Americans, Baby* (1974) and *Tales of Mystery and Romance* (1977) and Michael Wilding's (b.1942) *Living Together* (1974) mythologized these inner suburbs.

Melbourne writers began to migrate northwards: David Williamson (b.1942) and Peter Carey (b.1943) to Balmain, Barry Oakley to Paddington. Williamson's plays *Emerald City* (1987) and *Top Silk* (1989) capture the brash dynamic city of the 1980s. The declining dockyards of Balmain meant harbour views and cheap rents for the first wave of artists. It was also a suburb redolent of waterfront crime and corruption, and some of this found its way into Williamson's *Sons of Cain* (1985). Melbourne-born Morris West (b.1916), veteran novelist of Italian, Southeast Asian and North American corruption, also captured this Sydney world in *Cassidy* (1986).

For all the louche charm of its inner city nightlife, Sydney offered the attractions of splendid beaches and a climate rivalling the Cote d'Azur. West and Keneally both chose to live up the peninsula between the ocean and Pittwater, setting of Keneally's *Passenger* (1979). The poet Robert Adamson settled on the Hawkesbury River just north of Sydney, source of some of his most memorable poems. Les Murray (b.1938), the poet of rural values, lived in the suburb of Chatswood before heading out of Sydney for the bush at Bunyah. He shows the rural suspicion of Sydney in "Explaining to the Fencers:"

"Uncle Clarrie reckoned when he knew Sydney first, it was a lazy dangerous town five stories high/with razors up lanes, trams crushing stained corn, hawkers spitting/straw hats on the ferry, shopgirls indignant about everything..."

The *eminence grise* through many of these years was Nobel Prize-winner Patrick White (1912–90). Returning to Australia in the 1950s, he first settled at Castle Hill on the outskirts of Sydney and bred goats. *The Tree Of Man* (1955) portrays that district, the huge city encroaching on early settlements. Later he moved to 20 Martin Road, overlooking Centennial Park, scene of his play and

Peter Carey, above, *creates a postmodernly historical Balmain in the opening parts of his Booker Prize-winning novel* Oscar and Lucinda *(1988), before Oscar starts his trek to the North.*

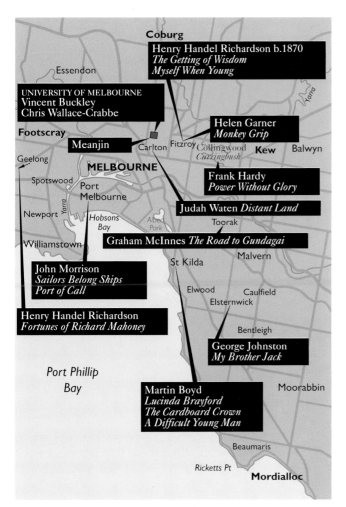

MELBOURNE: *As the inner-city working class suburbs of Melbourne,* above, *became first Bohemian, then gentrified, they passed through a literary incarnation. Neighbouring Fitzroy is the setting for Helen Garner's novel of sex and drugs,* Monkey Grip *(1977). The University and its environs are a recurrent landscape for the poems of Vincent Buckley and Chris Wallace-Crabbe.*

film *The Night the Prowler* (1978). His portrayal of Sydney ranges from colonial times with *Voss* (1957), the suburbs of *Riders of the Chariot* (1961) to the inner-city art world of *The Vivisector* (1970). He created Sarsaparilla, a particularly awful suburb, for his portraits of Australian middle class.

Where Sydney has the raffish quality of a cosmopolitan port, Melbourne boasts elegant European boulevards. One of the first crime novels, *The Mystery of the Hansom Cab* (1886), by Fergus Hume, was set in East Melbourne. Marcus Clarke (1846–81) celebrated the literary life of the 1880s in stories and journalism, though he's best-known for his novel of the convict system, *His Natural Life* (1874), mainly set in the prison settlement of Port Arthur in Tasmania. Convictism is also dealt with in Hal Porter's *The Tilted Cross* (1961), set in Tasmania, Keneally's *Bring Larks and Heroes* (1967), set in New South Wales and Robert Hughes's history *The Fabled Shore* (1987). One of the great Melbourne novelists was Henry Handel Richardson (1870–1946), born Ethel Florence at 1 Blanche Terrace, Fitzroy, and best remembered for her trilogy *The Fortunes of Richard Mahoney* (1917–29), mostly set in rural Victoria. Another is Martin Boyd (1893–1969), whose novels *The Cardboard Crown* (1952) and *A Difficult Young Man* (1955) explore middle class life in St. Kilda.

Of the many literary cafés and bars, the most famous from the 1890s to the 1920s was Fasoli's (first at 108 Lonsdale Street, then in King Street); later other haunts (the Swanston Family, Tattersall's and the Italian Society) flourished. Melbourne is also home to two key literary magazines, *Meanjin* and *Overland*. In the 1950s and 1960s the city had a strong left-wing literary group. John Morrison wrote about the docks in *Sailors Belong Ships* (1947) and *Port Of Call* (1950); Frank Hardy's *Power Without Glory* (1950) captured the inter-relation of politics and crime in Collingwood, fictionalized as Carringbush.

Melbourne, like Sydney, had its literary revival in the late 1960s and 1970s. Playwriting in particular thrived. Carlton, the suburb around the university, houses both the La Mama Theatre, and the Australian Performing Group at the Pram Factory, the theatre which performed the early work of David Williamson, John Romeril and Jack Hibberd. Williamson's *Don's Party* (1971) is a classic of Melbourne election night, while *The Club* (1977) looks at the Melbourne obsession with football, also the theme of Barry Oakley's novel *A Salute to the Great McCarthy* (1970).

Australia has always been a society of immigrants, who typically settled in the major cities where they landed. Judah Waten captured the life of Jewish migrants in Carlton in *Distant Land* (1960); Morris Lurie comically treats the same milieu in stories and novels from the early *Rappaport* (1966) to the later *Madness* (1991). Other cities too have their storytellers, like Tim Winton in Perth. So does the outback, so crucial to Australia's sense of place.

CONTEMPORARY ISRAELI WRITING

"This is the state of Israel: a refugee camp thrown together in a hurry. A place of wet paint. Remnants of foreign ways from Marrakesh, Warsaw and Bucharest and the godforsaken *shtetls* drying in the sun among the sand in the wretched new housing developments," noted one of Israel's leading authors, Amos Oz (b.1939). A State rebuilt by Jews seeking refuge in their homeland after 2,000 years of exile, their commitment to the national ideology coloured their initial reactions, of disappointment or enthusiasm, to the Land. In any event, the new life was seen as a wishful antidote to exile. The poet Avraham Shlonsky (1900–1973) sang praise to the roadbuilders and swamp-drainers. "My land is wrapped in light as in a/prayer shawl. The houses stand forth/ like frontlets; and the roads paved by/ hand, stream down like phylactery/straps." Worship of Land has replaced Worship to God; images from the religious world have been transferred to a secular one.

Israeli literature, especially since the 1980s, has attempted both to restore the lost paradise of the early Zionist settlers and decode the myth surrounding it. Life in Rosh Pinna in the north, at the turn of the century, is reconstructed by Shulamit Lapid (b.1934) in *Gai Oni* (1982), revealing the hardship and determination of a single-minded people conquering the landscape against all odds. Within the wild beauty of the Galilean mountains, dotted with bedouin tents and a few hostile Arab villages, the early pioneers struggle to establish their Jewish settlement. In *The Blue Mountain* (1991) Meir Shalev (b.1948) depicts the early settlements of the Yizre'el Valley, where legends flowered in riotous profusion, and the fantastic saga of lives and loves is unravelled.

In *After the Holidays* (1987), Yehoshua Kenaz (b.1937) conjures the heavily perfumed orange groves and tree-lined streets with their neigbourhood benches in a settlement in the coastal plain. Childhood in the south of the country, on the edge of the desert, has been reconstructed by S.Y. Yizhar (b.1916) in his two latest novels (*Mikdamot*, 1992 and *Zalhavim*, 1993). Even in 1948 in the midst of the War of Independence, Yizhar's protagonist sees the hills with their flocks and crops, as peaceful as in Biblical times, being invaded by Israeli soldiers.

Urban life in Israel began only in 1919 with the establishment of Tel Aviv, the first town built by Jews after their return to the Holy Land. Until then, it was Jerusalem and the life of the new settlements with the surrounding Arab world, exotic and repulsive at the same time, that appeared in the Hebrew literature of these

In the famous photograph above, *capturing the moment of Tel Aviv's birth, a few dozen settlers, dressed in European suits and hats, stand in the blazing sun to draw lots for the sandy plots about to be their homes. They look incongruous, but on the brink of transformation.*

European newcomers. But the new city, with its sand and its close proximity to the sea, soon became a new focus. Famous images of sun-swept young men and women, full of hope for new beginnings, posed against the empty horizons, began to appear in the works of the writers who celebrated the city. The poet Nathan Alterman (1910–70) describes the lure of the sea and imagines the city itself walking toward it: "From Allenby St to Herzl St the street was filled with rivers of perambulation and all rivers go to the sea." Alterman's books were illustrated by Nahum Gutman's naive drawings of donkeys and men in work clothes against a background of yellow sands, blue skies and sea, small, white buildings making a pleasing pattern. But sand and sea were also images of fragility and the hardships of conquering nature: "More like a stage set than a city. Nothing but a cardboard façade dividing the desert from the sea," says Amos Oz in "Late Love."

In Ya'akov Shabtai's (1934–81) stories of childhood memories of Tel Aviv (*Past Perfect*, 1987), open spaces and undeveloped coastline still survive, but with his adulthood the ugly, densely populated city emerges. Similar are contemporary descriptions of Haifa, the stronghold of the German cultured bourgeois community. In A.B. Yehoshua's (b.1936) *Five Seasons* (1990), indistinguishable apartment blocks standing on stilts on the edge of deep woods, neglected front gardens and crowded beaches are all we have of this beautiful hillside city overlooking the largest port of Israel. Tel Aviv has become a city forgetful of its romantic hopeful past. "Little Tel Aviv" has been swallowed by ugly buildings, fast food kiosks, supermarkets. Still, a live pulsating city has emerged: Tel Aviv is the base for the most of the country's entertainment life, as well as its cultural activities.

Jerusalem, Israel's capital, stands diametrically opposed: "far from the plains of citrus groves.... A shuttered, wintry city," writes Oz in *Under This Blazing Light* (1995). Geographically, Jerusalem is surrounded by mountains hanging above valleys and wadis built on stone. Historically, she has been the centre of Jewish consciousness for many centuries. "Blessed art thou, O Lord, who rebuilds Jerusalem," are the words daily recited in the prayers; the National Anthem of the State of Israel expresses the longing "to live in freedom in the land of Zion and Jerusalem."

In early Jewish sources, the city is described both as "Heavenly Jerusalem," mystical and metaphysical, and as "Jerusalem Below," dirty, ugly and sick. Uniting tensions of old and new, religious and secular, hope and despair, it is held holy by Christians, Muslims and Jews. This often creates a sense of ambivalence. Yoseph Haim Brenner (1881–

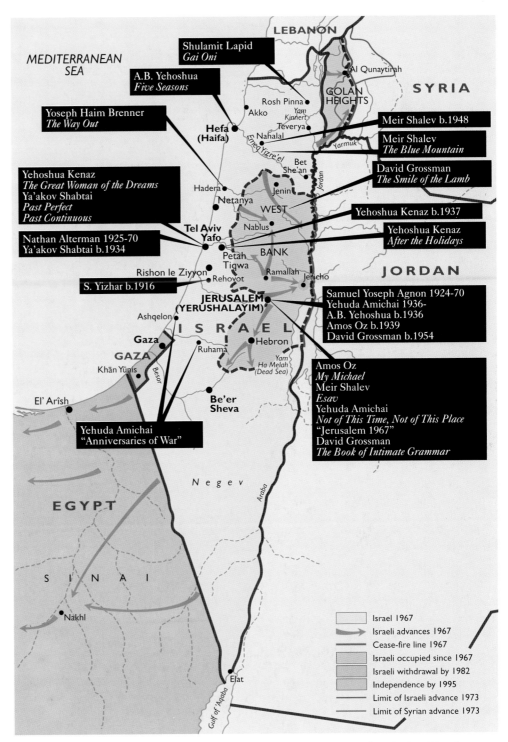

ISRAEL: *A succession of wars has meant that the boundaries of Israel are constantly changing. Although Jews first wrote about other lands after their return to the Holy Land in 1919, they soon focused their attentions on places nearer to their reclaimed home.*

1921), the Zionist ideologue, described the life of the Jewish inhabitants at the turn of the century as being one of "breakdown and bereavement," cruelly stripping the city of any hint of spirituality. Haim Hazaz (1897–1973) showed the mystic dreams of a messaniac age, but stressed the naivety and futility of their dreams. This polarity

The Old City of Jerusalem, shown above, *is a city of mosques, synagogues and churches, shrouded under a cloud of prophecy.*

between Holy and secular pervades the fiction of S.Y. Agnon (1888–1970). In the story "Thillah," walking in the Old City, along the street of the smiths, past shoemakers, basket weavers, and little shops selling food, one reaches the Street of the Jews: "Huddled in their tattered rags sat beggars, not caring even to reach a hand from their cloaks." Yet, seeing Jerusalem for the first time, the protoganist of "Just Yesterday" is ecstatic with excitement; even the air has a mysterious quality. This "Heavenly Quality" is still in contemporary writing. Jerusalemites are bent on symbols, consider themselves symbols, says the protagonist of A.B. Yehoshua's *Three Days and a Child* (1971).

Likewise the poet Yehuda Amichai contemplates Jerusalem with a mixture of love and exasperation:

"Jerusalem is a port city on the shore of an eternity/The Temple Mount is a huge ship, a magnificent/luxury liner. From the portholes of her Western Wall/cheerful saints look out, travelers. Hasidim on the pier/wave goodbye, shout hooray, hooray, bon voyage! She is/always arriving, always sailing away. And the fences and the piers/and the policemen and the flags and the high masts of churches/and mosques and the smokestacks of synagogues and the boats/of psalms of praise and mountain-waves. The shofa blows: another one has just left. Yom Kippur sailors in white uniforms/climb among ladders and ropes of well-tested prayers/And the commerce and the gates and golden domes/Jerusalem is the Venice of God."

The dust, stones and ghosts of barbed wire fences divide the city in two: the Old City with its old mosques; foreign consulates and the housing projects; the zealous black-coated Hasidim and the tourists; in the distance the spires of Bethlehem, the barren hillsides and the Dead Sea;

the New Jerusalem, Jewish and modern, outside the Old City Walls with its many different quarters.

No-Man's Land, which split the city in two between 1948 and 1967, is for the protagonist of Amichai's *Not of This Time Not of This Place* (1975), a constant reminder of the futility of wars, while the threatening barbed wire arouses fascination in Oz's hero in *My Michael*. The "other side" meant the Arabs: the enemy. In *Sleeping on a Wire* (1993), David Grossman (b.1954) sets out to discover the Israel where the Arabs live, political conflict obscuring the pastoral landscape. Driving from Nazareth along an entirely "Arab" route though villages on parched stone hills, seeing shepherds, hens and veiled women, or on the road in the "Little Triangle" (land between Jerusalem and Haifa), he has the urge "to peel this land of its names, designations, descriptions and dates, Israel, Palestine, Zion, 1987, 1929, 1936, 1948, 1967, 1987, the Jewish state, the Promised Land, the Holy Land, the Land of Splendor, The Zionist entity, Palestine.... I could again sense the simple and mysterious love of the land – that is, of the land itself, prior to any name or title – of this strip of the planet that fate has burdened us with, with its colors and aromas and land and trees and changing seasons."

In Israel geography is everything – a tiny piece of land, claimed by many nations since it was first settled; the scene of the bloodiest wars, a capital city, small and beautiful, the centre of three great religions, the site of bitter bloodshed. Its writing cannot but be read also as a chronicle of the continuous turmoils experienced during the wars. Not to write of this is as much a political statement as to tackle the issues head-on. Here as much as anywhere place and conflict are inextricably linked, as Yehuda Amichai poignantly expresses in one of his many poems about his beloved city: "Jerusalem stone is the only stone/that hurts. It has a network of nerves."

In his novels and short stories Amos Oz, right, describes Jerusalem as ephemeral, paradoxically mirroring the fragility of the national existence it was built to rebut.

IN SEARCH OF ANDALUSIA: ARABIC LITERATURE TODAY

The post-colonial Arab world is plagued with military conflicts, internal stagnation, economic under-development and political despotism. It is split between the nationalist – or Islamic – option and dependence on the West. The very identity of the Arab individual is challenged by historical events far beyond his or her control. With this loss of control over surroundings, the Arabic language becomes the last frontier. In this critical juncture, historical and geographical spaces become grounds contested through language in the pages of contemporary Arabic writing.

One of the difficulties of translating modern Arabic literature into vernacular is the language itself, which distinguishes between spoken and written forms, and is splitting into various sub-languages as a result of external and internal influences. Multi-layered texts with regional flavours, therefore, lose part of their richness in translation into English or other European languages. And the number of titles translated is very small; in 1988 only 29 Arab books were translated into French. As a result, old images of ancient cities tend to remain stagnant.

When a new collection of the poems by Constantine Cavafy, the Greek poet who spent much of his life as a civil servant in Alexandria, was published recently in France, Margaret Yourcenar explained its flavour in her introduction: "What is shocking about Cavafy's writing is the absence of a Mediterranean or eastern imagery.... He was cut off from the Arab and Islamic world, and his eastern side is suspended." He planted his Hellenism on Alexandria, and indigenous people, their language and culture, are almost non-existent. Much the same is true of Durrell's (1912–90) *Alexandria Quartet* (1957–1960), which had so much influence in the West. Durrell's quartet, or "relativity poem," emphasizes the mysterious, cosmopolitan nature of Alexandria, where European characters interact. It becomes an interpreted space emphasizing a

Images of ancient cities like Alexandria, depicted in the Latin manuscript, above, and created in Western languages by Shakespeare, Constantine Cavafy, E.M. Forster and Lawrence Durrell, endure beyond a normal life-span, holding the Arab world still, outside history and geography.

Eurocentric reading of history and geography. Such a fictive Alexandria is being challenged and replaced by narratives written in Arabic by Egyptian writers: above all by Naguib Mahfouz (b.1911), winner of the 1988 Nobel Prize for Literature.

In his novel *Miramar* (1978) Mahfouz uses techniques similar to Durrell, but to put the past in a different perspective. Durrell writes of the city's European community from before the Second World War to the mid-fifties; Mahfouz is concerned with the period that follows. In *Miramar*, Zohra, the peasant maid meticulously drawn by Mahfouz, is the central consciousness of the novel and is made to stand for Egypt. This spirited young Egyptian, with no foreign ancestors, is alien and inaccesible to foreign observers like Durrell. Meanwhile characters like Madame Mariana, who laments a past when foreigners "energized" Egyptian society, link the worlds described by the two writers. Mahfouz reclaims Alexandria and places it back in its Arab and Islamic history, identifying it with Princess Qatr el-Nada, daughter of the Sultan Ibn Tulun (864–905). Mariana, attached to the European-influenced past, is ageing, but Zohra is young and vivacious. Alexandria first becomes the Princess, then Zohra, then post-colonial Egypt in its own distinctiveness.

With yet greater awareness of decolonization, Edward el-Kharrat, another leading Egyptian writer, born in

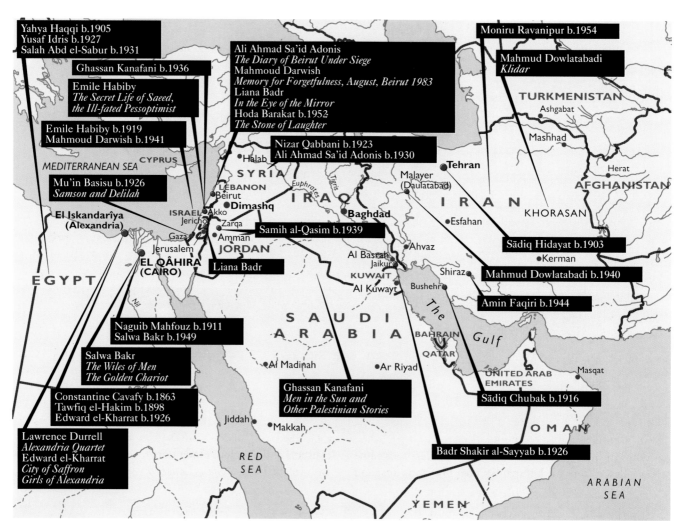

Yahya Haqqi b.1905
Yusaf Idris b.1927
Salah Abd el-Sabur b.1931

Ghassan Kanafani b.1936

Emile Habiby
*The Secret Life of Saeed,
the Ill-fated Pessoptimist*

Emile Habiby b.1919
Mahmoud Darwish b.1941

Mu'in Basisu b.1926
Samson and Delilah

Ali Ahmad Sa'id Adonis
The Diary of Beirut Under Siege
Mahmoud Darwish
Memory for Forgetfulness, August, Beirut 1983
Liana Badr
In the Eye of the Mirror
Hoda Barakat b.1952
The Stone of Laughter

Nizar Qabbani b.1923
Ali Ahmad Sa'id Adonis b.1930

Samih al-Qasim b.1939

Liana Badr

Naguib Mahfouz b.1911
Salwa Bakr b.1949

Salwa Bakr
*The Wiles of Men
The Golden Chariot*

Constantine Cavafy b.1863
Tawfiq el-Hakim b.1898
Edward el-Kharrat b.1926

Lawrence Durrell
Alexandria Quartet
Edward el-Kharrat
*City of Saffron
Girls of Alexandria*

Ghassan Kanafani
*Men in the Sun and
Other Palestinian Stories*

Moniru Ravanipur b.1954

Mahmud Dowlatabadi
Klidar

Sādiq Hidayat b.1903

Mahmud Dowlatabadi b.1940

Amin Faqiri b.1944

Sādiq Chubak b.1916

Badr Shakir al-Sayyab b.1926

*For Arab women writers resistance
to imperialism is linked to the fight
for their freedom of expression in a
contemporary, male-dominated society.*

Alexandria in 1926, claims the city was not only, as Westerners like Cavafy have thought, the heir to Greek colonial glories, but also to the ancient spiritual treasures of the age-old, long-protracted Pharaonic era. In his two novels *City of Saffron* (1989) and *Girls of Alexandria* (1993), el-Kharrat displays his emotional and cultural bonds to his birthplace; Alexandria is "a blue-white marble city woven and rewoven by my heart upon whose frothing incandescent countenance my heart is ever floating." The aim is not just to recover fictional territory, but to express the repressed history of his region and culture. Today's Alexandria is linked with Arab Islamic culture, as well as many mystic Mediterranean legacies (Christian, Jewish and Islamic)

THE ARABIC WORLD: *The Arab imagination has been drawn by lost maps. Palestinian writers like the late Ghassan Kanafani and Emile Habiby, poets like the late Muain Bisysu and Samih al-Qasim, and the woman writer Liana Badr, have all attempted to draw alternative literary maps of their own homeland, in order to preserve and recover it.*

the West has been inclined to forget. Yet, if Arab writers are reclaiming their heritage, that itself is disputed. Today modern Arabic literature, especially fiction, is in a transitional phase. Arabs were historically storytellers, as *The Arabian Nights* testifies. But for today's writer the task has become that of rethinking and reclaiming Arab terrain, and resisting the incorporation of Arab history and culture into the culture of the West – as has happened over so many centuries in the process of "Orientalism," which made the Arab world exotic space for the Western imagination.

This argument over the map of fiction can be seen in a good deal of the literature from the Arab world today. This is particularly true of Palestine, that most contested of places on the map of reality. Palestinian poet Mahmoud Darwish (b.1941, *Memory for Forgetfulness: August, Beirut, 1983*, 1995) is inevitably preoccupied with the homeland,

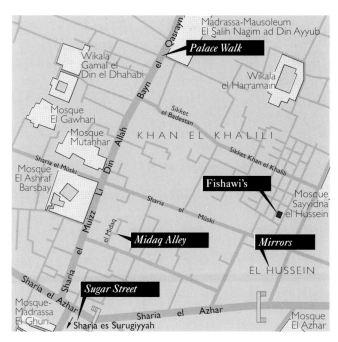

Cairo: In his Cairo Trilogy *and* Midaq Alley *Naguib Mahfouz draws on the history of the old part of the city.*

identity and Palestinian loss. Though Western poets may be free to write largely of private lives, Darwish turns the private lyric into a form of public declamation. Yet while he writes of his own troubled world, he no less sees himself as a descendent of the Spanish poet Garcia Lorca, and mentions him in many poems, so emphasizing his own Mediterranean and "Andalusian" identity.

Which takes us back to a key date in the Arab literary imagination: 1492, the year when, as Columbus voyaged to America, the Muslim Arabs surrendered Andalusia and the great red fortress of the Alhambra in Granada to Isabella and Ferdinand. The irrevocable loss of paradise, and the Mediterranean realm where Moorish or Islamic agriculture, trade and industry, architecture, literature and learning richly flourished, is probably one of the deepest scars in the Arab soul. It would happen a second time. Four hundred years later, Palestine was lost to the Zionists, and another disruption of history was inflicted.

In much Arab writing from 1500 on, that "Andalusian" space was to attain mythical dimensions – metaphorical, paradisical, larger than it ever was. It is a utopia where religions co-existed in harmony, the arts flourished and the Muslim Arabs' Golden Age prospered, winning the admiration of medieval Europe. The task of bidding farewell to Andalusia becomes an attempt to reclaim it, along with other lost lands. Mahmoud Darwish's "Eleven Stars Over Andalusia" (1994) is a vivid poetic evocation of the sense of loss and rupture, to memory and the soul. But the spirit of resistance in Arab writing has not been confined to reaction against fictional or very real imperialism. For women writers it is a fight for freedom. Andalusia for them is no remote place to search

for; it is here and now, as they try to carve a space in a language that is a tool of a dominant male culture. Salwa Bakr (b.1949), the Egyptian writer, is a pre-eminent practitioner of the colloquialized standard Arabic, especially in *The Wiles of Men* (1992), and *The Golden Chariot* (1994) where the voices of women, which most of the time cannot be distinguished from each other, are close to colloquial Egyptian, drawing on the long oral tradition. Their language is interwoven with the influence of *The Arabian Nights* and Arab folklore, creating profound political and social commentary where tale appears within tale.

Women writers have also had their own response to the bitter conflicts of the region. Hoda Barakat's (b.1952) *The Stone of Laughter* (1994) was hailed as the best novel written against the background of the Lebanese Civil War of 1975–79. To describe the ugly reality of a great Mediterranean city bent on self-destruction, she creates a new language, blasting the city with words, trying to betray it in order to reconstruct it.

In a world of fast-changing history, of lost maps and ravaged homelands, contested landscapes and competing versions of faith, politics and imagination, contemporary Arab literature still has many questions to ask. Questions not just about the images imposed on the Arab world by the West, but about all notions of identity and the shortcomings of grand rhetorics like pan-Arabism. If some writers still lament the loss of Andalusia, their attempt to claim this lost paradise may be, paradoxically, the last attempt to exorcise it from our collective memories and souls.

Mahmoud Darwish, top, *and Hoda Barakat,* bottom, *write of their homeland.*

SOUTH AFRICAN STORIES

Johannesburg is not a lovely city. To the South the mine dumps and yellow slag heaps are reminders of the gold mining industry which once flourished there, but now has largely moved on. The city itself is separated from the giant townships, very basic and functional dormitory cities, by these mine dumps and ring roads. To the north are the sprawling and comfortable suburbs, from where the mines and their tips cannot be seen at all. The city, although still the headquarters of the major mining houses and their satellite enterprises, is in a process of change – which means that after dark whites retreat to their suburbs and malls.

The Rand Club, which was once the centre of all activity and intrigue, is now more a museum than a way of life. Johannesburg is a city in search of an identity – yet it remains unquestionably the beating heart of South Africa. The Market Theatre and others, once beacons in the cultural darkness, fight on in a new era and a new South Africa, in which the old moral certainties have gone. After the Second World War the city was an unlikely place for a flowering of literature; yet it was here, from the townships of Sophiatown (now gone) and Vrededorp to the leafy suburbs of Parktown, that a vibrant literary life appeared to be emerging, along with lively new journalism and music.

Today the fifties in Johannesburg are seen as something of a golden age – with singers like Miriam Makeba and Dolly Rathebe, gangsters like the "Russian Gang" and journalists like Don Mattera, Nat Nakasa, Bloke Modisane, Can Themba and Ezekiel Mphahlele achieving celebrity, largely in the *Drum* magazine, still in existence under the editorship of Anthony Sampson, but also in *The Rand Daily Mail*, which was entering its heyday of opposition to an increasingly repressive apartheid government. This optimism and idealism was the mirror of the growing strength and assertiveness of the African political movements. Sophiatown – a ramshackle but bustling township near to the centre of Johannesburg – was the focus of this new life. Shebeens, like Aunt

In the bird's-eye view of Johannesburg, above, *reminders of the city's gold-mining past are clearly visible.*

Suzie's, were the meeting points at this time for writers, political activists and gangsters.

It was in this period that Nadine Gordimer (b.1923) emerged from the small nearby mining town of Springs. Her first collection of stories, *Face to Face*, was published in 1949. She has described her route to discovering her own country as being via Bohemia. This was an age of daring racial mixing, illicit drinking in shebeens, great expectations of revolutionary change, optimism and excitement. It ended effectively with the Sharpeville killings of 1960. The age of innocence was over. For many black writers disillusionment had set in far earlier. Now writing took a new turn, as journalists were "banned," political leaders went underground, and many South African writers including Bessie Head, Alex La Guma and Dan Jacobson left the country. Although those few years did not produce many great works, they poignantly suggest the cultural life that might have been.

The years that followed (which saw the Soweto Children's Uprising and the emergence of Steve Biko's "Black Consciousness") were called "the interregnum." The literature of this period is full of a sense that the process of liberation is unstoppable. The Market Theatre became an island of hope and cross-racial collaboration, almost a rehearsal for the new society. The interregnum ended in April 1994, with the first democratic elections.

Gerard Sekoto's painting, Yellow Houses: A Street in Sophiatown *(c.1940), left, portrays a Johannesburg township which has now disappeared.*

A peaceful protest at Sharpeville in 1960 against the Pass laws, organized by the Pan-African Congress, resulted in a massacre, below, when police opened fire, killing seventy protesters, and wounding a further two hundred. For many this put an end to the optimism of the 1950s.

In truth South African literature has always existed under the long shadow of racial conflicts and tensions. The near half-century since formal apartheid was introduced has produced some notable literature – known, perhaps dismissively, as "white writing." Black writing suffered disproportionately, through the denial of education, dispersal and exile. While Nadine Gordimer, André Brink, J.M. Coetzee and Athol Fugard emerged to articulate the white cultural and political dilemma with great force on the world stage, no like success has been enjoyed by black writers. Certainly none has appeared in South Africa to challenge Chinua

Achebe, Wole Soyinka or Ben Okri. White writers have felt the disparity keenly; many have tried to keep in close touch with the black community and political opposition, and Gordimer published a study of black South African writers, *The Black Interpreters* (1973). Some have turned to historicism, others to allegory, to avoid the taint of privilege.

The world became increasingly interested in South Africa and the appalling injustices to which those white writers who remained (many, like Christopher Hope, left) were testifying. Gordimer achieved world fame with her stories *Soft Voice of the Serpent* (1952) and novels like *The Late Bourgeois World* (1966) and *A Guest of Honour* (1970). Her novel *Burger's Daughter* (1979) was banned after the Soweto riots. André Brink, born in 1935 in Vrede, Orange Free State, has written prolifically in Afrikaans and

English; but it was when his novel *Looking on Darkness* (1974) was banned by the authorities that he attracted international attention. In the Eastern Cape the playwright Athol Fugard, born in 1932 in Middelburg, Cape Province, wrote *Blood Knot* (1960), starting a long career in theatre (The Serpent Players in Port Elizabeth, The Space Experimental Theatre in Cape Town and the Market Theatre in Johannesburg) which has attracted attention not only to him but to his actor-collaborators John Kani and Winston Ntshona. In Cape Town itself, new writers-in-opposition emerged, among them the novelist J.M. Coetzee (b.1940), whose novel *The Life and Times of Michael K* won the Booker Prize in 1983, and the poet Breyten Breytenbach (b.1939), to make their distinctive contribution to literature, some as part of the group Die Sestigers. Breytenbach was eventually imprisoned and

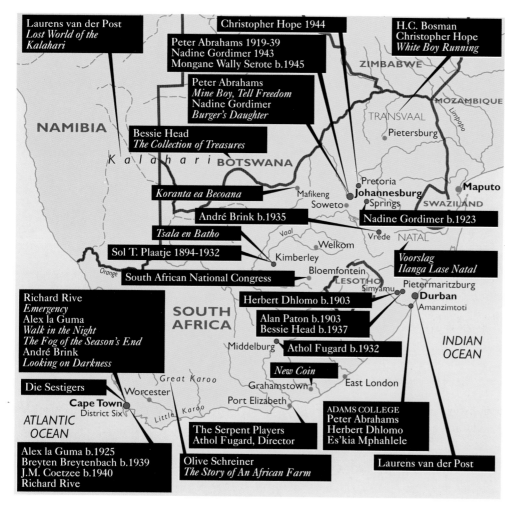

Laurens van der Post
Lost World of the Kalahari

Christopher Hope 1944

Peter Abrahams 1919-39
Nadine Gordimer 1943
Mongane Wally Serote b.1945

H.C. Bosman
Christopher Hope
White Boy Running

ZIMBABWE

Peter Abrahams
Mine Boy, Tell Freedom
Nadine Gordimer
Burger's Daughter

MOZAMBIQUE

TRANSVAAL

Pietersburg

NAMIBIA

Bessie Head
The Collection of Treasures

K a l a h a r i **BOTSWANA**

Koranta ea Becoana

Pretoria
Johannesburg
Maputo

Mafikeng
Soweto
Springs
SWAZILAND

André Brink b.1935

Nadine Gordimer b.1923

Tsala en Batho

Vaal
Vrede **NATAL**

Sol T. Plaatje 1894-1932

Orange
Welkom
Kimberley
Bloemfontein

Voorslag
Ilanga Lase Natal

South African National Congress

LESOTHO
Simyamu
Pietermaritzburg
Durban

Richard Rive
Emergency
Alex la Guma
Walk in the Night
The Fog of the Season's End
André Brink
Looking on Darkness

**SOUTH
AFRICA**

Herbert Dhlomo b.1903

Amanzimtoti

Alan Paton b.1903
Bessie Head b.1937

**INDIAN
OCEAN**

Middelburg
Athol Fugard b.1932

Die Sestigers

Great Karoo

New Coin

Cape Town
District Six
Worcester
Little Karoo
Grahamstown
East London

**ATLANTIC
OCEAN**

Port Elizabeth

The Serpent Players
Athol Fugard, Director

ADAMS COLLEGE
Peter Abrahams
Herbert Dhlomo
Es'kia Mphahlele

Alex la Guma b.1925
Breyten Breytenbach b.1939
J.M. Coetzee b.1940
Richard Rive

Olive Schreiner
The Story of An African Farm

Laurens van der Post

SOUTH AFRICA: *Johannesburg and Cape Town are the chief literary centres in the country, and house some of today's best-known writers.*

Born in the Orange Free State in 1876, he moved with his parents to a mission station of the Berlin Missionary Society near the diamond mining town of Kimberley as a child. Becoming a court interpreter, and starting the magazine, *Tsala en Batho*, he went on to keep an extraordinary diary of life in the besieged town of Mafeking, translate Shakespeare into Tswana, oppose the Natives Land Act of 1913 and to write *Native Life in South Africa* (1916). He helped found the South African Native National Congress in Blomfontein (which would become the ANC) and spent many years in London trying to persuade the Imperial Government to intervene in the destruction of African franchise rights. Today his life and work are undergoing long overdue revaluation.

In Natal between the wars three young writers – William Plomer (1903–73), Roy Campbell (1902–57) and Laurens van der Post (b.1906) – produced a short-lived but influential magazine called *Voorslag* (Whiplash) whose intent was "to sting with satire the hindquarters of the bovine citizenry of the Union." In a sense these writers sum up the dilemma of white South African writers, in their desire to be international in scope, yet to speak with a distinct South African voice. In 1825 Plomer wrote a key novel, *Turbott Wolfe*, attacking the "colour bar" as it was called, and he settled in England in the 1930s. Campbell went on to support Franco and eventually settled in France; he produced volumes of poetry (*The Georgiad*, 1931, is perhaps the most famous), a pro-Fascist poetic polemic, *Flowering Rifle* (1939), which damaged his reputation, and an autobiography, *Light on a Dark Horse* (1951). Van der Post, an Afrikaner, wrote an early novel *In a Province* (1934) attacking South African racism. After war service and imprisonment by the Japanese in the Far East, he went on to write about Africa, travel and anthropology, drawing on Jung and a degree of homegrown mysticism. His best-known books are *Venture Into the Interior* (1952) and *Lost World of the Kalahari* (1958).

returned to live in Paris; Coetzee is now South Africa's most refined literary voice. Alex La Guma, born in Cape Town's District Six in 1925, became a leading ANC official.

The first South African writer to become widely known was Olive Schreiner (1855–1920). She lived for many years in the Karoo, an arid sheep-farming district of the Cape. Her most famous novel *The Story of an African Farm* (1883) was written when she was only 21 and working as a governess. She went on to become deeply involved in social issues, particularly women's rights, and spent much time in England, where she was close to Havelock Ellis. She returned to South Africa in 1894 and completed only one other novel, *Trooper Peter Hallet* (1897), but wrote an enormous number of tracts. *The Story of an African Farm* still stands out in contemporary feminist literature. Schreiner died in 1920 in Wynberg, Cape Town.

Sol T. Plaatje (1876–1932) is considered to be South Africa's first black novelist to write in English. Like many South African writers, he was a political activist and journalist before turning to fiction. Still *Mhudi*, published in 1930, 15 years after it was written, was a considerable achievement. Plaatje's own life was the greatest testament.

Alan Paton's Cry, the Beloved Country *was a moving plea for racial understanding. It became a worldwide bestseller, and was also made into a successful film from which the still,* above, *was taken.*

Other writers recorded the South African experience more intimately. From a backward community in Northern Transvaal where he went as a young teacher in the 1920s, Herman Charles Bosman (1905–51) wrote tales of rural life that made no attempt to transcend national borders. Throughout his troubled life (including a spell in jail for murder, described in *The Stone Cold Jug*, 1949) he wrote of distinctively South African characters, with a shrewd understanding of underlying racial tension. Later he lived in Johannesburg, writing copiously for journals; *Mafeking Road* (1947) is his best-known collection of stories.

One of South Africa's most famous books appeared right after the Second World War, when Alan Paton (1903–88) wrote the worldwide bestseller *Cry, the Beloved Country* (1948), the sentimental but moving account of the sundering of a rural Zulu family. Paton himself was born in Pietermaritzburg and was educated at the University of Natal. He became governor of a reformatory in Durban, and a liberal-minded man, who wrote his masterpiece while on a sabbatical in the United States. Paton's autobiography *Towards the Mountain* was published in 1981 and his *Journey Continued* posthumously in 1988.

Writers in South Africa today have won a recognizable place. Their task is to deal with a fast-changing and confusing culture. Nadine Gordimer won the Nobel Prize for Literature in 1991. At the present moment, she, André Brink and J.M. Coetzee are the most widely-read of South African writers outside of their country, all of them dealing in different ways with the cultural and political demands of life in a radically altered country. South Africa now waits to see just what will emerge from its new freedoms. Poets like Mongane Wally Serote, Jeremy Cronin, Njabulo Ndebele and Sipho Sepamla

– all ideologically committed – have continued to make names for themselves. Protest poetry and declamation, popular in the townships, enjoy an ambivalent status, somewhere between literature and polemic.

The strength of community theatre together with the revival of interest in writers and campaigners like Bessie Head (1937–86), also from Pietermaritzburg, and the vigorous efforts of the Congress of South African writers: all these things testify to the understandable eagerness to value work that was produced in "the struggle." At the same time there is a competitive belief that the most distinctive work will come from a rejection of the past.

Still, there is a general faith in South Africa – fostered in the universities and magazines like *Staffrider* – that a literary flowering is well overdue. If it does happen, Johannesburg city, the bustling, crime-ridden, melting pot of South Africa, is the most likely locus. Nothing, however, will retrieve the lives and works lost to drink, exile, violence, suicide, repression and torture. The story of the writers of the last fifty years in South Africa is one of tragic lost opportunity; in that respect at least, it is a mirror of society.

South African poets Dennis Brutus and Sipho Sepamla and novelist J.M. Coetzee are shown above (from left to right) *at the 48th International Pen Convention in 1986, which was held in San Francisco.*

Nadine Gordimer, right, *is today one of South Africa's best-known writers. In recognition of her contribution to writing she was awarded the Nobel Prize for Literature in 1991.*

LATIN AMERICAN WRITING:
A LITERARY HERITAGE EXPLORED

Latin America embraces dozens of cultures, every possible kind of geography, an astonishing mixture of races and several important languages. It is a region without an orthodox interpretation of its own histories. The one thing everyone can agree on is that it is "a beggar sitting on a pile of gold" – in other words it has somehow lost its way on the path to becoming great, condemned to be less than it should have been. Because of its prodigal variety, it is misleading to generalize about anything Latin American: something to bear in mind when approaching its literature.

Two major tributaries flow into its stream: the heritage of Europe, and the legacy of the folk cultures of the original peoples and those who came from overseas. Latin American writing has been hardly influenced by that of the United States, perhaps because it is considered the neighbourhood bully, its political interference and economic sabotage long resented. The legends and myths of the indigenous peoples are widely enjoyed. Every child knows the story of how the armadillo knitted its own shell, or why the rabbit has long ears. Such tales evidence a metaphorical and poetic conception of the world (silver is the tears of the moon, gold the sweat of the sun), a view of it as wondrous and capricious, that has greatly enriched Latin American writing.

Although tales of the Andes have been widely popular, those of the jungle peoples of the Amazon have often been known mostly to the anthropologists. But one great and influential text captures the power and flavour of Amazonian myth: Mário de Andrade's *Macunaíma* (1928). More recently there have been Darcy Ribeiro's *Maíra* (1978) and João Ubaldo Ribeiro's masterpiece *An Invincible Memory* (1984). This

Latin America is a land of the fantastical, the mythological and the poetic – a world captured here by Mexican Diego Rivera's The Market at Tenochtitlan.

explores the legacy of the black peoples that the slavers brought in from West Africa, carrying with them a culture that in many places, especially Brazil, remains intact to this day. Conflating the Catholic saints with their own gods, and linking elaborate and beautiful myths with their systems of practical magic ("Santería"), they could follow their own religion even in white man's churches.

This influenced the work of Brazil's most popular novelist, Jorge Amado (b.1912). A Communist in his youth, Amado became more interested in the improvised and difficult lives of the poor people of Bahia. Their energy, humour and optimism are reflected in his novels: *Dona Flor and Her Two Husbands* (1966) and *Gabriela,*

Clove and Cinammon (1958), a cult among young women in Brazil, many of whom announce in all seriousness "I am Gabriela." Amado can be criticized for celebrating the lives of those (pimps, thieves, swindlers, gangsters) who make life hell for ordinary citizens and for losing his original political fire. But his works are in the Magic Realist vein, and his achievement in capturing the imagination of a nation for half a century is monumental.

The European influence owes much to the fact that many Latin American writers and intellectuals feel they actually are European. They are often more so than Europeans themselves, since they see Europe from the outside, as a whole. In fiction Miguel de Cervantes, with his baroque imagination, sympathetic humour and picaresque style, is the one unmistakable influence. But few major European writers have not fed the Latin American flame. Mario Vargas Llosa (b.1936) is a passionate admirer of

Gustave Flaubert and Isabel Allende (b.1942) surely read Lampedusa's *The Leopard* before writing *The House of the Spirits* (1982). Most have spent long periods in Europe, as well as in other Latin American countries, often combining writing with careers in diplomacy or journalism.

One result of this is that Latin American writers can be found to correspond to just about every phase and movement of European literature. It is important to stress this; we should not assume all Latin American writing is Magical Realist. This does not mean it is a subsidiary of European letters, however. In recent decades Latin American literature has been more influential than influenced. Writers like Jorge Luis Borges (1899–1986), Gabriel García Márquez (b.1928) and Alejo Carpentier (1904–79) have had enormous impact in places as diverse as India, Sierra Leone and Britain – not least because

LATIN AMERICA: *Latin America is literature's fascinating New World, a place for new and exciting imaginative voyages of discovery.*

Magical Realism has been a great liberator of the plot, and these exuberant styles appeal to all writers in love with language.

Of Magical Realism, that primal form of storytelling and myth making, there is no easy definition. In one sense it is straight-faced exaggeration. We do not say someone can jump a long way, we say they can fly. In another it means taking literally the beliefs and superstitions of one's ordinary characters. Above all it is a way narrative can explore, create, fantasize about possible worlds. It is the storytellers' approach to modal logic, which lends itself to considerable humour.

a truly amorous celebration of the baroque possibilities of the Castilian tongue. Márquez calls a character "a furtive angel with maritime eyes," Allende's *House of the Spirits* opens with the irresistible "Barabbas came to us by sea." Like Borges, Márquez is a very great poet who happens to write in prose; we read him with an intense pleasure that overlooks ramshackle narrative and neglect of characterization. However, the great phase of Magical Realism is probably over. The currency has been devalued, become self-conscious, self-mocking – as in Mexican Laura Esquivel's popular *Like Water For Chocolate* (1989).

Magical Realism is often also political realism. Foreign readers unaware of the region's history may not realize that every book sites itself within specific social, historical and political frameworks. In some writing – as with the Chilean playwright Ariel Dorfman (b.1942, *Death and the Maiden*, 1992) – this is plain enough. But we can read Márquez's wonderful, best-selling *One Hundred Years of Solitude* (1967) while totally unfamiliar with Colombia's hard past – or perhaps find it hard to understand that the Peruvian Vargas Llosa's masterpiece *The War of the End of the World* (1981) deals with a popular revolution in Brazil. Political writing has come from the liberation struggles of the nineteenth century and the equally radical struggles of the twentieth, most recently in Central America, but most is of historical rather than literary interest.

Today much of the finest writing there is in Spanish and Portuguese comes from the New World. If it drew on European traditions, it depended too on the break away from European parentage. The transition toward new confidence is seen in the work of fine writers like Joaquim Maria Machado de Assis (1839–1908), the Brazilian mulatto who wrote *Epitaph of a Small Winner* (1880) and *Don Casmurro* (1899). By the 1930s a regional literature wholly of its time and place began to flourish. In Venezuela Rómulo Gallegos (1909–67) portrays the hard life of the hinterland in his naturalistic *Doña Bárbara* (1929) and *Canaima* (1935). In Peru Ciro (1909–67) Alegría gives

HONORARY LATIN AMERICANS AND THEIR FICTIONS

1904 Joseph Conrad *Nostromo*
1904 W.H. Hudson *The Green Mansions*
1926 D.H. Lawrence *The Plumed Serpent*
1927 Thornton Wilder *The Bridge of San Luis Rey*
1940 Graham Greene *The Power and the Glory*
1958 Graham Greene *Our Man in Havana*
1983 Lisa St Aubin de Terán *Keepers of the House*
1990 Nicholas Shakespeare *The Vision of Elena Silves*
1990 Louis de Bernières *The War of Don Emmanuel's Nether Parts*

In the famous prologue to his novel *The Kingdom of This World* (1949), Alejo Carpentier provided a seminal account. He invokes the *Morte d'Arthur*, the Marquis de Sade, Rimbaud, the surrealists – but fails to find in any of them anything sufficiently marvellous to encompass Latin American reality. "What is the history of America if not a chronicle of the marvellous in the real?" he asks, and proposes the undeniable truth that Latin America is a land of the fantastical, a place where people have long searched for the Enchanted City of the Caesars. His argument is borne out by Eduardo Galeano's trilogy *Memory of Fire* (1982–86) worth consulting for a picture of Latin America's extraordinarily accidental history.

Allende, another prominent exponent of Magical Realism, is clearly influenced by Márquez, and both show us *Broad and Alien is the World* (1941). Brazil had Graciliano Ramos (*Barren Lives*, 1938) and João Guimarães Rosa, whose *The Devil to Pay in the Backlands* (1956) finds a style that is metaphysical, idiosyncratic and highly baroque. Even the self-conscious fiction of Borges mixes the European mannerism and the gaucho world of Argentina.

Regionalism, or *indigenismo*, fell into disfavour with many intellectuals, but re-emerged as recent political crises grew. There has been a large literature on dictatorship, abuse of power and terrorism, addressed by Carpentier, Augusto Roa Bastos, Márquez, Allende, Vargas Llosa and Omar Rivabella among others. If the normalization of Latin American politics continues, the writing of the immediate future may reflect a more personal and metaphysical tendency; and the work of women writers will increasingly come to the fore.

Prominent exponents of Magical Realist fiction (clockwise from top left) *are Isabel Allende, Gabriel García Márquez, Jorge Luis Borges and Mario Vargas Llosa.*

(1582–1658) and the magnificent Sor Juana Inés de la Cruz (1648–1695), a nun in Mexico, expert in astronomy, music and letters, driven to an early death by jealous religious superiors. More recently came Nicaraguan Rubén Darío (1867–1916), founder of Spanish "Modernism;" the surrealist Octavio Paz of Mexico (b.1914, *The Labyrinth of Solitude*, 1950), and the revered Pablo Neruda of Chile (1904–73). He was a genuine people's poet, whose *Twenty Love Poems and a Song of Despair* (1924) has affected the manner in which Latin Americans fall in love. Other great names are Gabriela Mistral of Chile, César Vallejo of Peru, Argentinian Ricardo Molinari and Borges whose *Ficciones* (1944) gave us perfect stories. Poetry in Latin America is not, as so often in Europe and America, for an elitist minority. As recent Central American political poetry

Latin America has a strong tradition of documentary non-fiction, owing much to the high standard of journalism that grew in the absence of tabloids. A seminal text was Euclides da Cunha's *Rebellion in the Backlands* (1902). Thought by many to be Brazil's greatest contribution to world literature, it details the progress of a brutal war against a band of religious mystics who began a new community at "Canudos." The book, dramatic, wise, bitter and humane, is of epic stature – a horrifying account of the atrocities the civilized can perpetrate against the half-civilized. More recently there have been small jewels like Carolina Maria de Jesús's *Child of the Dark* (1960), the diary of a desperately poor woman trying to survive in São Paulo's slums. Alonso Salazar's *Born to Die in Medellin* (1990) details the appalling way a generation of youth has been corrupted by the cocaine trade in Colombia.

Latin America has long produced notable poets. Early on were Peru's Francisco de Borja y Acevedo

shows (Roque Dalton, Claribal Alegría), it is a vibrant art, passionately pursued by almost everyone who can write, particularly in countries like Colombia, where the people are fabulously proud of the beauty, clarity and precision of their "Castellano."

Today the Latin American diaspora is producing its own literature. Luis Rodriguez's *Always Running* (1993) is an extraordinary memoir of gang life in chicano Los Angeles. Denise Chavez, a New Mexican writer, has broken new ground by writing an energetic, authentically Latino novel in English, *Face of An Angel* (1994). Notable Cuban exiles are Reinaldo Arenas and Guillermo Cabrera Infante, that wildly funny and linguistically exuberant writer (*Three Trapped Tigers*, 1967), who says he fell out with Castro because he would not smoke his own cigars. As the Mexican novelist Carlos Fuentes (*The Death of Artemio Cruz*, 1962) has argued, Latin America is still literature's fascinating New World, a place for new imaginative voyages of discovery.

THE WRITING OF AFRICA TODAY

The world spoke for so long of the "Dark Continent," full of "noble savages" beautiful in their animal-like grace and without history or culture, that correcting this calumnous impression became a key task for the new generation of black writers who emerged in the years up to and just following the era of post-colonial independence. Many were themselves products of a colonially based education, but this did not prevent independent thinking. In consequence schools like Government College, Umuahia, or universities like Ibadan became workshops for new writing and had their counterparts in Kenya and other parts of Southern Africa.

So the encounter with European and American culture greatly influenced the African writers who emerged in the 1950s. The early plays of Nigerian Wole Soyinka (b.1934) are indebted to the Greeks, to Bertolt Brecht and to Samuel Beckett. The first novels of fellow Nigerian Chinua Achebe (b.1930), *Things Fall Apart* (1958) and *No Longer At Ease* (1960), take their titles from poems by W.B. Yeats and T.S. Eliot. Paradoxically, these authors were at the same time determined to assess their own indigenous cultures which, as they could see with their own eyes and hear with their own ears, were far away from the uncreative heathenism ascribed to them in European books. They set about writing their own versions of the African past and present, derived from the stories, languages and festivals that surrounded them in their early lives.

Nigerian writers draw on the mythological history of their past when rivers like the one above *relied on the protection of gods.*

As Africa had few scripted languages before modern times, it was thought it had no literary inheritance. Yet oral traditions stretched back hundreds of years, expressed in a rich tapestry of story-telling, praise-poems, myths and proverbs. For domestic and celebratory occasions across the still largely rural continent, orality would be used in ways already faded or near-extinct in industrial societies. Though African writers felt potentially intimidated by the wealth of European literature when they expressed themselves in published form – usually in English, French or Portuguese – they quickly realized that their oral traditions more than compensated for their lack of written inheritance.

The first African novelist to make an international impact was Amos Tutuola (b.1920, Abeokuta, Nigeria), whose works imaginatively recreated stories literally heard at his Yoruba-speaking mother's knee. *The Palm-Wine Drinkard* (1952) required the support of no less than T.S. Eliot and Dylan Thomas to secure publication in a Britain suspicious of its unfamiliar grammatical constructions; it recounted the archetypal tale of a drunken man who follows his dead tapster into the next world and in his quest encounters scenes both comic and horrible, such as the deconstruction to a rolling skull of the "Complete Gentleman." Though later novels never had quite the same success, Tutuola has continued to be a prolific explorer of his story-telling culture in works like *The Witch-Herbalist of the Remote Town* (1981) and *Pauper, Brawler and Slanderer* (1987).

The oral tradition is such a living part of African life that it would be wrong to regard its permeating influence as nostalgic or artificial. African writers have sometimes been compared with Irish, but there has seldom been the conscious revival of old mythologies that writers like Yeats indulged. The animal tales and metaphors from the natural world that appear so often in Achebe's writing, the honouring of river deities in Elechi Amadi's, the storytelling framework of Ngugi wa Thiong'o's *Devil on the Cross* (1982) – all draw on a culture rooted in the present. The one major African author to set out to evoke a Golden Age partly of his own making was Léopold Sédar Senghor (b.1906), poet and later president of Senegal. A master of the French language, he saw, in ancient Egypt, in imported Hellenism and in the grand nobility of traditional African carving and bronzework, spiritual qualities which could be renewed as the continent sought to shape its post-colonial identity and culture.

Clockwise from top left: *Chinua Achebe, Wole Soyinka, Ngui wa Thiong'o and Amos Tutuola.*

Another important influence on African writing has been the popular literature sold cheaply in markets and on street corners. By the late 1940s this was vigorously evident in the main cities of East Africa. Though badly printed, with lurid titles (*How to Get a Lady in Love, Rosemary and the Taxi Driver*, and so on), these romances and moral homilies were important in developing the reading habit. Writers such as Nigerians Cyprian Ekwensi (b.1921) in *Jagua Nana* (1961), the tragic tale of a golden-hearted prostitute in Lagos, or Meja Mwangi (b.1948) in *Going Down River Road* (1976), set in the brothels of Nairobi, wrote about the risks of city life in a style both melodramatic and moralistic, vivacious and compassionate.

Two Nigerian writers raised modern African literature to a new level of popularity: Chinua Achebe (b.1930) and Wole Soyinka (b.1934). Achebe is best-known as a novelist, Soyinka as a playwright, but both have worked in many genres, particularly as poets and essayists, and supported the development of African writing. Both were politically active in opposing oppression in Nigeria: Achebe openly espoused the secessionist Biafra cause in the Nigerian Civil War (1967–70) and Soyinka was detained in prison for many months at this time (see his memoir *The Man Died*, 1973). Both live outside Nigeria, critical of the authoritarianism of the present military government. In 1986 Soyinka became the first African writer to win the Nobel Prize for Literature (subsequently won in 1988 by Naguib Mahfouz of Egypt and in 1991 by Nadine Gordimer of South Africa).

Achebe's quartet of early novels – *Things Fall Apart* (1958), *No Longer at Ease* (1960), *Arrow of God* (1964) and *A Man of the People* (1966) – can be read as a loose sequence spanning Nigerian history, from the first incursion inland by whites in the 1890s to the disillusioned aftermath of Independence in the mid-1960s. Each is different in form and language, but together with his novella *Girls at War* (1972) as a coda on the breakdown of civil order, they offer a potent critique of colonialism and self-rule. *Anthills of the Savannah* (1987) showed his narrative powers at their peak, in a masterly if pessimistic portrait of political implosion in contemporary Africa, with a faint hope offered by the role African women might play in the future. An Ibo speaker born at Ogidi, Eastern Nigeria, Achebe shows it is possible for English to be regenerated by the rhythms and similes of African language.

Soyinka's writings also scrutinize failures of leadership and political chaos, often with overt satirical intent. From *A Dance of the Forests* (1960), commissioned for Nigeria's Independence celebrations, to his *The Beatification of Area Boy* (1995), his plays have been devastating exposures of corruption in political affairs. Meticulous stagecraft and searing wit make him a major dramatist of modern times; he is also a novelist of philosophical interest,

Wole Soyinka's Beatification of Area Boy *was premièred, right, in England at the Leeds Playhouse in 1995.*

Lagos, above, is the setting for The Joys of Motherhood *by Buchi Emecheta (b.1944), the first novels of Ben Okri (b.1959) and Festus Iyayi (b.1947), and for a school of influential essayists led by Chinweizu (b.1943).*

notably in *The Interpreters* (1965), and a shrewd, tender autobiographer in *Aké: The Years of Childhood* (1981) and *Ibadan: The Penkelemes Years* (1994). The books are rooted in the places he knows best, the city of Abeokuta where he was born, and Ibadan. Most of his work, for all the network of other influences in it, is indebted to his Yoruba culture, which spreads across western Nigeria and is the source of much black expression globally.

Both writers belong to a generation of remarkable Nigerians writing around the time of Independence. It includes poets J.P. Clark (b.1935), Gabriel Okara (b.1921) and Christopher Okigbo (1932–67), whose death in the Civil War was recognized as a profound loss to modern poetry in English. Other leaders of this talented group of writers are Elechi Amadi (b.1934), whose stories like *The Concubine* (1966) about the river gods and village rivalries in the area near Port Harcourt derive from ancient customs and beliefs, and Flora Nwapa (1931–92), the first woman writer in Africa to be widely known. But West Africa is not confined to Nigeria. Ghana produced a

Ghana's Ayi Kwei Armah's most famous novel The Beautyful Ones Are Not Yet Born *(1968), near right, thinly disguises the Accra of Kwame Nkrumah's time in an abrasive, neo-existentialist critique of classical authority. Kenyan Ngugi' wa Thiong'o's* Grain of Wheat, *far right, was published in English in 1967.*

major novelist in Ayi Kwei Armah (b.1939), whose complex, often socialist yet metaphysical books are tragic statements about African sensibility. French-speaking Senegal not only produced in Senghor one of the great modern French-language poets, but novelists of stature, including two women, Aminata Sow Fall (b.1941), author of *The Beggars' Strike* (1979), and Mariama Bâ (1929-81), whose *So Long a Letter* (1979) is one of the most trenchant insights into the marital status of African women.

In East Africa the outstanding writer has been Kenya's Ngugi wa Thiong'o, formerly James Ngugi (b.1938). His work moved from a semi-Christian position to a committed Marxism; in consequence he has lived in exile for some twenty years. His fiction stays firmly derived from the landscape and village life of Kenya, particularly the Kikuyu-speaking area round Limuru, where he was born. After years of writing outstanding novels in English (*Petals of Blood*, 1977, is an epic description of political corruption and redemption), he turned to the Kikuyu language in later fiction like *Devil on the Cross* (1982) and *Matagari* (1987). His change of language became a *cause célèbre* in African literary debate, focusing attention on the authenticity of works written in European rather than indigenous languages.

Many feel that the real promise of African writing lies in southern Africa, especially in South Africa. During the struggle for independence in Zimbabwe most intellectuals fought in the bush or lived abroad, returning after 1980, almost immediately producing stimulating work. Most prominent was Dambudzo Marechera (1955–87), whose prize-winning story collection *The House of Hunger* (1978) reflected the violence of life in the township where he grew up. Wilson Katiya (b.1947), S. Nyamfukudza (b.1951) and Chenjerai Hove (b.1956) all made their mark writing of the tensions between generations and between tradition and modernity inherent in most societies, but especially those undergoing the turmoil of revolutionary change.

Ben Okri, far left, *who now lives in England, is the most impressive younger writer to have emerged from modern Nigeria, as much at home in an epic legend-based fantasy like the Booker Prize-winning* The Famished Road *(1991) as in some masterly short stories and his novel,* Songs of Enchantment *(1993), near left.*

New writers emerge all the time in Africa. In recent times those who have won attention include from Nigeria, the poet Niyi Osundare (b.1947) and the satirist Ken Saro-Wiwa (1941–95), whose unjust execution enraged international opinion; and from Ghana Kojo Laing (b.1946), and the Mauritian writer Lindsay Collen (b.1948), whose novel *The Rape of Sita* (1993) was banned in her country for offending Hindu fundamentalists. Challenges to African writers include severe censorship regulations and the poor circulation of books – making it likely that some of the best writers like Somalia's

Nuruddin Farah (b.1945), author of *Maps* (1986), and Tanzania's Adbulrazak Gurnah (b.1948), author of *Paradise* (1994), will live outside their countries, for protection or better publishing opportunities.

For a continent long dismissed as primitive, which has lately been largely interpreted in terms of its tyrannies, wars, famines and poverty, it is a marvellous corrective to see the first-rate literature which exists all over Africa. As African art and music has affected other world arts, so now its writers affect world literature. Yet every African writer identifies with a particular place with its own history and this is probably the greatest example it gives to increasingly deracinated and alienated Western authors.

AFRICA: *Many African writers draw on their native home for material. Chinua Achebe, for example, uses fictional names (shown in italics on the map) for real places in his novels.*

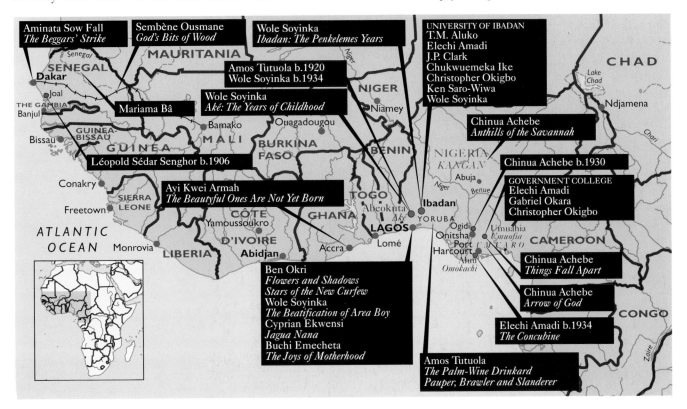

CANADIAN IMAGES

Some cities have had more than their share of literary luck. Inexplicable cultural forces mix with real historical and social change to create places where for a time the work of writers reaches critical mass, then transforms the whole language and cultural tradition. The New England of the American Renaissance and the Dublin of the Celtic Revival are notable examples. A recent case is Toronto, the young Canadian city on Lake Ontario where, from around 1967 into the eighties, an explosion of new literary talent occurred which has given it a noted place in any list of key centres of English-language writing.

The Toronto writers who came to maturity over this time include Margaret Atwood, Carol Bolt, Barry Callaghan, Austin Clark, Matt Cohen, Timothy Findley, David French, Joy Kogawa, Dennis Lee, Gwendolyn McEwen, Graham Gibson, Eli Mandel, Michael Ondaatje, Judith Thomson, George F. Walker and Richard Wright. Although she lived for a time on the Canadian West Coast, in Vancouver and Victoria, Ontario-born novelist and short story writer Alice Munro (b.1931) kept an office in Toronto and did some of her writing in the city.

Robertson Davies (1913–95) was an internationally known novelist and playwright and a fine, ironic Canadian chronicler well before the eighties. Between 1962 and 1980 he was Master of Massey College at the University of Toronto, a neo-Gothic campus founded in 1827, still pleasantly placed mid-town near the provincial Parliament buildings. An important centre of Canadian intellectual activity, Toronto has also had – as Davies's novels (some of them set there) suggest – a distinct flavour of conservatism. If a new breed of Canadian authors based largely in the city sought for the first time to tell overtly Canadian stories in a Canadian voice, this was scarcely noticed by the university's academics – with a few influential exceptions. The poet Earle Birney (b.1904) taught here in the 1940s, and

In the 1970s the distinctive silos and railroad tracks by the harbour in Toronto were knocked down to make way for Harbourfront, above, *a postmodern development of condominiums, hotels, stores, cafés and marinas. With government aid, it also suddenly became a centre for the seat-of-the-pants arts activity that was developing all over the city, and the most popular arts venue in Canada.*

encouraged a whole new generation of poets. So did Northrop Frye, author of *Anatomy of Criticism* (1957), who frequently turned his mind from studies of Blake and the *Bible* to his own country's literature (to the dismay of many of his academic colleagues). A fellow-professor was Marshall McLuhan (1911–80), author of *The Gutenberg Galaxy* (1962) and warm supporter of the *avant-garde*. Although he never directly engaged in the study of Canadian literature, he drew the attention of critics worldwide with his mysterious arguments and oracular pronouncements ("The medium is the message") and lent new Canadian writers a confidence that, without him, might have been a little shakier.

These new writers were driven by various emotions, some negative. They found it absurd that a city so materially wealthy and booming had remained culturally parochial. Toronto was, even in Canadian terms, a late-founded city, set up in 1793 as a defensive site to protect British Canada against its more powerful neighbour after the American Revolution. It was home to little more than a few Indian dwellings, a couple of log cabins and a tent; yet its founding governor and his wife both wrote poetry. By 1837 the city was large and noble enough to welcome its first eminent literary visitor, Captain Frederick Marryat, who, like many British travellers on the continent, found it a decided relief after touring the United States. Charles Dickens was glad to arrive there after his depressed American tour of 1842, praising it as "full of life and motion, bustle, business, and improvement" in his *American Notes* (1842).

As refugees from the Highland Clearances and the Irish potato famine swelled the population and city in the nineteenth century, the band of foreign literary visitors swelled too, including Mark Twain, William Dean Howells, Matthew Arnold, Henry James and Arthur Conan Doyle. Around the end of the century, a small band of Torontonians began to acquire a degree of literary fame: Robert Barr, Ernest Thompson Seton, Marshall Saunders, Sarah Jeannette Duncan. In this century writers with Toronto connections include novelists Morley Callaghan and Mazo de la Roche and poets E.J. Pratt and John McCrae.

But Toronto remained more notable for literary hospitality than for its own achievements. William Faulkner, who revered the Canadian war ace Billy Bishop, came as a twenty-year-old Southerner to Toronto in July 1918, to train as a pilot with the Canadian Expeditionary Force for the RAF. In order to appear Canadian (as an American he could not legally join up), he assumed a British accent, acquired a false family history and added an English "u" to the spelling of his name. Fortunately for literature, it was in Toronto that he turned from his first literary aim of writing Keatsian poetry to writing fiction. By the time he returned to Oxford, Mississippi, he had constructed several more stories about himself, including claims to various flying missions, even an account of himself as a wounded airman, which served him in great stead back home.

But Ernest Hemingway did win his wound, on the Italian front in 1918. After his return to Chicago as an unemployed hero, he went to Toronto (153 Lyndhurst Avenue) to take a job as a journalist on the *Toronto Star Weekly*. The *Star* sent him to Paris as European correspondent and so financed his early stories. After a couple of years he returned to Toronto and lived at 1599 Bathurst Street. Here Sylvia Beach, from the Shakespeare Bookshop in Paris, sent copies of James Joyce's *Ulysses*, then banned in the United States but not in Canada. From his Toronto cache of Joycean contraband, Hemingway smuggled in ones and twos all the copies of the first edition purchased by American subscribers. "Someday someone will live here and be able to appreciate the feeling with which I launched *Ulysses* on the States (not a copy lost) from this city," he was able to boast.

When Montreal, top, *hosted a world fair, Expo '67, it stirred national pride as nothing had before, and a people raised to middling self-esteem and culturally dominated not just by Britain but the nearby weight of the world's biggest mass-culture exporter acquired greater faith in their own worth. The concrete buildings in the photograph,* above, *where built for the Fair.*

Eventually Hemingway was glad to go back to Paris Bohemia, in part because Toronto still thought like a province. A Briton (or any citizen from a powerful country) can hardly imagine never having studied in school the national history or literature. Till the 1970s it was the norm in English-Canada, however, for students to know nothing about their nation's past. By not teaching these things, schools succeeded in making Canadians think they were culturally inferior, had little history, no stories worth telling. The cultural amnesia affected writing. Canadian poetry for the first half of the century generally moved down a single track: from imitation of British models to imitation of American ones. Into the 1960s older Canadian novelists would often set their

Margaret Atwood, above, and Michael Ondaatje, left, wrote their novels from the streets of Toronto in the 1970s and 1980s.

stories abroad, because of publishers' fears that a native setting would harm sales. Wyndham Lewis (1882–1957), Vorticist writer and painter, lived in Toronto in 1940–43, at the Tudor Hotel at 559 Sherbourne Street (it caught fire during his stay). He had mixed feelings about the city, and once called it a "sanctimonious icebox."

The literary revival of the sixties, which matched new artistic trends in other post-imperial countries, like Australia, was partly a reaction to this older arid Toronto, but also to the optimism produced by the Expo '67 Fair in Montreal. The Fair created a newly energized *zeitgeist* which entered writing, spawning a fresh generation of poets, playwrights, short story writers and novelists. Most were young, and able to explore a past largely denied them, a present which was virtually unwritten. The fact that Toronto was near-virgin literary ground proved a major stimulus. Groups formed, new magazines began. An early road-block was the attitude of established Canadian publishing houses, who seemed to believe that every good writer fled the country – Mavis Gallant, Brian Moore and Mordecai Richler all did in the 1950s – and any that remained were by definition second-rate. New writers started to publish themselves, learning how to typeset, print, bind, sell their own books. Young publishers sprang up; in the high-rise, downtown Toronto core were born Coach House Press, House of Anansi Press, new press, Press Porcepic, Black Moss Press, Lester & Orpen Dennys. With such houses writers like Margaret

Atwood (*The Circle Game*, 1966), Michael Ondaatje (*Coming Through Slaughter*, 1976), Matt Cohen (*Korsoniloff*, 1969), Graeme Gibson, and Timothy Findley (*The Last of the Crazy People*, 1967) published early books. An older house, McClelland and Stewart (on Hollinger Road), became committed, under Jack McClelland, to publishing newer Canadian writers; Macmillan of Canada supported Robertson Davies and Alice Munro. In response to the new wave, the big international publishing conglomerates began their own Canadian imprints.

Writers' institutions have always played a larger part in Canadian life than most, fighting for cultural funds from the federal and provincial governments. Most were in Toronto, now chief centre of the English-language culture. Here the League of Canadian Poets was conceived in 1967, and marked its birth a year later with the city's first Poetry Festival. In 1973 the Writers' Union of Canada and the Playwrights' Union were founded. All are located at 24 Ryerson Avenue, also home to the Writers' Development Trust, an offbeat literary funding agency, started by a small group of Toronto authors led by novelist Graeme Gibson. In the same building is Canadian PEN (an organization concerned with writers imprisoned for political reasons), revivified by Margaret Atwood.

Also born in the 1970s was Harbourfront, the federal government-created arts and recreation area on the Toronto waterfront. In June 1974 the Harbourfront Reading Series (235 Queen's Quay West) began a weekly programme. In 1980 it became the venue for an annual International Festival of Authors which to date has attracted more than 2,500 authors from over eighty countries.

The cultural developments of the sixties and seventies were sorely needed; the results have been formidable. The country now has forceful writers' organizations, a literary festival of world repute, publishers confidently printing its national authors, good literary magazines like *Exile*, fine bookstores on Queen Street West. Above all it has major and distinctive literary figures: Josef Skvorecky, Margaret Atwood, Michael Ondaatje, Timothy Findley, and new writers like Paul Quarrington (*Whale Music*, 1990), Barbara Gowdy and Katherine Govier (*Hearts of Flame*, 1991). They write of cultural struggle, complexity and difficulty: Atwood of the need to flee and surface again, Ondaatje (born in Sri Lanka) of the plurality of identities. Part of the story they tell is that cultural identity today is a struggle rather than fact, and Canada is fast-changing. A new Toronto now lies over the old one: the colonial city has become a cosmopolitan and multi-cultural place. Between 1967 and 1980 the whole nature of English-Canadian experience and its cultural texture transformed. The new writers were part of the cause of the revolution, and also its essential chroniclers.

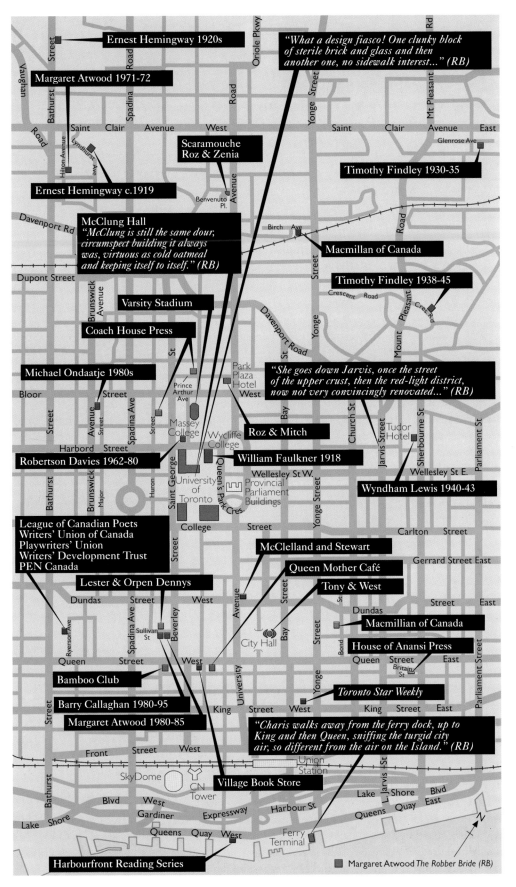

Ernest Hemingway 1920s

Margaret Atwood 1971-72

"What a design fiasco! One clunky block of sterile brick and glass and then another one, no sidewalk interest..." (RB)

Scaramouche
Roz & Zenia

Ernest Hemingway c.1919

Timothy Findley 1930-35

McClung Hall
"McClung is still the same dour, circumspect building it always was, virtuous as cold oatmeal and keeping itself to itself." (RB)

Macmillan of Canada

Timothy Findley 1938-45

Varsity Stadium

Coach House Press

Michael Ondaatje 1980s

"She goes down Jarvis, once the street of the upper crust, then the red-light district, now not very convincingly renovated..." (RB)

Roz & Mitch

Robertson Davies 1962-80

William Faulkner 1918

Wyndham Lewis 1940-43

League of Canadian Poets
Writers' Union of Canada
Playwriters' Union
Writers' Development Trust
PEN Canada

McClelland and Stewart

Queen Mother Café

Lester & Orpen Dennys

Tony & West

Macmillian of Canada

House of Anansi Press

Bamboo Club

Barry Callaghan 1980-95

Margaret Atwood 1980-85

Toronto Star Weekly

"Charis walks away from the ferry dock, up to King and then Queen, sniffing the turgid city air, so different from the air on the Island." (RB)

Village Book Store

Harbourfront Reading Series

Margaret Atwood *The Robber Bride* (RB)

Robertson Davies, above, published his first novel Tempest-Tost, *the opening volume of his* Salterton Trilogy *of Canadian life, in 1951. However, when he started his* Deptford Trilogy *with* Fifth Business *in 1970 he took on new literary energy.*

TORONTO: *As the critic Northrop Frye once said, writing always began with the local; and in the sixties, for the first time Canada was developing a confident and nationalistic literary culture. It had a series of writers' groups located at Ryerson Avenue and the Harbourfront cultural centre. Among the many writers who wrote of the city was Margaret Atwood – some key settings of* The Robber Bride (1993) *are shown here.*

Lake Ontario

EVERYWHERE THE WIND BLOWS: AFRICAN-AMERICAN WRITING TODAY

Ignited by the Harlem Renaissance of the 1920s, and the optimism for human and civil rights it embodied, the African-American writers of the modern period have sought to exercise the full dimensions of the long-promised equality. No longer is their literature confined in any geographical way. Indeed the twentieth century American technological revolution and the northward (and eventually westward) migration it spawned, coupled with increasing levels of educational achievement by greater numbers of African-Americans and the end of legal racial segregation after the Civil Rights struggles of the 1960s, gave to their fiction, poetry and drama a spirit not just of literary but of geographical diversity that is still evolving.

New York is still its locus, but contemporary African-American writers have grown up and written about their experiences throughout the United States. Of course there remains a rather strong connection to the American South – the place of transition and sorrow for many African-Americans. Much contemporary literature written by African-Americans is an attempt to recall and reconcile this history. The writers of the Harlem Renaissance were anxious to put slavery and its legacy behind them. And while the rural South continues to be of major interest to African-Americans, it is the urban Northeast and the industrial Midwest that have dominated much of their fiction. Indeed the juxtaposing of rural and urban experiences has typified a fair portion of this writing. James Baldwin's first novel *Go Tell It On the Mountain* (1953) is one example, moving effortlessly from New York City to Mississippi.

Sugar cane plantations, like the one above in Louisiana, remain a strong image in the minds of African-American writers. From Jean Toomer to Zora Neale Hurston to Ernest Gaines, sugar cane is as prominent a symbol as any in the urban environment.

No writer better shows the rise of the African-American voice than Toni Morrison, born in 1931 in Lorain, a small town in Ohio. Her novels – *Sula* (1973), *Song of Solomon* (1977), *Tar Baby* (1981) *Beloved* (1987) and *Jazz* (1992) – culminated in the first Nobel Prize in Literature awarded to an African-American writer. *Beloved*, although infused with all the southern energy of Jean Toomer's *Cane* (1924) or Zora Neale Hurston's *Their Eyes Were Watching God* (1934), takes place instead in America's heartland, Ohio. It documents the price of freedom, the run from slavery along the underground railroad, the struggles against the terrors of racism. Toni Morrison captures the challenge faced by African-Americans to take control of their own lives: in particular the triumph of black women over extraordinary obstacles.

The South still has its important African-American writers. Ernest J. Gaines (whose work is sometimes compared with Faulkner's) was born in 1933 in Oscar, Louisiana, a multi-cultured region where several of his novels are set. His *The Autobiography of Miss Jane Pittman* (1971) takes place in the earliest stages of the struggle for integration and civil rights. The story turns on a moment when a thirsty Jane Pittman bends down to drink from a "Whites Only" water fountain. Another book by Gaines, *A Gathering of Old Men* (1983), takes place in contemporary times (the 1970s), and is set on a Louisiana sugar cane

Toni Morrison, left, *brought the voice of African-American writers to a larger audience when she was awarded the Nobel Prize for Literature in 1993.*

plantation. It is interesting how many books by black authors, contemporary and historical, locate their stories amid the cane: one would think it would be cotton.

But African-American novels stretch now far beyond the boundaries of the plantation and the small southern town. There are many stories which chronicle the interactions of blacks in the white world. And this is a time when African-American literary critics with stature, such as Henry Louis Gates, Jr, Houston Baker, Jr, and Shirley Anne Williams, to name but a few, have validated the significance and essentiality of African-American literature as a fundamental aspect of the American canon.

The literature of African-Americans has been deeply influenced by social and political trends. For example, the Black Arts Movement of the mid–1960s through to the mid-1970s was infused with rising anger, as the patient wait for equality seemed destined for frustration. The staunch dependence on the non-violent push for Civil Rights espoused by Martin Luther King, Jr, was slowly given over to the militancy of political activists such as the Black Panther Party and Malcolm X (*The Autobiography of Malcolm X*, 1965). Le Roi Jones changed his name to Amiri Baraka and wrote plays for black audiences. Polemical books by Angela Davis, Eldridge Cleaver and Stokeley Carmichael explored political strategies.

From the 1940s on, important new work had already appeared. Books like Margaret Walker's (b.1915) poetic *For My People* (1942), Ann Petry's (b.1908) *The Street* (1942), a story of Harlem, the novels of Richard Wright (*Native Son*, 1940), Ralph Ellison (*Invisible Man*, 1952) and James Baldwin (*Another Country*, 1962) advanced African-American writing towards the seventies. John Oliver Killens' (1916–87) *And Then We Heard the Thunder* (1962) dealt with segregation in the army; Margaret Walker's

"This girl Beloved, homeless and without people, beat all, though he couldn't say exactly why, considering the coloured people he had run into during the last twenty years. During, before and after the War he had seen Negroes so stunned, or hungry, or tired or bereft it was a wonder they recalled or said anything. Who, like him, had hidden in caves and fought owls for food; who, like him, stole from pigs; who, like him, slept in trees in the day and walked by night; who, like him had buried themselves in slop and jumped in wells to avoid regulators, raiders, patrollers, veterens, hill men, posses and merry makers.... Only once had it been possible for him to stay in one spot – with a woman, or a family – for longer than a few months. That once was almost two years with a weaver lady in Delaware, the meanest place for Negroes he had ever seen outside Pulaski Country, Kentucky, and of course the prison camp in Georgia."

Beloved, Toni Morrison

Jubilee (1966) told of a people's history out of slavery. And when John A. Williams (b.1925) wrote *The Man Who Cried I Am* (1967) – a novel that traverses the globe, beginning in Manhattan in the 1960s, but more significantly taking in Leiden and Stockholm – he showed the world, as Richard Wright and James Baldwin had already, that African-Americans were no longer confined to city ghettos.

Ishmael Reed's (b.1938) satire *Mumbo Jumbo* (1972) takes place in 1920s New Orleans, and shows the spread of African-American culture as the people become infected by "Jes Grew," a kind of dance craze that takes over the body:

"With the astonishing rapidity of Booker T. Washington's Grapevine Telegraph Jes Grew spreads through America following a strange course. Pine Bluff and Magnolia Arkansas are hit. Natchez, Meridian and Greenwood Mississippi report cases. Sporadic outbreaks occur in Nashville and Knoxville Tennessee as well as St Louis where the bumping and grinding cause the Gov to call up the Guard. A mighty influence, Jes Grew infects all that it touches."

Reed has pioneered the development of characters and stories which defy any limitations. Indeed his use of history, time and location makes his stories special. From New Orleans to Richmond, Virginia, to Yellow Back Radio (*Yellow Back Radio Broke Down*, 1969) we are transported beyond the boundaries of realism. Ishmael extends our notion of who African-Americans are and where they live.

Recently there has been Randall Kenan (b.1963) who wrote *Let the Dead Bury Their Dead* (1992). He is another marvellous example of a contemporary writer who has managed to catch the rich texture of Southern experience. His collection of short stories is set in the North Carolina town of Tims Creek, and they capture all the magic and complexity of life there. John Edgar Wideman's (b.1941) *Philadelphia Fire* (1990) is closely set around West Philadelphia's University City neighbourhood, under the

John Edgar Wideman's Philadelphia Fire *concentrates on a tragedy in the history of Philadelphia, above, when the radical black back-to-nature movement was bombed by the city's police.*

shadow of the University. Then there's the National Book Award winner Charles S. Johnson's *Middle Passage* (1991), which starts in the steamy city of New Orleans and takes its central black character out to sea in one of the first successful novels about the traumatic journey African-Americans made across the Atlantic.

Recent African-American literature, especially in the eighties and early nineties, has been dominated by the women. Alice Walker (b.1944) with *The Color Purple* (1982; made into a feature film by Stephen Spielberg) told in its own distinctive language a story which underscored the struggle of black women in the rough, raw post-slavery South. Gloria Naylor (b.1950), with her *Women of Brewster Place: A Novel in Seven Stories* (1982; made into a television movie co-starring Ophrah Winfrey), set in a decaying apartment block, spoke about the urban struggle of black women to survive. Ntozake Shange (b.1948), in her seminal "choreopoem," *For Colored Girls Who Have Considered Suicide When the Rainbow Is Enuf*, produced on Broadway in 1976, captured the volatile issues nested in the relationships between black men and women, and explored the flavour of many regional influences, bringing blues together with salsa, Chicago jazz with urban New York funk. Maya Angelou's (b.1928) career began with her early life-story in *I Know Why the Caged Bird Sings* (1969) and maybe culminated in her poem, "In the Dawn of Morning," read at the inauguration of President Clinton. Rita Dove (b.1952) was appointed Poet Laureate of the United States in 1993, renewed in 1994 and 1995, and became a Pulitzer Prize winner for *Thomas and Bewlah* (1986), a series of poems following the title figures from Southern origins to Akron, Ohio.

Alice Walker is shown above *in 1986 being presented by singer Tom Waits with the Purple Globe Award in recognition of her contribution to literature. Her novels concentrate on the struggle by black women to survive in a hostile environment.*

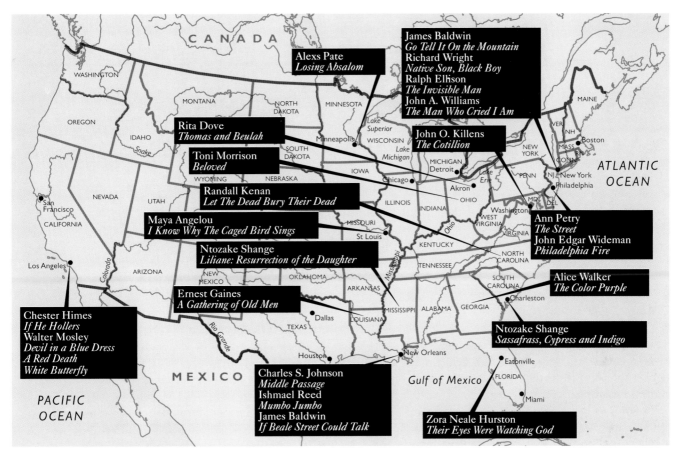

CANADA

James Baldwin
Go Tell It On the Mountain
Richard Wright
Native Son, Black Boy
Ralph Ellison
The Invisible Man
John A. Williams
The Man Who Cried I Am

Alexs Pate
Losing Absalom

John O. Killens
The Cotillion

Rita Dove
Thomas and Beulah

Toni Morrison
Beloved

Randall Kenan
Let The Dead Bury Their Dead

Maya Angelou
I Know Why The Caged Bird Sings

Ntozake Shange
Liliane: Resurrection of the Daughter

Ann Petry
The Street
John Edgar Wideman
Philadelphia Fire

Ernest Gaines
A Gathering of Old Men

Alice Walker
The Color Purple

Chester Himes
If He Hollers
Walter Mosley
Devil in a Blue Dress
A Red Death
White Butterfly

Ntozake Shange
Sassafrass, Cypress and Indigo

Charles S. Johnson
Middle Passage
Ishmael Reed
Mumbo Jumbo
James Baldwin
If Beale Street Could Talk

Zora Neale Hurston
Their Eyes Were Watching God

PACIFIC OCEAN

ATLANTIC OCEAN

Gulf of Mexico

MEXICO

THE UNITED STATES: *The map shows how contemporary African-American writers have widened the locale for their fictions to include the north of the United States as well as the south.*

By the mid-nineties, two African-American writers seem to have particularly captured the public's attention: Walter Mosley (b.1952) and Terry McMillan (b.1951). Mosley – President Clinton's favourite mystery writer – wrote *Devil in a Blue Dress* (1990, made into a feature film), *A Red Death* (1991) and *White Butterfly* (1992) which brought to life a time and the social circumstances of the black community in Los Angeles, little written of before.

Terry McMillan's *Waiting to Exhale* (1992) is one of the best-selling novels ever written by a black writer – a contemporary story of four women dealing with their families, loves and friendships. One striking thing is the strength of its location; it puts African-Americans in Phoenix and Denver among other places, while also underscoring the way the African-American "eye" still has a particular way of "seeing," no matter where it is located:

"My baby sister has also never appreciated or understood taking real risks, so she wasn't all that thrilled when I called her two weeks ago to tell her I was moving to Phoenix. 'Why would anybody in their right mind want to live in Arizona?' she asked me. 'Are there any black folks out there? And isn't it where that governor rescinded the King holiday after it had already been passed?' I had to remind her that my best friend, Bernadine – the girl who was my roommate in college, the girl

whose wedding I drove sixty miles in a snowstorm to get to because I was her bridesmaid — lives in Scottsdale. She been black all her life, and she seems to like it there. And as far as the King holiday goes, all I could say was that I'd be one of the first people at the polls when the time came."

In my own novel, *Losing Absalom* (1995), we first meet Absalom's son, Sonny, in an office in Minneapolis, and end up with the entire family in North Philadelphia. But the fact that Sonny now works in Minneapolis and has to come back home to Pennsylvania is the point. The experiences of today's African-American writers have taken them deeper into their communities and dispersed them further into the outer reaches of American society. From the abstract magic realism of Ishmael Reed to the largely white spaces of Terry McMillan's Phoenix, black writers are finding themselves and their energies focused on a new terrain.

Walter Mosley, shown above *reading from one of his books, wrote a series of novels set in the 1940s in the South Central Los Angeles black community.*

MANHATTAN TALES:
WHO'S AFRAID OF TOM WOLFE?

Our young novelist has made up his mind: enough procrastination. Tom Wolfe has thrown down the gauntlet, and our novelist intends to pick it up: he will write the New York Novel to End All New York Novels – from Wall Street to the Village to Midtown to Uppers East and West; to Harlem, to...anyway, he'll find out what comes after Harlem in the course of his research.

Our novelist has finally cringed in self-recognition at Wolfe's pivotal 1989 manifesto ("Stalking the Billion-Footed Beast") calling for fat, documentary, realistic, social novels (eerily like his own *Bonfire of the Vanities*). At first our novelist dismissed Wolfe's essay as a piece of unseemly triumphalism. No, he said to himself, he would stick to stories of the rural Midwest (he had looked out the window at vast tracts of rural Midwest while attending a creative writing programme), and to guys who pumped gas, gals who smoked menthols, and that frisson of trick banality near the end where the male protagonist drops his beer can and the reader realizes the poor slob's mother has been dying all along.

Our novelist thought Wolfe's presumption was patently offensive. Had James Joyce insisted that everyone spend the next 17 years writing huge volumes of impenetrable word-play about Ireland? Gradually, though, Wolfe's words had begun to sink in: "...a novel of the city, in the sense that Balzac and Zola had written novels of Paris and Dickens and Thackeray had written novels of London, with the city always in the foreground, exerting its relentless pressure on the souls of its inhabitants." His wrists ache just thinking about trying to describe the Manhattan skyline in prose to someone who has never seen it. Over coffee and bagels, his typewriter resonating with potential, he looks again at Wolfe's novel.

It isn't as if Wolfe's writing style needed a boost of adrenaline in the first place, but Manhattan does something to almost everyone's prose. The exclamation marks! *The italics!* The repetition, the restating of things, the refrains, the saying of things four times! And so, breathlessly, the reader is guided along the fateful path of Sherman McCoy, bond trader at a time when bond traders earned so much money it was almost impossible to look down on them any longer. It was also a time when the gap between rich and poor was less a "gulf," as it was usually called, than a Marianas Trench. Wolfe's coup, he would have our novelist believe, was to research the underbelly of New York, to go to the worst possible place, then write about it. No New Yorker would have had any

The awesome Manhattan skyline at night, left: our novelist resolves to refer allusively to "screaming spires."

MANHATTAN MID 1980S...*in two dimensions, a grid pulsating with potential for our novelist's masterpiece. In it, he will plagiarize Martin Amis's low-life, Jay McInerney's night-life, Tom Wolfe's world of high-finance, Paul Auster's aimless walks through the city, Brett Easton Ellis's unflinching violence.*

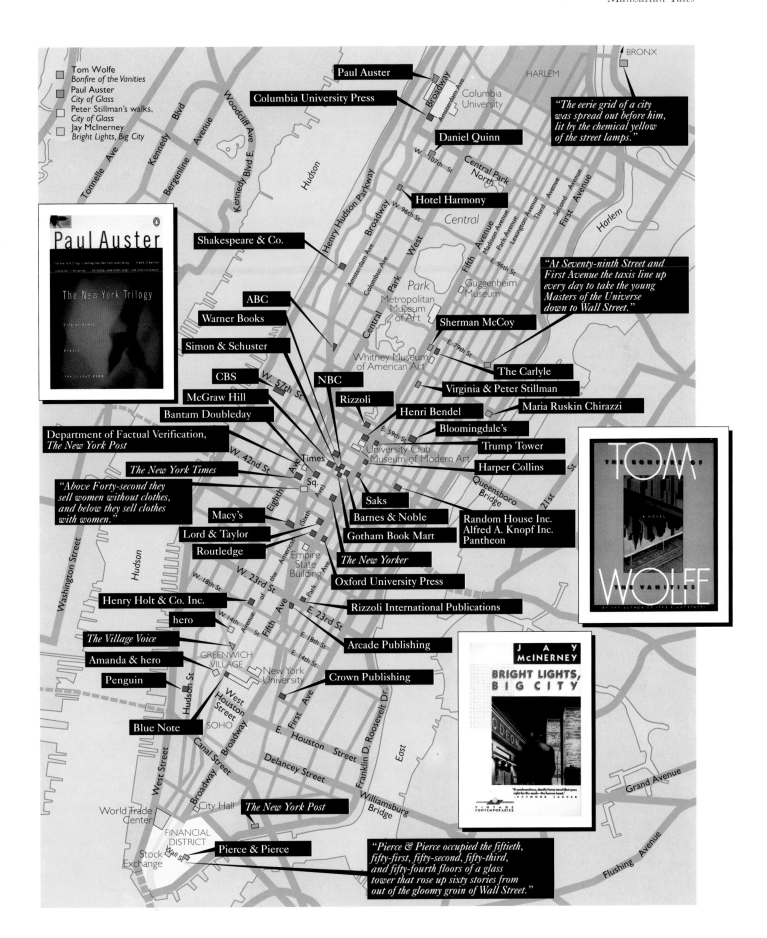

BRONX

HARLEM

□ Tom Wolfe
  Bonfire of the Vanities
□ Paul Auster
  City of Glass
□ Peter Stillman's walks,
  City of Glass
□ Jay McInerney
  Bright Lights, Big City

Paul Auster

Columbia University Press

Columbia University

Daniel Quinn

"The eerie grid of a city was spread out before him, lit by the chemical yellow of the street lamps."

Hotel Harmony

Central

Shakespeare & Co.

Guggenheim Museum

"At Seventy-ninth Street and First Avenue the taxis line up every day to take the young Masters of the Universe down to Wall Street."

Metropolitan Museum of Art

Park

ABC

Warner Books

Simon & Schuster

Sherman McCoy

Whitney Museum of American Art

The Carlyle

Virginia & Peter Stillman

CBS

NBC

McGraw Hill

Rizzoli

Maria Ruskin Chirazzi

Bantam Doubleday

Henri Bendel

Department of Factual Verification, *The New York Post*

Bloomingdale's

University Club
Museum of Modern Art

Trump Tower

The New York Times

Times Sq.

Harper Collins

"Above Forty-second they sell women without clothes, and below they sell clothes with women."

Queensboro Bridge

Saks

Macy's

Barnes & Noble

Random House Inc.
Alfred A. Knopf Inc.
Pantheon

Lord & Taylor

Gotham Book Mart

Routledge

Empire State Building

The New Yorker

Oxford University Press

Henry Holt & Co. Inc.

Rizzoli International Publications

hero

The Village Voice

Arcade Publishing

Amanda & hero

GREENWICH VILLAGE

Penguin

New York University

Crown Publishing

Blue Note

SOHO

Delancey Street

Williamsburg Bridge

Grand Avenue

World Trade Center

City Hall

The New York Post

FINANCIAL DISTRICT

Stock Exchange

Pierce & Pierce

"Pierce & Pierce occupied the fiftieth, fifty-first, fifty-second, fifty-third, and fifty-fourth floors of a glass tower that rose up sixty stories from out of the gloomy groin of Wall Street."

Flushing Avenue

Paul Auster

The New York Trilogy

THE BONFIRE OF THE VANITIES
TOM WOLFE
A NOVEL

JAY McINERNEY
BRIGHT LIGHTS, BIG CITY
ODEON

[315]

Tom Wolfe, near left has thrown down the gauntlet, calling for fat, documentary, social novels (writing of Wall Street, far left, for instance); our novelist has picked it up.

difficulty in agreeing with Wolfe that the South Bronx was the supreme candidate for that honour. The clash between Sherman and Manhattan's evil twin uptown drives the plot along through a circus of political, racial, financial and legal drama. Sherman is destroyed not so much by his own mistakes and hubris as by the relentless, chaotic machinery of the city itself. One passage from *Bonfire* is so central to understanding why Wolfe wrote the novel that he quotes it in his manifesto:

"The towers were jammed together so tightly, he could feel the mass and stupendous weight. Just think of the millions, from all over the globe, who yearned to be on that island, in those towers, in those narrow streets. There it was, the Rome, the Paris, the London of the twentieth century, the city of ambition, the dense magnetic rock, the irresistible destination of all those who insist on being where things are happening."

Our novelist agrees. It is thrilling to know that the material of a novel sprouts all around him, begging to be harvested. He decides to stretch his legs before writing his great masterpiece, the Dickensian opening line of which is already lodged in his mind: "Manhattan." He goes out to buy the *New York Post*, secret vice of the cognoscenti: WHALE SWALLOWS CABBIE! This reminds him of an earlier novel of the period, Jay McInerney's *Bright Lights, Big City* (1984), in which the *Post*'s headlines feature symbolically (COMA BABY LIVES). The novel's unnamed "hero," followed about somewhat jarringly in the second person plural, falls prey to the overly social Tad Allagash and, excused by cuckolding and bereavement, drinks booze and snorts cocaine, until his boss justifiably sacks him from his job as fact checker for a literary magazine indistinguishable from *The New Yorker*. Written in light, almost conversational prose, the novel gives the reader a glimpse – authentic, our novelist can attest – into the delectable and demeaning temptations of the Manhattan night when so many of the privileged young had too much money and too few original ideas about how it should be spent.

Our novelist walks uptown on the sunny side of Seventh Avenue South – recalling that characters do a lot of walking in Manhattan novels, calling out street and avenue names to themselves – and passes a pair of beautiful girls. One of them – wearing her father's Brooks Brothers button-down shirt, black leggings, white trainers and sunglasses – could be Alison Poole, from McInerney's second Manhattan novel, *Story of My Life* (1988). Twenty-year-old Alison narrates the story in a ghastly, hard-nosed, illiterate voice perfectly pitched to a would-be-actress daughter of oft-divorced, distant, *nouveau-riche* parents. Her preoccupations are men, cocaine, her bastard of a father, then men and cocaine again. Her New York, like that of her predecessor in *Bright Lights*, is nocturnal, subterranean and out of focus. Her breathtaking selfishness is as repellent as her depressing monologue is compelling. Our novelist resolves to make all his female characters vacuous, beautiful, promiscuous would-be actresses or models. And then kill them off, he thinks, remembering Bret Easton Ellis's *American Psycho* (1991).

Now, exactly what was Ellis *thinking*? Our young novelist had plunged right in on what appeared to be a spot-on satire of eighties' Manhattan no-one else had crystallized so perfectly: the obsession with outward appearances, physical fitness, banal popular music, up-to-the-minute restaurants, all conveyed through the faux sophistication of empty-headed young men earning fortunes for no reason. In measured, laconic prose and layer after layer of painstaking sartorial detail, Ellis sets in train a rhythm of narrative that could have sustained the novel to the end without...well, without the protagonist's cutting out Deranged Mendicants' eyeballs, without raping and chopping to pieces countless girls, without playing gynaecologist with a rat, without cooking brains and other organs and washing them down with blood, without page after page of some of the most horrific sexual violence ever imagined, much less written down, printed, bound and stacked in bookshops for sale. It *works*, thinks our novelist, praying that Ellis's violence is somehow metaphorical, girding himself for pornographic scenes of his own.

American Psycho's theme is overtly stated: "surface, surface, surface." Human interaction is superficial to the point where people are interchangeable – Patrick

Bateman, stylish serial murderer, is often mistaken for others; he himself confuses many of those around him. His bald confessions are taken in jest by his trendy friends. The novel ends uncompromisingly with Bateman still prospering, still unnoticed by the Chinese laundry where he takes his blood-soaked sheets, still casually slaughtering man, woman, child and beast on the slightest whim.

Ellis's original publishers, after paying him a large advance, decided not to issue the novel on the ludicrous grounds that it was offensive to women – a bit like saying nuclear weapons harm trees. Our novelist wants to avoid this inconvenience by including only a single random murderer and making that character female. Deranged Mendicants, drug abuse, mass murder, vacuous models – he can see his Manhattan novel taking shape already.

Heading east on 42nd Street, our novelist is reminded by the strip joints and porn emporia of a foreign interloper who also had his say about New York in the eighties. *Money* (1984) by Martin Amis, contains more than its share of Deranged Mendicants ("The city is full of these guys, these guys and dolls who bawl and holler and weep about bad luck all the hours there are, I read somewhere that they're chronics from the municipal madhouses. They got let out when money went wrong ten years ago..."), drug abuse ("Unless I specifically inform you otherwise, I'm always smoking another cigarette" – and this applies equally to drinking scotch), vacuous women, walking named-and-numbered streets, but, sadly, no mass murder. The protagonist, John Self, has an appetite for liquor and pornography that is enough to make the reader want to throw up and wash his hands.

Having read *Money* and digested its themes of avarice and modern degradation, our novelist makes a mental note to include at least passing references to the problems average New Yorkers face: parking, storage space, extreme and arbitrary weather, the tough, tough slog to work every morning. He also decides to have characters walk in Central Park on sunny spring days, in that miraculous green canyon between the cliffs of priceless apartment buildings. Really, Manhattan isn't *that* awful.

What is needed is a big novel about a big city. And it *is* big, thinks our author, underlooking the 59th Street Bridge. A Deranged Mendicant asks him if he can have three million dollars for dental work. A young man in an Italian suit, who might very well be Patrick Bateman, drives back and forth looking for a parking space. A fat, sweating, balding man carrying a plastic bag of bottles might as well be John Self on the make. Paul Auster himself chooses that moment to walk by. Our novelist, remembering *Bright Lights, Big City*, makes a mental note to end his towering *chef d'œuvre* with a Fitzgeraldian mention of Dutch settlers coming to these shores not so long ago, a virgin land theirs for the taking.

Heading home to his cramped apartment and his typewriter and his parking problem, dwarfed by skyscrapers, filled with Wolfe-inspired ambition, our novelist is ready to begin. He has his opening line – "Manhattan" – and may even have a title: *Dwarves of Babylon*. He wonders, with a shudder, what Tom Wolfe has been working on all these years.

Our novelist will, like Paul Auster, above, catalogue Deranged Mendicants: "Then of course, there are the tramps, the down-and-outs, the shopping bag ladies, the drifters, the drunks. They range from the merely destitute to the wretchedly broken. Wherever you turn, they are there, in good neighbourhoods and bad." (City of Glass)

"THIS GREY BUT GOLD CITY"
THE GLASGOW OF GRAY AND KELMAN

"...if a city hasn't been used by an artist not even the inhabitants live there imaginatively. What is Glasgow to most of us? A house, the place we work in, a football park or golf course, some pubs and interconnecting streets. That's all.... Imaginatively Glasgow exists as a music-hall song and a few bad novels. That's all we've given to the world outside. It's all we've given to ourselves."

This intriguing summary comes from Duncan Thaw, the artist-protagonist of Alasdair Gray's (b.1934) novel *Lanark* (1981), as he surveys the city from a hilltop above Cowcaddens in the 1950s. It is a statement which has come to prove over-convenient for purveyors of the myth of the artistic impoverishment of the urban west of Scotland, and those who have seized upon it have been slow to see the joke. The historical legacies of overseas trade, massive industrialization, a once-glorious collaboration in British imperial confidence, and potently radical political traditions continue to make Glasgow's civic culture one of the richest and most vibrant anywhere in these islands. It is a city whose socialist and populist energies continue to feed a vitality often strangely – and defiantly – at odds with the social and economic deprivations which have always plagued large sectors of its geography and population.

Duncan Thaw's "few bad novels" are, in fact, exceptions within a long and distinguished tradition of working-class, urban realism of which *Lanark* itself is a kind of apotheosis – hence another irony. The novel from which the statement comes was hailed as a literary landmark upon its publication for its unsurpassed imaginative transformation of the city, a transformation which continues to influence contemporary Scottish writing from Glasgow, and far beyond. Gray's daring synthesis of realism and fantasy within one text, in ways made familiar by a global postmodernism, remained faithful to Scottish traditions, and to its sense of place. Here was a formally adventurous and epic projection of Glasgow, on both the naturalistic and dystopian "sci-fi" planes, which created deep and disturbing metaphors for the city's recent history specifically, and apocalyptic warnings for a collapsing capitalist West in general.

Lanark detonated an explosion in the city's creativity whose shock-waves still reverberate; in his subsequent fictions Gray has continued to add after-shocks of his own. Though far-removed from the exuberance and powerful visual dimension of Gray, his contemporary James Kelman (b.1946) has had possibly even greater influence on younger writers, who have been eager to extend his combination of formal daring with a radically politicized aesthetic. Enacting the actual textures of urban life through refined techniques of linguistic hyper-realism, Kelman's novels and short stories pointedly reject authorial interference, and pursue an intense internalization fusing thought and speech, recreating the stark parameters which define and delimit his characters' lives; lives which Kelman sees as representative of political and social marginalization on a massive scale in contemporary Scotland.

Kelman's insistence on the authenticity of the inner voice makes the immediacy of his recurrent settings of the urban wastelands of Glasgow's peripheral housing schemes, forlorn pubs or betting-

Gray playfully combines artwork and text in his novels. Shown left *is the frontispiece (in actual fact a 3-D drawing of Scotland) to Book Four of* Lanark.

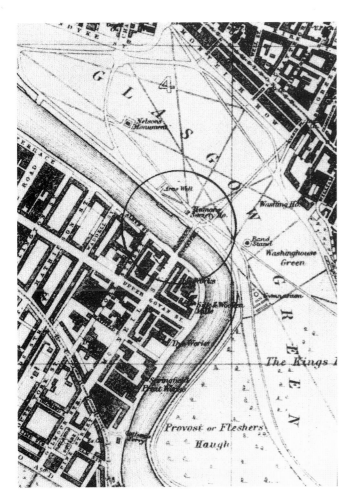

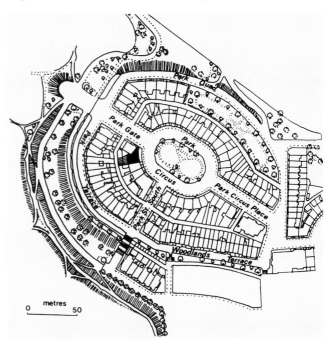

In his novel Poor Things *Gray combines "found" manuscripts, maps and historical documentation: the illustration from the book, left, shows Glasgow Green in 1880; "the circle surrounds the spot where Lady Victoria Blessington drowned herself." The black box on the map* below *indicates 18 Park Circus, a chief location in the book.*

shops frustratingly difficult to actualize: locality and identity become indissolubly fused in language. Yet Glasgow is very powerfully present as a force which determines the identity and consciousness of his protagonists. It is the redemptive "glimpses of the indefinite" to be discovered in "this grey but gold city" which sustain the eponymous "hero" of *The Busconductor Hines* (1984) in his imaginative attempts to escape the mindless repetitions of wage-slavery to municipal transport. Similarly, the anguished school-teacher Patrick Doyle in *A Disaffection* (1989) is seen in an early episode in feebly half-hearted flight on the urban motorway to England from his "palpably impalpable" Glasgow. The most intense and powerful exploration in Kelman's work yet of the paradoxical relationships between psychic and physical space is undoubtedly the Booker Prize-winning *How Late It Was, How Late* (1994), where the protagonist Sammy Samuels, blinded after police brutality, gropes and begs his stricken way home across a city which no other Glasgow novel has attempted to "see" with such a devastatingly simple sense of horror and defamiliarization. In forcing us through Sammy's predicament to listen to the city, Kelman reinvents it just as thoroughly as Gray has done.

Sheer stoicism, pride and determination get Sammy home: all three are conspicuous amongst Glasgow's civic virtues. A fourth, which possibly overshadows the others,

is a scintillatingly reductive wit, and not even the existential preoccupations of Kelman are strong enough to resist it. The most flagrant and ambitious Glasgow novel in this regard must surely be Alasdair Gray's *Poor Things* (1992), a riotous parody of English and Scottish Victorian fiction which lovingly recreates the fabric of imperial, nineteenth century Glasgow in the context of late twentieth century postmodern sophistication. Its detailed manuscripts, maps and historical documentation and beguiling fusion of facticity and fiction produce a text which is a teasingly delightful mindgame, but one which poses profound questions concerning the politics of race, gender and class.

In the now substantial *œuvres* of Gray and Kelman can be found ample proof that a Scottish writer need not devote creative energies towards a specific geographical locality at the expense of engaging with issues of global relevance. The process of reconfiguring literary Glasgow continues, mapping a fast-changing city in exciting new fiction alert to the avoidance of old and jaded stereotypes of violence and squalor. The different voices of novelists like Janice Galloway, A.L. Kennedy and Frank Kuppner envision an urban world stalked by loneliness and pain, yet still capable of yielding a transcendent, healing magic. Their continuing work emphatically gives the lie to Duncan Thaw's provocatively inaccurate diagnosis. Glasgow is as big as the imagination can make it.

LONDON: THE DISLOCATED CITY

"Why is London like Budapest?/Because it is two cities divided by a river." So begins Angela Carter's *Wise Children* (1991), one of the finest London novels of the last few years. It is much more than a "London novel," of course – a starry-eyed celebration of British music-hall history which delights in subverting the tired old distinction between "high" and "low" culture – but one of its most appealing elements is its vibrant portrait of family life in Brixton, south of the river, "on the left-hand side, the side the tourist rarely sees, the bastard side of Old Father Thames."

As Carter's narrator, Dora Chance, goes on to explain, the divide is not quite so clear cut any more: it used to be that "the rich lived amidst pleasant verdure in the North...while the poor eked out miserable existences in the South in circumstances of urban deprivation." Now, "there's been a diaspora of the affluent, they jumped into their diesel Saabs and dispersed throughout the city." But Carter's basic allegiances are never in doubt: like most of the best contemporary London writing, *Wise Children* is firmly on the side of the marginalized, the downtrodden, the underdog. The portrait of London to emerge from this book is emphatically "the side the tourist rarely sees."

This in itself is a problematic area: many of the most successful British writers live in London, command large advances for their novels, inhabit some of the capital's most gracious districts, and own substantial homes. But is this really the best vantage point from which to chronicle the lives of the underprivileged and the urban poor? It is not necessarily to the high-profile novelists, then, that the reader should turn for the most authentic accounts of modern London life.

For a remarkable description of conditions in a south London council block and the intertwining destinies of its residents, one could do no better than Carol Birch's *Life in the Palace* (1988), or the books of Martin Millar, whose evocations of Brixton subculture are even spikier and more bracing than Angela Carter's, and who brings healthy doses of wit and magic realism to bear on the lives of his squatters, buskers and

cheerfully impoverished dreamers. His best books are probably *Milk, Sulphate and Alby Starvation* (1987) and *Dreams of Sex and Stage Diving* (1994). What distinguishes both Millar's and Birch's work is the absence of condescension towards their characters: they refuse to pick them up with tweezers and regard them as an interesting social phenomenon. While we may admire the artifice and dazzling stylistics of Martin Amis, and while his descriptions of Ladbroke Grove's cavernous pubs and crumbling terraces may ring true, characters like Keith Talent, the grotesque darts-playing slob from *London Fields* (1989) seem, by comparison, to derive from a very detached and literary concept of "low life."

At any rate, the emerging consensus from the London novelists of the 1980s and 1990s is of a capital city in terminal decline. Acute housing shortages, severely underfunded public transport, rising pollution and traffic congestion, the presence of many mentally ill patients on the streets under the new "care in the community" scheme, the

MODERN LONDON: *The promiscuous intermingling of the poor and the affluent captured so keenly in Angela Carter's* Wise Children *is part of the recent fracturing of London portrayed in today's London novels.*

Carol Birch lived on a council estate like the one in Edmonton, left, *for six years, and says that she wrote* Life in the Palace, *out of "a sense of anger and injustice, and a desire to set the record straight" after seeing her home described as a "slum" and a "hellhole" in the London newspapers.*

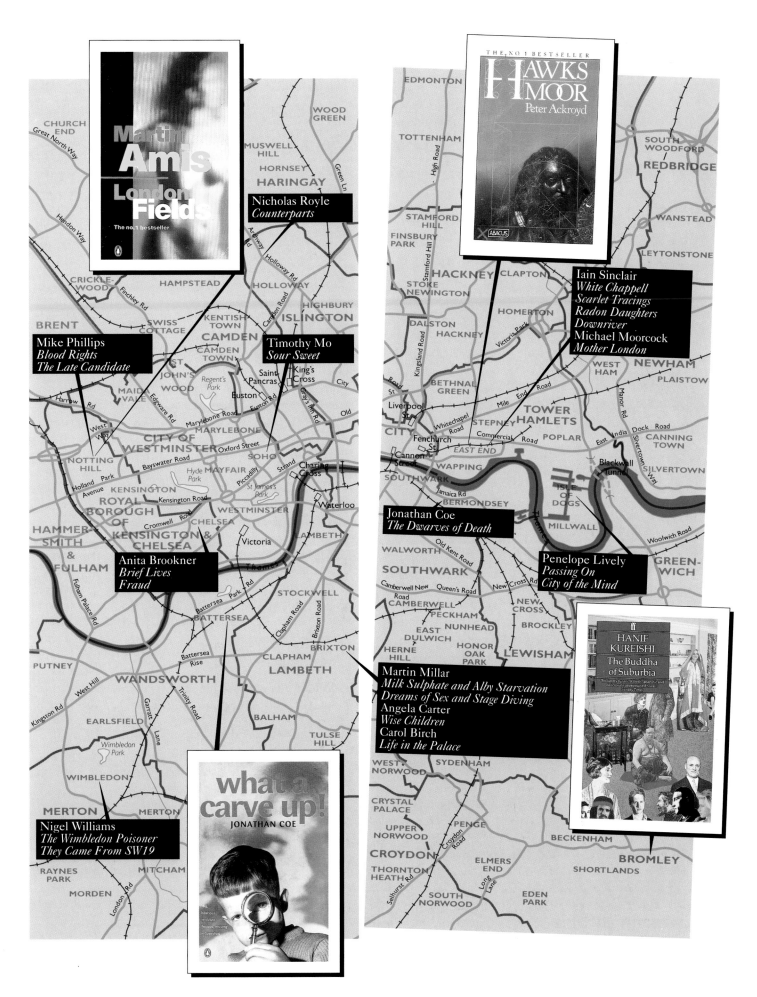

Nicholas Royle
Counterparts

Mike Phillips
Blood Rights
The Late Candidate

Timothy Mo
Sour Sweet

Iain Sinclair
White Chappell
Scarlet Tracings
Radon Daughters
Downriver
Michael Moorcock
Mother London

Anita Brookner
Brief Lives
Fraud

Jonathan Coe
The Dwarves of Death

Penelope Lively
Passing On
City of the Mind

Martin Millar
Milk Sulphate and Alby Starvation
Dreams of Sex and Stage Diving
Angela Carter
Wise Children
Carol Birch
Life in the Palace

Nigel Williams
The Wimbledon Poisoner
They Came From SW19

The Buddha of Suburbia, *by Hanif Kureishi,* left, *conveys a vivid sense of what it feels like to grow up just outside London, gazing longingly into its charmed inner circle.*

Nigel Williams writes about Wimbledon, that quiescent, leafy enclave, below, *where London proper shades into suburbia, and family tensions and potentially murderous passions are bubbling behind its placid façade of well-washed cars and neatly-clipped hedges.*

lack of an elected, centralized governing body since the ideologically-motivated abolition of the Greater London Council in 1986: all of these are reflected to some extent in the work of such recent observers of London life as Maggie Gee (*Lost Children*, 1994), Margaret Drabble (*The Radiant Way*, 1987) and Maureen Duffy (*Londoners*, 1983).

It's easy to become fixated on these images of decline and to forget that other, more stable and elegant versions of London continue to exist and to be recorded by some modern novelists. Anita Brookner is generally thought of as an introspective writer, but in novels such as *Brief Lives* (1990) and *Fraud* (1992) can be found a matchless recreation of the sad, stubbornly genteel milieu of Chelsea and South Kensington: quiet, tree-lined streets stretching between the Kings, Fulham and Old Brompton Roads, the fading grandeur of their Georgian terraces providing an appropriate setting for Brookner's stark little dramas of loneliness and unrealized hopes.

Nigel Williams is another writer who, like Brookner, has established a solid connection between London's cityscape and certain emotional states. Writing about Wimbledon, he exploits life in suburbia for comedy, and

through novels like *The Wimbledon Poisoner* (1990) and *They Came From SW19* (1992) has built up a devoted local following. However, Hanif Kureishi's *The Buddha of Suburbia* (1989) remains the definitive recent novel of life outside the inner city. Set largely in the unlovely suburb of Bromley, it follows the adventures of Karim as he dreams of becoming an actor, escaping from his stifling suburban lifestyle and gravitating towards the intellectual and glamourous (as he sees it) central London.

Kureishi's main theme is racial identity – Karim's mother is British but his father is Indian, and he regards himself as "having emerged from two old histories." This too is a pervasive concern of the modern London novel. By far the most ethnically diverse city in England, London is home, according to the *Evening Standard*, to 77% of the country's black Africans, 58% of its Caribbeans, 53% of its Bangladeshis, 41% of its Indians and 36% of its Chinese. This ethnic diversity is not reflected in the London publishing establishment. Figures like Kureishi are rare: writers from a mixed ethnic background who have achieved literary eminence and who choose to root their novels in contemporary London rather than treating themes such as exile and diaspora across a broader canvas.

The novels of Guyana-born Mike Phillips, one of London's best and most popular crime writers – *Blood Rights* (1989) and *The Late Candidate* (1990) – draw on his knowledge of Notting Hill and Camden Town. And this alerts us to another salient feature of the modern London novel: just as racial boundaries are beginning to dissolve, and as the geographical lines of demarcation between rich and poor become increasingly blurred, so too the hallowed distinction between "genre" and "literary" fiction is starting to collapse. For instance, *Counterparts* (1994) by Nicholas Royle has been acclaimed both as a horror novel and as a formally adventurous exploration of dual identity: whatever your interpretation, Royle's device of a tightrope-walking hero allows him to create some stunning set pieces, many set around the Archway area of North London. In a similar vein there is Barbara Vine, alias Ruth Rendell, who is often pigeonholed as a crime writer, but whose masterly thriller *King Solomon's Carpet* (1991) is by far the most sustained and serious attempt to probe the mysteries of the London Underground rail network and put them to artistic use.

Vine's novel has a thrilling archaeological quality, a fascination with London's most secret and deeply-buried histories, which is also shared by some more bookish writers. Several of them, such as Michael Moorcock, Iain Sinclair and Peter Ackroyd, tend to concentrate on London's East End, which is still haunted by memories of violent and unexplained crimes, in particular the Jack the Ripper murders. But the East End is also the site of one of

In Sour Sweet *(1982), Timothy Mo combines a
satirical account of the Chen family's attempts to
assimilate themselves into British society with a
darker subplot involving the Triad underworld,
set in Chinatown in London's Soho,* right.

the most grotesque architectural initiatives
of the 1980s: the commercial development
of the Docklands area on sites previously
given over to housing for local families.
Penelope Lively touches on this subject
memorably in her novels *Passing On* (1989)
and especially *City of the Mind* (1991),
which, though short, is one of the more
ambitious and wide-ranging London novels of the last few years. But the spirit of
this mad enterprise, with its post-modern sense of a history which has been papered over by modern aberrations, is
best captured by Peter Ackroyd in *Hawksmoor* (1984). Two
parallel narratives unfold in ingenious counterpoint: the
stories of Nicholas Dyer, an eighteenth century architect
(and closet satanist), and of Nicholas Hawksmoor, a mod-
ern-day detective investigating a series of murders
perpetrated in eighteenth-century churches.

The locations of these murders include Spitalfields,
Wapping and Limehouse – the familiar stamping-ground
of another East End literary excavator, Iain Sinclair.
Sinclair rarely strays off this territory in his novels *White
Chappell, Scarlet Tracings* (1987) and *Radon Daughters*
(1994), but his most famous and successful book is
Downriver (1991). In this novel he grasps the essential
formlessness of modern London, a city whose energies
can no longer be contained within the boundaries of a
neo-Dickensian linear narrative. To this end Sinclair's

book consists of twelve separate
short stories, tenuously linked by
theme and imagery rather than
plot or character. The stories
range widely in time, if not
location, taking in a Victorian
pleasure-boat disaster on the
river Thames, the nightmarish
world of a train driver who has
to drive nuclear waste through
Hackney, and an exuberant magical realist excursion in which the

Isle of Dogs is colonized by the Vatican and re-named the
"Isle of Doges." Threading these disparate episodes
together is the Thames itself – which, as Angela Carter
once eloquently observed, runs through the book "like a
great wet wound."

So is *Downriver*, with its fragmented, postmodern
technique, its violence, dark humour and knowing sense
of history, the definitive London novel of the last decade?
The only serious challenger is *Mother London* (1988), written by a friend and admirer of Sinclair's, Michael
Moorcock. The two books have a great deal in common:
both are long and episodic, both feature characters who
have made it their business to acquire an extensive, arcane
knowledge of London's secrets and subterranean mysteries, both are fuelled by anger at the damage done to
London in the 1980s by ignorant, unscrupulous develop-
ers. Moorcock's is the more accessible: his history of
London from the Blitz to the present day is centred
around just three characters,
Josef Kiss, Mary Gasalee and
David Mummery, each psy-
chologically damaged in some
way by wartime bombing. In its
scope, its confident splicing of
tragedy and farce, its intimate
knowledge of the city and its
occasional eruptions of political
anger, it can be seen as a worthy
companion piece to *Downriver*,
rather than its rival. Both of
these books, in any case, get
closer to the heart of England's
modern, fractured, bedraggled
capital city than almost any
novel written by their more
mainstream contemporaries.

THE WORLD AFTER THE WALL

In November 1989 the Berlin Wall, the most visible and oppressive remnant of the Iron Curtain that had once stretched from the Baltic to the Adriatic, came down. Over a tense few years, the former Soviet Union disintegrated, countries that had been members of the Soviet bloc declared their independence and the geo-political map of the world changed yet again. An era of over forty years of confrontation and division was replaced by new types of fragmentation; politicians declared the birth of a "New World Order," only to see it take on new forms of disorder. In the minds of most writers too, the world map had fundamentally changed.

One spectacular outcome was that some of the writers who had been political dissidents now became public figures. The playwright Václav Havel became president of Czechoslovakia – only to see that relatively new country, founded after the collapse of the Austro-Hungarian empire, dissolve into two. Alexsandr Solzhenitsyn returned as a moral hero from his Vermont exile to Russia, crossing the continent from Vladivostock to Moscow to inspect its condition in the age of the free market, economic crisis and rising crime. But freedom did not necessarily allow a suppressed literature to flourish; rather the ever more commercial conditions of the world publishing market asserted themselves in Central Europe as they had in the post-modern and culturally-glutted West.

On the eastern and southern borders of a Europe that had once been clearly defined, fragmentation and instability, rather than great economic development and innovation, grew. Meantime the rise of global communications, of multi-national corporations, the information super-highway, greater and easier human mobility, and fresh racial intermingling made the world seem different, and yet everywhere more the same. These forces, and in Europe the growth and expansion of the European Community, the super-sovereign state or federation of states, had a significant effect on the authority and confidence of those nation-states that, over the centuries, had been the foundations and the warring factions on the map of modernity.

The world after the wall has come to seem a much more varied and a much more confusing place.

It opened the international market place to new energies, not least those of the Pacific Rim. Nations like Japan, Singapore, Malaysia and China have turned into rising powers and centres of investment, development and innovation. Other states and regions, above all in the Islamic world, have asserted a different and more radical, more fundamentalist identity, turning to their faith to define their political and historical character. Further fundamentalisms and tribalisms have asserted themselves, even as, at the same time, the cities of the world become ever more polyglot and pluri-cultural and the intersections of cultures rapidly increased.

At the turn of the millennium, it's possible to see a number of powerful and often contradictory processes shaping the conditions of writing. With the relative weakening of the nation-state, and the growth of a new multi-culturalism, the literary identity of many of the more important and powerful nations on the grand map of literature has changed. As Salman Rushdie has said, many of the most interesting new fictions being produced in Britain today are "migrants' tales," written by authors from a wide variety of cultural origins who are using English as their language, but drawing on a great mix of traditions. In the United States, the powerful new writing of African-Americans and Native Americans has changed the emphasis and direction of the American tradition and re-evaluated the spirit of the American Dream.

The photograph, left, shows Germans taking down the Berlin Wall in November 1989.

Japan's stock exchange in Tokyo, above left, *is at the forefront of the financial world.*

Playwright Václav Havel, above right, *became president of Czechoslovakia in 1990, only to resign two years later in response to the impending dissolution of the Czech and Slovak Federation.*

An example of the rising popularity of computers are internet cafés, like the one above *in Paris, where conversation is no longer with people in the café, but on screen with the rest of the world.*

Indian and African writing has taken on a new cultural energy and authority; as have the voices of post-colonial writers throughout the entire world. At the same time there has been an intensification of regionalism, as writers in smaller nations and localities break free of the cultural norms and traditions to assert a more independent and positive cultural identity.

The growth of communications technologies has both encouraged the spread of narratives and weakened the authority of the book. Never were more books written, published and circulated freely through the world; at the same time the written word yields to the visual sign, the printed page to the flickering image of television, film and the VDU (Visual Display Unit). The Death of the Book has often been prophesied in modern times. What is truer is that the book takes its place in a world of ever-growing communications, where the transmission of narratives is no longer a local, regional or national affair, but part of a world of globally-transmitted images and hyper-realities.

The writers' task of capturing the fast-changing world in print and imaginative literature has probably never appeared harder – not least because as the second millennium ends the shape of the future is far less clear than our expectations and fantasies have led us to expect. The prospect of the future includes multiplying technologies, the growth of new genetic sciences, and no doubt adventures into other worlds. It also includes new tensions and conflicts, the decline or collapse of former nations and world-powers as well as the formation of new ones.

The map of writing, the atlas of literature, has been through many changes since its beginnings. Stories have always widened with a widening awareness of the world, the growth of pilgrimage, exploration and discovery, the founding of cities and the growth of new nations. Stories and books are themselves maps of the world; but the world they map is always changing. If literature itself is an atlas, an imaginative map of landscapes, cities, countries, voyages and fantastic journeys of utopian or dystopian discovery, that atlas needs constant updating. As the hero of Herman Melville's novel *Redburn* (1849) notes: "Every age makes its own guide-books, and the old ones are used for waste paper." But literature often prospects the maps of the future, and there will always be new guide-books – which is why the atlas of literature is never done.

Satellites circuit in space, above, *gathering information from the whole universe to be analysed on Earth.*

AUTHORS AND THEIR WORKS

The following authors are discussed but not featured in the essays and their dates and/or works have not been given elsewhere.

AMIS, KINGSLEY (1922–95) English novelist and poet. Best known for his satirical novel *Lucky Jim* (1953). His cultural and social disillusionment is apparent in his other works, which include *That Uncertain Feeling* (1955), *Take a Girl Like You* (1960), *Ending Up* (1974), *Stanley and the Women* (1985), the Booker Prize-winner, *The Old Devils* (1986) and *You Can't Do Both* (1994). Non-fiction works include *What Became of Jane Austen?* (1970) and *On Drink* (1972).

ATWOOD, MARGARET (1939–) Canadian novelist and poet born in Ottawa. Themes of her novels include such contemporary issues as feminism and the effect of mass society on the individual. She is best known for *The Handmaid's Tale* (1985), which has been adapted into a film. Among her extensive list of works are *The Edible Woman* (1969), *Cat's Eye* (1988), several volumes of poetry and a collection of short stories, *Wilderness Tips* (1991).

BALDWIN, JAMES (1924–87) American author from Harlem, New York City, where at 14 he became a preacher. Later, he lived in Paris where he wrote his first two novels *Go Tell It on the Mountain* (1953), based on his experience as a preacher, and *Giovanni's Room* (1955), in which he explored his homosexuality. His following novel *Another Country* (1962) received critical acclaim, as did his collection of essays *The Fire Next Time* (1963). Other novels are *The Devil Finds Work* (1976) and *Just Above My Head* (1979). He also wrote plays and short stories.

BECKETT, SAMUEL (1906–89) Anglo-French playwright and novelist. Born in Dublin, but settled in Paris after studying and teaching there. He wrote primarily in French, often translating his works into English himself. In 1969 he was awarded the Nobel Prize for Literature. His work often depicts the futility of life, which is especially evident in his well-known plays *Waiting for Godot* (1952) and *Endgame* (1957). His novels include *Murphy* (1938), *Malone Dies* (1951), *Watt* (1953), *How It Is* (1961) and *The Lost Ones* (1971). He also wrote a study of *Proust* (1931), a screenplay *Film* (1969) and numerous collections of short stories.

BELLOW SAUL (1915–) Born in Quebec, Canada, of Russian-Jewish parents, he grew up in the slums of Montreal and in Chicago. He won the Nobel Prize for Literature in 1976, and the Pulitzer Prize for *Humboldt's Gift* (1975). Taking Dostoevsky, D.H. Lawrence and Joseph Conrad as his mentors, he endeavoured to write novels to "instruct a young and raw nation." Titles include: *Dangling Man* (1944), *Seize the Day* (1956), *Henderson the Rain King* (1959), *Herzog* (1964), *Mr Sammler's Planet* (1970), *The Dean's December* (1982) and *More Die of Heartbreak* (1987). He has written short stories, a play, *The Last Analysis* (1965), and a memoir, *To Jerusalem and Back* (1976).

BENNETT, ARNOLD (Enoch Arnold Bennett) (1867–1931) One of the great twentieth century English novelists and dramatists, Bennett is famous for his stories about the Five Towns, which include *Anna of the Five Towns* (1902), *The Old Wives' Tale* (1908) and *Clayhanger* (1910).

BLAKE, WILLIAM (1757–1827) English poet and artist. Blake was born in London and lived most of his life there. Many of his works were illustrated with his own engravings. His book *Poetical Sketches* (1783) was the only work he had conventionally published during his lifetime. He is best known for his poems *Songs of Innocence* (1789) and *Songs of Experience* (1794), in which the world is seen from a child's perspective. Other works show his deep obsession with mysticism, among these are *The Book of Thel* (1789), *The Marriage of Heaven and Hell* (c. 1790) and *Jerusalem* (1804–20).

BOCCACCIO, GIOVANNI (1313–75) Italian poet and storyteller. Born in Paris, the illegitimate son of an Italian merchant and a French woman, he studied law before going to work at the court of Naples where he fell in love with Maria, the daughter of the King, who as "Fiammetta" was to inspire much of his work. His *Decameron* (1348–53), a hundred tales told by a group of people trying to escape the plague in Florence in 1348, is his greatest work, providing source material for, among others, Chaucer and Tennyson. In 1373 in Florence he gave the first lectures on Dante's *Divine Comedy*.

BÖLL, HEINRICH (1917–85) German novelist, short story writer and playwright. Nobel Prize-winner in 1972, he was critical of many elements of modern society including the Catholic church and contemporary German culture. His work includes the collection of short stories *Traveller, If You Come to Spa …* (1950) and the novels *Adam, Where Art Thou?* (1951), *Billiards at Half Past Nine* (1959), *Absent without Leave* (1964), *Group Portrait with Lady* (1971), *The Lost Honour of Katherine Blum* (1974) and two anthologies in English, *Eighteen Stories* (1966) and *Children Are Civilians Too* (1970).

BORGES, JORGE LUIS (1899–1986) Argentine poet, critic and short story writer. Born in Buenos Aires, he was educated in Switzerland, afterwards living in Spain. Considered the foremost contemporary Spanish American writer, he returned to Buenos Aires in 1921 as an *ultraísta* (Spanish Expressionist) poet, writing *avant-garde* poems based on daring metaphors. He shared the Formentor Prize with Samuel Beckett in 1961. A chief exponent of Magical Realism, his poetry collections include *Dreamtigers* (1964), *A Personal Anthology* (1967), *In Praise of Darkness* (1974); short story collections include the early *A Universal History of Infamy* (1935) and *Ficciones* (1944), *Labyrinths* (1953), *Extraordinary Tales* (1955), *The Book of Imaginary Beings* (1967), *Dr Brodie's Report* (1972) and *The Book of Sand* (1977).

BRECHT, BERTOLT (Eugen Berthold Friedrich) (1898–1956) German dramatist and poet. Under National Socialism in 1933 he went into exile, living in Denmark and the United States before returning to Germany to live in East Berlin in 1949 and establishing the Berliner Ensemble there. He is best known for his brilliant wit, outspoken Marxism and his revolutionary ideas in theatre. *The Threepenny Opera* (1928), his version of Gay's *The Beggar's Opera*, brought him success. Other plays include *Baal* (1919), *Drums in the Night* (1922), *Mother Courage* (1938), *The Good Woman of Setzuan* (1943) and *The Caucasian Chalk Circle* (1945).

BRINK, ANDRÉ (1935–) Born in Vrede, South Africa, where he still lives, he takes an anti-Apartheid stance in his writing and was the first Afrikaner writer to be banned under the 1963 censorship laws. His work, influenced by Camus and the Existentialists, includes the novels *Looking on Darkness* (1974), *Rumours of Rain* (1978), *A Chain of Voices* (1982), *A Dry White Season* (1984), *The First Life of Adamastor* (1993), *On the Contrary* (1993), *Imaginings of Sands* (1996) and an early collection of essays *Writing in a State of Siege* (1983).

BULGAKOV, MIKHAIL (1891–1940) Russian novelist and playwright. Officially criticized for several of his works. His novels include *The Deviliad* (1925), *The White Guard* (1925), *The Master and the Margarita* (tr. 1967) and *The Heart of a Dog* (1925).

BUNYAN, JOHN (1628–88) English writer. His constant study of the Bible intensified his religious beliefs and he began to act as a lay preacher in the Baptist church. In 1660 he was sent to prison for 12 years for unlicensed preaching where he completed nine books, including *Grace Abounding to the Chief of Sinners* (1666). When he was released he was a hero and continued to write and preach until his death. His book *The Pilgrim's Progress from This World to That Which is to Come* (1678–84) is considered one of the world's great works of literature.

BURNS, ROBERT (1759–96) Scottish poet. The son of a farmer who encouraged his children's education. His poems were circulated widely in manuscript form, but none were published until *Poems, Chiefly in the Scottish Dialect* (1786), which was an immediate success. His popularity is based on his ability to depict the lives of his fellow Scots. Two collections contain 268 of his songs – *George Thomson's Select Collection of Original Scottish Airs for the Voice* (1793–1811) and *James Johnson's Scots Musical Museum* (5 vols., 1787–1803).

CANETTI, ELIAS (1905–1994) Novelist and essayist born in Bulgaria from a Sephardic Jewish background. He spent his early life in Vienna and emigrated to England in 1939. He wrote in German, and was awarded the Nobel Prize for Literature in 1981. Novels include *Auto-da-Fé* (1935), *Crowds and Power* (1960) and *Earwitness* (1986). He also wrote plays, autobiographies and a study of Kafka.

CAREY, PETER (1943–) Australian novelist born near Melbourne. He confronts the social myths in Australian society through his writing. His novels include *The Fat Man in History* (1974), *War Crimes* (1979), *Bliss* (1981), *Illywhacker* (1985) and *Oscar and Lucinda* (1988), for which he won the Booker Prize, *The Tax Inspector* (1991) and *The Unusual Life of Tristan Smith* (1994).

CARTER, ANGELA (1940–1992) English author, who wrote in the Magic Realist style, where writing is characterized by images that portray the imaginary or fantastic in rational terms. Novels include *The Infernal Desire Machine of Doctor Hoffman* (1972), *Nights at the Circus* (1984) and *Wise Children* (1991). She also wrote short stories and plays for the radio.

CATHER, WILLA (1876–1947) American novelist and short story writer, born in Gore, Virginia. She worked as a teacher and journalist until the publication of her first collection of short stories, *The Troll Garden* (1905), when she joined the editorial department at *McClure's* magazine. In 1912 she left to dedicate herself to creative writing. From the age of nine she lived on the Nebraska prairie, and this landscape features prominently in her novels, which include *O Pioneers!* (1913), *My Antonia* (1918), the Pulitzer Prize-winning *One of Ours* (1922) and *A Lost Lady* (1923). Other works include *Lucy Gayheart* (1935), *The Old Beauty and Others* (1948), a collection of short stories *Youth and the Bright Medusa* (1920), and a number of essays.

CHEKHOV, ANTON (1860–1904) Russian short story writer, dramatist and physician, born in Taganrog. He began writing to support himself and his family while he studied for a medical degree in Moscow. His plays, which concentrate on the interaction between characters rather than dramatic action, had an enormous influence on both Russian and foreign literature. His first large collection of short stories, *Motley Stories* (1886), was followed by *At Twilight* (1887) and *Stories* (1888). His first major drama was *Ivanov* (1887). The Moscow Art Theatre dramatized his other key works, including *The Seagull* (1895), *Uncle Vanya* (1900), *The Three Sisters* (1901) and *The Cherry Orchard* (1904).

COCTEAU, JEAN (1889–1963) French writer, visual artist and filmmaker. A leader of the French *avant-garde* in the 1920s. His first major success was the novel *Les Enfants Terribles* (1929) which he later made into a film (1950). He relied on fantasy and the adaptation of classical myths like *Orpheus* and *Oedipus*. Works include the plays *Orphée* (1934) and *The Infernal Machine* (1934), ballets, sketches, monologues, drawings and the text that he wrote with Stravinsky for the opera-oratorio *Oedipus Rex* (1927).

COLETTE (Sidonie Gabrielle Colette) (1873–1954) French novelist particularly known for her sensitive observations of people, especially women. She published her early Claudine novels under the name of her first husband, Willy (Henry Gauthier-Villars), with titles like *Claudine at School* (1900) and *The Innocent Wife* (1903). Later she wrote novels under her own name, including *The Vagrant* (1910), *The Cat* (1933) and *Gigi* (1945).

COLLINS, WILKIE (William Wilkie Collins) (1824–89) English novelist. Trained as a lawyer, he is really only known today for his two mysteries *The Woman in White* (1860) and *The Moonstone* (1868), but he wrote some 30 novels. He is recognized as the first writer of full-length crime novels in English.

CONGREVE, WILLIAM (1670–1729) English dramatist born near Leeds and educated at Trinity College, Dublin. He wrote a novel – *Incognita* (1691) – and translations of Juvenal and Persius (1693). His plays include the comedies *The Old Bachelor* (1693), *The Double Dealer* (1694), *Love for Love* (1695) and *The Way of the World* (1700) and the tragedy *The Mourning Bride* (1697).

CONRAD, JOSEPH (1857–1924) English novelist. Born Josef Teodor Konrad Walecz Korzeniowski of Polish parents in Berdichev, Russia. He joined an English merchant ship in 1874 and often drew on his sailing experiences in his work. In 1886 he became a British citizen. His works include *The Nigger of the Narcissus* (1897), *Lord Jim* (1900), *Nostromo* (1904), *The Secret Agent* (1907), *Under Western Eyes* (1911), *Chance* (1913) and *Victory* (1915) and the novellas *Youth* (1902), *Heart of Darkness* (1902) and *Typhoon* (1903). He wrote two novels with Ford Madox Ford, *The Inheritors* (1901) and *Romance* (1903).

CRANE, HART (Harold Hart Crane) (1899–1932) American poet born in Garrettsville, Ohio. He published only two volumes of poetry during his lifetime, *White Buildings* (1926) and *The Bridge* (1930), but these established him as one of the most original and talented American poets of the twentieth century.

CRANE, STEPHEN (1871–1900) American novelist, poet and short-story writer. Born in Newark, New Jersey, he moved to New York City to pursue a career as a freelance writer. He helped introduce realism into American literature, basing many of his works on his own experiences. His novels include *Maggie: A Girl of the Streets* (1893), which he published himself, and *The Red Badge of Courage* (1895), his classic story of the American Civil War. Crane also wrote short stories and poems in *The Monster and Other Stories* (1899), *The Black Riders and Other Lines* (1895) and *War is Kind* (1899).

DE BEAUVOIR, SIMONE (1908–86) French author, leading exponent of the Existentialist movement and close friend of Jean-Paul Sartre. Best known for her analytical study of the status of women, *The Second Sex* (1949–50). Other work includes the novels *All Men Are Mortal* (1946), *The Blood of Others* (1946) and *The Coming of Age* (1970). Autobiographical writings include *Memoirs of a Dutiful Daughter* (1958), *The Prime of Life* (tr. 1962), *Force of Circumstance* (1963), *A Very Easy Death* (1964) and *All Said and Done* (tr. 1974).

DESAI, ANITA (1937–) Indian author, born in Mussoorie of a Bengali father and German mother. She writes in Urdu and translates the texts into English herself. *Clear Light of Day* (1980) and *In Custody* (1984) were short-listed for the Booker Prize. She received the Guardian Award for Children's Fiction for *The Village by the Sea* (1982), and the 1978 National Academy of Letters award for *Fire on the Mountain* (1977). Other novels include *Bye-Bye, Blackbird* (1971), *Cry, the Peacock* (1983), *Baumgartner's Bombay* (1988) and *Journey to Ithaca* (1995).

DICKINSON, EMILY (1830–86) American poet born in Amherst, Massachusetts, where she spent most of her life. Her bold and individual style ensured her status as one of the great American poets. Until the age of thirty she lived a busy life of friendships, parties and involvement in the church, after which she became increasingly withdrawn, until she became a recluse in her father's house. During her lifetime she published only seven poems, and only after her death did her sister find over 1,000 more hidden in her bureau. These were not published until 1955, in *The Poems of Emily Dickinson*.

DINESEN, ISAK (Baroness Karen Blixen) (1885–1962) Danish author who wrote primarily in English. She married and joined her husband on a coffee plantation in East Africa. She wrote a lyrical, autobiographical account of life in Africa entitled *Out of Africa* (1937), made into a film. Other work includes *Seven Gothic Tales* (1934), *Winter's Tales* (1943), *Last Tales* (1957), *Anecdotes of Destiny* (1958) and *Shadows on the Grass* (1960).

DOS PASSOS, JOHN (1896–1970) American novelist born in Chicago. Graduated from Harvard, he dealt in his early works with the First

World War. Novels include *Three Soldiers* (1921), *Manhattan Transfer* (1925) and the two trilogies *The Big Money* (1936) and *U.S.A.* (1937). His non-fiction includes *Tour of Duty* (1946), *Men Who Made the Nation* (1957), *Mr Wilson's War* (1963) and *Easter Island: Island of Enigmas* (1971).

DOSTOEVSKY, FYODOR (1821–81) Russian novelist born and raised in Moscow by Russian Orthodox parents. A profound writer, he depicted the depth and complexity of the human soul with remarkable insight. His vast body of works include *Poor Folk* (1846), *The Double* (1846), *The Insulted and The Injured* (1861-62), *The House of the Dead* (1862), *Notes from the Underground* (1864), *The Gambler* (1866), *Crime and Punishment* (1866), *The Idiot* (1868), *The Possessed* (1871–72), *Raw Youth* (1875) and *The Brothers Karamazov* (1879-80).

DURRELL, LAWRENCE (1912–90) British author born in India of Irish parents. He was very widely travelled, often working in diplomat positions. He set many of his works in exotic locations, writing about love and a sense of place, particularly in his masterpiece *The Alexandria Quartet* (1957–60). Among his other works are: *Reflections on a Marine Venus* (1953), *Bitter Lemons* (1957), *Esprit de Corps* (1957), *Stiff Upper Lip* (1958), *Tunc* (1968), *Nunquam* (1970), *The Avignon Quincunx* (1974–85), and the travel books *Prospero's Cell* (1945) and *Spirit of Place* (1969).

ELIOT, GEORGE (Mary Ann or Marian Evans) (1819–80) English novelist born in Arbury, Warwickshire. Brought up in an atmosphere of strict evangelical Protestantism, she rebelled and renounced organized religion altogether. She primarily wrote about life in small rural towns. She began her career as a sub-editor of the *Westminster Review*. Her work includes *Scenes of a Clerical Life* (1858), *Adam Bede* (1859), *The Mill on the Floss* (1860), *Silas Marner* (1861), *Romola* (1862–63), *Felix Holt* (1866), *Middlemarch* (1871–72), *Daniel Deronda* (1876) and the poem "The Spanish Gypsy" (1868).

ELIOT, THOMAS STEARNS (1888–1965) American-English poet and critic born in St Louis. One of the most distinguished literary figures of the twentieth century, he won the Nobel Prize for Literature in 1948. He began his literary career as an assistant editor of the *Egoist* (1917–19) and edited his own quarterly, the *Criterion* (1922–39). He started work for London publishers Faber and Faber in 1925 and became one of their directors. His early poems, *Prufrock and Other Observations* (1917) and *The Waste Land* (1922), express the anguish and isolation of the individual. Later work expresses hope for human salvation, particularly *Ash Wednesday* (1930) and *Four Quartets* (1935–42). He also wrote verse dramas, including the successful *Murder in the Cathedral* (1935) about the death of Thomas à Beckett, and the comedies *The Cocktail Party* (1950) and *The Elder Statesman* (1959).

FITZGERALD, F. SCOTT (Francis Scott Key Fitzgerald) (1896–1940) American novelist and short-story writer born in St Paul, Minnesota. He later moved to New York City with his wife Zelda. He is considered the literary spokesman of the "jazz age." He is best known for his novel, *The Great Gatsby* (1925), in which he explores the vacant myth of the American Dream. Other novels are *This Side of Paradise* (1920), *The Beautiful and the Damned* (1922), *Tender is the Night* (1934) and *The Last Tycoon* (1941). He also wrote collections of short stories, including *Flappers and Philosophers* (1920), *Tales of the Jazz Age* (1922), *All the Sad Young Men* (1926) and *Taps at Reveille* (1935).

FORD, FORD MADOX (Ford Hermann Madox Hueffer) (1873–1939) English author, poet and critic. Editor of the *English Review* (1908–11) and the *Transatlantic Review* (1924). His novels include *The Good Soldier* (1915) and *Parade's End* (1924–28), consisting of *Some Do Not*, *No More Parades*, *A Man Could Stand Up* and *The Last Post*.

FORSTER, EDWARD MORGAN (1879–1970) English writer who lived in Italy and Greece before returning to live the rest of his life in Cambridge. In his novels he often satirizes the atttitudes of English tourists abroad. His works, many of which have been filmed, include *Where Angels Fear to Tread* (1905), *The Longest Journey* (1907), *A Room with a View* (1908), *Howards End* (1910), *A Passage to India* (1924) and *Maurice* (post. 1971). His short stories are collected in *The Celestial Omnibus* (1911) and *The Eternal Moment* (1928).

FOWLES, JOHN (1926–) English novelist born in Leigh-on-Sea, Essex. His novels include *The Collector* (1963), *The French Lieutenant's Woman* (1969), made into a film, *The Magus* (1966), *Daniel Martin* (1977), *Mantissa* (1982) and *A Maggot* (1985). He has written a collection of short stories and some critical studies.

FRISCH, MAX (1911–1991) Swiss writer who trained as an architect. Work includes the novels *I'm Not Stiller* (1954), *Homo Faber* (1957), *A Wilderness of Mirrors* (1964) and the plays *The Firebugs* (1953) and *Andorra* (1961).

FUENTES, CARLOS (1928–) Mexican writer, editor and diplomat. His work, which seeks to understand and interpret his country and its people, includes *Where the Air is Clear* (1958), *A Change of Skin* (1967), *Old Gringo* (1986), *Distant Relations* (1980), *Christopher Unborn* (1987) and *Diana* (1995).

GARCIA LORCA, FEDERICO (1898–1936) Spanish poet and dramatist. Known for the passion and violence in his work, he was killed by Franco's soldiers at the outbreak of the Spanish Civil War. His *Gypsy Ballads* (1928) won him recognition as the most popular Spanish poet of his generation. Other work includes the poetry collections, *Lament for the Death of a Bullfighter* (1935) and *The Poet in New York* (1940), a book of prose, *Impressions and Landscapes* (1918) and his plays, *Blood Wedding* (1938), *Yerma* (1934) and *The House of Bernarda Alba* (post. 1945).

GIDE, ANDRÉ (1869–1951) French novelist and a leader of French liberal thought, and one of the founders (1909) of the influential *Nouvelle Revue française*. He was awarded the Nobel Prize for Literature in 1947. Novels include *Prometheus Unbound* (1899), *The Immoralist* (1902), *Strait is the Gate* (1909), *Lafcadio's Adventures* (1914), *The Counterfeiters* (1926) and an autobiography, *If It Die* (tr. 1935).

GRASS, GÜNTER (1927–) German novelist, lyricist, artist and playwright born in Danzig (now Gdansk). Principally deals with the social and political concerns Germany faced before reunification. Novels include *The Tin Drum* (1959), *Dog Years* (1963), *From the Diary of a Snail* (1972), *The Rat* (1987) and *The Call of the Toad* (1992). He has also written poems and plays and a collection of speeches and open letters entitled *Speak Out!* (tr. 1969).

GOLDING, WILLIAM (1911–93) English novelist principally concerned with the intrinsic cruelty of Man. Best known for his novel *The Lord of the Flies* (1954), later made into a film, he was the Nobel Prize-winner for Literature in 1983, and was knighted in 1988. He also received the Booker Prize in 1980 for his novel *Rites of Passage*. His other work includes *The Inheritors* (1955), *Pincher Martin* (1956), *Free Fall* (1959), *The Spire* (1964), *The Pyramid* (1967), *The Scorpion God* (1971), *Darkness Visible* (1979) and a maritime trilogy: *Rites of Passage* (1980), *Close Quarters* (1987) and *Fire Down Below* (1989).

GREENE, GRAHAM (Henry Graham Green) (1904–91) English novelist, playwright and journalist. His work combines elements of the detective story with psychological dramas. His novels include *Stamboul Train* (1932), *Brighton Rock* (1938), *The Power and the Glory* (1940), *The Ministry of Fear* (1943), *The Heart of the Matter* (1948), *The End of the Affair* (1951), *The Quiet American* (1955), *Our Man in Havana* (1958), *A Burnt-Out Case* (1961), *The Comedians* (1966), *Travels with My Aunt* (1969), *The Captain and the Enemy* (1980) and a short story collection *May We Borrow Your Husband?* (1967). He wrote plays, including *The Potting Shed* (1957) and *The Complaisant Lover* (1959) and, with Carol Reed, the film script for *The Third Man* (1950).

HAMSUN, KNUT (1859–1952) Norwegian novelist whose work often deals with the effect of materialism on the individual and a love of nature. He was awarded the Nobel Prize for Literature in 1920 for his novel *The Growth of the Soil* (1917). Other work includes *Hunger* (1890), *Mysteries* (1892), *Pan* (1894), a trilogy of plays and a volume of poems published in 1903.

HAVEL, VÁCLAV (1936–) Czech dramatist, essayist and former president. He was imprisoned in 1979 for four years by the Czechoslovak Communist regime and his plays were banned because he was the leading spokesman for the dissident group Charter 77. After the collapse of Communism in 1990 he was elected president of Czechoslovakia and he resigned in 1992. His works include *The Garden Party* (1963), *The Memorandum* (1965) and *Letters to Olga* (tr. 1989).

HEANEY, SEAMUS (1939–) Irish poet born in Londonderry, Northern Ireland, and winner of the Nobel Prize for Literature in 1996. His collections, which explore the issues that face contemporary Ireland, include *Death of a Naturalist* (1966), *North* (1975), *Field Work* (1979), *The Haw Lantern* (1987), *Station Island* (1984), *Selected Poems 1966–87* (1990) and *Seeing Things* (1991).

HESSE, HERMANN (1877–1962) German novelist and poet. At the outbreak of the First World War he went to Switzerland and obtained citizenship there. He won the Nobel Prize for Literature in 1946. His works include *Peter Camenzind* (1904), *Demian* (1919), *Siddharta* (1922), *Steppenwolf* (1927), *Narcissus and Goldmund* (1930), *Magister Ludi* (1943) and *The Glass Bead Game* (1943).

HOFMANNSTHAL, HUGO VON (1874–1929) Dramatist and poet and a key exponent of Romanticism in Austria. His first verses were published when he was 16 years old and his play *The Death of Titan* (1892) when he was 18. He worked on librettos for Richard Strauss, and after the First World War helped found the Salzberg Festival, where his plays, including his *Everyman*, are regularly produced.

HUXLEY, ALDOUS (1894–1963) English author educated at Eton and Oxford, he lived in Italy before settling in the United States. His works include *Crome Yellow* (1921), *Antic Hay* (1923), *Those Barren Leaves* (1925), *Point Counter Point* (1928), *Brave New World* (1932), now recognized as a classic in literature, *Eyeless in Gaza* (1936), *After Many a Summer Dies the Swan* (1939), *Ape and Essence* (1948), *The Devils of Loudun* (1952) and *The Genius and the Goddess* (1955). He also wrote collections of short stories and essays.

IONESCO, EUGÈNE (1912–1994) Born in Romania, he settled in France in 1938 and began writing *avant-garde* plays associated with the Theatre of the Absurd, including *The Bald Prima Donna* (1950), *Les Chaises* (1952) and *Rhinoceros* (1959).

KAWABATA, YASUNARI (1899–1972) Japanese novelist who in 1968 became the first Japanese author to receive the Nobel Prize for Literature. He was a leader in the school of Japanese writers that wrote with a lyrical and impressionistic style. His work includes *Snow Country* (tr. 1956), *Thousand Cranes* (tr. 1959), *The Sound of the Mountain* (tr. 1970), *The Lake* (tr. 1974) and *The House of the Sleeping Beauties and Other Stories* (1969).

KUNDERA, MILAN (1929–) Czech-born novelist and essayist who has lived in France since the 1968 Soviet invasion of Czechoslovakia. He is best known for his novel *The Unbearable Lightness of Being* (1984), which was made into a film. Other novels include *The Joke* (1967), *Life is Elsewhere* (1973), *The Book of Laughter and Forgetting* (1979), *Immortality* (1991) and *Slowness* (1995).

LAMPEDUSA, GIUSEPPE DI (1896–1957) Italian novelist. He was a wealthy Sicilian prince and drew on his family's history for his most acclaimed work, *The Leopard* (post. 1958). His only other work was *Two Stories and a Memory* (post. 1961).

LAWRENCE, D.H. (David Herbert Lawrence) (1885–1930) English author born in Nottingham. He began his career as a teacher, before writing. In 1912 he eloped to the continent with Frieda von Richthofen Weekley, a German noblewoman. During the First World War his outspokenness and Frieda's German birth aroused suspicion that they were spies. After 1919 they left England, only later returning for brief visits, spending time in Ceylon, Australia, the United States and Mexico. Lawrence died at the age of 45 of tuberculosis. His writing has often been criticized for its sexual frankness. An early work, *Sons and Lovers* (1913), is based on his own life. Other novels include *The White Peacock* (1911), *The Rainbow* (1915), *Women in Love* (1921), *Aaron's Rod* (1922), *Kangaroo* (1923) and *The Plumed Serpent* (1926). His most controversial novel, *Lady Chatterley's Lover* (1928), was banned in England and the United States because of its explicit sexual content. He also wrote travel books, literary criticism, poems, essays and plays.

LESSING, DORIS (1919–) Born in Persia to British parents, she moved with her family to Zimbabwe in 1925. After a career as a legal secretary and two failed marriages, she left for England with her son in 1949. Many of her novels take up African themes. They include *The Grass is Singing* (1950), a series of five novels collectively entitled *The Children of Violence*, including *Martha Quest* (1952), *Ripple from the Storm* (1958) and *The Four-Gated City* (1969), and another series of five science-fiction novels under the title *Canopus in Argos*. Among her other works are *The Golden Notebook* (1962), *Briefing for a Descent into Hell* (1971), *The Summer Before the Dark* (1973), *The Good Terrorist* (1985), *The Fifth Child* (1988) and *Love, Again* (1996).

LEVI, PRIMO (1919–87) Italian writer. A chemist of Jewish descent, he was sent to Auschwitz during the Second World War, the experience of which forms the themes in his work, *If This Is a Man* (1947), *The Truce* (1963) and *The Drowned and the Saved* (1986). Other work includes *The Periodic Table* (1975) based on the chemical elements.

LEWIS, WYNDHAM (Percy Wyndham Lewis) (1886–1957) English author and painter born in Maine in Canada. He was a leader of the Vorticist movement and co-founder and editor of the magazine *Blast* with Ezra Pound. His non-fiction work includes *The Art of Being Ruled* (1926), *Time and Western Man* (1927) and *The Writer and the Absolute* (1952). Fiction includes *The Apes of God* (1930), *The Revenge for Love* (1937) and *Self-Condemned* (1954).

LLOSA, MARIO VARGAS (1936–) Peruvian novelist and politician who made an unsuccessful run for president in the 1990 general elections. His novels, which can be seen as a chronicle of Peruvian life, include *The Time of the Hero* (1962), *The Green House* (1965), *Conversation in the Cathedral* (1970), *Aunt Julia and the Scriptwriter* (1977), *The War of the End of the World* (1981), *The Real Life of Alejandro Mayta* (1984), *Who Killed Palomino Molero?* (1987), *The Storyteller* (1987), *In Praise of the Stepmother* (1990) and his partly autobiographical *A Fish in the Water* (1993). He has also written plays, and criticism, including *The Perpetual Orgy: Flaubert and Madame Bovary* (1975).

LOWRY, MALCOLM (Clarence Malcolm Lowry) (1905–57) English novelist recognized as an important writer only after his death. He is best-known for *Under the Volcano* (1947). His first novel, *Ultramarine* (1933), was later reworked and published in 1962. Other work, all published posthumously, includes the novel *Dark As The Grave Wherein My Friend is Laid* (1968), collections of poems and short stories.

MAILER, NORMAN (1923–) American writer who graduated from Harvard in 1943. He served in the army during the Second World War and drew on his experiences for his novel *The Naked and the Dead* (1948). He was awarded the Pulitzer Prize in 1968 for *The Armies of the Night*. Other novels include *Barbary Shore* (1951), *The Deer Park* (1955), *An American Dream* (1965), *Ancient Evenings* (1983), *Tough Guys Don't Dance* (1984) and *Harlot's Ghost* (1991).

MANN, THOMAS (1875–1955) German novelist and essayist awarded the Nobel Prize for Literature in 1929. He was outspoken in his opposition to fascism and left Germany for Switzerland in self-imposed exile in 1933. He was particularly concerned with the intricacies of the relationship between art and society. His novels include *Buddenbrooks* (1900), *Tonio Kröger* (1903), the classic *Death in Venice* (1912), made into a film, *Royal Highness* (1915), *The Magic Mountain* (1925), *Doctor Faustus* (1947), *The Confessions of the Confidence Trickster Felix Krull* (1954) and an autobiographical essay *Reflections of a Nonpolitical Man* (1918). He also wrote political speeches and essays.

MAURIAC, FRANÇOIS (1885–1970) French writer who received the Nobel Prize for Literature in 1952. His work, imbued with Roman Catholicism, is often set in the area around Bordeaux. Novels include *The Desert of Love* (1925), *Thérèse* (1927), *Knot of Vipers* (1932) and *The Frontenac Mystery* (1933). Mauriac was also a distinguished essayist, and worked as a columnist for *Figaro* magazine after the Second World War. Collections of his essays and articles include *Second Thoughts* (1947) and *Cain, Where Is Your Brother?* (tr. 1962).

MELVILLE, HERMAN (1819–91) American author born in New York City, best-known for his masterpiece *Moby-Dick* (1851). He left school at 15, and after a variety of different jobs spent 18 months on a whaler, where he had many adventures including being captured by a tribe of friendly cannibals and spending some time in the Pacific Islands before finally being released. Although popular at the beginning of his writing career, he died in poverty and obscurity. His other novels include *Typee: A Peep at Polynesian Life* (1946), *Omoo: A Narrative of Adventures in the South Seas* (1847), *Redburn* (1849) and the novella *Billy Budd* (post. 1924). He also wrote short stories, including *The Piazza Tales* (1856), as well as volumes of poetry and essays.

MILLER, HENRY (1891–1980) American author born in New York City. He lived in Paris in the 1930s, before returning to settle in California. He had a close relationship with the writer Anaïs Nin, and lived a publicly rebellious and unconventional life. His first two novels (*Tropic of Cancer*, Paris, 1934, and *Tropic of Capricorn*, Paris, 1939) were denied publication in the United States until the early 1960s because of their alleged obscene sexual content. Other work includes a travel book of modern Greece, *The Colossus of Maroussi* (1941) and the *Rosy Crucifixion* Trilogy, *Sexus* (1949), *Plexus* (1953) and *Nexus* (1960).

MILTON, JOHN (1608–74) Blind English poet born in London and noted for his classic *Paradise Lost* (1667), now considered the greatest epic poem in the English language. He was educated at Christ's College, Cambridge, and wrote poetry in both English and Latin. After leaving Cambridge, he dedicated himself to writing poetry, producing the masque *Comus* (1634) and the poem *Lycidas* (1638) before leaving for Italy, where he met many notable figures including Galileo, returning to England in 1639. Other work includes *Paradise Regained* (1671), the poetic drama *Samson Agonistes* (1671) and many essays.

MISHIMA, YUKIO (Kimitake Hiraoka) (1925–1970) Japanese writer born in Tokyo to a samurai family, he had various jobs before he started writing. He wrote novels, short stories, essays and plays, and directed and starred in plays and films. Novels include the quartet *The Sea of Fertility* (*Spring Snow*, tr. 1972, *Runaway Horses*, tr. 1973, *The Temple of Dawn*, tr. 1973, and the *Decay of the Angel*, tr. 1974). Other novels are *Confessions of a Mask* (1949), *The Sound of Waves* (1954), *The Temple of the Golden Pavilion* (1956), *After the Banquet* (1960) and *The Sailor Who Fell from Grace with the Sea* (1963).

MOORE, MARIANNE (1887–1972) American poet born in St Louis, she worked in New York as a librarian before becoming editor of the *Dial* (1925–29). In 1951 she was awarded the Pulitzer Prize for her *Collected Poems*. Her poems are known for their idiosyncratic subject matter and the way they are composed for their visual effect on the page. Other works are *Poems* (1921), *Observations* (1924), *What are Years?* (1941), *O to Be a Dragon* (1959) and *Complete Poems* (1967). She has translated *The Fables of La Fontaine* (1954) and produced a selection of essays, *Predilections* (1955).

MURDOCH, IRIS (Jean Iris Murdoch) (1919–) British novelist and philosopher born in Dublin, Ireland, awarded the 1978 Booker Prize for her novel *The Sea, The Sea*. In 1948 she was made lecturer in philosophy at Oxford and in 1963 honorary fellow of St Anne's College, Oxford. Her other novels, often dealing with complicated and sophisticated relationships, include *The Flight from the Enchanter* (1956), *The Bell* (1958), *A Severed Head* (1961), *An Accidental Man* (1972), *Message to the Planet* (1989) and *The Green Knight* (1993). She has also worked on

several dramatizations of her novels and written several plays and critical works.

MUSIL, ROBERT (1880–1942) Austrian novelist whose writing is often compared to that of Marcel Proust. He is known for his two novels, *Young Törless* (1906), and the massive *The Man without Qualities* (1953–60). His short stories were published posthumously in *Tonka and Other Stories* (tr. 1965) and *Three Short Stories* (1970).

NABOKOV, VLADIMIR (1899–1977) Russian author born in St Petersburg, he emigrated to England in 1917 and graduated from Cambridge in 1922. He moved to the United States in 1940, where he became professor of Russian literature at Cornell University before moving to Switzerland in 1959. Until 1940 he wrote under the name V. Sirin. His early works were written in Russian and then translated into English with his collaboration. Titles include *The Real Life of Sebastian Knight* (1938), *Bend Sinister* (1947), *Lolita* (1955), *Pnin* (1957), *Ada* (1969) and *Look at the Harlequins* (1974). He also wrote poetry (*Poems and Problems*, 1970) and short story collections (*Nine Stories*, 1947, *Nabokov's Dozen*, 1958 and *A Russian Beauty*, 1973).

NERUDA, PABLO (Neftali Ricardo Reyes Basualto) (1904–73) Chilean poet, diplomat and Communist leader awarded the Nobel Prize for Literature in 1971. While he was in the consular service he lived in the Far East, Argentina, Mexico and Europe. He had a wide following in Latin America and his poems, often sensual and lyrical descriptions of people and places, were very popular. Among his volumes of poetry are *Twenty Love Poems and A Song of Despair* (1924), *Residence on Earth and Other Poems* (1933), *Elemental Odes* (1954), *Extravagaria* (1958) and *Fully Empowered* (1962).

ONDAATJE, MICHAEL (1943–) Poet and novelist born in Sri Lanka and educated there and in London before moving to Toronto, Canada. His early work consisted of volumes of poetry, including *Dainty Monsters* (1967) and *The Left-Handed Poems: Collected Works of Billy the Kid* (1970), but he gained recognition with his first novel, *Coming Through the Slaughter* (1977), which showed his interest in the grotesque in everyday life. He has also written *In the Skin of the Lion* (1987) and *The English Patient* (1992) for which he was awarded the Booker Prize.

ORWELL, GEORGE (Eric Arthur Blair) (1903–50) British novelist and essayist born in India. He is best known for his futuristic novels *Animal Farm* (1946) and *Nineteen Eighty-Four* (1949). The memoirs *Down and Out in Paris and London* (1933) describe his life as an impoverished writer in Europe. Other works include *Burmese Days* (1934), *A Clergyman's Daughter* (1935), *Keep the Aspidistra Flying* (1936), *The Road to Wigan Pier* (1937), *Homage to Catalonia* (1937) and *Coming Up for Air* (1939). He also wrote literary essays.

PASTERNAK, BORIS (1890–1960) Russian poet, prose writer and translator of Jewish descent. He was greatly influenced by the composer Scriabin and writer Leo Tolstoy, both of whom were family friends. He is best known for his masterpiece *Dr Zhivago* (Italy, 1957), adapted into a famous film. Popular in Russia, he was awarded the Nobel Prize for Literature in 1958. His early work includes the poetry collections *A Twin in the Clouds* (1914), *My Sister, Life* (1922) and *Second Birth* (1932), a collection of short stories, *The Childhood of Lovers* (1924) and the autobiographical *Safe Conduct* (1931). During the purges of the 1930s, he concentrated on making translations of Goethe, Shakespeare and other key writers. Later novels includes *On Early Trains* (1942) and *The Breadth of the Earth* (1945).

PETRARCH, FRANCESCO (1304–74) Italian poet born in Arezzo, but living in France until his return to Italy in 1353. His *Canzoniere* is an epic collection of love poems written in Italian to the unknown "Laura." Other works were mainly in Latin and include the epic poem *Africa*. In 1341 he was made Poet Laureate in Rome.

PINTER, HAROLD (1930–) English dramatist of Portuguese-Jewish descent. His plays are referred to as "comedies of menace," because of the characteristic "Pinteresque" style and tension that he builds up with silence and speeches. Plays include *The Room* (1957), *The Birthday Party* (1958), *The Caretaker* (1960), *The Collection* (1962), *The Homecoming* (1965), *Landscape* (1968), *Old Times* (1970), *Betrayal* (1978), *A Kind of Alaska* (1982), *Mountain Language* (1988) and *Party Time* (1991). He has also written the screenplays for British films *The Servant* (1963), *The Pumpkin Eater* (1964), *Accident* (1966) and *The Go-Between* (1971), a collection of *Poems* (1971) and a biography.

POE, EDGAR ALLAN (1809–49) American poet, short story writer and critic born in Boston, today acknowledged as one of the most talented writers in American literature. He was briefly educated in England and Scotland but later returned to the United States. He was editor of the *Southern Literary Messenger* in 1835 until his drinking lost him the editorship. He is principally known for his poem "The Raven," published in *The Raven and Other Poems* (1845), and his short story of Gothic horror, "The Fall of the House of Usher," which appeared in *Tales of the Grotesque and Arabesque* (1839).

POTTER, DENNIS (1935–1995) British playwright born in the Forest of Dean. He was educated at Oxford, where he was involved in left-wing politics. He later worked as a journalist and critic. He is best-known for his television dramas, *Pennies from Heaven* (1978), *Blue Remembered Hills* (1979), *The Singing Detective* (1986), *Blackeyes* (1987), *Brimstone and Treacle* (1978) and *Karaoke* and *Cold Lazarus*, both televised posthumously in 1996.

PROUST, MARCEL (1871–1922) French novelist born in Paris and considered one of the great literary figures of the modern age. Although he wrote other works (including *Pleasures and Regrets*, 1896), he is best-known for the 16-volume poetic *Remembrance of Things Past* (1913–27), of which the second volume, *Within a Budding Grove* (1919), won the Goncourt Prize.

POUND, EZRA (1885–1972) American poet, critic, and translator born in Hailey, Idaho. He left the United States to travel in Europe in 1907 and eventually settled in England where he published his poetry collections, *Personae* (1909), *Exaltations* (1909), *Canzoni* (1911) and *Ripostes* (1912). A leading exponent of the *avant-garde* in England and founder of the Imagist school of poets, he encouraged many writers, notably T.S Eliot and James Joyce. He left for Paris in the early 1920s, where he became associated with Gertrude Stein and Ernest Hemingway. He settled in Italy in 1925 and during the Second World War broadcast anti-Semitic and Fascist propaganda to the United States for the Italians for which he was indicted for treason. He was confined to a mental hospital in Washington after his trial (1946–1958) and returned to Italy after his release. His most ambitious achievement is his epic series of poems *Cantos* (1925–60).

RICHARDSON, HENRY HANDEL (Ethel Florence Richardson) (1870–1946) Australian novelist born in Melbourne. She studied the piano at Leipzig and later turned to writing. She lived in Germany, and England. Her novel *The Getting of Wisdom* (1910) is based on her school days at Melbourne's Presbyterian Ladies' College. Other works are *Maurice Guest* (1908), *The Fortunes of Richard Mahony* (1930), *The Young Cosima* (1939) and the autobiography *Myself When Young* (1948).

RILKE, RAINER MARIA (1875–1926) German poet born in Prague and considered one of the greatest lyric poets of modern Germany, creating the "object poem" which sought to capture the nature of a physical object. He did not enjoy his time at military and business school and lived an unsettled life with friends, including the sculptor Rodin, for whom he worked as secretary (1905–6). After extensive travel he settled in Paris in 1913, but was forced to return to Germany because of the First World War. After 1919 he lived in Switzerland where he died from blood poisoning after a prick from a rose thorn. His work includes the collections of poetry *Life and Songs* (1894), *Stories of God* (1904), *The Book of Hours* (1905) and *Duino Elegies* (1923). His only novel was *The Notebook of Malte Laurids Brigge* (1910).

SHAW, GEORGE BERNARD (1856–1950) Irish novelist, playwright and critic born in Dublin and awarded the Nobel Prize for Literature in 1925. He left school at 14 to work for an estate agent. In 1876 he moved to London where he spent nine years. He wrote five novels, several of which were published in small socialist magazines. An ardent socialist and a member of the Fabian society, he was also music critic for the *Star* (1888) and the *World* (1890), and after 1895, drama critic for the *Saturday Review*. Among his works are his early plays, published as *Plays Pleasant and Unpleasant* (1898), *Three Plays for Puritans* (1901), *Man and Superman* (1905), *Major Barbara* (1905), *Androcles and the Lion* (1912) and *Pygmalion* (1913), made famous when it was turned into the musical film, *My Fair Lady* (1956). Other plays include *John Bull's Other Island* (1904), *The Doctor's Dilemma* (1906), *Heartbreak House* (1920), *Saint Joan* (1923), *The Apple Cart* (1928), *To True to Be Good* (1932), *The Millionairess* (1936) and *Bouyant Billions* (1949).

SHELLEY, MARY WOLLSTONECRAFT (1797–1851) English author. She fell in love with the poet Percy Bysshe Shelley, whom she accompanied abroad and married after his wife's suicide in 1816. She is best-known for her Gothic thriller *Frankenstein* (1818). She also wrote *The Last Man* (1826) and the partly autobiographical *Lodore* (1835), and between 1839–40 she edited her husband's works.

SOLZHENITSYN, ALEKSANDR ISAYEVICH (1918–) Soviet writer born in Kislovodsk. He was awarded the Nobel Prize for Literature in 1970, but was forced to decline it under government pressure, although, later in exile in Stockholm, he was able to accept it in person. While he was serving on the German front he was arrested for criticizing Stalin in letters to a friend and sentenced to eight years in labour camps. On his release he was exiled to Kazakhstan, but after Stalin's death in 1956 his citizenship was restored. His novel *One Day in the Life of Ivan Denisovich* was finally published in 1962. With Khrushchev's deposition, Solzhenitsyn's succeeding works were banned. In 1974, he was arrested, formally accused of treason and stripped of his citizenship, and deported to the West, eventually settling in the United States. His other novels include *Cancer Ward* (1968), *The First Circle* (1969) and *August 1914* (1972). *The Gulag Archipelago* (1974) is a personal collection of documents and reminiscences of the oppressive Soviet totalitarian system between 1918 and 1956.

SPARK, MURIEL (1918–) Scottish novelist whose Roman Catholic upbringing is reflected in her work. Her novels, often eccentric and quirky, include *The Comforters* (1957), *Memento Mori* (1958), *The Bachelors* (1960), *Girls of Slender Means* (1963), *The Mandelbaum Gate* (1965), *The Public Image* (1968), *The Driver's Seat* (1970), *The Takeover* (1976), *Loitering with Intent* (1981) and the autobiographical *Curriculum Vitae* (1995). She has also written poems and short stories, critical studies of Mary Shelley (1951), John Masefield (1953) and a biography of Emily Brontë (1953). Her short novel *The Prime of Miss Jean Brodie* (1961) was made into a film.

STEIN, GERTRUDE (1874–1946) American author and patron of the arts born in Allegheny. She moved to Paris in 1902 where her home and salon became a literary meeting place for artists and writers of the *avant-garde*, attracting among others, Matisse, Picasso, Ernest Hemingway and Ford Madox Ford. She coined the phrase "lost generation" for post First World War expatriates. Her work includes the novels *Three Lives* (1909) and *The Making of Americans* (1925) and her memoir, *The Autobiography of Alice B. Toklas* (1933), written from the point of view of her close friend Alice. She has also written critical essays and a volume of "Cubist" poetic prose, *Tender Buttons* (1914).

STRINDBERG, JOHAN AUGUST (1849–1912) Swedish dramatist, playwright and novelist known for his innovative dramatic and literary styles. The unwanted son of a well-to-do father and his servant, related themes of his life appear in much of his work. Intensely pessimistic, this includes *The Red Room* (1879), a collection of bitter sketches and the plays, *Master Olaf* (1878), *The Father* (1887), *Miss Julie* (1888), *The Dance of Death* (1901), *The Dream Play* (1902) and *The Ghost Sonata* (1907).

STOPPARD, TOM (Thomas Straussler) (1937–) English playwright. He was born in Gottwaldov, Czechoslovakia, lived in India as a child and moved to Bristol where he worked as a journalist before moving to London in 1960. In London he wrote plays for radio and worked as a theatre critic. He gained recognition with his play *Rosencrantz and Guildenstern Are Dead* (1967). Other plays include *Travesties* (1974), *Dirty Linen* (1976), *The Real Thing* (1982), *Hapgood* (1988), *Arcadia* (1993) and *Indian Ink* (1995). He has also written a novel, *Lord Malquist and Mr Moon* (1966), short stories and screenplays.

SVEVO, ITALO (Ettore Schmitz) (1861–1928) Italian novelist born in Trieste from a Jewish background. His novels include *A Life* (1893) and *The Tale of the Good Old man and of the Lovely Young Girl* (1929). He was virtually unknown until James Joyce made him famous by helping him get his masterpiece *Confessions of Zeno* published in 1923. His writing career was cut short when he was killed in a car crash while working on his fifth novel, *The Grand Old Man* (post. 1967).

TOLSTOY, COUNT LEO (Lev Nikolayevich Tolstoy) (1828–1910) Russian novelist and philosopher born of a noble family at Yasnaya Polyana, his parents' estate near Tula. He was sent to university at the age of 16 to study languages and law but left without finishing his degree because he was bored. He joined the army in 1851 and took part in the defence of Sebastopol. His work includes the autobiographical trilogy, *Childhood* (1852), *Boyhood* (1854) and *Youth* (1857), but he is most famous for his masterpieces *War and Peace* (1864–69), an epic story set in Russia at the time of the Napoleonic wars, and *Anna Karenina* (1873–77), a moving study of an unhappy marriage. His conversion to Christianity is reflected in his later novels, including *Confession* (1879) and *Resurrection* (1899–1900). Plays include *The Power of Darkness* (1886) and *The Living Corpse* (post. 1911).

TROLLOPE, ANTHONY (1815–82) English novelist. He spent many unhappy years as a postal clerk until he transferred to Ireland and became a postal inspector. He continued to work for the postal service until 1867, introducing to Britain its landmark red pillar-box for posting letters. He was also responsible for introducing the novel sequence in British fiction, with his series of novels involving interconnecting characters and settings. He is best-known for his Barsetshire series, which includes the *The Warden* (1855), *Barchester Towers* (1857), *Doctor Thorne* (1858), *Framley Parsonage* (1861) and *The Last Chronicle of Barset* (1867). His other major series of novels, the Palliser books, began with *Can You Forgive Her?* (1864) and ended with *The Duke's Children* (1880). Other novels include *The Way We Live Now* (1875) and *The American Senator* (1877). He also wrote travel books and biographical works.

TURGENEV, IVAN SERGEYEVICH (1818–83) Considered one of the great Russian novelists. From a landowning family in Orel province, he studied in Moscow, St Petersburg and Berlin. An enthusiastic advocate of the Westernization of Russia, from around 1855 he lived in Western Europe, writing some of his best work. Novels include *On the Eve* (1860), *Fathers and Sons* (1860), *Smoke* (1865–6) and *Virgin Soil* (1877). He also wrote short stories and plays.

VALÉRY, PAUL (1871–1945) French poet and critic, he was a follower of the Symbolists and one of the great French poets of the twentieth century. His work includes the prose-style *An Evening with Mr Teste* (1896), and five collections of essays, all called *Variety* (1924–44). Among his poetry collections is *The Graveyard by the Sea* (1920).

WAUGH, EVELYN ARTHUR ST JOHN (1903–66) English writer, educated at Oxford. He is best-known for his novel *Brideshead Revisited* (1945), about "Oxbridge" and British aristocratic life, which was made into a successful British television mini-series. Among his novels are works of high social satire and comedy, including *Decline and Fall* (1928), *Vile Bodies* (1930), *Black Mischief* (1932), *A Handful of Dust* (1934), *Scoop* (1938) and *Put Out More Flags* (1942) and a series of novels about the Second World War comprising *Men at Arms* (1952), *Officers and Gentlemen* (1955) and *The End of the Battle* (1961).

WEISS, PETER (1916-82) German-Swedish dramatist, novelist, film director and painter whose work looks at the themes of exile and politics. He is most famous for his play, *The Persecution and Assassination of Jean Paul Marat as Performed by the Inmates of the Asylum of Charenton under the Direction of the Marquis de Sade* (1964).

WELLS, HERBERT GEORGE (1866-1946) English novelist best known for his science fiction. Apprenticed to a draper at the age of 14, he eventually managed to go to the University of London through grants and scholarships. He taught biology before dedicating himself to his writing in 1893. A mixture of fantasy and reality, his works include *The Time Machine* (1895), *The Wonderful Visit* (1895), *The Invisible Man* (1897), *The War of the Worlds* (1898) and *The History of Mr. Polly* (1910). Among his later works are *The Shape of Things to Come* (1933) and *Mind at the End of Its Tether* (1945).

WELTY, EUDORA (1909–) American author born in Jackson, Mississippi and winner of the Pulitzer Prize in 1972 for her novel *The Optimist's Daughter*. She wrote about the rural life of the people of Mississippi. Her work includes the collections of short stories, *A Curtain of Green* (1941), *The Wide Net* (1943) and *The Bride of Innisfallen* (1955), and the novels *Delta Wedding* (1946), *The Ponder Heart* (1954) and *Losing Battles* (1970). She also published an autobiographical work, *One Writer's Beginnings* (1984) and a novella, *The Robber Bridegroom* (1942).

WEST, MORRIS (1916–) Australian novelist born in Melbourne. His work reveals his interest in Roman Catholicism and international politics. Novels include the best-seller *The Devil's Advocate* (1959), *The Shoes of the Fisherman* (1963), *Harlequin* (1974), *The Clowns of God* (1981), *The World Is Made of Glass* (1983) and *Cassidy* (1986).

WILDE, OSCAR (Oscar Fingall O'Flahertie Wills Wilde) (1854–1900) Irish writer born in Dublin. He studied at Trinity College, Dublin, and at Magdalen College, Oxford. Known for his sophisticated and brilliant wit, he spent two years in jail for homosexual offences resulting from his relationship with Lord Alfred Douglas, after which he wrote *The Ballad of Reading Gaol* (1898). He spent the rest of his life ill and bankrupt in France. He is famous for his plays of shrewd social observation which include *Lady Windermere's Fan* (1892), *A Woman of No Importance* (1893), *An Ideal Husband* (1895) and his masterpiece, *The Importance of Being Earnest* (1895). Other works include a collection of fairy stories, *The Happy Prince* (1888), and his famous novel, *The Picture of Dorian Gray* (1891). He also wrote short stories and two historical tragedies *The Duchess of Padua* (1892) and *Salome* (1893).

WILLIAMS, TENNESSEE (Thomas Lanier Williams) (1911–83) American dramatist born in Columbus, Mississippi. He was awarded the Pulitzer Prize in 1947 for his autobiographical play, *A Streetcar Named Desire*, and again in 1955 for *Cat on a Hot Tin Roof*. Other plays include *The Glass Menagerie* (1945), *Summer and Smoke* (1948), *Sweet Bird of Youth* (1959), *Period of Adjustment* (1959), *The Milk Train Doesn't Stop Here Any More* (1963) and *The Seven Descents of Myrtle* (1968). One-act plays are collected in *27 Wagons Full of Cotton* (1946) and *The American Blues* (1948). Other works include short stories, a novel, *The Roman Spring of Mrs Stone* (1950), a volume of poems, *In the Winter of Cities* (1956) and a film script, *Baby Doll* (1956).

WOLFE, TOM (Thomas Kennerly Wolfe, Jr) (1931–) American journalist and novelist born in Richmond in the United States. His novels about contemporary American culture are written in a journalistic style, combining personal impressions with academic jargon and reconstructed dialogue. His first novel *The Bonfire of the Vanities* (1987) set around Wall Street, was highly successful and was also made into a film. His other works, essays of New Journalism, include *The Kandy-Kolored Tangerine-Flake Stream-line Baby* (1965), *The Electric Kool-Aid Acid Test* 1968), *The Right Stuff* (1975) and *From Bauhaus to Our House* (1981).

PLACES TO VISIT

Phone numbers and opening hours have been given where available. Please note that all the information was correct at the time of going to press, but visitors are advised to confirm details locally.

ARGENTINA

JORGE LUIS BORGES FOUNDATION CULTURAL CENTRE, Calle Florida 6, Avenida Córdoba, Buenos Aires, tel: 01 3155410
Cultural centre with exhibits relating to Jorge Luis Borges including his library. Open daily.

AUSTRALIA

Sydney

FORT STREET SCHOOL, Observatory Hill, Watson Road, tel: 02 258 0154
Now the headquarters of the National Trust, these buildings were once a school attended by many important writers. Open Monday to Friday, 9.00am to 5.00pm, Saturday and Sunday 12.00am to 5.00pm.
MARBLE BAR, Hilton Hotel, 259 Pitt Street
1950s Literary bar decorated with Norman Lindsay artwork, preserved intact inside the hotel.
WRITERS' WALK AROUND CIRCULAR QUAY
Paved walk from the Opera House to the Harbour and Rocks area with plaques along the way giving information about well-known writers. For information contact New South Wales Ministry of the Arts on 02 228 5533.

Outskirts

HENRY LAWSON FESTIVAL, Grenfell, tel: 063 43 7156
Held each June in Henry Lawson's birthplace, Grenfell, with recitals, dramatics and competitions.
NORMAN LINDSAY ART GALLERY AND MUSEUM, 14 Norman Lindsay Crescent, Faulconbridge, tel: 047 51 1065
Norman Lindsay's home for most of his life, includes a collection of his work; sculptures, novels and an exhibition of marionettes from The Magic Pudding. *Open daily, 11.00am to 5.00pm. Closed Tuesdays.*
SIR HENRY PARKES MEMORIAL SCHOOL OF ARTS, corner of Manners Street and Rouse Street, Tenterfield, tel: 067 36 1454
Memorabilia relating to politician and novelist Henry Parkes.
VARUNA WRITERS' CENTRE, 141 Cascade Street, Katoomba 2780, tel: 047 82 5674
Former home of Eleanor Dark, now a Writers' Centre offering residential fellowships to writers. Also publishes Varuna New Poetry.

Victoria

HENRY HANDEL (ETHEL) RICHARDSON'S HOUSE, Lake View, Victoria Street, Chiltern, tel: 057 261317
Childhood home of Henry Handel (Ethel) Richardson, described in her novel Ultima Thule. *Open weekends and Public Holidays.*

AUSTRIA

Vienna

CAFÉ CENTRAL, Herrengasse/Strauchgasse
Concert café where live music is played. Frequented by Robert Musil, Alfred Adler and Leon Trotsky in their time.
CAFÉ LANDTMAN, Dr-Karl-Lueger-Ring 4
Freud's favourite café.
CAFÉ MUSEUM, Friedrichstrasse 6
Gallery café showing young artists. Decorated by Adolf Loos.

FREUD'S HOUSE (Freud Haus), Bergasse 19, tel: 01 3191596
Sigmund Freud's consulting rooms and home, now the Freud Museum. Open daily.
SECESSION BUILDING, Friedrichstrasse 12, tel: 01 5875307
Home of the Secession movement and Ver Sacrum *magazine. Houses Gustav Klimt's newly-restored Beethoven Frieze. Closed Mondays.*
STATUE OF FRIEDRICH VON SCHILLER, Schillerplatz 3.
STATUE OF JOHANN WOLFGANG GOETHE, junction of Operning and Goethegasse.
WITTGENSTEIN'S HOUSE (Wittgenstein Haus) Kundmanngasse 19, tel: 01 7133164
Ludwig Wittgenstein's modernist house, now open to the public. Closed weekends.

CANADA

British Columbia

CATES PARK, Vancouver
The site where Malcolm Lowry had his Dollarton shack and where he wrote Under the Volcano. *The park now has a Malcolm Lowry Walk touring the country of his life and fiction.*

Newfoundland

L'ANSE AUX MEADOWS NATIONAL PARK, Box 70, Saint Lunaire-Griquet
Site of the only certain Viking habitation in North America, and the most likely setting for the Vinland adventures in The Greenland Saga *and* Erik the Red's Saga. *Open 15 June to early September.*

Nova Scotia

GREAT VILLAGE
This hamlet was the childhood home of American poet Elizabeth Bishop, and the setting of many of her poems.

Ontario

HARBOURFRONT, 235 Queen's Quay West, Toronto, tel: 416 973 4760
Home of the Harbourfront Reading Series which has weekly readings. Houses International Festival of Authors.
PLAYWRIGHTS' UNION OF CANADA, WRITERS UNION OF CANADA, 24 Ryerson Avenue, Toronto
Home to contemporary writers in Canada.
SUSANNA MOODIE'S HOUSE, 114 Bridge Street, Belleville
The home of Susanna Moodie, best known for her novel Roughing It In the Bush.
UNCLE TOM'S CABIN MUSEUM, 40 Country Road, Dresden
Houses the grave and home of Josiah Henson, the slave whose life was the direct inspiration for Harriet Beecher Stowe's Uncle Tom's Cabin.

Prince Edward Island

ANNE OF GREEN GABLES MUSUEM, Box 491, Kensington, PEI, COB 1MO
House where Lucy Maude Montgomery spent much of her childhood, now a museum in her honour. Open daily June to mid-October.
GREEN GABLES, Cavendish PEI, COA 1NO
Lucy Maude Montgomery's neighbours' house, which is "Green Gables" in her novels. For information write to: Parks and People Association, Box 1506, Charlotttown PEI, C1A 7N3. Open June to end of September.

Quebec

BEN'S RESTAURANT, Sherbrooke Street West, Montreal
A restaurant with its own Poet's Corner. A favourite hang-out for Montreal writers, its walls are covered with photographs of authors.

Yukon

THE DAWSON CITY MUSEUM, Dawson
Houses material and artifacts relating to the many local authors.

THE JACK LONDON CABIN, Dawson
Contains furniture, photographs and artifacts relating to Jack London's time in Dawson. Open May to early October.

CHILE

LA SEBASTIANA, Pasaje Collado 1, Cerro Florida, Valparaíso, tel: 032 256606
Former house of Pablo Neruda open to the public. Closed Mondays.
NERUDA HOUSE MUSEUM, Isla Negra, tel: 035 461284
Pablo Neruda's oceanic house, filled with memorabilia including his collection of bowsprits and nautical instruments. Open weekdays. Telephone for reservations.
NERUDA MUSEUM, La Chascona, Márques de La Plata 0195, Santiago, tel: 02 777 8741
Museum dedicated to the poet Pablo Neruda. Closed Mondays.

COLUMBIA

GABRIEL GARCÍA MÁRQUEZ BIRTHPLACE MUSEUM, Aracataca, nr Fundacion, Magdalena, N Columbia
House where Gabriel Garcia Márquez was born, now a small museum dedicated to the author. Viewing can be arranged on arrival.

THE CZECH REPUBLIC

Prague

EXPOSITION FRANZ KAFKA, U Radice 5, Prague 1
Birthplace and museum of Franz Kafka.
OLSANSKE CEMETERY, Vinohradska
Cemetery where Franz Kafka is buried.
U KALICHA (The Chalice), Na Bojisti 12, Prague 2
The Inn immortalized in Jaroslav Hasek's The Good Soldier Schweik. *Today it contains Hasek's birth certificate and memorabilia.*

FRANCE

Paris

AU LAPIN AGILE, 22 rue des Saules, 75018
Club popular with among others Guillame Apollinaire, and subject of paintings by Toulouse-Lautrec.
CAFÉ DES DEUX MAGOTS, 170 boulevard Saint-Germain, 75006
Famous literary haunt of Verlaine, Rimbaud, Simone de Beauvoir, Ernest Hemingway and Louis Aragon among others.
CAFÉ DE FLORE, 172 boulevard Saint-Germain, 75006
Haunt of Jean-Paul Sartre, Simone de Beauvoir and the Existentialists.
CIMETIÈRE DU MONTPARNASSE, 3 boulevard Edgar Quintet, Montparnasse
Burial ground of literary figures, including Maupassant, Sartre and Simone de Beauvoir.
CIMETIÈRE DU PÈRE LACHAISE, 16 rue du Repos
Burial ground of, among others, Marcel Proust, Oscar Wilde, Honoré de Balzac and Molière.
COMÉDIE FRANÇAISE, 2 rue de Richelieu, Tuileries, 75001
Home of Molière's old company since 1799.
FONTAINE MOLIÈRE, rue de Richelieu, Tuileries, 75001
A nineteenth century fountain marks the home of Molière.
L'HÔTEL, 13 rue des Beaux-Arts, 75006
The hotel where Oscar Wilde died, now houses memorabilia.
HÔTEL DU QUAI VOLTAIRE, 19 Quai Voltaire, Tuileries, 75007
Favourite haunt of Blondin, Baudelaire and Pissarro.
LA MAISON DE BALZAC, 47 rue Raynourd, Chaillot Quarter, 75016, tel: 1 42 24 56 38

Balzac lived here for seven years. Now open to the public, the library contains 10,000 books. Open daily 10.00am to 5.40pm. Closed Mondays and public holidays.
MAISON DE VICTOR HUGO, 6 Place des Vosges, the Marais, 75004, tel: 1 42 72 10 16
Hugo's house in Paris for 17 years, restored to its original character. Open Tuesday to Sunday from 10.00am to 5.40pm.

Alsace

AUBERGE AU BOEUF, 1 rue de l'Eglise, 67770 Sessenheim, Bas-Rhin, tel: 88 86 97 14
Exhibition containing documents about Goethe and Fréderique Brion. Closed 1 to 15 February and 1 to 15 August.
MÉMORIAL GOETHE, rue Fréderique Brion, 67770 Sessenheim, Bas-Rhin
Contains objects relating to Goethe's stay in Sessenheim, when he fell in love with the daughter of the pastor, Fréderique Brion. Open daily from 9.00am to 6.00pm.

Aquitaine

CENTRE FRANÇOIS MAURIAC DE MALAGAR, 139 boulevard du Président Wilson, 33200, Bordeaux, Gironde, tel: 56 17 00 59
Family home of François Mauriac, where he wrote Knot of Vipers *and* Flesh and Blood. *As it was when the author lived there, with a small museum devoted to the writer. Open 15 June to 30 September, Wednesdays, Saturdays and Sundays from 2.30pm to 6.30pm.*
MUSÉE ARNAGA, Route de Bayonne, 64250 Cambo-les-Bains, Pyrénées-Atlantiques, tel: 59 29 33 80
Built for Edmond Rostand between 1903 and 1906. Open 1 February to 30 April from 2.30pm to 6.00pm, 1 May to 30 September from 2.30pm to 6.30pm, from 31 October to 31 January, 2.30pm to 6.00pm.
TOUR DE MONTAIGNE, Saint-Michel de Montaigne, 24230 Velines, Dordogne, tel: 53 58 63 93
Home of Montaigne, where he wrote his Essays, *and where he died in 1592. Open every day in July and August, closed Mondays and Tuesdays the rest of the year. Closed 6 January to 18 February.*

Auvergne

CHÂTEAU DE SAINT-POINT, 71630 Tramayes, Saône-et-Loire, tel: 85 50 50 30
Favourite residence of poet Lamartine, bought by his father in 1801. Guided tours of the interior. Gardens unchanged since his death. Open 1 March to 15 November, every day except Wednesdays and Sunday mornings, from 10.00am to 12.00am and 4.00pm to 6.30pm.
CIRCUIT LAMARTINE, *a tour of Lamartine country, starting from Mâcon, where the musée Lamartine is at 41 rue Sigorgne.*
ESPACE JAMES JOYCE, 03150 Saint-Gérand le Puy, Allier, tel: 70 99 80 22
James Joyce stayed here between 1939 and 1940, and to mark his visit the building houses regular exhibitions relating to Ireland.
MAISON D'ENFANCE DE LAMARTINE, 71960 Milly-Lamartine, Saône-et-Loire, tel: 85 37 70 33
Childhood home of the poet, immortalized in his poems. Open from 2 April to 9 October. Closed Mondays and Fridays. Guided tours.
MUSÉE COLETTE. *Contact Mairie de Saint-Sauveruen Puisaye, rue Gerbaude, 89520 Saint-Sauveur-en-Puisaye, tel: 86 45 52 15*
A museum devoted to author Colette is being set up at her birthplace. Each year there will be an exhibition on a different aspect of her life.
LES ROUTES HISTORIQUES DE MME DE SÉVIGNÉ, Siége social Moulin de Lachereuil, 21500 Fresnes-les-Montbard, Côte d'Or, tel: 80 92 18 87
Covers almost 100 sites which Mme de Sévigné stayed at or visited.

Bretagne

CHÂTEAU DE COMBOURG, 35270 Combourg, Ille et Vilaine,
Côte d'Armour, tel: 99 73 22 95
*Fifteenth century castle. Childhood home of Chateaubriand and
remembered in his works. Contains memorabilia. From April to the
end of September house open every day except Tuesday from 2.00pm
to 5.30pm; in October from 2.00pm to 4.00pm. Park open every day
30 April to end of October.*

CHÂTEAU DES ROCHERS-SÉVIGNÉ, 35500 Vitré, tel: 99 75 04 54
*Mme de Sévigné's husband's family residence, where she spent time
when not in Paris. Contains memorabilia and portraits. Closed New
Year, Easter, All Saints Day and Christmas. From 1 October to 31
March closed Tuesdays and Saturday, Sunday and Monday mornings.*

ROUTE CHATEAUBRIAND, l'Association des Amis de la Route
Chateaubriand, CDT, tel: 99 02 97 43
Takes in 15 monuments and castles associated with the writer.

Centre

LA CHAPELLE SAINT-GILLES, 41800 Montoire-sur-le-Loir,
Loir-et-Cher, tel: 54 85 38 63
*Ronsard was prior of this chapel. Contains interesting murals.
Open 9.00am until dusk.*

MAISON DE GEORGE SAND, Nohant-Vicq, 36400 La Châtre,
Indre, tel: 54 31 06 04
*Home of George Sand's grandmother, Sand frequently visited the place
from the age of four, in later years accompanied by such notaries as
Chopin, Balzac, Flaubert and Gautier. Now a museum to the writer.
Open daily except Christmas, 1 January, 1 May and 11 November.*

MAISON DE GEORGE SAND, Villa Algira, 36190 Gargilesse-
Dampierre, Indre, tel: 54 47 84 14
*This small house was home to George Sand from 1857. Contains fami-
ly collections, documents and personal artifacts. Open daily 9.00am to
12.30pm, 2.30pm to 7.00pm, 1 October to 3 November. Saturdays,
Sundays and holidays, open 9.00am to 12.30pm and 2.30pm to 7.00pm.*

MAISON DE RABELAIS, "La Devinière," 37500 Seuilly, Indre et
Loire, tel: 47 95 91 18
Rabelais' birthplace, restored and now a museum containing his work.

MANOIR DE LA POSSONNIÈRE, Couture-sur-Loir, 41800
Montoire-sur-le-Loir, Loir-et-Cher, tel: 54 72 40 05
*Ronsard's birthplace, now restored to how it was at the time. Limited
visiting times.*

MUSÉE BALZAC, Château de Saché, 37190 Saché, Indre et Loire,
tel: 47 26 86 50
*Sixteenth century castle, now a museum devoted to Balzac, who
stayed here between 1829 and 1837. Closed December and January.*

MUSÉE MARCEL PROUST, 4 rue du Docteur Proust, 28120 Illiers-
Combray, Eure et Loir tel: 37 24 30 97
*The young Proust stayed here every Easter and Summer. Immortalized
as the home of his "tante Marie" in his work. Contains memorabilia.
Open 15 January to 15 June and 15 September to 15 December. Guided
visits at 2.30pm and 4.00pm. Closed Mondays. Extra summer tours.*

MUSÉE RENÉ DESCARTES, rue Descartes, 37160 Descartes, Indre
et Loire, tel: 47 59 79 19
Descartes' birthplace opening to the public in 1996.

MUSÉE RONSARD, Prieure Saint-Cosme, 37520 La Riche, Indre
et Loire, tel: 47 37 32 70
*Ronsard was Prior at this eleventh century priory from 1564. He died
here, and his remains are buried here.*

ROUTE GEORGE SAND, Contact the Office de Touisme de La
Châtre, tel: 54 48 22 64 for information
A tour of the George Sand area.

"SUR LES PAS DE RONSARD," L'Office de Tourisme de Vendôme,
Vendôme, Loir-et-Cher, tel: 54 77 05 07
A tour of Ronsard country between Vendôme and the Château du Loir.

Champagne-Ardenne

CHÂTEAU DE CIREY, Cirey-sur-Blaise, 52110 Blaiserives, Haute
Marne, tel: 25 55 43 04
*Home of the marquise du Châtelet, who Voltaire frequently visited.
Open daily 15 June to 15 September from 2.30pm to 6.30pm, October
10.00am to noon and 2.30pm to 6.30pm.*

MUSÉE-CAFÉ VERLAINE, 1 rue du Pont Paquis, 08310 Junivville,
Ardennes, tel: 24 72 72 16
*Ancient inn frequented by Verlaine between 1880 and 1882, restored
to its original character. Small exhibition about Verlaine.*

ROUTE RIMBAUD-VERLAINE, CDT, Ardennes, tel: 24 56 06 08
*Tour of Rimbaud country, including Rethel, Juniville, Coulommes,
Roches, Vouziers and Charleville-Mézières.*

Ile de France

CHÂTEAU DE BRETEUIL, 78460 Choisel, Yvelines, tel: 1 30 52 05 11
*Marcel Proust often stayed here with the Marquis de Breteuil. Open
daily 2.30pm to 5.30pm.*

CHÂTEAU DE MONTECRISTO, 1 avenue Kennedy, 78560 Port-
Marly, Yvelines, tel: 1 30 61 61 35
Home of Alexandre Dumas, where he wrote The Three Musketeers
and The Count of Montecristo. *Closed Mondays.*

GRANGES DE PORT ROYAL, 78470 Magny-les-Hameaux, Yvelines,
tel: 1 30 43 73 05
*Both Racine and Pascal spent time here. Now a museum. Open daily
except Tuesdays, 10.00am to noon and 2.00pm to 6.00pm.*

MAISON D'EMILE ZOLA, 26 rue Pasteur, 78670 Medan, Yvelines,
tel: 1 39 75 35 65
*Emile Zola's home from 1878. Now a musuem. Open Saturdays and
Sundays 2.00pm to 6.00pm.*

MAISON DES JARDIES, 14 Avenue Gambetta, 92310 Sèvres, Hauts
de Seine, tel: 1 45 34 61 22
Balzac lived here 1838–40. Open Mondays, Fridays and Saturdays.

MAISON LITTÉRAIRE DE VICTOR HUGO, 45 rue de Vauboyen,
91570 Bièvres, Essonne, tel: 1 69 41 82 84
*Victor Hugo stayed here with his friend Bertin before his exile to
Guernsey. Contains hundreds of original works and documents
relating to the poet. Open Saturdays and Sundays 2.30pm to 6.30pm
and weekdays by appointment.*

LE MONT-LOUIS, 4 rue du Mont-Louis, 95160 Montmorency,
Val d'Oise, tel: 1 39 64 80 13
*Rousseau's home between 1757 and 1762. Restored to its original state,
containing furniture, also from L'Hermitage. Houses an exhibition
of work by Rousseau. Open Tuesday to Sunday 2.00pm to 6.00pm.*

MOULIN DE VILLENEUVE, 78730 Saint-Arnoult-en-Yvelines,
Yvelines, tel: 1 30 41 20 15
*Second home of Louis Aragon and Elsa Triolet from 1951 now open
to the public. Contains over 30,000 books. Closed Mondays.*

MUSÉE FRANÇOIS MAURIAC, Château de la Motte, 5 rue Léon
Bouchard, 95470 Vémars, Val d'Oise, tel: 1 34 68 34 10
*The second home of Mauriac's wife now devoted to the writer. Open
by appointment only.*

ROUTE TOURISTIQUE DES ECRIVANS EN YVELINES,
tel: 1 39 02 78 78
A tour of places associated with writers from the Yvelines area.

LA VALLÉE AUX LOUPS, 87 rue Chateaubriand, 922290 Chatenay-
Malabry, Hauts de Seine, tel: 1 47 02 08 6
Chateaubriand lived here for ten years from 1807. Now faithfully

restored to how it was at the time. Open Wednesdays, Fridays, Saturdays and Sundays.

Languedoc-Roussillon

MUSÉE PAUL VALÉRY, 34 rue François Denoyer, 34200 Sète, Herault, tel: 67 46 20 98
A small musuem dedicated to the poet, who was born in the village. Open daily except Tuesdays, 10.00am to noon and 2.00pm to 6.00pm.

Normandy

CHÂTEAU DE MIROMESNIL, Tourville-sur-Arques, 76550 Offranville, Seine-Maritime, tel: 35 04 40 30
Birthplace of Guy de Maupassant, now houses memorabilia. Open 1 May to 15 October daily except Tuesdays.

MAISON DES BORDS DE SEINE, Pavillon Flaubert, 18 quai Gustave Flaubert, Dieppedalle-Croisset, 76380 Canteleu, Seine-Maritime, tel: 35 36 43 91
Contains memorabilia of Flaubert, who often brought friends to his father's house here. Open 10.00am to noon and 2.00pm to 6.00pm. Closed Tuesdays, Wednesday mornings and bank holidays.

MAISON DES CHAMPS, Musée Pierre Corneille, 502 rue Pierre Corneille, 76650 Petit-Couronne, Seine-Maritime, tel: 35 68 13 89
Corneille's home when not in Rouen. Open Easter to 30 September, 10.00am to noon and 2.00pm to 6.00pm. Closed Tuesdays.

MAISON NATALE ET MUSÉE FLAUBERT ET D'HISTOIRE DE LA MÉDECINE, 51 rue Lecat, 76000 Rouen, Seine-Maritime, tel: 35 08 81 81
Musuem and birthplace of Gustave Flaubert. Closed Sundays, Mondays and Bank Holidays.

MAISON NATALE DE PIERRE CORNEILLE, 4 rue de la Pie, 76130 Rouen, Seine-Maritime, tel: 35 71 63 92
Corneille's birthplace and main home for 56 years. Open daily except Tuesdays, Wednesday mornings and most public holidays, from 10.00am to noon and 2.00pm to 6.00pm.

Picardy

MUSÉE ALEXANDRE DUMAS, 24 rue Démoustier, 02600 Villers-Cotterêts, Aisne, tel: 23 96 23 30
Musuem devoted to Alexandre Dumas and Alexandre Dumas fils. Open 2.30pm to 5.00pm. Closed Tuesdays, bank holidays and the last Sunday of the month.

MUSÉE JEAN DE LA FONTAINE, 12 rue La Fontaine, 02400 Château-Thierry, Aisne, tel: 23 83 10 14
Fontaine's birthplace and museum. Closed Tuesdays and bank holidays.

MUSÉE JEAN RACINE, 2 rue des Bouchers, 02460 La Ferté-Milon, Aisne, tel: 23 96 77 77
Jean Racine's birthplace and museum. Open 1 April to 15 November, Saturdays, Sundays and bank holidays.

Poitou-Charentes

LE MAINE-GIRAUD, 16250 Champagne Vigny, Charente, tel: 45 64 04 49
Country retreat of Alfred de Vigny and now a musuem. Open every day from 9.00am to noon and 2.00pm to 6.00pm.

MAISON DE FAMILLE, 162 rue Bourbon, 86100 Chatellerault
Childhood home of Descartes now open to the public.

Provence, Alpes, Côte d'Azur

LE CIRCUIT "DANS LES PAS DE MARCEL PAGNOL," L'Office de Tourisme d'Aubagne, Bouches-du-Rhône, tel: 42 03 49 98
Organized tours to rediscover Pagnol's Provence.

MUSÉE PAGNOL, Esplanade Charles de Gaulle, 13400 Aubagne, tel: 42 03 49 98
Museum devoted to Marcel Pagnol who was born in the village.

Rhône-Alpes

LES CHARMETTES, Chemin des Charmettes, 73000 Chambéry, Savoie, tel: 79 33 39 44
Jean-Jacques Rousseau's home from 1736.

MAISON DU DOCTEUR GAGNON, 20 Grand Rue, 38000 Grenoble, Isère, tel: 76 42 02 62
Home of Stendhal's grandfather, now open to the public, containing memorabilia relating to the novelist. Closed Mondays, public holidays and 1 to 20 September.

MAISON DE VOLTAIRE, Château de Ferney, 53 rue Meyrin, 01210 Ferney-Voltaire, Ain, tel: 50 40 63 33
Voltaire's home from 1759 and now a museum. Open Saturdays, 2.30pm to 5.00pm in July and August only.

MUSÉE ALPHONSE DAUDET, Le Mas de la Vignasse, 07120 Saint-Alban Auriolles, Ardèche, tel: 75 39 65 07
Museum dedicated to Daudet, who stayed here with his uncle from 1849. Closed Tuesdays in May, June and September.

ROUTE HISTORIQUE JEAN-JACQUES ROUSSEAU, Centre d'Information dè la Caisse Nationale des Monuments Historiques et des Sites, 62 rue Saint-Antoine, 75004, Paris, tel: 1 44 61 21 50
Follows Rousseau's life from Genève to Paris, going across France.

ROUTE HISTORIQUE STENDHAL, Office de Tourisme de Grenoble, Isère, tel: 76 42 41 41
Traces the life and work of Stendhal in the area.

GERMANY

Berlin

BERTOLT BRECHT'S HOUSE (Brecht–Haus), Chausseestrasse 125, tel: 030 282 9916
Last home of Bertolt Brecht and Helene Weigel. Now the Bertolt Brecht Centre. Restored rooms, lectures and events connected to the author. Small tours Tuesdays to Saturdays, telephone to book.

CAFÉ ICI, August strasse 61
Café-gallery frequented by aesthetes and writers.

DOROTHEENSTADT CEMETERY (Dorotheenstädtisher Friedhof), Chausseestraße
Contains graves of many famous people including Heinrich Mann, Arnold Zweig and Bertolt Brecht.

THEATER AM SCHIFFBAUERDAMM, Bertolt-Brecht-Platz 1, tel: 030 2888155
Bertolt Brecht's Threepenny Opera *premièred here in 1928. Now home of the Berliner Ensemble showing Brecht's plays.*

Weimar

DOWAGER DUCHESS ANNA AMALIA'S RESIDENCE (Wittumspalais), Theatreplatz, tel: 03643 545377
Ducal palace where Duchess Anna Amalia lived. Also a museum devoted to Christoph Martin Wieland. Due to reopen in 1999.

FRAUENTOR CEMETERY (Historischer Friedhof), Karl Hausknechtstrasse
Goethe and Schiller buried with Duke Karl August. Closed Tuesdays.

FRIEDRICH VON SCHILLER'S HOUSE (Schillerhaus), Schillerstrasse 12, tel: 03643 545350
House where Friedrich von Schiller lived and died, and where he wrote Wilhelm Tell. *Closed Tuesdays.*

HERDER CHURCH (Herderkirche), Herderplatz
Church where Johann Herder was Pastor. Tomb inside.

JOHANN GOTTFRIED HERDER MUSEUM (Kirms-Krackow house), Jakabstrasse 10. Re-opens 1999, tel: 03643 545102 *for information.*

JOHANN WOLFGANG VON GOETHE'S HOUSE (Goethehaus), Am Frauenplan 1, tel: 03643 545300
House where Johann Goethe lived for fifty years. Closed Mondays. Parties over ten must book. Museum reopening in 1999.
JOHANN WOLFGANG VON GOETHE'S SUMMERHOUSE (Goethe's Gartenhaus), im Park an der Ilm, tel: 03643 545375
Home and summer retreat of Goethe, where he began Iphigènie.

GREAT BRITAIN
ENGLAND
London
BLUE PLAQUE HISTORICAL HOUSES
Houses around London with historical and literary connections which are marked by a blue plaque listed in Blue Plaque Guide to Historical Houses, *available from bookshops or English Heritage, tel: 01604 781163.*
CARLYLE'S HOUSE, 24 Cheyne Row, SW3 5HL, tel: 0171 352 7087
Thomas and Jane Carlyle lived here for 47 years. Now a museum. Open April to October, Wednesdays to Sundays.
DICKENS' HOUSE MUSEUM, 48 Doughty Street, WC1N 2LF, tel: 0171 405 2127
Former home of Charles Dickens where he wrote Oliver Twist *and* Nicholas Nickleby, *now a museum. Closed Sundays.*
DR JOHNSON'S HOUSE, 17 Gough Square, London, EC4A 3DE, tel: 0171 353 3745
Samuel Johnson lived here and wrote his Dictionary *from 1748 to 1759. Houses memorabilia and manuscripts. Closed Sundays.*
HIGHGATE CEMETERY, Swain's Lane, N6 6PJ
Among the famous buried in this beautiful cemetery are Karl Marx, George Eliot, Christina Rossetti and Sir Leslie Stephen. Open daily.
KEAT'S HOUSE, Wentworth Place, Keats Grove, Hampstead, NW3 2RR, tel: 0171 435 2062
House where Keats wrote his greatest "Odes" and fell in love with Fanny Brawne. Now a museum. Open daily 1 April to 31 October.
KELMSCOTT HOUSE, 26 Upper Mall, Hammersmith, W6, tel: 0181 741 3735
Home of William Morris and the Kelmscott press. Sample books on display. Open Thursdays and Saturdays, 2.00pm to 5.00pm.
LONDON WALKS, PO Box 1708, tel: 0171 624 3978
Visit places associated with Sherlock Holmes, Oscar Wilde, Shakespeare, Charles Dickens and the Bloomsbury group.
POPE'S GROTTO, Pope's Villa, Cross Deep, Twickenham, Middlesex, TW1 4QJ, tel: 0181 892 5633
The grotto and gardens are all that remains of Pope's villa in Twickenham. Open by appointment Saturday afternoons only.
SHAKESPEARE'S GLOBE EXHIBITION, New Globe Walk, Bankside, Southwark, tel: 0171 928 6406
Exhibition charting the research and progress of rebuilding Shakespeare's Globe theatre. Includes a guided tour of the theatre. Open daily.
SHERLOCK HOLMES PUBLIC HOUSE AND RESTAURANT, 10 Northumberland Street, WC2 5DA
Large selection of Holmes's memorabilia.
STRAWBERRY HILL, Saint Mary's College, Waldegrave Road, Strawberry Hill, Twickenham, TW1 4SX, tel: 0181 744 1932
Horace Walpole's Gothic creation. Open May to October, Sundays 2.00pm to 3.30pm.
WESTMINSTER ABBEY, Victoria Street, SW1P 3PE
Famous literary figures buried in "Poets Corner" include Chaucer, Charles Dickens, Robert Browning and Alfred Lord Tennyson, with memorials to Shakespeare, Keats and Shelley.

WILLIAM MORRIS GALLERY, Water House, Lloyd Park Forest Road, Walthamstow, E17, tel: 0181 527 3782
Former home of William Morris. Now houses a collection of his works. Open Tuesdays to Saturdays and first Sunday of every month.
YE OLDE CHESHIRE CHEESE, Wine Office Court, 145 Fleet Street, tel: 0171 353 6170
Bar and restaurant frequented by Dickens and Dr Johnson; home of the literary group the Rhymer's Club founded here by Yeats in 1891.
Bedfordshire
BUNYAN MEETING CHURCH AND MUSEUM, Mill Street, Bedford, MK40 3EU tel: 01234 213722/358870
Church where John Bunyan was minister for 16 years. Museum contains Bunyan memorabilia and editions of The Pilgrim's Progress *in more than 160 languages. Open daily April to October.*
BUNYAN TRAIL, telephone tourist office 01234 215226 for details
Visit sites associated with John Bunyan.
Buckinghamshire
MILTON'S COTTAGE, Deanway, Chalfont St Giles, Bukinghamshire, HP8 4JH, tel: 01494 872313
Home of John Milton in 1665, now open to the public. Open March to October, Tuesday to Sunday and Bank Holiday Mondays.
Cheshire
TABLEY HOUSE, Knutsford, Cheshire, WA16 0HB, tel: 01506 750151
Favourite childhood haunt of Elizabeth Gaskell. Open April to October, Thursdays to Sundays and Bank Holiday Mondays.
TATTON PARK, Knutsford, Cheshire, WA16 6QN, tel: 01565 654822
The house was the model for The Towers in Elizabeth Gaskell's Wives and Daughters. *House open April to September, Tuesdays to Sundays, in October weekends; grounds open April to October daily and November to March Tuesdays to Sundays.*
Cumbria
BRANTWOOD, *Coniston, Cumbria*, LA21 8AD, tel: 015394 41396
Home of John Ruskin from 1871 until his death in 1900, reconstructed to how it was during his life there. Open mid-March to mid-November daily and mid-November to mid-March Wednesdays to Sundays.
DOVE COTTAGE, Town End, Grasmere, LA22 9SH, tel: 015394 35547/35544
Former home of William and Mary Wordsworth, now a museum restored with Wordworth's furniture and belongings. Closed mid-January to mid-February.
HILL TOP, Near Sawrey, Ambleside, LA22 0LF, tel: 015394 36269
Beatrix Potter's hideaway which inspired much of her work was bought with the royalties from her first book, The Tale of Peter Rabbit. *Open 1 April to 3 November, Saturdays to Wednesdays.*
RYDAL MOUNT, Ambleside, LA22 9LU, tel: 015394 33002
William Wordsworth lived here from 1813 to 1850. Still a family house of his descendants, with period furniture. Open daily 1 March to 31 October. Closed Tuesdays 1 November to 28 February, and in January.
WORDSWORTH HOUSE, Main Street, Cockermouth, CA13 9RX, tel: 01900 824805
House where William Wordsworth was born in 1770. Open April to October, Mondays to Fridays, and Saturdays 29 June to 7 September.
Dorset
DORSET COUNTY MUSEUM, High West Street, Dorchester, DT1 1XA tel: 01305 262735
Museum contains a collection of Thomas Hardy memorabilia and a reconstruction of his study at Max Gate. Closed Sundays.
HARDY'S COTTAGE, nr Dorchester, DT2 8QJ, tel: 01305 262366
Telephone for appointment with custodian. Open daily April to October except Thursdays.

THE HARDY SOCIETY, PO Box 1438, Dorchester DT1 1YH, tel: 01305 251501
Provides walking maps tracing locations that appear in Thomas Hardy's work. Available from the Dorchester tourist information centre, tel: 01305 267992, or from the society.
STINSFORD CHURCHYARD, Stinsford, East of Dorchester
Thomas Hardy's heart is buried in his wife's grave, adjacent to graves of other members of his family.

East Sussex
BATEMAN'S, Burwash, TN19 7DS, tel: 01435 882302
Home of Rudyard Kipling for over thirty years from 1902 until his death. Furnished with Kipling's old furniture with the study how he left it. Open April to end October, closed Thursdays and Fridays.
CHARLESTON FARMHOUSE, Firle, nr Lewes, BN8 6LL, tel: 01323 811626
Former home of Vanessa Bell, Duncan Grant, Clive Bell and Maynard Keynes and retreat and meeting place for the Bloomsbury Group. Restored interior and garden with collection of paintings. Open April to October, Wednesdays to Sundays and Bank Holiday Mondays 2.00pm to 5.00pm. From July to August, Wednesdays to Saturdays 11.00am to 5.00pm, Sundays 2.00pm to 5.00pm.
LAMB HOUSE, West Street, Rye, East Sussex. tel: 01892 890651
Home of Henry James from 1898 to 1914 and where he wrote The Wings of a Dove, The Golden Bowl *and* The Ambassadors. *Open April to October, Wednesdays and Saturdays 2.00pm to 6.00pm.*
MONK'S HOUSE, Rodmell, nr Lewes, BN7 3HF, tel: 01892 890651
Home of Virginia Woolf from 1919 to 1969. Open Wednesdays and Saturdays from 2.00pm to 5.00pm.

Gloucester
KELMSCOTT MANOR, Kelmscott, nr Lechlade, GL7 3HJ, tel: 01367 252486
Summer residence of William Morris, house contains personal relics. He is buried in the local churchyard. Open April to September, Wednesdays only and Thursdays and Fridays by appointment.

Hampshire
CHARLES DICKENS'S BIRTHPLACE MUSEUM, 393 Old Commercial Road, Portsmouth, PO1 4QL, tel: 01705 827261
Charles Dickens's birthplace. Open from April to September.
JANE AUSTEN'S HOUSE, Chawton, Alton, GU34 1SD, tel: 01420 83262
Jane Austen wrote Mansfield Park, Emma *and* Persuasion *while living here. Now a museum. Open daily March to December, at other times weekends only.*
WINCHESTER CATHEDRAL, Winchester Cathedral Close, Winchester, tel: 01962 853137 for guided tours
Jane Austen and Izaak Walton are buried here.

Hertfordshire
SHAW'S CORNER, Ayot Saint Lawrence, nr Welwyn, AL6 9BX, tel: 01438 820307
George Bernard Shaw lived here from 1906 until his death in 1950. Unchanged house contains literary and personal relics. Open March to October, Wednesdays to Sundays and Bank Holiday Mondays 2.00pm to 6.00pm, parties by written appointment March to November.

Kent
BLEAK HOUSE MUSEUM, Fort Road, Broadstairs, CT10 1HD, tel: 01843 862224
Holiday home of Charles Dickens for 15 years and where he wrote David Copperfield. *Open daily March to mid-December.*
CANTERBURY CATHEDRAL, The Precincts, Canterbury
Chaucer's pilgrims journeyed here to visit shrine of Saint Thomas à Becket who was murdered on the altar in 1170. Setting for T.S Eliot's Murder in the Cathedral.
CANTERBURY TALES, Saint Margaret's Church, Saint Margaret's Street, tel: 01227 454888
A re-creation of Chaucer's Canterbury Tales *using a combination of sound, smell and wax figures.*
GAD'S HILL PLACE, Higham, nr Rochester, ME3 7PA tel: 01474 822366
Home of Charles Dickens from 1857 to 1870, now a school. Part of house and conservatory open to the public. Open April to October.
PENSHURST PLACE, Penshurst, nr Tonbridge, TN11 8DG, tel: 01892 870307
Former home of Sir Philip Sidney, still owned by the family. Open daily September to March, and April to August weekends only.
SISSINGHURST CASTLE AND GARDENS, Sissinghurst, Cranbrook, TN17 2AB, tel: 01580 715330
Vita Sackville-West lived here from 1932 until her death. Open April to October. Closed Mondays.

North Yorkshire
SHANDY HALL, Coxwold, nr York, YO6 4AD, tel: 01347 868465
Former home of Laurence Sterne. His books and manuscripts are on display. Open June to September, Wednesday and Sunday afternoons.

Nottinghamshire
D.H. LAWRENCE BIRTHPLACE MUSEUM, 8A Victoria Street, Eastwood, Nottingham, NG16 3AW, tel: 01773 763312
Former home of the Lawrence family. House restored as a miner's cottage with a museum and exhibition dedicated to D.H. Lawrence. Open daily. Local librarian provides a pamphlet that lists walks visiting locations included in Lawrence's novels.
NEWSTEAD ABBEY, Newstead Abbey Park, Linby, NG15 8GE, tel: 01623 793557
Owned by the Byron family for 350 years, Lord Byron lived here from 1798 to 1817. Now a museum. House open daily April to September, noon to 5.00pm. Gardens open daily.

Oxfordshire
MANOR HOUSE and POPE'S TOWER, Stanton Harcourt, nr Witney, OX8 1RJ, tel: 01865 881928
Alexander Pope stayed here while he translated the fifth volume of Homer's Illiad. *Open April to September, Thursdays and Sundays, 2.00pm to 6.00pm, telephone for specific dates.*

Somerset
COLERIDGE COTTAGE, 35 Lime Street, Nether Stowey, Brigwater, TA5 1NQ. tel: 01278 732662
Former home of Coleridge; house contains memorabilia. Open from April to September, Tuesdays, Wednesdays, Thursdays and Sundays 2.00pm to 5.00pm.

Staffordshire
SAMUEL JOHNSON BIRTHPLACE MUSEUM, Breadmarket Street, Lichfield, WS13 6LG, tel: 01543 264972
The house where Samuel Johnson spent his first 26 years, now a museum with restored interior. Open daily.

Warwickshire
ARBURY HALL, Nuneaton, CV10 7PT, tel: 01203 382804
Former home of George Eliot. Open April to September, Sundays and Bank Holidays only. Private parties by arrangement.
ANNE HATHAWAY'S HOME, Cottage Lane, Shottery, Stratford-Upon-Avon, CV37 9HH, tel: 01789 292100
Family home of Shakespeare's wife, Anne Hathaway. Open daily.
MARY ARDEN'S HOUSE, Station Road, Wilmcote, Stratford-Upon-Avon, CV37 9UN, tel: 01789 293455

Childhood home of Shakespeare's mother, Mary Arden, now a museum. Open daily.

NUNEATON MUSUEM AND ART GALLERY, Riversley Park
Has a room depicting a specific time in George Eliot's life and contains much of the original furnishings of her home in Regent's Park.

WILLIAM SHAKESPEARE'S BIRTHPLACE, Henley Street, Stratford-Upon-Avon, CV37 6QW, tel: 01789 204016
House restored to as it was in Shakespeare's time. Open daily.

West Yorkshire

BRONTË SOCIETY AND BRONTË PARSONAGE MUSEUM, Haworth, Keighley, BD22 8DR, tel: 01535 642323
Lifelong home of Charlotte, Emily, Anne and Branwell Brontë, filled with books, manuscripts and personal memorabilia that belonged to the Brontës. Closed 15 January to 9 February.

BRÖNTE WAY, tel: 01535 642323
A forty mile walk in four sections to sites associated with the Brontës including the birthplace of the Brontë sisters.

OAKWELL HALL COUNTRY PARK, Nutter Lane, Birstall, tel: 01924 474926
House features as "Fieldhead" in Charlotte Brontë's Shirley.

THE RED HOUSE MUSEUM, Oxford Rd, Gomersal, Cleckheaton, tel: 01274 872165
House appears as "Briarmains" in Charlotte Brontë's Shirley.

WUTHERING HEIGHTS WALK, tel: 01535 642323
Six mile walk to Top Withins, the setting for Wuthering Heights.

SCOTLAND
Edinburgh

ROBERT LOUIS STEVENSON'S CHILDHOOD HOME, 17 Heriot Row
Enquiries and bookings: Macfie Trading Co., tel: 0131 556 1896.

THE WRITERS' MUSUEM, Lady Stair's Close, Lawnmarket, tel: 0131 529 4901
Includes momentoes of Robert Louis Stevenson, Sir Walter Scott and Robert Burns. Closed Sundays.

Elsewhere in Scotland

ABBOTSFORD, Melrose, Roxburghshire, TD6 9BQ, tel: 01896 752043
Sir Walter Scott's home for twenty years. Scott's study and library open for viewing. Open daily mid-March to October.

BURNS COTTAGE, Alloway, Ayr, KA7 4PY, tel: 01292 441215
Birthplace of Robert Burns, now a museum. Open daily.

BURNS HOUSE, Burns Street, Dumfries, Dumfries and Galloway, DG1 2PS, tel: 01387 25529
Former home of Robert Burns and where he died in 1796, now a museum. Open October to March, closed Sundays and Mondays.

WALES

DYLAN THOMAS'S BOAT HOUSE, Dylan's Walk, Laugharne, Dyfed, SA33 4SD, tel: 01994 427420
Favourite home of Dylan Thomas. Restored interior and small gallery showing Thomas's paintings. Open daily.

IRELAND
Dublin

ABBEY THEATRE, Lower Abbey Street, tel: 01 8787222
W.B. Yeats and Lady Gregory were the first directors. Now the National Theatre showing Irish theatrical classics.

DUBLIN WRITER'S MUSEUM, 18 Parnell Square, tel: 01 8722077
Memorabilia and exhibits of famous literary figures including G.B. Shaw, Samuel Beckett, W.B. Yeats, Jonathan Swift and James Joyce. Literary lectures and seminars. Open daily.

GEORGE BERNARD SHAW BIRTHPLACE MUSEUM, 33 Synge Street, tel: 01 4750854
First home of the Shaw family. Open daily May to October.

JAMES JOYCE CENTRE, 33 North Great Georges Street, tel: 01 8788547
In the summer it organizes tours of Dublin given by descendants of the writer. November to April closed Mondays.

LITERARY PUB CRAWLS, tel: 01 4540228
Visit pubs associated with James Joyce, Samuel Beckett and Oscar Wilde with actors highlighting points of interest. Easter to October, tours daily. November to Easter no tours on Mondays, Tuesdays or Wednesdays.

OLD LIBRARY, TRINITY COLLEGE, College Green, Dublin 2, tel: 01 6082320
Contains The Book of Kells, *one of the oldest books in the world, dated at around 800 AD. J.M. Synge's tiny typewriter is also on display along with the* Book of Durrow. *Open daily.*

ULYSSES MAP OF DUBLIN, or JOYCE'S DUBLIN, Dublin Tourist Board, Suffolk Street, Dublin 2, tel: 01 6057789
A Walking Guide to Ulysses, *retraces the journey of Joyce's characters around Dublin as featured in the novel.*

Outskirts of Dublin

JAMES JOYCE MUSEUM, Martello Tower, Sandycove, Dun Laoghaire, tel: 01 2809265
Tower appears in the first chapter of Ulysses. *Museum, opened by Sylvia Beach, first publisher of* Ulysses, *in 1962, contains Joyce memorabilia and letters. Open daily April to October, and by appointment from November to March.*

Galway

W.B. YEATS HOUSE, Thoor Ballylee, 4 miles NE of Gort, tel: 091 31436
Former home of W.B. Yeats. Interior restored with a museum. Open daily Easter to 30 September.

ISRAEL
Jerusalem

AGNON'S HOUSE, Klausner 16, tel: 02 716498
Home of the novelist and Nobel Prize-winner, Shmuel Yosef Agnon, now open to the public. Open Sundays to Thursdays 9.00am to noon.

Tel Aviv

Bialik House, 22 Bialik Street, tel: 03 5254530
Home of Haim Nachman Bialik, Israel's national poet. Contains memorabilia and temporary exhibits. Closed Saturdays.

HABIMA THEATRE, 2 Tardat Boulevard, tel: 03 5266666
Israel's national theatre, all performances are in Hebrew.

OLD CEMETERY, Trumpeldor Street
Poets Haim Nachman Bialik and Saul Tchernichovsky are buried here.

Galilee

KINNERET CEMETERY, Kibbutz Kinneret, Ṣ of Tiberias, Sea of Galilee.
Among those buried here are poetess "Rachel" and poet "Elisheva."

ITALY
Rome

KEATS AND SHELLEY MEMORIAL HOUSE, Piazza di Spagna 26, tel: 06 6784235
House where Keats died. Now a museum dedicated to Keats, Shelley and Lord Byron. Closed Saturdays and Sundays.

PROTESTANT CEMETERY (Cimilerio Acattolico) Via Caio Cestio 6
Cemetery contains Keats's grave and Shelley's ashes.

Florence

BAPTISTERY OF SAN GIOVANNI, Piazza San Giovanni
Inspiration for Dante's poetry and where he was baptized.
Open daily from 1.00pm to 6.00pm.

CASA DI DANTE, Via San Margherita, tel: 055 219416
Site of Dante's birth. Reconstructed as a Dante museum in 1895.
Closed Tuesday and Sunday afternoons.

ELIZABETH AND ROBERT BOWNING'S APARTMENT, Casa Guidi,
Piazza S. Felice 8, tel: 055 284393
The Brownings lived here after their secret marriage in 1846 and
were visited by, among others, Nathaniel Hawthorne and Anthony
Trollope. Includes library and Robert Browning's study. Open
Mondays, Wednesdays and Fridays from 3.00pm to 6.00pm.

ENGLISH CEMETERY (Cimitero Protestante), Piazzale Donalerlo
Elizabeth Browning's grave is designed by Frederick Leighton.
Walter Savage Landor and Frances Trollope are also buried here.

Outskirts of Florence

BOCCACCIO'S TOMB, Church of S.S. Jacopo E Filippo, Certaldo.

CASA DEL BOCCACCIO, Via Boccaccio 18, Santa Andrea
Inpercussina, Sasciano, tel: 055 828471
Reconstruction of Boccaccio's house. Open Mondays and Thursdays
from 4.30pm to 7.30pm and Wednesdays from 9.00am to noon.

Venice

BYRON MUSEUM, Mechitar Monastry (Monastero Mekhitarista),
San Lazzaro degli Armeni, tel: 041 5260104
Lord Byron stayed here while learning Armenian. Now a museum
with Byron memorabilia. Open daily 3.00pm to 5.00pm.

HARRY'S BAR, San Marco 1323, Calle Vallaresso.
Haunt of artists and writers in the 1940s and 1950s. Still the place
to see and be seen. Closed Mondays.

LOCANDA CIPRIANI AT TORCELLO (six miles NE of Venice)
Favourite hang-out of Ernest Hemingway. Open March to October,
Wednesdays and Sundays.

JAPAN

Tokyo

MUSEUM OF MODERN JAPANESE LITERATURE, 4–3–55 Komaba,
Meguro-ku, Tokyo 153, tel: 03 3468 4181
Museum devoted to Japanese literature. Lectures also held. Closed
Sundays, last day of every month and national holidays.

Honshu Island

TAKUBOKU ISHIKAWA MEMORIAL MUSEUM, 9 Shibutami,
Tamayama, Iwate-gun, Iwate-ken 028–41, tel: 0196 83 2315
Museum devoted to Takuboku Ishikawa. Nearby is the temple
where the poet grew up and the old school house where he used to
teach. Open daily, closed at the end and beginning of the year.

JUNICHIRO TANIZAKI MEMORIAL MUSEUM, 12-5 Ise-chou,
Ashiya-shi, Hyogo 659, tel: 0796 23 2319
Museum contains over 2,000 items relating to the life of Junichiro
Tanizaki. Closed Tuesdays.

KENJI MIYAZAWA MEMORIAL MUSEUM, 1-1 Yazawa,
Hanamaki-shi, Iwate-ken 025, tel: 0198 31 2319
Museum dedicated to Kenji Miyazawa. Open daily, closed at
the end and beginning of the year.

LAFCADIO HEARN (YAKUMO KOIZUMI) MEMORIAL MUSEUM,
322 Okutani-chou, Matsue-shi, Shimane-ken 690,
tel: 0852 21 2147
Museum contains an exhibition, study and store room with 1,000
items relating to Yakumo Koizumi. Open daily.

NATSUME SOSEKI LIBRARY IN LIBRARY OF TOHOKU UNIVERSITY,
Kawauchi, Sendai-shi, Miyagi-ken 980, tel: 0222 22 1800
Constructed by Natsume Soseki's eldest son, Jun'ichi, it
contains about 3,000 books, diary entries and memorabilia.
Open academic terms.

YASUNARI KAWABATA LITERARY MUSEUM, Kaminakajo,
Ibaraki-shi, Ibaraki-ken 567, tel: 0726 25 5978
Museum contains exhibition, gallery and rooms relating
to the work of Yasunari Kawabata. Closed Tuesdays and
Sunday afternoons.

YASUNARI KAWABATA MEMORIAL MUSEUM, 1-12-5 Hase,
Kamakura-shi, Kanagawa-ken 248, tel: 0467 22 5978
Former residence of Yasunari Kawabata. Now a museum containing
manuscripts, letters and memorabilia. Introduction required.

Kyushu Island

HAKUSHUU KITAHARA'S BIRTHPLACE, 55 Ishiba, Okinohata-
chou, Yanagawa-shi, Fukuoka-ken 832, tel: 0944 72 6773
Contains items relating to Hakushuu Kitahara's youth including
his old desk. Open daily, closed at the end and beginning
of the year.

NATSUME SOSEKI HOUSE, 4-22 Tsuboi-chou, Kumamoto-shi,
Kumamoto-ken 860, tel: 0963 25 6773
Former residence of Natsume Soseki; the reception room houses
an exhibition. Closed Mondays, Thursday afternoons and
national holidays.

NORWAY

Oslo

IBSEN'S APARTMENT, Arbiens gate 1, 0253 tel: 22552009
Henrik Ibsen's last home. Now a museum with his original study as
one of the exhibits. Open Tuesdays to Sundays from noon to 3.00pm.

OSLO IBSEN ANNUAL FESTIVAL, National theatre, Stortings gate
15, 0161
Theatre shows special performances of Ibsen's plays.

Elsewhere in Norway

HAMSUN CHILDHOOD HOUSE, 8294 Hamarøy, tel: 75770294
Knut Hamsun's former home, now a small museum. Open daily
mid-June to mid-August, 10.00am to 8.00pm. Other times by
appointment.

IBSEN'S CHILDHOOD HOME, Venstøp, 3700 Skien, tel: 35581000
Contains an exhibition of Ibsen's family and childhood experiences.
Open 15 May to 31 August.

IBSEN'S HOUSE, 4890 Grimstad, tel: 37044653
Now a museum dedicated to Henrik Ibsen with the world's
largest collection of Ibsen memorabilia. Open 15 April to
15 September.

SKIEN IBSEN ANNUAL FESTIVAL, Skien, tel: 35581910
Events connected to Henrik Ibsen. Usually at the end of August.

SOUTH AFRICA

Johannesburg

MARKET THEATRE, Bree Street, tel: 011 832 1641
Developed in old, converted market buildings the complex
contains four live theatre venues showing as part of the programme
sharply critical contemporary plays.

Northern Cape Province

SOL T. PLAATJE'S HOUSE, 32 Angel Street, New Park, Kimberley,
tel: 0531 32526
Home of the novelist Sol T. Plaatje for many years, now a national
monument. Open daily from 8.00am to 2.30pm.

SPAIN

Madrid

CAFÉ GIJÓN, Paseo de Recoletos 21
Famous as a literary meeting place and location of literary events.
CERVANTES' BIRTHPLACE (Museo Casa de Cervantes), Calle
Mayor 48, Alcalá de Henares, 28801, tel: 91 889 9654
*Site where Miguel de Cervantes was born, a replica house contains
a small Cervantes museum. Closed Mondays.*
CERVECÉRIA ALEMANA CAFÉ, Plaza Santa Ana 6
*Famous as a literary haunt frequented by Ernest Hemingway.
Still attracts many writers and poets.*
HOUSE OF LOPE DE VEGA, Calle Cervantes 11, tel: 91 429 9216
*Home of Lope de Vega for 25 years, now a museum. Open Tuesdays
to Saturdays, 9.30am to 2.30pm.*

Elsewhere in Spain

HOUSE OF MIGUEL DE CERVANTES (Casa de Cervantes), Calle
Rastro 7, Vallodolid tel: 983 308810
*Former home of Miguel de Cervantes, restored with period furniture
and a display of Cervantes' books. Closed Mondays.*
DULCINEA'S HOUSE, Calle Jose Antonio, El Toboso tel: 95 819 7288
*House where Miguel de Cervantes' mistress, Ana Zarco de Morales
(the real Dulcinea), lived. Closed Sunday afternoons and Mondays.*

UNITED STATES OF AMERICA

New York City

ALGONQUIN HOTEL, 50 W44th Street, tel: 212 840 6800
Dorothy Parker attended the literary luncheon club The Round
Table *held here in the 1920s. Now a favourite literary haunt.*
CHUMLEY'S, 86 Bedford Street, Greenwich Village
*Saloon where Dylan Thomas, John Steinbeck, Ernest Hemingway,
William Faulkner, Jack Kerouac, John Dos Passos and Theodore
Dreiser drank. Book jackets of famous patrons cover the walls.*
THE EAR INN, 326 Spring Street, Soho
A bar since 1812, it is still a popular haunt for poets and writers.
GOTHAM BOOK MART, 41 W47th Street
*Foremost literary bookshop in New York which stocked James Joyce
and Henry Miller when they were banned in the United States.*
POE COTTAGE, Poe Park, Grand Concourse and Kingbridge
Road, The Bronx, tel: 718 881 8900
Edgar Allen Poe lived here while he wrote Ulalume *and* The Bells.
Period furniture and memorabilia. Open weekends only.
WHITE HORSE TAVERN, 567 Hudson Street, Greenwich Village
Favourite haunt of Dylan Thomas. Still attracts a literary crowd.

California

CAFÉ TRIESTE, 609 Vallejo Street, North Beach, San Francisco
Popular café with San Francisco's literary crowd.
CITY LIGHTS BOOKSTORE, 261 Columbus Avenue, San Francisco,
tel: 415 362 8193
*The first all-paperback bookshop in the United States established in
1953. Still owned by poet and novelist Lawrence Ferlinghetti, it has
a vast collection of avant-garde, contemporary and Beat writing.*
Dashiell Hammett Tour. For bookings tel: 650 873 1803
*Three-mile walking tour of sites around San Francisco associated with
Dashiell Hammett and his novels.*
FORMOSA CAFÉ, 7156 Santa Monica Boulevard, Hollywood
*Longtime film industry watering-hole. Photographs and memorabilia
of famous customers cover the walls.*

JOHN'S GRILL, 63 Ellis Street, San Francisco, tel: 415 986 0069
Restaurant frequented by Dashiell Hammett; contains memorabilia.
MANN'S CHINESE THEATER, 6925 Hollywood Boulevard, Hollywood
*Built by Sid Grauman in 1927, the oriental decor is intact. Still shows
films. Pavement outside has hand- and footprints of the famous.*
MUSSO AND FRANK'S, 6667 Hollywood Boulevard, Hollywood
*The oldest restaurant in Hollywood. Frequented by F. Scott
Fitzgerald, William Faulkner and Ernest Hemingway in the 1940s.*
SHERLOCK HOLMES PUBLIC HOUSE, 13th floor, Holiday Inn –
Union Square, 480 Sutter Street, San Francisco
*Bar with Victorian decor, Holmes memorabilia and a replica of
Holmes's Baker Street sitting rooms.*
STEINBECK CENTER FOUNDATION, 371 Main Street, Salinas,
tel: 408 796 3833
*Exhibits on Steinbeck. Open Mondays to Fridays 8.00am to 5.00pm.
In June to August also open Saturdays 10.00am to 3.00pm.*
STEINBECK HOUSE, 132 Central Avenue, Salinas, tel: 408 757 3106
John Steinbeck's birthplace restored and run as a restaurant.
VESUVIO'S, 255 Columbus Avenue, North Beach, San Francisco
*Bar frequented by Dylan Thomas and Jack Kerouac next to the City
Lights bookstore. Photographs and memorabilia cover the walls.*

Connecticut

HARRIET BEECHER STOWE HOUSE, Forest Street, Hartford
*Next to Twain's house, details as below, Harriet Beecher Stowe
lived here for thirty years.*
MARK TWAIN'S HOUSE, 77 Forest Street, Hartford, tel: 860 493 6411
*Former home of Samuel Clemens (Mark Twain). Open daily
November to May, closed Mondays and Sundays before 1.00pm.*

Florida

ERNEST HEMINGWAY HOUSE, 907 Whitehead Street, Key West,
tel: 305 294 1575
Former home of Hemingway, where he wrote For Whom the Bell
Tolls *and* A Farewell to Arms. *Open daily.*

Maryland

EDGAR ALLAN POE HOUSE AND MUSEUM, 203 North Amity
Street, Baltimore, tel: 410 396 7932
House where Edgar Allan Poe lived and wrote Berenice.
*Open October to July, Wednesdays to Saturdays, noon to 3.45pm,
from August to September also open Saturdays.*

Massachusetts

CONCORD MUSEUM, 200 Lexington Road, Concord,
tel: 978 369 9763
*Museum includes Ralph Waldo Emerson's study and artifacts and
furnishings of Henry David Thoreau. Open daily.*
CUSTOM HOUSE, 178 Derby Street, Salem, tel: 978 740 1660
*Nathaniel Hawthorne worked here, his office and desk are preserved.
Open daily.*
HAWTHORNE'S BIRTHPLACE, 54 Turner Street, Salem,
tel: 978 744 0991
*House restored with some family furniture. "The House of the Seven
Gables," the setting of Nathaniel Hawthorne's novel of the same name
is also at this location. Open daily.*
HENRY WADSWORTH LONGFELLOW'S HOUSE, 105 Brattle Street,
Cambridge, tel: 617 876 4491
Received as a wedding present, Henry Wadsworth Longfellow lived

here for *45 years, writing* Evangeline *and* The Song of Hiawatha. *Open daily.*

LONGFELLOW'S WAYSIDE INN, off route 20, Sudbury, Concord
Oldest inn in the country; Longfellow's Tales of Wayside Inn *set here.*

THE OLD MANSE, Monument Street, Concord, tel: 978 359 3909
Ralph Waldo Emerson and Nathaniel Hawthorne both lived here. Restored interior with memorabilia. Open mid-April to October, Thursdays, Saturdays and Mondays, Sundays 1.00pm to 4.30pm.

ORCHARD HOUSE, 399 Lexington Road, tel: 978 369 4118
Former home of Louisa May Alcott. Open daily from April to October, from November to March, Saturdays and Sundays only.

RALPH WALDO EMERSON HOUSE, 28 Cambridge Turnpike, Concord, tel: 978 369 2236
Home of Ralph Waldo Emerson for 47 years with original interior. Open mid-April to October, Thursdays, Saturdays and Sundays, 2.00pm to 5.00pm.

SLEEPY HOLLOW CEMETERY, Bedford Street, Concord
Nathaniel Hawthorne, Louisa May Alcott and family, Ralph Waldo Emerson and Henry David Thoreau are buried here.

THOREAU LYCEUM, 156 Belnap Street, Concord, tel: 978 369 3565
Replica of Thoreau's cabin. Open daily from March to December, Sundays 2.00pm to 5.00pm.

WALDEN POND RESERVATION, Walden Street, Concord, tel: 978 369 3254
Cabin gone but possible to follow trail to the place where David Thoreau lived and wrote.

THE WAYSIDE, 455 Lexington Rd, Concord, tel: 978 369 6975
Louisa May Alcott and Nathaniel Hawthorne lived here. Open from mid-April to October, Fridays to Tuesdays.

Minnesota

SINCLAIR LEWIS BOYHOOD HOME, 812 Sinclair Avenue, Sauk Centre, St Cloud, tel: 320 352 5201
Open daily May to September.

SINCLAIR LEWIS MUSEUM, Routes Interstate 94 and Highway 71, Sauk Centre, St Cloud, tel: 320 352 5201
Open daily.

Mississippi

FAULKNER'S HOUSE, Rowan Oak, Old Taylor Road, Oxford, tel: 601 234 3284
Former home of William Faulkner, where he wrote the Snopes *trilogy and* Absalom, Absalom! *Closed Mondays.*

Missouri

MARK TWAIN'S BIRTHPLACE, 208 Hill Street, Hannibal, tel: 573 221 9010
A museum with personal items including an early handwritten manuscript of Tom Sawyer. *Open daily.*

New Jersey

FENIMORE COOPER'S HOUSE, High Street, Burlington tel: 609 386 4773
James Fenimore Cooper's birthplace, now a museum. Open Mondays to Thursdays, 1.00pm to 4.00pm, Sundays 2.00pm to 4.00pm.

New York State

FENIMORE COOPER'S HOUSE, Lake Road, Cooperstown, Otsego, tel: 607 547 1400
Site where James Fenimore Cooper once lived, now a museum with Cooper memorabilia. Open daily.

JAMES FENIMORE COOPER TRAIL, Cooperstown, Otsego Lake
Contact New York State Historical Association Research Library, Route 80, Lake Road, Cooperstown, Otsego, tel: 607 547 4701.

WALT WHITMAN'S BIRTHPLACE, 246 Old Walt Whitman Road, Huntington Station, Suffolk tel: 516 427 5240
The house has been restored to how it was when Walt Whitman was a boy. Open Wednesdays, Thursdays, Fridays, 1.00pm to 4.00pm, Saturdays and Sundays, 10.00pm to 4.00pm.

WASHINGTON IRVING'S HOUSE, Sunnyside, West Sunnyside Lane and Route 9, Tarrytown, Westchester, tel: 914 591 8763
Open March to December, closed Tuesdays.

RUSSIA

Moscow

DOSTOEVSKY HOUSE MUSEUM (Muzey-kvartira F.M.Dostoevskovo), Ulitsa Dostoevskovo 2, tel: 095 2811085
Home of Dostoevsky for 16 years, now a small museum. Closed Mondays, Tuesdays and last day of the month.

NEW CONVENT OF THE VIRGIN (Novodevichiy Monastyr), Novodevichiy Proezd 1
Cemetery where Gogol and Chekhov are buried.

TOLSTOY ESTATE MUSEUM (Muzey-Usadba Lva Tolstovo), Ulitsa Lva Tolstovo 21, tel: 095 2469444
Winter home of Tolstoy. One of Russia's best museums with an extensive collection of memorabilia and personal relics belonging to the author. Closed Mondays.

TOLSTOY MUSEUM (Muzey L.N. Tolstovo), Ulitsa Prechistenka 11, tel: 095 202190
Manuscripts, photographs and paintings associated with Leo Tolstoy. Closed Mondays.

Outskirts of Moscow

GOGOL'S HOUSE, Nikitskiy Bulvar 7A, Arbatskaya
Gogol spent his last years here finishing Dead Souls. *Houses a small museum. Open Thursday and Saturday afternoons.*

TOLSTOY BIRTHPLACE AND COUNTRY ESTATE, Yasnaya Polyana
Tolstoy's house for sixty years. Closed Mondays.

St Petersburg

ALEXANDER NEVSKIY MONASTERY (Aleksandro-Nevskaya Lavra), Reki Monastyrki Naberezhnaya 1
Dostoevsky, Tchaikovsky and Rimsky-Korsakov are buried here.

DOSTOEVSKY HOUSE MUSEUM (Muzey-kvartira F.M. Dostoevskovo), Kuznechniy Pereulok 5, tel: 812 311403
Dostoevsky spent his last three years here writing The Brothers Karamazov, *now a museum. Closed Mondays and last Wednesday of every month. Telephone to book tours.*

PUSHKIN HOUSE, Museum of Literature, Naberezhnaya Makarova 4
Collection of first editions, pictures and personal possessions associated with leading Russian literary figures including Pushkin, Gogol and Dostoevsky. Closed Mondays and Tuesdays.

PUSHKIN HOUSE MUSEUM (Muzey-kvartira A.S. Pushkina), Reki Moyki Naberezhnaya 12, tel: 812 3140006
House where Pushkin died after a duel, now a museum which contains his study and personal possessions. Closed Tuesdays.

Outskirts of St Petersburg

PUSHKIN'S DACHA, Pushkinskaya Ulitsa 2, Pushkin (Tsarskoe Selo)
Pushkin and his wife, Natalya, spent the summer of 1831 here. Restored interior includes Pushkin's study and personal possessions. Closed Mondays and Tuesdays.

PUSHKIN'S SCHOOL, Alexander Lycée (Memorialniy Muzey Litsey), Komsomolskaya Ulitsa 2
School rooms and dormitory are preserved. Closed Tuesdays.

FURTHER READING

AFRICA AND SOUTH AFRICA

Chinua Achebe, Jomo Kenyatta and Amos Tutuola, *Winds of Change: Modern Stories from Black Africa* (1977)

Chinua Achebe and C.L. Innes, eds, *African Short Stories* (1985)

Ulli Beier, ed, *An Introduction to African Literature: An Anthology of Critical Writing* (1967)

J.M. Coetzee, *White Writing on the Culture of Letters in South Africa* (1990)

Nadine Gordimer and Lionel Abrahams, *South African Writing Today* (1967)

Nadine Gordimer, *The Black Interpreters: Notes on African Writing* (1973)

Oona Strathern, *Traveller's Literary Companion: Africa* (1994)

Landeg White and Tim Couzens, eds, *Literature and Society in South Africa* (1990)

AUSTRALIA AND NEW ZEALAND

Murray Bail, ed, *The Faber Book of Contemporary Australian Short Stories* (1988)

D.M. Davin, ed, *New Zealand Short Stories* (1953)

Ken Goodwin, *A History of Australian Literature* (1986)

H.M. Green, *A History of Australian Literature* (1962: rev. 1984)

Rodney Hall, ed, *The Collins Book of Australian Poetry* (1983)

Laurie Hergenhan, *The Penguin New Literary History of Australia* (1988)

Robert Hughes, *The Fatal Shore* (1987)

Leonie Kramer, *Oxford History of Australian Literature* (1981)

Mary Lord, ed, *Australian Writers and Their Works* (1974); *Best Australian Short Stories* (1991)

Peter Pierce, ed, *The Oxford Literary Guide to Australia* (1987)

C.K. Stead, ed, *New Zealand Short Stories: Second Series* (1966)

John Tranter and Philip Mead, eds, *Bloodaxe Book of Modern Australian Poetry* (1994)

William Wilde and Joy Hooton, *The Oxford Companion to Australian Literature* (1986)

Michael Wilding, ed, *The Oxford Book of Australian Short Stories* (1995)

CARIBBEAN

Marcela Breton, ed, *Rhythm and Revolt: Tales of the Antilles* (1995)

David Dabydeen, *A Handbook for Teaching Caribbean Literature* (1988)

Louis James, ed, *The Islands In Between* (1968)

V.S. Naipaul, *A Way in the World* (1995)

EUROPE (General)

J.A. Bede and W.B. Egerton, eds, *The Columbia Dictionary of Modern European Literature* (rev. 1980)

Malcolm Bradbury and James McFarlane, eds, *Modernism: A Guide to European Literature 1890-1930* (rev. 1991)

Simon Cheetham, *Byron in Europe* (1988)

Stephen Coote, *Keats: A Life* (1995)

Godfrey Hodgson, *A New Grand Tour* (1994)

Richard Holmes, *Footsteps: Adventures of a Romantic Biographer* (1995)

James Joll, *Europe Since 1870: An International History* (rev. 1983)

James Naughton, ed, *Traveller's Literary Companion: Eastern Europe* (1994)

Andrew Sinclair, ed, *The War Decade: An Anthology of the 1940's* (1989)

Monroe K. Spears, *Dionysus and the City: Modernism in 20th-Century Poetry* (1970)

Norman Stone, *Europe Transformed: 1878–1919* (1983)

Nigel West, *The Faber Book of Espionage* (1993)

AUSTRIA, CENTRAL AND NORTHERN EUROPE

Alan Janik and Stephen Toulmin, *Wittgenstein's Vienna* (1973)

Barbara Jelavich, *Modern Austria: Empire and Republic, 1815-1986* (1987)

Ivan Klima, *The Spirit of Prague* (1994)

James McFarlane, *Ibsen and the Temper of Norwegian Literature* (1960)

Claudio Magris, *Danube* (1989)

C.E. Williams, *The Broken Eagle: The Politics of Austrian Literature from Empire to Anschluss* (1974)

FRANCE

Shari Benstock, *Women of the Left Bank: Paris 1900–1940* (1987)

James Campbell, *Paris Interzone* (1994)

D.G. Charlton, ed, *A Companion to French Studies* (1972)

John Cruikshank, ed, *French Literature and its Background* (5 vols., 1968–69)

Michael Fabre, *From Harlem to Paris: Black American Writers in France, 1840–1980* (1991)

Noël Riley Fitch, *Literary Cafés of Paris* (1989)

J.E. Flower, *Writers and Politics in Modern France* (1977)

P. Harvey and J. E. Heseltine, *Oxford Companion to French Literature* (1959)

Ian Higgins, ed, *Anthology of Second World War French Poetry* (1982)

George Lemaitre, *From Cubism to Surrealism in French Literature* (1941)

Ian Littlewood, *Paris: A Literary Companion* (1987)

James R. Mellow, *Charmed Circle: Gertrude Stein and Company* (1974)

Roger Shattuck, *The Banquet Years: The Origins of the Avant Garde in France, 1885 to World War I* (rev. 1968)

George Wickes, *Americans in Paris* (1980)

William Wiser, *The Crazy Years* (1990)

GERMANY

Alan Bance, ed, *Weimar Germany: Writers and Politics* (1982)

Keith Bullivant, ed, *The Modern German Novel* (1987)

Gordon Craig, *Germany, 1866–1945* (1978)

Henry and Mary Garland, eds, *The Oxford Companion to German Literature* (1986)

Peter Gay, *Weimar Culture: The Outsider as Insider* (1968)

Michael Hamburger, ed, *German Poetry, 1910–1975: An Anthology in German and English* (1977)

C.W. Haxthausen and H. Suhr, eds, *Berlin: Culture and Metropolis* (1990)

Victor Lange, *The Classical Age of German Literature* (1982)

Dorothy Reich, ed, *A History of German Literature* (1970)

John Willet, *Art and Politics in the Wiemar Period: The New Sobriety 1917-1933* (1978)

C.E. Williams, *Writers and Politics in Modern Germany* (1977)

GREAT BRITAIN (General)

Bill Brandt, *Literary Britain* (1986)

David Daiches and John Flower, *Literary Landscapes of the British Isles: A Narrative Atlas* (1979)

Margaret Drabble, *The Oxford Companion to English Literature*

(1985); *A Writer's Britain: Landscape in Literature* (1979)

Dorothy Eagle, Hilary Carnell and Meic Stephens, *The Oxford Illustrated Guide to Great Britain and Ireland* (rev. 1992)

R. Lancelyn Green, *Authors and Places* (1963)

Kate Marsh, ed, *Writers and Their Houses* (1993)

Frank Morley, *Literary Britain: A Reader's Guide to Writers and Landmarks* (1980)

Ian Ousby, ed, *The Cambridge Guide to Literature in English* (rev. 1993)

Francesca Premoli-Droulers, *Writers' Houses* (1995)

Gillian Tindall, *Countries of the Mind: The Meaning of Place to Writers* (1991)

England

Peter Ackroyd (Intro), *Dickens's England: An Imaginative Vision* (1986)

Bryan Appleyard, *The Pleasures of Peace: Art and Imagination in Postwar Britain* (1989)

John Atkins, *The British Spy Novel: Studies in Treachery* (1984)

Paul Bailey (ed), *The Oxford Book of London* (1995)

F.R. Banks, *The Penguin Guide to London* (1960)

Anne Oliver Bell, ed, *The Diary of Virginia Woolf* (5 vols. 1977–87)

Malcolm Bradbury, David Palmer and Ian Fletcher (eds), *Decadence and the 1890s* (1979)

Derek Brewer, *Chaucer in His Time* (1963)

Humphrey Carpenter, *The Brideshead Generation: Evelyn Waugh and His Generation* (1989)

David Cecil, *A Portrait of Jane Austen* (1980)

Hugh Cecil, *The Flower of Battle: British Fiction Writers of the First World War* (1995)

Graham Chainey, *A Literary History of Cambridge* (1995)

Mark Cocker, *Loneliness and Time: British Travel Writing in the 20th Century* (1994)

Millie Collins, *Bloomsbury in Sussex* (1989)

Robert M. Cooper, *The Literary Guide and Companion to Southern England* (1985)

Valentine Cunningham, *British Writers of the Thirties* (1988)

David Dabydeen and Paul Edwards, eds, *Black Writers in Britain: An Anthology* (1992)

Andrew Davies, *Literary London* (1988)

A.M Edwards, *In the Steps of Thomas Hardy* (1989)

Iain Findlayson, *Writers in Romney Marsh* (1986)

Geoffrey Fletcher, *Pocket Guide to Dickens' London* (1976)

Paul Fussell, *Abroad: British Literary Travelling Between the Wars* (1980); *The Great War and Modern Memory* (1975)

Martin Green, *Dreams of Adventure, Deeds of Empire* (1980)

Thomas Hardy and Hermann Lea, *Thomas Hardy's Wessex* (1913)

Humphrey House, *The Dickens World* (1941)

John Dixon Hunt and Peter Willis, *The Genius of Place* (1975)

Samuel Hynes, *The Auden Generation* (1976)

Holbrook Jackson, *The Eighteen-Nineties* (rev. 1988)

Peter Keating, *The Haunted Study: A Social History of the English Novel, 1875–1914* (1989)

Peter Lewis, *The Fifties* (1978)

Grevel Lindop, *A Literary Guide to the Lake District* (1993)

Roger Loomis, *A Mirror of Chaucer's World* (1965)

Howard Loxton, *Pilgrimages to Canterbury* (1978)

John Lucas, ed, *The 1930s: A Challenge to Orthodoxy* (1978)

Luree Miller, *Literary Villages of London* (1989)

Alan Myers, *Myers' Literary Guide: The North East* (1995)

Norman Nicholson, *The Lakers: Adventures of the First Tourists* (1995)

F. B. Pinion, *A Hardy Companion* (1968)

Roy Porter, *London: A Social History* (1994)

V.S. Pritchett, *London Perceived* (1962)

S. Schoenbaum, *William Shakespeare: A Documentary Life* (1977)

Miranda Seymour, *Ring of Conspirators: Henry James and His Literary Circle, 1895-1915* (1988)

Alan Sinfield, ed, *Society and Literature, 1945–1970* (1983)

Terence Spenser, ed, *Shakespeare: A Celebration* (1964)

John Sutherland, *The Longman Companion to Victorian Fiction* (1988)

Peter Vansittart, *London: A Literary Companion* (1992)

Ian Watt, *The Rise of the Novel* (1957)

George G. Williams, *Guide to Literary London* (1973)

Scotland

Alan Bold, *Modern Scottish Literature* (1983); *Scotland: A Literary Guide* (1989)

Cairns Craig, ed, *The History of Scottish Literature* (4 vols., 1987–89)

Andrew Lownie, *The Edinburgh Literary Guide* (1992)

Andrew Pennycock, *Literary and Artistic Landmarks of Edinburgh*, 1973

Trevor Royle, *Precipitous City: The Story of Literary Edinburgh* (1980); *The Macmillan Companion to Scottish Literature* (1983)

Gavin Wallace and Randall Stevenson, *The Scottish Novel Since the Seventies* (1993)

Roderick Watson, *The Literature of Scotland* (1981)

Wales

Meic Stephens, *The Oxford Companion to the Literature of Wales* (1986)

IRELAND

E.A. Boyd, *Ireland: Literary Renaissance* (1916)

Susan and Thomas Cahill, *A Literary Guide to Ireland* (1973)

Seamus Deane, ed, *A Short History of Irish Literature* (1986); *An Anthology of Irish Writing* (1991)

Richard Ellmann, *Ulysses on the Liffey* (1972); *Four Dubliners: Yeats, Wilde, Joyce and Beckett* (1986)

Vivien Igoe, *A Literary Guide to Dublin* (1994)

P.J. Kavanagh, *Ireland: A Literary Companion* (1994)

Sheelagh Kirby, *The Yeats Country* (1962)

William Trevor, *A Writer's Ireland: Landscapes in Literature* (1984)

Robert Welch, *Oxford Companion to Irish Literature* (1996)

ITALY

Peter Bondanelli and Julia Conway, *The Macmillan Dictionary of Italian Literature* (1979)

Van Wyck Brooks, *Dream of Arcadia: American Writers and Artists in Italy, 1760-1915* (1958)

Francis King, *Florence: A Literary Companion* (1992)

Mary McCarthy, *Venice Observed* (1982)

Carl Maves, *Sensuous Pessimism: Italy in the Work of Henry James* (1978)

S. Pacifici, *A Guide to Contemporary Italian Literature* (1962)

Peter Quennell, *Byron in Italy* (1951)

John Varriano, *Rome: A Literary Companion* (1992)

RUSSIA

Vera Alexandrova, *A History of Soviet Literature 1917–1964* (1964)

Edward Brown, *Russian Literature Since the Revolution* (1963)

Ronald Hingley, *Russian Writers and Soviet Society, 1917–1978* (1979)

Y. Yevtushenko, A.C. Todd, M. Hayward, D. Weissbort, eds, *Twentieth Century Russian Poetry* (1994)

SPAIN

Gerald Brenan, *The Spanish Labyrinth: An Account of the Social and Political Background of the Spanish Civil War* (1943)

Valentine Cunningham, ed, *Spanish Front: Writers on the Spanish Civil War* (1986)

Philip Ward, *The Oxford Companion to Spanish Literature* (1977)

INDIA

Aditya Behl and David Nicholls, eds, *The Penguin New Writing in India* (1995)

Arjun Dangle, ed, *Poisoned Bread, Translations from Modern Marathi Dalit Literature* (1992)

K.R. Srinivasa Iyengar, *Indian Writing in English* (1962)

Adil Jussawalla, *New Writing in India* (1974)

Bruce Palling, *India: A Literary Companion* (1992)

Alan Sandison, *The Wheel of Empire: A Study of the Imperial Idea in Some Late 19th and early 20th Century Fiction* (1967)

Simon Weightman, ed, *Traveller's Literary Companion: The Indian Subcontinent* (1993)

Angus Wilson, *The Strange Ride of Rudyard Kipling* (1977)

JAPAN AND SOUTH EAST ASIA

Alastair Dingwell, ed, *Traveller's Literary Companion: South East Asia* (1993)

Harry Guest, ed, *Traveller's Literary Companion: Japan* (1993)

LATIN AMERICA

David W. Foster, ed, *Handbook of Latin American Literature* (1987)

Jean Franco, *An Introduction to Spanish-American Literature* (1995)

D.P. Gallagher, *Modern Latin American Literature* (1973)

Jason Wilson, *Traveller's Literary Companion: South and Central America* (1993)

UNITED STATES OF AMERICA

Daniel Aaron and Robert Bendiner, eds, *The Strenuous Decade: A Social and Intellectual Record of the 1930s* (1970)

Jervase Anderson, *This Was Harlem: A Cultural Portrait 1900–1950* (1981)

Houston A. Baker, Jr, *Modernism and the Harlem Renaissance* (1987)

Bernard W. Bell, *The Afro-American Novel and its Tradition* (1987)

Malcolm Bradbury, *Dangerous Pilgrimages: Trans-Atlantic Mythologies and the Novel* (1995)

Van Wyck Brooks, *The Flowering of New England: 1815–1865* (1936)

Ann Charters, *Beats and Company: Portrait of a Literary Generation* (1986); *Scenes Along the Road* (1970)

Peter Conn, *Literature in America: An Illustrated History* (1989)

Malcolm Cowley, *Exile's Return: A Literary Odyssey of the 1920s* (1934)

Morris Dickstein, *Gates of Eden: American Culture in the Sixties* (1977)

Ann Douglas, *Terrible Honesty: Mongrel Manhattan in the 1920s* (1995)

Susan Edmiston and Linda D. Cirino, *Literary New York: A History and a Guide* (1976)

Federal Writers Project, *New York Panorama* (1938)

Gene Feldman and Max Gartenberg, eds, *The Beat Generation and the Angry Young Men* (1958)

Lawrence Ferlinghetti and Nancy J. Peters, *Literary San Francisco* (1980)

Otto Friedrich, *City of Nets* (1986)

Edwin Fussell, *Frontier: American Literature and the American West* (1965)

Martin Green, *The Problem of Boston* (1966)

Ian Hamilton, *Writers in Hollywood 1915-1951* (1990)

John Harris, *Historic Walks in Old Boston* (1982); *Historic Walks in Cambridge* (1986)

Don Herron, *The Literary World of San Francisco and its Environs* (1986)

Eric Homberger, *The Historical Atlas of New York City* (1995)

Hugh Honour, *The New Golden Land: European Images of America from the Discoveries to the Present Time* (1976)

William Howarth, *The Book of Concord: Thoreau's Life as a Writer* (1983)

James de Jongh, *Vicious Modernism: Black Harlem and the Literary Imagination* (1990)

Alfred Kazin, *A Writer's America: Landscape in Literature* (1988)

Richard H. King, *A Southern Renaissance: The Cultural Awakening of the American South, 1930-55* (1980)

Marcia Leisner, *Literary Neighbourhoods of New York* (1989)

Alain Locke, *The New Negro* (1925)

Leo Marx, *The Machine in the Garden: Technology and the Pastoral Ideal* (1964)

Fred McDarrah, *Greenwich Village* (1963)

Fred W. McDarrah and Patrick J. McDarrah, *The Greenwich Village Guide* (1992)

Luree Miller, *Literary Hills of San Francisco* (1992)

Ethan Mordden, *The Hollywood Studios* (1988)

Toni Morrison, *Playing in the Dark: Whiteness and the Literary Imagination* (1992)

George and Barbara Perkins and Philip Leininger, *Benet's Reader's Encyclopedia of American Literature* (1987)

Gil Reavill, *Hollywood and the Best of Los Angeles* (1994)

Jack Salzman, ed, *Years of Protest: A Collection of American Writings of the 1930s* (1967)

Henry W. Sams, ed, *Autobiography of Brook Farm* (1958)

Henry Nash Smith, *Virgin Land: The American West as Symbol and Myth* (1950)

Harvey Swados, *The American Writer and the Great Depression* (1966)

F.W. Volpe, *A Reader's Guide to William Faulkner* (1964)

Caroline Ware, *Greenwich Village 1920-30* (rev. 1994)

Steven Watson, *Strange Bedfellows: The First American Avant-Garde* (1991)

Henry Wiencek, *The Smithsonian Guide to Historic America: Southern New England* (1989)

Elias Wilentz (ed), *The Beat Scene* (1960)

WRITING OF THE FIRST AND SECOND WORLD WARS

Ronald Blythe, ed, *Components of the Scene: An Anthology of the Prose and Poetry of the Second World War* (1967)

Paul Fussel, *The Great War and Modern Memory* (1975)

Brian Gardner, ed, *Up the Line to Death: The War Poets 1914-1918* (1964)

Brian Gardner, ed, *The Terrible Rain: The War Poets 1939-45* (1966)

M.S. Greicus, *Prose Writers of World War 1* (1973)

Holger Klein, ed, *The First World War in Fiction: A Collection of Critical Essays* (1976)

I.M. Parsons, ed, *Men Who March Away: Poems of the First World War* (1965)

Andrew Sinclair, ed, *The War Decade: An Anthology of the 1940s* (1989)

INDEX

References to illustrations are in *italic*; maps in ***bold italic***; chapter headings and main entries in **bold**. Authors are in [brackets] following their works.

Abse, Dannie 243
Abstraction 159
Absurd, Theatre of 226
Acevedo, F. de B. y 301
Achebe, Chinua 302-3, *303*,
Ackroyd, Peter 96, 99, 323
Adam, Villiers de l'Isle 129
Adamov, Arthur 226
Adams, Henry 154
Adamson, Robert 286
Addison, Joseph 50
Aesthetic movement 144-5
Africa 302-5, *305*
African-American writing *190*, **190-93**, *192*, *193*, 205, *310*, **310-13**, *312*, *313*
After the Wall (Malcolm Bradbury) **324-5**
Agathon (Wieland) 74
Agee, James 199
Agnon, S.Y. 290
Akhmatova, Anna *262*, 263
Albee, Edward 226
Albert, Prince Consort 87
Aldington, Richard 173
Alegría, Ciro 300-301
Alemán, Mateo 29
Alexandria, Egypt 291-2
Allen, Walter 209
Allende, Isabel 299, 300, *301*
Allfrey, Phyllis S 283
Altenberg, Peter 160
Alterman, Nathan 288-9
Althusser, Louis 226
Alton Locke (Kingsley) 114
Amadi, Elechi 303, 304
Amado, Jorge 298-9
Ambassadors, The (James) 131, 132
America, see Latin America; African-American Writing, United States of America
Amichai, Yehuda 290
Amis, Kingsley 216, 219, 237, *243*, 274, 326
Anderson, Sherwood 156, 176, 186, 189, 194-6, 197
Andrade, Mário de 298
Angelou, Maya 312
Antigua 283
Apollinaire, Guillaume 171
Arabic literature **291-3**, *292*
Arden, John 236
Arenas, Reinaldo 301
Armah, Ayi Kwei 304, *304*
Arnim, Achim von 77
Arnold, Matthew 61, 100, 113-14, 115, 307
Aron, Raymond 224
Arrowsmith, Aaron *56-57*
Art Nouveau 160
Assis, Joachim Maria Machado de 300

Atwood, Margaret 308, *308*, *326*
Auden, W.H. *112*, 183, *211*, 213, 214-15
Audobon, James 85
Austen, Jane 45, **66-9**, *66*, *68*
Auster, Paul 315, 317, *317*
Australian Images: Sydney and Melbourne (Michael Wilding) **284-7**
Austria 160-62, 170-71
Authors and their works **326-32**
Ayckbourn, Alan 243

Bâ, Mariama 304
Babbitt (Lewis) 194
Bacon, Francis 11
Bainbridge, Beryl 243
Bakr, Salwa 293
Baldwin, James 193, 225, 310, 311, 326
Ballantyne, R.M. 150
Balsdon, Dacre 275
Balzac, Honoré de 72, 84, *92*, 93-5, *93*, *94*
Banville, John 277
Baraka, Amiri 311
Barakat, Hoda 293, *293*
Barbados *282*
Barbusse, Henri *171*, 172-3
Barstow, Stan 242
Barthes, Roland 226
Bartholomew, Atlas of Commercial Geography *116-7*
Bassani, Giorgio 234
Bates, H.E. 220
Bates, Ralph 213
Bath, Avon 66-8, *67*
Jane Austen's, *69*
Baudelaire, Charles 128
Bay Psalm Book 34
Beach, Sylvia 176, *177*, 307
Beardsley, Aubrey 145, *155*
Beat Generation (Eric Homberger) **252-5**
Beat poets 226, **253-5**
Beauvoir, Simone de 224, *225*
Becher, Johannes R. 228
Beckett, Mary 279
Beckett, Samuel 45, 168, 214, 217, 220, 221, 226, 277, 302, 326
Bede, Cuthbert (Edward Bradley) 274
Beerbohm, Max 145, 274
Beggar's Opera (Gay) 49,*49*
Behan, Brendan 166, 236, 277
Behn, Aphra 42, *42*
Bell, Vanessa *and* Clive 178-80, *178*
Bellow, Saul 156, 219, 326
Bely, Andrei 183
Benchley, Robert 200
Benn, Gottfried 185, 228, *228*
Bennett, Alan 242, 326
Bennett, Arnold 103, 144, 145
Bentley, Phyllis 209
Benton, Kenneth 259
Bergen, Norway 18, *138*
Bergerac, Cyrano de 40

Berkeley, George 52
Berlin ***184-5***, **231**
between the wars **182-5**
post-war **228-31**, 229, *230*
Russian emigré writers 183
Wall *230*, 231, *256*, **257**, *324*, *324*
Berlin: the Centre of German Modernism (Heinz Ickstadt) **182-5**
Bernstein, Leonard *247*
Bierce, Ambrose 124
Bingham, John, Madeleine *and* Charlotte 258
Bird, Isabella 149
Bird, Robert Montgomery 124
Birney, Earle 306
Black Arts Movement 311
Blake, William 49, 99
Bleasdale, Alan 243
Blois, France 25
Bloomsbury **178-81**, *179*
Blunden, Edmund 171
Blythe, Ronald 243
Boccaccio, Giovanni 16, 19, 326
Bohemians 126-9
Bolger, Dermot 277
Böll, Heinrich *228*, 230, *231* 326
Bombay, India **266-9**, *268*, *269*
Booth, General William 145
Bordeaux, France 24-5, *25*, *27*
Borges, Jorges Luis 234, 299, *301*, 326
Bosman, Herman Charles 297
Boston, Massachusetts **108-11**, *109*
Boulle, Pierre 219
Boyd, Martin 287
Bradbury, Malcolm 274, *274*
Bradford, William 34
Bragg, Melvyn 61, 243
Braine, John 242
Brand (Ibsen) 139
Brandes, Georg 137
Brantôme, Pierre de 24
Brathwaite, Edward Kamau 283
Brazil 298, 300
Brecht, Bertolt 183, *183*, 184-5, 202, 228-9, *230*, 231, 236, 302
Brennan, Christopher 285
Brenner, Yoseph Haim 289
Brentano, Clemens 77
Breytenbach, Breyten 295-6
Brierley, Walter *208*
Brink, André 295, 297
Britain,
American writing; effect on 78-81
"Birmingham Group" 209-10
civic theatres *241*, 243
"Condition-of-England Question" 100-101
Depression 208, **208-11**, *209*, **210**
industrialism 99, **100-103**, *103*

modern universities 274-5, **275**
northern England towns 101-2, *101*, *102*
provincial writing **240-43**, *241*
see also London
British Empire,
American colonies 34
explorer adventurers 148-51
extent of 148, **149**
Broadway (Arthur Miller) **244-7**
Broch, Hermann 162
Brod, Max 164-5
Bromfield, Louis 200
Brontë family 102, *104*, **104-7**
Bronze Horseman, The (Pushkin) 90
Brooke, Rupert 115, 170, *172*
Brookner, Anita 322
Brougham, Henry (Lord Brougham and Vaux) 54
Brown, Dr John 58
Brutus, Dennis 297
Bryant, William Jennings 186
Buchan, John 256
Bulgakov, Mikhail 262, 326
Bunting, Basil 243
Bunyan, John 19, 326
Burgess, Anthony 216
Burke, Edmund 46, 52, *52*
Burney, Fanny 66
Burns, Robert 54, 142, 326
Burroughs, William S. 226, 253, 255
Burton, Richard 149
Byron George Gordon, 6th Baron 54, *62*, *63*, 63-5, *65*, 68, 114

Cable, George Washington 125, 197
Cain, James M. 200
'Caine' Mutiny, The (Wouk) *219*
Cairo, Egypt *293*
Caldwell, Erskine 199, 205
Callow, Philip 208
Calvin, Jean 25
Calvino, Italo 232, 234, *234*
Cambridge University **112-15**, *115*, 178
Campbell, Roy 296
Campus Fictions (D. J. Taylor) **274-5**
Camus, Albert 217, 220, 221, 224, *226*
Canadian Images (Greg Gatenby) **306-9**
Candide (Voltaire) 40
Canterbury Tales (Chaucer) 16-19, **17**
Capek, Karel 163
Capote, Truman 199
Carey, Peter 286, *286*, 327
Caribbean *280*, **280-83**, *281*
Carlyle, Thomas 54, 100, 101, 102, 103, 108
Carpentier, Alejo 299-300
Carr, John Dickson 258
Carroll, Lewis (C.L. Dodgson) 112, 113, *113*

Carson, Ciaran 279
Carter, Angela 320, 323, 327
Cassady, Neal 253, 254, *255*
Categorical Imperative 75
Cather, Willa 188, 327
Catholicism 50-51, 53, 112, 129, 166-7, 276-9
Cavafy (Greek poet) 291, 292
Cazalis, Maria 224
Celati, Gianni 234
Cervantes, Saavedra, Miguel de **28-31**, 42
Cervantes' Spain (Patricia Shaw) **28-31**
Césaire, Aimé 280-81, *282*
Champlain, Samuel de 34
Chandler, Raymond 200
Chandos Letter (Hofmannstal) 161
Chandra, Vikram 267
Chaplin, Sid 208
Chateaubriand, F.-R. de, Vicomte 70, *70*, 71-2
Chaucer, Geoffrey **16-19**, *16*
Chaucer's England (Malcolm Bradbury) **16-19**
Chavez, Denise 301
Chawton, Hampshire 68
Chekov, Anton 327
Chesterfield, Philip D. Stanhope, Earl of 50
Chesterton, G.K. 146, 147
Chicago in the 1890s *157*
Chicago's World Fair (Malcolm Bradbury) **154-7**
Childers, Robert Erskine 256
Chopin, Kate 125, 197
Le Cid (Corneille) 38
cinema,
Hindi 267, *267*
Italian 233-4
screenplays 200-203
Clarissa (Richardson) 45
Clark, J.P. 304
Clarke, Marcus 287
Claudel, Paul 129
Cobbett, William 114
Cocteau, Jean 175, 176, 327
Coetzee, J.M. 295, 297, *297*
Cohen, Matt 308
Cold War Tales (Nigel West) **256-9**
Coleridge, Samuel Taylor 58, *60*, 60-61, 62, 79, 108, 114
Colette 327
Collen, Lindsay 305
Collins, Wilkie 45, 147, 327
Columbus, Christopher 32, *33*, 79-81, 154, 293
"*Comédie humaine*" (Balzac) 93-5
Communism,
Bolshevik Revolution 172
post-war 159, 229
Spanish Civil War **212-15**, *215*
Communist Manifesto (Marx/Engels) 102
Concord, Massachusetts 110-11
Congreve, William 49, 50, 66, 327
Conrad, Joseph 131-2, *132*, 144, 151, *151*, 284, 327

Constant, Benjamin 72
Contemporary Israeli Writing (Risa Domb) **288-90**
Cook, Captain James 37, *56-7*
Cooper, James Fenimore 81, *82*, *83*, **82-5**, *85*, 149, 186
Cooper, Leslie 209
Cooper, William 239, 240-42
Corneille, Pierre 38-9
Cornwell, David 257
Corso, Gregory 226, 253, *254*, 255
Cosa, Juan de la the New World *33*
Country Wife (Wycherley) 49
Courbet, Gustave 128
Cowley, Malcolm 186
Cowper, William 48
Crane, Hart 327
Crane, Stephen 124, 131, 144, 180, 188, 327
Creech, William 54
Crime and Punishment (Dostoevsky) 88, 90, *90*, 91, *91*
Cross, Eric 276
Cruz, Sor Juana Inés de la 301
Crystal Palace, London 87, 100, *101*
game **86-7**
Cubism 159, 189
Cullen, Countee 192, *192*
cummings, e.e. 173, 176, 186
Cunha, Euclides da 301
Curran, John Philpot 52
Czechoslovakia 264, 265

Dabydeen, David 283
Dada movement 171, 175, 177, 189
D'Aguiar, Fred 283
Dalton, John 58
Dampier, Captain William 37
Dangerous Liaisons (Laclos) 41
Daniel, Yuliv 264, *264*
Dante Aligheri 12, *12*
Dante's Italy *15*
Dante's Worlds (Patrick Boyde) **12-15**
Danube, The (Magris) 160
Dário, Rubén 301
Dark, Eleanor 286
Darwin, Charles 114, 128, 149
Darwish, Mahmoud 292-3, *293*
D'Aubigné, Agrippa 26
Davie, Donald 243
Davies, Robertson 306, 308, *309*
Davies, W.H. 209
Day Lewis, Cecil 214, 217
de Quincey, Thomas 58, 60-61
Deane, Seamus 279, *279*
Death of a Salesman (Miller) 244, *244*, *245*
Decadence movement 129
Decameron (Boccacio) 16
Defoe, Daniel 42, *42*, 48, 49, 150

Deighton, Len 258, 259
Delaney, Shelagh 236
Dell, Floyd 186, 188, 189
Depression America (Chris Bigsby) **204-7**
Depression Britain (D. J. Taylor) **208-11**
Derrida, Jacques 226
Desai, Anita 266, 267, *267*
Descartes, René 24, 39
Dexter, Colin 275
Dickens, Charles 19, 45, 58, 61, 79, *96*, **96-9**, 101-3, 118, 146-7, 284, 307
Dickens's London *99*
Dickens's London (Malcolm Bradbury) **96-9**
Dickie, James 199
Dickinson, Emily 111, 327
Dictionary of the English Language (Johnson) 46, *46*
Diderot, Denis 38, *40*, 40-41
Dineson, Isak 327
Discovery of the New World: Arcadia and Utopia (Malcolm Bradbury) **32-5**
Disraeli, Benjamin 101, *102*, 103
Divided Ireland (Glenn Patterson) **276-9**
Divine Comedy (Dante) *12*, 12-15
Döblin, Alfred 184-5, 202, 228
Dr Jekyll and Mr Hyde (Stevenson) 143, *143*, 146
Doctor Zhivago (Pasternak) 263-4, *264*
Dodge, Mabel 189
Dombey and Son (Dickens) 100
Dominica 283, *283*
Don Quixote (Cervantes) *28*, **28-31**, *29*
Don Quixote's Spain **30-31**
Donleavy, J.P. 226
Doody, Margaret 274
Dorchester, Dorset 136
Dorfman, Ariel 300
Dos Passos, John 173, 186, 189, 200, 205, 213, 254, 327
Dostoevsky, Fyodor 88, 90, *90*, 91, 328
Douglas, Frederick *123*
Douglas, Keith 218-19, 220
Dove, Rita 312
Doyle, Roddy 277-9, *277*, *279*
Doyle, Sir Arthur Conan 147, *147*, 307
Drabble, Margaret 240, 322
Drayton, Michael 34
Dreaming Spires: Nineteenth Century Oxford and Cambridge (Jon Cook) **112-15**
Dreams of Empire (Malcolm Bradbury) **148-51**
Dreiser, Theodore 154, 155, 156, 186, 188, 189, 200-201

Du Bellay, Joachim 27
du Maurier, Gerald 129
Dublin,
eighteenth century *50*, **50-52**, *51*
Joyce's **166-9**, *168-169*
see also Ireland
DuBois, W.E.B. 190, 192, *192*
Duffy, Maureen 322
Dumas, Alexander (*pére*) 92
Duncan, Robert 255
Dunciad (Pope) 46-7
Durrell, Lawrence 291, 328
Dylan Thomas's Wales (Russell Celyn Jones) **248-51**

Eastern Europe *265*
Eastman, Max 188-9
Eco, Umberto 232, *234*, 235, *235*
Edinburgh,
eighteenth century *53*, **53-5**, *55*
and Stevenson **140-43**, *143*
Edinburgh Review 54
Eich, Günter 229
Eichendorff, J.F. von 77
Eighteenth Century Dublin (Owen Dudley Edwards) **50-52**
Eighteenth Century Edinburgh and Scotland (Owen Dudley Edwards) **53-5**
Eighteenth Century London (Roy Porter) **46-9**
Eisler, Hanns 228
Ekwensi, Cyprian 303
Eliot, George 100, 103, *103*, 328
Eliot, T.S. 17, 81, 120, 156, 175, 176, 181, 239, 302, 328
Ellis, Bret Easton 316-17
Ellison, Ralph 193, 311
Emerson, Ralph Waldo 87, 108-11
Emerson's and Hawthorne's New England (Malcolm Bradbury) **108-11**
Emile (Rousseau) 40
Encyclopaedia Britannica 54
Encyclopedia 40, 41
Endo, Shusaku 272, *272*, *273*
Engels, Frederick 102
Enlightenment,
in France **38-41**
in Germany 75
in Scotland **53-5**
Enzensberger, Hans 230
Esquivel, Laura 300
Essays (Montaigne) 24, 24-7
Etherege, Sir George 49
Eugene Onegin (Pushkin) 89-90
Europe,
Grand Tour 78-9 *79*
Romantics *64-5*
transatlantic novels **78-81**, **130-33**
Washington Irving's *80*
European Apple: Henry James's International Scene (Malcolm Bradbury) **130-32**

Everywhere the Wind Blows: African-American Writing Today (Alexs Pate) **310-13**
Ewart, Gavin 218
Existentialism **224-7**, 237, *238*, 239, 253
Existentialist Paris and Beyond (Ian Littlewood) **224-7**
Expressionism 170, 177, 182
Ezekiel, Nissim 268

Fall, Aminata Sow 304
Fanon, Frantz 280-81
Fantasywallas of Bombay (Githa Hariharan) **266-9**
Farah, Nuruddin 305
Farewell to Arms (Hemingway) 173
Farquhar, George 52
Farrell, James T. 156, 205
Faulkner, William 125, 133, *197*, **197-9**, *198*, *199*, 201, 205, 307
Faust (Goethe) 75, *75*, 75
Fergusson, Robert 54-5
Ferlinghetti, Laurence 255, *255*
Festival of Britain 236, *236*
Fichte, Johann 76
Fielding, Henry 42, 43, 49
Findley, Timothy 308
Fischer, Samuel 185
Fitzgerald, F. Scott 176, 177, 196, 200-201, *201*, 205, 328
Flaubert, Gustave, 24, 126, *126*, 130, 299
Fleming, Ian 256, 259, *259*
Florence, Italy *12-13*, *13*
Fontane, Theodor 182, 229
Ford, Ford Maddox 131, 145, 173, 175-6, 328
Forest, John William de 125
Forster, E.M. 112-13, 151, 170, 178-81, 226, 328
Foucault, Michel 226
Fowles, John 328
France,
Age of Enlightenment **38-41**, *41*
American colonies 34
courtly love 16
Louis-Philippe's reign 92
in Montaigne's time **24-7**, *26*
Napoleonic Wars 62, 66, 72
Philosophes **38-41**, *40*
regional novel 95
Revolution (1789) 62, 71-2, *72*
Revolution (1848) 126, *126*
Romantic movement **70-73**, 92
Third Republic 126
World War I writers 171
France of the Enlightenment (John Fletcher) **38-41**
Franklin, Miles 284
Fremont, John Charles 85
Freud, Sigmund 160, 162
Friel, Brian 279, *279*
Frisch, Max 226, 328
Fry, Roger 180
Frye, Northrop 306

Fuentes, Carlos 301, 328
Fugard, Athol 295
Fuller, Roy 220
Füssli, Johann Hei 77
Futurism 159, 170, 177

Gadda, Carlo Emilio 232
Gaines, Ernest J. 310-11
Galeano, Eduardo 300
Gallegos, Rómulo 300
Lorca Garcia, Frederico 293, 327
Gardner Smith, William 225
Garland, Hamlin 154
Garland, Judy *247*
Garnett, David 178
Gaskell, Elizabeth 101, *101*, 104, 107
Gates, Henry Louis 311
Gautier, Théophile 72
Gay, John 49, *49*
Gee, Maggie 322
Genet, Jean 224
Germany,
between the wars **182-5**
book-burning *182*, 185
exile literature 228
Group 47 **229-31**, *231*
Kultur 75
Modernism 182-5
Neue Schule 75-7
rise of Hitler 182-3
post-war **228-31**, *229*
Romantic movement **74-7**, *76*, *77*
"Rote Kapelle" 228
World War I 213
writers fighting in Spain 213
Writers' Union 231
see also Berlin
Germany After the War (Heinz Ickstadt) **228-31**
Germinal (Zola) 128, *128*
Ghosh, Amitav 268
Gibbons, Grassic 209
Gibson, Grahame 308
Gide, André 24, 132, 176, 328
Gilpin, William 58
Ginsberg, Allen 226, 253-5
Ginzburg, Natalia 234
Giraudoux, Jean 246
Gissing, George 99, 103, 144-5
Glasgow 53, 318-19, *318*, *319*
Glasgow, Ellen 124, 125, 197
Globe theatre, London 22, *22*
Goethe, Johann Wolfgang von 65, 74-7, *75*, 108
Gogol, Nikolai 73, 88-90
Golding, Louis 209
Golding, William 216, 237
Goldsmith, Oliver 46, 52, *52*, 66
Goldwyn, Sam 200
Goncourt, Edmond *and* Jules 128, 130
Gone With the Wind (Mitchell) 124, 199
Gongora, Luis de 29
Good and Bad Government in Siena (Lorenzetti) 12, *13*
Good Soldier Schweyk (Hasek) 164, *164*, 173

Gordimer, Nadine 294-5, 297, *297*, 303
Gorky, Maksim 262
Gough, Medieval world map *18*
Government Inspector, The (Gogol) 90
Grapes of Wrath (Steinbeck) **204-7**, *206*, *207*
Grass, Günter 219, 220, 230, 231, 328
Grattan, Henry 52
Graves, Robert 173
Gray, Alasdair **318-19**, *318*, *319*
Gray, Thomas 58, 60
Great Exhibition (1851) **86-7**, 97, 100, *101*, *103*, 236
Great Gatsby, The (Fitzgerald) 196
Greco, Juliette 224, *225*
Green, Martin 188
Greene, Graham 214, 218, 257-8, *259*, *300*, 328
Greenwich Village **186-7**
Greenwich Village (Eric Homberger) **186-9**
Greenwood, Walter 208, 209
Gregory, Lady Augusta 152-3, *152*
Grenfell, Julian 170
Grimm, Jacob *and* Wilhelm 76, 77
Grossman, David 290
Grosz, George 182, 183, *183*, 184-5
Grotewohl, Otto 228
Group 47 229-31, *231*
Guernica (Picasso) *214*
Gulliver's Travels (Swift) 43, *43*, 51
Gurnah, Abdulrazak 305
Gurney, Ivor 171
Gutenburg, Johannes 11
Guttuso, Renato *233*
Guyana 283

Haggard, H. Rider 150
Hakluyt, Richard 33
Halley, Edmund 37
Halward, Leslie 208
Hammett, Dashiell 200
Hampson, John 209
Hamsun, Knut 137
Hard Times (Dickens) 97-8, 102
Hardy, Frank 287
Hardy, Thomas 103, 113, 114-15, **133-6**, *133*, 144, 284
Hardy's Wessex *134-5*
Harlem in the 1920s *191*
Harlem's Renaissance (Eric Homberger and Chris Bigsby) **190-93**
Harmsworth's political map *158-9*
Harris, Joel Chandler 122
Harris, William 283
Hasek, Jaroslav 163, 164-5, *164*, 173
Havel, Hippolyte 189
Havel, Václav 226, 265, 324, *325*
Haworth, West Yorkshire **104-7**

Hawthorne, Nathaniel 110, *110*, 124
Hazaz, Haim 289
Head, Bessie 297
Heaney, Seamus 152, 243, 277, 279, 329
Hearn, Lafcadio 270
Heart of Midlothian (Scott) 53
Heath, Roy A.K. 283
Hecht, Ben 156, 200
Hegel, Friedrich 75
Heller, Joseph 216, 219
Hellman, Lilian 199, 200, 246
Hemingway, Ernest 81, 132, 156, 172, 173, 175-7, 183, 196, 205, 213-14, *213*, 307
Henry of Navarre (Henry IV, King of France) 25
Henry VII, Holy Roman Emperor 13
Henty, G.A. 151
Herder, Johann Gottfried 74, 75
Hermlin, Stefan 231
Heslop, Harry 209
Hesse, Heinrich 228
Hesse, Hermann 228, 230, 329
Hewitt, John 276
Heym, George 182
Heym, Stefan 231
Heyward, DuBose 199
Hill, Abram 192
Hill, Geoffrey 243
Himes, Chester 193, 225
Hines, Barry *240*, 242
History Man, The (Bradbury) 275
Hitler, Adolf 162, 182, 184, 228
Hoffman, E.T.A. 77, 182
Hofmannsthal, Hugo von 160-61, 329
Hogarth, William 47, *48*
Hogarth Press 181, *181*
Hoggart, Richard 242
Hölderlin, Friedrich 75
Höllerer, Walter 231
Holmes, John Clellon 252
Hopper, Edward 196
Hornung, E.W. 147
House for Mr Biswas, A (Naipaul) 282
Howells, William Dean 124, 307
"Howl" (Ginsberg) 253-5
Huckleberry Finn (Twain) 118-19, *118*
Hudson, Henry 34
Hughes, Langston 192
Hughes, Robert 287
Hughes, Ted 242
Hugo, Victor *71*, 72, 73, *73*, 92, 126
Hume, David 54
Hume, Fergus 287
Humphry Clinker (Smollett) 48
Hungary 265
Hurston, Zora Neale 310
Huxley, Aldous 181, *201*, 202, 329

Ibsen, Henrik **137-9**
Imagism 180, 188

Impressionism 144-5
In Search of Andalusia: Arabic Literature Today (Fadia Faqir) **291-3**
India **266-9**, *269*
    East India Company *148*
    Parsis 266-7
Industrial Revolution 57, 79, 86, 99
Infante, Guillermo Cabrera 301
Interpretation of Dreams (Freud) 160
Ionesco, Eugene 219-20, 226, 236
Ireland,
    divided **276-9**, *278*
    eighteenth century **50-52**
    Field Day 279
    Literary Revival 167
    "Troubles" **276-9**, *277*
    Yeats's land *153*
    see also Dublin
Irish Revival, The (Frank Delaney) **152-3**
Irving, Washington 77, 78-81, *78*
Isherwood, Christopher 183, 202, 208, *211*
Israel **288-90**, *288*, *289*
Italy,
    fascist censorship 232-3
    Jewish writers 234
    in time of Dante **12-15**, *15*
    Montaigne's visit 26-7
    post-war fiction **232-5**, *235*
    Romantics attachment to 63-5
    wartime devastation *232*

J'Accuse (Zola) 128
Jackson, Holbrook 144
Jacobson, Howard 275
Jahnn, Hans Henry 231
James, C.L.R. 281
James, Henry 79, 81, **130-33**, *130*, 144, 166, 170, 171, 175, 180, 186, 188, 307
    transatlantic themes *131*
James Fenimore Cooper's Frontier (Malcolm Bradbury) **82-5**
James Joyce's Dublin (Desmond Hogan) **166-9**
Jane Austen's Regency England (Malcolm Bradbury) **66-9**
Japan *270*, *271*, *325*
    early writers 270
    modern novels **271-3**
    theatre 271
Japan: Land of Spirits of the Earth (Kazumi Yamagata) **270-73**
Jefferson, Thomas 84, 122, 123
Jeffrey, Francis 54
Jellicoe, Ann 236
Jerusalem 289-90, *290*
Jésus, Carolina Maria de 301
Johannesburg, South Africa 294-6, *294*, *295*
Johnson, Charles S. 312
Johnson, James Weldon 192
Johnson, Samuel 46, *46*, 55

Johnson, Uwe 230, 231
Johnston, Jennifer 279
Journal Tel Quel 226
journalism 46-7, 48-9, 145
Journeys of the Age of the Novel (Malcolm Bradbury) **42-5**
Joyce, James 45, 162, **166-9**, 170, *166*, 175, 176, *177*, 188, 277, 314
    Dublin **168-9**
Jünger, Ernst 185, 228
Jussawalla, Adil 268
Kafka, Franz **163-5**, *163*, 173, 183
    Prague *165*
Kafka's Prague (Malcolm Bradbury) **163-5**
Kanga, Firdaus 266, 267
Kant, Immanuel 75
Katiya, Wilson 304
Kavanagh, Patrick *276*, 277
Kawabata, Yasunari 271, 329
Keats, John 58, 61, 62, 63, 65
Kenan, Randall 312
Keillor, Garrison 196
Kelman, James 318-19
Kenaz, Yehoshua 288
Keneally, Thomas 284, 286-7
Kennedy, John Pendleton 122
Kerouac, Jack **252-5**, *252*
Kessler, Harry Graf 185
Keynes, John Maynard 178, 180
el-Kharrat, Edward 291-2
Kidnapped (Stevenson) *142*, 143
Kierkegaard, Søren 137
Killens, John Oliver 311
Kincaid, Jamaica *282*, 283
King Solomon's Mines (Haggard) 150
Kingsley, Charles 103, 114
Kipling, Rudyard 150-51, *150*
Kirchner, Ernst-Ludwig 182
Kisch, Egon Erwin 184
Kleist, Heinrich von 75
Knight, Maxwell 258
Knopf, Alfred 192
Koeppen, Wolfgang 230-31
Koun, Karolos 21-2
Kraus, Karl 161-2
Kreymborg, Alfred 188
Kristeva, Juila 226
Krolow, Karl 230
Kundera, Milan 31, 329
Kureishi, Hanif 322

la Boétie, Etienne de 24
la Fontaine, Jean de 39
La Guma, Alex 296
La Mancha, Spain 28-9, *29*
Lacan, François 226
Laclos, Choderlos de 41
Laing, Kojo 305
Lake District of the Romantics (Melvyn Bragg) **58-61**
Lake District *59*
Lamantia, Philip 255
Lamartine, Alphonse de 73, 92
Lamb, Charles 49
Lamming, George 281
Lampedusa, Giuseppe Tomasi di 234, 299, 329

Lanier, Sidney 197
Lapid, Shulamit 288
Larkin, Philip 240, 242
Lasker-Schüler, Else 185
Last Tycoon, The (Fitzgerald) 201
Latin America 34, *298*, **298-301**, *299*
Latin American Writing: A Literary Heritage Explored (Louis de Bernières) **298-301**
Lawrence, D.H. 170, 171, 180-81, 242, 284, 329
Lawson, Henry 284-5
Lazarillo de Tormes 29
le Carré, John 257-9, *258*, *259*
le Queux, William 256
Leatherstocking Saga (Cooper) 82-5, *82*, *83*, *85*
Lee, Nathaniel 46
Lehmann, John 208
Leitch, Maurice 279
Lennox, Charlotte 42
Lepanto, Battle of (1571) 28
Lermontov, Mikhail 90-91
Les Miserables (Hugo) *71*, 73, *73*
Lessing, Doris 239, 329
Let Us Now Praise Famous Men (Agee/Evans) 205
Levi, Carlo 234
Levi, Primo 217, 221, 234, *234*
Lévi-Strauss, Claude 226
Lewis, Sinclair 183, 189, 194-6, *194*
Lewis, Wyndham 180, 308, 329
Liebermann, Max 182
Liebknecht, Karl 182-3
Life on the Missippi (Twain) 120
Lillo, George 49
Lindsay, Norman *and* Jack 285-6
Lindsay, Vachel 188, 196
Littlewood, Joan 236
Lively, Penelope 323
Liverpool, England 243, *243*
Livings, Henry 242
Livingstone, David 149, *149*
Llosa, Mario Vargas 299, 300, *301*, 329
Lochhead, Liz 243
Locke, Alain 192
Lockhart, J.G. 114
Lodge, David 242, 274-5
London,
    in 1890s **144-7**
    in 1950s **236-9**, *238*
    Bethlem Hospital 46
    Bloomsbury **178-81**, *179*
    Festival of Britain 236
    Campaign for Nuclear Disarmament 237, *237*
    Centre 42 237
    coffee houses 48, *48*
    Dickens's **96**, 96-9, 97, 98-9
    East End **145-7**, *146*, *146*, 322-3, *323*
    eighteenth century **46-9**, *47*, *48*
    growth of 100, 144
    Grub Street 46-7
    Henry James's residence in 130-32, 144
    Johnson on 46

literature of **144-7, 236-9, 320-23**
medieval 16, *16*
modern **320-23**, *321*
modern novelists **320-23**
National Theatre 236-7
"New Look" 237
Royal Court Theatre 236-7 *237*
Shakespeare's **22-3**, *23*
Stendhal's visits 92
theatres 49
West End **146-7**, *147*
London, Jack 145, 284
London: The Dislocated City (Jonathan Coe) **320-23**
London in the Fifties (Malcolm Bradbury) **236-9**
London in the 1890s (Malcolm Bradbury) **144-7**
Longfellow, Henry Wadsworth 108
Longley, Michael 277
Look Back in Anger (Osborne) 236-7, *237*
Lord of the Flies (Golding) 237
Lorenzetti, Ambrogio 12, *13*, *14*
Lost Generation 189
Louis XIV, King of France 38-40
Lowry, Malcolm 329
Lucky Jim (Amis) 237, 274
Lurie, Morris 287
Luther, Martin 25
Luxembourg, Rosa 183
Lyme Regis, Dorset 67, *68*, *69*

McAlmon, Robert 183
McClure, Michael 255
McCullers, Carson 199
McGahern, John 276
McInerney, Jay 316, 317
McLuhan, Marshall 306
McMillan, Terry 313
McNeice, Louis 213, 214-15, 276-7
Macaulay, Thomas Babington 54, 100, 114
Macdonald, Alexander 55
MacInnes, Colin 239
Mackenzie, Compton 256, 274
MacLaverty, Bernard 279
Macpherson, James 55
Macintyre, White Duncan 54-5
Mach, Ernst 161
Madame Bovary (Flaubert) 126
Maeterlinck, Maurice 200
Magic Mountain, The (Mann) 170
Magical Realism 299-300, 313
Magris, Claudio 160
Mahfouz, Naguib 291, 303
Mahler, Gustav 160
Maid of Buttermere (Bragg) 61
Mailer, Norman 203, 219, 252, 329

Main Street (Lewis), 194, 195
Main Street, USA (Malcolm Bradbury) **194-6**
Malberba, Luigi 234
Mallarmé, Stephane 129, 285
Malraux, André 213, 214, 225
Manchester, England 101
Manganelli, Giorgio 232
Manhattan Tales: Who's Afraid of Tom Wolfe? (Paul Micou) **314-17**
Mankiewicz, Herman J. 200, *200*
Mann, Heinrich 185, 202, 228-9
Mann, Klaus 185
Mann, Thomas 170, 183, 184, 202, 228, 329
Manning, Frederick 173
Manning, Olivia 219
Mappa mundi 14, *14*
Marechera, Dambudzo 304
Marguerite de Navarre 25
Marinetti, F.T. 170
Mark Twain's Mississippi (Malcolm Bradbury) **118-121**
Márquez, Gabriel Garcia 299-300, *301*
Marryat, Captain Frederick 306-7
Martellus, Henricus **10-11**
Martineau, Harriet 100, 107
Marx, Karl 43, 102, 239
Masses, The (New York magazine) 188-9, *188*
Massie, Alan 243
Masterman, John 258
Masters, Edgar Lee 195, 196
Matthiessen, Peter 226
Maturin, Charles 45
Maugham, Somerset 145, 256
Maupassant, Guy de 128, 130
Mauriac, François 175, 214, 330
Melbourne, Australia **286-7**, *287*, **287**
Melville, Herman 102, 186, 325, 330
Mencken, H.L. 194, 196, 200
Meneghello, Luigi 234
Meredith, Christopher 251
Mérimée, Prosper 70, *70*, *72*, *73*, 92
Merleau-Ponty, Maurice 224
Merry Wives of Windsor (Shakespeare) 21
Middle Ages 10-35
Midnight's Children (Rushdie) 266, 267, 268
Millar, Martin 320
Miller, Arthur 190, 204-5, 206, **244-7**, *244*
Miller, Henry 330
Milton, John 330
Le Misanthrope (Molière) 39, *39*
Mishima, Yukio 272, 330
Mississippi River **118-21**, *119*, *120*
Mark Twain's *121*
Mistral, Gabriela 301

Mistry, Rohinton 266-7
Mitchell, Margaret 124, 199
Modernism,
in America 155-6
in England 131-2, 147, 172, 181
German **182-5**
Italian *233*
in Paris 129, 175-6
Spanish 301
in Vienna 160-62
Molière (Jean-Baptiste Poquelin) 38-9
Molinari, Ricardo 301
Moll Flanders (Defoe) 42
Monluc, Blaise de 24
Monroe, Harriet 156, *156*
Montaigne, Michel de **24-7**, *24*
Montaigne's France (James Supple) **24-7**
Montesquieu, Charles Louis de Secondat 40
Montreal, Canada *307*, 308
Moorcock, Michael 323
Moore, Brian 277
Moore, G.E. 178
Moore, George 145, 153
Moore, Marianne 186, 188, 189, 330
Moorhouse, Frank 286
Moraes, Dom 268
Moravia, Alberto 233, 234, *234*
More, Sir Thomas 32
Morrell, Lady Ottoline 180-81
Morris, William 146
Morrison, Danny 279
Morrison, John 287
Morrison, Tony 310
Moser, Kolomon 160
Mosley, Walter 312, *312*
Mottram, R.H. 173
Muldoon, Paul 243, 279
Munch, Edvard 137, *137*
Murasaki, Lady 270
Murder in the Cathedral (Eliot) 17
Murdoch, Iris 237, 330
Murray, Les 286
Musil, Robert 160, 162, 184 330
Musset, Alfred de 70, *70*, 72, 92, 95
Mwangi, Meja 303

Nabokov, Vladimir 183, 226, 330
Naipaul, V.S. 281, 282, *282*
Napoleon Bonaparte 62, 66, 70-72, 84, 92, 93, 126
Naturalism movement 129, 189
Naylor, Gloria 312
Neo-Realism 233
Neruda, Pablo 301, 330
New England **108-11**, *108*, *109*, *111*
New Negro, The (Locke) 191
New World **32-5**
Voyages of Discovery *33*
New York,
"The Eight" 188
Greenwich Village **186-9**, *186-7*, *253*, 254

Harlem **190-93**, *190*, *191*, *192*, *193*, 310
Liberal Club 189
Lower East Side *253*
magazines 188-9
Manhattan **314-17**, *314*, *315*, *317*
theatre on Broadway **244-7**, *245*
Wall Street novels 314-17
Washington Square Bookshop 188-9, *189*
see also United States of America
Newman, Henry, Cardinal 112
Newton, Isaac 37
Nicholson, Norman 58, 61, 243
Nicolson, Harold 181
Nigeria *302*, **303-4**, *304*, 305
Nodier, Charles 72
Novalis (Friedrich von Hardenberg) 76
Nwapa, Flora 304
Nyamfukudza, S. 304

O Neachtain, Sean (John Neville) 51
Oakley, Barry 286, 287
O'Brien, Flann 276, 277
O'Casey, Sean 153, 246
O'Connor, Flannery 199
O'Connor, Frank 276
O'Connor, Joseph 277
Odets, Clifford 204, 244, 246
Oe, Kenzaburo 273, *273*
Okara, Gabriel 304
Okigbo, Christopher 304
Okri, Ben 295
Old Curiosity Shop (Dickens) 97, 102-3
Old Goriot (Balzac) **93**
Olivier, Sir Laurence (later Lord) 236, 246
Olympia Press 226
Ondaatje, Michael 308, *308*, 330
O'Neill, Eugene 186, 188, 192, 244
Oppenheim, E. Phillips 147, 256
Orlovsky, Peter 226
Oroonoko (Behn) 42
Orwell, George (Eric Blair) 208, 209, *209*, *213*, 214, 330
Osborne, John 236-7
Osundare, Niyi 305
Our Town (Wilder) 196
Owen, Wilfred 171, 172, 220
Oxford Movement 112
Oxford University **112-15**, *112*, *113*
Oz, Amos 289-90, *290*

Paine, Tom 38, 186
Paris,
in 1830s **92-5**, *93*
in 1920s **174-5**, *175-7*
American presence 175-7, 225-6
avant-garde 126
Balzac's *93*
Beat poets 226

bellé epoque 129
Bohemian **126-9**, *127*
clubs *224*
Comédie Française 38, *38*, *39*, 73
Eiffel Tower 129, *129*
Existentialist **224-7**, *227*
experimental presses 177
internet cafés *325*
Montparnasse 177
nouveaux romanciers 226
Pont Neuf 25
publishing houses 226
rebuilding 117, 126
Romantic writing **70-73**, *71*
Sacre Coeur *129*
salons 176
structuralism 226-7
theatres 38-9, 226
Paris as Bohemia (John Fletcher) **126-9**
Paris in the Twenties (Malcolm Bradbury) **174-7**
Paris of the French Romantics (Douglas Johnson) **70-73**
Parker, Dorothy 200
Parkman, Francis 85
Pascal, Blaise 24, 39
Pasolini, Pier Paolo 235
Passage to India (Forster) 170
Pasternak, Boris 262, 263-4, *264*
Patchen, Kenneth 255
Pate, Alexs 313
Patel, Gieve 268
Pater, Walter 100
Paton, Alan 296, *296*
Patterson, Banjo 284-5
Paulin, Tom 279, *279*
Pavese, Cesare *233*
Paz, Octavio 301
Peer Gynt (Ibsen) 138
Percy, Walter 199
Peregrine Pickle ... (Smollett) 44
Peter the Great, Tsar of Russia 88, *88*
Petrarch, Francesco 330
Petry, Ann 193, 311
Philby, Kim 258
Phillips, Caryl 283
Phillips, Mike 322
picaresque novel 29, *31*, 43, 209
Picasso, Pablo *214*
Pilgrim Fathers 34, *34*
pilgrimages **17-19**, *18*
Pilgrim's Progress (Bunyan) 19
Pinter, Harold 226, 257, 330-31
Plaatje, Sol T. 296
Plater, Alan 242-3
Plimpton, George 226
Plomer, William 296
Poe, Edgar Allen 108, 122, 123, 128, 129, 186, 331
Poole, Alison 316
Pope, Alexander 40, 46-7, *47*
Porter, Hal 287
Portrait of the Artist as a Young Man (Joyce) 167-8

Post-War Italian Fiction
  (Guido Almansi) **232-5**
Postmodernism 226
Potter, Beatrix 58
Potter, Dennis 243, 331
Pound, Ezra 81, 156, 171,
  175-6, 180, 188, 214, 331
Powell, Anthony 208, 216,
  239
Prague **163-5**, *163*, *164*, **165**
Pre-Raphaelite
  Brotherhood 112
**Precipitous City: Robert
  Louis Stevenson's
  Edinburgh** (Gavin
  Wallace) **140-43**
Priestley, J.B. 209, *210*, 211,
  242
Principia Ethica (Moore) 178
Pritchett, V.S. 145
Protestantism 25-6, 52,
  53, 112, 276-9
Proust, Marcel 129, 132,
  170, 175, 177, 331
Pudd'nhead Wilson (Twain)
  118-20, *119*
Pudney, John 220
Pushkin, Alexander 73, **88-
  91**, *89*

Quarrington, Paul 309
Queneau, Raymond 224
Quevedo, Francisco 29

Rabelais, François 25, *25*,
  42
Racine, Jean 38, 39, 40, 92
racism 190-93
Rackham, Arthur *43*, *81*
Ramos, Graciliano 301
Ramsay, Allan 54
Rastafarian movement
  280-81, *281*
Rathenau, Walter 183
Raven, Simon 275
Ravenna, Italy 12
Reade, Charles 103
Réage, Pauline 226
Realism movement 92-3,
  117, 128, 130
Reason, Age of **36-55**
Reed, Ishmael 311-13
Reed, John 189, 254
Reinhardt, Max 184
Remarque, Erich Maria 173,
  184
Remembrance of Things Past
  (Proust) 170, 175, 177
Renaissance **10-35**
Restoration theatre 49
Rexroth, Kenneth 255
Reynolds, Sir Joshua 46, *46*
Rhys, Jean 283
Ribeiro, Darcy 298
Richardson, Henry Handel
  287, 331
Richardson, Samuel 42, *45*
Richelieu, A.J. du
  Plessis, Cardinal 38, *38*
Richter, Hans Werner 229,
  231
Richter, Johann Friedrich
  (Jean Paul) 75, 79
Rights of Man (Paine) 38
Rilke, Rainer Maria 331
Rimbaud, Arthur 129, 300
Rip Van Winkle (Irving)
  79-81

Road to Wigan Pier
  (Orwell) 208-11
Roberts, Kate 251
Robertson, William 53
Robinson Crusoe (Defoe)
  42-3, *43*, *44*, 150
Roderick Random ...
  (Smollett) 44
Rodman, Henrietta 189
Rodriguez, Luis 301
Romance of the Rose 16
Romantic movement 49, 57,
  70-73, **74-7**, 92
nouveaux romanciers 226
Romantics Abroad (Rupert
  Christiansen) **62-5**
Rome 63, *63*
Scandinavian writers 137
transatlantic novels 131, *131*
Ronsard, Pierre de 25-6
Room at the Top (Braine)
  242
Room With a View
  (Forster) 178-80
Roque, John *47*
Rosa, J. G. 301
Rosenberg, Isaac 171
Rossellini, Roberto 233, *233*
Roth, Henry 190
Roth, Joseph 162, 184
Rousseau, Jean Jacques 38,
  40, *40*, *41*, 71
Royal Shakespeare Company
  236
Royal Society 37, 51
Royle, Nicholas 322
Rushdie, Salman 266-8,
  267
Ruskin, John 61, *112*, 115
Russell, Bertrand 181
Russell, George ("AE") 153
Russell, Willie 243
Russia,
  Booker Prize 265
  Cold War **256-9**
  emigré writers 183
  glasnost policy 265
  Moscow *263*
  post-war **262-5**, *265*
  Revolution (1917) 160,
    183
  St Petersburg *91*
  World War II writers 217
  Writers' Union 262-5
**Russia and Eastern Europe
  After the Second World
  War** (Arch Tait) **262-5**
Rutherford, Mark 103
Rye, Sussex 131, *132*

Sachs, Nelly 217, 219, 230
Sackville-West, Victoria
  Mary ('Vita') 181
Sade, Donatien A.F.,
  Marquis de 41, 300
Saint Bartholomew's Day
  Massacre (1572) 27
Saint-Exupéry, Antoine de
  213
St Petersburg **88-91**, *89*,
  90, *91*
Salazar, Alonso 301
Salem, Massachusetts 110
San Francisco, California
  253
Sand, George 72, 95, *95*
Sandburg, Carl 156, *156*,
  188, 196

Sarang, Vilas 268
Sarashina, Lady 270
Saro-Wiwa, Ken 305
Sartre, Jean-Paul 217,
  224-5, *225*
Sassoon, Siegfried 171, *172*,
  173, 181
Satellite map *260-1*
*Saturday Night and Sunday
  Morning* (Sillitoe) 242
Savinio, Alberto 232
Scandinavia *139*
**Scandinavia: the Dark and
  the Light** (James
  McFarlane) **137-9**
Scarlet and the Black, The
  (Stendhal) 92-3
**Scenes from Provincial
  Life** (Malcolm
  Bradbury) **240-43**
Schelling, Friedrich 76
Schiller, Friedrich von
  74, *74*, 75-7
Schlegel, August Wilhelm
  and Friedrich 75-6, 77,
  182
Schlondorf, Volker 244
Schmidt, Arno 231
Schnitzler, Arthur 161
Schoenberg, Arnold 202
Schreiner, Olive 296
Sciascia, Leonardo 234
Scotland,
  eighteenth century **53-5**
  Gaelic language 54-5
  Glasgow **318-9**
  Robert Louis Stevenson
    140-44
  Scott's romanticizing 79
Scott, Sir Walter 45, 53,
  53, 54, *54*, 55, 68, 69,
  72, 77, 79, *79*, 135
Secession movement
  160-62
Secret Agent, The
  (Conrad) 144
Seghers, Anna *228*, 228-9
Selvon, Samuel 281
Senex, John *36-7*
Senghor, Léopold Sédar 303
Sentimental Education, The
  (Flaubert) 126
Sentimental Journey ...
  (Sterne) 45
Seth, Vikram 268
Shabtai, Ya'akov 289
Shakespeare, William 20,
  20-23, 92
**Shakespeare's Stratford
  and London** (Terry
  Hands) **20-23**
Shalev, Meir 288
Shange, Ntozake 312
Sharpe, Tom 275
Shaw, George Bernard 52,
  146, 262, 277, 331
Shelley, Mary 45, 63, 331
Shelley, Percy Bysshe 57,
  63-5, *63*, 115
Sheridan, Richard
  Brinsley 52, 66, 246
Sheridan, Thomas 52
Shlonsky, Avraham 288
Sica, Vittorio de 233
Sidhwa, Bapsi 266-7, *266*
Sidney, Sir Philip 32
Silence (Endo) 272, 272-3
Sillitoe, Alan 208, 242

Silone, Ignazio 232
Simms, William Gilmore 122
Sinclair, Iain 323
Sinclair, Upton 124, 156,
  156, 189
Sinyavsky, Andrei 264, *264*
*Sketch Book of Geoffrey
  Crayon, Gent* (Irving) 78-9
slavery 118-20, **122-5**,
  123, **124**
**Sleeping Giant: Pushkin's,
  Gogol's and Dostoevsky's
  St Petersburg** (Arch
  Tait) **88-91**
Slessor, Kenneth 284
Smart, Kit 46
Smellie, William 54
Smith, Adam 32
Smith, Captain John 34
Smith, Sydney 54
Smollett, Tobias 42, *42*,
  43-4, 48
Snow, C.P. 239, 240-42, 274
Snyder, Gary 253, 255
Social Contract
  (Rousseau) 40
Socialism 146, 160, 182, 185
Sollers, Philippe 226
Solzhenitsyn, Aleksandr 264,
  332
Sondheim, Stephen *247*
Sorrows of Young Werther
  (Goethe) 74
Soseki, Natsume 270-71
**South, Slavery and the
  Civil War** (Chris
  Bigsby) **122-5**
South Africa 294-7, *294*,
  295, *296*, 304
South African Stories
  (Justin Cartwright) **294-7**
Southey, Robert 61, 62
Soyinka, Wole 302, *303*, 303-4
Spain,
  Andalusia 291-3
  in Cervante's time
    28-31, **30-31**
  Civil War **212-15**, *215*
  New World discoveries
    and settlement 32, 33, 34
Spanish Civil War
  (Valentine
  Cunningham) **212-15**,
Spark, Muriel 237, *237*
Spectator 50
Spender, Stephen 183, 208,
  213, 217, 220
Spenser, Edmund 50
Spicer, Jack 255
spy fiction **256-9**
Stadler, Ernst 182
Staël, Madame de (A.L.G.
  Necker) *70*, 70-71, *74*
Starvinsky, Igor 202
Stead, Christina 284
**Steaming Chimneys:
  Britain and Industrialism**
  (Malcolm Bradbury)
  100-103
Steele, Richard 50, *52*
Stein, Gertrude 132, 156,
  176, *176*, 177, 225
Steinbeck, John **204-7**, *206*
Stendhal, Henri Beyle 92,
  92-5, *93*
**Stendhal's Balzac's and
  Sand's France** (Douglas
  Johnson) **92-5**

Stephen, Virginia 178
Stephens, James 153
Sterne, Laurence 42, *42*, 45,
  45
Stevens, Wallace 156
Stevenson, Robert Louis
  53, 140-43, *140*, 144,
  146, *150*, 284
Stoppard, Tom 332
Storey, David 242
Stowe, Harriet Beecher
  111, 124
Strachey, Lytton 178, 181
Strangers and Brothers
  (Snow) 240
Stratford-Upon-Avon,
  Warwickshire **20-22**,
  20
Shakespeare's Stratford
  21
Streetcar Named Desire
  (Williams) 246, *246*
Strindberg, Johan August
  137, 138
structuralism and post-
  structuralism 226-7
Der Sturm (Berlin
  periodical) 184, *184*
Sturm und Drang 74
Summer and Smoke
  (Williams) 246
Surkov, Alexei 263
Surrealism 175, 177
Sussex *180*
Svevo, Italo 232, 332
Swift, Jonathan 42, 43,
  50-51, 52, *52*
Swiss family Robinson
  (Wyss) 150
Sybil ... (Disraeli) 101
Sydney, Australia **284-7**,
  285, *286*
Symbolist movement 129,
  177
Synge, J.M. 153

Tabard Inn, Southwark 16,
  17
Tale of Beryn (anon.) 19
Tanizaki, Junichiro 271
Tel Aviv, Israel *288*,
  288-9
Tempest, The
  (Shakespeare) 33
les Temps Modernes
  (journal) 225
*Ten Days That Shook the
  World* (Reed) 254
Tennyson, Alfred, Lord
  100, 112-13, *114*
Thackeray, William
  Makepeace 45, 101, 114
Tharoor, Shashi 266, 267
Thaw, Duncan 318
theatre,
  Absurd 226
  Aristotelian unities 39
  Broadway **244-7**, *245*
  civic *241*, 243
  classical tragedy 38
  comedies 39
  Dublin 52
  Japan 271
  London 22, *22*, 49, 236-7
  Paris 38-9, 226
  Restoration 49
Thiong'o, Ngugi wa 303,
  303, 304

"This Grey But Gold City":
the Glasgow of Gray
and Kelman (Gavin
Wallace) **318-19**
Thomas, Dylan 239, *248*,
248-51, 302
Thomas, G.C.H. 283
Thomas, Gwyn 251
Thomas, R.S. 251
Thomas-à-Becket, Saint 17,
17
Thomas Hardy's Wessex
(Michael Millgate)
133-6
Thoreau, Henry David
110-11, *111*
Thurber, James 189, 194
Tieck, Ludwig 76, 77, 79,
182
Todorov, Tzvetan 226
Toller, Ernst 213
Tolstoy, Count Leo 332
Tom Jones ... (Fielding)
43, *43*, **44**
Tomlinson, H.M. 171
Tone, Theobald Wolfe 52
Toomer, Jean 191, 310
Toronto, Canada **306-8**, *309*
transatlantic novels
78-81, 130-33
Transcendentalism 108-10
travel and discovery 33-4,
37, 42-5, 84-5
Treasure Island
(Stevenson) 150, *151*
Trevor, Elleston 257
Trilling, Lionel 189
Trinidad 282
Tristram Shandy ...
(Sterne) 45, *45*
Trollope, Anthony 45, 101,
135
Trollope, Frances 100
Trotsky, Leo 160
Tucker, Reverend Josiah 48
Turgenev, Ivan 88, 90, 130,
330
Turner, Frederick Jackson
154
Tutuola, Amos 302, *303*
Tvardovsky, Alexsandr *262*,
263
Twain, Mark *118*, **118-21**,
125, 182, 186, 307
Tytler, James 54

Ulbricht, Walter 228
Ulysses (Joyce) 162, 166-7,
170, 172, 175, 176, *177*,
189, 307
Unanisme 177
Uncle Tom's Cabin (Stowe)
111, 124, *125*
Under Fire (*Le Feu*)
(Barbusse) 171-2, *171*
Under Milk Wood (Thomas)
250, 251
United Nations *222-3*
United States of America,
African-American
writing *190*, **190-93**,
192, 193, 205, *310*,
310-13, *312, 313*
Americans in Paris
175-7, 225-6
Amerindian literature
34, 71-2

Beatniks **252-5**, *254,
255*
black writing **190-93**
Broadway theaters *244*
"Chicago Renaissance"
154-7, *154, 155*, **157**
Civil War 120, 124-5,
197
Cold War 225
Constitution 40
Declaration of
Independence 38, 74
Depression **204-7**, *204,
205, 207*
Dickens's tours 97, 99,
118, 307
discovery of New World
35, *32-5*
Federal Writers'
Project 205-6
frontier novels 118-20
Harlem **190-3**, *191*
Hollywood **200-203**, *201,
202*, **202-3**
Louisiana Purchase 84
Manhattan **314-7**, *315*
New England writers *108*,
108-11, *109*
1950s 252-5
1920s writers in Paris
176-7
Revolution (1776-83) 57,
78
Route 66 *206-207*
San Francisco *253*
settlement of 34
slave states *124*
slavery 118-20, **122-5**
small-town values 194-6
Southern writing **122-5**,
197-9, *199*
suburban 252-5
Thomas's reading tours
251
transatlantic novel
78-81, 130-33
Transcendentalism 108-10
West, myth of 82-5 **83**,
84, 85, 154
Westward expansion, *83*
World Fair (1893) *154*,
154-7, *155*
World War I 172
World War II writers 216
Yoknapatawpha County,
Missippi **197-9**, *199*
see also New York

Valéry, Paul 129, 175,
176, 177, 332
Vallejo, César 301
Van der Post, Laurens
296
Vanburgh, Sir John 49
Vega, Lope de 29
Verlaine, Paul 129
Verne, Jules 149
Vespucci, Amerigo 32,
33
Vian, Boris 224
Vienna **160-62**, *161*
Vigny, Alfred de 73, 92
Vine, Barbara 322
Virginia, USA 34
Visconti, Luchino 234
Vita nuova (Dante) 12
Vittorini, Elio 233

Voltaire (F.-M. Arouet)
38, 40, *40*, 182
Vonnegut, Kurt 219
Vorticism 170, 180, 308

Wackenroder, Wilhelm 76
Wainwright, John 58
Waiting for Godot
(Beckett) 220, 221, 226
Walcott, Derek 283
Waldseemüller, Martin 32
Wales **248-51**, *249, 250, 251*
Walker, Alice 312, *312*
Walker, Margaret 311
Walpole, Horace 66
Ward, Mrs Humphry 115
Ward, Ned 48-9
Warren, Robert Penn 198
Washington, Booker T.
190
Washington Irving's Europe
(Malcolm Bradbury)
78-81, *80*
Waste Land, The (Eliot)
175, 176, 181
Waten, Judah 287
Waterhouse, Keith 242
Waugh, Alec 208
Waugh, Evelyn 202, 208,
214, 216, 218-19, 226,
274
Wealth of Nations (Smith)
32
Wegel, Helen 229
Weimar and the German
Romantics (Rudiger
Ahrens) **74-7**
Weimar
Eighteenth Century *76*
Weisenborn, Günter 228
Weiss, Peter 332
Welles, Orson *200*, 225
Wells, H.G. 99, 146
Welty, Eudora 199
Werfel, Franz 202
Wesker, Arnold 236, 237
Wesley, Mary 217
Wessex 133-6, *133-6*
West, Morris 286
West, Nathanael 201, *202*
West, Father Thomas 58
West, Arthur Graeme 171
West Indies 280-83
Whalen, Philip 255
Wharton, Thomas, Earl of
50
Whistler, James McNeill
145
White, Patrick 286-7
Whitman, Walt 124
Wideman, John Edgar 312,
312
Wieland, Christopher
Martin 74
Wiesel, Elie 217, *217*
Wild Yorkshire: the
Brontës of Haworth
(Jane Sellars) **104-7**

Wilde, Oscar 108, 114,
115, 144-5, 277, 332
Wilder, Thornton 176, 196,
246
Wilding, Michael 286
Wilhelm Meister ...
(Goethe) 75, 76
William Faulkner's New
South (Malcolm
Bradbury) **197-9**
Williams, Eric 281
Williams, John A. 311
Williams, Nigel 322
Williams, Raymond 243
Williams, Tennessee 125,
199, 204, 244-6, *246*, 332
Williams, William Carlos
188, 255
Williamson, David 286,
287
Williamson, Henry 173
Wilson, Angus 217, 239
Wilson, Colin 239
Wilson, Edmund 129,
189
Winckelmann, Johann
75
Winesburg, Ohio
(Anderson) 194-5,
196
Winthrop, John 34
Wittgenstein, Ludwig 161,
162
Wittgenstein's Vienna
(Malcolm Bradbury)
160-62
Wolf, Christa *84*, 231
Wolfe, Thomas 183, 189,
254
Wolfe, Tom 314-17, *316*,
332
Women in Love (Lawrence)
170
Woolf, Adrian 178-81,
183
Woolf, Virginia (née
Stephen) 24, 132,
178-81, *178, 181*
Wordsworth, Dorothy 49,
58, *58*, 60, 114
Wordsworth, William 49,
58, *58*, **60-61**, 62
World After the Wall, The
(Malcolm Bradbury)
324-5
world atlases *10, 14, 36,
44, 56, 86-7, 116-17,
158, 222-3, 260-61*
World of Bloomsbury
(Malcolm Bradbury)
178-81
World War I 132, 163
post-war Germany 182
trench warfare *170*, 171
writers **170-73**, *173*
World War II,
atom bomb *221*, 224
atrocities 217, *218*, 220

bombing *219*
elegies 220
ending Depression 206-7,
211
Europe and North Africa
218
events of 216
fiction **217-19**
German resistance 228
Jewish writers 217
Pacific *221*
poetry 219, **220-21**
writers **216-21**
writers in action
216-21
post-war literature 223
Wright, Richard 156,
192-3, 205, 225, 311
Writers Go to War
(Valentine
Cunningham) **216-21**
Writers' Hollywood (Paul
Levine) **200-203**
Writers of the Great War
(Malcolm Bradbury)
170-73
Writing of Africa Today
(Alaistair Niven) **302-5**
Writing of the Caribbean
(Lucretia Stewart)
280-83
Wuthering Heights
(Brontë) 104, 107,
107
Wycherley, William 49
Wyeth, Andrew 196

X, Malcolm 311

Yeats, W.B. 144-5, *144,
152*, **152-3**, 168, 171,
246, 302
Yeats' land *153*
Yehoshua, A.B. 289, 290
Yellow Book 145, *145*
Yevtushenko, Yevgeney *262,
263, 264, 265*
Yizhar, S.Y. 288
Yoknapatawpha County,
Mississippi **197-9**, *198,
199*
Yorkshire
Brontë's *105*
Young, Arthur 58
"Young Vienna" movement
162
Younger, William 258
Yourcenar, Margaret 291

Zangwill, Israel 145
Zhukovsky, Vasily 89, 90
Zola, Émile 128, *128*, 145
Zoshchenko, Mikhail 263
Zuleika Dobson (Beerbohm)
114
Zweig, Arnold 173, *228*,
229
Zweig, Stefan 160, 162

ACKNOWLEDGMENTS

The Publishers would like to thank Justine Bell, Phil Rose of Lovell Johns, Cynthia Howell for her cartographic editorial help, David Bowron for indexing the book, Rachel Wearmouth at Lonely Planet Guide books for supplying us with a number of their guides, Nouvelles France for their help with literary places to visit in France and the numerous tourist boards throughout the world who gave us help and information.

PICTURE CREDITS AND ACKNOWLEDGMENTS

Illustrations courtesy of: Abacus Books illustration by Nick Bantock: 321tr, **AKG London**: 16b, 41, 65, 75t, 76tl, 80l, 81br, 83, 101t, 114tr, 118t, 139tr, 146t, 163tr, b, 164bl, 183tr, 185, 217, 256, 292, /Axel Lindahl: 138, /Berlinische Galerie, Berlin/©DACS 1996: (Self portrait by George Grosz 1928) 183tl, /Bibliothèque Nationale, Paris: 38b, /Blerancourt, Musée de l'Amitie Franco-Americaine: 122, /Detroit Institute of Arts: ('Die Nachtmahr' by Fussili) 77br, /Jamestown-Yorktown Foundation, ML Holmes: 32, /Paul Mellon Collection: (Scene from the 'Beggar's Opera' by William Hogarth) 49t, **Al Hayat**: 293cr, br, **Alinari**/Pinacoteca Nazionale, Siena: (Citta sul mare by Ambrogio Lorenzetti) 14t, **Archivio IGDA**: 164br, 174t, 209tr, /Musée d'Art Africaine, Paris: 33cl, /Museo della Marina, Lisbon: 33tl, **Beacon Communications/20th Century Fox** (courtesy Kobal): 277b, **Bertram Rota**/©Angelica Garnett: 181tl, **Bildarchiv Preussischer Kulturbesitz**: 183b, 184, 228cl, 230b, **Bodleian Library, University of Oxford**: (MS Gough Gen.Top.16): 18t, 213b, /©HarperCollins Cartographic 1996. Reproduced with permission: 222-3, **The Bostonian Society/Old State House**: 109, **Bridgeman Art Library**/Ackermann & Johnson Ltd, London: (View of Pope's Villa on the River Thames at Twickenham by Samuel Scott) 47t, (Christchurch, Oxford by J Murray Ince) 112tr, /Beamish, North of England Open Air Museum, Durham: (Old Hetton Colliery, Newcastle, Anon) 100, /British Library: (Murder of Thomas à Becket, by John of Salisbury, Latin Life of Becket) 17tl, (The Travellers, or a Tour Through Europe, publ by William Spooner) 79t, /Christie's, London/©DACS 1996: (Sacre Coeur, Montmartre by Maurice Utrillo) 129, /City of Edinburgh Museums & Art Galleries: (Sir Walter Scott and his Literary Friends at Abbotsford (study) by Thomas Faed) 79b, (View of Edinburgh from from the top of the Calton Hill by Nelson's Monument, litho) 140b, /Fine Art Society/Arthur Rackham illustration used with the kind permission of his family©: 81bl, /Giraudon: (Voltaire, aged 23 by Nicholas de Largilliere) 40tr, (George Sand (AAL Dupin) by Auguste Charpentier) 95t, Giraudon/Maison de Balzac, Paris: (Honore de Balzac from daguerreotype) 92tr, /Giraudon/Musée Antoine Lecuyer, Saint-Quentin, France: (Jean Jacques Rousseau by Maurice Quentin de la Tour) 40tc, /Giraudon/Musée des Beaux Arts, Lille: (The Republic, 1848 by Jules Claude Ziegler) 126b, /Giraudon/National Palace, Mexico City © Instituto Nacional de Bellas Artes: (Market at Tenochtitlan by Diego Rivera) 298, /Guildhall Library, Corporation of London: (Map of London as surveyed and published by John Roque) 47b, (Portsmouth St, Lincoln's Inn Fields by John Crowther) 97tl, /Hermitage, St Petersburg: (Actors from the Comédie Française by Antoine Watteau) 39b, /Hirshhorn Museum, Washington DC: (Slave Market by Friedrich Schulz) 123tl, /Johannesburg Art Gallery, S Africa: (Yellow Houses: a street in Sophiatown by Gerard Sekoto ©) 295tr, /Lauros-Giraudon: (Henri Marie Beyle (Stendhal) by John Olaf Sodermark) 92tl, /Manor House, Stanton Harcourt, Oxon: (Alexander Pope by Sir Godfrey Kneller) 47c, /Musée Condé, Chantilly: (Michel Montaigne, French School) 24t, /Musée d'Orsay, Paris: (Emile Zola by Edouard Manet) 128l, /Museo Nacional Centro de Arte Reina Sofia, Madrid/©Succession Picasso/DACS 1996: (Guernica 1937 by Pablo Picasso) 214t, /Museum of Fine Arts, Budapest/©DACS 1996: (Appropriating land in Sicily by Renato Guttuso) 233b, /National Gallery, London: (Triple portrait of the head of Richelieu by Philippe de Champaigne) 38t, /National Museum of Wales, Cardiff/©Julius White: (Dylan Thomas by Augustus John) 248, /National Portrait Gallery, Smithsonian Institution: (Pocahontas, after the engraving by Simon van de Passe) 34t, /New York Historical Society: (Scene from 'The Last of the Mohicans' by Thomas Cole) 85, /Palazzo Pubblico, Siena: (Good Government in the City, (detail) (fresco) by Ambrogio Lorenzetti) 14t, /Petit Palais, Geneva: (The Seine at Argenteuil by Renoir) 132tr, /Private Collections: (View of London by Cornelius de Visscher) 23t, (Denis Diderot by Jean Baptiste Greuze) 40tl, (The Doubling Room, Dean Mills, Anon) 101c, (Cover of 'The Yellow Book' 1894 by Aubrey Beardsley) 145b, (Sherlock Holmes (litho) after Roy Hunt) 147t, (Mountains and coastline, view from '36 Views of Mount Fuji' by Utagawa or Ando Hiroshige) 270b, (Eight Huts in Haiti by D Roosevelt ©) 280, /Roy Miles Gallery, London: (Lord Byron reposing having swum the Hellespont by Sir William Allan) 62, /Stadtische Museum, Vienna: (Café Griensteidl, Vienna by Reinhold Volkel) 162t, /Tate Gallery, London: (Nocturne in Blue and Gold: Old Battersea Bridge by James McNeill Whistler) 145t, /Towner Art Gallery, Eastbourne/©Angelica Garnett: (8 Fitzroy Street by Vanessa Bell) 178b, /Victoria & Albert Museum, London: (Scene from 'Le Bourgois Gentilhomme' by Charles Robert Leslie) 39t, (The Harbour and the Cobb, Lyme Regis, Dorset, by Moonlight by Copplestone Warre Bamfylde) 68b, (Cover of 'The Chap Book' 1894 by William Bradley) 155t, (Lovers from 'Poem of the Pillow' by Kitagawa Utamaro) 270tr, /Victoria Art Gallery, Bath: (Milsom Street, Bath (aquatint) by John Claude Nattes) 67t, (The Pump Room, Bath (aquatint) by John Claude Nattes) 67b, /Walker Art Gallery, Liverpool: (The Funeral of Shelley by LEP Fournier) 63b, /Wallington Hall, Northumberland: (Industry of the Tyne: Iron and Coal by WB Scott) 102t, /Waterman Fine Art Ltd, London/©Michael Chase: (Worms Head, Gower Peninsula by Sir Cedric Morris) 251b, /Wordsworth Trust, Grasmere: (William and Mary Wordsworth by Margaret Gillies) 58, **British Library**: (World Map by Aaron Arrowsmith K.Top.4.36.1 11Tab) FCt, 56-7, (Map of Spain by Pedro de Medina C62 f.18) 30, (Crystal Palace Game Map, Maps 28.bb 7) 86-7, **Brontë Society**: 105t, c, b, 106, 107tr, l, **Camera Press**: 264t, 282c, /Jane Bown: 267bc, 286b, /Gerald Cubitt: 294, /Karsh of Ottwawa: 309, /L Polyzkova: 262tl, /Pressens Bild: 282tr, /Jean Schmidt: 225c, /Bernard G Silberstein: 307t, /Lennox Smillie: 281, /Gavin Smith: 308c, /Sally Soames: 308t, /Sharron Wallace: 282b, **Jonathan Cape**: 219b, /Illustration by Jo Agis 305tr, **J Allan Cash**: 142t, **Jean-Loup Charmet**: 171, **Christie's Images**/©Angelica Garnett: (Portrait of David Garnett by Vanessa Bell) 179tl, (Portrait of Lytton Strachey reading by Vanessa Bell) 179br, /©1978 Estate of Duncan Grant: (Portrait of Vanessa Bell by Duncan Grant) 179tr, **Collections**/Alain le Garsmeur: 167, 168 bkgd, 169r, 169b, 323r, /Geoff Howard: 322c, **Collins Associates**: 279cl, **Thomas Cook Travel Archive**: 131tc, **Corbis-Bettmann**: 108, 118b, 123tr, 152tl, 162b, 175b, 177c, 186, 189b, 190, 192tr, 192tl, 193t, 194, 201bl, 203, 206cl, 216, 221, 230t, 247b, 254, 297b, 307c, 312b, /Brady: 110l, **Dorset County Museum**/Thomas Hardy Memorial Collection: 133b, ©**Douglas Brothers**: 305tl, **ET Archive**: 69 bkgd, 128r, 150tl, /Birmingham City Art Gallery: (Grasmere by the Rydal Road by Francis Towne) 61, /British Library: (World Map by Henricus Martellus Add.15760) 10-11, /British Museum: (Cottonian World Map) 14b, (Globe Theatre by JC Visscher) 22, /Canterbury Cathedral: 19, /Christchurch College, Oxford: 114tl, /Courage Breweries: (Dr Johnson by Sir Joshua Reynolds) 46t, /India Office Library: 148, /Museum für Gestaltung, Zurich: 160b, /National Gallery, London: (Weymouth Bay by Constable) 136t, /Naval Museum, Genoa: (World Map by Juan de la Cosa) 33tr, /Private Collection: (Music Hall, Fishumble Street, Dublin by FW Fairholt) 50, /Strindberg Museum, Stockholm: 139c, /Victoria & Albert Museum, London: (Facsimile of the Ellesmere Manuscript) 16t, 17b, 18bl, br, **Mary Evans Picture Library**: 20t, 23b, 27t, 42cr, 43tl, 45t, 45b, 46b, 49b, 52tl, 53, 54b, 66, 74b, 76tr, 96tl, 101b, 103, 104r, 110r, 111r, 114br, 125t, 149, 150tr, 150b, 151b, 151b, 177t, 126t, **Excelsa/Mayer Burstyn** (courtesy Kobal): 233t, **Explorer**: 42tl, **Faber & Faber Ltd**: /©Barney Cokeliss: 79tl, /Illustration by Peter Blake: 321br, **Farrar, Straus & Giroux**: 315cr, **Field Day Theatre Co**: 279cr, **A Frajndlich**: 316tr, ©**Allen Ginsberg** as taken by Peter Orlovsky: 255, **Goethe-Museum, Düsseldorf**/Anton-und-Katharina-Kippenberg-Stiftung: (View of Weimar by Georg Melchior Kraus) 74t, **Ronald Grant Archive**: /British Lion: 257, 297t, /RKO: 200, ©**Alasdair Gray**/: "Lanark"/Cannongate Books: 318, /Bloomsbury Publishing: 319tl, tr, **Sonia Halliday Photographs**/Bibliothèque Nationale, Paris: 291, **Hamish Hamilton/Penguin**: 26, **Harbourfront Centre**/Michael Cooper: 306, **Robert Harding Picture Library**: 134 bkgd, 249, 274b, 302, 304tl, 323b, /David Beatty: 251t, /E Simanor: 290t, /JHC Wilson: 267cr, /Adam Woolfitt: 132tl, **Heinemann African Writers Series**: 303tl, cr, 304br, bc **Hulton Getty**: FCcr, b, BC, 20b, 42tr, 54t, 59 bkgd, 70tl, 73t, 78, 80b, 93tr bkgd, tl, b, 95b, 98, 104l, 107cr, 121t bkgd, 123cr, 125c, 131r, 140tl, 144, 152b, 155b, 172tl, tr, 174b, 178tl, 208, 209b, 210tl, tr, bl, 211, 213t, 219t, 220, 232, 236, 237t, 238 bkgd, 240, 241bl, 242, 243t, b, 250, 259tl, tr, 266, 268, 278tr, **Images of India**/DPA: 269tr, bl, **Imperial War Museum, London**: 170, **Israel Press & Photo Agency Ltd**: 288, **Japan Information and Cultural Centre**: 272tl, **Kobal Collection**: 201c, 202, **London Borough of Camden/Keats House, Hampstead**: 63t, **Magnum Photos**: /Ian Berry: 241tr, 282tc, 295b, /Rene Burri: 234tr, /Henri Cartier-Bresson: 226, /Bruce Davidson: 317br, /Eliott Erwitt: 252, /Philip Jones Griffiths: 316tl, /Thomas Hoepker: 314, /David Hurn: 276, /Herbert List: 209tl, /Peter Marlow: 320, /Inge Morath: 297c, /Martin Parr: 278br, /Gilles Peress: 267cr, 277t, /Eli Reed: 311, 317bl, /Sebastiao Salgado: 234cr, **Mansell Collection**: 17tr, 80t, 111l, 133t, /Beaconsfield: 102c, **National Portrait Gallery, London**: (Henry James by John Singer Sargent) 130, (Samuel Taylor Coleridge by Peter Vandyke) 60bl, **Network**: Michael Abrahams: 313, /Chris Davies: 287, Jack Picone: 284, /Steve Pyke: 274t, 322tl, **Neue Constantin/ZDF** (courtesy Kobal): 235, **New York Public Library**: 156bl, /Eliz Buehrmann: 156tr, /Schomburg Center for Research in Black Culture, Astor, Lennox & Tilden Foundations: 192b, 193b, /Underwood & Underwood: 156tl Peter Newark's Pictures: 48, 82b, 84t, 119c, 121b bkgd, 146b, 147b, 172tc, 195b, /Dorothea Lange: 205 **North Wind**: 34b, 84bl, bc, br, 96b, 97t, 154, 157bkgd, cl, c, cr, 198b, 199tr, **W W Norton & Co, Inc.** Reproduced from 'The Portable Faulkner', edited by Malcolm Cowley. ©1946 by Viking Press, Inc/199tl, **Novosti/Russia**: 88, 89b, 90tr, **Oklahoma Historical Society**/Archives & Manuscripts Division: 206-7t bkgd, **Paramount**: (courtesy Kobal): 258, /Talent Associates (courtesy Kobal): 300, **Penguin UK**: 321bl, /©Douglas Brothers: 321tl, **Penguin USA**: 196, 315tl, **Photofest**: 244b, 246tl, 247t, /Friedman-Engeler: 246tr, /Martin Harris/Pix: FCbc, 244tl, **Pictorial Press**/Pix: 201br, **PLAYBILL®** cover printed by permission of PLAYBILL Inc. PLAYBILL® is a registered Trademark of PLAYBILL Incorporated, New York, NY: 245, **Polygram Pictures**: 283, **Popperfoto**: 42cl, 52tr, cl, cr, 89t, 165, 204, 214c, 237t, 239t, 239b, 241tl, 286c, **Princeton University Libraries**/Sylvia Beach Papers, Dept of Rare Books & Special Collections: 175t, **Arthur Rackham** illustration used with the kind permission of his family© 43b, **Real Academia Española**: 28t, **Rex Features**: 259c, /Action Press: 301tl, /Marina di Crollalanza: 234tl, /Fotex/M Hoffmann: 290b, /Geraint Lewis: 301cl, /Michael Powell: 234cl, /Sipa: 301cr, 324b, 325tl, tr, /Sipa/D Hulshizer: 312t, /Peter Trievnor: 273c, **Roger-Viollet**: 70tr, 70cr, 82tl, /©Harlingue-Viollet: 70cl, /©Lipnitzki-Viollet: 225t, **Royal Geographical Society**: (World map of Commerical Geography pl.15 publ Bartholomew): 116-7, (Political World Map from Harmsworth New Atlas) 158-9, **Scala**: /Duomo, Florence: (Dante (fresco) by Domenico di Michelino) 12, /Museo del Bigallo, Florence: (Madonna della Misericordia (fresco) anon) 13b, /©The Munch Museum/The Munch-Ellingsen Group/DACS 1996: (Ibsen at the Grand Cafe, Oslo by Edvard Munch) 137, **Science Photo Library**/Dr Gene Feldman NASA GSFC: 260-1 **SCR Photo Library**: 262tr, bl, br, 264b, /Tretjakoff Galerie, Moscow: 90tl, **Shakespeare Birthplace Trust**: 21tr, **Frank Spooner Pictures**: /Chiasson: 310, /Gamma: 325b, Gamma/Frederic Reglain: 302, /Jordan: 301tr, /Thomas Toucheteau: 325cl, **State University of New York at Buffalo**, The Poetry/Rare Books Collection: 188, 189t **Stiftung Weimarer Klassik**/Goethe-Nationalmuseum: (Goethe by Georg Melchior Kraus): 75b, **Sygma**: 279tr, /Keystone: FCcl, 224, 227t bkgd, 227b, **Topham-Picturepoint**: 160tl, **20th Century Fox** (courtesy Kobal): 207c, **Ullstein**: 182, 228tl, 231, /Fritz Eschen: 228cr, Eva Siao: 228tr, **Ulysses**/©Angelica Garnett: 181tl, 181cl, cr, **University College Dublin**, Library, Special Collections: 166, **University of Chicago Library**: 156br, ©**University of Mississippi**/Center for the Study of Southern Culture/Cofield Collection: 197, 198tl, tr, **Vintage Books**, cover design by Lorraine Louie, cover photo illustration by Marc Tauss: 315b, **Harland Walshaw**: 21b, 136b, **Simon Warner**: 303b, **West Africa**/Caroline Forbes: 303cl, **Peter Whitfield**: 4-5 bkgd, 36-7, **Whitney Museum of American Art, New York, Josephine N Hopper Bequest/Photograph ©1996**: (Railroad Crossing 1922-23 (oil on canvas) by Edward Hopper 70.1189,) 195t, **Michael Woods**: 174r bkgd, **Wordsworth Trust, Grasmere**: 60tr, 172tl, **Yale University**, Beinecke Rare Book & Manuscript Library: 176.

While every effort has been made to trace the present copyright holders we apologize in advance for any unintentional omission or error and will be pleased to insert the appropriate acknowledgment in any subsequent edition.

The Publishers would like to thank the following for their help in preparing this book: the staff of the London Library, Peter Ellis at Ulysses and Martin Batty at Bertram Rota antiquarian booksellers, Joanna Hartley at the Bridgeman Art Library and the staff of the Hulton Getty Collection.

[352]